This book belongs to:

Anthony Anecito

DB2® High Performance Design and Tuning

Richard Yevich

Susan Lawson

ISBN 0-13-203795-5

90000

Prentice Hall PTR
Upper Saddle River, NJ 07458
www.phptr.com

9 780132 037952

Library of Congress Cataloging-in-Publication Data

Yevich, Richard.
  DB2 high performance design and tuning / Richard Yevich, Susan Lawson.
    p. cm.
  ISBN 0-13-203795-5
    1. IBM Database 2. 2. Database management. I. Lawson, Susan. II. Title.

QA76.9.D3 Y48 2000
005.75'65--dc21

00-055810

Editorial/Production Supervision: *Precision Graphics*
Interior Compositor: *Precision Graphics*
Acquisitions Editor: *Tim Moore*
Editorial Assistant: *Julie Okulicz*
Marketing Manager: *Bryan Gambrel*
Buyer: *Maura Zaldivar*
Cover Design Director: *Jerry Votta*
Cover Design: *Nina Scuderi*
Project Coordinator: *Anne Trowbridge*

Prentice Hall books are widely used by corporations and government agencies for training, marketing, and resale.
The publisher offers discounts on this book when ordered in bulk quantities.
For more information, contact:
Corporate Sales Department
Prentice Hall PTR
One Lake Street
Upper Saddle River, NJ 07548
Phone: 800-382-3419; Fax: 201-236-7141; E-mail: corpsales@prenhall.com

Printed in the United States of America
10 9 8 7 6 5 4 3 2

ISBN 0-13-203795-5

Prentice-Hall International (UK) Limited, *London*
Prentice-Hall of Australia Pty. Limited, *Sydney*
Prentice-Hall Canada Inc., *Toronto*
Prentice-Hall Hispanoamericana, S. A., *Mexico*
Prentice-Hall of India Private Limited, *New Delhi*
Prentice-Hall of Japan, Inc., *Tokyo*
Pearson Education Asia Pte. Ltd.
Editora Prentice-Hall do Brasil, Ltda., *Rio de Janeiro*

To my family for their love and support,
and to Susan for her patience,
understanding, and fortitude.
                                                    —Richard

To my husband and family for their support,
and to Richard for his guidance
and encouragement.
                                                    —Susan

Contents

Foreword

$\mathbf{D}$B2 for OS/390 is growing fast. The growth comes from current applications scaling up, from vendor applications, and from new customers. There have been many changes in the past 17 years and 10 releases. Version 7 is coming soon. The use of DB2 has changed a lot. The initial query or decision support applications were very small and simple, but they have grown from megabytes to gigabytes to terabytes and continue to grow in size and complexity. Business intelligence adds many options for mining, OLAP, and content management.

We have partnered with many vendors that are growing rapidly, such as SAP, PeopleSoft, Siebel, and Ceres. These applications are demanding for a DBMS, and they also require a very close partnership to provide the best scalability and availability. In the business intelligence area, some of the key partners are Hyperion, ETI, Vality, MicroStrategy, SAS, Cognos, Brio, and Business Objects. We work with Tivoli and deliver management tools in "coopetition" with many others, including Candle, Compuware, Computer Associates, and BMC.

Traditional OLTP has changed dramatically. The batch work has increased in volume and in the need to be concurrent with other work. The applications have grown much more complex. OLTP has changed into e-business and e-transaction processing. In some ways, e-business is very simple. The customers want the best of everything, and they want it now. If yours is not the best, the competition is only a mouse click away. For e-business applications, the demands are similar: they must be fast, scalable, available, and flexible to usable information. E-transaction processing builds upon many of the traditional transaction-processing strengths of DB2. Data management for web transactions has changed from simple transactions, accessing a few files in one DBMS, to much more complex federated work. One web click can drive a dozen transactions across several subsystems, so the user interface is simpler. That's what it takes to make the data more usable.

A successful e-business must be able to scale without limits. Instead of just company employees, every person with a web connection is a potential user. They will connect when it's convenient for them, so you need to be ready for performance peaks that are hard to imagine. We think there were more than 142 million people online in 1998. This number is expected to leap to 502 million worldwide by 2003. Are you ready for the peak load? Imagine millions of servers connecting billions of people and trillions of devices.

Another factor in the growth is connection to other web devices and appliances. I received my IBM WorkPad recently. DB2 Everywhere runs on Palm Pilot, IBM WorkPad, and Windows CE devices. Mobile telephones must similarly accommodate a variety of devices. As microprocessors become more and more pervasive, the ability to communicate becomes more important. We expect storage capacity to grow at an astonishing compound rate of 90% a year. At that rate, the current 1 TB application will become 24 TB in five years. Data is being kept much longer, especially in the business intelligence world. The growth rate might be even faster, especially if your application is successful.

One web click may drive a dozen transactions to deliver a customer response, adding another factor in the calculations. Scalability must include the ability to scale in processors, I/O, memory, utilities, and applications that include transactions, batches, and queries. The numbers of users and the volume of data must be able to be scaled. While we support terabytes today, every limit must increase exponentially. The key DB2 scaling improvements enhance performance by a factor, rather than a percentage. For example, parallelism improvements in SQL and utilities deliver performance that is several times faster.

As soon as your application is on the web, it must be continuously available. If your application is not up, you've shut the customer out of your store. If the customer starts using a competitor, you might lose all of that business. Availability is not perfect for any application. The best availability is a carefully engineered compromise to meet the service-level agreement for continuous availability and costs. Often very high availability needs substantial redundancy, additional servers, and the ability to switch part of the application to another server or work in read-only mode. For continuous operation the application must be minimal, flexible, and consistent with high performance.

Information is one of the dominant factors in being competitive. The e-business click stream has extremely high volume and high value. The ability to collect, organize, and use the information for competitive advantage is critical for success. The data needs to be combined with other application data and external data. Business intelligence requires much more space and processing to convert data into information. The information lets you improve your business and grow even faster.

The DB2 advantages for business intelligence begin with very strong optimization of the use of the hardware and operating system. DB2 SQL performance improvements continue, with stronger optimization in each release. The optimization has been cost based since 1983. More complex customer queries and larger amounts of data have been processed. As customers found problems, they provided information for more improvements. This cycle has improved use of indexes, reduced processing times, and increased use of parallelism. Star schema optimization, index ANDing and ORing, summary tables, improved buffer management, and more sophisticated query rewrite continue to deliver substantial increases in every release.

So that's all we need to do. Provide the best of everything. Deliver fast. Make the information usable. Make the application fun to use. Be able to scale and provide fast access. Always be available. Use the information from the click stream to improve the business. When our customers are asked, "Why DB2?" they often respond, "Because it works!"

The Experience Shows

DB2 does not work by itself. Building a high-performance application requires skill, teamwork, knowledge, judgment, and experience. While our customers have shown that they can build large, high-volume applications, they have also learned some hard lessons. It's much easier to learn those lessons in a class or from a book, rather than when angry customers are waiting. Using the design and tuning lessons for some other product is sometimes part of the problem instead of the solution. Richard and Susan are very experienced with large, complex applications that need very high performance. They have worked with very large tables and high-availability needs. As you read this book, you will see that their experience shows.

It Depends

My favorite answer for most performance and availability questions is, "It depends." Most of the interesting questions do not have a simple answer. We'd like to have simple, objective answers to our complex, subjective questions. The only problem is that the simple answer is wrong. Performance experts know the right answer: "It depends."

Sometimes the pressure is so great that we oversimplify and give a simple answer, even though it's only partially correct. Our facts are uncertain, because the measurements are difficult and we are often working on the uncertain future. While "it depends" is completely correct, it is also completely useless unless we go on to explain more about the dependencies and issues. Richard and Susan explain what it depends upon.

ROGER MILLER,
IBM LEAD DB2 STRATEGIST

Preface

What's the one thing I can do to fix the performance problems in my DB2 systems?

D B2 came, saw, and conquered on the mainframes or enterprise servers, better known today as the S/390. Just take a look at the some of the enormous database sizes and heavy workloads that DB2 is currently supporting in production. Here are a few examples: a single database table of six billion rows, an online system achieving over 1,200 transactions per second, batch systems exceeding 80 million update transactions per day and turning out approximately 1.3 million reports daily, and insert programs pushing 300+ inserts per day. These database systems are in existence today and are growing and pushing the envelope in new ways. These numbers may seem astonishing to some, but they show the capabilities of the DB2 engine and set the stage for larger databases and more complex applications. Take, for example, a major service firm that is in the planning stages of creating a 130-billion-row table, which we like to call a VLTB (very large table), to be implemented in the near future. These figures will probably be exceeded greatly by the time you read this material. Even with all these success stories and reports of the amazing accomplishments of these large-database and high-transaction-volume systems, many organizations are still failing to meet their service-level agreements. Why? It is not DB2 that has failed at these sites, but the design and implementation of the applications being implemented in DB2 and the care and feeding of the subsystem and its surroundings. To build a system of large magnitude such as those mentioned earlier, organizations are faced with several new challenges. Many of these challenges need to be met head on with knowledge and expertise that often is lacking, making this task virtually impossible.

Technical specialists such as database administrators, database designers, system programmers, and application programmers often are expected to perform miracles and are all too often limited in the resources available to accomplish the difficult task at hand. "Develop a large database with several large tables with no outages allowed, to support a complex application with several thousand SQL statements, running millions of transactions per day with excellent response time. By the way, we have no time for additional education, design reviews, or SQL performance tuning because we have a deadline to meet." Sound familiar? Many organizations have found that it is very easy to implement DB2 applications, which is one of the best features of the product, but without careful planning and attention to performance, these easy-to-implement applications can soon become performance nightmares. This fact could be best emphasized with a quote from IBM lead DB2 strategist Roger Miller: "The rule is not to bite the hand that you expect to feed you."

Many organizations have had their share of experience with poorly performing applications in the past, and the reason is probably that it is easy to implement a database application poorly when critical phases of system development are rushed or skipped altogether. No one goes into systems development with the goal of developing a poorly performing application. Often, however, there are design, development, and programming standards and practices in place that seem to force poor performance due to a lack of understanding about all the elements that affect performance in DB2. Even worse is the adherence to old performance myths that have been propagated through the years. This book is designed both to try to destroy the bad practices and to direct focus on more efficient and effective ways of viewing performance in DB2. DB2 works exactly the way it is directed, good or bad. The good news is that it is a proven fact that we can accomplish amazing feats with DB2 if we understand how it works and what is needed to make it perform.

Purpose of this Book

The title includes the words "high performance." Today, there are many books, papers, and especially IBM manuals that contain mountains of material on performance. But when technical people are faced with the development of a high-performance system, who has time to climb those mountains? As a result, many systems achieve what is deemed as acceptable performance based upon the best efforts of the technical staff with the resources available to them. The problem of less-than-optimal performance has existed in the past, but something is happening today to change the perspective of what is acceptable: the "e" stuff and to a lesser degree the "BI" stuff. For example, one company was very happy with its data-sharing complex's achieving 1,000 transactions per second, but the movement to support web-based clients changed all that. In a traditional application, a terminal operator may place an order using one or more transactions. But when an order is placed from the web, it may spawn 10 of those traditional back-end transactions. Prior to the web phenomenon, there were a fixed number of terminal operators, but the web opens up an unlimited number of users issuing transactions to place orders. What was acceptable performance in the past is now simply inadequate because you are not just dealing with your internal company personnel (who may have not complained or were ignored about system response time) taking orders. The rules have changed; with e-business you open the doors of your company to the world. You might say that you expose yourself, and any performance problems you had in the past will now be magnified.

So what can be done to take an existing application to a level far above what is achieved today, and how do we develop a new application that can perform at or above expectations? Too often this question is answered by adding additional CPUs. Sure, that makes vendors happy, but is that really how to address performance problems? This is short-term, quick fix, but it often is not the answer because the dollar costs related to this solution are often too high, and in the long run the application may not be scalable because the underlying problems have not been addressed.

What needs to be done is to remove code length at all of the 50 or more pressure points within the DB2 environment and within the application. It is the task of the person responsible for performance to find these key points and determine the best way to improve performance, through either subsystem tuning, database tuning, or application tuning. It is truly amazing what can be done by identifying a few key points and tuning them, and the benefits gained by such efforts are definitely worth it. We have seen simple system changes increase the number of concurrent threads by a factor of 4. SQL tuning dropped an application from 400 hours a month to less than 7. While some areas may seem miniscule by themselves, it is the combined benefits that will provide your database systems with optimal performance. By performing several small changes, it is possible for a 100-transaction-per-second OLTP application to become a 400-transaction-per-second OLTP application on the same hardware and operating environment. The challenge lies with the "bloodhound" skills to find the performance problems and the proper knowledge and resources to fix them. There are also many problems that can be fixed quite easily, bringing large performance gains immediately.

This book focuses on identifying these key pressure points, determining what is necessary to improve them, and taking a little code length out of each one. Suppose that you could remove 0.10 CPU seconds from 40 different pressure points. That equates to 4 CPU seconds for allowing more transactions to complete. Since the average OLTP system handles between 8,000 and 12,000 SQL statements per second, it is easy to figure out just how significant a series of minor changes can be. Add this type of change to other tuning efforts, and the results of the overall combined effort can be truly amazing.

Keep in mind there is no "silver bullet" in DB2 performance. Optimal performance comes from a combination of proper design, subsystem implementation, application coding, and customizing DB2 for your organization's specific requirements.

Maximum performance cannot be achieved without a full understanding of how each component interrelates with the others, such as how a simple SQL statement can use or abuse all the resources of the system and take literally hours to run but, with a minor change, take fewer resources and complete in seconds. Every design issue in DB2 is a trade-off. DB2 must be viewed as a delicate balance of issues and techniques, where pushing down on any single point increases pressure on another point somewhere else. High-performance design and tuning require a delicate balance, and therefore each balance/counterbalance situation will be discussed. It is important that all technical support personnel understand how and why these trade-offs occur and, more important, what they can do in their particular area to achieve high performance.

There are many rules of thumb and guidelines for DB2. Unfortunately, sometimes these guidelines become standards of practice. Each of these "rules" must be examined, explained, and accepted or rejected. Mostly, they represent valid "day 1" starting points and nothing else. Worse, any "rule" is subject to change during any maintenance release of the DB2 software and must be reviewed or analyzed on an ongoing basis.

Often this question arises: "Since my system is relatively small with only a handful of users and a small amount of data, should I be concerned with *all* of these issues?" The answer is, "Yes, especially if you want to succeed by giving your applications the ability to integrate with others and to grow in both scope and scale." This can truly be achieved by striving for optimal performance in the implementation, which requires an overall understanding of the critical issues. Keep in mind that almost all systems expand, regardless of the initial plan or scope. It appears that the word "archive" has been removed from the dictionary, along with the phrase "We will never need that old data again." Once a system comes online in DB2, the data's life seems to become eternal. This is understandable, because we really don't deal with simple data anymore. We deal in information, and information must be viewed as a fixed asset with a real dollar value. For instance, when two old, seemingly unimportant pieces of data become "related" and then become an "atomic particle of information," the data will never again be just old and unnecessary; it now has become information that needs to be stored indefinitely.

Therefore, it is important that we strive to do it right the first time, or at least try to design the system to handle growth without degrading performance. Several years ago, a one-million-row table was considered enormous. Currently, a retailer has a six-billion-row table that has been estimated to reach ten billion rows (probably a very conservative estimate). A service organization is achieving 1,200 transactions per second, with each transaction comprising multiple SQL DML statements; however, these are designed transactions. A major financial company is viewing an EIS database that is being estimated in petabytes (1,000 TB or 1,000,000 GB, and too long to list in megabytes or bytes). Today, we talk about terabyte disk storage servers and storage area networks (SANs) housing massive amounts of data and turning that data into "information," and we are increasing the size of the data stores. Two traditional rules of thumb still apply:

> Rule of Thumb: It depends.
>
> Rule of Thumb: Always design for performance.

These two rules will never change, although there is an important corollary:

> Rule of Thumb: If you do not design for performance, then by default you are designing for poor performance.

Think about that for a while: designing for poor performance intentionally.

As an example of designing for poor performance, many places assume that all SQL gets written the best way possible, by all personnel, the first time! Unfortunately, this is not often the situation. In fact, the two most important areas of abuse that cause poor performance are improper use of SQL and improper physical design. Combine these two areas and you have a formula for disaster. This is not just opinion but comes after years of analysis by many who routinely address performance problems in real-world DB2 applications. Performance improvements of 240 to 1 have been achieved by simply correcting poor SQL and COMMIT strategies and minor tweaking of the relational design. Batch jobs have been reduced from 4 hours to 10 minutes and from 2 hours to 55 seconds. In one case an 85–95% reduction in run time was achieved on a system that would have required

400 hours of elapsed time to run each month (along with some hardware changes); this application now runs in 7 to 15 hours. These are significant numbers, and if you apply a cost factor to this, the dollar figures are impressive. A common problem in achieving a proper database design occurs when an improper system design is forced to be accepted, even though it could never support the application requirements. Even with this knowledge, the attitude seems to be, "Just fix it later; we have a deadline to meet, and we have already started coding." Unfortunately, and most of the time as predicted, the application's transactions cannot complete in the time allotted, and the database cannot handle the load. The most detrimental fact here is that design flaws are hardest, if not impossible, to fix, regardless of the amount of system or SQL application tuning. Sometimes this can result in the worst of all fates, moving the application logic into the program and simply using a DB2 file system. When this happens, the power of DB2 is completely inhibited, and any further growth of the application becomes a daunting task.

Without fail, in every organization where the issues and resources of DB2 have been discussed at any managerial level, a common reaction is, "DB2 implementation is easy and should not take many resources." Often this statement is based upon what is expected of DB2, without taking into consideration what needs to be given to the processes using DB2 to meet those expectations. For example, it is often said that "SQL is easy to learn and code; it must be DB2 that is causing the problem," when the truth is that SQL can be extremely difficult to learn to use properly. Today we are reviewing 10-page SQL statements that do the processing of several hundred lines of COBOL. This is a little more complicated than a single SQL select statement on a small PC-based database. This misperception often leads to SQL performance tuners being very undervalued, if they exist within the organization at all.

There is a big difference in performance between work done using SQL and work done after the SQL in the application code. Typically, SQL is used as "just another access method." SQL is *not* an access method! The number of ways that SQL can be used to navigate relational structures is mind-boggling. The DB2 SQL optimizer is one of the most powerful and robust optimizers in existence today, with amazing query rewrite capabilities. The more you can drive through the engine and allow the optimizer to help, the better your performance will be. Why have DB2 do a little work, incur all of the overhead to pass massive amounts of data back to the program, only to have to process it there? There have been several instances where pages—yes, pages—of C or COBOL code containing multiple cursors, fetching rows, and building complex linked lists for further processing other tables were replaced with one SQL statement. In every case where this was possible, there was a significant reduction in processing time.

These are some of the types of problems and issues that are addressed in the following chapters. All components of making DB2 work well are addressed, from system administration to physical design, down to a single SQL statement.

It is very difficult to investigate any type of problem in DB2 without offending hardworking technical support folks who have implemented what they truly believed to the correct method or who were limited by time or resources. It is important to understand that what was implemented in an earlier release of DB2 may not be optimal or applicable with the current release. This often is overlooked, resulting in less-than-optimal performance standards carried though DB2 releases. Every installation is different, and every installation has different problems. What is done at ABC Company, while it sounds wonderful, will not necessarily work at DEF Company and in fact might bring DEF Company to its knees if attempted! The topics presented in this book should help anyone make such determinations before disaster occurs. Remember the prime rule of DB2: "It depends!" This book helps identify what it depends upon, so that you can make informed performance decisions and achieve the desired results.

Organization of this Book

The book is organized from the broad to the narrow—from the overall environment to the inside of DB2 itself, from the application programs that use DB2 to the specific pieces used to build the applications. We found composing chapters on CPU, I/O, and memory difficult, since parts of this material come from so many different areas, covering all aspects of DB2 and its use. We decided to present this information in a hierarchical structure. The material is divided into six sections:

- Section 1 is an overview of DB2 performance issues and a list of the top 20 performance myths that we most often encounter when identifying performance problems. These myths involve areas of performance that are most commonly misunderstood or misinterpreted. The resolutions of these myths are found throughout the various chapters, with additional information to help avoid problems associated with the myths and to fix existing problems.

- Section 2 begins at the top of the DB2 hierarchy by discussing the system performance aspects of DB2, such as I/O and storage management, CPU, and memory. We look at such items as DFSMS usage, new disk storage devices, and detailed buffer pool design strategies.
- Section 3 takes you into the aspects of physical design. Topics here include designing database objects, such as indexes, and discussing tricks and techniques for special situations, such as code and reference tables. This section also includes information on how to best support the DB2 catalog and directory, which contains all the information about physical objects.
- Section 4 goes into application programming topics. These chapters cover proper application design, commit strategies, application interfaces, SQL coding tips, and examples of coding complex SQL statements. We also take a look at the latest enhancements in Version 6 and have a brief look at what is coming in Version 7.
- Section 5 covers using several of the new, and not so new, features of DB2, such as stored procedures, triggers, user-defined functions, LOBs, and Java.
- Section 6 is optional for many readers, because it covers an optional feature of DB2 called data sharing. This section addresses issues about migrating to a data-sharing environment, tuning your current environment prior to the migration, physical design considerations, and how to monitor and tune in this new environment.

Each chapter contains more information explaining the details of the areas we cover, as well as performance design strategies, tuning tips, and even critical roles and responsibilities critical for today's high-performance environment.

Audience for this Book

This book is for database designers, database administrators, architects, application designers, programmers, and anyone else who has the responsibility to ensure that DB2 systems meet or exceed their stated performance objectives. The four stages of building systems have always been

1. Make it work.
2. Make it work right.

3. Make it work fast.
4. Make it work all the time and be continuously available.

This book focuses mainly on the third category and a little on the fourth. The third category is often passed over in the real world of business applications. In most of these cases, failure to meet performance objectives often lies with the database design. Most often it lies with the physical database design and its implementation of programming paradigms and data access.

The book specifically addresses correctness of physical database design in DB2 and implementation strategies for application design and information access, along with some advanced SQL. We have attempted to leave no stone unturned. As you will see from the war stories throughout the text, we take no prisoners when it comes to eliminating performance problems.

We have presented this material several times all over the world and many times got the same two responses: either excitement from now knowing where to look for problems where tuning will pay off or concern about how to fix problems that have become imbedded in the organization throughout the years. The good news is that much of the information in this book comes from our real-life work and experience. We have worked with several large DB2 clients, we have seen what works and what does not, and in many cases we have seen tremendous improvements just by following high-performance design strategies.

Acknowledgments

There are many people to thank for assisting in the creation of this book, and many more who have provided information over the years, and it would impossible to name everyone. We would like to extend a very special thank you to all the IBM DB2 developers in the Silicon Valley Labs, and a special nod to Roger Miller and Jeff Josten for their technical reviews. For assisting in reviews, answering questions, and providing guidance, we thank Michael Hannan, Joel Goldstein, Kathy Komer, Klaas Brant, Jan Henderyckx, and Jeff Vowell. We also would like to thank our many clients who have allowed us to share their experiences.

Setting the Stage

 It is always necessary to set the tone for a book, and that is what this chapter is about: reality, opinions, and projections with a little bit of humorous observation, real world pain, complaining, and truth. It is critical when talking about DB2 to remember that what has bit us in the past can resurface in the future, and we must take with us into the world of relational DB2 the experiences of our past. Even with all of the benefits of a relational database environment and DB2 itself, we must remember that careful planning, attention to detail, and informed decisions are still very critical in this environment. One common mistake is the underestimation of the effort required to implement a high-performance system to meet today's processing and data requirements. We can achieve our performance goals by building upon the lessons learned in the past and integrating those with the new knowledge required to construct high-performance systems based upon today's technology. We do not have to reinvent the wheel, just give it some new high-performance treads, because it's all about going farther, lasting longer, and performing better.

Many pioneering companies found out the hard way that many of the past best practices were not only sound, but are still required today to milk every last ounce of performance from the large DB2 systems they are implementing. For some reason, in the data-processing professions, there seems to be the philosophy that we can simply start over again with each new advance, that somehow the new products will supply the intelligence necessary to overcome what caused us grief in the past. This is most prevalent with relational database implementations, where the hope is that the relational database will provide the magic that is necessary to build and maintain a high-performance system. Our successes in the relational environment depend on how well we can incorporate our past experiences, both good and bad, with the continual growth of our knowledge about the relational environment and current technology. There really is no magic—the rabbit has always been in the hat; it is up to us to pull him out either by his ears or by his tail.

The Legacy

Relational databases were such a new concept that we all wanted to believe the hype: more productivity with less effort and less cost. Information systems management was excited that perhaps this would allow some downsizing of the programming staff and shorten the development time by an incredible factor. These results would give a much needed boost to the perception of the IS department and help it succeed. "Yes, Virginia, there is a Santa Claus." The promoters promised increased productivity, easier adaptability to any future change or modification, lower development cost, instant answers to any complex ad hoc question, immediate implementation of decision support systems (DSS), executive information systems (EIS) overnight, true data independence, full data integrity, the removal of the backlog of maintenance, and the proof that Oswald acted alone! The reality is that after more than 15 years of DB2, we are beginning to realize at least some of those promises through advances in technology and a better understanding of how to properly implement in a relational environment. As for Oswald, many now believe that he did not act alone, but as for the rest, we still need more time.

Performance Does Not Come Easy

History taught us that to achieve good performance in any computer application, we had to do the following tasks:

- Apply many skilled techniques.
- Understand the underlying architecture of all the components.
- Spend time researching and benchmarking to see what approaches were best.
- Install all kinds of performance tools and perform benchmarking.
- Train, train, train the application, database, and systems personnel.
- Hope for the best.

It is often a mystery as to why the first five items are often overlooked today, except that we are becoming more of a "mouse-click" society that expects a magnitude of results with minimal effort. We still adhere to the last point, and we do all hope for the best. But in order to achieve high performance in DB2, we have to apply skilled techniques and understand the underlying architecture of the database engine, language components, 4GLs, CASE tools, utilities, and operating systems. We must spend time researching all the papers and presentations on the technical issues. This also includes attending many of the yearly conventions where the true in-depth information is presented and real-life experiences are shared. Benchmarking is required to determine which of several approaches will provide the best performance. Then the performance tools must be installed and tested, both for the operating and database environments. However, we somehow have seem to have skimped a lot on the training in the applications area, because somewhere along the way we have missed the information that showed how performance in the relational world is no longer the exclusive domain of the systems people, but now also lies in the hands of the applications developers and programmers. This programming and application group is the same group that we were hoping to downsize when we moved into the relational world, and often the education dollars are not spent here. In many organizations, applications people are never given an overabundance of credit or responsibility for performance but are viewed as just coders, not as valuable resources who, if given the proper resources, such as education and training, can become valuable soldiers in the performance war.

In reality, when we look back, it is safe to say that IS managers were often misled. But was it really their fault? Not at all. By the time DB2 was introduced, IS was hungry for a database system that could deliver ad hoc, batch, and OLTP systems that could also be changed easily, so hungry that they believed DB2 could change their world, but the perception was that the change could come at little or no cost, with little or no effort.

When DB2 was first released in 1983 with Version 1, Release 1, it was just that, a first release. DB2 has come a long way since its inception and initial implementation adventures. With several reductions in CPU and more efficient I/O capabilities, DB2 has evolved into a database management system capable of achieving its true batch and online processing potential, far surpassing what was expected and delivered in the early years. With its evolution we have also seen improved scalability, by a factor of more than 100, and a significant reduction in planned and unplanned outages. DB2 continues to improve with each release, adding more functionality and improved performance. Many of these enhancements are so significant that we will someday look back on where it is today just as we today look back on where it was in the beginning.

The industry has pushed DB2 far beyond the stated expectations of most industry experts of the time, then and throughout its history. Those in the industry who have been able push DB2 to the limits were able to do so by applying the techniques and principles learned in the past, coupled with an understanding of the internals of DB2 and how to properly design both objects and applications. Many of those techniques are explored in this book. Our goal is to provide information that will help all organizations move toward the success that they hear about at trade shows, conferences, and user groups but that they themselves have been unable to achieve.

The Realization

Information systems have come from an environment in which performance was truly in the hands of the systems personnel; even if the application developers did a less-than-optimal job, performance could always be improved by tweaking the operations system or the specific subsystem components. In the DB2 world, systems can do very little to improve performance if applications are poorly constructed. On the other hand, a highly tuned application can run so well that systems people can do little to improve its performance. This is a complete turnaround, and one that requires management to have an open mind in order to achieve a good balance of expertise and support. Expectations depend on the emphasis given to training applications personnel in the use of the database engine and allocating enough hardware resources that the engine can run as expected. Unfortunately, many companies have approached DB2 as buying a large corporate yacht but keeping it in dry dock because they cannot afford the gas or the in-water anchorage slot. DB2 requires disk and memory in order to deliver what we want it to deliver: robust applications that are easily adaptable with true ad hoc capability. A robust database engine that can do anything we ask it to can do it on limited resources. If DB2 is given enough resources to work, even minimally, the systems it can deliver are more than enough to meet any realistic expectations.

With the implementation of DB2 UDB for OS/390 Version 6 and the announcement of Version 7, significant enhancements have been made in functionality, scalability, and performance. For example, more parallelism is now used in the product in several areas, such as utilities. This allows several processes to run in parallel, significantly reducing the elapsed time of utility execution. The utilities have also been greatly enhanced with additional functionality that used to be the realm of the third-party vendors. Version 6 also provides enhanced distributed capabilities at many levels and support for object-relational technology. It is difficult to imagine what kind of impact this will have on the corporate environment, as these improvements are coming at a faster pace than business applications have been able to keep up with. But with the advent of e-commerce, e-business, and business intelligence, the whole world of processing data and information is changing as we drive towards solutions that did not even exist before.

How far are we really from output from data mining queries that drive declarative business rules in the object-relational database to dynamically change the processing for web-based systems based on changing customer patterns? Maybe a year or two!

Why the Myths Arose

DB2 appeared in 1983, and pseudo-expert advice appeared about one hour later. Unfortunately, this type of advice evolved into absolute truths early on and was based on too little information, incomplete information, or sometimes real information that was valid only for the current release but was stated in such a way as to become a hard and fast rule. This led to a lot of rules and standards in the beginning, and some have become so ingrained that they have become almost bylaws of systems development. Before we move on, we need to remember the only two true rules in DB2.

1. Anyone who says something is "always this way" is probably wrong.
2. There are no always rules in DB2 except one: it depends!

The purpose of this book is not to emphasize past mistakes but to try to set the correct perspective on information passed on through the years and evaluate its applicability today. No two systems are exactly the same, where everything is done exactly the same. Sure, some myths may appear to be nice starting points, and perhaps some of them are. But a starting point means that we must move on from there. Some systems today are operating as expected in terms of their service-level agreements, but if you examined them, you would find that the resources consumed far exceed those required to drive a system 10 times as complex. Since the system is working as expected, nothing appears to be wrong, and if the particular method that achieved that "result" is shared with many others, it could also become a new "rule," though it is more likely a myth! This particular method may have worked and produced adequate results in this particular environment, but it surely is not appropriate for all environments and could even prove harmful. Don't believe everything you hear (or read). Take all implementation and performance recommendations with an open, yet cautious, mind and then evaluate them against your environment.

Now it is time to take a quick look at the top 20 performance myths. Additional information regarding each myth and its reality is further detailed in the chapter reference provided after each one.

Top 20 Myths

1. Logical design should *always* map exactly to the physical.

   Reality: Physical design should remain as close as possible to the logical structure, but changes in the physical design mandated by performance should never be ignored just because they didn't come from the logical.

   Reference: Chapter 5, "Physical Database Objects"

2. Put everything in one buffer pool (BP0) and let DB2 manage it.

   Reality: While this is stated in the DB2 manuals and other places, you want to do this *only* if your memory is limited (10,000 4K pages or less), you do not have the time to manage it, and you are also not at all concerned with performance. It is better stated this way: *never* put anything but the DB2 catalog and directory into BP0.

   Reference: The section "Buffer Pools" in Chapter 3, "Memory"

3. DSNDB07 is always 100% sequential.

   Reality: Almost never is DSNDB07 100% sequential, as there is random activity to the pages in the work files. Random activity can be as much as 45%, but normally it is in the range of 3% to 10%.

   Reference: The section "DSNDB07: A Different Kind of Buffer Pool" in Chapter 3, "Memory"

4. VARCHARs should always be placed at the end of the row.

   Reality: It is the word *always* that is the real problem. If a table is almost always read and very seldom updated, then yes, this would reduce CPU, but in almost all other cases it is the worst thing to do, even if the table is compressed. It should be at the end only if it is heavily updated, but this is often not the case.

Reference: The section "VARCHAR Usage and Placement" in Chapter 5, "Physical Database Objects"

5. Applications should be coded to follow the logical process.

   Reality: Pseudo-code or a logical process diagram never takes into account coding methods for performance. This is most dramatic in OLTP transaction coding.

   Reference: Chapter 12, "Program Design and Processing"

6. Most processes cannot be performed in SQL.

   Reality: Actually, the reverse is generally true. SQL is a very rich language that can perform most processes. The real difficulty is that SQL is often approached as an I/O handler instead of a set processor.

   Reference: Chapter 16, "SQL"

7. Code and reference tables should be used with DB2 declared referential integrity (RI).

   Reality: RI should not be used as a shortcut for edit validations, which generally belong elsewhere, but should be used for true parent-child relationships.

   Reference: The section "Referential Integrity" in Chapter 5, "Physical Database Objects"

8. Tables should have only one or two indexes at most.

   Reality: Tables should have as many indexes as required to provide the performance necessary.

   Reference: Primarily the section "Indexes" in Chapter 5, "Physical Database Objects"

9. Nonpartitioning indexes (NPIs) should not be used, especially on large tables.

   Reality: There are "numerous problems involved," which can generally be overcome, but NPIs are quite necessary for proper access and performance.

   Reference: The section "Indexes" in Chapter 5, "Physical Database Objects," and the section "Nonpartitioning Indexes" in Chapter 6, "VLDBs, VLTBs, and Warehouses"

10. Large tables should be split.

    Reality: This is a legacy fear that too much data in a table means performance degradation. With several tables of over 6 billion rows in production, this myth has been laid to rest.

    Reference: The section "Tables" in Chapter 5, "Physical Database Objects," and Chapter 6, "VLDBs, VLTBs, and Warehouses"

11. DB2 defaults are okay.

    Reality: Defaults are generally never okay, since they can and do change over versions and releases. Consider, for example, the bind parameter CURRENT-DATA.

    Reference: All sections where parameters are discussed.

12. Never use negatives in SQL WHERE predicates.

    Reality: Another one of those generic rules that was never fully stated correctly. If and only if the only predicate is a negative, then the SQL access path could be using an unnecessary table space scan. But in almost all other cases, additional filtering would be done inside the DB2 engine, which is good.

    Reference: Chapter 16, "SQL"

13. I can rely on just EXPLAIN to determine whether the access path is good.

    Reality: EXPLAIN does not show the order in which the query blocks are executed, tells you nothing about stage 1 or stage 2 predicates, and never tells how often a block is executed. Basically, EXPLAIN just dumps some data in a table that takes a lot of additional explaining through competent analysis in conjunction with other information. There are some tools to help with this process (such as Visual Explain), but there also are some that can do more harm than good if all the facts are not considered.

    Reference: Chapter 22, "EXPLAIN"

14. Do not make the EDM pool so large that it pages.

    Reality: The EDM pool generally gives much better performance through paging (referring to paging to expanded storage, not disk) rather than being too small and having to constantly rebuild internal structures due to page stealing and other factors.

    Reference: The section "EDM Pool" in Chapter 3, "Memory"

15. Extents do *not* matter anymore.

    Reality: Since when? At some point in the future, when the world is fully SAN and ESS, then maybe. The impact of extents has been lessened quite a bit with the new disk cache controllers, but there is still some additional checking and processing required to manage them.

    Reference: Chapter 1, "I/O and Storage Management"

16. Relational division has no use in DB2.

    Reality: Relational division has been used in many systems in the past and can be effectively implemented by both database designers and application developers. In the current world of business intelligence (BI) and marketing systems, it probably is used in every single application, several times.

    Reference: Chapter 16, "SQL"

17. Bind all packages into two plans: one batch and one online.

    Reality: This was an unfortunate statement made at the introduction of packages in DB2. There are many reasons that this generic approach is wrong, besides just being generic.

    Reference: The section "Binding" in Chapter 10, "General Program Design Issues"

18. Uncommitted read is a dirty word.

    Reality: Uncommitted read is not a four-letter word but a very nice performance enhancement that can be used in far more places than often realized.

    Reference: The section "Isolation Level" in Chapter 10, "General Program Design Issues"

19. There are no locking problems since there are no timeouts and deadlocks.

    Reality: The fact that a particular problem does not occur does not mean that there is not a performance issue to be investigated. Often locking is not perceived as a problem due to focusing on reactive tuning measures (counting the number of deadlocks or timeouts), not on proactive tuning (monitoring lock wait time).

    Reference: The section "Locking and Lock Avoidance" in Chapter 13, "Locking and Concurrency"

20. ESA data compression is always good.

    Reality: While compression can provide benefits in many areas, there are a few situations where it can hurt. Each scenario must be evaluated to determine if compression is appropriate. This is not an option that should be mandated or rejected at a high level.

    Reference: The section "Compression" in Chapter 1, "I/O and Storage Management"

21. There are only 20 myths about DB2 performance.

    Reality: There are hundreds.

    Reference: The 2nd edition, 3rd edition, 4th edition.

Environment and Tuning

I/O and Storage Management

CPU

Memory

I/O and Storage Management

D B2 stores data and delivers it to applications for processing. So it seems logical that first we need to take a hard look at exactly how and where we store this data and how we manage it. At the highest level of performance engineering, we will make sure that data is stored properly, so that I/O will not be the preferred method of access. Some I/O costs more from a performance perspective than other I/O. You need to differentiate between them, based on the metrics at your own organization.

Data Facility Storage Management Subsystem (DFSMS)

The Data Facility Storage Management Subsystem (DFSMS) can be used to manage DB2 data sets automatically and reduce the amount of administrative work for database and system administrators. DFSMS allows easier allocation and movement of data, better availability and performance management, and automated space management. More important, performance is improved because performance goals can be set for each class of data, thereby reducing the need for manual tuning. This environment also utilizes the cache provided by the various levels of storage hardware.

In the past, DFSMS has been avoided by many organizations because of the interaction necessary between the database administrator (DBA) and the storage management group. This interaction was necessary in order to set up the groups for proper placement of DB2 data sets. DFSMS can be managed through the use of storage pools for a majority of the DB2 data sets, helping to ease the amount of interaction between the groups. It is possible to reach data placement objectives established by the database administration group by taking advantage of DFSMS.

Regardless of the amount of interaction necessary and time needed for proper setup of storage pools, DFSMS is going to become not only necessary for data-set management in DB2, but in many cases mandatory (refer to the section "Extended Addressability" in this chapter).

DFSMS implementation is often difficult (and sometimes feared) because DB2 DBAs are sometimes not fluent in the terms and capabilities of DFSMS or not involved or influential in the definition and implementation of DFSMS. By understanding the constructs of DFSMS, a DB2 DBA can work very well with the storage management group in order to define proper classes and groups to most optimally support the needs of the DB2 data sets. This becomes most critical in a high-performance, high-availability system. This section is not intended to walk you through how to implement DFSMS, but rather to give you some information and recommendations about the opportunities available for optimizing the data sets behind your DB2 data and the data sets used in the DB2 recovery process.

DFSMS consists of several constructs. Together these define how DFSMS stores and manages the data sets. Data classes are defined for organization, storage classes are defined for performance, management classes are defined for availability, and storage groups are defined for location. The classes manage the data sets, and the storage groups manage the underlying volumes.

Data Classes

By using data classes in DFSMS, you can specify a set of space and allocation attributes for DB2 data sets. This data class is then used during allocation so that all attributes for data-set creation do not have to be individually specified for each allocation. You can have different data classes established for the different types of data sets you may need to allocate. Attributes of data classes include space requirements, organization, and volume specifics. Data classes are optional but highly recommended.

Storage Classes

It has always been recommended in DB2 that critical data sets be specifically allocated to volumes to ensure optimal performance. This was often a manual process and sometimes implemented by defining one volume for one DB2 storage group (not to be confused with a DFSMS storage group, discussed later). Storage classes are provided by DFSMS to help achieve the separation necessary for critical data sets with specific performance requirements.

The performance characteristics for a data set are defined in a particular storage class. The target I/O response time allowed for a request to the disk controller is also defined for the class. DFSMS selects a volume based upon these objectives and tries to meet them, but they are not always guaranteed.

Attributes for the storage classes include performance objectives, availability objectives, accessibility characteristics, and caching options.

Here are examples of storage-classes for user data sets:

- Test class: A class where the requirements for performance and availability are low. Defined for development and test databases.
- Mission-critical class: A class where the requirements for performance and availability are very high. The class may provide volumes with characteristics critical for availability, such as RAID support or dual-copy capability.
- General class: A catch-all class for normal processing requirements with decent performance and availability requirements.

These are examples of storage-classes for recovery data sets:

- High-priority recovery critical class: This class would be used for the active log data sets and the BSDSs. These data sets are critical and require high performance and availability as well as guaranteed space.
- High-priority recovery class: this class could be used for archive log data sets. These data sets also have high availability and performance requirements but are not required to have guaranteed space.
- High-priority copy class: This class should be used for image copy data sets that have high performance and availability needs.
- Low-priority copy class: This class is the catch-all for all other image copy data sets.

Management Classes

A management class controls the following criteria for managing a set of data sets:

- Space management
- Retention
- Migration
- Expiration
- Backup

For data sets with specific similar availability requirements, a management class should be defined. For example, test data sets that could be controlled by hierarchical storage management (HSM) could be assigned to a particular management class.

These are examples of management classes for user data sets:

- Low-activity/inactive class: This class contains data sets that could be migrated after a given period of inactivity. It could be used for test and development data sets that are not used continually.
- High-availability class: This class is for data sets with high availability requirements, such as production.

Here are examples of management classes for recovery data sets:

- Daily copy class: This class can be used to manage image copy data sets that are taken daily but expire in seven days.
- Monthly copy class: This class can be used to manage image copy data sets that are taken monthly and expire in three months.
- Secondary copy class: This class can be used to manage backup, or secondary, archive log data sets or bootstrap data sets (BSDSs).

Storage Groups

Volumes are allowed to be pooled together with DFSMS. This relieves the previous problem of having to manually control the volumes in order to lessen the possibility of I/O contention and volume-full conditions. The storage group allows the placement of a data set on a volume in its pool based on the storage class defined, the status of the storage group, the volume, and the amount of available free space. Attributes for the storage groups include space thresholds, migration, and backup.

Storage groups must contain whole individual volumes that cannot be shared among groups, and the data sets cannot be shared nor multivolume. Volumes are selected from a list built, based upon several criteria.

It is recommended that production data sets and data sets used for backups be assigned to a particular storage group.

STOGROUPs used by DB2 can define a group of volumes available for use.

Example:

```
CREATE STOGROUP VOLUMES(VOL1, VOL2, VOL3)
```

DFSMS storage groups could be defined to match the volume list of these STOGROUPs during an initial conversion to DFSMS, and then the STOGROUP could be defined with VOLUME(*) to allow DFSMS to further handle allocation among the group of volumes defined in the DFSMS storage group. It does this assignment based on DFSMS classes used for the data sets.

Example:

```
CREATE STOGROUP VOLUMES('*')
```

However, it is important to understand the difference between DB2 STOGROUPs and DFSMS storage groups. DB2 STOGROUPs refer to a particular collection of volumes on which to create DB2 data sets, and different STOGROUPs can point to the same volumes, whereas DFSMS storage groups refer to grouping of volumes based upon a specific set of criteria, and a volume can belong to only one storage group.

Not using a guaranteed-space storage class is recommended, in order to give DB2 the ability to specifically select a volume for data-set allocation. Having DFSMS select a volume from a given storage class that has not been defined this way is recommended, to better take advantage of the capabilities of DFSMS. If space requirements do not change and are small, then guaranteed space is okay, but this is usually not the case.

Storage group characteristics can be changed without an outage to DB2. This can be useful if the hardware changes and a reconfiguration of volume placement is necessary.

Here are examples of storage groups for user data sets:

- Placement-critical group: This storage group assigns volumes that have specific requirements for data-set placement. This may be the case for critical table spaces or large, partitioned table spaces.
- Low-priority group: This storage group is for data sets that do not have high availability or performance needs and that could be migrated if necessary.
- High-performance group: This storage group provides volumes for data sets that require high performance and availability (no migration allowed).
- General group: This storage group is a catch-all for the majority of data sets, providing average performance and no migration.

These are examples of storage groups for recovery data sets:

- Low-priority group: This group is defined for the archive log data sets (primary and secondary) as well as backup, or secondary, image copies. These data sets can be migrated.
- High-performance/availability group: This group is used for the active logs and BSDSs of the production subsystems.
- Low-performance/availability group: This group is used for the active logs and BSDSs of the nonproduction subsystems.
- High-priority copy group: This group manages all image copies with high availability and performance requirements.
- Low-priority copy group: This group manages all image copies with low availability and performance requirements or is just a catch-all group for the other image copies.

The assignment of table-space, index-space, and recovery data sets to DFSMS classes and storage groups needs be well thought out and planned and in most cases requires strict adherence to data-set naming conventions, depending on the method used for assignment. In most cases, to implement DFSMS optimally, it is recommended that DFSMS codes defined for classes be used in the naming conventions of the index spaces and table spaces.

Note: The book does cover how to set up DFSMS naming conventions or how to implement classes and groups in DFSMS. For details on this and other DFSMS/DB2 topics, refer to the IBM Redbook SG24-5462-00 (Storage Management with DB2 for OS/390).

Reclaiming Space

DFSMS automatically reclaims space that was allocated to now unused or old (based upon specific criteria) data sets, making this space available for new allocations. You do not want to use DFSMS DEFRAG to eliminate secondary extents. Although it will work, you can easily get into trouble when running utilities that reallocate the space. As a result, you may suddenly find that a table space that previously fit into one extent is scattered all over in multiple extents or, even worse, doesn't fit in the maximum number of extents anymore.

Disk Storage

Tape versus Disk

There are different costs associated with backing up to magnetic tape and to disk. While it is less expensive to back up to tape, in a high-performance, high-availability environment tape backup can most certainly have a negative effect and prevents DB2 Version 6 from using additional parallelism in the recovery process, which affects availability.

Data-Set Allocation and Placement

With the new disk architectures, the rules we used to follow for data-set placement are less important, due to new large cache structures and log structured files (i.e., RVA devices), which do not maintain the physical location of data during updates. This makes the execution of the REORG utility less important for reclaiming fragmented space. Sequential prefetch prestages logically sequenced tracks in the cache for I/O improvement during the prefetch operation.

If you still desire to control data-set placement, DFSMS can be used to meet placement requirements of DB2 data sets. However, separation of volumes is beneficial only if you have separate paths in order to achieve high parallel transfer rates.

Extents

Even though a logical view of the data is maintained with the new devices, extents still do matter. Each extent on a disk file has different control blocks controlling access, and there is extra logic to determine the correct data area to access. In addition, there are defined thresholds for when sequential prefetch will be turned off due to the distance between two successive pages. The bottom line is that there is extra code length, one way or the other, with extents. When you are trying to reduce code, extents are just another place that can contribute some extra code.

Extended Addressability

In order to support many of the new features in DB2 Version 6, such as table spaces requiring the use of data sets larger than 4 GB (for more information on large table spaces, refer to Chapter 5, "Physical Database Objects"), DFSMS 1.5 is required.

Optimizing Data-Set Placement for Parallelism

When optimizing parallelism for SQL queries, data-set placement may play a role, depending on the hardware levels utilized. To obtain maximum parallelism across data sets, it is very important to ensure that the data sets (partitions) of the table spaces be placed on separate disk volumes (and if possible, on separate controllers). If not enough volumes are available (e.g., 50 partitions for a table space, but only 20 volumes available for the data sets), the data sets need to be placed on the volumes in a round-robin fashion (refer to Chapter 21, "Parallelism"). This allows better parallelism of the query across the data. With the new Enterprise Storage Server (ESS) hardware technology, this has become less of an issue, maybe not even an issue at all. See the section "Enterprise Storage Server" later in this chapter.

I/O Subsystem

Avoiding I/O altogether is the best option for performance. The next best option would be not to perform the I/O to disk but to cache. Many factors are involved in optimizing and eliminating I/O operations. We must first find where and why I/O occurs by monitoring the subsystem and the application, and we must then control the I/O, eliminating unnecessary I/O that adds overhead to our applications.

Understanding I/O

DB2 uses buffer pools, hiperpools, and group buffer pools to cache data and help minimize I/O to disk. (For more details on buffer pools, refer to Chapter 3.) Many disk device
storage controllers also provide an additional cache for intermediate data storage. These
controllers can perform read-ahead operations if they detect that pages are being sequentially accessed, allowing a better cache hit ratio on the device.

There are different methods of bringing pages into the DB2 virtual buffer pools
from disk. If the application needs a few pages, or just one, it performs a synchronous
(normal) read. If the application is requesting several pages with sequential prefetch, the
pages are read into the buffer pool in a single I/O, prestaging them for read operations
yet to come. This is known as a asynchronous read and often occurs concurrently with
the application process. Dynamic prefetch can occur at execution time, which provides
the same basic process as sequential prefetch and gets invoked when a process called
sequential detection has determined that the pages are being accessed in sequential
order. The last method is list prefetch. This method operates with a RID (row identifier)
list that is built from the index. The RIDs are sorted, and then the pages can be accessed
in order.

The prefetch operations are limited by the characteristics of the buffer pools. Be
careful when defining the size of your buffer pools; you can inadvertently cause more I/O,
because the prefetch operation quantity is directly related to the buffer pool size. Normal
prefetch I/O (for 4K pages) is 32 pages per I/O. If your buffer pool is less than 1,000
pages, you may be getting only 16 or 8 pages per I/O, depending on the exact size, so you
would be doing more I/O if your buffer pool is too small. Note that the prefetch quantities
vary by page size as well.

There are also various methods for writing data out to disk after it has been updated.
The majority of writes from DB2 are done asynchronously, independently of the applications. For information on when writes occur, see Chapter 3, "Memory." The other type of
write is the synchronous write, which causes an application to wait for the completion of
the write. Synchronous writes can occur when exception conditions are encountered, such
as when passing two DB2 checkpoints in a unit of work before an updated page is externalized, or when the virtual buffer pool that was holding the updated page is too small or
its immediate write threshold is reached.

Logging also is a source of I/O operations that needs to be monitored and controlled.
Information on logging is provided later in this chapter.

I/O Scheduling Priority

DB2 can schedule single-page synchronous read and write I/O, sequential prefetch, list sequential prefetch, and sequential detection using the application address space's I/O scheduling priority. In order to use this facility, MVS I/O priority scheduling must be enabled by specifying IOQ=PRTY in the IEAIPSxx member of SYS1.PARMLIB.

The IOP parameter must also be used to set the I/O priority for the address space of a performance group. The IOP parameter is in the IEAIPSxx member of SYS1.PARMLIB. When these settings are used, the I/O scheduling priority for asynchronous write I/O is determined by DBM1 address space. This is the strategy that is recommended for organizations that need to favor OLTP systems over other address spaces for I/O processing.

Cache Considerations

In order to avoid excessive I/O, it is important to take advantage of all the caching abilities available in both DB2 and the disk I/O subsystem. DB2's internal caching abilities come mainly through the implementation of buffer pools (virtual, hiper, and group). There are also options in DB2 to help optimize use of external cache.

SEQCACH

The DSNZPARM SEQCACH gives us the ability to control DB2's interaction with the disk I/O subsystem's cache when performing read operations. There are two options for this parameter: SEQ or BYPASS. BYPASS is the default and was often the preferred option with older, second-generation disk controllers because their cache storage was rather small. However, with newer disk controllers with larger cache, the SEQ option is better because it allows DB2 to use the disk caching for sequential operations (sequential prefetch and dynamic prefetch, but not list prefetch). The performance gains from using this parameter vary, based on the model, the size of the cache, and the brand of the hardware.

In order for the cache to be effective in most cases, it needs to be large. If the cache is not large enough or if there is extensive use of the cache by concurrent processes, for example, it is possible to overload the cache and degrade system performance. One very important situation to watch for is large sorts, as they can easily overload the cache. It is generally better to allocate work files to volumes where cache is disabled.

Enterprise Storage Server (ESS)

Not only is more and more disk storage required, but with all the new styles of processing (legacy, e-business, business intelligence) and with the integration of many types of platforms, more sophisticated storage hardware is required. The Enterprise Storage Server (ESS) from IBM is a smart data storage device, introducing appliance-like intelligent storage, which can be served by a storage area network (SAN). This means that we have a new style of disk device that can provide storage for heterogeneous servers and platforms (S/390 with OS/390, RS/6000 with AIX, others with UNIX, and so on) at the highest level of performance. But the importance of this to the DB2 world is that almost everything changes when it comes to placement of data and how data is served to DB2, because with the S/390 new performance features can significantly reduce execution times.

An ESS hardware solution can provide up to 11 TB of storage with 16 3990 control unit images, providing up to 256 devices per control unit image (4,096 volumes) and 2,048 logical paths mapped over 32 ESCON ports. Also, there can be up to 16 fiber channel ports, providing support for FICON for the S/390 servers, which is the newest and fastest method of transferring data. Data is striped across RAID ranks (a rank is a collection of disks), which achieves significantly high device performance.

Features Benefiting DB2

For DB2 there are many benefits to using an ESS for high-performance systems because there are advanced features that work in DB2's favor. Parallel enhancements require significantly fewer resources than with previous devices, up to seven times less hardware investment. The ESS implements something called PAV (parallel access volume), which allows multiple concurrent I/O on a given device and multiple partitions of a table space on the same volume without any perceivable loss of performance. This works well with DFSMS, in that it is possible to turn over almost complete control of data storage to DFSMS and ESS. This was not possible in the past; if partitions were on the same volumes before, IOSQ (I/O subsystem queue) times would be high, which in most cases doubled the elapsed time for a query. This PAV feature in conjunction with another feature called multiple allegiance allows concurrent access to the same volumes from different systems and almost eliminates IOSQ and PEND time, yielding lower elapsed time for transactions and queries. This is especially critical in data sharing, where without the ESS one member must wait for another member's I/O to complete before it can start its work.

The interaction between large DB2 buffer pools and controller cache has been eliminated by the ESS. When a large buffer pool is used, most often controller cache hit ratio for synchronous reads is poor. The read misses in the cache can become a problem, increasing the time it takes to service the request. In the ESS, the disk arrays comprise seven disks, which, when used in conjunction with the PAV feature, can be used to dramatically increase the throughput to a device.

Heavy update workloads, large query processing, and DB2 utilities all have performance gains when using the ESS. Of course, it is very important to complete all other tuning strategies prior to using the ESS. With a large workload of heavy update/insert/delete activity, the deferred write queue thresholds are constantly exceeded, causing heavy random I/O updates to the database. Workloads trying to read data during this time are delayed behind the writes that have been queued to the unit. The accumulated time for these delays is shown in IOSQ time. But in the ESS, with the combination of I/O priority queuing and PAVs, the read data requests are satisfied while the writes are continuing. The same performance benefit occurs when checkpoints cause the updated buffers to be flushed out to disk. The ESS comes with a larger sequential bandwidth and can complete large queries much more rapidly than previous I/O subsystems. The features also significantly reduce elapsed times for utilities. Elapsed times for reorganizations, image copies, and loads often are reduced by more than 50%. With the movement toward high availability and shorter windows for maintenance, the ESS can be a major component in the solution.

Tuning I/O and Caching

I/O, from a DB2 perspective, is the movement between the buffer pool and disk. However, a little more is involved with the additional I/O operations, and there are many areas for performance degradation and improvement. These areas include the paths from the hosts to the storage server, the caching of the storage server, and the internal activity between the cache and the physical server.

In order to monitor I/O, a DB2 monitor such as DB2PM can be used. Statistics for the various read and write operations can be viewed. You can view these statistics in total for the subsystem or by individual buffer pool. When attempting to tune a process that appears to be I/O bound, you need to have the objects separated into their own buffer pools so that you can properly analyze the operations against the data and indexes used by the application. For more information, refer to Chapter 3, "Memory." You can also easily view, by data set, the delays caused by I/O operations by performing a `DISPLAY BUFFERPOOL DETAIL` command.

When you monitor cache hits, it is important to understand what *cache hit* means. A cache hit occurs when the requested record is found in the cache, a memory resource of the storage server, and this cache hit takes a small amount of time for reads/writes and data transfer. Data not found in the cache (a cache read/write miss) requires the same response time as noncached data. A high cache hit rate provides faster I/O response time, because the number of accesses to the disk is minimized.

Performance of cached data depends on the reference of other records in the same track and the amount of re-reference of the same record. These dependencies are directly related to the application process. DB2 monitors can report I/O activity against a variety of page sets. For each buffer pool, you can report such activities as I/O request, prefetch reads, writes, and castouts.

Another way to monitor I/O performance is through the SMF (System Management Facility) 42-6 record. This record reports I/O activity by data sets. Information in the record includes

- Volume number
- Access intensity (I/O rate $\times$ disk response)
- Disk response time (average)
- I/O rate
- Connect and disconnect time (average)
- Ratio of reads to writes
- Pending time (average)
- Number of I/O operations
- Overall cacheable I/O
- Read cache hits
- Write cacheable I/O
- Fast write cache hits
- Number of sequential I/O operations
- Record cache read requests

You should monitor these records for peak workloads and identify the most critical data sets and those most in need of performance help. It is easy to identify these data sets, because the records can be sorted by access intensity, which brings to the top the most active data sets. These are the ones to focus on. The cache read hits can be measured as follows:

- 50% or greater—high
- 20–50%—medium
- 0–20%—low

A very high activity cache read hit percentage for a data set means that the data is frequently referenced; if you have enough central or expanded storage available, consider increasing the buffer pool that supports this data set. A low hit percentage points toward more random access and low reference. If you have a low cache hit percentage and the access intensity is high, consider placing the objects defined by these data sets in their own buffer pool, separate from those with high cache hit percentages.

You can look at a few more fields in the SMF 42-6 record to help tune I/O and buffer pools. As a quick example using Figure 1.1, which shows just a few fields from an example report, you can quickly observe that there is probably a problem with V10001 because it has very high queuing and response times. This is usually a problem with the volume having a heavy workload. Another observation is that the read-to-write ratio and cache hit rate are very high for the data set TBSP02DS. A large buffer pool with a high write threshold would be best for this page set because its pages are highly re-referenced. This would help decrease the high I/O rate.

I/O and Caching Summary

The balancing of the buffer pools, the cache, and the type of disk can result in a 50-fold decrease in elapsed time for an I/O-bound job, depending on the situation.

Data Set ID	VOLSER	Access Intensity	I/O Rate	RESP	QUE	CON	R/W	CHIT
TBSP1DS	V10001	0.457	11.01	52.3	32.0	1.7	2.4	40.1
TBSP2DS	V10007	0.334	6.01	10.1	8.9	1.4	91.5	69.1

Figure 1.1   SMF 42-6 Output Example

The more you can do to reduce I/O, the better. One way to reduce I/O that is not discussed in this chapter is to push the logic of the application into SQL and let the DB2 engine do the processing, eliminating excessive I/O to retrieve data only to process it in the program. This is further discussed in Chapter 10, General Application Design.

Compression

DB2 introduced data compression back in Version 3. Data quantities in tables had just begun a dramatic increase, and I/O subsystem storage was becoming a significant part of the cost of a DB2 system. Since that time, data storage cost has fallen dramatically, and newer devices that also compress and cache data under the control of unit processors have changed the issue. Many organizations have stopped looking at DB2 data compression as a feature, while others are still operating under the myth that DB2 compression is always beneficial. The true story is that DB2 data compression can be a major player in improved performance and storage savings, but also can have a negative effect on performance by relying too heavily on the CPU and by increasing disorganization in certain types of tables.

DB2 Compression Methods

There are actually two methods used for DB2 compression. One is software compression, which is delivered as part of the DB2 product. This software compression should never be used on purpose in a production environment, as it is incredibly CPU intensive. It is okay to use for evaluation or as a backup in case the other method fails, which is unlikely. This other method is implemented through IBM's synchronous data-compression hardware. Most of the current generation of machines, both IBM's and other vendor's, have this feature, although each implements it in a slightly different fashion. Even at the microcode level among the different vendors, the difference is negligible. When DB2 starts, it looks at an OS/390 control block called the CVT (communications vector table). If the CVTCMPSH indicator bit is turned on in CVT field FLAG2, DB2 uses hardware compression, meaning that it issues the machine instruction for hardware compression. If for some reason that instruction fails, upon sensing the error, DB2 resorts to software compression.

The DB2 compression is based on the Lempel-Ziv-Welch algorithm, which is a dictionary-based algorithm similar to the familiar zip format on the PC; if you zip a group of files and then unzip them, you should notice that unzipping is considerably faster than zipping. The same is true for the DB2 compression: more CPU overhead is used to compress the data than to decompress it. It is important to understand just how this compression works, at least conceptually. Processes build a nonadaptive static dictionary of the most common recurring patterns of data. Once the dictionary is built, it is optimized. Basically, a larger-than-allowed dictionary can be constructed using the most frequently occurring patterns. The algorithm by default reduces the dictionary tree to 1,024 nodes. It is rumored that there are ways to change this default number, but I am not aware of anyone who has attempted it. Once the dictionary has been optimized, the data can be compressed.

What Is and Is Not Compressed

Only application table-space page sets are subject to compression. Index spaces, the catalog, the directory, and the work files are not subject to compression. In addition, not all the data in a table space is compressed. The compression dictionary, which is stored in the table space, is not compressed, and neither are the space map pages, header information for the table space, or individual pages. The unit of compression is not a page, as was true with older algorithms, but a data row. Even data rows are not always compressed, since DB2 does not compress any row that cannot be compressed to a shorter length than the original. A flag bit in the row prefix is used to indicate that a row is compressed. Figure 1.2 shows compressed page and row format. Since a row may or may not be compressed, compression should never be used as an encryption method for security or any other reason. Even if a row is marked as compressed, that only means that there is compressed data somewhere in the row. Since the compression method depends on repetitive data, a lot of data contained in rows is not likely to be compressed. Figure 1.3 is a high-level diagram that gives you a general idea of how the compression dictionary works. The dictionary is shown as an abstract set of trees, where each tree has a root node from the 256-character alphabet. Each node on the tree represents a string, with the node number actually showing the end of the string. In the figure, you can see the tree under the character C with limbs for

CALIFORNIA—node 275

CALL

COLUMN

COLUMBIA

COLD—node 264

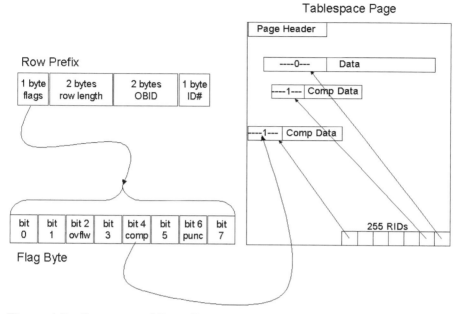

Figure 1.2   Compressed Page Format

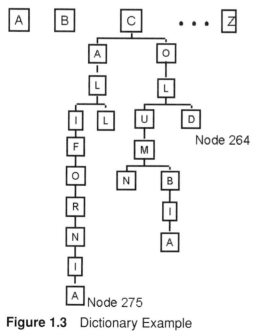

Figure 1.3   Dictionary Example

The dictionary is really made up of two parts: a fixed number of alphabet entries and a variable number of dictionary entries. Each node can be represented by 12 bits. The actual number of entries in the dictionary is either 512, 1,024, 2,048, 4,096, or 8,192, but in most cases, with normal data volume it is 4,096. As new data rows are added or existing rows are updated, the data in the row must be matched against existing tree limbs to see if there is a node that can replace the string in the data row. For example, assuming that there are rows that contain the data in our example tree, in the output compressed row, 12 bits for node 275 would represent CALIFORNIA, and 12 bits for node 264 would represent COLD, that is, in effect, 3 bytes of compressed data (24 bits) instead of 14 bytes of decompressed data.

The matching of inserted or updated data against the existing tree obviously require some code length and therefore add some CPU overhead, but it is truly minimal when using hardware-assisted compression. Compare this to the overhead when the row is read, however. When an indicator in the row shows that the following data is a dictionary entry (e.g., 275), as the row is expanded, the 275 is simply replaced with entry 275 from the dictionary. That is a very short code length and is negligible in terms of CPU overhead. Data is more often fetched than manipulated, and that is why this algorithm represents a very good tradeoff for performance.

Performance Issues

Once compression has been enabled for either a table space or a partition by changing or altering the DDL, there are many issues regarding compression and performance, and each of these is examined in the following sections:

Expectations

Disk device compression

Binding and access paths

Compression ratio

Data disorganization

CPU overhead

Locking impacts

Logging impacts

Expectations

DB2 compression is used for two reasons: storage savings and I/O improvement. Compression can be used so that more rows fit onto a page, allowing you to store more data on the same amount of disk. Fitting more rows on a page allows better performance when reading data and a better hit ratio in the buffer pools. In some instances, compression can be less than optimal, depending on the usage of the data. Like any technique, it should be tested for both scenarios. Some organizations thought compression would only incur overhead and not provide the expected benefit due to the heavily random nature of the processing, but testing proved the exact opposite. Dynamic prefetch was invoked, and the dramatic reduction in I/O cut the elapsed time by over 50%, with no perceivable increase in CPU time. As usual, it depends.

Virtual Buffer Pool Impact All data pages belonging to the compressed table space are still compressed in the buffer pool. When rows are inserted or updated, they are stored compressed in the buffer pool. Rows are decompressed only as they are processed on behalf of the requesting application. For any compressed table space, less space is required in the buffer pool, so not only is disk storage possibly saved, but memory for the buffer pools is saved. Additionally, since there are now more rows on a page and more rows in the buffer pool, hit ratio is potentially improved. Hiperpools, buffer pools in data spaces, and global buffer pools also realize this advantage.

Storage Improvement As a general rule, it is safe to say that 40% to 50% savings are average. But savings of what? If that number is of pages saved, 40% to 50% fewer pages need to be processed. Disk storage could be another matter, because most disk subsystems today support an additional hardware compression technique. The bottom line here is to expect disk storage savings that can be very dramatic.

The following story explains the relationship of storage size to compression. There was a table that was compressed in testing. The total volume of the table was calculated, and disk storage was ordered to meet the requirement, almost 750 TB. The disk storage was the RVA type, which was generally sized at 4 to 1—100 cylinders of data could be stored in 25 cylinders due to the internal hardware compression. However, when loading started for the production data, that ratio was not achieved. The organization experienced only about a 2-to-1 ratio. The problem was that the 4-to-1 ratio was based on raw data, not DB2 compressed data, for which the average compression is 2 to 1, and even less in some cases. Caveat emptor!

I/O Improvement   I/O is where you should expect the most benefit. In most cases, I/O should be reduced as more data is read and written per I/O. This yields higher buffer page hits because more data is held in memory. The more the data is accessed sequentially, the bigger the benefit. On certain tables, there may be little or no benefit if the data is always accessed randomly without any underlying sequential retrieval (dynamic prefetch).

One area to pay close attention to is data rows that are very long. When the data rows are compressed, there may be no improvement in the number of rows on the page because the length of the compressed row is still quite large. But if these were moved to 8K or 16K page sizes and then compressed, the benefit could be large. This again depends on whether processing of the data is sequential or random.

Device Compression

Newer disk storage devices and subsystems normally compress data by a 4-to-1 ratio (25 real cylinders emulate 100 logical cylinders). When you use ESA compression for DB2, which puts more dense data on a single page, the ratio on these disk devices drops to an average of 2 to 1 (25 real cylinders emulate 50 logical cylinders). These two methods of compression cannot be compared, as they provide entirely different benefits. They are compatible and in most cases should be used together.

Effects on Access Paths

When compression is turned off or on, the number of rows per page changes, and this affects the calculation used by the optimizer in determining access paths, since fewer rows are now transferred per I/O. Most of the time, although you will not see any change, this dependency exists. Therefore, if you turn compression on or off on a table space, any plans or packages that depended on those objects must be rebound.

There is one other time that rebinding might be necessary, and that is if the percentage of rows compressed changes significantly, since this can also affect query optimization. We have witnessed only a couple of access path changes. In the first, list prefetch was selected after compression. The density of the rows changed the ratio of access over the cardinality to such a degree that the access path changed. In the other case, dynamic prefetch was used, due to the closer proximity of the rows. But in general, we see very few changes that could possibly be attributed to selecting from very few possible access paths.

Compression Ratio

Both REORG and LOAD build compression dictionaries. For best performance, use only the REORG dictionary. While there are cases where the level of compression is the same, the difference tends to increase the larger and more partitioned the tables get. The percentage of compressed rows after a REORG is greater for several reasons. The way that the compression dictionary is built during the execution of the REORG utility always provides the best possible dictionary, and this dictionary is always better than the one built during the LOAD utility. Also, after a table is compressed, there is normally data maintenance (inserts, updates, deletes) that do not necessarily match the existing dictionary. As these updates accumulate in the table, the percentage of rows actually compressed goes down. It is better to have a ratio decrease from a REORG dictionary than from a LOAD dictionary.

To measure the benefits you are achieving by compression, you can look in the DB2 catalog. The column PAGESAVE in the table SYSTABLEPART shows the percentage of pages saved in either the table space or the partition. This percentage should be monitored, and if it moves downward, the dictionary is becoming less effective, and perhaps it is time to rebuild. The column PCTROWCOMP in the tables SYSTABLES (table level) and SYSTABSTATS (partition level) shows the percentage of rows that are compressed. This percentage is used by the optimizer during access path selection and helps determine CPU cost.

One small note regarding the statistics collection for a compressed table space: RUNSTATS always decompresses each row. If your data is not changing that dramatically and no statistics are really changing, why run RUNSTATS? The logging implications are discussed in Chapter 5, but it is worth noting here that using compression on a DB2 table causes logging according to the rules for variable length rows, but the data is compressed, so the log records are smaller. While this is not a problem itself, there are other performance considerations. Benchmark time again!

Data Disorganization

Indirect references, where an index points to one page but instead of a row there is a pointer to another page, can cause serious degradation under certain circumstances. Basically, two GETPAGEs instead of one are required, which could in many cases cause two I/O operations, one of them probably synchronous. This is a potential problem with the compressed page format. When performing updates to rows, two situations can cause data to become disorganized and to increase the NEARINDREF and FARINDREF:

- Updates to variable character columns in a table
- Updates to tables in compressed table spaces

When a row's length changes, it might increase in size due to an increase in the length of a variable-length column, and when compression is used, it can have the same effect on the storage of the data. The updated row cannot fit on the current page, so it is relocated to a page that has the space required. On the original page, the row points to the RID (row ID) on the page now storing the data. If that page is within 32 pages of the original page, the NEARINDREF count increases. If it is not stored within 32 pages, the FARINDREF count increases.

In most situations, this is not a significant problem, assuming that free space has been increased to minimize the impact. But, we have seen one situation where the increase in indirect references degrades performance considerably. A certain type of table, called various names, stores temporal data that will be edited, validated, and eventually used to populate the primary operational tables. This short-lived data can be volatile. The more volatility, the greater the increase in the indirect references, and eventually the process to retrieve the data to populate the permanent tables requires twice as many GETPAGEs and perhaps twice the I/O. The information in figure 1.4 shows this more dramatically. In this particular case, the updated data was eventually removed by using INSERT into SELECT, which would require two GETPAGEs for the number of entries in the indirect reference columns. It is safe to assume that the far indirect reference will result in two physical I/O operations.

CPU Overhead

While this point has been mentioned several times already, it is worth repeating: where the hardware assists compression, there is generally negligible increase in CPU overhead. Rows inserted and updated incur a small penalty, but rows fetched incur very little. Scanning a table repeatedly certainly incurs measurable overhead, but the highest CPU increase we have measured at production sites was about 3%. This was in a fairly normal OLTP environment and holds true for the majority of cases. The bottom line is not to fear CPU overhead but, at the same time, run a valid test to measure the results.

Indirect	Refs			Row	Count
Near	Increase	Far	Increase	# Rows	Increase
0		0		6,606,093	0
38,622	38,622	82,048	82,048	6,967,418	361,325
38,638	16	185,339	103,291	6,977,109	9,691
38,645	7	243,914	58,575	6,988,602	11,493

Figure 1.4　Compression and Indirect References

Locking Impacts

While the possibility of an impact on locking is very remote, it needs to be mentioned. In certain situations where the density of the rows increases considerably on a page, concurrency could become a problem. Normal performance measurement and tuning rules apply.

Logging

Every system has some component that eventually becomes the final bottleneck. Logging is not to be overlooked when trying to get one more transaction through the system in a high-performance environment. Logging can be tuned and refined, but the synchronous I/O will always be there. We control logging and response time in various ways, depending on the issue we are trying to address. Logging is affected by several factors. Following is a list of the key people responsible for the various aspects of the logging process.

1. The table designer determines the size of the records written to the log via table/column design.
2. The data designer determines the size of the records written to the log.
3. The application programmer determines the size of the records written to the log.
4. The application designer determines the commit frequency.
5.   The DBA determines the size and number of log buffers.

It appears that the greatest percentage of logging overhead is in the application developer's hand. For information on how to tune areas 1 and 2, refer to Chapter 5, "Physical Database Objects," and for tuning 3 and 4, refer to Section 4, "Application Design and Tuning." Here we focus on what the system administrator and database administrator can do to improve the performance of the logging process.

Log Reads

When DB2 needs to read from the log, it is important that the reads perform well because reads are normally performed during recovery, restarts, and rollbacks—processes that you do not want taking forever. An input buffer must be dedicated for every process requesting a log read. DB2 first looks for the record in the log output buffer. If it finds the record there, it can apply it directly from the output buffer. If the record is not in the output buffer, DB2 looks for it in the active log data set and then in the archive log data set. When the record is found, it is moved to the input buffer so that it can be read by the requesting process. You can monitor the success of reads from the output buffers and active logs in the statistics report (figure 1.5). These reads are the better performers. If the record has to be read from the archive log, the processing time is extended. For this reason, it is important to have large output buffers and active logs. You also should make sure that you have a large enough input buffer; the default of 60 K is usually adequate.

Log Writes

Applications move log records to the log output buffer using two methods: no wait or force (figure 1.6). The no-wait method moves the log record to the output buffer and returns control to the application; however, if no output buffers are available, the application waits. If

LOG ACTIVITY	QUANTITY
READS SATISFIED-OUTPUT BUFFER	109011
READS SATISFIED-OUTP. BUF(%)	100
READS SATISFIED-ACTIVE LOG	0
READS SATISFIED-ACTV.LOG(%)	0
READS SATISFIED-ARCHIVE LOG	0
READS SATISFIED-ARCH.LOG(%)	0
TAPE VOLUME CONTENTION WAIT	0
WRITE-NOWAIT	5678K
WRITE OUTPUT LOG BUFFERS	**822K**
BSDS ACCESS REQUESTS	3
UNAVAILABLE OUTPUT LOG BUFFER	**0**
CONTR. INTERV. CREATED-ACTIVE	34902
ARCHIVE LOG READ ALLOCATION	0
ARCHIVE LOG WRITE ALLOCAT.	0
CONTR. INTERV. OFFLOADED-ARCH	23904

Figure 1.5   Log Statistics

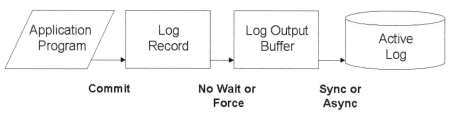

Figure 1.6 Log Writes

this happens, it can be observed in the statistics report when the UNAVAILABLE OUT-PUT LOG BUFFER (figure 1.5) has a nonzero value. This means that DB2 had to wait to externalize log records due to the fact that there were no available output log buffers. Successful moves without a wait are recorded in the statistics report under NOWAIT requests.

A force occurs at commit time, and the application waits during this process, which is considered a synchronous write.

Log records are then written from the output buffers to the active log data sets on disk either synchronously or asynchronously. To know how often this occurs, you can look at the WRITE OUTPUT LOG BUFFERS in the statistics report.

There are a few options to improve the performance of log writes. First, we can increase the number of output buffers available for writing active log data sets. The size of the output buffer can be 40K to 400,000K (in Version 6). It can be changed in DSNZPARM OUTBUFF. You should increase this if you see that buffers are unavailable. A large buffer improves performance for log reads and writes.

Active Logs

Sizing

You should make your active logs large enough that they do not interfere with other processes. If your active log data sets are too small, active log switches occur often. When an active log switch takes place, a checkpoint is taken automatically. Even if your write thresholds (DWQT/VDQWT) are set properly, as well as your checkpoints, you may still see an unwanted write problem. Your logs could be driving excessive checkpoint processing, resulting in constant writes. This would prevent you from achieving a high ratio of pages written per I/O, because the deferred write queue in the buffer pool would not be allowed to fill properly.

Dual Logs/Placement

Your active log should reside on a fast device, because if you have a high write I/O rate, you could directly affect the response time of your application. You also want to avoid disk contention on the devices where the active log data sets reside. In order to do this, you should have separate access paths for the primary and secondary active log data sets and define these data sets on dedicated volumes. The logs should be placed on disk devices that are on the same channel or controller, where other busy data sets do not exist. The system logs are critical for performance. The commit process waits for a successful write to the active log, and if there is contention on the logs, performance suffers.

You need a minimum of three volumes of the active data sets so that you can have sequential sets of active log data sets on different access paths and avoid contention during the log archive process.

Archive Logs

It is best to have your archive logs on disk, not on tape if possible. A recovery process with archive logs on tape would have to serialize with all other processes needing to read the tape. You cannot run multiple recovery jobs in parallel if the archive logs are on tape, and of course you have the normal tape processing drawbacks (mounting, rewinding, etc.). If you must archive to cartridge, make sure that you fill up the cartridge (about 200 MB for a normal cartridge). Also, make sure that you have enough active logs to allow archive failure or large rollbacks. In order not to introduce a single point of failure, the active logs have to be dual. A minimum for a system log is $200 \times 2 \times 3 = 1200$ MB. They should be large enough to keep archiving as low as possible; the appropriate size depends on the amount of system activity.

CPU

T uning CPU in the non-DB2 world is very different from tuning CPU for DB2. For DB2, CPU consumption tends to be controlled mostly by the applications; however, this often gets overlooked. If we remember that DB2 is just a server, albeit a very powerful one, we must also take responsibility for its resource consumption. As you can see in Chapter 3, "Memory," and Chapter 1, "I/O and Storage Management," when it comes to managing memory and I/O, the systems area is primarily responsible for the tuning efforts. But when it comes to CPU resource consumption, although there are some issues that the systems area can address, this is primarily an application issue, as will be evident in various topics throughout this book. In this chapter we examine some of the most common areas where CPU overhead can be reduced, but in reality, almost every topic covered in this book reduces CPU consumption to some degree.

CPU and SQL Design Issues

The primary areas of CPU consumption exist in the use of SQL and application design. All the issues discussed in this chapter can lead to extensive unnecessary resource consumption, and all are major tuning points for the most CPU reduction. In this chapter we bring to light the issue of just how important SQL is in terms of CPU usage. Each of the different resolutions depends on the structure and use of the individual applications, since the approach for a warehouse transaction might be different from that for an OLTP transaction.

All the categories and examples in this section are looked at in detail in chapters to follow, but here we set the stage for why the tuning of applications is critical for reducing CPU. Generally, it is either application CPU time or DB2 CPU time on behalf of an application that is excessive. In this chapter we look specifically at CPU use and consumption by various activities in the system.

Number of SQL Statements

The number of SQL statements issued can be a very significant consumer of resources, especially when they are repetitive and retrieve data from the same row. Quite often this is directly related to poor design and ineffective usage guidelines. Some code generators repeatedly ask for the same row but different columns through the course of a single process. For example, this is a scenario that we call "Have you seen Jones?" The logic of the program issues a SELECT for several columns from Jones's row and proceeds through some logic. Then a check is made to see if Jones's data will fall through for the major path or drop out the side, where the process will simply complete or get another account. Most of the time, the process continues, and another SELECT is issued for more columns from Jones's row. Another check is made to see if Jones's data will continue down the major path or drop out the side. Then another check is made, and so on. At one company, we have seen this occur for every account processed during an online day. Over 90% of the time more than five SELECTs, sometimes as many as seven SELECTS, were issued against the same row.

The staff members who were monitoring the subsystem were delighted, because they saw a wonderful hit ratio on the account table, as would be expected since there were five to seven GETPAGEs issued for the five to seven SELECTS for the same page, which was definitely staying cached in memory. There are several problems with this scenario:

1. Each unnecessary call was additional overhead for the entry and exit code surrounding a call to DB2.
2. Each time a call was made, not only was the data page requested, but there were redundant GETPAGEs to the index also, all totally unnecessary, that caused additional I/O due to the activity in the system on the index.
3. Each SELECT had to use the same three columns to drive the index, so an average of 18 extra predicates were processed.

4. Each time DB2 was unnecessarily servicing this redundant request, it was not able to use those resources for truly necessary requests.

This last point is critical to make clear to all developers: when DB2 is performing unnecessary work, it cannot perform necessary work, and it is not the issuer of the SQL statement that gets punished, but rather the others on the system that are waiting for those resources.

The net effect of fixing unnecessary SQL statements can be seen by the following metrics, which were common in this case and others that used a particular code generator.

- Average of 21 transactions per second
- Average of six SELECTs for the same row (five unnecessary)
- 16-hour average online day
- $21 \times 5 \times 60 \times 60 \times 16 = 6,048,000$ unnecessary calls to DB2
- $6,048,000 \times 15 = 90,720,000$ extra predicates processed
- $6,048,000 \times 3 = 18,144,000$ GETPAGEs (some requiring I/O)

In summary, put a millisecond number to any of those figures, add a few microseconds for the additional I/O, and see what the savings could be if this process was changed. Put another way, figure out how many more transactions, sales, or produced widgets could have occurred by using those resources productively.

Unfortunately, that is not the end of this story, as some locking occurred on some of the data being processed, adding to the overhead as well. Where there was locking, there was a lot of time spent waiting for those locks by other processes, so that's even more overhead to add. These are the applications that see five times the amount of work go through the system when tuned, and such tuning is not difficult to do.

Part of the difficulty is that the process is implemented as it was diagramed and supplied to the tool. It is exceedingly difficult to get high performance when the code has to be programmed to follow a logical path instead of a path that considers performance factors.

Number of Rows Retrieved

The actual number of rows that need to be updated, inserted, or deleted in an application is based on a combination of design and business requirements, which are physical design issues. However, the actual number of rows retrieved is generally more a programming and SQL issue, since it basically comes down to where the rows are filtered from the result set required. The overhead for retrieving one additional row can be very high, depending on how many times it is done, similar to the SQL statement overhead scenario discussed in the preceding section. Every unneeded row that is brought to a program generally causes the following unnecessary events to occur:

- GETPAGEs, which might require additional I/O for both data and index
- Movement of the columns selected from the page buffer into a work area
- Passing the work area through to stage 2
- Transferring the data cross-memory to the program
- Extra code execution in the program to test whether or not to filter

This is actually the short list describing some of the areas of higher overhead in resource consumption. There are many different reasons that programs retrieve unneeded rows and many design issues that affect the proper solution, but here we are concerned only with checking whether unnecessary retrieval occurs and planning to change it.

One simple technique to find out whether unneeded row retrieval is occurring is to verify code by looking for IF statements after an SQL statement that do filtering that should have been done within the SQL. Many times we see prefetch enabled when a single row is retrieved and when simple existence checking is performed. Another way to view this problem that requires more overhead is by using a performance trace to show the number of rows that were qualified in stage 1 and stage 2 and those returned to the program. By matching the results from the traces to the application program requirements, large discrepancies tend to jump off the page.

Number of Columns Retrieved

Every column selected has to be moved from the buffer pool to a user work area, which gets passed through stage 2 and eventually passed cross-memory to the application memory area. Even though there are times when individual columns are passed together in a single cross-memory call, it is best to view this as one cross-memory move per column, as this is generally the case. There is also overhead when all the columns "retrieved" get to the stage 2 relational data services layer in DB2 only to be filtered out; in many cases that could have been done in the stage 1 data manager layer.

This overhead is illustrated in this scenario. We know how much it costs to retrieve a single row and return it to the application. Suppose that row had 30 columns in it; that would be similar to one column retrieved unnecessarily 30 times.

This is an area for significant CPU reduction in some cases, and it is very easy to prove that this is a problem in almost every application. When an application is being coded, the SQL most often has to be completed to some degree first. This is especially true for SQL SELECTs, since they retrieve the data that the rest of the code will use. So let us assume that an application selects 17 columns in 17 host-program structures. But if you examine that code more closely, you might find that only 12 or 16 of the actual host variables ever get used during the process. Even one extra column is one column always retrieved for no reason, consuming CPU unnecessarily.

This cannot be discovered by using programs or queries to see if the plan or package has a dependency on a column. This cannot be determined by tools that analyze the code, since the column is "used." It cannot be determined by a tool that traps and traces the host variable that received the column value, since the entire use of the variable could be to simply move it to another variable that also never gets used. A host variable trace tool cannot determine it, since the data could have been moved into a structure comprising many variables.

We have polled a large number of people at conferences and seminars, and to this day the percentage of places that certify that no unnecessary columns are retrieved is less than 0.01%. In addition, every time we have taught application developers SQL, they have agreed that in many cases columns are retrieved into host variables that never get used. They also admit to not going back and removing them, mostly due to time constraints or because they just did not consider it an issue.

Unnecessary Repetitive Processes

Many times when performing a performance audit, we find a critical process that is repeated for every occurrence of an event. For example, one organization in the transportation industry, a railroad, was doing scheduling for boxcars. This is a complex process; trains are built, broken apart, and reorganized as boxcars for customers move across the system. When putting a train together, the selection of each boxcar's route is based on many factors. In this particular process, SQL accessed many tables, and each boxcar drove the process. This system had been in production for quite a while and was considered acceptable until a CPU transaction audit was done. High CPU usage was expected for this process, but not to the degree that was found. A very simple change reduced the overhead by a significant number of MIPS.

When the process was designed, it seemed straightforward by the business rules, and it was: there was nothing wrong with the way it was implemented. But the small change—checking whether the next boxcar was going to the same place for the same customer as the last one—resulted in a significant reduction in processing (over 10 MIPS), since this particular railroad generally moved an extremely large number of cars for most of its customers. No knowledge of this was given to the programmer when the code was written. The programmer was given only the input, process, and output specifications. For performance, we need much more than just that basic type of information. Entire orders for additional mainframes have been suspended for a year by performance audits. Even though what the system delivers is acceptable, it might not being delivering it efficiently enough.

Referential Integrity

Implementation of referential integrity (RI) may have implications from a CPU resource perspective, especially when RI is used across the board without performance certification, that is, as a design default method. This applies to both defined (declarative) and application program RI, where all the relationship checking is done in the program code.

DB2 declarative RI is phenomenally efficient and uses all sorts of techniques to avoid unnecessary overhead, but that does not mean that it is efficient in every case. When declarative RI is used, in one or two places it can still be potentially abusive, such as when an extremely large number of child rows are inserted for a single parent or when a cascade delete goes down many levels in a parent-child hierarchy, with each level having a larger number of deletes. When application RI is used, it generally is not efficient at all for a high-performance application. Application RI requires SQL in the application to do the interrogation as if it were just normal SQL not using any specific techniques. Quite often the existence-checking SQL causes many GETPAGEs and much physical I/O just to see if something exists. But we are not concerned so much with the SQL here as with the all-or-nothing philosophy and its inherent overhead. Many application code generators allow only one or the other to be used for all situations.

We need to be precise in the design and use of RI, deciding which type to use in each specific instance, and we should be prepared to change the type, since enhancements in systems can dramatically change the ratio of data covered by a parent-child relationship.

There are no hard and fast rules for making the RI process decision, except "Don't *always* do it one way." Previous guidelines for RI simply don't apply anymore, such as don't use declarative RI if it covers more than three levels in a hierarchy, and don't use declarative RI if more than a hundred child inserts are done for a single parent. This last guideline is still followed but is far out of date. DB2 uses several techniques to speed the various RI checks; the most important is that RI checks are done inside DB2, not with data or SQL from an application. Triggers can be also used for effective application-controlled RI, while declarative RI can be used in other situations. Sometimes it is very important to break apart large RI structures, so declarative RI is used in some cases and application RI in others. We cover various other solutions when we discuss code tables and application design. The issues are that RI can consume unnecessary amounts of CPU and that a specific process needs to be in place to evaluate which type is used, where it is used, and whether it is coded and certified.

Sorting

Many sorts are unneeded and yet never get removed or corrected. Many times an index not only can do away with the sort but can dramatically improve response time and reduce overhead. It is common for many more columns than necessary to be included in a sort. There are ways of adjusting some of these sorts by reconstructing the SQL as well. One of the methods is to remove sort overhead in general by running queries against the output of EXPLAIN and reviewing all the SQL that uses a sort. It is often quite an amazing exercise, since significant abuses in sorting appear. Generally, this is a problem of ineffective SQL, as there are ways of minimizing both the data sorted and the length of the sort key. Since the key is extracted from the data, those columns are actually in the sort row twice.

Sometimes an external sort method is better, and sometimes the internal sort is better. But often a mythical guideline says to do it only one way, whether there are 100 rows in the sort or 10,000,000 rows. The sort method needs to be balanced with buffer pools, work files, sort memory area, and so on; these topics are discussed extensively in Chapter 3.

Physical Design Issues

Unnecessary CPU overhead can sometimes be the result of poor index design or lack of appropriate indexes. This and other issues of database design are discussed in Chapter 5.

Application Design Issues

Application design obviously can contribute to unnecessary CPU overhead, specifically when it comes to SQL syntax and SQL guidelines. Stories about the application program that used to run in two hours but now runs in under one minute are commonplace at conferences and on the DB2-L Internet list server. We take a look at several application issues for achieving high performance in Section 4, "Application Design and Tuning."

I/O Layers

I/O layers always contribute to CPU overhead, not because they are APIs but because they are a generic, unnecessary addition to the code length for a process. APIs and functional layers are a different story. Often heard is the statement, "We might use a different database or data store some day, and we want to be able to convert easily." The correct interpretation of that statement is, "We want to have lousy performance for the next several years, perhaps even slowing up business processing and growth, so that we can hold on to the concept that we might save money doing a conversion that may or may not happen." We need to look at the real issues.

Linear VSAM is the actual I/O, and SQL is already the "I/O layer." We have discussed the problem of retrieving unnecessary columns and rows, and the whole philosophy behind an I/O layer is to take SQL down to a unit record method, constantly retrieving unnecessary columns and rows. I/O layers have one characteristic in common, which is four starting routines for almost every major table:

- A generic select module
- A generic update module
- A generic insert module
- A generic delete module

It tends to degrade from there. At one organization it was common to have 16 to 32 modules for each major table. Imagine the difficulty for the programming staff alone to try to figure out which of the 32 modules to use for a given process. In addition, the constant calling of each of the various layers requires significant code length to complete a simple process.

There are many discussions of this issue in later chapters as it affects other areas, but consider the simple problem in the following real-world scenario. A retail system required approximately seven I/O modules for purchase orders. A program to insert a purchase order had to call seven different programs. Each program had the same beginning SQL statements for status checking and so forth prior to the SQL for the actual data. The overhead for the insert was

- Seven times the same SQL status checking
- Seven times the complete entry and exit code execution in the module
- Seven times the generic SQL for retrieving all the columns
- Seven times the generic updating of all the columns, whether changed or not
- Seven times the overhead required

At the same time, purchase order updates and changes occurred. Some would change the quantity of a purchase order, some would add line items to a purchase order, some would delete line items from a purchase order. Most would time out after waiting a long time for locks they couldn't get. Most would abend with deadlocks when they finally got some of the locks but could not get the others. Modules were called in no prescribed order, so each process was constantly getting locks for one table, while another process already had locks on the other necessary tables, while each was waiting for the locks held by the other.

The entire system was so convoluted that it had to be scrapped after being custom built; one of the ERP packages that did not have nearly enough customization for the business units was brought in instead. A better solution would have been to simply create three modules to insert, update, and delete purchase orders that had all the specific SQL necessary to perform the function; most (if not all) of the overhead could have been eliminated, including the timeouts and the deadlocks.

I/O layers generally prevent functionally specific SQL, which means that they do not perform as well as they could by design (designing for poor performance). Sometimes I/O layers are used because "SQL is too difficult for my programmers." This attitude is disappointing. If your programmers are competent enough to write the processes for your business, they certainly can handle anything required to complete that goal via more complex SQL programming.

The guideline is simple: never use generic I/O modules. In fact, never do generic anything with DB2, since generic means less than the best performance. We are trying to shorten code length, not lengthen it.

Benefits of SQL Tuning for CPU

When you look for CPU improvements, we want you to think about each little pressure point in DB2. Is it the best? Can it be better? Is it hurting? If you change it, can you allow more work? Take, for example, a system named "Black Hole" by the DBAs at particular organization. It was "working" according to all business units, but the DBAs knew something was wrong. So they first simply examined the SQL. They determined whether each SQL statement and process could be made better, and if so, they costed it the old way and the new way (modeling with DB2 Estimator). They determined how many times the statement, process, or transaction would be executed per second, hour, day, and year. They multiplied that factor against the per-MIP cost, compiled a summary, and then went to management for permission to tune. The savings were over a million dollars a year. Another company delayed the upgrade to a new mainframe by over a year through SQL tuning, and there are many similar stories.

One more little problem was found in the "Black Hole." One ugly transaction took about eight minutes to run, which was only once or twice a day, so the business unit was happy with the output. When the programmers fixed the a join, making it a non-Cartesian join, the transaction completed in less than a second.

Life of xPROCs

As part of the performance optimization for packages and plans, DB2 builds internal procedures to reduce the CPU overhead for repetitive SQL. The procedures are called SPROC (select procedure), IPROC (insert procedure), and UPROC (update procedure). DB2 monitors SQL activity during run time, watching for iterative looping processes against the same table. After the third same process, an internal executable procedure is created that performs the same work at about 30% the cost of the interpretive procedure used normally. SQL statements that fetch a large number of rows and columns generally show the largest benefit from these procedures and therefore are the ones that consume the most overhead if the procedures are not used.

A problem can occur that invalidates these packages and plans with no outright indication that this has happened. As a result, needless CPU time is again being used. If packages and plans have xPROCs that have been invalidated, you can rebind the appropriate plans and packages to once again take advantage of the optimization.

The only way to determine if the optimization has been invalidated is to check the BYPASS COL field in the Miscellaneous section of the DB2PM statistics report, which is from field QISTCOLS in IFCID 2. If this field is nonzero, you need to use IFCID 224 to get the names of the plans or packages that need to be rebound, since this IFCID is written whenever maintenance invalidates the xPROCs. The rebinding enables the procedures to be rebuilt and removes the excess overhead. Other considerations about these procedures are discussed in later chapters on COMMIT strategies and use of the RELEASE DEAL-LOCATE bind parameter.

Address Space Priority

A general recommendation for how to establish the OS/390 address space dispatching priorities is for the IRLM address space to be placed above IMS, CICS, and DB2, with DB2's MSTR and DBM1 address spaces placed above CICS. Here is a recommended priority listing:

- MVS monitor with IRLM capabilities
- IRLM
- DB2 performance monitors
- DBM1
- MSTR
- CICS

DB2 locks are set and released with excessive wait time if the IRLM address space is not at the top of the dispatching priorities. A warning message is issued if the IRLM is not above DBM1 at DB2 start-up. It is important to pay attention to the dispatching recommendations of the vendor of the various performance monitors. Each has one or more address spaces and always recommends specific dispatching priorities. If a performance monitor that can analyze problems in the IRLM is used, dispatching IRLM before a DB2 or MVS monitor could be a problem. If a performance monitor can't get dispatched ahead of IRLM, you cannot find or analyze the problem. Note that under OS/390, the DPRTY parameter is no longer valid, and all priorities have to be set using the MVS parameters in either the IPS/ICS table or the program priority table. If the IPS/ICS table is used to define relative priorities, the priorities can be changed dynamically.

Mixed Workloads and WLM

Test and Production Mix

Production workloads are normally moved into a separate DB2 subsystem. This is a requirement for performance, security, and service-level agreements that is normally different from that for test environments. New applications generally don't work at optimal performance because the proper tuning has not been performed yet. Tuning a new application would take resources away from other production workloads and have a negative effect on the new application's own performance. Many ZPARMs have to be tuned differently, depending on whether they run in a test or production environment. Test and production subsystems are combined at some businesses, which may also use a single subsystem to volume-test and certify the system. This is never an advisable strategy. Test and production environments should always be separated.

WLM

When it comes to mixing environments and determining who gets the CPU, the WLM (Workload Manager) component lets you set separate priorities based on plan, package, AUTHID, or transaction ID. WLM also nicely manages the dramatically fluctuating workloads associated with ad hoc use and end-user computing. With more resources and more powerful machines, it makes more sense to consolidate workloads than to have multiple servers. WLM can be viewed as a means to save CPU.

OLTP and Warehouses

Many workloads are quite different from just simple test and production, for example, warehouse systems. Many myths are perpetrated about warehouses, such as that data marts are always separate, isolated databases and that data warehouses and operational systems cannot exist together. It is also frequently stated that users do not need to have highly responsive systems and do not need to have access to operational data. The reality of existing implementations shows quite the opposite to be true, specifically for larger warehouses. These business systems are required to shape competitive analysis, make critical and time-dependent financial decisions, and adapt to changing market pressures. Those realities dictate responsive, scalable systems that can easily manage a growing number of users and handle very large data stores that are constantly changing in structure. In the movement toward these enterprise warehouses, the blueprint is integration—not separation—of data, information, servers, and user facilities.

As these systems are constructed, end-user access often requires many different architectures, networks, and client topologies (for example, online terminal and browser access). Enterprise warehouses and large data marts need the best to provide the information necessary to move a business forward.

One of the more difficult problems in building today's enterprise data warehouses has been the perceived requirement to build totally isolated database systems, due primarily to the myth from the olden days that mixed queries and data cannot coexist in a single box or be handled by a single DBMS engine.

OS/390 and DB2 both support just about any type of mixed environment that can be constructed. WLM has managers for controlling components such as CPU, I/O, and storage. These controls allow a full range of workload prioritization, such as time-based aging or favoring critical functions. These controls are dynamic and at any point can be redirected to a particular required result. Normal OLTP activity tends to move in a straight line of resource consumption, while warehouse activity bounces from one extreme to the other. The WLM truly proves its worth in the mixed environment of OLTP and warehouse, preventing the OLTP from being influenced by the extremities of resource consumption from warehouse queries or processes. On the other hand, if a critical warehouse query does arrive, the OLTP can be downgraded to allow the warehouse process to complete as rapidly as required. Since DB2 can handle up to 25,000 clients per SMP node, a Sysplex could conceivably handle 800,000 clients, with up to 64,000 concurrent clients (threads) over 32 DB2 subsystems. These client processes can come from locally attached stations or through the network, using either dynamic SQL database access or static preprogrammed SQL.

IRLM

A simple IRM guideline is that you should not share IRLMs between DB2 subsystems. In some circumstances, sharing is not even impossible. The main reason for this guideline is that the IRLM is crucial for DB2 operation and performance. IRLM sharing might give the other subsystems, DB2 or IMS, for example, the potential to harm it, degrading performance through extensive resource sharing within the IRLM.

To keep CPU overhead at a minimum, the general guideline is to specify the parameter PC = NO. This allows IRLM locks to be maintained in ECSA, which does not have the cross-memory problems of the alternative. When PC = YES is used, there is cross-memory work and additional CPU use, because the locks are stored in the IRLM private area. Some of the CPU overhead of the IRLM can be minimized by application-locking strategies. Often too much data is locked unnecessarily. Reduction of locking reduces CPU overhead in the IRLM. However, the ECSA is generally the best option to hold the IRLM locks. Because ECSA storage can be accessed with fewer instructions, this option is the fastest. However, this is also the most dangerous option. ECSA is not protected by OS/390 and can be destroyed by other misbehaving system tasks. Another danger is that the IRLM may take too many locks and use all of the ECSA available in the system, destroying OS/390 in the process. Be careful when using ECSA, and make sure that the locks are limited and monitored. If IRLM puts its locks in the private area, these dangers do not apply. However, if private-area locks are used excessively, performance degrades. This is a trade-off, and the proper decision is not always easy. It comes down to trying to solve the resource usage problem by adjusting the IRLM. The bottom line is that no general rule applies in every case. This decision needs to be made precisely.

Thread Reuse

In any kind of OLTP where there are constantly repeating transactions, thread reuse must be enabled to improve performance. The overhead of thread creation is dramatically depicted in figure 2.1, a chart of performance pressure points that are addressed in many later chapters. These performance pressure points are applicable for both CICS and IMS.

CICS

Thread reuse can be specified for CICS through parameters in the RCT for pool and entry threads. Thread reuse should be specified for any transactions that are repeated with a consistent frequency that is less than the time the thread would be deallocated if not reused.

Sign-On/Identify
    AUTHID is passed to DB2
    Catalog access for authorization
    check (with catalog lock)
 	
Check Max Users
    "WAITS" if at maximum number of
    threads (ZPARM)
 	
Thread Creation
    SKCT Directory and Header are
    loaded
    CT (Cursor Table) is created
    Directory Access for PLAN parts
 	
Check Plan Authorization
    Catalog access - check AUTHID (with
    catalog lock)
    Catalog access - objects AUTH
    checked (with catalog lock)
    Automatic rebind occurs here if
    required - (with catalog locks)
	Resource Allocation
	    Load DBDs
	    Allocate and open all datasets (underlying
	    VSAMs)
	    Acquire locks - (tablespace, index space
	    locks)
	
	Process SQL
	    EDM process
	    RDS process
	    DM process
	    BUFMGR process
	    Data access (Index access)
	    Predicate processing
	    Sorting
	
	COMMIT Processing
	    Log buffers are written to DASD
	    Locks are released
	
	Thread Termination
	    Accounting records are written
	    Storage is freed
	    Objects are closed (CLOSE = YES [maybe])

Figure 2.1   Thread Creation

IMS

The cost of thread creation and termination can be shared in IMS among multiple transactions. You should set the PROCLIM greater than 1 to allow processing multiple input messages in one scheduling of the program and then use class priority scheduling. IMS fast path and class scheduling can also be used to achieve the same result if you reuse threads with WFI (wait for input).

Traces

DB2 traces cause overhead, period. But should they be turned off? Many installations turn off traces as well as SMF recording because they are trying to get as much work as possible through the system. However, in many cases, they would be better advised to take a more proactive approach and turn on some of the traces to find out where they can get a larger benefit by tuning the subsystem and applications. Many times when asked to conduct a performance audit we have not been allowed to collect any of the metrics that would truly show what is happening but only to conduct a random point walk-about.

But there are some real guidelines here, since traces such as the global trace can require 20% to 100% additional CPU overhead. The global trace should always be turned off unless a particular reason demands it, normally an extremely rare situation.

Accounting classes 1 and 3 should generally be left on, and if additional information is required for performance tuning, accounting class 2 provides detail on thread-level entry into and exit from DB2, which allows you to separate DB2 times from application times. It generally adds about 3% overhead to OLTP and as much as 10% to heavy batch jobs. If you are interested only in getting more information from CICS, the overhead is not worth it, since the same information is available from the class 1 time. Accounting class 7 and 8 can be used if you want to collect information about packages and stored procedures. If you are already using 2 and 3, then the overhead for 7 and 8 are negligible.

The performance trace is an exception trace, which you should use only when you are looking for something particular. It should never be left on. Use it to isolate a specific performance problem, and use it only briefly. The entire performance trace can consume the entire CPU. We saw one case where the performance problem could not be found because the trace was taking so many resources; the trace was the real problem. A minimal performance trace includes classes 1 through 3, but even then the overhead can be as high as 25%, and we have heard of cases where it approached 40%.

The audit trace generally is not run, but when it is used for auditing purposes, it generally carries about a 3% to 5% cost, depending on what is audited and the volatility of the system. The audit trace is normally used only in exceptional cases to try to find suspected security violations or to try to find out all access and types of access for a given table. In general, we do not recommend turning it on unless a real, solid business reason demands it. However, since the word *audit* is in its name, the IS audit department often requests it to be turned on. This is not a valid business reason unless there is a specific security violation must be audited based for business reasons. It is not a date audit trace.

If you are concerned about performance and throughput, when everything is working, do not use the IRLM, MVS, IMS, and CICS trace options.

Memory

O nce upon a time, back when memory meant the actual physical memory available, understanding and tuning memory was easy. Then came paging. Paging allowed virtual memory (which meant that we could pretend we had a lot of memory, when in actuality the only memory in use was real physical memory or real storage). However, there were limitations in the size of the real memory (central storage, main storage, main memory, or random access memory [RAM]), so a method to extend this memory was introduced, giving us extended memory (expanded storage). But all information stored in pages in expanded storage must be moved back to central storage to be addressable by the processors. Ironically, to comply with this main storage/expanded storage of the old bipolar machines, portions of main storage are set aside to act as expanded storage (the G series CMOS machines do this). While this is not a problem in CMOS machines, since all memory is accessed in nanoseconds (billionths of a second), the older machines with true expanded storage served up data in only microseconds (millionths of a second). This central storage/expanded storage is simply referred to as processor storage. Now we have software of any size, using whatever portion of this processor storage that we allow, sharing it with every other process running in whatever virtual machine (LPAR, or logically partitioned mode, which is manipulated by a microcode process called PR/SM, for Processor Resource/Systems Manager) that we have set up in the real machine. Got it?

So with DB2 we need to understand how the storage is used, how to control how much of it gets used, how to determine what is real or virtual, and how much gets paged.

This involves some of the most important tuning efforts within the engine that we can do, involving the caches (buffer, EDM, sort, RID).

Virtual Storage

Address Spaces

Address spaces in OS/390 are limited to 2 GB until 64-bit addressing is introduced and fully utilized (then we don't have to worry about central storage and expanded storage anymore, since all memory is directly addressable by the processors). In the past, everything was written in 24-bit mode, and for a long time 16 MB was the largest address space allowed for 24-bit mode. Today, most code is written in 31-bit mode, which allows 2GB addressing. However, even today with the 2GB address space, there are still some constraints for existing code written in 24-bit mode. The phrase "below the line" refers to code that needs to run below the 16MB line within the address space. There is no performance degradation in accessing code and data in the memory area above the 16MB line. The 16MB line is a hard and fast line that gives rise to many problems.

Cross-memory services (XMS) for the most part did away with the overhead of communicating between address spaces, and DB2 makes use of this. The DB2 DBAS, SSAS, IRLM, SPAS, DDF, and user address spaces work together to provide what cannot be accomplished in a single address space. Each must deal with the memory area below the line and above the line, so in essence the limitations of the 16MB line are extended by the number of address spaces working together to provide the solution. In the OS/390 world, address spaces working together are often called horizontal memory expansion. What is called vertical memory expansion is the movement of code and data above the 16MB line, up to the 2GB limit.

The big reduction in virtual storage constraint came through horizontal expansion with hiperpools (up to 4×2 GB hiperspaces), which is now being further enhanced through the use of data spaces (up to 256 GB) for buffer pools and the EDM pool.

Below the 16MB Line

Currently, the 16MB line does not limit the majority of DB2's capabilities, and each new release removes more of the constraint. However, today one major culprit and a couple of minor ones make watching the 16MB line still necessary. VSAM open-data-set control blocks and working storage to support threads still require memory below the line. While it is always difficult to state a hard numerical requirement, we need to provide some recommendations. These numbers should be close to true on your system. Remember that what is important is not whether the actual numbers are correct, but the impact of abusing the memory lines by ignoring guidelines for usage. Assuming that the SWA (system work area) is set to be above the line (as is normally done), the following numbers are in effect for the DB2 virtual storage requirement below the 16MB line:

- DB2 base requirements
  - Approximately 600 K below the line
- Working storage for threads (DSNZPARM CTHREAD)
  - Approximately 40 K for each thread on average; it can be as low as 10 K and higher than 80 K. Static SQL tends to be in the 20K to 49K area, and dynamic SQL tends to be in the 60K to 80K area.
  - 1 K below the line is always required for the thread
- VSAM open-data-set control blocks (DSNZPARM DSMAX)
  - Approximately 1.8 K for each open data set
  - 0.3 K below the line

Open-Data-Set Guidelines

Currently, 32,767 open data sets are possible in DB2, the current DSMAX maximum setting. This many open data sets would consume 10 MB of the storage below the 16MB line, which is way too much. But there is a need to balance the memory requirement with the number of open data sets. Some systems may need to have more than 10,000 data sets open all of the time (some enterprise resource planning [ERP] applications perhaps), but currently most environments do not have that kind of dependency. DSMAX needs to be set so that the most frequently used data sets remain open. This needs to be balanced with the time required to start DB2 after an abnormal end or to stop DB2. This time will lessen with future DB2 and operating system improvements. The number of open data sets affects checkpoint overhead.

The issue of the number of open data sets drives the recommendations for segmented table spaces. Most ERP systems with a vast number of physical objects already package their tables in segmented table space. But many organizations overlook code, reference, decode, and lookup tables: quite often these tables are not segmented, and simple addition shows a potential problem. One client used 280 tables with 425 supporting indexes for a total of 705 VSAM open control blocks. But if the 280 tables are placed into, say, only three segmented tables packed by similar use and structure, we are now down to only 428 VSAM open control blocks. We just gave back some real and virtual memory for something more important. Checkpoint time may improve, the DB2 system will shut down more quickly, and so on. It is very easy to tune and achieve a large overall benefit if you just look for all the little places where resources can be freed.

Concurrent Threads

In addition, the number of concurrent threads needs to be carefully monitored, and perhaps CTHREAD may need adjustment. One of the major impacts here is that when parallelism is used for applications or utilities, each parallel task is a thread. Not only can this be a problem if CTHREAD is too small, but additional memory is required below the line for parallelism.

One other impact area is for systems such as ERP systems, which are almost 100% dynamic SQL. Since dynamic SQL has a much higher requirement for working storage, there is a much higher below-the-line requirement than for a normal, static SQL system.

Buffer Pools

Before we start to discuss buffer pools, it might be helpful to take a look at figure 3.1, showing the relationship of all the memory components, since we need to make some decisions regarding DBM1, data spaces, and hiperspaces.

Overview

Buffer pools are areas of virtual storage that temporarily store pages of table spaces or indexes. When a program accesses a row of a table, DB2 places the page containing that row in a buffer. When a program changes a row of a table, DB2 must (eventually) write the data in the buffer back to disk, normally either at a checkpoint or a write threshold. The write threshold is either a vertical threshold at the page-set level or a horizontal threshold at the buffer-pool level. Storage for buffer pools is backed by memory in the DBM1 address space (virtual storage of 2 GB); this can be extended to hiperspace (normally expanded memory), or buffer pools can exist in a data space (virtual storage of 2 GB).

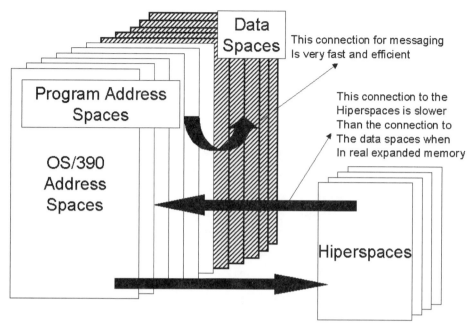

Figure 3.1 Buffer Pools, Hiperpools, Data Spaces

This section covers how to design a buffer-pool strategy to best suit the type of processing required for an object. Information on how to separate and tune buffer pools via thresholds and how to best control write operations is examined. Three different strategies for the two different types of storage are evaluated, with guidelines for when each is appropriate.

How buffer pools work is fairly simple by design, but tuning these simple operations can make all the difference in the world to the performance of applications. The data manager issues GETPAGE requests to the buffer manager, which hopefully can satisfy the request from the buffer pool instead of having to retrieve the page from disk. We often trade CPU for I/O in order to manage our buffer pools efficiently. Buffer pools are maintained by subsystem, but individual buffer-pool design and use should be by object granularity and in some cases also by application.

DB2 buffer-pool management by design allows the ability to ALTER and DISPLAY buffer pool information dynamically without a bounce of the DB2 subsystem. This improves availability by allowing you to dynamically create new buffer pools when necessary and also to dynamically modify or delete buffer pools. You may need to ALTER buffer pools a couple times during the day because of varying workload characteristics. We discuss this when we look at tuning the buffer-pool thresholds. Initial buffer-pool definitions are set at installation or migration but are often hard to configure at this time because the application process against the objects is usually not detailed at installation. Regardless of what is set at installation, you can use ALTER any time after the install to add or delete new buffer pools, resize the buffer pools, or change any of the thresholds. The buffer-pool definitions are stored in the BSDS, and we can move objects between buffer pools via an ALTER INDEX or ALTER TABLESPACE command and a subsequent START or STOP command on the object.

Several processes are involved in the GETPAGE operation to move a requested page into the buffer pool, such as OPEN and CLOSE operations, invocation of read or write engines, interfacing with the disk cache, and management of the buffer space and hiperspace (figure 3.2). The GETPAGE process finds or triggers a move of the page to the buffer pool, which can reside in space backed by the DBM1 address space, or to an area

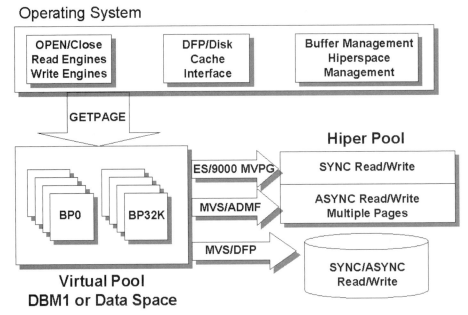

Figure 3.2   Buffer Manager Overview

of memory backed by a data space. A hiperpool may be used behind the buffer pool to allow pages to remain cached longer in the event that they begin to fall off the LRU (least recently used) queue. The pages are moved to or from the hiperpool either one at a time using a MVPG (move page) hardware instruction or several at a time using ADMF (asynchronous data mover facility) hardware facility. Pages that need to be externalized are written to disk via DFP.

All virtual address spaces are 2 GB each. All buffer pools are backed by virtual memory in the DBM1 address space, which is a 2GB address space. In reality, you have only 1.6 GB to use (400,000 4K pages), as the other space is set aside for DB2 process usage. It is worth noting that only a few organizations have been able to achieve quality performance with buffer-pool allocations over 1 GB. The reason for this should be intuitively obvious: not enough room is left over for core processes, EDM, RID, sort caches, and so forth. This creates interesting problems as you begin to run out of space for buffer pools, because DBM1 is responsible for several activities in the DB2 subsystem, such as management of the EDM pool, RID pool, sort pool (these are discussed in detail in the next sections of this chapter), DB2 catalog and directory, and application programs. We later discuss in detail some relief that came about through the implementation of data spaces in version 6 to help with a constrained DBM1 address space. Data spaces allow buffer pools to be backed by an area of memory not in the DBM1 address space (horizontal memory expansion). Hiperpools are implemented in their own address space, normally expanded memory, and you can have up to four hiperspaces of 2 GB each (8 GB total) to support them (figure 3.3).

You have to make decisions based upon your environment constraints and object usage to determine where your buffer pools should reside and whether or not you should have them backed by a hiperpool. A page can reside in a virtual pool (buffer pool) backed by DBM1, a hiperpool, a buffer pool backed by a data space, a group buffer pool (figure 3.4), or on disk. How you design and implement your buffer pools becomes critical and often takes careful planning and a good understanding of exactly how the data is processed.

Note: When we say that something is backed by DBM1 (virtual storage), that means it could be backed by real memory behind DBM1, expanded memory, or paging (disk).

Note: A new IFCID in version 6 helps determine where a page resides: IFCID 198.

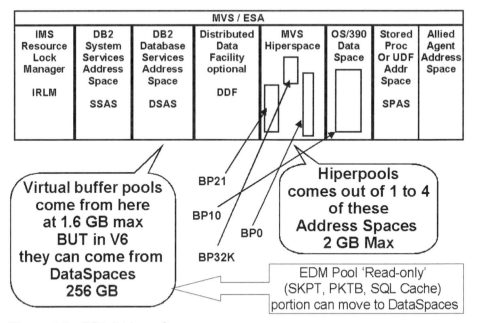

Figure 3.3   DB2 Address Spaces

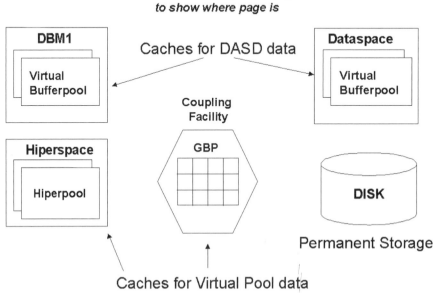

Figure 3.4   Page Residence

Pages

There are three types of pages in virtual pools:

- Available pages: pages on an available queue (LRU, FIFO, MRU) for stealing
- In-use pages: pages updated or currently in use by a process that are not available for stealing. In-use counts do not indicate how to accurately ????? the size of the buffer pool, but this count can help determine residency for initial sizing.
- Updated pages: these pages are not "in use" and not available for stealing and are considered "dirty pages," waiting in the buffer pool to be externalized (figure 3.5).

The data manager issues GETPAGEs to the buffer manager as required or forced. A GETPAGE is the process of getting a new page into the buffer pool for use. The process may obtain the page from various places: virtual pool or data space, hiperpool, group buffer pool, or disk. You want to do GETPAGEs without additional I/O, and I/O can be avoided if a strategy is in place for a good hit ratio. Hiperpools can help in many scenarios (figure 3.6).

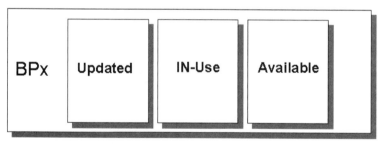

Figure 3.5   Bufferpool Pages

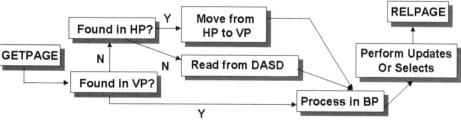

Figure 3.6   GETPAGE/RELPAGE Process

As of version 6, we have four page sizes to use:

BP0–BP49	4K pages
BP8K0–BP8K9	8K pages
BP16K0–BP16K9	16K pages
BP32K0–BP32K9	32K pages

The new 8K and 16K page sizes are logical constructs of physical 4K pages (figure 3.7), as is the 32K page size.

Index page sizes have not changed and are still 4K pages. Work-file table space pages are still only 4K or 32K pages also. The number of asynchronous page writes per I/O changes with each page size accordingly.

4K pages	32 writes per I/O
8K pages	16 writes per I/O
16K pages	8 writes per I/O
32K pages	4 writes per I/O

With these new page sizes you can achieve better hit ratios and have less I/O because you can fit more rows on a page. For instance, if you have a 2,200-byte row (for a data warehouse) a 4K page would be able to hold only one row, but an 8K page could fit three rows on a page, one more than if 4K pages were used and one less lock also, if locking is required. However, we do not want to use these new page sizes as a Band-Aid for what may be a poor design. You may want to consider decreasing the row size based upon usage to get more rows per page (refer to Chapter 5, "Physical Database Objects," for more information).

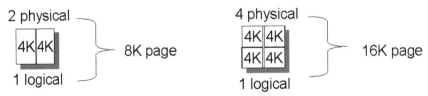

Figure 3.7   Logical Page Sizes

Virtual Buffer Pools and Hiperpools

We can allocate up to 80 virtual buffer pools (in version 6). This allows up to fifty 4K-page buffer pools (BP0–BP49), up to ten 32K-page buffer pools (BP32K–BP32K9), up to ten 8K-page buffer pools, and up to ten 16K-page buffer pools. Up to 80 hiperpools can be allocated to support the virtual buffer pools.

When a hiperpool should be used is always a question. You should use MVS ESA (extended storage area) hiperspaces for hiperpools to improve the buffer hit ratio (referenced pages found in the buffer pool). You should also use hiperpools when you see that paging is high in the virtual buffer pool, you need to increase the number of pages available to the application, and no additional central storage is available. You should also use hiperpools when a larger area for random processing is required and the virtual pool is mostly sequential.

Hiperpools allow additional caching of data to keep it around longer for application usage. Use of a hiperpool requires ADMF (asynchronous data movement facility) and up to a 2GB ESA. Data movement by the system service ADMSERV is performed in 4K blocks. Sometimes a single page may be moved between the virtual buffer pool and the hiperpool using the MVPG command. ADMF is used at other times and can move up to 125 pages in one ADMF request (figure 3.8). Only clean pages are stored in the hiperpools, those that are falling off the available queues in the virtual buffer pool. Hiperpools can be backed by auxiliary storage, meaning paging to disk.

Performance can be improved by using hiperpools when there is a low hit ratio in the virtual pool due to pages needed by the application being written out to disk before they can be referenced (figure 3.9).

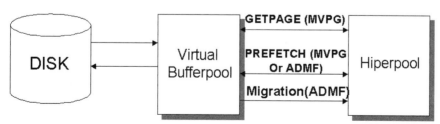

Figure 3.8   Hiperpools and Page Transfer

HIT RATIO		PERFORMANCE	
Virtual Pool	Hiper Pool	CPU Cost	Elapsed Time
HIGH	-----	SMALL	REDUCED, LOWER I/O
LOW	HIGH	SMALL	REDUCED, LOWER I/O
LOW	LOW	INCREASE	INCREASE

Figure 3.9 Buffer Pool and Hiperpool Performance

When you use hiperpools, 128 to 256 pages are maintained in a free queue (FQ) in the virtual pool. This area is kept free for pages moved between the hiperpool and virtual pool so that pages in the virtual pool are not stolen simply to support the use of a hiperpool.

Buffer Pool Queue Management

Pages used in the buffer pools are processed in two categories: random (pages read one at a time) or sequential (pages read via prefetch). These pages are queued separately in the LRU (random least-recently-used queue) or SLRU (sequential least-recently-used queue; prefetch steals only from this queue). The percentage of each queue in a buffer pool is controlled via the VPSEQT (sequential steal threshold) parameter (figure 3.10). VPSEQT is a hard threshold to adjust and often requires two settings, for example, one setting for batch processing and a different setting for online processing. The way data is processed often differs between batch and online processes. Batch processing is usually more sequential, whereas online processing is more random.

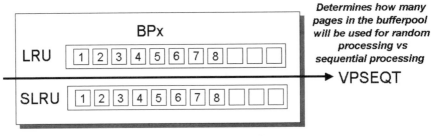

Figure 3.10 Random and Sequential Page Queue

Since version 5, DB2 breaks up these queues into multiple LRU chains. Thus, there is less overhead for queue management. The latch that is taken at the head of the queue (actually on the hash control block, which keeps the order of the pages in the queue) is latched less because the queues are smaller. Multiple subpools are created for a large virtual buffer pool, and the threshold is controlled by DB2 and does not exceed 4,000 VBP buffers in each subpool. The LRU queue is managed within each of the subpools in order to reduce the buffer-pool latch contention when concurrency is high. These buffers are stolen in a round-robin fashion through the subpools (figure 3.11).

In version 6, a new page-stealing option was introduced with a new method of queue management. FIFO can now be used instead of the default of LRU. With this method, the oldest pages are always moved out. This decreases the cost of doing a GET-PAGE operation and reduces internal latch contention for high concurrency. This should be used only where there is little or no I/O and where table space or an index is resident in the buffer pool. Separate buffer pools for LRU and FIFO objects can be set via the ALTER BUFFERPOOL command with a new PGSTEAL option for FIFO. LRU is the PGSTEAL option default (figure 3.12).

I/O Requests and Paging

In synchronous reads, one physical 4K page is read per I/O. In synchronous writes, one page per I/O is written. You should use only truly necessary synchronous reads and writes. If you do not, you may begin to see buffer pool stress (maybe too many checkpoints). DB2 begins to use synchronous writes if the immediate write threshold (IWTH) is reached

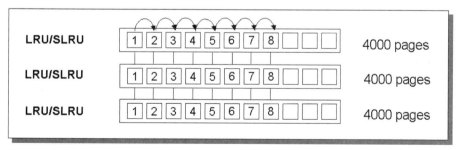

Figure 3.11 Multiple LRU Chains

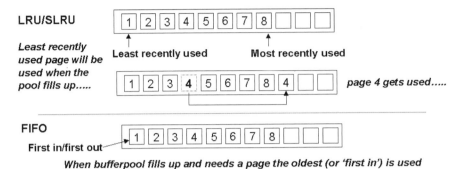

LRU/SLRU

Least recently used page will be used when the pool fills up.....

Least recently used   Most recently used

page 4 gets used.....

FIFO

First in/first out

When bufferpool fills up and needs a page the oldest (or 'first in') is used

Figure 3.12   Page-Stealing Option

(more on this threshold later in this chapter) or if two checkpoints pass without an updated and not yet committed page being written.

In asynchronous reads, several pages are read per I/O for prefetch operations such as sequential prefetch, dynamic prefetch, or list prefetch. In asynchronous writes, several pages are written per I/O for such operations as deferred writes.

Before data can be used, it must be in central storage. After an I/O brings the page in, it can be migrated out to a page data set (OS/390 paging), to expanded storage (DB2 or OS/390), or to disk (via a DB2 write; see figure 3.13). You want to eliminate paging to auxiliary storage. From a statistics report, you can easily find how much paging is occurring. You want to keep the ratio of the number of page-ins for read I/Os to the total number of

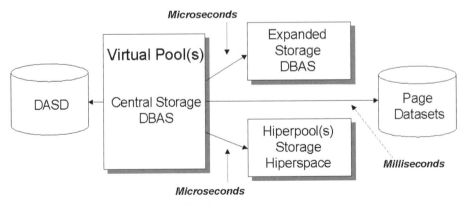

Figure 3.13   Buffer Pools and Paging

page requests below 5%. Figure 3.14 shows a sample calculation for determining the paging percentage. We often see paging in buffer pools when they are overallocated and there is not enough memory to support them.

Page Externalization

Pages are externalized to disk when any of the following events occur.

- DWQT threshold is reached.
- VDWQT threshold is reached.
- Data set is physically closed or switched from R/W to R/O.
- DB2 takes a checkpoint (LOGLOAD is reached).
- QUIESCE (WRITE YES) utility is executed.
- A page is at the top of LRU chain, and another update is required of the same page by another process.
- A process COMMITs.

You should control page externalization via your DWQT and VDWQT thresholds for best performance and to avoid surges in I/O (figure 3.15). You do not want page externalization to be controlled by DB2 system checkpoints, because too many pages would be written to disk at one time, causing I/O queuing delays, increased response time, and I/O spikes. During a checkpoint, all updated pages in the buffer pools are externalized to disk, and the checkpoint is recorded in the log (except for the work files, DSNDB07).

PAGEINS FOR READ I/O

/

(SYNC READ I/O +
SEQUENTIAL PREFETCH PAGES READ +
LIST PREFETCH PAGES READ +
DYNAMIC PREFETCH PAGES READ)

Figure 3.14 Paging Calculation

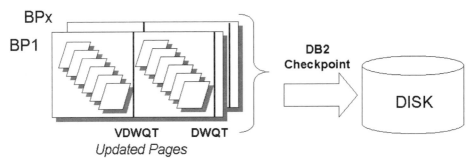

Figure 3.15   Page Externalization: Writes vs. Checkpoint

Checkpoint and Buffer Pool Issues

DB2 checkpoints are controlled through the DSNZPARM LOGLOAD. The LOGLOAD parameter is the number of log records written between DB2 checkpoints. The default was changed from 10,000 to 50,000 in a recent version, which can be too low for some production subsystems. Often you may need different settings for this parameter, depending on your workload. For example, you may want it higher during batch processing. However, this is a hard parameter to set often, because to take effect it requires a bounce of the DB2 subsystem. Recognizing the importance of the ability to change this parameter based on workloads, IBM included in version 6 a SET LOG LOGLOAD command to dynamically set the LOGLOAD parameter. This is *not* a dynamic DSNZPARM; the original DSNZPARM takes effect again if DB2 is bounced. Other options have been added to the SET LOG command to SUSPEND and RESUME logging for a DB2 subsystem. SUSPEND causes a system checkpoint to be taken in a non-data sharing environment. Obtaining the log-write latch prevents any further log records from being created and causes any unwritten log buffers to be written to disk. Also, the BSDS is updated with the high-written RBA. All further database updates are prevented until update activity is resumed by issuing a SET LOG command to RESUME logging, or until a STOP DB2 command is issued. These are single-subsystem-only commands, so they must be entered for each member in a data sharing environment.

In general terms, during online processing, DB2 should take a checkpoint about every 10 to 15 minutes, or some other period based on investigative analysis of the impact of restart time after a failure. Two real concerns influence how often to take checkpoints:

- The cost and disruption of the checkpoints
- The restart time for the subsystem after a crash

Hundreds of checkpoints per hour is definitely too many, but the general guideline (four to six checkpoints per hour) is likely to cause problems in restart time, especially if it is used for batch update timing. After a normal QUIESCE STOP, there is no work to do. The real concern for checkpoints is in DB2 ABEND situations or when a MODIFY *irlm*,ABEND command is issued, which also requires DB2 to be restarted.

The costs and disruption of DB2 checkpoints are often overstated. A DB2 checkpoint is a tiny hiccup; it does not prevent processing from proceeding. A LOGLOAD setting that is too high, along with large buffer pools and high thresholds, such as the defaults, can cause enough I/O to make the checkpoint disruptive. In trying to control checkpoints, some of our clients increased the LOGLOAD value and made the checkpoints less frequent, which in effect made them much more disruptive. The problem is corrected by reducing the amount written and increasing the checkpoint frequency, which yields much better performance and availability. It is possible, and has occurred at some installations, that a checkpoint every minute did not affect performance or availability. The write efficiency at DB2 checkpoints is the key factor to observe to see whether LOD-LOAD can be reduced. If the write thresholds (DWQT and VDQWT) are doing their job, there is less work to perform at each checkpoint. Using the write thresholds to perform I/O in a level, nondisruptive fashion is also helpful for the nonvolatile storage in storage controllers.

However, even if the write thresholds (DWQT and VDQWT) and checkpoints are set properly, you can still have an unwanted write problem. This problem can occur if the log data sets are not properly sized. If the active log data sets are too small, active log switches occur often. When an active log switch takes place, a checkpoint is taken automatically. Therefore, logs could be driving excessive checkpoint processing, resulting in constant writes. Constant writes prevent a high ratio of pages written per I/O, because the deferred write queue is not be allowed to fill as it should. Refer to Chapter 1, "I/O and Storage Management," for additional information on log data sets.

Buffer Pool Parameters

The best opportunity for effective tuning is through the manipulation of the buffer-pool threshold values. Most threshold values can be changed dynamically, and they can and should be different for each buffer pool, with several fixed settings per day, week, month, quarter, and year.

Buffer Pool Size

Buffer pool sizes are determined by the VPSIZE parameter. This parameter determines the number of pages to be used for the virtual pool. The virtual pool (but not hiperpool or data spaces) has an upper limit of 400,000 4K pages total (1.6 GB) in the DBM1 address space for the entire subsystem. This must be shared among all buffer pools (and everything else) in the DBM1 address space. If you are using data spaces to back the virtual pools, you have more space available to use on other critical components (more on this later).

First set the buffer pool to a size that seems valid, and then monitor the actual usage. A starting formula for sizing is the pages written into buffer pool in writes per second times the number of seconds that pages should stay resident. This will give you the number of pages to start with.

Example:

2,100 writes/second × 3 seconds = 6,300 pages
Start with at least 6,300 pages.

The hardest part with this formula is to determine the page residency time. This is extremely dependent on the objects in the buffer pool and how the objects are accessed by the various applications. The question you should start with is, "How quickly is this page referenced by the application?"

One traditional rule for determining whether a buffer pool is sized correctly is to increase the size of the buffer pool until no more hit ratio improvements or paging problems occur. This is a valid rule, but it is not optimal. A better rule would be to reduce virtual pools and back the buffer pool with main memory only. You can then use large hiperpools if there is still not enough memory to keep the paging down and to provide a decent hit ratio. However, this may not be so effective when using CMOS OS/390 machines, as discussed in the first paragraph of this chapter.

Sequential versus Random Processing

VPSEQT is the percentage of the virtual buffer pool that can be used for sequentially accessed pages. It prevents sequential data from using all the buffer pool and keeps some space available for random processing. The value is 0 to 100%, with a default of 80%. The default value indicates that 80% of the buffer pool is to be set aside for sequential processing and 20% for random processing. This threshold needs to be set according to how objects in that buffer pool are processed.

One tuning option often used is setting VPSEQT to 0 to set the pool up for just random use. When VPSEQT is 0, the SLRU is no longer valid, and the buffer pool is totally random. Since only the LRU is used, all pages on the SLRU have to be freed. This also disables prefetch operations in this buffer pool, which is beneficial for certain strategies. It turns off the CPU for each GETPAGE (up to 10% GETPAGE overhead reduction). However, there are problems with this strategy for certain buffer pools, which are addressed later.

Writes

The DWQT (deferred write threshold), also known as the horizontal deferred write threshold, is the percentage threshold that determines when DB2 starts turning on write engines to begin deferred writes (32 pages/asynchronous I/O). The value can be from 0 to 90%, with a default of 50%. When the threshold is reached, write engines (up to 300 write engines as of this publication) begin writing pages out to disk. DB2 can run out of write engines if the write thresholds are not set to keep a constant flow of writing of updated pages to disk. If this shortage is uncommon, it is okay, but if it occurs daily, you have a tuning opportunity. DB2 turns on these write engines, basically one vertical page set queue at a time, until a 10% reverse threshold is met. You can detect when DB2 runs out of write engines by the WRITE ENGINES NOT AVAILABLE indicator in the statistics report.

A high value for the DWQT threshold helps to improve the hit ratio for updated pages but increases I/O time when deferred write engines begin. We use a low value to reduce I/O length for deferred write engines, but this increases the number of deferred writes. This threshold should be set based on the referencing of the data by the applications.

If you set DWQT to 0 so that all objects defined to the buffer pool are scheduled to be written immediately to disk, DB2 actually uses its own internal calculations for exactly how many changed pages can exist in the buffer pool before it is written to disk (figure 3.16). Thirty-two pages are still written per I/O, but it will take 40 "dirty pages"

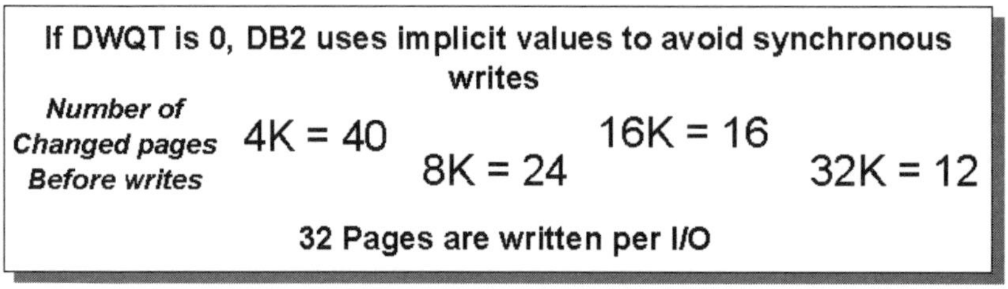

If DWQT is 0, DB2 uses implicit values to avoid synchronous writes

Number of Changed pages Before writes

4K = 40

8K = 24

16K = 16

32K = 12

32 Pages are written per I/O

Figure 3.16   Default Writes

(updated pages) to trigger the threshold, so highly re-referenced updated pages, such as space map pages, remain in the buffer pool.

When implementing LOBs (large objects), a separate buffer pool should be used, and this buffer pool should not be shared (backed by a group buffer pool in a data sharing environment). DWQT should be set to 0 so that force-at-commit processing occurs for LOBS with LOG NO and the updates continually flow to disk instead of surges of writes. For LOBs defined with LOG YES, DB2 could use deferred writes and avoid massive surges at checkpoint.

The DWQT threshold works at a buffer-pool level for controlling writes of pages to the buffer pools, but for a more efficient write process, you should control writes at the page-set or partition level. This can be controlled via the VDWQT (vertical deferred write threshold), the percentage threshold that determines when DB2 starts turning on write engines and begins the deferred writes for a given data set. This threshold helps to keep a particular page set or partition from monopolizing the entire buffer pool with its updated pages. The value can range from 0 to 90%, with a default of 10%. VDWQT should always be less than DWQT.

A good rule of thumb for setting VDWQT is that if fewer than 10 pages are written per I/O, set it to 0. You may also want to set it to 0 to trickle-write the data out to disk. It is normally best to keep this value low to prevent heavily updated page sets from dominating the section of the deferred write area. As of version 6, both a percentage and a number of pages from 0 to 9,999 can be specified for the VDWQT. You must set the percentage to 0 to use the number of pages specified. If you set VDWQT to 0,0, the system uses MIN(32,1%) for good trickle I/O.

If you set VDWQT to 0, 32 pages are still written per I/O, but it will take 40 "dirty pages" to trigger the threshold, so highly re-referenced updated pages, such as space map pages, remain in the buffer pool.

It is a good idea to set the VDWQT using a number rather than a percentage, because an increase in the buffer pool with VDWQT as a percentage means that more pages for a particular page set can occupy the buffer pool, which may not always be optimal or desirable.

In any performance report showing the amount of activity for VDWQT and DWQT, you want to see VDWQT being triggered most of the time (VERTIC.DEFER.WRITE THRESHOLD) and the DWQT much less frequently (HORIZ.DEFER.WRITE THRESHOLD). There can be no general ratio guidelines, since triggering depends on both activity and the number of objects in the buffer pools. The bottom line is that you want to control I/O by the VDWQT and use the DWQT to watch for and control activity across the entire pool and in general to write out rapidly queuing pages. This also assists in limiting the amount of I/O that a checkpoint would have to perform.

Parallelism

VPPSEQT (virtual pool parallel sequential threshold) is the percentage of VPSEQT that can be used for parallel operations. The value ranges from 0 to 100%, with a default of 50%. If VPPSEQT is set to 0, parallelism is disabled for objects in that particular buffer pool. This can be useful in buffer pools that cannot support parallel operations. VPXPSEQT (virtual pool sysplex parallel sequential threshold) is the percentage of VPPSEQT to use for inbound queries. It also defaults to 50%, and if it is set to 0, sysplex query parallelism is disabled. In affinity data sharing environments, VPXPSEQT is normally set to 0 to prevent inbound resource consumption of DSNDB07 and work files. The buffer pool parameters for parallelism are discussed further in Chapter 21, which covers parallelism in depth.

Hiperpool Size

HPSIZE is the size (in 4K pages) of the hiperpool. This generally needs to be greater than VPSIZE; a good starting size is at least double the size of the virtual pool. If the hiperpool is too small, too much overhead is incurred maintaining queues, which defeats the purpose of having a hiperpool. Hiperpools still take some memory in the DBM1 address space (about 2% of the defined hiperpool size). A 2GB hiperpool requires about 40 MB of memory for hash blocks that contain information about all pages in the hiperpool.

Hiperpool Thresholds: HPSEQT and CASTOUT

HPSEQT (hiperpool sequential steal threshold) is the percentage of the hiperpool that can be used for sequentially accessed pages. The value ranges from 0 to 100%, with a default of 80%. If HPSEQT is set to 0, sequential pages are not moved to the hiperpool from the virtual pool. HPSEQT is normally a low number, often near 0, because random pages primarily benefit from a hiperpool (i.e., index non-leaf pages). Only virtual pools dedicated to heavily scanned objects with frequently re-referenced pages benefit from a high sequential hiperpool.

CASTOUT tells whether or not MVS should protect DB2 pages in hiperspace. A value of YES lets MVS steal the pages if usage is occasional; NO tells MVS to try to protect the pages, unless MVS determines stealing is absolutely necessary or when response time is critical.

DBM1 or Data Space

Version 6 introduced the VPTYPE (virtual pool type) parameter and data spaces as a method for caching data. VPTYPE specifies the type of virtual buffer pool to allocate: DBM1 memory or an associated data space. VPTYPE (PRIMARY) allocates the buffer pool in DBM1, where the maximum limit is 1.6 GB (or less if data space buffer pools are allocated). VPTYPE (DATASPACE) allocates the buffer pool in a data space. Buffer control storage is still in the DBM1 address space, but there is now a maximum limit of 32 GB for 4K page size when data spaces are used (versus the 1.6GB maximum when not used). Hiperpools are not used with data spaces. More on data spaces appears later in this chapter.

LRU or FIFO

Version 6 also introduced a new queuing method, VPSTEAL, which allows a choice of queuing method for buffer pools. The default is LRU (least recently used). The FIFO option was covered in more detail earlier in this chapter in the section "Buffer Pool Queue Management."

Figure 3.17 summarizes the buffer pool thresholds. With each new release we have been given more control over the management and administration of buffer pools. If you are wise, you will learn how to take advantage of these tuning capabilities based upon your knowledge of the application's use of objects, knowledge that DB2 lacks.

Internal Thresholds

The following thresholds are percentages of unavailable (either updated or in use by a process) pages to total pages.

THRESHOLD NAME	THRESHOLD ID	V6 VALUE	V5 VALUE	V3 VALUE	V2 VALUE
IMTH	Immediate Write	97.5%	97.5%	97.5%	97.5%
DMTH	Data Manager	95%	95%	95%	95%
SPTH	Seq Prefetch	90%	90%	90%	90%
VPSEQT	VP Seq Steal	0 - 100%	0 - 100%	0 - 100%	80%
HPSEQT	HP Seq Steal	0 - 100%	0 - 100%	0 - 100%	---------
DWQT	Deferred Write	0 - 90%	0 - 90%	0 - 90%	50%
VDWQT	Data Set DW	# pages	0 - 90%	0 - 90%	10%
VPPSEQT	VP Parallel Seq Steal	0 - 100%	0 - 100%	0 - 100%	---------
VPXPSEQT	VP Sysplex Par Sq S	0 - 100%	0 - 100%	-----------	---------
VPTYPE	Bufferpool Type	Pr/DtSP	-----------	-----------	---------
PGSTEAL	Queuing Method	LRU/FIFO	-----------	-----------	---------

Figure 3.17   Threshold Summary

SPTH

SPTH (sequential prefetch threshold) is checked before a prefetch operation is scheduled and during buffer allocation for a previously scheduled prefetch. If SPTH is exceeded, prefetch either is not scheduled or is canceled. PREFETCH DISABLED—NO BUFFER on the statistics report is incremented every time a virtual buffer pool reaches 90% of active stealable buffers, disabling sequential prefetch. This value should always be 0. A nonzero value is an indication of probable degradation in performance due to disabling of all prefetch. To eliminate this problem, you may want to increase the size of the buffer pool (VPSIZE). Another option may be more frequent commits in the application programs to free pages in the buffer pool, as this will put the pages on the write queues.

DMTH

DMTH (data manager threshold, also referred to as buffer critical threshold) occurs when 95% of all buffer pages are unavailable (in use). This event can also be seen as unaccounted-for I/O in a user's task control block (TCB). The buffer manager will request all threads to release any possible pages immediately by setting GETPAGE/RELPAGE processing by row instead of by page. After a GETPAGE processes a single row, a RELPAGE is issued. This procedure causes CPU overhead to become high for objects in that buffer pool, and I/O-sensitive transactions can suffer. This problem can occur if the buffer pool is too small. A sign of a problem is a nonzero value in the DM THRESHOLD REACHED indicator on a statistics reports. DMTH is checked every time a page is read or updated. If this threshold is not reached, DB2 accesses the virtual pool once for each page (no matter how many rows used). If this threshold has been reached, DB2 accesses the virtual pool once for every *row* on the page that is retrieved or updated. This can lead to serious performance degradation.

IWTH

IWTH (immediate write threshold) is reached when 97.5% of buffers are unavailable (in use). If this threshold is reached, synchronous writes begin, which present a performance problem. For example, if there are 100 rows in page and 100 updates, 100 synchronous writes occur, one by one for each row. Synchronous writes are not concurrent with SQL, but serial, so the application must wait while the writes occur (including 100 log writes that must occur first). This causes large increases in I/O time. When the IWTH is reached, it is not recorded explicity in a statistic reports, but DB2 will appear to hang, and synchronous writes begin when this threshold is reached. Be careful with certain monitors that send exception messages to the console when synchronous writes occur; they may refer to this condition as "IWTH reached," but not all synchronous writes are caused by reaching this threshold. Synchronous writes are simply being reported incorrectly.

> Note: Be aware that the IWTH counter can also be incremented in some performance reports when dirty pages on the write queue have been re-referenced and caused a synchronous I/O before the page could be used by the new process. This threshold counter can also be incremented if more than two checkpoints occur before an updated page is written, since this causes a synchronous I/O to write out the page.

Buffer Pool 0 (BP0)

Buffer pool 0 is the least understood and most abused buffer pool in DB2. DB2 uses this buffer pool for its catalog and directory. This use cannot be changed, but just because DB2 has designated BP0 for its objects does not mean that BP0 has "special" abilities or privilege in the subsystem. It has no special significance; it just happens to be the first buffer pool, but it needs to be left alone and not contaminated with objects. DBD (database descriptor) and DBRM (database request module) plan and package segments are loaded into the EDM pool through BP0, and this use also cannot be changed. You directly affect the performance of this DBD and plan and package loading as well as all access to the catalog and directory when you create other objects in BP0. Other types of catalog access, such as for dynamic SQL, authorization checking, and many others, can also be affected.

This is such an important fact that version 6 now has a new DSNZPARM to assign both tables and indexes to other default buffer pools to keep them out of BP0. The biggest culprits of BP0 abuse are vendor utilities and proprietary products that do not specify a buffer pool for their objects because they do not try to guess where the user would like them. Too often they simply are allowed to default to BP0, the absolute worst place for them.

It would be ideal if we could simply revoke use of BP0 to prevent explicit specification. Many years ago it was mistakenly advised to use BP0 for everything, and unfortunately, many companies are still following that rule. But if you want high performance, it is time to change. *Do not use BP0;* leave it for DB2 use only.

A good starting guideline for BP0 size is about 2,000 pages. This pool normally does not have to be large. Set VPSEQT at 45% to 50% for a buffer pool that can adequately handle both random and sequential processing of these objects. You should monitor your own usage to determine the best mix, but you should always adjust the thresholds from the defaults.

Keep in mind that the default buffer pool for the work files used for sorting and other materializations (DSNDB07) is BP0. If you allow the work files to default to BP0, you are almost intentionally placing performance roadblocks in your DB2 subsystem. The buffer pool necessary to support the work files and the buffer pool necessary to support BP0 have totally different processing characteristics and must have different thresholds. Also, performance using catalog and directory objects and sort work files is the most critical in the subsystem. It makes perfect sense not to let one contaminate the other (e.g., stealing pages from each other).

Virtual-Pool Design Strategies

At one time the general rule was one buffer pool for best overall performance, This old, misinterpreted guideline is totally incorrect, because this almost guarantees that you will never get decent performance out of your subsystem and was only a guideline if you generally use fewer than 10,000 total pages. It is disturbing that the DB2 manuals recommend using only one buffer pool if you do not have the time or personnel to perform tuning operations, which implies that you are not concerned with performance. Most of us are concerned seriously. You need several buffer pools to improve performance of selected page sets, and more buffer pools allow finer tuning and monitoring. By developing a strategy for proper sizing and object placement, you can reduce application response time, optimize usage of memory resources, and save CPU through I/O reduction.

Figure 3.18 shows how to start breaking your objects into buffer pools based upon the type of their use by applications. Each one of these buffer pools has its own unique settings, and the type of processing may differ even among batch cycles and the driving online day. These are very generic examples. Actual definitions would be much more finely tuned and less generic.

More-Detailed Example of Buffer Pool Object Breakouts

BP0	DB2 catalog and directory use only
BP1	DSNDB07: cursor tables, work files, sorts
BP2	Heavily accessed code and reference tables
BP3	Small tables, heavily updated transition tables, work tables
BP4	Basic tables
BP5	Basic indexes
BP6	Special large-clustered, range-scanned table
BP7	Special master table full index (randomly searched table)
BP8	Entire database for a special application
BP9	Derived tables and "saved" tables for ad hoc queries
BP10	Staging tables (edit tables for short-lived data)
BP11	Staging indexes (edit tables for short-lived data)

DSNDB07: A Different Kind of Buffer Pool

The DSNDB07 table space *must* be separated into its own buffer pool. Its unique set of characteristics is unlike that of any of the other buffer pools. All the pages at one time could be dirty, updated, and referenced. If pages are externalized and read back in they can be stolen. Another myth that we need to dispel is that it is 100% sequential. Due to some of the processing that takes place is the work files (e.g., sort and merge, sparse indexes for noncorrelated subqueries), some of the processing in this buffer pool may be random. In fact, in certain environments, it may be very random. VPSEQT could start at 90% and must be monitored to determine whether it should be lower. VDWQT can start at 90%, because you want to keep the pages around (especially when sorting). DSNDB07 pages are *not* written to disk at checkpoint, and you *never* want this buffer pool to hit the DM

➤ **Memory resident, table and indexes, random**
➤ **Memory resident, sequential tables**
    ➤ **It's indexes**
➤ **Read-only, random**
    ➤ **It's indexes**
➤ **Read-only, sequential**
    ➤ **It's indexes**
➤ **Lightly updated, no re-reference**
    ➤ **It's indexes**
➤ **Lightly updated, high re-reference**
    ➤ **It's indexes**
➤ **Heavily updated, no re-reference**
    ➤ **It's indexes**
➤ **Heavily updated, high re-reference**
    ➤ **It's indexes**
	➤ **LOBs read only**
	    ➤ **It's indexes**
	➤ **LOBs updated**
	    ➤ **It's indexes**
	➤ **Special indexes**
	➤ **Special tablespaces**
	➤ **Special databases**
	➤ **QMF**
	➤ **Vendor Objects**
	➤ **DB2 Catalog/Directory**
	➤ **Troubleshooting**
	➤ **FIFO**
	➤ **ROLAP/MOLAP**
	➤ **Shared Data (Sysplex)**
	    ➤ **Cached**
	    ➤ **Non-cached**

Figure 3.18   Guidelines for Designing Buffer Pools

critical threshold. However, there are some potential problems with these settings. If you set VDWQT and DWQT to 90% and the actual writing of updated pages to a particular disk slows down, the queues get long, the I/O does not complete fast enough, the queue of updated pages in the pool passes the 90%, 95%, and 97.5% thresholds (SPTH, DMTH, WITH), and things can get exceedingly ugly. As with all values, DSNDB07 data sets need to be sized and placed properly on the right types of devices, the DSNDB07 buffer pools need to be large enough to accommodate the processes, and applications need to be tuned so that they are not abusing the resources. It is a delicate balancing act, but you can set DSNDB07 and work files to a proper level and greatly improve performance.

In one case, we rapidly adjusted several buffer pool parameters but paid special attention to the buffer pool for DSNDB07 and reduced warehouse queries from hours to minutes. This short example illustrates the importance of tuning this buffer pool.

DSNDB07 and Hiperpool Usage

Should the DSNDB07 buffer pool be backed by a hiperpool? Generally no, but in special situations you may want to add a hiperpool to a virtual pool. As a general guideline, no hiperpool should be defined for DSNDB07 unless pages are being paged out and read back in continually. If you think that a hiperpool will help, then define it behind the DSNDB07 virtual buffer pool, but set VPSEQT to 50%, and set HPSIZE to twice the size of the DSNDB07 buffer pool VPSIZE. Then immediately monitor its use, and start making adjustments. If the hiperpool is truly being used at better than 10% efficiency, start to reduce the real pool and the hiperpool by the same ratio, watch all ratios, and adjust accordingly. In certain unusual cases, with a highly mixed mode of sorts and large results sets—as in large enterprise warehouses using certain types of OLAP, ROLAP, MOLAP, and other multidimensional query tools—this might provide a big benefit.

DSNDB07 Buffer Pool Hit Ratio

The hit ratio for this buffer pool needs to be calculated a bit differently from that of other buffer pools (discussed later), because some SQL statements utilize a special GETPAGE request that reserves an empty buffer even before the page in brought in from disk. During the sort input processing, a GETPAGE is issued for each empty work file page without a read I/O. Because of this fact, when we calculate the hit ratio for the buffer pool supporting the work files, we divide the number of GETPAGEs by 2.

The hit ratio calculation for the DSNDB07 buffer pool is

$$(\text{GETPAGES}/2 - \text{pages read})/(\text{GETPAGES}/2)$$

If the work files are not isolated to their own buffer pool, it is impossible to calculate the hit ratio due to the unique nature of the work-file usage of the buffer pool.

Code, Decode, Reference, and Lookup Tables

Code, decode, reference, and lookup tables all have unique characteristics. They should be placed in their own buffer pool. For design recommendations for these tables, refer to the examples in Chapter 5, "Physical Database Objects": reduce the quantity of physical objects, reduce memory below the line, and use a table of tables by adding a column.

You want to pin these objects in memory because they are often small and highly re-referenced. They are also generally read-only. A buffer pool tuning technique is to first make the buffer pool large enough to fit all of the code and reference tables, or at least sets of constantly used ones. Then turn on the new FIFO queuing in version 6 to kill the CPU overhead for LRU management. There is no need to manage a queue for objects that will be totally memory resident. Then set VPSEQT to 0, and kill the overhead for sequential prefetch management (figure 3.19).

Other techniques have been tried in the past to pin these objects in memory, such as scanning the table and indexes during a start-up period to stage all of the pages in the buffer pool. However, if you use the technique to stage pages, you will be unable to turn off the prefetch management by setting VPSEQT to 0. If you initially set VPSEQT to get 0 then perform a scan, the scanned pages will never get on the queue and will not get staged. If you scan the objects, stage the pages, and then ALTER the table space to VPSEQT = 0, DB2 frees all the sequential pages. Either way, you are not staging the pages nor turning off prefetch management overhead. The only way to turn off this overhead is to set VPSEQT to 0 and let the pool fill with pages naturally.

Dynamic Threshold Setting

We have discussed all the buffer pool thresholds and how to break objects out into separate buffer pools based on usage. Now give some thought having multiple sets of thresholds for each buffer pool, based upon usage. This usage can vary among daytime (online) processing, nighttime (batch) processing, weekend (summary report) processing, and so on.

An ALTER BUFFERPOOL command could be issued before each change in processing to properly configure the buffer pool for the upcoming usage. It could then be ALTERed back to its original settings when the process has completed.

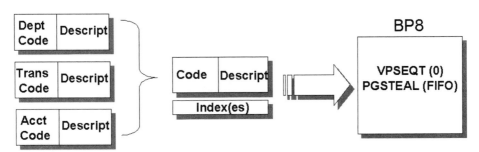

Figure 3.19   Code, Decode, Reference, and Lookup Tables

Example:

A buffer pool containing just a critical, large customer table that is heavily randomly updated with little or no re-referencing during the day but that is constantly scanned at night for batch purposes would have different processing characteristics in the day and at night.

Daytime settings:

$$VPSIZE = 1000 \qquad VPSEQT = 20 \qquad DWQT = 10 \qquad VDWQT = 2$$

Nighttime settings:

$$VPSIZE = 5000 \qquad VPSEQT = 90 \qquad DWQT = 10 \qquad VDWQT = 2$$

The Hit Ratio

Buffer Pool Hit Ratio

A buffer pool hit ratio is defined as the percentage of times the page was found in the pool. However, the hit ratio calculation GETPAGE/read I/O is not generally meaningful. Would 50:1 be a good number or maybe 70:1, and what would that really mean? This really is an application hit ratio or "read efficiency" from your monitor; it is only useful if your data access is almost all *random* and is not meaningful if the same page is constantly re-reading.

A more accurate hit ratio would be this system hit ratio:

$$(GETPAGEs - pages\ read)/GETPAGEs$$

The pages read are the synchronous I/O operations plus all pages read by prefetch, list prefetch, and dynamic prefetch.

This ratio can also be calculated for every application execution from the Accounting 101 record data for random access, sequential access, or both. Be very cautious when using a monitor that displays the buffer pool hit ratio. Find out what calculation is behind the hit ratio that your particular performance monitor reports. If the monitor shows a good hit ratio, you may have a problem and not know it.

A negative hit ratio can happen when prefetch pages are brought into the buffer pool and are never referenced. The pages may not get referenced for a couple of reasons: (1) the query ended, or (2) the prefetch pages were stolen for reuse before they could be used and had to be retrieved from disk again. We have seen one other situation that caused a negative hit ratio: sequential detection kept turning on dynamic prefetch, and very few of the pages were used from each prefetch stream.

The calculation of the hit ratio for the buffer pool that holds the DSNDB07 work files is a bit different from the aforementioned calculation. Refer to the section 'DSNDB07' earlier in this chapter for this calculation.

Hiperpool Hit Ratio

The hiperpool effectiveness ratio is calculated a bit differently.

Pages read from hiperpool/Pages written to hiperpool

One percent or 2% is not good, since the hiperpool is not really providing a benefit. Many pages are being moved to the hiperpool for no reason, and that is wasted overhead. ten percent or greater is a very good effectiveness percentage, until it gets too high. Effectiveness approaching 40% to 60% becomes a problem, because that percentage represents too many pages brought back to the virtual pool too quickly. This generally means that the underlying pool is not sized correctly or the VPSEQT ratio is incorrect. In most cases, it means that the underlying pool does not have enough room in the random area. Keep in mind that you will apply this percentage to the activity to determine the true I/O savings, which is in essence the measure of the effectiveness of the hiperpool.

Tuning with the DISPLAY BUFFERPOOL Command

In several cases the buffer pools can be tuned effectively using the DISPLAY BUFFER-POOL command. When a tool, such as the excellent DB2 Buffer Pool Tool, is not available for tuning, the following steps can be used to help tune buffer pools.

1. Use command and view statistics.
2. Make changes (to thresholds, size, object placement).
3. Use command again during processing and view statistics.
4. Measure statistics.

The output contains valuable information such as prefetch information (sequential, list, dynamic requests), pages read, prefetch I/O, and disablement (no buffer, no engine).

Figures 3.20, 3.21, and 3.22 show the DISPLAY BUFFERPOOL LSTATS option, DETAIL option, and version 6 enhancements.

This information can be used with spreadsheets that you create yourself to tune your buffer pools. The spreadsheet in figures 3.23-1 and 3.23-2 shows how to lay out your buffer pool information from the DISPLAY command to view the sizes and thresholds of your buffer pools. You can put calculations in your spreadsheets to help you determine how many pages are available in each buffer pool for certain operations such as parallelism. You also need a spreadsheet showing what is in each buffer pool (figures 3.24-1 through 3.24-3). You can download the spread sheets that we use from our web site, www.ylassoc.com. There is much more information on the web site that explains how the spreadsheets are used, what all the columns mean, and indications that point to potential problems.

Keep in mind that, although you can get good information from the DISPLAY BUFFERPOOL command, the incremental detail display shifts the time frame every time you perform a new display. Figures 3.25 and 3.26 contain information in the spreadsheets along with some notes on exactly what those figures mean and where some problems might occur.

```
-DISPLAY BUFFERPOOL(BP1) LIST LSTATS

DSNB401I - BUFFERPOOL NAME BP1, BUFFERPOOL ID 1, USE COUNT 2
DSNB402I - VIRTUAL BUFFERPOOL SIZE = 2000 BUFFERS
            ALLOCATED       = 2000  TO BE DELETED = 0
            IN-USE/UPDATED  =  300
DSNB403I - HIPERPOOL SIZE 4000 BUFFERS, CASTOUT = YES
            ALLOCATED       = 4000  TO BE DELETED = 0
            BACKED BY ES    = 2890
DSNB404I - THRESHOLDS -
            VP SEQUENTIAL   = 80    HP SEQUENTIAL = 80
            DEFERRED WRITE  = 50    VERTICAL DEFERRED WRT = 10
            PARALLEL SEQUENTIAL = 50
DSNB405I - HIPERSPACE NAME - @001SSOP
DSNB455I - SYNCHRONOUS I/O DELAYS -
            AVERAGE DELAY = 2 MAXIMUM DELAY = 32
            TOTAL PAGES    =25
DSN9022I - DSNB1CMD '-DISPLAY BUFFERPOOL' NORMAL COMPLETION
```

Figure 3.20   DISPLAY BUFFERPOOL LSTATS

```
-DISPLAY BUFFERPOOL(BP1) DETAIL

DSNB401I - BUFFERPOOL NAME BP1, BUFFERPOOL ID 1, USE COUNT 2
DSNB402I - VIRTUAL BUFFERPOOL SIZE = 2000 BUFFERS
               ALLOCATED       = 2000  TO BE DELETED = 0
               IN-USE/UPDATED  =  300
DSNB403I - HIPERPOOL SIZE 4000 BUFFERS, CASTOUT = YES
               ALLOCATED       = 4000  TO BE DELETED = 0
               BACKED BY ES    = 2890
DSNB404I - THRESHOLDS -
               VP SEQUENTIAL   = 80    HP SEQUENTIAL = 80
               DEFERRED WRITE = 50     VERTICAL DEFERRED WRT = 10
               PARALLEL SEQUENTIAL = 50
DSNB405I - HIPERSPACE NAME - @001SSOP
DSNB409I - INCREMENTAL STATISTICE SINCE 11:48:34 JAN 11, 2000
DSNB411I - RANDOM GETPAGE     = 400 SYNC READ I/O(R) = 280
           SEQ. GETPAGE       = 540 SYNC READ I/O(S) =  30
           DMTH HIT           = 0
DSNB412I - SEQUENTIAL PREFETCH -
               REQUESTS        = 0      PREFETCH I/O  = 0
               PAGES READ      = 0
DSNB413I - LIST PREFETCH -
               REQUESTS        = 0      PREFETCH I/O  = 0
               PAGES READ      = 0
```

Figure 3.21   DISPLAY BUFFERPOOL DETAIL

```
DSNB414I - DYNAMIC PREFETCH -
               REQUESTS        = 0      PREFETCH I/O        = 0
               PAGES READ      = 0
DSNB415I - PREFETCH DISABLED -
               NO BUFFER       = 0      NO READ ENGINE      = 0
DSNB420I - SYS PAGE UPDATES    = 0      SYS PAGES WRITTEN   = 0
           ASYNC WRITE I/O     = 0      SYNC WRITE I/O      = 0
DSNB421I - DWT HIT             = 0      VERTICAL DWT HIT    = 0
           NO WRITE ENGINE     = 0
DSNB430I - HIPERPOOL ACTIVITY (NOT USING ASYNCHRONOUS
           DATA MOVER FACILITY) -
               SYNC HP READS  = 200  SYNC HP WRITES    = 0
               ASYNC HP READS =   0  ASYNC HP READS    = 0
               READ FAILURES  =   0  WRITE FAILURES    = 0
DSNB431I - HIPERPOOL ACTIVITY (USING ASYNCHRONOUS
           DATA MOVER FACILITY) -
               HP READS       = 230  HP WRITES         = 3
               READ FAILURES  =   0  WRITE FAILURES    = 0
DSNB440 - PARALLEL ACTIVITY -
               PARALL REQUEST =   0  DEGRADED PARALL   = 0
```

Figure 3.21   DISPLAY BUFFERPOOL DETAIL *(cont.)*

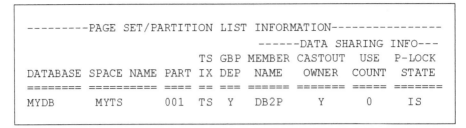

```
---------PAGE SET/PARTITION LIST INFORMATION---------------
                              -----DATA SHARING INFO---
                   TS GBP MEMBER CASTOUT  USE  P-LOCK
DATABASE SPACE NAME PART IX DEP  NAME    OWNER  COUNT  STATE
======== ========== ==== == === ======= ======= ===== =======
MYDB     MYTS        001 TS  Y   DB2P      Y       0    IS
```

Figure 3.22 DISPLAY BUFFERPOOL Version 6 Enhancements

	Pages	Numb Pages	% total	Getpages Random	Getpages Seq	Total Getpages	Sync I/O Random	Sync I/O Seq	Total Sync I/O
System Hit Ratio									
(Getpages-(SIO+PfPgs+LpfPgs+DynPfPgs))/Getpages * 100									
BP0	10,000	1,183	0	1,821,414	161,559	1,982,973	1,601	793	2,394
BP1	10,000	5	0	2,640	5,875	8,515	402	214	616
BP2	30,000	38	0	63,021	8	63,029	3	2	5
BP3	10,000	175	0	283,325	9,719	293,044	2	0	2
BP4	45,000	66,054	27	106,931,000	3,795,664	110,726,664	3,795,664	1,528	3,797,192
BP5	20,000	67,570	27	112,905,000	362,578	113,267,578	362,840	130	362,970
BP6	25,000	24,895	10	41,443,355	287,659	41,731,014	2,956,991	35	2,957,026
BP7	20,000	0	0	1	1	2	1	1	2
BP8	20,000	40	0	0	66,708	66,708	0	4,664	4,664
BP9	10,000	72,426	29	1,530,201	119,878,000	121,408,201	84	36	120
BP10	30,000	14,615	6	24,162,048	336,530	24,498,578	1,570,220	286	1,570,506
BP11	5,000	0	0			0			0
BP12	5,000	0	0			0			0
BP30	1,000	0	0			0			0
BP31	1,000	0	0			0			0
BP32K	5000	0	0	24	3	27	2	1	3
Totals	247,000	247,000		289,142,029	124,904,304	414,046,333	8,687,810	7,690	8,695,500

Figure 3.23-1 Buffer Pool Spread Sheet

				Async Seq PF	Async List PF	Async Dyn PF	Total Async I/O		BP Hit Ratio	GP/IO Ratio
BP0				36,170	0	594	36,764		98.03%	51
BP1				7,341	10	26	7,377		6.13%	2
BP2				146	0	0	146		99.76%	418
BP3				0	0	0	0		100.00%	146522
BP4				1,302,785	21,744	621,329	1,945,858		94.81%	20
BP5				1,434	0	53,926	55,360		99.63%	271
BP6				289,411	0	277,100	566,511		91.56%	12
BP7							0		0.00%	1
BP8				99,620	0	0	99,620		-56.33%	1
BP9				2,568	0	8,081	10,649		99.99%	11274
BP10				333,876	17,898,544	1,637,860	19,870,280		12.48%	2
BP11							0			
BP12							0			
BP30							0			
BP31				1,113,961	0	0	1,113,961			
BP32K				0	0	0	0		88.89%	9
Totals				3,187,312	17,920,298	2,598,916	23,706,526		92.17%	13

Figure 3.23-2 Buffer Pool Spread Sheet

HP Effectiveness Ratio
Pages Read from the HP/Pages Written to the HP
This is the effectiveness (benefit) ratio, and is the most meaningful

	HP				Reads Sync	Async	ADMF	Total Reads	Sequential Use	Random Use	Effective Ratio	Hit Ratio
BP 0	0							0				0.0%
BP 1	0							0				0.0%
BP 2	15,000				0	0	0	0				0.0%
BP 3	0							0				0.0%
BP 4	5,000				139,051	53,051	44,464	236,566	41%	59%	0.2%	0.2%
BP 5	10,000				829,693	25,029	13,068	867,790	4%	96%	67.5%	0.8%
BP 6	15,000				319,607	1,456	6,760	327,823	3%	97%	8.5%	0.9%
BP 7	16,170							0				
BP 8	15,000				19	407	4,363	4,789	100%	0%	4.8%	-12.7%
BP 9	0							0				0.0%
BP 10	50,000				199,381	945,697	329,805	1,474,883	86%	14%	23.0%	48.2%
BP 11	0							0				
BP 12	0							0				
BP 30	0							0				
BP 31	0							0				0.0%
BP 32K	0							0				0.0%

Figure 3.24-1   Buffer Pool Spread Sheet

	HP				Writes Sync	Async	ADMF	Total Writes	Total Reads	Effectiveness Ratio
BP0	0							0	0	
BP1	0							0	0	
BP2	15,000				0	0	0	0	0	
BP3	0							0	0	
BP4	5,000				758	123,451	134,904,407	135,028,616	236,566	0.2%
BP5	10,000				0	105,691	1,180,090	1,285,781	867,790	67.5%
BP6	15,000				0	185,370	3,665,738	3,851,108	327,823	8.5%
BP7	16,170							0	0	
BP8	15,000				0	44,504	55,926	100,430	4,789	4.8%
BP9	0							0	0	
BP10	50,000				0	1,202,300	5,200,288	6,402,588	1,474,883	23.0%
BP11	0							0	0	
BP12	0							0	0	
BP30	0							0	0	
BP31	0							0	0	
BP32K	0							0	0	

Figure 3.24-2   Buffer Pool Spread Sheet

HP Hit Ratio
HP Reads/(Getpages - Synch Reads - Asynch Reads)
This is the % of BP Hits found in HP

	HP				HP Reads	Getpages	Sync Reads	Async Reads	HP Hit Ratio
BP0	0				0	1,982,973	2,394	36,764	0.0%
BP1	0				0	8,515	616	7,377	0.0%
BP2	15,000				0	63,029	5	146	0.0%
BP3	0				0	293,044	2	0	0.0%
BP4	5,000				236,566	110,726,664	3,797,192	1,945,858	0.2%
BP5	10,000				867,790	113,267,578	362,970	55,360	0.8%
BP6	15,000				327,823	41,731,014	2,957,026	566,511	0.9%
BP7	16,170				0	2	2	0	
BP8	15,000				4,789	66,708	4,664	99,620	-12.7%
BP9	0				0	121,408,201	120	10,649	0.0%
BP10	50,000				1,474,883	24,498,578	1,570,506	19,870,280	48.2%
BP11	0				0	0	0	0	
BP12	0				0	0	0	0	
BP30	0				0	0	0	0	
BP31	0				0	0	0	1,113,961	0.0%
BP32K	0				0	27	3	0	0.0%

Figure 3.24-3   Buffer Pool Spread Sheet

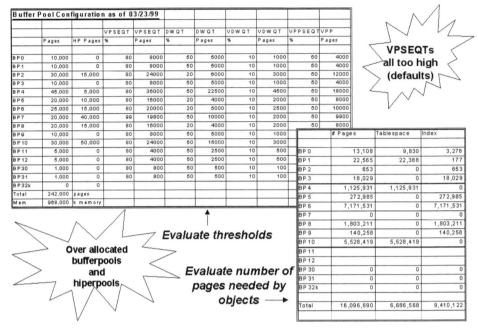

Figure 3.25 Example Buffer Pool Layout (Prior to Tuning)

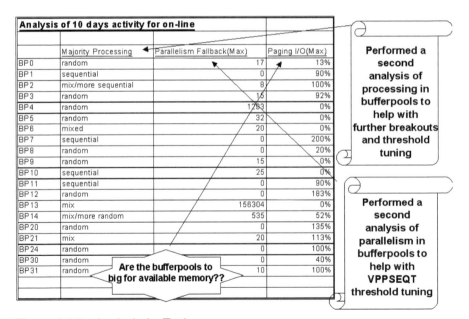

Figure 3.26 Analysis for Tuning

Tuning Buffer Pools with the Buffer Pool Tool®

There is only one tool on the market for tuning buffer pools and providing predictive analysis for buffer pool changes. This tool is the DB2 Buffer Pool Tool from Responsive Systems, also part of the IBM suite of tools for DB2 (figures 3.27-1 through 3-27-3).

Data Spaces

As of version 6, we now can define buffer pools in data spaces. Data spaces are basically buffer pools defined in a separate area of memory. Data spaces are defined as address spaces of up to 2 GB that can hold only data. These address spaces are not allowed to execute program code. The resources to back data spaces are the same as those used for normal address spaces, which are the same as for any virtual storage: a combination of central

```
Statistics for Table Space.....................DB2PO.SOLNSORD

Number of GetP..............690,589   29.0% of pool GetP
 Number of Sequential Access.634,019  91.8% of GetP         <<< Note
 Number of Random Access......56,570   8.2% of GetP
 Number of RID_List...............0    0.0% of GetP

 Number of Random Misses......27,438        7.6 Misses per Sec
 Number of Misses (others)....19,740        5.5 Misses per Sec
 Number of No_Reads...............0    0.0% of GetP
 Number of Hits..............643,411  95.2% of GetP (Appl. HIT
RATIO)
 System HIT RATIO..............-1.9 %
 Avg. Page Residency.............0 Seconds
```

Figure 3.27-1   Buffer Pool Tool—Object Statistical Analysis

```
Number of Pages Read.................704,258     195.6 Pages per Second
 Number of Sync  Pages Read.........27,938    4.0% of Pages Read
 Number of SPref Pages Read........654,078   92.9% of Pages Read
 Number of LPref Pages Read..............0    0.0% of Pages Read
 Number of DPref Pages Read.........22,242    3.2% of Pages Read
Number of Read I/Os.................49,414       13.7 Read I/Os per Sec
 Number of Sync  Read  I/Os.........27,938   56.5% of Read I/Os
 Number of SPref Read  I/Os.........20,735   42.0% of Read I/Os
 Number of LPref Read  I/Os..............0    0.0% of Read I/Os
 Number of DPref Read  I/Os............741    1.5% of Read I/Os
 Delay  of Sync  Read  I/Os.............21   Avg. MSeconds (Max 239)
 Delay  of SPref Read  I/Os.............38   Avg. MSeconds (Max 250)
 Delay  of LPref Read  I/Os..............0   Avg. MSeconds (Max 0)
 Delay  of DPref Read  I/Os.............43   Avg. MSeconds (Max 183)
```

Figure 3.27-2   Buffer Pool Tool—Object Statistical Analysis

```
Number of SetW (Updates)............14,443   8.5% of pool SetW

Number of Pages Written.............8,055        2.2 Pages per Sec
   Number of Sync  Pages Written ..........1   0.0% of Pages Written
   Number of ASync Pages Written ......8,054 100.0% of Pages Written

Number of Write I/Os................4,833        1.3 I/Os per Sec
   Number of Sync  Write I/Os..............1   0.0% of Write I/Os
   Number of ASync Write I/Os..........4,832 100.0% of Write I/Os
   Delay  of Sync  Write I/Os..............6   Avg. MSeconds (Max 6)
   Delay  of ASync Write I/Os..............4   Avg. MSeconds (Max 219)
```

Average Pages/Write (Asynch): 1.67

Figure 3.27-3   Buffer Pool Tool—Object Statistical Analysis

storage, expanded storage frames, and auxiliary storage. There can be paging activity between the paging device and central storage; when paging is used, low-use pages are paged out.

Virtual buffer pools use virtual storage space in the DBM1 address space, hiperpools take virtual storage from expanded memory, and virtual pools in data spaces take advantage of MVS data space. Data spaces still require a small amount of memory in DBM1 (each buffer requires 128 bytes), but using data spaces frees up memory in DBM1 for other uses. Data spaces allow up to 32 GB of storage (for 4K pages). You can have more space in a data space if you have larger page sizes (e.g., 32K), but the limitation is currently fixed at a total of 8 million pages (regardless of size; see figure 3.28). You define a buffer pool to use data space by specifying VPTYPE(DATASPACE). The default, of course, is VPTYPE(PRIMARY), which is what DB2 has always used.

I/O processing can directly address the buffers in a data space. An MVCL machine instruction (MOVE LONG) is used to move a data page into and out of a look-aside buffer in DBM1 before it can be referenced or updated. Page movement between buffers in the data space and the look-aside pool occurs at GETPAGE when DB2 uses the MVCL to COPY data into a look-aside pool and at RELPAGE when DB2 uses the MVCL to COPY the changed data page back to buffers in the data space (figure 3.29). The implementation of the data spaces is limited because 64-bit addressability is not available (though it is tentatively scheduled for OS/390 Version 2 Release 10). The memory where data spaces reside is not directly addressable, thus the need for the look-aside pool. When this feature is available, we will be able to fully implement data spaces without the use of a look-aside

Buffers size	Total amount of data space
4 KB	32 GB
8 KB	64 GB
16 KB	128 GB
32 KB	256 GB

Figure 3.28   Data Space Sizes

During a Getpage operation DB2 copies the data via a MVCL to the lookaside pool.

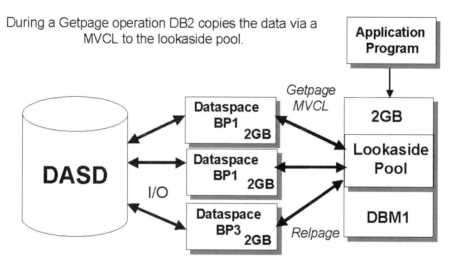

During a Relpage operation DB2 copies the changed data back to the bufferpool.

Figure 3.29   Data Spaces: 32-Bit Addressability

pool, since all memory will be directly addressable (figure 3.30). Until then, use buffer pools in data spaces only if you are constrained in the DBM1 address space or have large objects and cannot achieve an optimal hit ratio.

Keep in mind that data space are not hiperpools, nor are they necessarily a replacement for hiperpools. Hiperpools are generally for random use and are used to cache pages that fall off the LRU queue so that they can be re-referenced. Hiperpools cache only clean

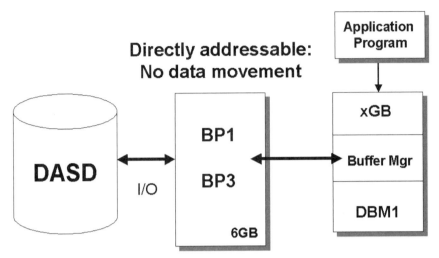

Figure 3.30   Data Spaces: 64-Bit Addressability

(not updated) pages. Data spaces work just like buffer pools, except they take up a different area of memory. They can cache clean or dirty pages and have direct access to disk. There is still a use for hiperpools, as data spaces simply offer more room for buffer pools. You can do I/O on a data space, whereas for a hiperpool, the pages must be moved back to the virtual buffer pool to do this.

One of the most important benefits of data spaces is that you can move the read-only portion of the EDM pool to a data space (via a DSNZPARM). This allows you to move objects such as the dynamic SQL cache to a data space, relieving the pressure on the EDM pool in the DBM1 address space. You can implement this by specifying a nonzero value for EDMPOOL DATA SPACE SIZE in the DB2 install panels.

Data spaces provide a foundation for DB2 to exploit large real storage when 64-bit addressability is implemented. With real storage support greater than 2GB coming in future generations of CMOS processors, DB2 will be able to scale by caching more data in memory and performing I/O directly against buffers in data spaces. This will help support more parallel queries and utilities, help changed data stay in memory longer, reduce write I/O for frequently updated data, and also help avoid write I/O for sort work files.

Buffer Pool Effects on Optimization

The optimizer can be affected by the virtual buffer pool and hiperpool definitions. The access path selection process may be affected; for example, inner and outer table selection for joins can be influenced by which table fits best into memory.

RID Pool

The RID (row identifier) pool is used for storing and sorting RIDs for operations such as

- List prefetch
- Multiple index access
- Hybrid joins
- Enforcing unique keys while updating multiple rows

The optimizer looks at the RID pool for prefetch and RID use. The full use of the RID pool is possible for any single user at run time. Run time can cause a table space scan if not enough space is available in the RID. For example, if you want to retrieve 10,000 rows from a 100,000,000-row table and no RID pool is available, a scan of 100,000,000 rows can occur at any time and without external notification. The optimizer assumes that physical I/O is reduced with a large pool.

Size

The default size of the RID pool is currently 4 MB unless otherwise specified. The size can be set from 16 K to 1,000 MB. If the size is set to 0, DB2 does not use the RID pool, which prevents list prefetch and multiple-index access operations. The size is set with an installation parameter. The RID pool is created at start-up time, but no space is allocated until RID storage is actually needed. It is then allocated above the 16MB line in 16K blocks as needed, until the maximum size specified in installation panel DSNTIPC is reached. There are a few guidelines for setting the RID pool size. You should have as large a RID pool as required, because it is a benefit for processing, especially with the recently added index screening as part of the RID selection process.

For example, suppose a process needs 1.5 million rows prefetched from a table with 100,000,000 rows. The optimizer calculates the RID pool size for this single query as follows:

1.5 million	number of rows
× 4	RID size in bytes (5 bytes for LARGE tables)
× 2	RID sort needs twice the raw data
12.0 MB	
× 2	assumes maximum size is half of RID pool
24.0 MB	

That means that at least a 24.0MB RID pool is required to support list prefetch processing for this one user query. But other users (many closely monitored systems show up to 10,000 SQL statements per second) are also doing list prefetch, multiple-index access, and hybrid join operations that need to use the RID pool. It is better to oversize the RID pool than to deal with access path failures when the RID pool cannot accommodate a particular critical query. The general formula for RID pool storage is

> Number of concurrent RID processing activities
> × Average number of RIDs
> × 2
> × 4 (bytes per RID, or 5 if LARGE or DSSIZE)

Statistics to Monitor

There are three statistics to monitor for RID pool tuning opportunities (figure 3.31).

RIDs over RDS Limit
RIDs over the RDS limit is the number of times list prefetch is turned off because the RID list built for a single set of index entries is greater than 25% of the number of rows in the table. If this is the case, DB2 determines that instead of using list prefetch to satisfy a query, it would be more efficient to perform a table space scan, which may or may not be good, depending on the size of the table accessed. Increasing the size of the RID pool

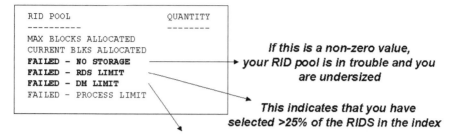

```
RID POOL                  QUANTITY
----------                --------
MAX BLOCKS ALLOCATED
CURRENT BLKS ALLOCATED
FAILED - NO STORAGE
FAILED - RDS LIMIT
FAILED - DM LIMIT
FAILED - PROCESS LIMIT
```

*If this is a non-zero value,
your RID pool is in trouble and you
are undersized*

*This indicates that you have
selected >25% of the RIDS in the index*

*Indicates that you have selected
over 16 Million RIDs*

Figure 3.31 RID Pool Statistics Report

will *not* help in this case. This application issue for access paths needs to be evaluated for queries using list prefetch.

There is one critical issue regarding this type of failure. The 25% threshold is actually stored in the package or plan at bind time; therefore, it may no longer match the real 25% value and in fact could be far less. It is important to know what packages and plans are using list prefetch, and on what tables. If the underlying table is growing, the packages and plans that are dependent on it should be rebound after a RUNSTATS utility has updated the statistics.

RID over DM Limit

RIDs exceed the DM limit when over 16 million RIDs are required to satisfy a query. Currently, DB2 has a 16-million RID limit. The consequence of hitting this limit can be falling back to a table space scan. To control this, you have a couple of options:

- Fix the index by doing something creative.
- Add an additional index better suited for filtering.
- Force list prefetch off, and use another index.
- Rewrite the query.
- Maybe the query simply requires a table space scan.

Insufficient Pool Size

Insufficient pool size indicates that the RID pool is too small.

Effects on Optimization

If the optimizer has determined that a RID pool is too small to build a RID list for a query, it will use an alternative access path. Be sure that the RID pool is the same size between test and production, or you could see different results in your EXPLAIN output and in your query execution.

SORT Pool

DB2 and Sorting

Sorts are performed in two phases (figure 3.32):

1. Initialization: DB2 builds ordered sets of runs from the given input.
2. Merge: DB2 merges the runs together.

At start-up, DB2 allocates a sort pool in the private area of the DBM1 address space. DB2 uses a special sorting technique called a tournament sort. During sorting processes, it is common for this algorithm to produce logical work files called *runs,* which are intermediate sets of ordered data. If the SORT pool is large enough, the sort completes in that

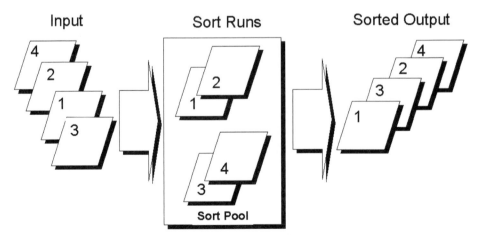

Figure 3.32 Basic SORT Pool Operation

area. More often than not, the sort cannot complete in the SORT pool, so the runs are moved into DSNDB07. These runs are later merged to complete the sort. When DSNDB07 is used for holding the pages that make up the sort runs, you can experience performance degradation if the pages are externalized to the physical work files, since they have to be read back in later to complete the sort.

Make sure that you assign an adequately sized SORT pool to your system and avoid really large SQL sorts in programs that need to execute fast. Overflow to DSNDB07 is reported in IFCID (traces), and your performance monitor can report these events.

Size

The sort pool size defaults to 1 MB unless otherwise specified. It can range in size from 240 K to 64 MB and is set with an installation DSNZPARM. The larger the SORT pool (sort work area), the fewer sort runs are produced. If the SORT pool is large enough, the buffer pools and DSNDB07 are not used. If buffer pools and DSNDB07 are not used, performance is better due to less I/O. You should make the SORT pool and DSNDB07 large, because you do not want sorted pages written to disk (figure 3.33).

DSNDB07 Work Files

For your DSNDB07 table space, you should have a minimum of five work data sets that are all equally large. Generally, you do not want secondary extents on these files. DB2 allocates the data sets for use in a round-robin fashion over the volumes. If the sizes are different, you will experience poorer performance in certain situations. The same is true

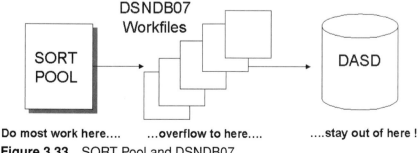

Do most work here....   ...overflow to here....   ....stay out of here !
Figure 3.33   SORT Pool and DSNDB07

when you have secondary extents; you should put secondary extents either on all the volumes or on none. For example, do a massive GROUP BY with different sizes, and compare the code length for processing with that of a GROUP BY with equal sizes. You will notice a difference.

As an analogy, pretend that you are on the beach and you have five empty buckets of different sizes. You have 5,000 requests for temporarily storing sand. You have to allocate a portion of each for each user and each suballocation for groups, sorts, and so on. As you move along from bucket to bucket, you have to check whether any of the different-sized buckets are full. If any are, you must skip them, record this exception information, and so on.

The same is true for secondary extents: each extent on a disk file has a different control block controlling access, and extra logic determines the correct data area to access. If everything is equal, you can optimize your approach. Different sizes cause problems. If needed, put secondary extents on all work files.

You should also allocate these data sets on separate I/O paths and volumes. This helps to minimize I/O contentions against the data sets. Keep in mind that DB2 does not give any special priority to these data sets or recognize their importance and usage. It is up to you to be sure that these data sets are placed and sized in the most optimal manner so that performance does not suffer. If you are constrained to only one disk volume, it would be better to have one large work file rather than many small ones on the same volume.

These work-file data sets in DSNDB07 are used for more than just sorting. They are also used for view materialization, temporary table materialization, nested table expression materializations, noncorrelated in-lists, and more. So by not properly tuning your sort processes and the data sets supporting them, you can negatively affect these other operations as well.

To determine whether your sort pool is being monopolized by the materialization of global temporary tables, you can run performance class 8 trace using IFCID 311. If you determine that this is the case, one option is to use declared temporary tables, which are not materialized in DSNDB07 (more on temporary tables in Chapter 14).

Application Impacts

Sorts can be caused by ORDER BY, GROUP BY, DISTINCT, UNION (except UNION ALL), joins (all methods), noncorrelated subqueries, or CREATE INDEX on existing data.

These are some options you can implement in your application to obtain optimal performance from the SORT pool and to avoid abusing it.

- Do not retrieve columns in your SQL statement that are unnecessary, because if they have to be sorted, this increases the total amount of data to be sorted.
- Do not unnecessarily select variable-character columns, because they are padded to their maximum length and can cause very large, cumbersome sorts.
- Do not code unnecessary ORDER BY, GROUP BY, or DISTINCT clauses.
- Do not sort rows that are greater than 4 K, because DB2 has to invoke a tag sort. RDS sorts do not use 32K work files, so if the row is larger than 4 K, a tag sort is performed, which increases the processing time for the query. A tag sort does a preliminary scan of the data and extracts the sort key and the RID. The tags are then sorted and linked up with the data via the RID. You can see whether this is occurring in your DB2 subsystem by monitoring the SORT TYPE field for the value ESA-TAG.

As an example of how applications affect sort, take a look at figure 3.34. The first query is a SELECT *, and the second query selects just a few necessary columns. When the data is sorted for each of the queries, there is a big difference. Notice the first query requires four work files and a merge and has a larger average elapsed time, all because of the larger row size. This adds time to the SQL statement execution. This information can be obtained through a performance trace: class 3 IFCID 63 and 96.

EDM Pool

Size

The EDM pool (environmental descriptor manager) contains many items, including these:

- DBDs: database descriptors
- SKCTs: skeleton cursor tables
- CTs: cursor tables (copies of the SKCTs)
- SKPTs: skeleton package tables

```
SELECT * FROM LARGE_TABLE ORDER BY NON_INDEX_COL

SORT ACTIVITY

TOTAL SORTS     :      1        AET/SORTS      :      .390489
WORKFILES       :      4.00     RECORDS        :      5089
INIT.WRKFILE    :      3.00     KEY SIZE       :      12.00
ROWS DELETED    :      0.00     DATA SIZE      :      518.00
MERGE PASSES    :      1.00     RECORD SIZE    :      530.00
SORT COLUMNS    :      31       SORT KEYS      :      1.00


SELECT COL1, COL2 FROM LARGE_TABLE ORDER BY NON_INDEX_COL

SORT ACTIVITY

TOTAL SORTS     :      1        AET/SORTS      :      .190338
WORKFILES       :      1.00     RECORDS        :      5089
INIT.WRKFILE    :      1.00     KEY SIZE       :      12.00
ROWS DELETED    :      0.00     DATA SIZE      :      40.00
MERGE PASSES    :      0.00     RECORD SIZE    :      62.00
SORT COLUMNS    :      2        SORT KEYS      :      1.00
```

Figure 3.34   Sort Trace Output

- PTs: package tables (copies of the SKPTs)
- Authorization cache block for each plan, except those with CACHESIZE set to 0
- Skeletons of dynamic SQL for CACHE DYNAMIC SQL

If the pool is too small, you will see increased I/O activity in the following DB2 table spaces, which support the DB2 directory:

DSNDB01.DBD01

DSNDB01.SPT01

DSNDB01.SCT02

Our main goal for the EDM pool is to limit the I/O against the directory and catalog. If the pool is too small, you will also see increased response times due to the loading of the SKCTs, SKPTs, and DBDs and the re-preparing of the dynamic SQL statements because they could not remained cached. If your EDM pool is too small, you will also see fewer threads used concurrently because DB2 knows that it does not have the appropriate resources to allocate or start new threads. If you increase the EDM pool, you may see an immediate increase in the number of threads allowed.

By correctly sizing the EDM pool, you can prevent unnecessary I/O from accumulating for a transaction. An SKCT, an SKPT, or a DBD that has to be reloaded into the EDM pool requires additional I/O. Reloading can happen if the pool pages are stolen because the EDM pool is too small. Pages in the pool are maintained on an LRU queue, and the least recently used pages are stolen if required.

You can save some space in the EDM pool if your plans are granted to public, because you can specify a CACHESIZE of 0 in the BIND statement.

If you are operating in a data sharing environment, you also have to increase the size of the EDM pool on each member in the data sharing group. Because changes to the DBD are not invalidated through the coupling facility, when a DBD changes, all other members are notified to load a fresh DBD when a new transaction starts. Current transactions use the old DBD (this is not a problem). To account for this, you should enlarge the EDM pool by at least 10% for normal systems. This increase depends on frequency of CREATEs, ALTERs, and DROPs, due to the way DB2 performs cross invalidations of objects between members for consistency.

However, when a plan or package is bound or rebound, there are no multiple copies of SKCTs and SKPTs in the EDM pool. The binder waits for all users to finish using these objects and then binds the plan or package. The member notifies all other DB2s via the coupling facility's shared communication area (SCA) to invalidate their copy in their EDM pool. EDM pools are not backed in the coupling facility because the change is not as frequent as for normal data. For more information about data sharing, refer to Section 6.

Another item to keep in mind regarding EDM pool size is that it may need to be increased during a release migration, because when plans or packages are rebound in the new release, an internal optimization process may increase their size. Be sure to monitor the efficiency of the EDM pool during a release migration.

Scared of oversizing the EDM pool? Don't be. The EDM is a fixed chunk of memory, and the worst that could happen is some paging. But if the EDM pool is too small, the consequences are poor performance in your application due to extra I/O required to load the package and plan components. You can monitor the FREE PG IN CHAIN parameter in the statistics report. If it is more than 20% of the total number of pages in the EDM pool during peak processing periods, it may be okay to reduce the size.

EDM Pool Efficiency

You can measure the following ratios to determine whether your EDM pool is efficient. Think of these as EDM pool hit ratios:

- CT requests versus CTs not in EDM pool
- PT requests versus PTs not in EDM pool
- DBD requests versus DBDs not in EDM pool

What you want is a ratio of 1 out of 5 for each of these. An 80% hit ratio is what you are aiming for (figure 3.35).

Some issues surrounding the management of the EDM pool storage relate directly to how you are managing your programs (packages). First of all, you want to use packages, not DBRMs bound to plans. You also want to keep in mind that using

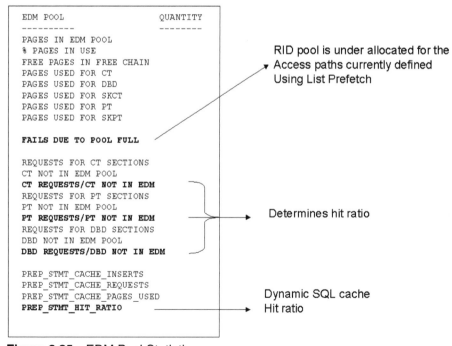

Figure 3.35   EDM Pool Statistics

DEGREE(ANY) increases EDM pool size (because it requires two access paths for each bound SQL statement). DB2 keeps one access path when parallelism is chosen and one access path when it is not. As you know, the decision to use parallelism is both a bind-time and run-time decision. So at run time, if the resources (i.e., buffer pool) are not there to support the parallelism, DB2 falls back to the nonparallel alternate access path. (For more information on parallelism, refer to Chapter 21). If you are not using parallelism or do not have the resources to support it, do not bind your packages with DEGREE(ANY), because you would be wasting storage in the EDM pool. You can use AVGSIZE in SYSPLAN or SYSPACKAGE to determine the increase necessary to support DEGREE(ANY). You also want to use RELEASE(COMMIT) only when appropriate and only for infrequently used packages and plans to get them out of EDM pool more quickly and free up the memory. Also, do not forget that as of version 6, you can move the dynamic statement cache as well as other read-only portions of the EDM pool into a data space.

Keep in mind that when a thread is created for the first time, the plan causes its related SKCT to be read in from DSNDB01 (the directory) to BP0 and then moved to the EDM pool. What if your BP0 is cluttered with other objects that do not belong there or is not properly tuned? Thread-creation performance could suffer. DBDs, plans, and packages are all loaded into the EDM pool via BP0, so keep it clean! For information on how to tune BP0, refer to the section "Buffer Pool 0 (BP0)" earlier in this chapter.

EDM Pool Issues

Dynamic SQL Caching

When statement caching is active, DB2 stores the header information in an EDM pool block and the SQL statement in one or more EDM pool blocks (figure 3.36). Skeleton copies of cached dynamic statements are kept in the EDM pool. But keep in mind that your static SQL statement components were already there, and so are the DBDs. If you are going to use dynamic SQL caching, you have to pay attention to your EDM pool size, because an EDM pool that is too small can affect the performance of static SQL also. Cached statements are not backed by disk. If its pages are stolen and the statement is reused, it will have to be prepared again. Static mini-binds can be flushed from EDM by LRU but are backed by disk and can be retrieved when used again. Statistics on the statistics long report (figure 3.37) help to monitor cache use, and trace fields show the effectiveness of cache.

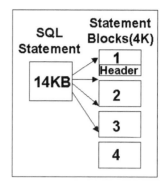

A single block of EDM storage
For both header and cached statement

Figure 3.36   Dynamic SQL Caching

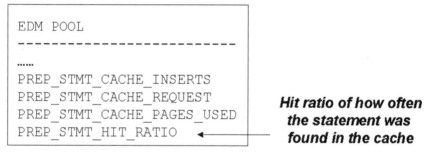

*Hit ratio of how often
the statement was
found in the cache*

Figure 3.37   Measuring Dynamic SQL Caching

DBD Growth

If left unchecked, some DBDs can grow to the point that they consume too much of the EDM pool and one day may not even be able to load. As an example, we can look at systems that use QMF.

QMF (Query Management Facility) has a SAVE DATA function to create an immediate table to save results of a query. These tables are usually used and then DROPped. DB2 always has to be able to recover, and the data is in the log, even though in this case there is no image copy of table. DB2 has stored the DDL (data definition language) of the table in a DBD so that it can reconstruct the table if necessary. The DBD now grows with every SAVE DATA command issued in QMF. To control this, you must use the MODIFY utility to reclaim the space and shrink the DBD size. This is almost never done, although it is common to create all sorts of tables for short use and then drop them. One day DB2 will try but not be able to load the DBD into the EDM pool due to size thresholds.

Some relief was introduced with version 6, which allows the DBD to be split into more manageable 32K chunks, but that does not solve the problem of unnecessary DBD growth. Splitting assists in loading the larger DBDs that are becoming more common with systems that have an extremely large number of objects, such as SAP systems.

> *Note: DBDs created before version 6 are not automatically stored in 32K pieces in the EDM pool until a DDL change causes the DBD to be written out.*

Just one more thought on this DBD and QMF issue. If the QMF objects are in BP0, they can steal pages that are truly needed by DB2, not exactly an ideal practice for good overall performance.

Unnecessary Packages in Pool

Another issue with the EDM pool and performance is that the EDM pool can often get flooded with unnecessary packages, due to the implementation of the myth that we should bind all online packages into one plan and all batches in another. Wrong! This technique requires more storage in the EDM pool; if you specify RELEASE(DEALLOCATE) for plans with a large number of packages, the space in the EDM pool is expanded greatly. This technique also generally takes away storage from other potential uses and uses more CPU processing to manage the storage and the longer chains. Also, increases in EDM pool storage may force you to use RELEASE(COMMIT) where you should otherwise use RELEASE(DEALLOCATE). Build plans by application and use.

Release Parameter

If you are experiencing constraints in the EDM pool and have already evaluated other tuning options, you can consider using RELEASE(COMMIT) for some of your infrequently used packages. This allows objects to be released earlier from the EDM pool. However, use of this parameter somewhat contradicts other performance considerations, so be careful with this. For more information on the RELEASE parameter, you can refer to Chapter 10, General Application Design.

Thread Storage

If you are seeing a constant growth problem in the EDM pool, you may want to specify YES for the DSNZPARM CONTSTOR (contract thread storage). For best performance, this parameter usually should be NO. This is to be used only on systems with long-running threads that are absolutely constrained by storage and need some relief. This allows DB2 to release unused thread storage at commit points rather than at thread deallocation. Be careful, as this may have an adverse effect on performance. Use this only if you are constrained in the EDM pool and absolutely cannot increase its size, have exhausted other tuning options, and cannot move the read-only object to a data space.

Database Design and Tuning

Catalog and Directory

Physical Database Objects

VLDBs, VLTBs, and Warehouses

Large Objects (LOBs)

Special Tables

Roles in Database Implementation

## CHAPTER 4

Catalog and Directory

Overview

The DB2 catalog and directory act as central repositories for all information about the objects in the subsystem, authorizations, and communications necessary to support DB2. A brief description of both the DB2 catalog and directory is provided in this chapter, but more important are the explanations of their usage, including some of the issues surrounding maintenance, access, and the physical placement of objects. The DB2 catalog and directory are the repository for all information about all databases, tables, table space, and indexes and need to be given consideration in terms of performance also. There are things we can do to the physical objects and the surrounding environment to help with performance for objects in the directory and particularly in the Catalog. Performance of the catalog and directory is important because constant access occurs daily in a normal environment for such things as authorization checking, data definition language, dynamic SQL, reoptimizations of SQL, and package binding and rebinding and many other needs.

This chapter also includes some catalog queries for executing reports from the DB2 catalog to extract object information to be used in different aspects of performance analysis. These query results can be used for design reviews, troubleshooting, and integrity checking and can be very useful in conjunction with EXPLAIN output.

Catalog

The DB2 catalog is composed of over 60 DB2 tables and supporting indexes and can be accessed by SQL. The catalog contains details about DB2 objects obtained from the DDL (data definition language) when an object is created or altered or from the DCL (data control language) when an authorization is granted on an object or group of objects. The catalog also contains information about communications with other DB2 and non-DB2 databases through the use of the communications database (CDB), which contains information about VTAM and TCP/IP addresses. It is critical that access to the catalog be as optimal as possible, and that includes proper care and maintenance of the structures supporting the catalog.

Storage and Maintenance

Data Sets

It is important to take into consideration proper allocation and placement of the data sets supporting the DB2 catalog. If you are using DFSMS for data-set management, you should assign the data sets to classes and groups that are defined for high performance and high availability with no migration allowed. (Refer to Chapter 1, "I/O and Storage Management," for information on DFSMS usage.) If the catalog for a heavily used production subsystem is in DFSMS multivolume data sets, there is a high potential for performance problems. It is recommended that large, contiguous data sets be used for heavily accessed, critical DB2 resources. Multivolume, multiextent data sets take more time and I/O than single-volume, single-extent data sets, which could affect the performance of processes accessing the catalog. Allowing these data sets to go into secondary extents could cause an increase in I/O against the catalog. If data set extents are common for any catalog table space, that table space's size allocation should be increased by executing the RECOVER utility on the appropriate catalog database or executing the REORG utility on the appropriate table space.

Recovery

Due to relationships and dependencies in the catalog, there is a specific order to recovering catalog datasets.

1. DSNDB01.SYSUTILX
2. DSNDB01.DBD01
3. SYSUTILX indexes
4. DSNDB06.SYSCOPY
5. SYSCOPY (3) indexes (IBM only)
6. DSNDB01.SYSLGRNX

7. SYSLGRNX indexes

8. DSNDB06.SYSDBAUT

9. SYSDBAUT (3) indexes (IBM only)

10. DSNDB06.SYSUSER

11. DSNDB06.SYSDBASE

12. SYSDBASE indexes (IBM only)

13. SYSUSER (3) indexes (IBM only)

14. All other catalog and directory table spaces and indexes

15. Catalog indexes (user-defined)

16. System utility table spaces, such as QMF

17. Communications database

18. Object and application registration tables

19. Resource limit specification tables

20. User table spaces

RUNSTATS

RUNSTATS should be run frequently on the DB2 catalog. The frequency depends on the amount of DDL, DML (data manipulation language), and other activities that update the catalog tables. Activities that update, insert, and delete rows in DB2 catalog tables can cause fragmentation and indirect references. DB2 cannot appropriately optimize queries against the catalog without having RUNSTATS current on the catalog table spaces and index spaces, and without current RUNSTATS it is difficult to determine when a REORG is necessary. The same principles apply for the DB2 catalog objects and DB2 user-defined objects.

Reorganization

You can also determine when to reorganize the DB2 catalog table spaces and index spaces by using the same techniques used for application table spaces and index spaces. First, ensure that statistics are kept current by using RUNSTATS based upon the frequency of changes in the catalog, so that decisions for reorganizations are based on current numbers. A reorganization can also be used if the objects are in extents or if unused space needs to be reclaimed. Extents in the catalog tables can cause additional I/O on the tables. In this situation, the catalog space should be increased by using REORG or by running the RECOVER utility (see the section "Recovery" in this chapter) on the appropriate database. DFDSS and HSM are shortcuts that can offer immediate relief to the problem and can quickly combine all the space into a single extent. When you have the space elsewhere, you can use the utility DFDSS to copy it to another location that combines all the space used into a single primary extent. The DB2 subsystem needs to be shut down to use this approach, which should be used only as a temporary measure and only when the normal procedures cannot be followed. Also, you can use HSM to perform a simple migrate and restore, which will remove any extents. This also requires the DB2 subsystem to be shut down.

DB2 catalog reorganizations have been possible only since version 4, due to complicated list structures, linkages, and internal hashing in the catalog. Prior to version 4, the RECOVER utility was the only option for reorganizing the indexes. If the catalog is not reorganized on a regular basis, the performance of both user and system queries against the catalog begins to suffer in any application to varying degrees. Every table space in the DSNDB06 database is eligible for reorganization.

DB2 directory reorganizations are also important, because the directory contains critical information regarding internal DB2 control and structures. These are important to DB2 processing because they affect application plan and package execution, utility execution, and database access. Allowing these table spaces to become disorganized can seriously affect transaction and utility performance. Many of our clients have seen significant performance improvements through catalog and directory reorganizations, especially in batch processes and dynamic SQL.

Keep in mind the relationships between the DB2 catalog and some of the DB2 directory tables. For instance, you should reorganize the directory table DBD01 when you reorganize catalog table SYSDBASE. Directory tables SCT01 and SCT02 need to be reorganized with SYSPLAN and SYSPACKAGE, respectively.

User Indexes

Beginning with DB2 Version 4, we have the ability to create our own indexes on the DB2 catalog to assist with both performance and object-reporting queries that access the DB2 catalog. Often this opportunity is overlooked or not deemed important. Consider that all the catalog tables come with a couple of standard indexes and these may or may not be the most optimal indexes for your most frequent catalog access needs. By determining what type of access you most frequently use, for example, through several binds during the day or multiple authorization checks, you can determine where you could most benefit from creating indexes. These indexes can be very important for performance, especially if your catalogs have become rather large.

Large and Consolidated Catalogs

Many times maintenance and user indexes get put aside or discarded because they are seen as unnecessary overkill. But if your environment has several processes that must access the catalog or you have a large number of objects in the catalog, these user indexes can make a large difference. Take, for example, a multiple-member data sharing environment where all objects for all subsystems are kept in the shared catalog. This one catalog can become rather large, and it is accessed by several DB2s. Performance is critical, and the maintenance and implementation of user indexes should not be overlooked.

It is also important to keep your catalog clean of unnecessary objects and authorizations. Refer to the section "Catalog Queries" in this chapter for some suggestions on how to find unused objects.

Directory

The DB2 directory is not accessible via SQL but does contain vital information regarding the operation and maintenance of the DB2 subsystem and its objects. The directory contains information required to start DB2, and activities and utilities in the DB2 environment actually update and delete table entries in the DB2 directory. The DB2 directory contains five tables, and a description of each is given in the following sections.

SPT01 Skeleton Package Table (SKPT) and SCT02 Skeleton Cursor Table (SKCT)

The SKPT table contains information about the access paths and the internal form of the SQL for a package at bind time. Table entries are made during bind time (BIND PACKAGE) and are deleted when a package is freed (FREE PACKAGE). Components from these tables are loaded into memory at execution time through buffer pool BP0 and moved into the EDM pool. The SKCT also is loaded into memory at execution time of the underlying SQL. It contains information regarding access paths and the internal form of the SQL for an application plan. The entries in this table are made when a plan is bound (BIND PLAN) and deleted when a plan is freed (FREE PLAN).

Refer to Chapter 3, "Memory," for information on tuning the buffer pool and EDM pool to ensure proper performance for operations using these tables.

DBD01 DBDs

These are the internal control block representations of the database. Each DB2 database has one DBD for its objects (table spaces, indexes, tables, RI constraints, and check constraints). Updates to this table are made when a database is created or altered. The DBD is loaded into the EDM when first required and is accessed by DB2 in place of continually using the DB2 catalog. This allows faster, more efficient access to this information by DB2 without contending with user or application access to the DB2 catalog. The information in the DBD01 directory table is also contained in the DB2 catalog.

SYSLGRNX and SYSUTILX

The SYSLGRNX table is referred to as the log range table, and it contains information obtained from the DB2 logs regarding the RBA (relative byte address) range for updates. This allows DB2 to efficiently find the RBAs needed from the DB2 logs for recovery purposes. A row is inserted every time a table space or partition is opened or updated, and it is updated when the object is closed or when a switch from read/write to read-only occurs. You can minimize the amount of data in the SYSLGRNX by controlling the frequency of opening and closing data sets if that is a concern, although you will have little control over the number of entries due to read/write to read-only switches. But let's look at the other side of having all these entries. These entries minimize the time it takes to recover, restart, roll back, or roll forward. Even though the number of entries may seem to be a problem, in a high-performance application, it is the number of entries that minimize outage time that is a more important concern.

The SYSUTILX table stores information about the execution of DB2 utilities, including the status and the steps of execution. This information is added when a utility is started, and the entry is removed when the execution has ended. These entries in SYSUTILX are used in the event that a utility needs to be restarted.

Shadow Catalog

If you are experiencing contention against the catalog and want better performance for critical operations during heavy access, a shadow catalog is a worthwhile option to consider.

For better performance for inquiries against the catalog from programmers, developers, DBAs, and vendor utilities, having a shadow copy of the DB2 catalog may also be a benefit. A shadow copy can help to reduce bottlenecks caused by these types of inquiries. However, one complication associated with a shadow copy of the catalog is keeping both catalogs synchronized. To ensure that the queries against the shadow catalog get current information, a refresh process is necessary to keep the tables in sync.

ODBC Catalog

Prior to version 6, a problem with ODBC client application workloads caused contention with DB2 processes that need to access the DB2 catalog, and the overhead for these clients was high. Many desktop tools need to obtain information by calling interfaces in the ODBC driver that retrieve data from the DB2 catalog. Access to the DB2 catalog by remote applications can be expensive. Performance problems can arise from remote applications' inefficient data access to the DB2 catalog tables, which are not specifically designed for ODBC access. The catalog tables are composed of several columns that are not required by the ODBC driver, which caused earlier versions of DB2 to retrieve a lot of extraneous data when reading the DB2 catalog. This fact also causes the ODBC driver to frequently join multiple catalog tables in order to produce the output needed by the ODBC driver's callable interfaces.

Other problems include lock contention. The ODBC driver collects data from the catalog, which acquires locks on pages in the DB2 catalog tables. Program binds and DDL operations can begin to time out when large numbers of end users access the catalog via ODBC and obtain locks. The catalog can essentially become unavailable for normal DB2 processing due to incoming ODBC requests. Also, data volume constraints are a concern. Some organizations have very large DB2 catalogs (especially in data sharing environments), with hundreds or even thousands of objects defined in the catalog tables. The majority of ODBC requests require access only to a very small subset of the tables defined in the DB2 catalog. But often the entire catalog is queried and returned to the calling program, increasing the response time of the end-user application and causing network delays due to the large amount of data being returned over the network. Out-of-memory conditions can also occur when an end user's personal computer attempts to display this large amount of data.

ODBC catalog replication provides remote application access to a shadow catalog (figure 4.1). The DB2 ODBC catalog is a new set of pseudo-catalog tables, which the IBM ODBC driver is enhanced to understand. This new catalog has been designed to improve the performance of ODBC requesting applications. The ODBC catalog tables include only the columns necessary to support ODBC operations and are defined to represent objects in the normal DB2 catalog. These new catalog tables have been prejoined, and they are specifically indexed to provide fast, efficient access to the DB2 catalog data required for ODBC applications.

IBM's ODBC driver was also enhanced to support multiple views of the DB2 ODBC catalog. Users have the ability to select the portion of the DB2 ODBC catalog that they want to view by choosing a view through the new CLISCHEMA option within the DB2CLI.INI file. This option must be specified in the DSN or common section of this file. The use of CLISCHEMA is totally transparent to the ODBC application program and is available to most desktop tools. Also, a system administrator can create DB2 ODBC catalog views to limit the view by different areas.

To implement this limited catalog view, use `ALTER TABLE xxx DATA CAPTURE CHANGES` to accept the name of a DB2 for OS390 catalog table (SYSIBM.xxx in system database DSNDB06). Logged DB2 changes against the DB2 catalog are augmented with changed data capture information. These log records look like current log records of user tables as mapped by DSNDQJ00. The records are marked in the log so that DPROPR can detect them in the log stream.

Other requirements needed to use this feature include using DROPR for MVS V5 (plus PQ16905), DROPR Apply for MVS V5, and DB2 Connect. DPROPR has also been enhanced to support this feature in both the CAPTURE and APPLY process, allowing it to

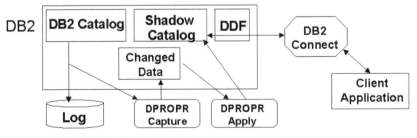

Figure 4.1   ODBC Catalog

keep the data in the DB2 ODBC catalog tables in sync with the data in the normal DB2 catalog tables. Users can specify how often the APPLY process should run, depending on the activity against the DB2 catalog. This method, known as the automatic mode, is the recommended approach to maintaining the ODBC catalog. Note that utility activity against the catalog is not captured in the CAPTURE process.

You could also implement the synchronization in manual mode by using the DB2 ODBC catalog tables without implementing automatic capture of changed catalog data. The drawback, of course, is finding a way to keep the DB2 ODBC catalog data current. A tool provided by IBM helps set up the tables, but keeping them in sync is a very difficult task.

Reducing Catalog Contention

If you are experiencing slow response time from operations that must access the catalog or queries running against the catalog tables and you have tried performance maintenance or adding indexes, there may be contention for the catalog resources. If there is contention, consider the following options (not in any particular order):

- Schedule catalog-intensive utilities for off-peak periods.
- Schedule operations such as execution of DDL for off-peak periods. (Version 6 offers some relief for DDL contention because the internal plan for DDL is now bound with an isolation level of RS [read stability] instead of RR [Repeatable Read].
- Develop canned queries or views for most optimal access.
- Verify that all indexes on the DB2 catalog tables are type 2.
- Use a shadow copy of the DB2 catalog.
- Use an ODBC catalog for distributed queries.
- Make sure that the catalog is reorganized regularly, depending on activity affecting the catalog.
- Keep statistics in the catalog current by running RUNSTATS on a predetermined basis so that dynamic queries use the latest statistics.
- Reduce the scope of the BIND operations by using packages.

Manually Updating Catalog Statistics

A few statistics in the DB2 catalog can be modified for query performance. This can be done to simulate production statistics in a test environment to get a feel for how queries will optimize in the production environment or to influence access paths.

Very large tables (VLTBs) are in a category all their own, because they do not usually have the luxury of regular RUNSTATS executions. It may be decided early in the development cycle that the VLTB will have fixed access path statistics (and this works well). You need to track all catalog fields and develop a method to easily change the statistics that you learn more about. These statistics may need to be tweaked (e.g., the top 10 values and their corresponding percentages). Some heavily accessed columns can really benefit from increasing the top 10 values to the top 100 values. Key correlation statistics also greatly influence access paths. Values can be added for all of the non-FULLKEYCARD combinations. Multicolumn statistics should also be collected and allowed for highly correlated nonkey columns that are usually specified together in SQL predicates.

Key Correlation Statistics

Correlation statistics were introduced in version 5, providing DB2 the ability to gather statistics when one column's value is related to the value of another column. Prior to this enhancement, the only cardinalities were first key column and full key (with limited information), and only the full key columns were correlated. This provided no second or third key cardinality, and multikey cardinality was considered independently, often leading to inaccurate estimation of filter factors, join size, join sequencing, and join methods and to inefficient access path selection.

The key correlation statistics are collected by the RUNSTATS utility with minimal additional overhead and can provide big CPU and elapsed-time reductions through improved cost and resource estimations. These key correlation statistics play a major role in access path selection by providing the optimizer with new columns of information on multicolumn cardinalities and multicolumn frequent values. This new feature gives you the ability to specify the number of columns on which to collect statistics (NUMCOLS) and the number of values to collect for nonuniform distribution statistics (COUNT). These keywords are used in the RUNSTATS utility (figure 4.2). The KEYCARD parameter indicates

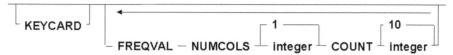

Figure 4.2   Key Correlation Statistics

that cardinalities for each column, concatenated with all previous key columns, are to be collected. This gives you the option to build the frequency values for critical, concatenated key columns, such as the first and second and even third columns. See Chapter 23 for more information on how the statistics can be best used and manipulated for access path selection.

Catalog Queries

We include here a large number of less common catalog queries. There may be some differences in the syntax represented here and what works in your environment. There are also differences in column names between versions of DB2. These queries will work in any environment but might require a little syntax tweaking. Also, notice that often a variable appears as *variable* or *variable%*. You will need to substitute the correct constants in these locations or change them to fit the objects for which you are looking.

Queries to Use with EXPLAIN Output

Plan table data from the EXPLAIN output by itself can be pretty meaningless, especially with complex queries and large amounts of data. To properly interpret EXPLAIN output and determine whether the access paths are optimal, you can run certain catalog queries to produce reports that enhance your ability to make performance decisions using EXPLAIN output. We have provided some examples. In Chapter 22, "Access Paths, Predictive Governing and Tuning," you can see a real-life example where the data from EXPLAIN was interpreted by itself (without supporting or corroborating details) according to all the standard rules of thumb for access path performance but was very misleading because crucial information was not taken into account.

Finding Extraneous Authorizations

When DB2 must perform authorization checking during plan, package, or query execution, it must internally query different tables to determine the appropriate level of authority against the objects. Tables that are very large and contain duplicate authorizations can begin to affect the performance of processes that require authorization checking. The following query produces a report that displays, by object, any duplicate authorizations where a privilege has been given to the same authorization ID by different users.

```
SELECT 'PLAN AUTHORIZATIONS', GRANTEE, NAME, COUNT(*)
FROM SYSIBM.SYSPLANAUTH
GROUP BY GRANTEE, NAME
HAVING COUNT(*) > 2
-- MULTIPLE GRANTS OF SAME PLAN AUTHORIZATION
UNION
SELECT 'PACKAGE AUTHORIZATIONS', GRANTEE, NAME, COUNT(*)
FROM SYSIBM.SYSPACKAUTH
GROUP BY GRANTEE, NAME
HAVING COUNT(*) > 2
-- SHOWS MULTIPLE GRANTS OF SAME PACKAGE AUTHORIZATION
UNION
SELECT 'DATABASE AUTHORIZATIONS', GRANTEE, NAME, COUNT(*)
FROM SYSIBM.SYSDBAUTH
GROUP BY GRANTEE, NAME
HAVING COUNT(*) > 2
-- SHOWS MULTIPLE GRANTS OF SAME DATABASE AUTHORIZATION
UNION
SELECT 'TABLE AUTHORIZATIONS', GRANTEE, TTNAME, COUNT(*)
FROM SYSIBM.SYSTABAUTH
GROUP BY GRANTEE, TTNAME
HAVING COUNT(*) > 2
-- SHOWS MULTIPLE GRANTS OF SAME TABLE AUTHORIZATION
UNION
SELECT 'SYSTEM AUTHORIZATIONS', GRANTEE, NAME, COUNT(*)
FROM SYSIBM.SYSRESAUTH
GROUP BY GRANTEE, NAME
HAVING COUNT(*) > 2
```

```
ORDER BY 1,3,4 DESC
-- SHOWS MULTIPLE GRANTS OF SAME SYSTEM AUTHORIZATION
```

Note: SYSTABAUTH may have different authorizations in each "duplicate" row that is not strictly a duplicate.

Identifying Partitioning Keys

In version 6 you have the ability to rebalance your partitioning keys. To do this, you need to determine the current partitioning keys and which partition keys need to be changed. (For more information on rebalancing partitions, refer to Chapter 5, "Physical Database Objects.") The following query can help by providing a view of the values allowable for each partition of all partitioned table spaces within a given database. The LIMITKEY field from SYSTABLEPART contains the actual values allowed in a given partition as they were defined in the CREATE INDEX statement when the partitioning index was defined. After the keys have been redefined, you may want to execute this query again to ensure that you have defined the keys as planned.

```
SELECT TBS.DBNAME, TBS.NAME, TP.PARTITION, TP.LIMITKEY
   , TP.CARD, TP.FARINDREF, TP.NEARINDREF, TP.FREEPAGE
   , TP.PCTFREE, TP.COMPRESS, TP.PAGESAVE,
DATE (TP.STATSTIME)
FROM SYSIBM.SYSTABLESPACE TBS, SYSIBM.SYSTABLEPART TP
WHERE TBS.DBNAME = database-name
AND TBS.NAME = TP.TSNAME
ORDER BY TBS.NAME
```

Determining When to REORG an Index

It is critical for performance that our indexes be in shape. When indexes become disorganized, access and other processes such as inserts may suffer. To determine when an index needs to be reorganized, you need to collect information about each partition in the index or about entire nonpartitioned indexes. The following query provides details such as leaf distribution, free space, cluster ratio, and cardinality of each partition for all indexes in a given database. From these statistics you can determine whether your index is in need of a reorganization. For an explanation of how to determine this, refer to Chapter 5.

```
SELECT IX.IXNAME, IX.PARTITION, IX.PQTY, IX.SQTY, IX.LEAFDIST,
    IX.FAROFFPOSF, IX.NEAROFFPOSF, IX.FREEPAGE,
    IX.PCTFREE, IX.CARDF, IT.KEYCOUNT, I.COLCOUNT,
    I.CLUSTERING, I.CLUSTERED, I.FIRSTKEYCARDF, I.FULLKEYCARDF,
    IT.NLEAF,
    IT.NLEVELS, IT.CLUSTERRATIO, SUBSTR(CHAR(I.STATSTIME),6,5)
FROM SYSIBM.SYSINDEXPART IX, SYSIBM.SYSINDEXES, I,
SYSIBM.SYSINDEXSTATS IT
    WHERE IX.IXNAME = I.NAME
        AND IX.IXNAME = IT.NAME
        AND IT.NAME = I.NAME
        AND IX.PARTITION = IT.PARTITION
        AND I.DBNAME = database-name
ORDER BY IX.IXNAME, IX.PARTITION
```

Determining Foreign Keys without Indexes

It is recommended that all foreign keys have indexes in order to provide optimal performance for delete and update operations. Several tables in the DB2 catalog must be joined together to find foreign keys that do not support indexes. The following query can help you identify tables with foreign keys that do not have corresponding indexes.

```
SELECT SR.TBNAME, SR.RELNAME
    FROM SYSIBM.SYSRELS SR, SYSIBM.SYSTABLES TB
        WHERE SR.TBNAME = TB.NAME
            AND TB.DBNAME = database-name
            AND TB.CREATOR = creator
            AND TB.CREATOR = SR.CREATOR
            AND NOT EXISTS
                (SELECT *
                FROM SYSIBM.SYSFOREIGNKEYS FK,
                    SYSIBM.SYSINDEXES IX,
                    SYSIBM.SYSKEYS SK
```

```
          WHERE SR.RELNAME = FK.RELNAME
          AND FK.CREATOR = TB.CREATOR
          AND IX.TBCREATOR = TB.CREATOR
          AND IX.CREATOR = SK.IXCREATOR
          AND SR.TBNAME = FK.TBNAME
          AND SR.TBNAME = IX.TBNAME
          AND IX.NAME = SK.IXNAME
          AND FK.COLSEQ = SK.COLSEQ
          AND FK.COLNO = SK.COLNO
          AND FK.COLNAME = SK.COLNAME)
ORDER BY SR. TBNAME, SR.RELNAME
```

Showing Foreign Keys Fully Supported by Indexes

It is just as important to produce a result that shows all index-supported foreign keys for all columns. This query produces that result (a classic relational division query).

```
SELECT F2.CREATOR, F2.TBNAME, F2.RELNAME, F2.COLSEQ,
F2.COLNAME
     ,I.NAME AS IXNAME
  FROM SYSIBM.SYSFOREIGNKEYS F2
     ,SYSIBM.SYSINDEXES  I
  WHERE F2.CREATOR = creator
  AND  I.TBCREATOR = F2.CREATOR
  AND  I.TBNAME = F2.TBNAME
  AND  NOT EXISTS
     (SELECT 1 FROM SYSIBM.SYSFOREIGNKEYS F
        WHERE F.CREATOR = F2.CREATOR
        AND  F.TBNAME = F2.TBNAME
        AND  F.RELNAME = F2.RELNAME
        AND  NOT EXISTS
           (SELECT 1 FROM SYSIBM.SYSKEYS K
              WHERE K.IXCREATOR = I.CREATOR
              AND  K.IXNAME = I.NAME
              AND  K.COLSEQ = F.COLSEQ
              AND  K.COLNAME  = F.COLNAME))
  ORDER BY 1,2,3,4,
  WITH UR;
```

The preceding query works best when there are special user indexes on the catalog tables to support this kind of query. A better example is a query using outer joins that does not rely on special catalog indexes:

```
SELECT X.CREATOR
    , X.TBNAME AS CHILD_TBL
    , SUBSTR(X.TBNAME,1,9) AS CHILD_TBL
    , X.RELNAME, SUBSTR(Y.IXNAME,1,8) AS FK_IXNAME
    , DIGITS(DECIMAL(F.COLSEQ,2)) AS SEQ
    ,F.COLNAME
    ,VALUE(DIGITS(DECIMAL(Y.MP,2)),'--') || ' / ' ||
    DIGITS(DECIMAL(X.CNT,2)) AS #MTCH_SEQ
    ,SUBSTR('X ', VALUE((X.CNT-Y.MP)/(X.CNT-Y.MP),2), 1)
    AS BAD_SEQ
    ,F.TBNAME AS PARENT_TBL
  FROM
  (SELECT F.CREATOR, F.TBNAME, F.RELNAME, COUNT(*) AS CNT
  FROM SYSIBM.SYSFOREIGNKEYS F
  WHERE F.CREATOR LIKE creator%
  GROUP BY F.CREATOR, F.TBNAME, F.RELNAME
  ) AS X
  FULL JOIN
  (SELECT F.CREATOR, F.TBNAME, F.RELNAME, K.IXNAME, I.INDEXTYPE,
    COUNT(*) AS CNT
  , SUM((F.COLSEQ/K.COLSEQ)*(K.COLSEQ/F.COLSEQ)) AS MP
  , MAX(K.COLSEQ) AS MAXSEQ
  FROM SYSIBM.SYSFOREIGNKEYS F
    ,SYSIBM.SYSKEYS K
    ,SYSIBM.SYSINDEXES I
  WHERE F.CREATOR LIKE creator%
  AND  F.CREATOR    = I.TBCREATOR
  AND  F.TBNAME    = I.TBNAME
  AND  F.COLSEQ    = K.COLSEQ
  AND  K.IXCREATOR = I.CREATOR
  AND  K.IXNAME    = I.NAME
  AND  F.COLNO     = K.COLNO
  GROUP BY F.CREATOR, F.TBNAME, F.RELNAME, K.IXNAME, =
```

```
I.INDEXTYPE
    HAVING MIN(K.COLSEQ) = 1
 ) AS Y
 ON   Y.CREATOR    = X.CREATOR
 AND  Y.TBNAME     = X.TBNAME
 AND  Y.RELNAME    = X.RELNAME
 AND  Y.CNT        = X.CNT
 AND  Y.MAXSEQ     = X.CNT
 FULL JOIN
 (SELECT CREATOR, TBNAME, RELNAME, COLNAME, COLSEQ
   FROM SYSIBM.SYSFOREIGNKEYS
   WHERE CREATOR LIKE creator%
 ) AS F
 ON   F.CREATOR = X.CREATOR
 AND  F.TBNAME = X.TBNAME
 AND  F.RELNAME = X.RELNAME
 WHERE X.TBNAME IS NOT NULL
 ORDER BY 1,2,3,4,5;
```

Identifying Index Columns

You need to analyze your indexes to determine which ones are being used most efficiently and which can be adjusted by adding or reordering columns. The following query can help you determine what columns compose each index.

```
SELECT I.TBCREATOR, I.TBNAME, I.NAME,
   I.UNIQUERULE, I.CLUSTERING, I.COLCOUNT, K.COLSEQ,
   K.COLNAME, K.COLNO, K.ORDERING
FROM SYSIBM.SYSINDEXES I,SYSIBM.SYSTABLES T
  ,SYSIBM.SYSKEYS K
    WHERE I.TBCREATOR   = table-creator
    AND I.TBCREATOR   = T.CREATOR
    AND I.TBNAME      = T.NAME
    AND T.DBNAME      = database-name
    AND I.NAME        = K.IXNAME
    AND K.IXCREATOR   = index-creator
ORDER BY I.TBNAME, I.NAME, K.COLSEQ
```

Primary Key Information

```
SELECT I.TBCREATOR  CONCAT '.' CONCAT I.TBNAME AS TABNAME
     , I.CREATOR     CONCAT '.' CONCAT I.NAME IXNAME
     , I.UNIQUERULE
     , K.ORDERING, K.COLNAME, K.COLSEQ, K.COLNO
     , I.CLUSTERING CONCAT I.CLUSTERED, I.FULLKEYCARDF
     , C.LENGTH, C.COLTYPE, C.COLCARDF
FROM SYSIBM.SYSKEYS   K
   , SYSIBM.SYSINDEXES I
   , SYSIBM.SYSCOLUMNS C
WHERE I.DBNAME       = database-name
  AND I.CREATOR      = K.IXCREATOR
  AND I.NAME         = K.IXNAME
  AND I.TBCREATOR    = C.TBCREATOR
  AND I.TBNAME       = C.TBNAME
  AND K.COLNAME      = C.NAME
  AND I.UNIQUERULE   = 'P'
ORDER BY TABNAME, IXNAME, K.COLSEQ;
```

Tables to Index to Keys to Columns

```
SELECT SUBSTR(TB.NAME,1,18) AS TABLE_NAME
   , INTEGER(TB.CARDF) AS TABLE_ROWS
   , SUBSTR(IX,NAME,1,15) AS INDEX_NAME
   , SUBSTR(IX.UNIQUERULE,1,1) AS UNIQUE
   , SUBSTR(IX.CLUSTERING,1,1) CONCAT SUBSTR(IX.CLUSTERED,1,1) AS
   CL_CD
   , INTEGER(IX.FIRSTKEYCARDF) AS FIRST_KEY_CARD
   , INTEGER(IX.FULLKEYCARDF) AS FULL_KEY_CARD
   , SK.COLSEQ, SK.COLNAME
   , INTEGER(CO.COLCARDF) AS COLUMN_CARD
   , CO.COLTYPE, CO.NULLS
FROM SYSIBM.SYSTABLES TB
   , SYSIBM.SYSINDEXES IX
   , SYSIBM.SYSKEYS    SK
   , SYSIBM.SYSCOLUMNS CO
WHERE TB.NAME = IX.TBNAME AND TB.CREATOR = IX.TBCREATOR
   AND IX.NAME = SK.IXNAME AND IX.CREATOR = SK.IXCREATOR
```

```
   AND CO.TBNAME = TB.NAME AND CO.TBCREATOR = TB.CREATOR
   AND CO.COLNO = SK.COLNO
   AND CO.COLNAME = SK.COLNAME
   AND TB.DBNAME = database-name
   AND TB.CREATOR = table-creator
ORDER BY TABLE_NAME, INDEX_NAME, SK.COLSEQ
```

Determining RI Relationships

```
SELECT R.CREATOR CONCAT '.' CONCAT R.TBNAME AS TABNAME
   , R.RELNAME
   , R.REFTBCREATOR CONCAT '.' CONCAT R.REFTBNAME AS
   REFTABNAME
   , CASE R.DELETERULE
     WHEN 'C' THEN 'CASCADE'
     WHEN 'R' THEN 'RESTRICT'
     WHEN 'N' THEN 'SET NULL' END AS RULE
   , F.COLNAME, F.COLSEQ, F.COLNO
   , C.LENGTH, C.COLTYPE, C.COLCARDF, I.FULLKEYCARDF
FROM SYSIBM.SYSFOREIGNKEYS F
   , SYSIBM.SYSTABLES   T
   , SYSIBM.SYSRELS     R
   , SYSIBM.SYSCOLUMNS C
   , SYSIBM.SYSINDEXES I
WHERE T.DBNAME = database-name
   AND T.CREATOR = F.CREATOR
   AND T.NAME = F.TBNAME
   AND T.CREATOR = R.CREATOR
   AND T.NAME - R.TBNAME
   AND F.RELNAME = R.RELNAME
   AND T.CREATOR = C.TBCREATOR
   AND T.NAME = C.TBNAME
   AND F.COLNAME = C.NAME
   AND I.TBCREATOR = R.REFTBCREATOR
   AND I.TBNAME = R.REFTBNAME
   AND I.UNIQUERULE = 'P'
   AND R.DELETERULE IN ('C', 'R', 'N')
ORDER BY TABNAME, REFTABNAME, R.RELNAME, F.COLSEQ
```

Synonyms Not Used

```
SELECT 'NON USED SYNONYMS: '
  , NAME, TBCREATOR, TBNAME
FROM SYSIBM.SYSSYNONYMS SY
WHERE NOT EXISTS
  (SELECT *
  FROM SYSIBM.SYSPACKDEP PK
  WHERE SY.NAME = PK.BNAME
  AND SY.CREATOR = PK.BQUALIFIER
  AND PK.BTYPE = 'V')
AND NOT EXISTS
  (SELECT *
  FROM SYSIBM.SYSPLANDEP PL
  WHERE SY.NAME = PL.BNAME
  AND SY.CREATOR = PL.BCREATOR
  AND PL.BTYPE = 'V')
ORDER BY TBCREATOR, NAME
```

Displaying Multicolumn Cardinalities

```
SELECT SUBSTR(K.IXNAME,1,8) AS IXNAME, A.TYPE AS T,
    DIGITS(DECIMAL(NUMCOLUMNS,2)) AS NC,
    K.COLNO, A.CARDF, HEX(COLGROUPCOLNO), A.NAME,
    HEX(SUBSTR(COLGROUPCOLNO,NUMCOLUMNS*2-1,2)),
    K.COLNAME
  FROM SYSIBM.SYSCOLDIST A, SYSIBM.SYSKEYS K
    ,SYSIBM.SYSINDEXES I, SYSIBM.SYSKEYS K2
  WHERE 1 = 1
  AND A.TBOWNER = table-owner
  AND A.TBNAME = table-name
  AND A.TYPE = 'C'
  AND I.TBCREATOR = A.TBOWNER
  AND I.TBNAME = A.TBNAME
  AND K2.IXCREATOR = I.CREATOR
  AND K2.IXNAME = I.NAME
  AND K2.COLSEQ = 1
  AND K2.COLNAME = A.NAME
  AND K.IXCREATOR = I.CREATOR
  AND K.IXNAME = I.NAME
```

```
AND K.COLSEQ = A.NUMCOLUMNS
AND SUBSTR('0123456789ABCDEF',K.COLNO-(K.COLNO/16)*16+1,1)
= SUBSTR(HEX(A.COLGROUPCOLNO),K.COLSEQ*4,1)
AND NOT EXISTS
(SELECT 1 FROM SYSIBM.SYSKEYS K3
WHERE K3.IXCREATOR = K2.IXCREATOR
AND K3.IXNAME = K2.IXNAME
AND K3.COLSEQ < A.NUMCOLUMNS
AND K3.COLSEQ > 1
AND (SUBSTR('0123456789ABCDEF',K3.COLNO-
(K3.COLNO/16)*16+1,1)
 <> SUBSTR(HEX(A.COLGROUPCOLNO),K3.COLSEQ*4,1)
 OR SUBSTR('0123456789ABCDEF',K3.COLNO/16-
(K3.COLNO/256)*16+1,1)
 <> SUBSTR(HEX(A.COLGROUPCOLNO),K3.COLSEQ*4-1,1)
 OR SUBSTR('0123456789ABCDEF',K3.COLNO/256-
(K3.COLNO/4096)*16+1,1)
 <> SUBSTR(HEX(A.COLGROUPCOLNO),K3.COLSEQ*4-2,1) )
 )
ORDER BY IXNAME, COLNO ;
```

Validating Manually Updated Multicolumn Cardinalities

To validate multicolumn cardinalities and to guarantee that they are not corrupt after manual population, use the following query. This is very important to prevent major DB2 system problems.

```
SELECT A.TBCREATOR
  ,A.TBNAME
  ,A.NAME
  ,A.NUMCOLUMNS
  ,SUBSTR(HEX(COLGROUPCOLNO) CONCAT ' ',1,64)
  AS COLGROUPCOLNO
  ,C.COLNAME
  ,C.COLNO
  ,A.HEXCOLNO
  ,MINSEQ AS POS
  ,CASE WHEN C.HEXCOLNO IS NULL THEN 5
  WHEN MINSEQ = 1 AND C.COLNAME <> NAME THEN 6
```

```
   ELSE 7 END AS ERR
   ,CASE
   WHEN ERR=1 THEN 'NUMCOLUMNS TOO HIGH'
   WHEN ERR=2 THEN 'NUMCOLUMNS DOESN''T MATCH GROUP
LENGTH'
   WHEN ERR=3 THEN 'DUPLICATE COLUMNS IN GROUP POSITIONS
'
        !!DIGITS(MINSEQ)!!' AND '!!DIGITS(MAXSEQ)
   WHEN ERR=4 THEN 'DUPLICATE ROWS'
   WHEN C.HEXCOLNO IS NULL THEN 'HEX COL NO. IN GROUP IS
INVALID
   WHEN MINSEQ = 1 AND C.COLNAME <> NAME
      THEN '1ST COL IN GROUP DOES NOT MATCH NAME'
   ELSE 'COLUMN NOT FOUND IN INDEX'
   END AS ERR_MSG
   FROM
(SELECT A.TBCREATOR
   ,A.TBNAME
   ,A.NAME
   ,A.NUMCOLUMNS
   ,A.COLGROUPCOLNO
   ,MIN(A.COLSEQ) AS MINSEQ
   ,MAX(A.COLSEQ) AS MAXSEQ
-----------------------------------
-- 1 MEANS TOO MANY COLUMNS IN COL GROUP
-- 2 MEANS NUMCOLUMNS DOESN'T MATCH LENGTH
-- 3 MEANS DUPLICATE COLS IN COL GROUP
-- 4 MEANS DUPLICATE ROWS
-----------------------------------
   ,CASE
   WHEN ERR > 0 THEN ERR
   WHEN MIN(A.COLSEQ) <> MAX(A.COLSEQ) THEN 3
   WHEN COUNT(*) > 1 AND MIN(A.COLSEQ) = 1 THEN 4
   ELSE 0 END AS ERR
   ,A.HEXCOLNO
   FROM
(SELECT
   A.TBOWNER AS TBCREATOR,
   A.TBNAME,
   A.NAME,
```

```
  A.NUMCOLUMNS,
  A.COLGROUPCOLNO,
  T.COLCOUNT,
  CASE WHEN NUMCOLUMNS*2 <> LENGTH(COLGROUPCOLNO) THEN 2
    WHEN COLCOUNT < NUMCOLUMNS THEN 1
    ELSE 0 END AS ERR
  ,HEX(SUBSTR(COLGROUPCOLNO,COLNO*2-1,2)) AS HEXCOLNO
  ,S.COLNO AS COLSEQ
  FROM SYSIBM.SYSCOLDIST A, SYSIBM.SYSTABLES T
  ,SYSIBM.SYSCOLUMNS S
WHERE 1 = 1
  AND T.CREATOR LIKE table-creator%
  AND (LENGTH(A.COLGROUPCOLNO) > 0
  OR NUMCOLUMNS <> 1)
  AND T.CREATOR = A.TBOWNER
  AND T.NAME = A.TBNAME
  AND S.TBCREATOR = T.CREATOR
  AND S.TBNAME = T.NAME
  AND S.COLNO <= A.NUMCOLUMNS
  AND (NUMCOLUMNS <= COLCOUNT
    AND NUMCOLUMNS*2 = LENGTH(COLGROUPCOLNO)
  OR S.COLNO = 1)
) AS A
GROUP BY
  A.TBCREATOR
  ,A.TBNAME
  ,A.NAME
  ,A.NUMCOLUMNS
  ,A.COLGROUPCOLNO
  ,A.ERR
  ,A.HEXCOLNO
) AS A
FULL JOIN
(SELECT
  TBCREATOR
  ,TBNAME
  ,COLNO
  ,HEX(COLNO) AS HEXCOLNO
  ,NAME AS COLNAME
  FROM SYSIBM.SYSCOLUMNS
```

```
    WHERE TBCREATOR LIKE table-creator%
) AS C
ONC.TBCREATOR = A.TBCREATOR
AND  C.TBNAME = A.TBNAME
AND  C.HEXCOLNO = A.HEXCOLNO
WHERE (C.HEXCOLNO IS NULL OR A.ERR > 0
   OR A.MINSEQ = 1 AND C.COLNAME <> A.NAME
   OR A.HEXCOLNO IS NOTNULL AND NOT EXISTS
     (SELECT 1
     FROM SYSIBM.SYSINDEXES I
     ,SYSIBM.SYSKEYS    K
     ,SYSIBM.SYSKEYS    K2
   WHERE I.TBCREATOR = A.TBCREATOR
   AND  I.TBNAME = A.TBNAME
   AND  I.COLCOUNT > A.MINSEQ
   AND  K.IXCREATOR = I.CREATOR
   AND  K.IXNAME = I.NAME
   AND  K.COLSEQ = 1
   AND  K.COLNAME = A.NAME
   AND  K2.IXCREATOR = I.CREATOR
   AND  K2.IXNAME = I.NAME
   AND  K2.COLSEQ = A.MINSEQ
   AND  K2.COLNAME = C.COLNAME
   AND  K2.COLNO = C.COLNO )
   )
ORDER BY TBCREATOR, TBNAME, NAME, NUMCOLUMNS, POS
WITH UR;
```

Re-engineering DDL from the Catalog

Many times we would like to be able to recreate an object or an entire system's objects. This is a real hassle when you need to move several hundred objects to a consolidated catalog in a data sharing environment. Not all of us keep all our original DDL current, as we should. There is no easy way to re-engineer DDL from the catalog without a third-party tool. That being said, one brave soul has developed a methodology for just this task. Michael Hannan has agreed to let us share this tool and method with you. Because the necessary JCL and SQL are rather lengthy, you can find the complete package on our web site at www.ylassoc.com.

Physical Database Objects

T his chapter covers several aspects of designing the physical, not the logical, objects in DB2. There are many issues to be concerned with in physical database design. A physical object design for maximum concurrency must minimize lock contention, avoid deadlocks, reduce lock wait time, and enhance performance through the use of partitions, indexes, pieces, and more.

Constructing a well-represented logical design is the key to being able to migrate into a physical design that meets your business requirements. However, it is the physical design of the database that determines how well the application performs and how easily the database can be used and maintained. When the physical design is well done and its environment has been considered, high performance is possible, which means doing more for the business. When the design is poor and doesn't consider its environment, it is difficult or sometimes impossible to tune for optimal performance. A good design has no potential for update anomalies; it is also relational, with relations based on the data and not on processes or shortcuts.

It is very important to make the correct design choices for physical objects such as tables, table spaces, and indexes: once a physical structure has been defined and implemented, it is generally difficult and time-consuming to make changes to the underlying structure. The best way to perform logical database modeling is to use strong guidelines developed by an expert in relational data modeling or one of the many relational database modeling tools available. But it is important to remember that just "pressing a button" to have a tool migrate your logical model into a physical model does not make the physical model optimal for performance. There is nothing wrong with twisting the logical design to improve performance as long as the logical model is not compromised or destroyed.

DB2 objects need to be designed for availability, ease of maintenance, and overall performance as well as for business requirements. There are guidelines and recommendations for achieving these design goals, but how these goals are measured depends on the business and the nature of the data.

Guidelines for Optimal Design

Guidelines for optimal design include suggestions for the reduction of CPU processing, I/O, memory, and all other system resources. Following are some points to consider when designing for high performance.

The number of SQL statements is directly related to design, not to the application itself. When the design allows navigating the data or using too many access modules, unnecessary SQL statements need to be used, driving up the resource cost of running the application. The design should allow much of the processing complexity to be encapsulated into SQL statements that do not require repetitive use. The cost of the system is directly related to how the data is stored and what SQL can be used to retrieve all the necessary data easily. There are more details on this in Chapter 16 on SQL.

The number of rows or columns retrieved is also related to the physical design, because while updates are an application requirement, the number of rows retrieved in support of updates and deletions is a design consideration. Retrieving unnecessary rows and columns drives up the cost of processing, generally many times that required by a proper design.

Sorting is also a physical design issue, most often related to the use and number of indexes, since some sorts would not be necessary if the proper physical indexes were defined. Sorting is also an application design issue, since it also depends on the proper use of SQL, which may be able to minimize sorts.

All designs should minimize locking contention so that concurrency is not an issue and the data is fully available to applications. Keep data currency and availability in mind during the design process. Design the database to minimize lock contention and avoid deadlocks, and design the applications with all the concurrency issues in consideration.

Table Spaces

The design and structure of the table spaces is critical to performance and manageability. The table space is the most accessed physical component in the database. It is the ultimate object for locks, volatility, utility use, and application performance. Some of the parameters involved in the definition are fairly straightforward, but many require very specific design strategies in order to achieve an acceptable level of performance.

Table Spaces per Database

The number of table spaces per database can vary greatly. Many shops have one database per application, since in DB2 a database is a logical construct. However, another technique often used in support of 24×7 operations is to have one table space per database. This is done to remove DBD locking problems when altering data structures in a database. It also reduces the contiguous memory required for loading a single DBD structure into the EDM pool (although this has been lessened in version 6) and reduces the amount of logging that occurs when changes are made to the DBD. However, it requires much more effort on the part of the administrative staff. The total number of pages from all the DBDs is larger than required in a single DBD, due to the DBD header pages. This is not a problem, just a point to remember. As a general rule, it is best to limit the number of table spaces in a database to a manageable number. The guideline in the past was generally about 30 to 50 table spaces and associated tables per database. However, as of the changes in version 6, the actual size is no longer the concern that it once was, since the loading of the DBD into the EDM pool is now done in manageable 32K chunks. The table spaces are still a concern if they are very large and full of nonreferenced objects, because they occupy valuable space in the EDM pool that could be used by other objects. The concern now focuses on the number of regularly occurring DDL changes and the impact on concurrency and continuous availability. Again, the overriding goal here is establishing the proper granularity of objects to achieve performance and availability, which varies dynamically for each business.

Segmented Table Spaces

In cases where a table is not partitioned, you should use segmented table spaces, never simple table spaces. A segmented table space organizes pages into segments, and each segment contains only the rows of one table. Segments can be composed of 4 to 64 pages each, and each segment has the same number of pages.

There are several advantages to using segmented table spaces. Since the pages in a segment contain only rows from one table, there is no locking interference with other tables. In simple table spaces, rows are intermixed on pages; if one table page is locked, it can inadvertently lock a row of another table just because it is on the same page. When you have only one table per table space, this is not an issue; however, there are still several benefits to having a segmented table space for one table. If a table scan is performed, the segments belonging to the table being scanned are the only ones accessed; empty pages are not scanned. If a mass deletion or a DROP table occurs, segment pages are available for immediate reuse, and it is not necessary to run a REORG utility. Mass deletions are also much faster for segmented table space, and they produce less logging. Also, the COPY utility does not have to copy empty pages left by a mass deletion. When inserting records, some read operations can be avoided by using the more comprehensive space map of the segmented table space. By being able to safely combine several tables in a table space, you can reduce the number of open data sets necessary, which reduces the amount of memory required in the subsystem (see Chapter 3, "Memory").

When using a segmented table space to hold more than one table, make sure the tables have very similar characteristics in all categories, including size, volatility, locking needs, compression, and backup and recovery strategies.

Guidelines for how many tables to have in a segmented table space are based upon the number of pages in the table space, but number of pages is not the only consideration. Following are very generic thresholds.

Number of pages	Table space design
Over 100,000	Consider partitioning
Over 10,000	One-table segmented table space
Over 128 but under 10,000	Multiple-table segmented table spaces
Under 128	Multiple-table segmented table spaces

SEGSIZE

SEGSIZE is what tells DB2 on OS/390 how large to make each segment of a segmented table space, and it determines how many pages are contained in a segment. The SEGSIZE varies, depending on the size of the table space. Recommendations are as follows:

Number of pages	SEGSIZE
28 or less	4 to 28
Between 28 and 128	32
128 or more	64

Tables per Table Space

One table per table space is still a good rule of thumb, because the individual needs of tables can be defined. Free space, locking, size, and volume placement can be addressed on a per-table basis if you have one table per table space. However, with the industry movement toward ERP software packages such as SAP and PeopleSoft, we find that this is sometimes not feasible due to the large number of tables. It would not be manageable to have each table in its own table space, because the maximum limit of open data sets would be exceeded. In cases like these, it is best to group the tables together based on their usage (for example, read-only tables or static code tables in one table space) or on application function.

Partitioning

There are several advantages to partitioning a table space. For large tables, partitioning is the only way to store large amounts of data, but partitioning also has advantages for smaller tables. DB2 allows you to define up to 254 partitions of up to 64 GB each. Non-partitioned table spaces are limited to 64 GB of data. Partitioning allows you to take advantage of query, CPU, and sysplex parallelism. Even a table with one partition allows a query that involves a join to enable CPU parallelism. You can take advantage of the ability to execute utilities on separate partitions in parallel and the ability to access data in certain partitions while utilities are executing on others. In a data sharing environment, you can spread partitions among several members to split workloads. You can also spread your data over multiple volumes and need not use the same storage group for each data set belonging to the table space. This also allows you to place frequently accessed partitions on faster devices.

However, even with all the advantages of having partitioned table spaces, you must keep a few potential disadvantages in mind when deciding about partitions. For instance, unless you use version 6, you cannot use the ALTER statement to change the partitioning key ranges. More important is the fact that you still cannot add additional partitions to a table (although this is a high-priority DB2 enhancement that we hope to see in the future). This could be a problem if your tablespace has run out of space, because it would force you to drop, recreate, and reload. Also, normally more data sets are opened for partitioned table spaces, which decreases available memory, and a table space scan for a partitioned table space may be less efficient than one for a segmented table space (unless the SQL is coded to allow the optimizer to use page-range scans).

Partitioning Strategies

There are several strategies for partitioning your data. You need to choose a partitioning strategy based on the nature of the data being stored and its intended use. We look at some of the more popular partitioning strategies:

- Linear
- Ascending sequence
- Archiving and rolling
- Single partition

Linear Distribution   You can design partitions to allow linear distribution of data, although this can be difficult with mismatched-size partitions, and partitions can run out of space. To use linear distributions requires a truly random key and a well-thought-out design. One option is to use the ROWID column data type (introduced in version 6 for support of LOBs) for random distribution of partition values. For additional information on the ROWID, refer to Chapter 7, "Large Objects (LOBs)."

The value of ROWID is a random value, from a low value to a high values (hexidecimal 0000 . . . through FFFF . . .). Therefore, if using a ROWID as the high-level column of a partitioning key, you can have linear distribution over the partitions in a partitioned table space.

There is one very serious disadvantage to random distribution due to the key normally used for linear distribution. Most often this random key is some type of surrogate key (refer to the section "Surrogate-Key Indexes" later in this chapter), meaning that it has no natural key value for the row. While this might work in OLTP environments, it normally gives rise to "death by random I/O" for any kind of work involving sets of data from the table. In two common scenarios, OLTP can suffer dramatically when sets of data are required. One scenario is when result sets are retrieved for scrolling, a technique used in almost every application. The other is where sets of data are required for any transaction. One common design strategy that mandates this kind of access is where updates are not applied but stored as a new record with a forward-ascending time stamp. Another situation is where the most current row needs to be retrieved from a set of like rows. Only one row is returned, but many rows need to be examined to return that one row. As tables get larger and larger, the linear distribution is potentially the worst method for adding additional data.

Ascending Sequence DB2 handles ascending sequence very well, and there are generally no problems with hot data areas. If data is always added to the end, this strategy can remove maintenance problems with older partitions, which is very useful when dealing with large tables. For an example, refer to Chapter 6, "VLDBs, VLTBs, and Warehouses."

While an ascending sequence works extremely well for inserts, there can be a problem when multiple-update processes and delete processes reference these new rows. This occurs, for example, when the data that has been inserted needs to be validated, edited, and updated before being used. In addition, when staging tables are used in this way, the difficulty is compounded by adding deletes to the mix. In this case, where there are many multiple-insert, -update, and -delete processes on or near the same area, row-level locking might be required. Some extreme techniques can be used for data spreading to eliminate this problem, but they can have a negative effect on sequential processes. This is another case where the primary use needs to be the driving factor of the physical design, not the logical design key construct.

Archiving and Rolling If you use each partition to hold a period's worth of data, for example, a month per partition, and later archive the older partitions as a new period begins, you have several issues to deal with. Please refer to Chapter 8, "Special Tables," for a discussion of design and SQL processing with cyclical partitioned tables.

One-Partition Table Strategies A one-partition table was necessary in version 5 for the table to qualify for query parallelism (figure 5.1), since there was no parallelism for

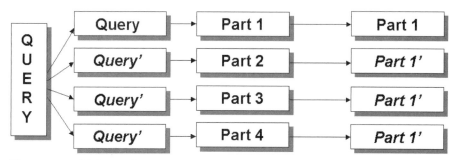

Figure 5.1   Using a One-Partition Table for Parallelism

segmented or simple table spaces. This was useful when a table was used in any joins, because DB2 split the query into multiple queries and ran them in parallel. In version 6 and beyond, this is not necessary, since all tables can participate in parallelism.

Selecting a Partitioning Key

The selection of a partitioning key is based upon the strategy you have chosen for implementation of your table space. Note that as of version 6, you can update partitioning keys through an SQL update rather than by performing an INSERT and DELETE. An SQL update should not be used often, and you should aim to use a partitioning key strategy that does not need to be updated. You should not update partitioning keys often because DB2 has to determine into which partition the new value needs to go, so it drains the range of partitions affected and the entire nonpartitioning index (NPI) on the table space (figure 5.2). This could cause major performance problems in a high-volume OLTP environment. This impact may be lessened if the column being updated is not one that controls the partitioning strategy, that is, not one of the leading columns that will be compared to the key range.

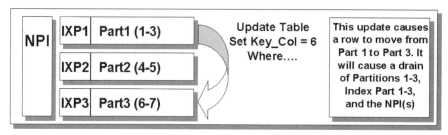

Figure 5.2   Update of a Partitioning Key

The guideline here for high performance is to use the SQL INSERT/DELETE strategy in a single UOW (unit of work) when you can. The SQL UPDATE is a nice feature for code-generated systems and other systems that might deal with data that could or could not be partitioned. Many times a system was developed using normal SQL UPDATE statements but grows in size so that it needs to be converted to partitioned table spaces. With this new feature, the code does not have to be changed, which also increases the portability of the application. But here we are dealing with performance, and if you want high performance and high availability, use the INSERT/DELETE strategy, especially if you have NPIs on the table space.

Rebalancing Partitioning Keys

Prior to version 6 there was a problem sometimes referred to as "ballooning partitions." This would occur when the data simply outgrew the key range defined for the partition, and there was no easy way to enlarge the partition or to redistribute the key values. With an enhancement that arrived in version 6, you can redefine the range values of partitions. Then through a subsequent reorganization of the table space, you can redistribute the data (figure 5.3). This ability gives rise to some new design strategies. Quite often, just simply having the ability to rebalance is not enough. You still cannot add partitions, but if individual partition growth becomes a problem, it can be handled by creating a table space with free partitions and redistributing the data into free partitions, thus accommodating the expansion.

With the introduction of partitioning key rebalancing come new issues. Rebalancing causes an outage, because the partitions are placed in REORG pending status and the range must be reorganized before the table space can be fully used by the applications. Depending on the altering of the key ranges, this may affect several partitions and associated NPIs.

```
ALTER INDEX SYMPOSIUM PART3 VALUES ('CHICAGO'),
                      PART 4 VALUES ('KUALA LUMPUR'),
                      PART 5 VALUES ('LUXEMBOURG'),
                      PART 6 VALUES ('NEWYORK');
```

Figure 5.3   Rebalancing Partitioning Keys

Table Space Compression

Using DB2 compression on a table space generally reduces the data storage required. The amount of reduction is determined by the frequency of patterns in the data. Predominantly character data tables average about 60% reduction, while heavily arithmetic data tables have average reductions in the 10% to 20% range. Before using COMPRESS (YES), it is possible to use a compression analysis tool (DSN1COMP) to determine what the compression will be.

When compression is used in conjunction with the hardware-assist feature, there is almost no measurable overhead for retrieval and only minimal overhead for compression in most cases. In some situations, compression overhead can be problematic, but normally only in applications that comprise data updates and inserts almost totally. If the hardware-assist feature is not used, the software emulation for compression carries significant CPU overhead, the amount varying for each table and its associated use. With compression, I/O overhead is also reduced, since more logical data is transferred per I/O. Generally, it is beneficial to use compression on most large tables.

A couple of caveats to compression include increased concurrency problems because you have more rows per pages. Also, if you do a lot of updates, you run the risk of driving more reorganizations of the table space (see Chapter 1 for information on compression).

Segmented Table Space Using Compression

When you compress a table space with multiple tables, improvements include reducing the space required and increasing the amount of data transferred on each I/O due to the larger number of rows per page. The one general difficulty with compressing multiple-table table spaces is that the compression dictionary is not based on a specific table's data, but on data from all the tables. Depending on the size of the tables, a single large table in the segmented table space may get good compression, while other smaller tables get none, due to the dictionary's matching the increased frequency of occurrences in the larger table. A compression dictionary should never be built using a load utility for a multiple-table table space, as this would create a dictionary based on the single table being loaded.

Free Space

The FREEPAGE and PCTFREE clauses help improve the performance of updates and insertions by allowing free space to exist on table spaces or index spaces. Performance improvements include improved access to the data through better clustering of data, less index page splitting, faster insertions, fewer row overflows, and a reduction in the number of REORGs required. Some trade-offs include an increase in the number of pages (and therefore more auxiliary storage needed), fewer rows per I/O, less efficient use of buffer pools, and more pages to scan. As a result, it is important to achieve a good balance for each individual table space and index space when deciding on free space, and that balance depends on the processing requirements of each table space or index space. When insertions and updates are performed, DB2 uses the free space defined and thus can keep records in clustering sequence as much as possible. When the free space is used up, the records must be located elsewhere, and this is when performance can begin to suffer. Read-only tables do not require any free space, and tables with a pure insert-at-end strategy generally don't require free space. Exceptions to this are tables with VARCHAR columns or tables using compression that are subject to updates.

The FREEPAGE amount represents the number of full pages inserted between each empty page during a LOAD or REORG of a table space or index space. The trade-off is between how often reorganization can be performed and how much disk can be allocated for an object. FREEPAGE should be used for table spaces so that inserts can be kept as close to the optimal page as possible. For indexes, FREEPAGE should be used for the same reason, except the improvement is in keeping index page splits near the original page instead of at the end of the index. FREEPAGE is useful when inserts are sequentially clustered.

PCTFREE is the percentage of a page left free during a LOAD or REORG. PCTFREE is useful when you can assume an even distribution of inserts across the key ranges. It is also needed in indexes to prevent all random inserts from causing page splits.

Data-Set Closure

DB2 defers closing and deallocating table spaces or indexes until the number of open data sets reaches the current limit or until the number of open data sets reaches 99% of the value specified for DSMAX (a DSNZPARM). If the DSMAX limit is reached, DB2 closes 3% of the data sets not in use. The CLOSE parameter identifies whether the table space should be closed when the table space is not used and the limit on the number of open data sets is reached.

Using CLOSE YES allows the table space to be closed. CLOSE NO means that under normal circumstances the table space is to be left open. However, if DSMAX is reached and no CLOSE YES page sets have been defined, CLOSE NO data sets will be closed. There have been many changes to the CLOSE YES/NO code in DB2, and as of version 5 the difference between CLOSE NO and CLOSE YES is hardly worth mentioning, even in data sharing. But if you are constantly hitting the threshold and cannot raise it, it would be better to have noncritical data sets defined as CLOSE YES so that they would be picked first for closure. Admittedly, this is very fine tuning, but we have seen cases where this technique was necessary.

The actual number of concurrently open data sets cannot exceed the MVS limit. This default limit was raised in to 32,767 in V6 from 10,000 in previous versions.

LOCKSIZE

Although LOCKSIZE ANY is the default, which allows DB2 the final choice in the size of a lock during execution, a better choice is the most suitable lock for the table, considering the application's needs. In the majority of cases, to achieve maximum concurrency with the least amount of overhead, LOCKSIZE PAGE is best. For more on locking options and implications, refer to Chapter 13, "Locking and Concurrency."

The LOCKSIZE LOB option supports LOBs (large objects). For more information on this option, refer to Chapter 7, "Large Objects (LOBs)."

MAXROWS 1 or LOCKSIZE ROW

DB2 supports row-, page-, table-, and table-space-level locking. You can specify `LOCKSIZE (ROW)` on your CREATE TABLESPACE statement to use row-level locking or `MAXROWS 1` to essentially provide the same concurrency benefits by locking on a single row only. MAXROWS 1 can result in an overallocation of space if you have a small row size, but it is preferable when using row-level locking for tables in a data sharing environment for reducing overhead for the additional page p-locks propagated to the coupling facility. The MAXROWS parameter can be altered (values 1 to 255) and takes effect immediately for all newly added rows; however, it is recommended that you reorganize the table space after an alteration of this nature.

Row-level locking should be used only in special cases when multiple users simultaneously need a page of data but each user is in update mode on different rows. Use row-level locking only if the increase in the cost of locking (CPU overhead) is tolerable and the need for that level of currency is real, not a result of design problems. The more rows per page, the more users per page, and the higher the resource overhead of locking. There are several situations when row-level locking has high overhead. One is in data sharing when the page p-locks have to be used for each row locked, and another is when a large number of threads on the same page perform inserts, updates, and deletes there at the same time.

If the users' interest is in the same rows, referred to as "hot rows," row-level locking does not have any positive impact on concurrency and only increases the CPU overhead used for locking. In this case, it would be better to use page-level locking. For actual CPU usage numbers and more information on the CPU processing necessary for row-level locking, refer to Chapter 13.

You also can potentially increase the locking cost for sequential update processing and introduce more possibilities for deadlocks. Increased locking occurs when a table is sequentially processed, row by row, and row-level locking is used. If there are 100 rows on a page, then 100 locks are required for row-level locking, versus a single lock if page-level locking is used. If multiple processes use the data, the possiblilty of deadlocks and time-outs increases.

Use of row-level locking in a data sharing environment can have a negative impact without any benefit, due to the amount of excess overhead it causes. (Refer to Chapter 31 for more information.) The bottom line is that row-level locking should be used only as a last resort in high-update, high-concurrency applications where it can be proven as a benefit.

Lock Escalation

Lock escalation can be turned off by setting the LOCKMAX parameter to 0 in the CREATE TABLESPACE statement.

```
CREATE TABLESPACE tablespace-name
IN database-name . . . LOCKMAX 0

ALTER TABLESPACE tablespace-name.database-name LOCKMAX 0
```

The object must be stopped (using STOP) and restarted (using START) for the ALTER to take effect.

To use LOCKMAX effectively, the lock size must be set to either LOCKSIZE PAGE or ROW. This option can be used for user tables or catalog tables. The one caution is to make sure that applications are committing frequently enough, else there is a chance of violating the NUMLKTS (locks per table space) DSNZPARM. Other options for the LOCKMAX parameter that are less severe include LOCKMAX x, where you can set x to be the maximum number of page or row locks held by an application before lock escalation can occur, and LOCKMAX SYSTEM, which allows lock escalation only when the NUMLKTS DSNZPARM is reached.

Selective Partition Locking

By using the LOCKPART YES parameter in the CREATE TABLESPACE statement for a partitioned table space, you enable selective partition locking (SPL). This setting moves the table-space lock to the partition level. This allows only the partitions being accessed to be locked, instead of all the partitions in the table space, and when lock escalation occurs, it occurs only on the partition, not on the entire table space. There are conditions that must be met for selective partition locking to work. For instance, partition-level locking will not work if there is a type 1 index used in the access path, if the plan is bound with ACQUIRE (ALLOCATE), if the table space was created with LOCKSIZE TABLESPACE, or if LOCK TABLE IN EXCLUSIVE MODE is used without the PART keyword. This parameter can be altered by using the ALTER TABLESPACE parameter, and the entire table space must be stopped using the STOP DATABASE command. Selective partition locking can be helpful in a data sharing environment.

Reorganizing Table Spaces

For any table space, a REORG is needed if any of the following conditions apply (using statistics from the clustering index):

- Any data set behind the table space has multiple extents.
- Whenever CLUSTERRATIO is less than 90%. However:
  - Keep very small tables clustered at 100% (cheap and easy).
  - Medium tables should be reorganized below 98%.
  - Large tables should be reorganized below 95%.
  - From 90% to 95% can cause very poor performance.
- (NEARINDREF + FARINDREF)/CARD > 10%
- FAROFFPOS/CARD > 5%
- NEAROFFPOS/CARD > 10%

These recommendations for the clustering ratio are not those in the manual but figures based on real situations. The best ratio depends on the frequency and type of data used. We have seen significant performance degradations at the 97% clustered level. The 90% figure is an absolute mandate for reorganization. No clustered table should ever fall below the 90% clustered threshold when the access paths in the system are built.

Table Space REORG Triggers

New triggers in the REORG utility determine when reorganization is necessary. These triggers can be used to automatically execute the REORG utility or, using the REPORTONLY options, to report on which table spaces need to be reorganized. The REPORTONLY options are OFFPOSLIMIT and INDREFLIMIT, and the SQL behind the triggers can be seen in figures 5.4 and 5.5.

Tables

DB2 tables are the basic construct for storing data. While the whole concept of storing data in a row and column format is not new or complex, it is important to understand the vast number of implications of various aspects of table design.

```
SELECT CARDF
      , (NEAROFFPOSF + FAROFFPOSF) * 100 / CARDF
FROM SYSIBM.SYSINDEXPART
WHERE CARDF > 0
AND (NEAROFFPOSF + FAROFFPOSF) * 100
      / CARDF > :offposlimit
```

Figure 5.4   REORG Trigger OFFPOSLIMIT

```
SELECT CARD
      , (NEARINDREF + FARINDREF) * 100 / CARD
FROM SYSIBM.SYSTABLEPART
WHERE CARD > 0
AND (NEARINDREF + FARINDREF * 100
      / CARD > :indreflimit
```

Figure 5.5   REORG Trigger INDREFLIMIT

- The contents of each table
- Organization of the columns in the table
- Organization of the data in the table
- Relationships among the tables
- Choice of primary key from candidate keys
- Order of columns in primary or unique keys

These are just a few of the many design issues we look at in this chapter.

Normalization

Normalization is a process of applying specific rules to a design that help you avoid inconsistencies and redundancies in the data. Normalization is necessary to process your data with SQL. If the data is not properly designed, the power of SQL is useless. You should always use the third normal form to get all the benefits of SQL. Many papers have been written on normal form, but a simple rule applies. Every attribute (column) should be fully dependent on the whole key and nothing but the key—there can be no dependency among its attributes. A design that is not in third normal form can cause update anomalies (because the same data appears in more than one place), and these anomalies have to be handled in the programs. This results in poor design and difficulty in ensuring data integrity.

Normalization has five levels of rules for relational design, and these five levels together are called normal forms. Generally, taking a design to the third normal form results in a good relational design. Third normal form is optimal for the majority of relational database designs because at this level the data depends solely on the key, and redundancies, which can cause update anomalies, have been eliminated. A modified third normal form, called the *Boyce-Codd normal form* (BCNF), requires every column to be functionally dependent on any possible candidate key. In certain situations, however, there are reasons to go to the fourth and sometimes fifth normal forms, which define how multivalued dependencies and join dependencies are handled.

It literally takes chapters on data modeling to explain all the details of the normal forms, but in most situations, simply following the rule for third normal form is sufficient.

For reference, these are the problems that the five normal forms remove from a design:

- First normal form removes repeating groups.
- Second normal form removes attributes (columns) that depend on part of a composite key.

- Third normal form ensures that nonkey columns are not functionally dependent on other nonkey columns.
- Fourth normal form removes multiple independent multivalued data.
- Fifth normal form removes interdependent columns.

Denormalization

There are trade-offs to be made when normalizing tables. While the rules of normalization tell us to break tables apart to avoid redundancies and inconsistencies, regularly joining these normalized tables together may have performance implications. However, there is basically no need for OLTP denormalization today. There are instances where OLTP denormalization is a performance benefit, but if it is a benefit, there are probably problems elsewhere that need to be addressed (design, SQL use, etc.). OLTP denormalization must be proven as an effective performance method and must be modeled to prove its cost. Keep in mind that denormalization causes anomalies, less-reliable data, and more-difficult coding.

In the past, if tables were joined together on a regular basis, you would have considered denormalizing them (joining them together in one table) to avoid the overhead of the join process during each SQL execution. There are reasons to join tables together, and often such joining is referred to as denormalization, when in fact it is not. Tables in a one-to-one relationship can be merged together even if the relationship is optional. This is not denormalization but rather just an alternative design. There are many ways that data can be modeled. During a normal process of moving from a logical data model to a logical database design, the iterative process can result in many different database designs. It is the maturing of the design to match the business and performance objectives that is important.

However, with the more recent releases of DB2, the engine has evolved to support very sophisticated joining methods and improve performance. Despite these advances, there is still overhead to join a row. For example, there is a 0.1-ms overhead per outer row in a nested loop join. When you consider splitting tables in a one-to-one relationship for performance, you need to make sure that the tables are not joined together the majority of the time. Splitting tables for performance means that the split should be required only a small percentage of the time. Denormalization should not be needed for performance reasons today. In the few rare cases where denormalization is necessary, such as in a read-only data warehouse environment, denormalization should not be considered an overall performance fix. Many ill-advised denormalizations actually cause worse overall performance. Occasionally, it is beneficial to keep derived or duplicated data.

Splitting Tables Based on Usage

There are some performance considerations for splitting tables based upon the way the columns in the tables are used. The goal here is to reduce the row size and the amount of data to be handled by the application. Smaller rows mean that more rows can fit on a page. Therefore,

- more data is returned for prefetch operations;
- more data can fit in the buffer pool reducing GETPAGEs;
- less locking overhead reduces CPU use; and
- real I/O is reduced.

An example of splitting tables is shown in figure 5.6. Splitting tables this way can lead to other benefits, such as compressing the infrequently used data table while leaving the critical data uncompressed when there is compression overhead. It also leads to smaller table sizes, which could lead to a reduced set of partitions, smaller NPIs, and reduced utility runs yielding smaller outages. This topic comes up several times throughout this book, such as in the discussion on handling VARCHAR columns and performance techniques for OLTP systems.

Auditing

The AUDIT parameter in the CREATE TABLE statement allows you to audit activity on a table. You can audit just changes, or you can audit all activity on a table (options are NONE, CHANGES, or ALL). The audit function is active only when you start an audit

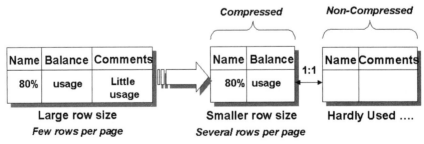

Figure 5.6   Splitting Tables Based on Usage

trace, and it can be performed for individual IDs, if necessary. There is overhead from using the AUDIT feature, so it should be used only in exceptional cases.

Columns

There is nothing complex about defining columns. However, the attributes of the column and the ordering of the columns in the table based upon their attributes and their usage considered need to be given. Column design may not seem important but improper column design can have a negative effect on your application's performance through excessive logging and overhead. A column should have a single purpose. Any column containing subsections (e.g., when the first 3 bytes are a type code, the second 3 bytes are a key code, and the next 4 bytes are a number) should be split into multiple columns to avoid the need to extract the subsections. However, when you integrate some legacy applications, you might need to carry both the composite column and the individual columns. It depends!

Ordering

The order of columns in the physical table is of critical importance for logging performance. Due to the way updates are logged, a specific order is recommended for creating columns in a table. This is most important for tables with variable-length rows (rows containing a VARCHAR or using compression). A variable-length row is logged from the first data byte updated through the end of the row, so why would you want to put the variable-length column at the end of the row? This just adds more overhead every time the row is updated, yet a majority of tables and tools that generate physical models and DDL place variable characters at the end of the row.

It makes more sense to place the most heavily updated columns toward the end so that less is logged (figure 5.7). Variable-character columns are rarely updated; they represent mainly descriptions or comments that are rather static. Figure 5.8 is a very common example of a table layout that follows a "logical" row construct produced by the logical model. It shows a typical account transaction table that must track the date and time a change was made and who made the change for auditing purposes. Tables such as these sometimes are modeled without consideration of the placement of each column. In this

Infrequent Updated	VARCHAR		Regularly Updated
	Non-updated	Updated	

Figure 5.7   Column Ordering Strategy

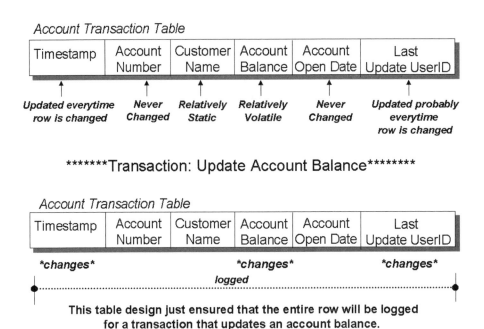

Account Transaction Table

Timestamp	Account Number	Customer Name	Account Balance	Account Open Date	Last Update UserID

| Updated everytime
row is changed | Never
Changed | Relatively
Static | Relatively
Volatile | Never
Changed | Updated probably
everytime
row is changed |

*******Transaction: Update Account Balance********

Account Transaction Table

Timestamp	Account Number	Customer Name	Account Balance	Account Open Date	Last Update UserID

changes   *changes*   *changes*

logged

This table design just ensured that the entire row will be logged
for a transaction that updates an account balance.

Figure 5.8   Column Ordering Common Problem

example, the row construction is the worst case for logging overhead, because DB2 will log from the first byte changed to the last byte changed. Figure 5.9 shows an example of a row that was constructed by ordering the columns according to their usage. By placing the more frequently updated columns at the end, DB2 will log less data when the row is changed. It is not a pretty, "logical" layout, but so what? We use SQL for retrieval of the data values, and it is not necessarily important to have the data in a particular "logical" physical sequence. But, although the physical ordering (storing) of the data during retrieval is not a huge concern, that too is based on the host variables for whom data is retrieved and into what it is deposited. Unless you are trying to shave milliseconds off of

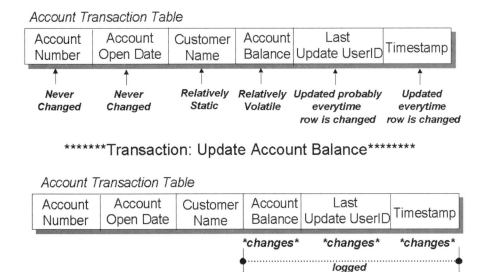

Account Transaction Table

Account Number	Account Open Date	Customer Name	Account Balance	Last Update UserID	Timestamp
↑ Never Changed	↑ Never Changed	↑ Relatively Static	↑ Relatively Volatile	↑ Updated probably everytime row is changed	↑ Updated everytime row is changed

********Transaction: Update Account Balance********

Account Transaction Table

Account Number	Account Open Date	Customer Name	Account Balance	Last Update UserID	Timestamp
			changes	*changes*	*changes*

logged

This table design reduced the amount of data to be logged by this transaction – this can be significant depending on the row size and the frequency of updates.

Figure 5.9 Column Ordering Alternative Example

high-volume transactions, you may not need to plan the column ordering in the table. But under certain conditions, the SQL SELECT could matter. If it exactly matches the contiguous area of the host variables receiving the column values, the columns could be transferred cross-memory together instead of individually. There is no way to guarantee that this will occur, but trying to match host-variable order might improve performance in extreme situations.

Figure 5.10 shows how adhering to a logical model in the physical design can potentially have an impact on the performance of the application and even the system. For example, let's say we have a tool that generates the DDL of the physical model from the logical model at the push of a button, and the standard is not to deviate from this. The column ordering is determined by the tool and not by physical performance criteria. By logging more bytes than necessary, we are recording unnecessary bytes in the log (twice with dual logging), which can fill our logs more quickly than necessary and cause more frequent log switches when logs fill up. When a log switch occurs, DB2 takes a checkpoint that flushes all updated pages in the buffer pool to disk. Now we might have to read those

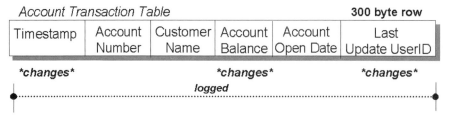

Account Transaction Table   **300 byte row**

Timestamp	Account Number	Customer Name	Account Balance	Account Open Date	Last Update UserID

    changes   **changes**   **changes**

logged

"No Changes. It is our standard to implement was comes out of the logical design without change"

IMPACT:

1 million trans Per day X 300 Bytes Logged X 2 (Before/After) + 2 Serial Sync I/O for each record	Logs fill quicker Must be switched more often More CHECKPOINTS Bufferpools get flushed	More Log Datasets to handle More waits in application Potential for poor performance

Figure 5.10   Death by Logical Modeling

pages back in and have pretty much squandered the efforts given to buffer pool tuning (see Chapter 3 for more about buffer pool and checkpoint tuning). Adherence to the logical model in this case causes the excess overhead to the application. By minimizing the amount of data logged, we can lessen the overall impact of the log process.

VARCHAR Columns

In general, the VARCHAR (variable character) data type is preferred over the CHAR (character) data type only if the amount of space saved is significant (only in the table space, not in indexes). VARCHAR should be used for columns whose values vary considerably in length. Keep these points about VARCHAR columns in mind:

- Do not use VARCHAR columns unless modeling shows that it provides a benefit.
- Do not use VARCHAR columns for disk savings.

- If an EDITPROC is in place for disk compression, VARCHAR is not needed for space savings.
- If you are using DB2 compression (hardware only), VARCHAR is not needed for space savings.

There is a strong overriding principal of use and performance. We don't split tables when they always have to be joined because the data in both is always needed. We don't create new tables where the data is always needed. These decisions involve a trade-off.

These points are not guidelines so much as ideas to think about.

- Consider putting the variable data into a separate table, linked via primary- or foreign-key indexes.
- Consider using multiple rows of fixed length with a sequence number in a child table instead of VARCHAR to allow textual data of any length to be handled.
- Consider using a single long VARCHAR in a separate table (or even in the same table).
- Consider using a LOB (if the reference to the LOB value is infrequent).
- Consider using a fixed-length column instead of VARCHAR for most uses, and put the overflow in another table. This works where the data is usually nearly the same length. (An amazing study that we did years ago on VARCHAR columns used for descriptive data showed that operators can describe almost anything in 37 bytes and rarely need 254 bytes. No keyboarder likes to type long descriptions.)
- Consider using a fixed-length column instead of VARCHAR for all uses, but make it the maximum required length (such as 37 bytes as in our study).
- Keep in mind that VARCHAR has a 2-byte overhead per value and requires some additional processing. It is also messy to handle in some languages.
- Almost never use VARCHAR for a column that could conceivably be indexed. But if you do and the column is searched, consider using the fix that allows index-only access with a VARCHAR, and pay the penalty of program code that is a bit more difficult.

Note: Beware of updates that involve putting text into empty lengthy VARCHAR columns (as can happen in the catalog). The indirect references of row relocation cause data scans to do synchronous I/Os, and performance can suffer greatly. Lengthy updatable VARCHARs have other impacts, such as more frequent reorganizations, that adversely affect high availability.

Do not expect the preceding design tactics to come from logical design. These are physical design issues. You do not update the logical design with these physical design techniques; however, you should update the data dictionary to reflect these changes.

VARCHAR Placement

The placement of VARCHAR columns in a table is critical for two reasons: to avoid the additional CPU use required for retrieving columns after the VARCHAR column in the physical row and to avoid unnecessary logging overhead.

VARCHAR columns should be placed near the end of the row, before all the frequently updated columns, because of logging overhead and because all columns accessed for selection that follow a VARCHAR column require additional instructions to determine the column mapping, which is based on the actual length of the VARCHAR column in the particular row.

One rare situation calls for placing the VARCHAR columns at the end of the row, and that is where the table is primarily read only and most columns are retrieved. This end-of-row placement here reduces CPU processing in stage 2. This placement just makes sure that the VARCHAR comes after all the columns that are regularly read.

Determining the Row Length

Make sure you do not define the length of the columns to be just slightly longer than a half or a third of a page. (On OS/390, a full page is 4 K or 32 K through version 5 and 4 K, 8 K, 16 K, or 32 K in version 6.) This length allows only one row to fit on each page, leaving the rest of the page empty and unused. A column length of less than half a page allows more rows to fit on the page in tables that are not compressed. When figuring out how long your row should be, do not forget to add in the DB2 overhead on each page. The best way to determine exactly what the page will look like based on row sizes is to use the DB2 Estimator product from IBM. It takes all the guesswork out of determining the row size and the number of rows on any type of page or table space.

Logging

When you design table columns, you need to keep the size of the record in mind because record size determines how much logging takes place. The longer the log records, the more data is in the log buffers, the longer is the wait for SYNC I/O at COMMIT, the longer is the second wait for the SYNC I/O at the dual log, and the worse is the response time. Refer to the section on column ordering for more details.

COMMENT ON Clause

Sometimes usage requires adding a more detailed description to an object by adding comments or labels to a table or a particular column. Be cautious when adding comments to a table or columns or when performing ALTERs using COMMENT ON and LABEL ON. The fields that store the values of labels or comments are stored as VARCHAR columns in the catalog. These fields come with a length of 0 and can cause fragmentation in the catalog and more frequent catalog REORGs when data is placed in them.

Many columns in the catalog are actually VARCHAR columns, and altering any of them can cause this type of fragmentation. In particular, changing them can increase the indirect references. Catalog REORGs are more important than many people realize, in part because the increased lengths of the VARCHAR columns cause indirect references.

NULL Usage

A null value is a way to represent the absence of any value. A null is not the same as a zero value for arithmetic data or a blank value for character data. Nulls should not be used for everything, but they do have their place. (This hot debate has been raging in the industry for 20 years.)

For example, if a full-time employee record has a HIRE_DATE field and a RELEASE_DATE field, the value for RELEASE_DATE of a current employee is neither NOT NULL (because you do not want to have to supply the employee's last day) nor NOT NULL WITH DEFAULT (because defaulting to the day the employee record was entered does not make sense). Therefore, the only valid value for this RELEASE_DATE is a NOT NULL value. Some applications use 12/31/9999 as a default end date, which can cause other problems, but using 12/31/9999 can make the SQL range searches easier and can allow increased access. As usual, it depends, and the trade-offs need to be examined both from an SQL perspective and from a business data integrity perspective.

DB2 does not calculate NULLs in functions such as averages, minimums, and maximums, which is good, but an additional byte in the table holds the null flag for each null column, and that can be a problem. In tables with billions of rows, the null flag represents billions of extra bytes. It also necessitates extra coding in the program to check for the possibility of NULLs being returned instead of valid data. This additional code can potentially be eliminated; it is just another performance pressure point.

The use of nulls can affect the results of queries. NULLs are not used in normal arithmetic comparisons, and you should use outer joins when joining columns that contain

NULLs. NULLs should never be the default for column values. They should be used only when fully justified, and all the implications must be fully understood. For example, what should a true or false test return if a column value is NULL?

There is one place that NULLs are required. When a foreign-key column references an optional parent relationship, the SET NULL referential rule is needed, and hence NULLs are required. These relationships exist when the parent row can be deleted but the child data must be maintained.

Distinct Data Types

You can create custom data types, called distinct types or user-defined data types (UDT), to enhance DB2 built-in data types. A distinct type is based on a DB2-supplied data type (source type) but has uniquely defined rules for comparisons and calculations that are more applicable to your data. A UDT can be created for decimal data types, text objects, image objects, or any other definition based on a DB2 data type. A UDT provides a way to differentiate one LOB from another LOB, even of the same base type such as BLOB or CLOB. A UDT is not limited to objects and can be created for standard data types as well as LOBs. LOB columns of binary data (BLOBs) don't really describe the data type, since a BLOB could hold X-rays, audio, or video, so you can create a data type for each of these and define the column using those terms. Even for normal data this is a benefit. For example, unique data types could be defined for U.S. dollar or euro for a decimal column to prevent SQL comparisons between unlike currencies. UDTs are created by the SQL CREATE DISTINCT TYPE statement. Distinct types are kept in the DB2 catalog table called DATATYPES and can be given a description in this table. For example, to create a distinct type called CURRENCY, based on the decimal data type, you could use the following statement:

```
CREATE DISTINCT TYPE CURRENCY
AS DECIMAL(6,2) WITH COMPARISONS
```

The distinct type CURRENCY is based on the decimal data type, but it is comparable only with another occurrence of the same distinct type. The WITH COMPARISON clause tells DB2 that this distinct type can be used in comparison operations with other occurrences of data using the same distinct type. The names of the distinct types must be unique within a schema.

While a euro, an Australian dollar, and a U.S. dollar can share the same base data type—fixed decimal (9,2), for example–each could be considered a distinct new data type.

```
CREATE DISTINCT TYPE EURO
AS FIXED DEC(9,2) WITH COMPARISONS;
CREATE DISTINCT TYPE AUSTRALIAN_DOLLAR
AS FIXED DEC(9,2) WITH COMPARISONS;
CREATE DISTINCT TYPE US_DOLLAR
AS FIXED DEC(9,2) WITH COMPARISONS;
```

These types are actually defined objects but are known only within the DB2 subsystem where they were created. Even within the same subsystem, there could be two definitions of the same UDT with variations, since they are qualified with the schema name.

Casting

Casting functions are supplied with DB2 to allow operations between different data types, for example, comparing a EURO UDT to an expression. We must CAST the expression to EURO for the comparison to work. Some casting functions are supplied with DB2 (CHAR, INTEGER, etc.), and some are created automatically whenever a UDT is created with CREATE DISTINCT TYPE.

Identity Columns

Identity columns were introduced with the refresh of version 6. An identity column is a special data type that guarantees a new, unique, ascending sequence value for a row. Previously, you had to use sequential number control tables or time stamps (refer to Chapter 8 for issues about those techniques). Now, with the use of the identity column, a value is based upon the store-clock value in the sysplex timer and is therefore unique across the sysplex as well. There can be only one identity column defined in the table, but this should always be used instead of any control mechanism that can process requests only in a serial fashion, such as a table controlling the sequential value.

Another feature of the identity column is a cache option that allows a large number of predetermined values in memory to speed up the insertion process. The minimal value of the cache is 2, and the maximum is the largest number than an integer can store. The default is 20, but the best value has to be determined for each application that does a large number of rapid inserts. For more information, see Chapter 11, "Version 6 Late Additions and Version 7."

Nonattribute Columns

Nonattribute columns are columns that contain derived data, aggregated data, or calculated values, columns that never come from the logical design. These are the columns that we add during the physical design to achieve particular performance goals. If these columns came from a logical design, it is clear that the logical design is a process design and should *not* be implemented in a relational database.

> *Note: The primary rule of physical design for performance is quite simple: Do whatever is necessary to achieve performance by manipulating the physical design without destroying the integrity of the logical design.*

Indicator Columns

Our definition of an indicator column is simply a column in a row that indicates whether a relationship exists between another table and the data contained in this row. For example, an indicator of Y (or any similar value) could be used if child rows exist for the parent or N if they do not. The logical model generally never contains these types of columns, since they are not attributes and do not define the primary key of the entity. These columns are used to determine relational existence without having to look elsewhere, so that in many cases unnecessary I/O does not occur, unnecessary SQL statements do not have to be issued, and unnecessary application code does not have to be used. This results in returning resources to the system and dramatically improving responsiveness.

The logical model shown in figure 5.11 is primarily a central table surrounded by eight other tables. The eight other tables contain optional data. This particular model exists in many applications. The application, such as an online account description, often issues an SQL statement for the account and then eight additional SQL statements. To improve performance, converting to an eight-table outer join is preferable in most situations when data is required from the optional tables. But often that data is simply not necessary. It would be impossible to construct a join based on indications that a row did exist in a child table, but often the related data is simply not needed.

As a simple example of how a process can dramatically change physical design, assume that the central table is a customer account table, and the associated tables hold data

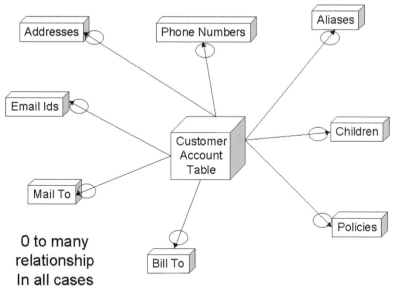

Figure 5.11   Central Table and Optional Tables

such as additional addresses, additional phone numbers, optional residential information, and so on. Assume that the online system is similar to a customer inquiry screen, and the screen is normally displayed as shown in figure 5.12. This screen displays all the information about the customer, but at any given time, the request deals with only one of the optional items. To answer the query, however, all data from all optional tables is necessary. If the query is run only once a day, it would not be a problem. However, several online assistance personnel use this query several times a minute. The screen was reconstructed as shown in figure 5.13 to display just an indication when other data exists. If the incoming query has to do with an area where no additional information exists, then no additional data is required, and a single retrieval of the base account is enough. But if the indicator column shows that additional data exists in the area being examined, simply clicking on that area causes the retrieval of that single area's additional data, without access to any of the other tables. The reduction of resource consumption in this particular application is quite significant. The reduction in the amount of overhead for the complete query is dramatic.

It is easy to change a system to get this kind of benefit. By using insert stored procedures or better insert triggers if available, the indicator columns can be maintained with-

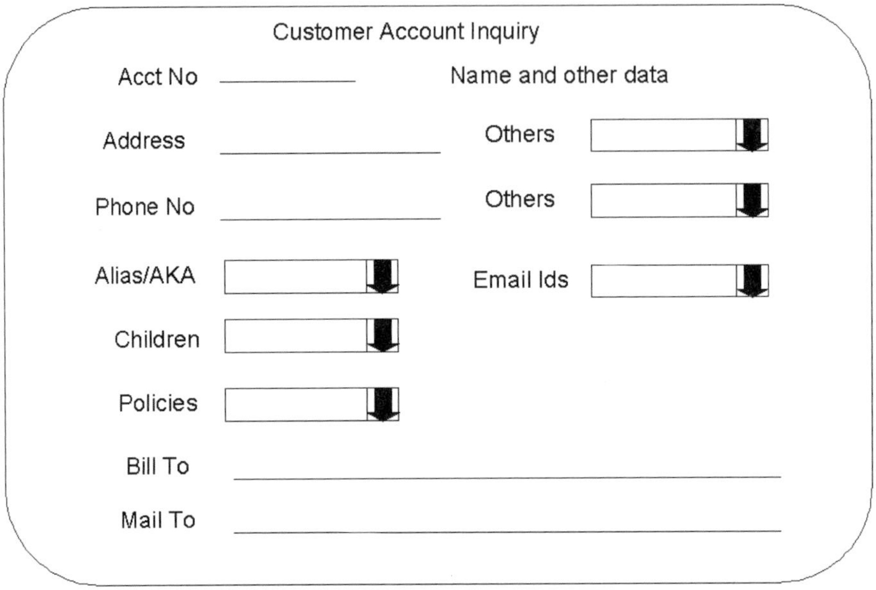

Figure 5.12   Customer Account Inquiry

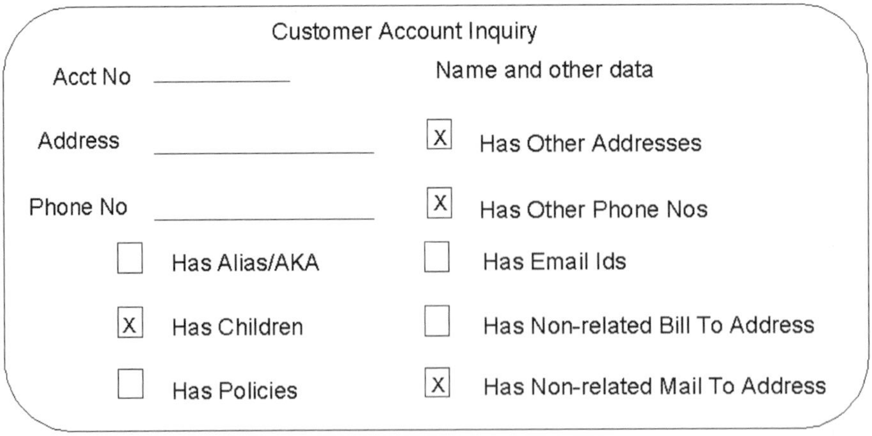

Table Column Format

Name	Address	Phone	Ind1	Ind2	Ind3	Ind4	Ind5	Ind6	Ind7	Ind8
Jones	Chicago	12-1223		X		X	X			X

Figure 5.13   Reconstructed Customer Account Inquiry

out risk of missing relationships. If the indicator columns need to be maintained by pure main-line application code, it might be necessary to write a little synchronization tool to run checks on relationships and make sure that all indicator columns are either set or cleared correctly, but this type of processing should be avoided.

These types of designs often exist where a logical design was forced to become physical design without change. In such cases, the implications of SQL and I/O were not considered, which caused a performance problem. As long as you remain true to the logical model, adding columns for the sole purpose of improving performance should not be prevented but mandated. Just because display screens are put together based on all the relationships does not mean that all these relationships are needed in every case. It is just as important to walk through the design of displays as it is to walk through the SQL and to review the code. Simple team reviews often turn up this type of improvement.

Aggregated or Calculated Columns

Another type of nonattribute column that we can add to tables in some cases to improve performance is calculated columns or aggregations, such as balance columns, totals columns, and composite columns. These additional calculated columns for totals are often required by applications on a regular basis and are generally calculated by summing data in another table and posting the results in a parent table. Suppose a bank allows any of its business accounts to call in on the phone and get the current balance and a list of all items posted against the account in the last cycle. (Bank processing is no longer done this way, but it does demonstrate the point.) When a business calls in, the query lists all activity since last night's cycle and then runs a balance since the last statement. It takes time and resources to aggregate all that data over that many days. Businesses make such queries more than one time per statement cycle. It would be more effective if the nightly batch cycle process just calculated the balance to that point and recorded it in the customer master table as an additional column. Then when the activity for each day is posted, the calculation requires only the new items by date calculated with the existing balance. If no work came in overnight, the query would have to retrieve only the balance column. Removing these repetitive types of queries can return large amounts of resources back to the system. There are many examples where extraneous calculations are done repetitively and do not need to be. A search should be made for all repetitive types of aggregations, both this kind and the simpler kind where SQL just repeats a non-data-driven calculation. Repetition is a waste of good resources.

Aggregated columns can have even a greater value when they are used in conjunction with a time stamp to identify when they were aggregated. Many times events do not require reaggregation, but reaggregation is performed even though nothing has changed. Using a time-stamp column in conjunction with perhaps an item-count column removes the iterative practices and can make further reductions.

We need to learn to adapt whatever physical design issues are required in order to meet the objective of the application and the performance criteria. There is nothing wrong with twisting the logical design to improve performance, as long as the logical model is not destroyed.

Multifunctional Columns

In many transactional systems, data arrives in batches from the outside and ends up in a staging or edit table. Eventually this data moves on to normal entity tables. Other similar processes collect different types of data in one phase, process it in another, then move it into proper tables. For a simplified example taken from a financial application, look at the rows in figure 5.14. Each row represents an incoming transaction. There is a large amount of unused space and fewer than necessary rows in the table space. This affects data transfer and the number of I/O operations issued on behalf of the application—overhead and more overhead.

Instead of a column for each type of data, we could use a type column to indicate the data contained in the next data column (variable), as in figure 5.15. This example demonstrates a different design but truly only scratches the surface of what a multifunctional column can do. Yes, once again we have offended the data designers who made the logical model, and yes, once again we have perhaps dramatically improved the performance of the system. However, you need to justify such trade-offs.

Account	Checks	Deposits	Wires	Adjustmt
12345	1234.56			
64789				3456.89
36980		34765.98		
84735			8500.00	

Figure 5.14   Incoming Transaction Table

Account	TransCd	Amount
12345	100	1234.56
64789	150	3456.89
36980	125	34765.98
84735	200	8500.00

Figure 5.15 Multivalued Column Table

Repeating Fields (Column-Forced Arrays)

It is safe to say that every application needs repeating fields. It is also true that effective relational design, driving through the first normal form, removes all repeating fields. So where is the middle ground here, and can you use repeating fields in a relational design? The answer is yes, you can use them when they are actually not repeating fields but separate fields, even if by name only. There are only 12 months in a year, seven days in a week, and 24 hours in a day, and these are not about to change. So why not have a table whose columns might be identified by "JAN, FEB, MAR" or "MON, TUE, WED" and so on? The point is that a month column might not be the lowest level of normalization, but the individual months might be.

Sometimes storing the data horizontally is much better from a performance perspective than storing the data vertically (figure 5.16). We could pull the vertical data out in a horizontal fashion through SQL or program code, but should we? It depends on the percentage use. If 90% of the time we use the data in a horizontal fashion, then store it horizontally. If 90% of the time we use the data in a vertical fashion, then store it vertically. If we need it another way, we do that through transformation in the SQL or in the code. This improves performance at the cost of program complexity, but performance is the goal, not simplistic programming. At times this is a difficult trade-off and can be very difficult to sell to higher levels in the organization. However, programs can be complex if that is what is required to meet the performance objectives. Complex does not mean unintelligible. We should always have code reviews in place to find the SQL problems and resolve them. Control tables can be used to describe how the data is stored or to direct the retrieval of the data, such as identification of which columns are populated, which columns have sums that need to be recalculated, and so on. Control tables enforce a level of data integrity.

GL_CODE	MONTH	AMOUNT
1350010	1	3644.00
1350010	2	25678.00
3450010	3	4129.00
4560020	2	678.00
4560020	4	344561.00
6780030	1	99786.00
1350010	3	796857.00

GL_CODE	JAN	FEB	MAR	APR
1350010	3644.00	25678.00	796857.00	353535.00
3450010	86666.00	13579.00	4129.00	45.00
4560020	74682.00	678.00	12.00	344561.00
6780030	99786.00	89786.00	3566.00	753.00

Figure 5.16   Vertical and Horizontal Data Storage

A certain business had to justify a very large financial application and do fiscal comparisons of current to past periods on a regular repetitive basis. If the data was stored vertically, many rows had to be retrieved, and many columns had to be sent cross-memory to the application. The application then put the data into a horizontal format for display and analysis. This particular client had to carry three years of financial data. In addition, often the comparison was not just of one month to a prior month, but of particular quarters to prior quarters and particular years to prior years. The amount of data retrieval and calculation was rather significant.

When we conducted a performance walk-through of the application, this heavy data retrieval process jumped into focus. We suggested that the data for three years, with group calculations, be stored horizontally (figure 5.17). Now, with a single row retrieval, all the data for the financial comparisons for a ledger can be retrieved with a single I/O. Only the columns required are lifted from the rows and returned to the program. In fact, some of the comparisons were moved into the SQL rather than moving more data into the program just for comparison.

Again, we might have offended the data designers who made the logical model, but we have perhaps dramatically improved the performance of the system with the twisting

GL	9801	9802	98Q1	98YTD	99xx	00xx	3YR_YTD
135	3644	25678	796857	1353535			
345	86666	13579	764129	1343245			
456	74682	678	567612	344561			
678	99786	89786	763566	753			

> Contains – 12 months for 3 years
> Contains Quarterly Totals
> Contains Year-To-Date Yearly Totals
> Contain 3 Year-To-Date Grand Total

Figure 5.17 Horizontal 3-Year Data and Subtotals

of the relational model. We got 10 more transactions per second through the system and reduced one eight-hour batch job to less than one hour and another from two hours to 20 minutes.

Referential Integrity

Mapping Logical Relationships to Physical RI Relationships

Not all physical designs map to the original logical designs; additional relationships are sometimes created to make the system functional. Physical designs that map completely to logical designs tend to be "performance-challenged" physical designs. Other tables can be defined in a logical model but never appear in the physical model, such as code tables that might have only a few values. Rather than build a physical table to hold those values, you should implement them through SQL DDL table check constraints. The physical design conforms to the logical model but does not implement the model precisely.

When to Use Declarative RI

Everything is good in moderation. DB2 declarative RI is no exception. RI should be used as much as possible to define the relationships that business processes depend on. It is much safer to use declarative RI than application-controlled RI, since in most pro-grammed RI situations, ghost data (missing dependencies) gets into the database. Items such as code tables and reference tables are not a good choice for RI, since these usually require large RI trees containing many tables to be built. Data validation by code tables should be handled through some other means than RI. Trees with many levels can also be difficult to handle, so you should also watch for tree depth. If it is necessary for a tree to extend to many levels, there is probably an overnormalization of the data. If the depth of the multilevel tree is valid but has too many levels, the RI tree should perhaps be broken into two, using a common program (such as a stored procedure or trigger) to maintain the relationships between the two trees.

If data is read-only, as in data warehousing, it may not be necessary to enforce RI during insert, update, and delete operations. However, some data warehouses are refreshed with loaded data that is not necessarily pure; we feel this is a mistake in design, but in some of those cases, declarative RI is used. With read-only systems, RI can be more in the way than beneficial. But with systems where the data gets updated, it is good practice to implement physical declarative RI and to use triggers for the exception cases when RI cannot be declared in the DDL (declarative RI).

Table Check Constraints

Benefits of using table check constraints include

- Making it very difficult via normal DML processing to get inconsistent data in the table
- Making programming easier by eliminating validation routines or logic to enforce constraints
- Ease of adding and removing without invalidating plans or packages
- Enforcement by LOAD with ENFORCE CONSTRAINTS, SQL INSERT, and SQL UPDATE
- Applicability to views on the table

Tables check constraints should not be used when RI is already performing a check, as this doubles overhead. However, you may want to evaluate the use of the declarative RI. If RI is being used to perform a code check, remove it and implement the code check by either a check constraint or a trigger. At one client we evaluated over 50 RI relationships and determined that 21 of those were basically code checking; they were converted to table check constraints, which of course eliminated the unnecessary RI hassles of abnormally large RI trees and recovery difficulties. Table check constraints are not necessary on history tables, since the data has already been "checked."

RI or Table Check Constraints

Physical DB2 RI should be used to maintain parent-child relationships but should *never* be used for edit validation (code or reference tables). RI is for checking parent-child relationships, not for providing a shortcut to coding edit validation. Table check constraints provide the ability to better control the integrity of your data, as do referential constraints and unique constraints. Sometimes a business rule cannot be enforced through a referential or unique constraint because a more complex type of integrity is needed. Table check constraint integrity ensures that every row conforms to a check constraint that is defined on a table.

Application-maintained RI can be dangerous to use and worse to maintain and should be used only in specific situations. Triggers and stored procedures can be used for more complex RI and instead of application-enforced RI.

Table check constraints can be used for enforcing some business rules not enforced by RI. These are also great for validating edit check of codes that are not volatile. An example of where a table check constraint may be used in place of a referential constraint is small code tables, where the RI is there simply to check code compliance (which is not a good use of RI). These codes, if relatively small in number and static, could be more efficiently verified in a check constraint on the table. For example, if yes or no are the only valid values for a column, you can and should create a check constraint to enforce this.

To summarize,

- Use declarative RI wherever possible for parent-child relationships.
- Do not use declarative referential integrity for edit validations, as this produces large RI trees and difficult utility usage.
- Use table check constraints for edit validations where the values are fixed.
- Use triggers for all other edit validations.
- Use application RI for very special performance situations, such as hundreds of inserts for a single parent.

Indexes

While indexes are key for query performance, they have performance implications for other DML functions, not to mention causing additional headaches in maintenance. Inserts and deletes have to be maintained in each index, as do updates if they involve index keys. The volume and sequence of inserts and updates have a direct impact on the maintenance of the index and the frequency of reorganizations. The more indexes on the tables, the more index REORGs are necessary. If no time is available for REORGs, performance for selects, updates, and inserts suffers. Choose indexes wisely based on frequent data access, and evaluate index usage after definition. A good philosophy is to add indexes until it hurts and then remove the last one. There are OLTP systems in place with over 20 indexes on the primary table, which often are necessary for performance. In data warehouses, especially with designs beyond the simplistic star schema, it is often necessary to have a large number of indexes on many tables. Remember that the optimizer can choose only from the indexes you create. If you create only two indexes and neither is truly optimal, the optimizer is stuck with choosing one of your poor choices. Relief has already come to the other platforms for DB2 with the Index Wizard, which will soon be available on OS/390. This little wizard can analyze all the queries and *assist* in predicting what indexes are truly necessary.

Clustering Index

The clustering index is *not* generally the primary key but a sequential range retrieval key and should be chosen by the most frequent range access of the table data. Range and sequential retrieval are the primary requirements, but partitioning is another, sometimes more critical, requirement, especially as tables get extremely large (refer to Chapter 6 for a case study). If you do not specify an explicit clustering index, DB2 clusters by the index that is the oldest by definition (often referred to as the first index created). If the oldest index is dropped and recreated, that index is now a new index, and clustering is now by the next oldest index.

We have seen many problems where an access path in testing was exactly the opposite in production, simply because the indexes on the tables were created in a different sequence. In these cases, no clustering index was defined, so the range retrieval index in testing was different from the range retrieval index in production.

Highly clustered secondary indexes should be constructed in certain situations, although this generally is not possible and can take considerable effort in physical design. But consider an index that has a high number of duplicates. If a scan is required for a set of like data and the index is highly unclustered (a high far-off position statistic), the amount of random I/O is high because index-driven random data access must be used. This contributes to a slower response. Index-only access is generally chosen by the optimizer if the data required is completely contained within the index. Index-only access might be a design option for highly unclustered data, but generally it is not possible. You can often use a method to pick columns for this type of high-clustered nonclustering index that more closely match the actual ordering of the data in the table. Such a method allows the index to be selected by the optimizer as an access path, reducing the amount of I/O. Finding this method is not intuitive nor easy but can be necessary for performance.

When processing an insert, DB2 chooses the defined clustering index for insertion order. However, if a clustering index has not been explicitly defined, DB2 uses the current oldest surviving index. Some people call this the first index created, but contrary to popular belief, the default index chosen for insert processing is not the first index created on the table nor the index with the lowest OBID (object identifier) (figure 5.18). For example, if indexes A, B, C, and D were defined in that order on a table and none was defined as the clustering index, index A would be chosen for inserts. If index A was dropped and redefined, it would become the "newest" index on the table, and index B would now be used for inserts. During the execution of the REORG utility, DB2 chooses the index to use for clustering the data in the same manner.

Bottom line: Always explicitly define a clustering index on any table. A REORG does not cluster the table space unless a clustering index is defined.

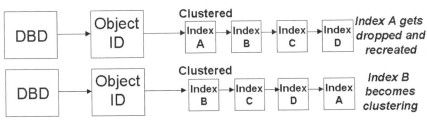

Figure 5.18 Clustering Index

Primary-Key Indexes

The primary key is *not* always the clustering index and generally should not be the range retrieval index. The primary key should generally be a unique, natural key. Every system based on a thorough logical design has unique, natural keys defined on all parent tables and on most other tables as well. A unique, natural key is the key that uniquely identifies the row and in most cases provides entity integrity (uniqueness). It generally is not just a single column but quite often is a single key in the parent tables at the top level, for example, the customer number or account number.

For high performance, you definitely need a unique index, although it does not have to be defined as the primary-key index, which has implications for referential integrity. For any application that uses a large quantity of random access, it is the unique indexes that provide the best access. If there is no natural key that can provide a unique index, often adding another column to the natural key provides uniqueness. Many times a time-stamp column added to the key provides uniqueness. Some sequencing mechanism is required when we don't want the original data rows updated, but would rather have an additional row added reflecting any change in the information and providing an audit trail.

Surrogate-Key Indexes

A surrogate key, or substitute primary key, can be used to avoid having to construct a primary key when one is not readily present. Surrogate keys can provide some flexibility in design but must also be used wisely and not as a de facto standard. Some "standards" say to never use the natural key but to always use a surrogate key. This standard ignores performance and always uses the worst design. If surrogate keys must be used for valid reasons, the creation of the value becomes a primary performance issue. We have seen various extremely strange methods of creating a surrogate key. Some very simple ways of dealing with this issue are discussed in Chapter 12.

Indexes on Foreign Keys

In the majority of cases, an index is necessary on a foreign key. It is advisable to have indexes' leading columns match the column definition of the foreign key. DB2 uses these indexes when validating constraints and enforcing referential integrity rules. Without the index to support the foreign key, DB2 would have to use a table space scan, adversely affecting performance except in very small child tables.

The performance of a DELETE operation can be significantly affected when a referential constraint is involved. For example, checking for dependent rows when a parent row is to be deleted could cause a relational scan if the dependent table has no index on the foreign key with the starting columns of the index. The index can contain more columns than are defined in the foreign key, and it will still be used as long as the foreign-key columns match the first columns of the index. This index is even more important when a cascading deletion could involve several tables. Depending on the rules in place for referential integrity, it is sometimes necessary to exactly match the columns in the foreign key to the primary key (or unique key used as the parent key). This is generally a good rule to follow.

By creating indexes for foreign-key columns, you can dramatically improve performance. Although an index is not required on a foreign key, it is highly recommended, because some RI operations can result in multiple scans of multiple tables; depending on the size of the tables, this could be very costly. Chapter 4 gives a query that can help you find foreign keys without corresponding indexes.

Nonpartitioning Indexes

Partitioning indexes are sometimes used for all data access of a partitioned table and other times are used for a partitioning sequence solely to enable ease of use, growth, and maintenance. It is very rare that a single index suffices for both random and sequential access to a partitioned table space in support of both OLTP and batch access. There is often a strong need for nonpartitioning indexes (NPIs), and yet as tables get larger and larger, NPIs are feared and in many cases not allowed. Remember, no rule is absolute, but in many places we have found an absolute ban on NPIs, normally as the result of a bad experience with NPIs. It is easy to have a bad experience with NPIs, since they need extensive planning to be effective.

NPIs can be good or bad, depending on whether or not the keys are ever updated. Another dependency is whether or not PIECESIZE is used and the definition of the pieces, which is discussed a little later. The maintenance of NPIs and the underlying table spaces is quite different, since a partition and a partition index are the granularity for utilities, but an NPI's granularity is the entire index. The larger the table space the more difficult it is to deal with utilities and partition independence, recovery, and online REORGs. Many of the problems with NPIs can be alleviated by designing the underlying table space and the partitioning key in such a way that the NPI is built using key columns that are permanent and not updatable. Future enhancements for NPIs will make them less difficult to deal with, but until that time, it just takes planning to outweigh the difficulties.

PIECESIZE

The PIECESIZE option on an index creation allows you to break a nonpartitioning index into several data sets (or "pieces"). Using pieces allows better performance of INSERT, UPDATE, and DELETE processes by eliminating the bottleneck previously caused by having only one data set behind the index. See figures 5.19 and 5.20 to observe how pieces helped with this bottleneck. The use of pieces is essential for nonpartitioning indexes that support large tables, but it can also be helpful for concurrency performance of heavy INSERT, UPDATE, and DELETE processing against any size partitioned table space with NPIs.

An individual piece can be as large as 64 GB (figure 5.21), and you can have up to 254 pieces (making a 16,256GB NPI); however, for practical purposes, the PIECESIZE is normally set so that a piece will fit on one disk volume. This allows more appropriately

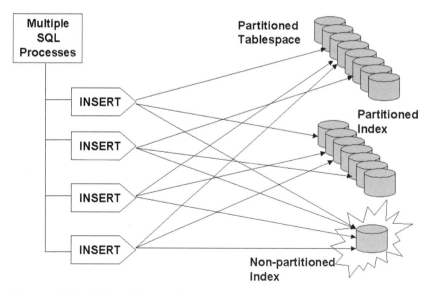

Figure 5.19   Before Pieces: Contention

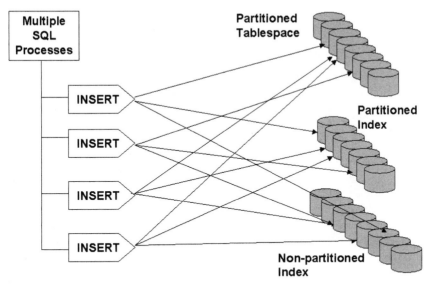

Figure 5.20   After Pieces: Reduced Contention

Non-LARGE	2 GB
LARGE	4 GB
DSSIZE	64 GB

Figure 5.21   Piece Sizes

placed data sets on different disk volumes to relieve contention when the index is accessed. Currently, the use of the piece is limited to physical partitioning and parallel access only.

When a load is performed and the nonpartitioning indexes use PIECESIZE, the entire piece is filled up to the amount specified in the PIECESIZE definition during the creation of the NPI. DB2 uses the primary space quantity and as many secondary extents as necessary to fill up to the PIECESIZE. During later processing, when an extent is necessary, the extent is taken at the end of the nonpartitioning index.

Sizing Pieces

To set the primary quantity space definition for a piece of an NPI, first you need to set the size for a piece of an NPI. To do this, you need to determine the number of pieces and set the PIECESIZE value. To choose a PIECESIZE value, divide the size of the non-partitioning index by the number of data sets that you want, which is different for every NPI in every application and is based on I/O configuration, the sizes of the disk devices, and the size of the NPI.

Once the number of pieces and the PIECESIZE are determined, you can define the proper primary and secondary space quantities. The primary and secondary quantities should be evenly divisible by PIECESIZE or else there will be wasted space in the NPI.

Based on user experiences, it is best to make the primary quantity equal to the PIECESIZE and keep the secondary quantity relatively small since it should never be used.

$$\text{PRIQTY} + (\textit{max-extents} \times \text{SECQTY}) => \text{PIECESIZE}$$

Also, for efficient use of space, size the NPI by the number of data sets desired. There is a maximum of 32 data sets for non-LARGE indexes.

Reorganizing Indexes

For any index space, a REORG is needed if any of the following conditions apply.

- Any data set behind the index space has multiple extents.
- LEAFDIST > 200 if FREEPAGE is not equal to 0; LEAFDIST can be higher otherwise.
- LEVELS have been increased, and LEVELS > 2.

Note: Other than an ascending index, which is inserted only into in ascending sequence, FREEPAGE should never be 0, since any page split would require the new page to be built at the end of the index space.

Index REORG Trigger

The LEAFDISTLIMIT option of the REORG utility helps determine when reorganization is necessary. A trigger can be used to automatically execute the REORG utility or, if you use the REPORTONLY options, to report which indexes need to be reorganized.

```
SELECT LEAFDIST
FROM SYSIBM.SYSINDEXPART
WHERE LEAFDIST > :leafdistlimit
```

Figure 5.22 REORG Trigger LEAFDISTLIMIT

LEAFDISTLIMIT and the SQL issued behind it are shown in figure 5.22. You should be careful with this trigger if you have a FREEPAGE of 0, because in that case the LEAFDIST is not a valid indicator for a REORG.

Views

Base Table Views

Base table views were common in the very early days of DB2. Today's recommendation is that base table views should be used only in very special situations. A base table view is a view containing all the columns in the table on which the view is based, or the primary subset of those columns. Base table views are used where columns need to be hidden from users and applications, such as security validation columns. In these cases, no authorizations for the base tables are granted to users or programs, only the authorizations for the views, because the security columns need to be protected from unauthorized use. Base table views can sometimes be more descriptive and meaningful if a lot of end-user ad hoc queries are used. For example, a column might be TR_ACCT_CD, and the view name for that same column could be TRACK_ACCT_CODE. By using fully defined names, ad hoc users don't have to depend on looking up the base column names, which could be confusing and misleading.

Views versus Direct Table Access

Use views to simplify queries or to implement security for end-user access. Queries, such as certain joins, can be complex, but a standard development technique using view definitions to handle the joins and allowing the outer referencing SQL to supply the restrictions permits both end users and development staff to use complex joins. This technique is *critically* important where a defined access path can be driven by the view but could be missed by hard-coding the SQL in a different form.

Here is a simple example of a three-table join to define a standard business relationship:

```
CREATE VIEW ACCT_INVOICE_ITEMS
AS
(SELECT ACCT_NO, ACCT_NAME, INV_NO,
    INV_DATE, ITEM_NO, ITEM_AMT
FROM ACCTS, INVOICES, ITEMS
WHERE ACCTS.ACCT_NO = INVOICES.INV_ACCT_NO
AND INVOICES.INV_NO = ITEMS.ITEM_INV_NO)
```

This SQL used by the users is more meaningful and easier to write:

```
SELECT ACCT_NO, INV_NO, ITEM_NO
FROM ACCT_INVOICE_ITEMS
WHERE ACCT_NO BETWEEN 10 AND 100
AND INV_DATE BETWEEN '1991-01-01' AND '1991-01-31'
```

Schemas

A schema is a logical group of named database objects. The schema name is used to qualify these database objects. Schemas extend the concept of qualifiers for tables, views, indexes, and aliases by enabling the qualifiers for distinct types, functions, stored procedures, and triggers to be called by schema names. Schemas then can be used to group all objects for and by an application or a functional grouping. For example, you could create a schema called INVENTORY using the following statement as input to the schema processor (in version 6):

```
CREATE SCHEMA AUTHORIZATION INVENTORY
```

You can then qualify all objects used in the inventory application with the schema name (for example, INVENTORY.PARTS). If you do not specify a schema on an object when it is created, it is qualified with your authorization ID. Schemas can be used to qualify all objects except databases. There are some subtle differences between OS/390 and other platforms. Under OS/390 we create an input stream with the DDL for the objects following a CREATE SCHEMA AUTHORIZATION statement. All the objects in the input stream to the schema processor inherit the qualifying name of the schema. While this is not much different from the way normal objects are qualified, it is very important for procedural and object enhancements.

## CHAPTER 6

VLDBs, VLTBs, and Warehouses

Very Large Databases (VLDBs)

What is large anyway? You could say that large is anything you are developing that is larger than anything you have developed in the past; large is relative. However, today when we talk about VLDBs, we are talking about hundreds of objects and terabytes (even petabytes) of data. What is a VLDB? In practice, it is at least approximately two to four times the average large database. Today many terabyte-sized databases serve as examples of VLDBs, but somewhere an even larger one is in the works. A VLDB is truly any database that is magnitudes larger than anything that particular business has handled before.

Some firms are looking at petabyte-sized database warehouses of historical items. Some people think such databases contain only "summarized" or "aggregated" data. Wrong! There is sometimes strong reason for detailed data and strong reason for aggregated BI (business intelligence) data stores. Suppose you stored every single item sold in every single store for 10 or 15 years. And suppose that you processed that data, grouping and adding value, into another structure. Would any business strategy look at only one of the databases? No!

At any point in time during the business day, the operational data that does not paint a picture of anything, as it is incomplete. But at the end of the business day (or business cycle), the complete details now present three distinct pictures. The pile of details can show various patterns. Processed as an aggregate, this data can paint another picture of the business at the close of the business cycle. Processed differently, this data can be aggregated to present various groupings and cross groupings to store as base data in the DDS system, and this data again can be grouped to higher levels and stored as group data in the BI system. This group data represents a stored form that otherwise would need to be continually grouped if simply left as base data (figure 6.1). These base-data and group-data databases are still a relatively new concept in most businesses. The base data does not represent a business entity with attributes, but more correctly represents a business information object. There are no design principles or guidelines for the proper design of either of these types of databases yet (e.g., no normal form for BI, warehouse, or dimensional design). There are many published strategies for determining the data needed in BI systems, but most assume that a fixed strategy will work for everyone. If two companies competing for the same business used the same model, neither would truly gain a competitive advantage, as information to drive the marketing strategy is the number one deliverable.

Data must be put into a form that fits whatever strategies analysts need for their unique perspective on the company. That is why there is BI base data and BI group data in the same database. The base data can be derived by rules from the operational data. These

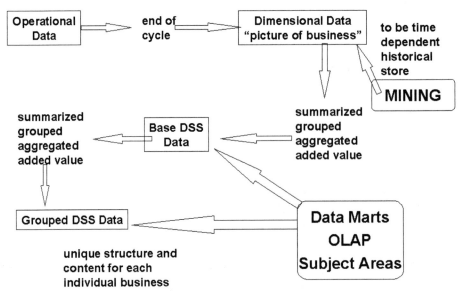

Figure 6.1   From Operational Data to Warehouse

rules are basically the same for every type of business. But the group data, or dimensional, or OLAP data, is the unique data mandated by the analysts.

Using base and group data in the same database is not theory. It is being done already, quietly. Marketing and strategic analysts have information so fast and so powerful, it has astounded them. The databases are so large that they truly are VLDBs, but VLDBs that support ad hoc relational queries from personnel both within and outside the IS department, using several different types of end-user tools. (Some of these tools are much better for these types of systems than others, as such systems really deal with business objects stored in relational tables.) These systems, regardless of cost, are giving their businesses incredible advantages in target marketing and competitive strategies.

Very Large Tables (VLTBs)

What is a large table today? Maybe somewhere near a billion rows, but as we know, multi-billion-row tables are becoming more popular. We have several clients with tables nearing 20 billion rows in production. But regardless of whether a table has 2 billion rows or 25 billion rows, there are some new things to think about. Design criteria change with tables of this size. They have to be designed differently if they are going to be maintained. Sequential range retrieval and SQL access become a secondary design issue, and maintenance, recovery, and utility use become the primary focus.

Partition strategies need to be carefully thought out, and these are *not* something you will see ever come out of a data-modeling tool. You may want to consider using an ascending key for data over time, using the identity column for sequential number generation, or using the ROWID for random linear distribution (refer to Chapter 5 for additional information on partitioning strategies).

Nonpartitioning Indexes

For large tables, NPIs *do work!* The trick is designing them properly so that they do not become a maintenance nightmare. The following case study is an example of how NPIs were used on a very large table.

We need to take advantage of pieces for best performance and manageability. NPIs can now be up to 16 TB in size, or 64 GB per data set for up to 256 data sets. (Refer to Chapter 5 for more information on pieces.)

Case Study: Implementation of a Six-Billion-Row Table

The best way to talk about how to implement VLTBs is to discuss an actual implementation and all the considerations surrounding it.

We had the opportunity to design and implement one of the first VLTBs: a six-billion-row table that went into production in July 1998. Now that number seems low, but the issues that we came across and some of the techniques that we used are still very applicable when implementing tables of this size and beyond.

Version 5 and Earlier Versions   Large table spaces have a significant impact on the database world. In the past, a technique commonly used to implement tables larger than 64 GB was to allow several physical tables to implement a single logical table (figure 6.2). While this technique worked, it was cumbersome to implement, because it required some

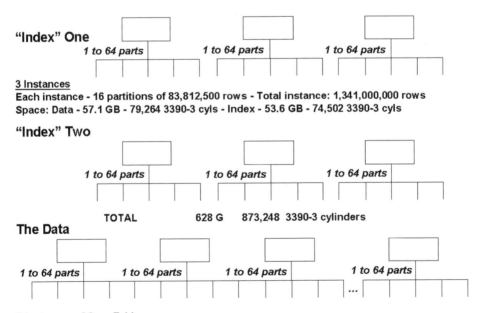

Figure 6.2   Original Logical/Physical on DB2 V4

kind of finder table in front of the process or direct processing to the appropriate physical table space. In addition, there could not be a real index, as each of the physical tables acting as logical indexes (figure 6.3) had its own partitioning index, and there was no method for defining an NPI over this logical structure. The requirements for something like an NPI were to have additional tables serve as logical indexes into the multiple physical table spaces, but each of the "index" tables also required its own index. All in all, this got quite messy, as the code to navigate through these layers had to be finely tuned, and most coding had to be encapsulated in application functional modules (figure 6.4).

You also had to make extensive use of SET PACKAGE to move through the layers; this required having different collections point to different databases and, in some cases, attaching synonyms or aliases to physical objects in the other databases (figure 6.5). If this sounds confusing, you should see the diagrams and object definitions! With the arrival of version 5, these problems were alleviated, as long as you had time to move through the UNLOADS, DROPS, REDEFINES, and RELOADS. But it was worthwhile, especially for systems that were hitting either the 64GB table limit or the partition-size limits of 1, 2, or 4 GB. Both those constraints are gone for 1TB table spaces as of version 5.

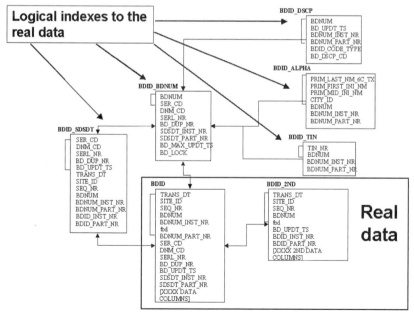

Figure 6.3 Physical Tables in V4 or Larger Than 1 TB in V5

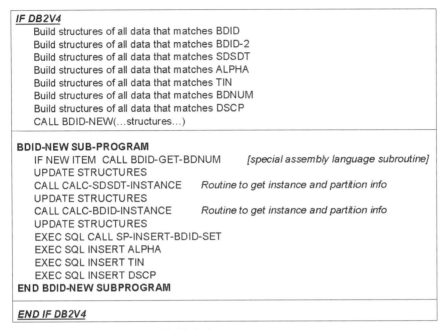

IF DB2V4
    Build structures of all data that matches BDID
    Build structures of all data that matches BDID-2
    Build structures of all data that matches SDSDT
    Build structures of all data that matches ALPHA
    Build structures of all data that matches TIN
    Build structures of all data that matches BDNUM
    Build structures of all data that matches DSCP
    CALL BDID-NEW(…structures…)

BDID-NEW SUB-PROGRAM
    IF NEW ITEM CALL BDID-GET-BDNUM   *[special assembly language subroutine]*
    UPDATE STRUCTURES
    CALL CALC-SDSDT-INSTANCE   *Routine to get instance and partition info*
    UPDATE STRUCTURES
    CALL CALC-BDID-INSTANCE   *Routine to get instance and partition info*
    UPDATE STRUCTURES
    EXEC SQL CALL SP-INSERT-BDID-SET
    EXEC SQL INSERT ALPHA
    EXEC SQL INSERT TIN
    EXEC SQL INSERT DSCP
END BDID-NEW SUBPROGRAM

END IF DB2V4

Figure 6.4   INSERT with Multiple Instances

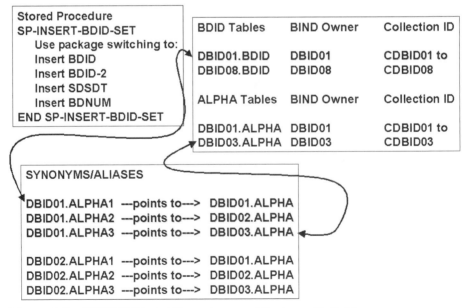

Figure 6.5   INSERT Stored Procedure and Package Switching

To define a large table of just 100 GB using the old method required an NPI. We had to define two partitioned table spaces, two partitioning indexes, an "index" table for the NPI, a real index on the NPI, and a finder table in front with its own index—a total of seven objects!

As of version 5, we need only three objects: the 1TB table space, its partitioning index, and the NPI. But if we apply the same example to the implementation of a core table that is initially loaded with 5.3 billion rows, the true value of the large table space becomes readily apparent. This table has well over 130 partitions, more than 130 partitioning-index partitions, and two NPIs of significant size. Also, prior to version 5, the NPIs were a real problem, since regardless of the number of partitions, the NPI was a single object; this made it "performance challenged." One of the NPIs for the six-billion-row table was close to 200 GB.

Designing the Table Probably the most interesting parts of this system were not only that it had a core table of six billion rows, but that there would be heavy usage of OLTP queries, BI queries, OLCP (online complex) queries, and concurrent batch and online programs. Regularly we were told that this could not be done, so it became a small challenge.

The core table had to be defined as a LARGE table space of 254 partitions. Each partition would hold approximately 40 million rows, and the key would be based on date ranges to control the sequencing. The dates of the data to be loaded went back to the 1950s, and we picked date ranges up to 2018 for the partitions to be filled in the future. Data would be added off the upper end, so only a few partitions would have actively inserted data (figure 6.6). The other partitions would not be active in terms of new insertions of data. But this is not the way the data was accessed. What about the queries? At this point, we did not care. The table had to be designed with a partitioning scheme that allowed proper care and maintenance of a table of this size. If the table had been designed solely for proper access, it would have been a maintenance nightmare and would never have worked.

We thought about carry a partition ID in the table to help allow dynamic control without ballooning partitions, but when we considered the disk space required to carry this ID, it simply was not a wise option.

The initial loading of the data would occupy the first 134 partitions, even though all 254 were defined to allow growth. The last few partitions were the only ones with active insertion of data, and as time progressed, they would become inactive as new partitions

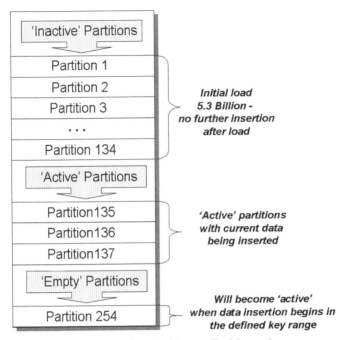

Figure 6.6   Partitioning for Upper-End Insertions

began to fill (partitions were based on data sequence and held approximately a month's worth of data). Figure 6.7 shows a catalog report with some statistics about this table. You can see that there are around 40 million rows per partitions.

The access to the table would be through two nonpartitioning indexes.

Clustering Index   The clustering index was designed solely for partitioning, not access. In other words, the partitioning scheme was designed so that all new data was inserted off the upper end; only a few partitions would be active with new data and therefore would require the most attention. The other less active partitions would require only infrequent copies (if updates were made) but would not need to be reorganized.

Because no access was done via the clustering or partitioning index, all access would use the nonpartitioning indexes.

Implementing the Nonpartitioning Indexes   For this table we implemented two NPIs. The NPIs were used for *all* access to the table. The clustering index was not used to access the table, and a table-space scan would not work, since it would require over seven days to complete.

NAME	PART	LOCK RULE	# T B L S	NACTIVE	C L O S E	S SIZ	SEG MAX	LOCK MAX	P E	T Y P E	MAX ROWS	CARD	FRE PGE	PCT FRE	C O M P	PAGE SAVE
OS2BBD01	254	P	1	60595770	N	0	0	L			255	37430813	0	0	Y	37
		P	1	60595770	N	0	0	L			255	41139590	0	0	Y	37
		P	1	60595770	N	0	0	L			255	38599808	0	0	Y	37
		P	1	60595770	N	0	0	L			255	40088888	0	0	Y	37
		P	1	60595770	N	0	0	L			255	38488070	0	0	Y	37
		P	1	60595770	N	0	0	L			255	33986142	0	0	Y	37
		P	1	60595770	N	0	0	L			255	34728639	0	0	Y	37
		P	1	60595770	N	0	0	L			255	32484798	0	0	Y	37
		P	1	60595770	N	0	0	L			255	41112217	0	0	Y	35
		P	1	60595770	N	0	0	L			255	35006958	0	0	Y	37
		P	1	60595770	N	0	0	L			255	34489551	0	0	Y	37
		P	1	60595770	N	0	0	L			255	37076087	0	0	Y	37

Row Counts per Partition →

Figure 6.7   Table Statistics

We made extensive use of piecesize with the NPIs. When the table was loaded, it filled up 78 pieces of the large NPI and 12 of the smaller one. In this implementation, the pieces were sized to fit one per physical volume; using user-defined methods, flexibility in placement was assured.

While building this 1TB table, we discovered a couple of issues with NPI pieces. When the NPI is built, each piece is loaded up to the maximum size defined, regardless of the definition of primary and secondary quantities. Processes such as page splits in the index still require some analysis and careful definition of free space. Both LOAD and REORG fill the pieces to their maximum size, so it is imperative to have the space definitions match the piecesize definition for proper utilization of the direct-access storage device (DASD).

We discovered another wonderful feature of type 2 indexes while constructing this system: the incredible ability of the index to handle a nonunique RID chain of over 600 million duplicates (one key with that many duplicates). It not only works, it works well!

Free Space   When designing a table of this size and its indexes, guessing at free space can cost a lot of disk space. The PCTFREE and FREEPAGE become a big issue.

Because processing was not fully understood prior to the start-up of the production environment, the free space was initially set to 10% PCTFREE and 0 FREEPAGE on both the NPIs but had to be redefined soon after production processing started. After we saw how and where the insertions were occurring, PCTFREE was dropped to 5%, and FREEPAGE was adjusted. The smaller NPI had its FREEPAGE set to 31 to keep the pages in the prefetch ranges but allow more FREEPAGEs, because the data in this index was inserted in clumps. The other index had insertions all over, so its FREEPAGE was left at 0.

Free space for the table-space partitions was an interesting issue. The table was designed so that all data would be inserted in date order in the last active partition, but that did not quite happen, because of where the data was coming from; data did not always arrive in the sequence that was anticipated by the table. So the last four partitions actually became the active partitions that allowed inserts, and we also had to account for this in the free space. All nonactive partitions in the table had no free space at all. The last four partitions now had to have FREEPAGE of 20 to allow the nonsequential insertions in this upper end and avoid having to do REORGs on the partitions. The free space was then removed when the partition became inactive. The lesson to be learned here is "designer, beware": know your data and how it is processed.

Loading the Data   Figures 6.8 through 6.10 show an overview of the high-level process of getting data from its source to the DB2 table. This is the process of loading a large table from converted data coming from one or more source systems. This parallel process can be used anytime a large amount of data needs to be loaded and a singular process would exceed all resources. The trick to make the process parallel was to allow all data coming out of conversion to be archived, since it might need to be input again to a loading. After writing the data to the archive, each row of data for the table was passed to a sort routine, not to sort it, but only to *split* the conversion data into logical groupings of 125 million rows each. These 125-million row files were then split into separate 25-million-row files for the actual loading into partitions of 125 million rows.

The purpose of the overlap was to free disk space and start each successive load process. This is a stepwise parallel process, freeing resources as it moves along. The first loads would use disk space from what would become the high end of the real table. You cannot normally have all the disk space needed to hold the table, hold all the input data, and sort six billion rows at the same time.

The first step was to take the 125-million-row set and split and sort it into the key ranges for each partition. The sorting of all this data was deferred until this step. The

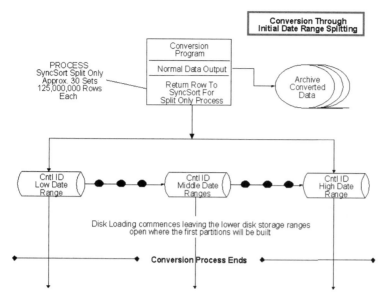

Figure 6.8   Load Process Part 1

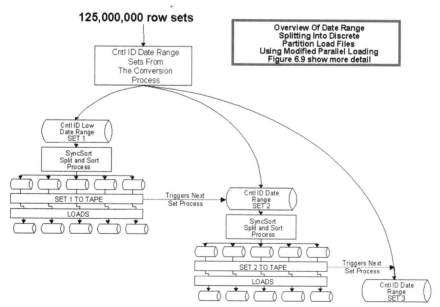

Figure 6.9   Load Process Part 2

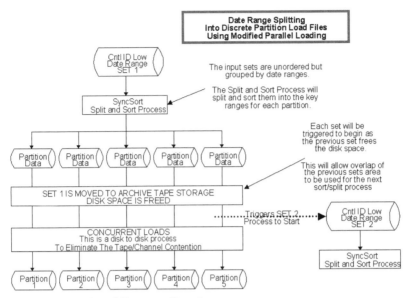

Figure 6.10 Load Process Part 3

sorted, split output now was five separate load files on disk. Each set was archived to tape, then the original disk from the 125-million-row file was freed, and the next parallel load process was triggered to begin.

We deviated a little from the initial design for loading due to some physical constraints. The initial conversion processed 3.1 billion rows in approximately 40 individual loads processes then into DB2 loadable data sets. The loads occurred in two groups: the first group loaded 3,135,772,036 rows, and then updates were performed to a few previously loaded partitions for correction processing. Then the second group loaded 1,613,572,458 rows, for a grand total of 4,749,344,494 rows. Three loads were executed at a time. The largest partitions averaged one hour each and were performed using a third-party load utility. At the same time, REORGs, RUNSTATS, and IMAGE copies were performed. Three partitions were copied in parallel, with the largest averaging 12 to 15 minutes each with a third-party utility.

When that data initially was loaded, the compression ratio was 38% to 48%. A REORG was then run on each partition to build a better compression dictionary. After the reorganization, a 99% compression ratio was achieved, with an average of 37% page savings. These partition-level REORGs were done before the NPIs were built. This reorganization also needed to occur for each new partition when its data records were inserted. The fact that the NPIs would already exist at that time would become an issue.

Building the Indexes   The partitioned index was a duplicate, clustering index and was built during data loading. The NPIs were built after the data was loaded. The larger of the two indexes was 78 pieces. This index was actually built after the first group was loaded so that some updates could be performed, but was dropped before the rest of the data was loaded. The keys were unloaded prior to the build, which took approximately four hours for four partitions in one job, with 150 million rows per job. Three jobs executed in parallel on four partitions each. This took about 30 hours for unloading and sorting index keys and then another 30 hours for index rebuilding (recovery build phase). Then the smaller NPI was built, using 12 pieces; it did not take nearly as long as the other to build.

Maintaining the Data   After the first load, RUNSTATS was executed with 10% sampling across table space. Only after an entire table space's RUNSTATS could partition-level RUNSTATS be taken, because at the time DB2 had to collect statistics for the entire table space first. This execution took 84 hours and 45 hours of CPU time. The RUNSTATS utility was performed during the first test building of this large table. The table was not dropped, but rather the data was deleted, so during final production load it was not necessary to run the RUNSTATS utility on the entire table space because the statistics still existed. Partition-level RUNSTATS could then be used thereafter, and each partition RUNSTATS took approximately 30 minutes. These partition-level RUNSTATS were executed in tandem with the partition-level image copies.

The partitioning index RUNSTATS took approximately 30 minutes per partition. The larger nonpartitioning index took 10 hours for the entire RUNSTATS, and the smaller index averaged around 8 hours.

A third-party check utility checked RI and table constraints after the load. The largest partitions averaged around 1 hour each for a total of 95 hours. However, it was determined that running the load with ENFORCE CONSTRAINTS was faster, and this method was performed during the production load. A check index for the largest NPI took 4 hours.

Reorganization of the nonpartitioning indexes using the REORG utility was not possible, due to the size of the required sorts. The indexes were recovered instead. To do this in a somewhat timely manner, the unloaded key files were kept, and no updates were allowed to the partitioning indexes. (This is a key point regarding NPIs on large tables: if they are designed and used properly, they do not cause the maintenance issues everyone fears.) Unloads were performed periodically on the last four partitions to keep the keys current. Reorg of the larger NPI had an elapsed time of 30 hours (provided the unload keys were current and available). For the partitioned index, the reorg took an average of 7–11 minutes per partition.

The table-space partition reorganization provided us with some tense moments. Each partition REORG took approximately 26–30 hours for a full (40-million-row) partition with a third-party utility. This was painful, because the actual reorganization of the data took only 2–3 hours, but the rest of the time was spent updating the NPIs. The IBM-supplied REORG took approximately 17 hours. Even though the data was loaded in sequence for the most part, we still had to do REORGs on newly used partitions in order to get a better compression dictionary, and then we had to also remove the free space when the partition was no longer receiving insertions. It is important to remember that we were using the early release version 5 and its utilities, not the more sophisticated utilities now available.

Buffer Pools   Now we confronted the question of how to size the buffer pools that had to support these large objects. Isn't there some rule of thumb that says to make the index buffer pool size large enough to hold all nonleaf pages plus 20% of the leaf pages? Okay, that's around 400,000 nonleaf pages from the three indexes, even without the 20%. And what about the other rule of thumb that says to size a buffer pool large enough to hold the entire index? For the larger NPI on this table, that is over eight million pages (figure 6.11 shows the index pages of the large NPI obtained via DB2 Estimator). Such a size is not possible, and even version 6 with data space support for buffer pools would provide only some

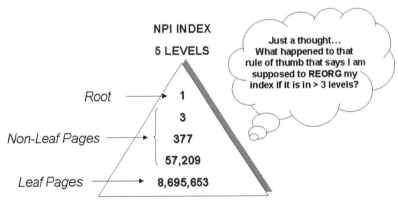

Figure 6.11   Large NPI Index Levels

minor relief. These guidelines simply cannot work for these large objects. So we had to experiment and make the best of what we had (which, by the way, was about 400 MB of total real memory).

First we had to take our best guess at the buffer pool sizes. In figure 6.12 you can see day 1 production processing of the large objects. This figure also shows which buffer pools held the large objects. After evaluating the processing, we determined how to better adjust the thresholds because our data was being mainly inserted and not referenced. We decided to lower the buffer pool sizes and let the pages participate in a continual flow to disk to minimize I/O spikes. We also adjusted the system checkpoint interval. In figure 6.13 you can see that we lowered the number of pages and adjusted the write thresholds. This worked very well.

But the next issue was parallelism and having enough buffers to support it. We started looking into query parallelism and noticed a good deal of fallback due to lack of buffers. We also observed that the degree of parallelism achieved at run time was often degraded from what was planned at bind time. (We found this information in the EXPLAIN output [degree determined at bind], the statistics report [fallback due to lack of buffers], and the performance trace with IFCID 121 and 122 [showing the degree at run time].) This led us to look into what degrees had been chosen at bind time, and we discovered that the degree of parallelism of all access against the large table where parallelism was applicable was 88.

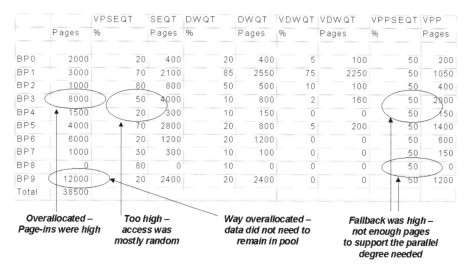

	Pages	VPSEQT %	SEQT Pages	DWQT %	DWQT Pages	VDWQT %	VDWQT Pages	VPPSEQT %	VPP Pages
BP0	2000	20	400	20	400	5	100	50	200
BP1	3000	70	2100	85	2550	75	2250	50	1050
BP2	1000	80	800	50	500	10	100	50	400
BP3	8000	50	4000	10	800	2	160	50	2000
BP4	1500	20	300	10	150	0	0	50	750
BP5	4000	70	2800	20	800	5	200	50	1400
BP6	6000	20	1200	20	1200	0	0	50	600
BP7	1000	30	300	10	100	0	0	50	150
BP8	0	80	0	10	0	0	0	50	0
BP9	12000	20	2400	20	2400	0	0	50	1200
Total	38500								

Overallocated –
Page-ins were high

Too high –
access was
mostly random

Way overallocated –
data did not need to
remain in pool

Fallback was high –
not enough pages
to support the parallel
degree needed

Figure 6.12   Initial Buffer Pool Settings

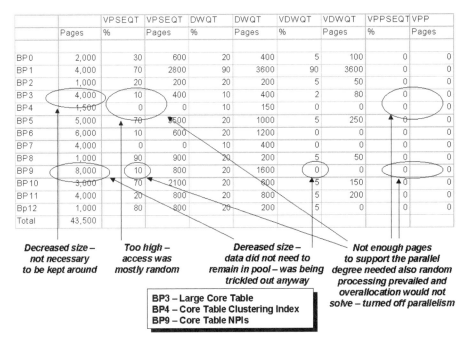

	Pages	VPSEQT %	VPSEQT Pages	DWQT %	DWQT Pages	VDWQT %	VDWQT Pages	VPPSEQT %	VPP Pages
BP0	2,000	30	600	20	400	5	100	0	0
BP1	4,000	70	2800	90	3600	90	3600	0	0
BP2	1,000	20	200	20	200	5	50	0	0
BP3	4,000	10	400	10	400	2	80	0	0
BP4	1,500	0	0	10	150	0	0	0	0
BP5	5,000	70	3500	20	1000	5	250	0	0
BP6	6,000	10	600	20	1200	0	0	0	0
BP7	4,000	0	0	10	400	0	0	0	0
BP8	1,000	90	900	20	200	5	50	0	0
BP9	8,000	10	800	20	1600	0	0	0	0
BP10	3,000	70	2100	20	600	5	150	0	0
BP11	4,000	20	800	20	800	5	200	0	0
Bp12	1,000	80	800	20	200	5	0	0	0
Total	43,500								

Decreased size – not necessary to be kept around   *Too high – access was mostly random*   *Dereased size – data did not need to remain in pool – was being trickled out anyway*   *Not enough pages to support the parallel degree needed also random processing prevailed and overallocation would not solve – turned off parallelism*

BP3 – Large Core Table
BP4 – Core Table Clustering Index
BP9 – Core Table NPIs

Figure 6.13   Buffer Pool Settings Postproduction

How were we getting 88 degrees of parallelism at bind time when we had only two CPUs? With CPU parallelism, anything is possible. We found that the figure of 88 comes from how DB2 initially determines the degree at bind time. DB2 takes the total number of active pages in the entire table and divides this by the total number of active pages in the largest partition of the table. For our large table, this was $60,655,478/691,126 = 88$.

Fallback was high, overhead for fallback was high, and we had a tremendous problem tuning buffer pools for parallelism. Many buffer pools (NPIs, etc.) were defined for random access. The VPSEQT was set low, and because the VPPSEQT is a percentage of VPSEQT and therefore there is no room for parallelism, we had more fallback problems. We tried inflating the number of pages in buffer pools to try to support the parallel requirements, but this was not enough. Our final solution: we turned parallelism off because the system could not support it. We did worry that access against the large table would suffer, but that was not the case. The applications were not suffering, and now the overhead was down.

SQL and the Beast   The system is now in production, and you might wonder about the impacts of SQL processing on a table that large. We were concerned with this also but found that extensive use can be made of the enhancements of page-range scanning. The major enhancement is the introduction of nondiscrete partitions to be identified for scanning, but the actual scanning in the partitions is performed by an NPI. This is where the optimizer can identify the partitions to be processed: by comparing key data against the key ranges and using the NPI as the access method. Of course, this requires using a new technique in the SQL of allowing multiple OR conditions or IN list predicates against the higher-order columns in the clustering index; in the past, this was usually avoided since it caused a table-space scan. As is usual with the growth of DB2, what was bad in the past now becomes good.

We also made use of key correlation statistics. The KEYCARD parameter on RUNSTATS indicates that cardinalities for each column, concatenated with all previous key columns, are to be collected. If KEYCARD is not specified, only FIRSTKEYCARD and FULLKEYCARD are collected. KEYCARD builds the frequency values for critical concatenated key columns: first and second columns and first, second, and third columns. This was important for us because the large NPI often was accessed using only the first three columns of the five-column index, which would have resulted in a three-column matching scan without knowing the extent of the scan. So by giving DB2 full key cardinality on all three columns with correlation statistics, we obtained a very accurate filter factor.

SQL performance analysis should start as early as possible in the development life cycle. We used exact index and table catalog statistics in the test and acceptance environments that were updated to mimic production for the purpose of validating the access paths. In addition to the statistics, the system DSNZPARMS, buffer pools, and RID, EDM, and sort pools were made the same so that the optimizer could react consistently among these environments. If the environments were inconsistent, the access path analysis would have been inaccurate, and we could have had some surprises in production.

Prior to production, the queries were reviewed for their adherence to best SQL access path selection. This was done by using a system developed inhouse to run EXPLAINs on the SQL in every program and analyze the access paths chosen. A full description of this system is described in Chapter 22, "Predictive Analysis, Governing and Tuning."

Warehouses

What warehouses are and are not has been explained in more ways than any other technology trend since the dawn of computers. This simple explanation will serve as the basis for discussion: a method of storing and using all the data that we have captured with existing systems and the voluminous amount of business data that we never captured before. Industry experts put warehouses into many practical categories, from enterprise warehouses to data islands. Software vendors in this arena seem to have a new offering almost daily, on machines from desktops to high-end mainframes. Hardware vendors seem to easily explain why their approach at clustering and parallelism is the ultimate solution to the growing demands of warehouse access and presentation of answers. Data warehouses present two types of information that are critically important for businesses to stay competitive: the noncomputerized information always used to mold business direction and new information that businesses literally could not benefit from before.

There are many myths perpetuated about data warehouses, such as that data marts are always separate, isolated databases and that data warehouses and operational systems cannot exist together. It is frequently stated that warehouse users do not need to have highly responsive systems and do not need to have access to operational data. The reality of existing implementations shows quite the opposite to be true, specifically for larger warehouses. These warehouses are business systems required to shape competitive analysis, make critical and time-dependent financial decisions, and adapt to changing market pressures. Those realities dictate responsive, scalable systems that can easily manage a growing number of users and handle very large data stores that are constantly changing in structure. In the movement toward these enterprise warehouses, the blueprint is integration—not separation—of data, information, servers, and user facilities.

It is not important for this discussion to consider all the possible subdivisions of warehouses. We define three very broad categories: operational data warehouses, data marts, and VLDB warehouses.

Operational Data Warehouses

An operational data warehouse is a system that is both a classic operational system and also the storage and service layer for historical data in whatever form required (detailed, summarized, added value, mined, etc.).

There are many disagreements on this definition, but such systems are used today at many large businesses that have discovered the benefits of data/information integration under a single complex with minimal data or system redundancy.

Data Marts

Data marts are defined theoretically as warehouses containing a subset of information that relates to a very specific business department. These are generally thought to be small, isolated warehouses, and in many aspects they have become dangerous, nonintegrated data islands.

VLDB Warehouses

While hardware processors may be shrinking, data storage is not. The growth in the amount of information stored appears to be exponential, as billions of rows and terabytes of data are not uncommon. One particular warehouse is growing at the rate of 150–200 GB per month, others at rates of millions of items per day. Access to these systems by business analysts and other interested parties is expanding just as rapidly, with more demands for faster access. The growth of information discovery from data mining is requiring more powerful engines and sophisticated parallelism, both in hardware and in database engines. As these systems are constructed, end-user access is requiring many different architectures, networks, and support of different client topologies (for example, online terminal and browser-type access). Enterprise warehouses and large data marts need the best if they are to provide the information necessary to move a business forward. The best is obvious to many: DB2 and OS/390.

Today, 390 is just another server, stand-alone or clustered, hanging on a network. It is no longer the "mainframe" hiding in a secured room somewhere, consuming outrageous dollars, requiring a mystical staff of gurus, and supporting legacy, uneasily modified systems. It is the premier server offering more capabilities than any other server, since it can easily support multiple client-server structures and networks and at the same time handle multiple mission-critical, terminal-based OLTP systems. As a server on the network, it can peacefully coexist with any other server on the network running any other operating environment (UNIX, Solaris, NT, etc.).

The Sysplex is IBM's architecture of clustering SMP (shared memory processors) systems into a NUMA-like (nonuniform memory architecture) (massively parallel processing) MPP environment. The current SMP systems built by IBM are CMOS-based machines supporting 10 or more processors of up to 200 usable MIPS each. An SMP machine is generally referred to as a CPC, or central processor complex. As a stand-alone machine, it is as powerful as the older bipolar mainframes. But today it is possible to cluster up to 32 of these SMPs together to form a Parallel Sysplex supporting up to 320 processors (limits are very temporal in the IBM world and have probably already increased). These 32 CPCs share physical data storage, so that in essence up to 320 processors could be directed at a massive VLDB, running in parallel to support a critical data-mining function or answering the infamous WQFH (warehouse query from Hell). These data farms, disk storage acres, are also theoretically unlimited in size.

The importance of Sysplex to data warehouses is twofold. It is now possible to picture a client-server system with all the client and network access supported by a single server. The truth behind that server is that it is not a single server but a Sysplex acting as a server in support of all types of connections and business systems. Reality shows us that not many queries use 320 processors, but many queries that require 10 processors each could be running together, in support of entirely different requirements, but each getting the level of support required.

The larger benefit from the large table support for data warehouses is not that massive data quantities need to be supported, but that lesser data stores can be split into more functional arrangements, such as by time series. By utilizing the change to the number of partitions that can be handled, benefits in query support, data archiving or purging, and parallelism are readily apparent. Data will not be maintained online in warehouses forever. There comes a point when some types of data outlive their usefulness and can either be purged or archived. If data is arranged by time, the table can be designed for partitions that can be cycled or easily reused. When verification queries are processed, they can be easily broken up into parallel processes by partitions, either by DB2 or programmer's design. DB2 allows unlimited variations when it comes to structuring data warehouses. Even star schemas, sometimes difficult in large warehouses, can be constructed and supported by DB2 using different types of horizontal or vertical partitioning and the increased number of large-table partitions supported.

As the industry has moved toward BI and data warehouses, so have the features of DB2. DB2 has always been an industrial-strength engine that can support the user population, handle the data growth, and still remain responsive enough to drive hundreds and in some cases thousands of transactions per second. The key, of course, comes from proper design and use. DB2 can handle not only OLTP and BI, but also the integration of these in two specific areas: (1) operational data warehouses (often referred to as ODS, operational data stores) where the data is contained in a single logical database and (2) combined systems that support both OLTP-designed databases and warehouse-designed databases.

Data Warehouse and OLTP

One of the more difficult problems in building today's enterprise data warehouses has been the perceived requirement to build totally isolated database systems, due primarily to the myth that mixed queries and data cannot coexist in a single box or be handled by a single DBMS engine. Man was never meant to fly either, right? DB2 is enabled to support just about any type of mixed environment that can be constructed. This has been proven through real production systems at several locations. We are able to manage, distribute, and balance our workloads very well with the WLM (Workload Manager), which controls resources within a single SMP or within the clustered Sysplex by ensuring that established goals and objectives are met. WLM has managers for controlling components such as CPU, I/O, and storage. These controls allow the full range of workload prioritization, such as time-based aging or favoring critical functions. These controls are dynamic and at any point can be redirected to change to a particular result required.

Normal OLTP activity tends to move in a straight line of resource consumption, while warehouse activity bounces from one extreme to the other. Where the WLM truly proves its worth is in the mixed environment of OLTP and warehouse, to prevent the OLTP from being influenced by the extremities of resource consumption from warehouse queries or processes. On the other hand, if a critical warehouse query does arrive, the OLTP can be downgraded to allow the warehouse process to complete as rapidly as required. Since DB2 can handle up to 25,000 clients per SMP node, a Sysplex could conceivably handle 800,000 clients, with up to 64,000 concurrent clients (threads) over 32 DB2 subsystems. These client processes could come from locally attached stations or through the network, using either dynamic SQL database access or static, preprogrammed SQL.

The WLM is the outer layer of control, while additional controls within DB2 allow the proper separation and integration of function. WLM is capable of managing each process according to its defined importance, regardless of where the workload originates. The dynamic nature of WLM and its relatively simple controls allow policies to be defined and adjusted to meet the normally scheduled demands or immediately adapt to unscheduled requirements. In any situation, especially with the change for the WLQH, WLM has controls that prevent any query from monopolizing the system. On the opposite end, it has controls for the permanently predictable short queries. WLM has additional controls that allow it to adjust, start, and stop additional DB2 stored procedure address spaces in order to meet the defined service-level goals.

The DB2 optimizer has changed significantly over the last several releases, specifically in the areas of parallelism. The management of resources by the WLM along with the optimized parallel support provides the resources necessary to do complex data mining in support of discovery and long-running verification queries.

While OLTP SQL tends not to be complex in construction, warehouse queries are complex. The filtering, joining, and aggregation common in warehouse queries could present difficulty in some DBMS systems, but not in DB2. The optimizer in DB2 is cost based, taking into consideration the I/O and CPU capabilities of the target system or clustered Sysplex. The optimizer does depend on accurate statistics, and keeping these current was always a problem in the past, since these were often collected only on columns present in indexes. Warehouse queries do not follow the predictable pattern of filtering based only on index columns, but use many more columns. It is critical to have statistics on all columns, especially in more dynamic SQL environments. RUNSTATS can capture these statistics by sampling the nonindex columns (for more information, refer to Chapter 23). Additionally, once these statistics have been collected on older data partitions, they probably do not have to be captured again. To get the best method of accessing the warehouse, calculated costing must be accurate. Support for dynamic SQL optimization includes the ability to optimize at run time, which also requires accurate statistics. Warehouses often contain nonuniformly distributed data, even if accurately designed, nonuniform data exist within a partition. Where one query might require a scan due to the values used, another might require an index. By optimizing these specific queries at run time, you can choose either access type. This feature must be regarded as dynamic, static SQL. But this is only half the battle with warehouse queries. The data used to produce aggregate results often requires data in related columns in the indexes providing the access path. RUNSTATS has the capability of collecting statistics on correlated index columns. This feature especially helps those generated queries coming from client-side tools.

Designing Warehouses

Star Schemas

A star schema design is used to represent data for OLAP (online analytical processing) systems or multidimensional analysis. You have a large table with data that you want to investigate. This table is called the fact table. The primary key of this table consists of

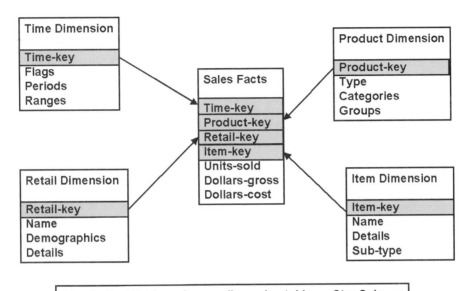

Classic Fact Table and many dimension tables -- Star Schema

Figure 6.14 Star Schema

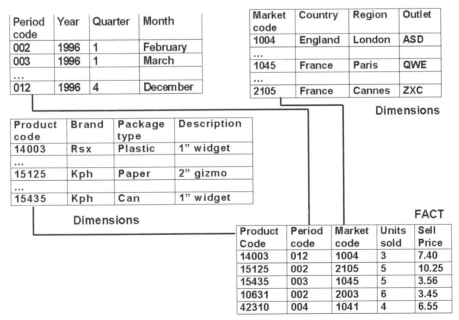

Figure 6.15 Example Star Schema

foreign keys that point to dimensions of the data (figures 6.14 and 6.15) Popular dimensions are time, geographic location, branch, channel, customer type, and so on. With OLAP tools, you can slice and dice the data into multiple dimensions, such as average sales per region by month by customer type. Once you find anomalies, you can go deeper into a dimension (for example, to look at the data by month instead of by week).

Star schemas are not appropriate for all data, though. If dimensions get too large, the processing gets too heavy and produces too many results. At that point, the concept doesn't work anymore. DB2 supports OLAP processing by means of CUBE and ROLLUP SQL functions.

Snowflake Schemas

A snowflake is a special form of a star schema where the dimensions, instead of being single tables, have relations with dependent tables (hierarchical parent-child relationships). A diagram of the design looks like a snowflake. These additional hierarchies generally cause difficult table joins to be used during processing.

If the dimensions have too many relations, you might have overnormalized the model. In that case, consider denormalizing, because the SQL to be coded can get very complex. In relational database design, the word *relation* is used to represent a relationship between two entities. In simpler terms, a parent table has a child table. For example, a parent table could be about your bank account, and the child table could be your checking transactions. The information in the child table contains the account number relating the child to the proper account information in the parent table.

Multistar Schema

A multistar schema is the opposite of a snowflake. The primary key has multiple relations from the same key or attributes (table columns) that do not point to other tables. Normally, this schema is the result of improper design or denormalizing. You should be able to recognize this kind of design; it should be redesigned to follow a more appropriate model.

Snowball and Dirty Snowball Schemas

When you put together a star schema whose relationships comprise multiple tables for the dimensions and whose fact table comprises multiple dimensions, you have been hit in the head with a chunk of ice called a snowball. If you then add multistar characteristics on top of this, the snowball starts to get really dirty. We are sure that somewhere out there someone has invented good, solid, theoretical definitions for these two constructs, but let's bring it back to reality. There is no effective way to query them and get any kind of meaningful results in any reasonable amount of allotted time. They cause the same problems as process design that starts to override relational design. It becomes impossible to form anything but simple relationships, which drives up the resource cost.

The bottom line with VLTBs, VLDBs, warehouses, ODSs, and so on is proper design. If the design works, there is a good chance that you can achieve some level of acceptable performance. If the design is better than just adequate, if it is good, then you can achieve high performance.

## CHAPTER 7

Large Objects (LOBs)

P lanning is required to avoid unnecessary over-
head in many situations in DB2. The implementation and use of LOBs are just another
item in a long list of performance considerations, but not one to be taken lightly. In the
past, it has been possible to get away with improper tuning and less than optimal performance. However, with the implementation of LOBs, there really is no room for error.

DB2's support of object orientation includes large objects (LOBs), user-defined
types (UDTs), user-defined function (UDFs), additional built-in functions, and triggers.
The introduction of LOBs, binary LOBs (BLOBs), and character LOBs (CLOBs) allows
columns to logically hold data up to 2 GB in length and support many LOB columns per
table. The LOB content is not actually stored in the table in which it is modeled (referred
to as the base table), but is represented in the table by a large object descriptor, called an
indicator, in conjunction with a column defined as the new data type of ROWID. The LOB
itself is logically stored in a separate object, linked to the base table. Normally, the physical LOB data is stored in a separate table space, but there are options for storing the data
in many native formats supported for each object type.

Since dealing with LOBs can often be difficult, depending on their content, IBM also
provides DB2 extenders that enable applications to exploit object-relational features for very
specific data types, such as pictures and video. The extenders provide all the definitions and
logic to allow applications a single point of access to all data, namely, SQL. (Refer to Chapter 18 for information on extenders and issues surrounding programming with LOBs.)

There are many parts to the implementation of LOBs in any system, both on the system side, where the impacts of memory, recovery, concurrency, and performance are

issues, and on the application side, where many new constructs, SQL changes, and coding procedures are issues. In this chapter we look at the physical aspects of LOBS and their individual components. To implement LOBs without experiencing performance problems, there are a few areas you need to consider:

- Where the LOB data is physically stored
- Loading and inserting LOBs
- Buffer pool impacts
- Logging and recovery impacts
- Locking changes and options
- Manipulating LOBs with SQL

In this chapter we focus on the first five issues, because these are addressed through the physical design and implementation of LOBs. The use of SQL for LOB manipulation is covered in Chapter 18, "LOBs and Extenders."

LOB Data Types

Three new data types have been added to DB2.

- BLOB data type (binary large object)
  - Binary strings (not associated with a CCSID)
  - Good for storing image, voice, and sound data
- CLOB data type (character large object)
  - Strings made of single-byte characters or single- or double-byte characters with an associated CCSID
  - Use if data is larger than VARCHAR allows
- DBCLOB data type (double-byte character large object)
  - Strings made of double-byte characters with an associated CCSID

Each of these types can contain up to 2 GB of data, although in most cases the amount of storage for individual columns is considerably less (depending on the type of data stored). There is a large use today of the 32K VARCHAR column, which has limitations in both size and functionality. Most of this use will probably be replaced by using LOBs in the future, certainly for new applications and functions. In many ways this should be considered a performance design move.

LOB Support for Multimedia Objects

To design a table to hold multimedia objects, such as medical X-rays or videos, you need to create columns using the LOB data types. The following example shows how to define a table to hold an audio message.

```
CREATE TABLE voice_response
    (call_option char(1),
    audio_response blob(10M) NOT LOGGED COMPACT)
```

The options NOT LOGGED and COMPACT tell DB2 not to log updates to the field and to decrease the amount of space required to hold the object, respectively. These options are discussed in detail later.

The maximum size of LOBs is 2 GB per column. LOBs can be used to support a variety of items, such as check images, audio, video (a 2 GB LOB could hold up to two hours), or lengthy documents. When a LOB column is defined, special functions are needed to handle the processing; for text, image, audio, and video, a special set of extenders is available. These extenders are for data definition, UDFs, and special processing programs such as search engines to make dealing with these data types easier for users.

LOB Table Spaces

You need to create a LOB table space for each column (or each column of each partition) of a base LOB table (base tables are described later). This table space contains the auxiliary table. This LOB table space has a new structure up to 4,000 TB in size. A new storage model is used for LOB table spaces. This linear table space can hold up to 254 data sets, which can be up to 64 GB each. The LOB table space is implemented basically in the same fashion as pieces are implemented for NPIs. You can have 254 partitions of 64 GB each, allowing a total of 16 TB, and one partition for each LOB column up to 254 partitions, which make up to 4,000 TB possible (figure 7.1).

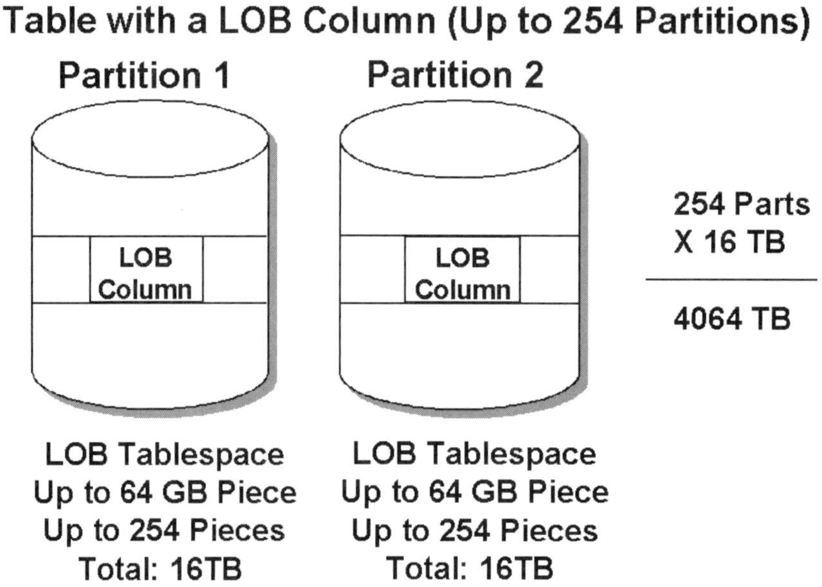

Table with a LOB Column (Up to 254 Partitions)

Partition 1   Partition 2

254 Parts
X 16 TB
_____
4064 TB

LOB Tablespace   LOB Tablespace
Up to 64 GB Piece   Up to 64 GB Piece
Up to 254 Pieces   Up to 254 Pieces
Total: 16TB   Total: 16TB

Figure 7.1   LOB Tablespace Size

The LOB table space has a new recovery scheme, and logging is optional. Changes to LOBs are never logged for UNDO and REDO (more on this log impact later). There is also a new locking option for the LOB table space, LOCKSIZE(LOB).

Partitioned base tables can each have different LOB table spaces. A LOB value can be longer than a page in a LOB table space and can thus span pages.

Page Sizes

With LOB page sizes, there is a trade-off between minimizing the number of GETPAGES and not wasting space (not really a new concept). Only one LOB value is stored in a given page in a LOB table space; any space unused by one LOB remains unused, and some space is also used for control information by DB2. For example, if you are using a 32K page size but your LOB is only 15K, you have a lot of wasted space. So you need to consider the page size used and the actual size of the LOB.

All LOBs usually are not equal, but if you know your LOBs' average size, you can choose a better page size. You can take the average size of the LOBs and add a percentage to account for the space used by control information.

```
Average LOB Length X 1.05 = Size of LOB
```

Some suggestions for page sizes for LOBs that are not the same size are as follows:

Average LOB size (x)	Page size
$x <= 4$ K	4 K
4 K $< x <= 8$ K	8 K
8 K $< x <= 16$ K	16 K
16 K $< x$	32 K

Some suggestions for page sizes for LOBs that are the same size are as follows:

LOB size (x)	Page size
x $<= 4$ K	4 K
4 K $< x <= 8$ K	8 K
8 K $< x <= 12$ K	4 K
12 K $< x <= 16$ K	16 K
16 K $< x <= 24$ K	8 K
24 K $< x <= 32$ K	32 K
32 K $< x <= 48$ K	16 K
48 K $< x$	32 K

LOB Tables

LOB data is not actually stored in the table in which it is defined. The defined LOB column holds information about the LOB, while the LOB itself is stored in another location. The normal place for this data storage is a LOB table space defining the physical storage that holds an auxiliary table related to the base column and table (figure 7.2).

Because the actual LOB is stored in a separate table, if a large, infrequently accessed, variable-character column is in use, you may be able to convert it to a LOB so

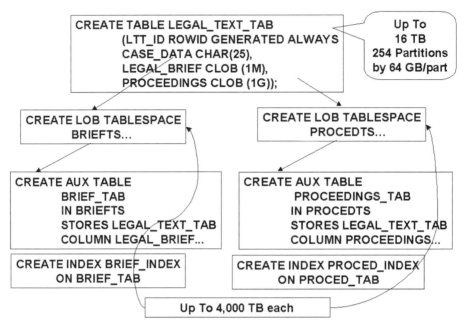

Figure 7.2   Large Object Tables

that it is kept separately. This could speed up table space scans on the remaining data, because fewer pages would be accessed.

NULL is the only supported default value for a LOB column. If the value is NULL, it does not take up space in the LOB table space.

Indicator Columns

The LOB indicator is a 6-byte field represented as a VARCHAR(4). It contains a 2-byte flag, with only the first two bits used for the NULL flag bit and the zero-length flag bit. It also contains a 2 byte field that indicates the version number for detection of any mismatches between the base table and the auxiliary table.

ROWID

The ROWID is a mechanism for handling LOBs. A LOB column in a table contains information about the LOB and does not hold the LOB data. This data is stored in other containers or table spaces. In the table that defines the LOB column, there is also a column called a ROWID. DB2 uses this data to point to the LOB data in the LOB storage object. The ROWID is a variable-length character-string representation 40 bytes long, but it is stored as if it were a VARCHAR of 17. The column is actually 19 bytes in length internally.

The ROWID column must exist in the base table before a LOB column can be defined, and there is one ROWID column per base table. All LOB columns in a row have the same ROWID, which is a unique identifier for each row in the table and is part of the key for indexing the auxiliary table.

ROWIDs are not the same as the RIDs (row identifiers). In most cases, DB2 generates the value if you specify GENERATE ALWAYS.

If SQL selects a row from a LOB table, the ROWID can also be selected. Since the ROWID implicitly (not explicitly) contains the location of the row, it can be used to navigate directly to the row, such as in a direct UPDATE statement. This type of access method is called direct row access and bypasses the need for an index or either a table-space scan (refer to Chapter 23 for more information). Another use of the ROWID is as the partitioning key (refer to Chapter 5).

LOB Indexes

There must be an index on each auxiliary table. No columns are specified when the index is created. The index itself consists 19 bytes for the ROWID and 5 bytes for the RID. No LOB columns are allowed in the index.

LOB Implementation

As you can see in figure 7.3, the implementation of LOBs can get rather complex. The base table LEGAL_TEXT_TAB defines the logical rows, which contain a CASE, LEGAL_BRIEF, and PROCEEDINGS. Since LEGAL_BRIEF and PROCEEDINGS are LOBs, they have corresponding LOB table spaces or tables and indexes. The physical implementation of this table includes a ROWID, which in this example is the LLT_ID that acts as the key. The LEGAL_BRIEF and PROCEEDINGS columns are physically implemented as indicators that point to the actual LOB data.

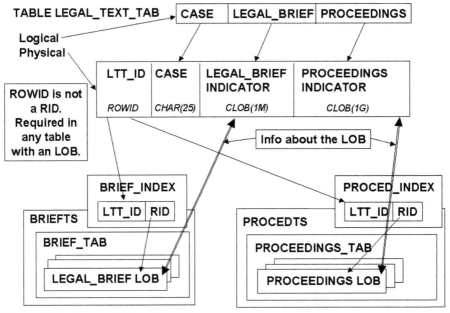

Figure 7.3   Large Object Implementation

Automatic Creation of LOBs

If a table contains a LOB column and the plan or package is bound with SQLRULES(STD), DB2 implicitly creates the LOB table space, the auxiliary table, and the auxiliary index. DB2 chooses the name and characteristics for these, thus implicitly creating these objects. This implicit creation is not a good idea, because naming standards and placement of these objects are critical for management and performance.

LOB Restrictions

There are some physical restrictions on LOBs and LOB table spaces.:

- No data compression
- No check constraints
- Only the LOB indicator is captured with DATA CAPTURE

- No EDITPROCs or FIELDPROCs
- No LOB columns in index keys
- No primary or foreign keys
- No unique attribute
- No DpropR replication allowed
- No partitioning or segmenting

Inserting and Loading LOBs

No single storage method fits all. The same is true for how LOBs are loaded and inserted. The methods here are entirely different depending on whether extenders are used or not. Without extenders, some real limitations need to be addressed when inserting LOB data, primarily the 32K limit and logging impacts. If the total length of the LOB column and the base table row is less than 32 K, the LOAD utility can insert the LOB column. When the limits of LOAD are exceeded, SQL INSERT or UPDATE statements need to be used. But the SQL INSERT has its own limitations: enough memory needs to be available to hold the entire value of the LOB. The limitation here is the amount of memory available to the application and the amount of memory that can be addressed by the language used. If the LOBs are all small, memory is not as much of an issue, because memory and language constructs are available. But when dealing with very large LOBs, the differences can be seen easily when comparing the C language construct with COBOL.

Here is a C language statement for a LOB host variable:

```
SQL TYPE IS CLOB(20000K) my_clob;
```

This construct is generated by DB2 as

```
Struct { unsigned long length;
  Char data[20960000];
  } my_clob;
```

Here is a COBOL language statement for a LOB host variable:

```
01 MY-CLOB USAGE IS SQL TYPE IS CLOB(20000K).
```

It is generated by DB2 as

```
01  MY-CLOB.
   02 MY-CLOB-LENGTH PIC 9(9) COMP.
MY-CLOB-DATA.
49  FILLER  PIC X(32767).
49  FILLER  PIC X(32767).
49  FILLER  PIC X(32767).
```

This code is repeated 622 times.

This is another problem that extenders assist in solving . When a table and column are enabled for an extender, the whole process changes. An INSERT statement can be used in the program to contain extender functions (UDFs) that allow an image, for example, to be loaded into the database directly from an external file. Actually, the image extender, the image content is inserted into an administrative support table, and another record is then inserted into another administrative table describing the attributes of the image, such as number of colors, thumbnail-sized version, and format characteristics (JPEG, TIFF, etc). The extenders require WLM to be installed to support the extender UDFs and stored procedures and to be used specifically in goal mode for performance reasons.

Buffer Pool Impacts

Buffer pools are required for caching LOBs only in certain situations. For example, if a LOB is inserted by an SQL INSERT in a program without an extender, the LOB must be moved through the buffer pools. Any single LOB is made up of one or more physical 4K pages, with a logical page size of 4 K, 8 K, 16 K, or 32 K. As the LOB is retrieved, it is moved into the buffer pool, and the buffer pool definition must match the logical page size that is most effective for the LOB with the least amount of wasted space. Obviously, these LOB buffer pools must not be shared with other objects, not only due to the size of the data being moved through it, but for the write thresholds as well. There is no reason for LOB data to remain resident in a buffer pool, so normally a VDWQT of 0 is used. This applies no matter what logging option is chosen for the LOB. With luck, most of the time the data is inserted through extenders, and retrieval is only of LOB locators (pointers) that allow extender functions to manipulate the data.

A new memory usage issue with LOBs does not involve the buffer pools, but rather normal data spaces. Many times when using LOBs, they must be materialized in contiguous storage. DB2 defers LOB materialization until absolutely necessary, but when it must materialize, it uses data spaces, if any are available. As with any memory use, a certain amount is set aside. If this amount is exceeded, the application SQL gets a –904 SQLCODE. The amount of storage that is used for data spaces to support materialization depends on the size and number of the individual LOBs that require materialization at any single instant. DB2 uses an internally defined number of data spaces for LOB materialization. LOB materialization is normally avoided when using locators in the programs and when using some extender functions. However there are times when materialization must occur and cannot be avoided:

- Conversion of a LOB from one code page to another
- Using a LOB as an input or output parameter for a stored procedure
- Using a LOB as a parameter to a user-defined function
- Moving data into a LOB host variable

Because these objects are large, you need to be able to control the amount of memory they can occupy so that they do not cause problems elsewhere in the subsystem. There are two DSNZPARMs that affect how the LOBs are materialized. The first is the USER LOB VALUE STORAGE (defined on install panel DSNTIP7). This is the upper limit for the amount of storage per user for storing LOB values. The default is 2 MB but can go up to 2 GB. The other is the SYSTEM LOB VALUE STORAGE. This is the upper limit for the amount of storage per system that can be used for storing LOBs. This can be up to 50 GB, with a 2GB default. *If there is not enough memory for a particular LOB, it will not be materialized.* If you need to see the amount of storage used by LOBs, you can view the MAX STOR LOB VALUES in the accounting report.

Logging Options

The logging for LOBs is optional. LOB table spaces can be defined with LOG NO or LOG YES. In addition, if there is logging, only redo log records are produced, no undo records, and redo records cannot exceed 1 GB. Therefore, recovery of LOB objects needs to be carefully planned. However, rollback is not affected, because you have the shadow of the LOB, and the space map pages are still logged. Even if a LOB is defined with LOG NO, the effects of insertions, updates, and deletions are still backed out if a unit or work is rolled back.

More frequent image copies for LOB tables are mandated, unless the LOB is truly read-only and the data has been sourced from a medium that still exists and can be used to repopulate the LOB. LOBs support both incremental and full image copies. LOBs are still recoverable in the event of a media failure, because enough information is recorded in the log about the LOB (even if it is LOG NO and no data is logged) to ensure the physical consistency of the pages.

LOG NO is a general recommendation, along with VDWQT 0 in the buffer pool. This combination works because the LOG NO uses the force-at-commit strategy, which immediately moves the data to disk. Thus any changes that are made to the LOB are written before the end of the phase 1 or the commit process (if they were not written before). This ensures that if an abnormal termination occurs, the LOB values are consistent with their corresponding base table.

Locking Options

LOBs also introduce changes to locking. There is a new lock mode for LOBs called a LOB lock. There is no row or page locking with a LOB. The locking for LOBs is not at all like traditional transaction-level locking. Since LOBs are in an associated object, concurrency between the base table and the LOB must be maintained at all times, even if the base table is using UR (uncommitted read). A LOB lock still needs to be held on the LOB to provide consistency and, most important, to maintain space in the LOB table space. LOB locks avoid conflicts between readers and deleters or updates. A SELECT or DELETE acquires a share-mode LOB lock, which doesn't prevent the DELETE but does prevent the reuse of the deallocated pages until all LOB locks are released. A shadow copy of the LOB exists until the LOB locks are released. INSERTs acquire exclusive LOB locks on new LOBs (an UPDATE is basically a DELETE followed by an INSERT). The LOCK TABLE statement, which produces a gross lock on the object, can still be used and does not require individual LOB locks to be acquired.

The ACQUIRE option of BIND has no effect on when the LOB table space lock is taken. Locks on LOB table spaces are acquired when they are needed. The table space lock is released according to the value specified on the RELEASE option of BIND with a couple of exceptions:

1. When a cursor is defined WITH HOLD
2. When a LOB locator is held

When a cursor is defined WITH HOLD, LOB locks are held through commit operations. When a LOB value is assigned to a LOB locator, the lock acquired remains until the application commits. If the application uses HOLD LOCATOR, the locator and the LOB lock must be held and cannot be freed until certain conditions exist. The locks are held until the first commit operation after a FREE LOCATOR statement is issued or until the thread is deallocated. Using LOB columns generally requires an increase in the number of locks held by a process. As a starting point for preventing unforeseen problems, LOCK-MAX should be nonzero on the LOB table spaces. An even better strategy is to use the gross locks during heavy inserting processes, which prevents most locking difficulties.

LOBs require a change in everything in the physical world, and they certainly have an impact on the use of the SQL language. Refer to Chapter 18, "LOBs and Extenders."

LOBs and Data Sharing

In most cases, modified LOB table-space pages are written to disk at a commit point unless you use GBPCACHE CHANGED or GBCACHE ALL, in which case the LOB pages are written to the group buffer pool. This is not an ideal option for large LOBs.

A better option is the use of GBPCACHE (SYSTEM) on the group buffer pool. This allows only the space map pages to be dependent on the group buffer pool, and all other pages are written directly to disk. This option is applicable only to LOBs, because you do not want these extremely large objects to use the coupling facility. Or better yet, try not to have LOBs participate in a data sharing environment if it is not necessary.

LOBs and User-Defined Types

Being able to store LOBs and manipulate them through extenders is only part of the story. You can also define new, distinct data types based on the needs of particular applications.

A user-defined type (UDT), also known as a distinct type, provides a way to differentiate one LOB from another LOB, even of the same base type, such as BLOB or CLOB. A UDT is not limited to objects and can be created for standard data types as well as LOBs. For more information on other uses of UDTs, refer to Chapter 5, "Physical Database Objects."

Even though stored as LOBs (binary or character), image, video, spatial, XML, and audio objects are treated as types distinct from BLOBs and CLOBs and from each other. For example, suppose an application that processes spatial data features needs a polygon data type. You can create a distinct type named *polygon* for polygon objects as follows:

```
CREATE DISTINCT TYPE polygon AS BLOB (512K)
```

The polygon-type object is treated as a distinct type of object, even though internally it is represented as a 512K binary object (BLOB). UDTs are used like SQL built-in types to describe the data stored in columns of tables as shown in the following code. The extenders create distinct data types for the objects they process, such as image, audio, and video, which makes it easier for applications to incorporate these types of objects.

```
CREATE TABLE DB2_MAG_DEMO
  (GEO_ID CHAR(6),
  EURO_ANNUAL      EURO_DOLLAR,
  OZ_ANNUAL        AUSTRALIAN_DOLLAR,
  US_ANNUAL        US_DOLLAR,
  DEMO_GRAPHIC   POLYGON)
```

Casting functions allow operations between different data types, for example, comparing a slide from a video UDT to an expression. You must CAST the expression to a UDT type (video in this example) for the comparison to work. Some casting functions are supplied with DB2 (CHAR, INTEGER, and so on), and others are created automatically whenever a UDT is created with the CREATE DISTINCT TYPE statement.

LOBs and User-Defined Functions

For LOBs, each DB2 extender delivers a package of UDFs for the type of object that it defines. Each UDF is object specific, delivering a process unique to the distinct type. The full name of a DB2 function is *schema-name.function-name*. Schemas are new to DB2 on

OS/390 and provide schema names to be used as identifiers for logical groupings of SQL objects. The extenders use the particular schema name MMDBSYS for all UDFs and UDTs. Since it is difficult and senseless to make all programs use the qualified name (MMDBSYS.udf), the schema name can be omitted when these are referred to by using the current path to determine the function or distinct data type required. The CURRENT PATH is a new register that identifies the path of schemas to be searched in serial fashion for the particular object, and its value can be set by the SET CURRENT PATH SQL statement. When using the extenders, it is almost always a requirement to add MMDBSYS to the CURRENT PATH, as follows:

```
SET CURRENT PATH = mmdbsys, CURRENT PATH
```

Special Tables

T here are several types of tables that you have to
define in DB2 for very specific purposes. In this chapter, we look at some of these special
tables and what makes them unique in terms of definition and in terms of support.

Code, Reference, and Decode Tables

Code tables, reference tables, and decode tables are usually used to store information such
as codes and descriptions, for both look-up and data validations. They are used to decode,
code, and find descriptions such as "25 means Sales Department" and sometimes ridicu-
lous things like "Y means yes" and "F means female." (We do away with those logical
tables that were implemented when they shouldn't have been.) These tables have unique
characteristics. They are generally static, relatively small, and referenced randomly by
several processes at the same time. Given these facts, they need to be handled differently
from other tables if you wish to get optimal performance out of the processes that reference them. In the following sections, we look at issues such as table design, locking,
access, and buffer pools.

Table Design

Sometimes logical design produces several tables to represent various codes and descriptions. These small tables are generally not necessary and cause additional overhead. The

more small tables and indexes, the more open data sets (for information on open data set overhead, refer to Chapters 1 and 5), and greater the potential for massive referential integrity trees (even though generally you should not use RI for code checking). This overhead can be reduced by combining multiple code and reference tables into one table or table space (figure 8.1). You can combine like code types (e.g., character or integer) into a single table for much easier, centralized manageability and programming. You can then get a better buffer pool hit ratio from the table by staging it in the buffer pool and eliminating sequential prefetch overhead. (Refer to Chapter 3 on buffer pools for more information.) A unique, clustering index on the code column can then provide quick access to the codes and their descriptions from one place and also disburse the data for one table throughout the object for better concurrency. Following the code column are the type of code, the description, and optional columns of various types that can be NULL. No processes have to deal with columns that can contain NULLs.

You should consider carrying the code or description in heavily accessed tables to avoid the join to another table. This rare situation has all the inherent problems of denormalization. Often, it is simply better in these cases to have a code that is so similar to the description that any programmatic display formatting can state it correctly if required. Such

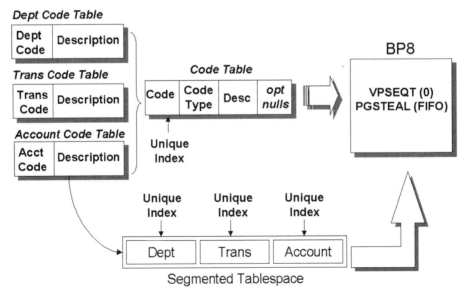

Figure 8.1   Code Tables

codes include state or province abbreviations. For example, in Australia, NSW or VIC is immediately recognizable, so there is no reason to carry a table and index for six codes.

One of the best ways to design code tables is to get rid of them. This is discussed at length in other chapters, such as Chapter 5, but table check constraints can remove dependency on some code tables. Code checks can be defined in a trigger, which removes dependency on code tables. Loading flat files into memory can get rid of code tables. Just because code tables come from a logical design does not mean that they have to occupy two physical data sets and require buffer pool management, I/O overhead, and control block memory.

Locking

Code tables, reference tables, decode tables, and edit tables are mostly static and generally accessed as read-only. Even if not static, they are generally only updated through very specific controls. So to avoid locking overhead, they should be accessed using uncommitted read (UR) when possible. Now, immediately you might say, "But they are not updated, and therefore lock avoidance is taking care of avoiding locking." True, so let's avoid the overhead of lock avoidance, say maybe around 60 instructions per access. Lock avoidance is always assumed to remove all the overhead of locking, when, in fact, it adds a little overhead in front to determine whether to lock or not. If locking is required, that is only more overhead. It is also assumed that the appropriate bind parameters are in effect for all processes using these tables. Be safe and smart: use UR for accessing these read-only, non-volatile tables. Refer to Chapter 13, "Locking and Concurrency," for more information.

Buffer Pools

Code tables, reference tables, decode tables, and edit tables should be isolated to their own buffer pool because their characteristics are unique. The tables and their indexes, if appropriately designed, are always accessed exactly the same way—randomly. So contrary to normal object separation for buffer pools, you should put both the indexes and the tables in the same buffer pool. The buffer pool should be large enough to hold all of the pages for the objects and allow them to remain resident in memory for access by all applications.

When access patterns against the data are known, not all of the data in the tables and indexes has to be loaded. For example, in most systems some reference tables have entries that might not be accessed for months. So if there is a way to group these code rows together by pages, you could reduce the number of pages in the buffer pool required to hold them.

You can also avoid overhead in managing buffer pool queues when dealing with these tables by using the FIFO queuing method along with some other disciplines. For more information on how to manage this type of buffer pool and some of the issues surrounding it, refer to Chapter 3.

Logical Locking and Checkout Tables

Logical locking tables, sometimes referred to as checkout tables, can become a real design and performance headache because of their unique processing requirements. These tables are used to "logically lock" an item that may hold some type of transaction-specific sequencing information or locking-associated information that cannot be locked by any other means. For example, the checkout processing often required in multi-tier environments requires this table (figure 8.2). Even more common is holding a lock on multiple occurrences of time-sensitive data held noncontiguously in a table space. Oftentimes these tables can become very large, and because of their high concurrency requirements, row-level locking is implemented. This locking solution, of course, can lead to more performance degradation in terms of locking overhead (refer to Chapter 13). These tables should be implemented with MAXROWS 1 if concurrency is a large problem, because the CPU overhead of row-level locking could hurt the applications. In a data sharing environment, if a table of this nature is implemented with high concurrency requirements, regardless of size, the use of row-level locking would be detrimental. If disk storage is a concern, the trade-off needs to be evaluated.

Number Control and Sequencing

Often tables are constructed to help applications assign sequential numbers (e.g., to funnel all work through a single toll gate, have only one open checkout counter in the grocery store, have only one door into the football stadium). There are many schemes used with one-row, sequence-number-control tables, but basically the MAX function is performed to get the highest number used from the table; it is incremented by 1, and then the row is updated with that number. The application then uses this number for its needed value (e.g.,

Account History Table

Acct Number	Acct Balance	Transaction Description	Transaction Date
1234	1.00	Deposit	1/1/2000
1234	2.00	Deposit	1/2/2000
1234	1.00	Withdrawl	1/5/2000
5678	5.00	Deposit	1/8/2000
5678	2.00	Deposit	1/10/2000

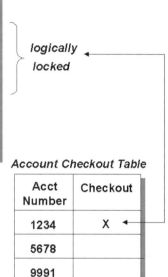

logically locked

The Account Checkout Table 'logically locks' the record in the Account History Table because before another process can use the records in the Account History Table it must check them out of the Account Checkout Table.

Account Checkout Table

Acct Number	Checkout
1234	X
5678	
9991	

Figure 8.2   Logical Locking Table Implementation

account number). The tables used to determine the next number are often hot spots for deadlocks and time-outs (almost 100% of the time).

Some options in the past have been to use time stamps to obtain the next highest value. However, during periods of high insert activity, a time stamp may not always be guaranteed to be unique (Chapter 12 shows how likely this might be). The refresh release of version 6 introduced identity columns. These columns guarantee uniqueness in numbering in a table and are based on the store clock value in the Sysplex timer and therefore are guaranteed to be unique across the Sysplex. Other design options for avoiding this kind of sequential control table and much more on identity columns are discussed in Chapter 12.

Heuristic and Dynamic Control Tables

Heuristic control tables are implemented to allow great flexibility in controlling concurrency and restartability. We have been developing restart and control tables for some time now to help with this, but let's take this a step further. Processing has become more complex, tables have become larger, and requirements are now 99.999% availability. To manage environments and their objects, you need dynamic control of everything. How many different control tables and what indicator columns you put in them vary, depending on the objects and the processing requirements.

Control and Restart Tables

Control and restart tables have rows unique to each application process to assist in controlling the commit scope using the number of database updates or time between commits as their primary focus. There is normally an indicator in the table to tell an application that it is time to stop at the next commit point. Each application or batch job has its own unique entry or entries (figure 8.3).

These tables are accessed every time an application starts a unit-of-recovery (unit-of-work), which is a process initiation or a commit point. The normal process is for an application to read from the table at the very beginning of the process to get the dynamic parameters and commit time to be used. The table stores information about the frequency of commits as well as any other dynamic information that is pertinent to the application process, such as the unavailability of some particular resource for a period of time. Once the program is running, it both updates and reads from the control table at commit time. Information about the status of all processing at the time of the commit is generally stored in the table so that a restart can occur at that point if required, without redoing processing that was already completed.

Control Table

JOB Name	Commit Frequency	Stop Indicator	Commit Counter	Last Commit	Restart Info
JOB1	50	Y	400	12:10	
JOB2	10	Y	100	02:00	
JOB3	10		2000	14:19	

Rows updated between commits   *Commits since start of job*   *Time of last commit*

Figure 8.3   Control/Restart Table

Values in these tables can be changed either through SQL in a program or by a production control specialist dynamically accounting for the differences in processes through time. For example, you would probably want to change the commit scope of a job that is running during the online day from its commit scope when running during the evening.

Partition Availability and Access

Partition availability and access extends control and restart tables by adding indicators to let applications know which partitions are available for use. This concept is used when utility processing needs to be performed at the same time as all other processes, for example, in a 24 × 7 environment. Actually, there can be many reasons to take a partition offline. The requirement is to take a partition offline but let all processes continue. This often requires not only an indicator of the state of the partition, but also maintaining the key ranges so that an application can determine whether it needs to access an unavailable partition. Inserts could be bucketed, to be applied after the partition becomes available. Inquiries could simply allow a response back to a process, allow the user to try again later, or trigger the process to use an alternative source for the information, such as "yes, you are a valid account, but details are unavailable at this time." There can be an infinite number of variations on this theme. Figure 8.4 shows an example of a table used for this purpose. We have discussed a few possibilities for these types of tables. With a good imagination and a need for dynamic control, the possibilities are endless.

Access Table

Table Name	Partition Number	Availability Indicator	Shadow Indicator		
TAB1	1	Y	N		
TAB1	2	N	N		
TAB2	10	Y	Y		

Whether or not the partition is available for use

If a shadow table is to be used

Figure 8.4   Partition Access/Availability Table

Historical Tables

The issue of storing and accessing historical data is very complex, since most systems are developed and installed without any quantity of historical data to contend with, leading to several difficult scenarios. The most common situation is that the performance and maintenance of a system with historical data is trivial in the beginning, because everything always works fast with minimal data. It is not until the data volume starts to grow beyond normal bounds that performance problems begin, and naturally, these problems are not discovered until the system is well in production. Then as the volume grows, the patterns of true access begin to develop, which will change not only the physical design, but probably also the application programs.

At some point in time, the data volume hits a threshold that requires either purging or archiving the oldest data, which in most cases requires additional program changes. The need for access does not go away just because we feel that the data could be archived. Depending on the type of historical data being maintained, either query access to the data goes away completely, or the data has to be maintained in such a fashion as to always be available. This archived availability presents yet another set of problems, simply because data structures tend to change over time and the data structure for the archived data may no longer match the current data structure.

We need to look at techniques for physical implementation and query access involving historical data tables. There are four primary areas to discuss:

- Types of applications and their respective differences
- Physical structuring of historical data
- SQL access
- Restoring Archived Data

Applications

Historical data is a very general term and truly means different things for each company and application within a company. Different types of historical data need to be handled by various applications. The underlying physical structure of the different types is predominately the same when it comes to the types of table spaces. The structuring of table spaces depends on volume, access characteristics, and total longevity. However, accessing the data in these stores is functionally dependent on the type of information being stored, and the differences in ease and performance of access are critical. Most corporations want all data instantly accessible all the time. In reality, this is simply not possible when you are dealing with large amounts of historical data. Not all data has a life expectancy of "forever"; some data must be updated while it is still considered history, and some data moves from constant access to almost nonexistent access. These dependencies emanate from the underlying operational nature of the data.

In a human resource application, the goal is to accurately picture the life of an employee within a corporate entity, which crosses many boundaries, from simple changes in salary to gross changes in occupational position and even movement across companies within an enterprise. Over time, many changes occur that change the picture represented by the historical data: management organizations change, departments come to life and disappear, salary classifications are restructured, and employee benefit plans are completely replaced. The simple query to show the life cycle of an employee over time can become extremely complex. Try to imagine your own picture within your organization. What is your salary today versus your salary before prior changes? What departments did you work for? Were the department classifications and employee benefit plans of today in existence at some earlier point in time in your career picture? This is an example of historical data that can last "forever," meaning that it cannot or should not ever be deleted, only archived after some significant event (e.g., changing jobs or being removed).

There is a major difference between human resource applications and applications that store financial data for a prescribed fiscal period, such as by month for three years. While having a fixed life cycle, any data can have very different access patterns and is not subject to change. The underlying structure for this data can be either vertical or horizontal, depending again on the requirements of retrieval and inquiry. We present an example of this type of partitioning later.

The most difficult historical data to store is data coming from certain service industries. This kind of data can be subject to change (reversal or correction of a past event) or just kept for inquiry purposes. In most instances, this data can have a fixed life cycle, but there are emerging requirements for this type of data to be maintained forever for certain types of inquiries. Take, for example, a utility company that supplies services to a home. Line items appear on the monthly bill for the types of services delivered. A mistake can be made that may not get noticed for a long period. For example, several charges on a phone bill recently were found after over one year to be incorrect due to a reporting error from one country to the originating country. Inquiry was required, and line item after line item had to be examined over the phone by the customer and the service representative. As a result of this, prior year's phone bills were then called into question. In past years, this type of service would have required long periods of correspondence through the mail to determine the errors and correct them. However, with access to the historical data, the items in question could be examined mutually and proper adjustments could be made immediately and satisfactorily.

Some applications of this nature, rather than posting an adjustment, add a correction entry to the data with a different set of effective dates. Yet other applications correct the original line items with an "as of" date.

In all these applications, the life cycle of the data and the access types of the data are functionally dependent not only on the types of systems, but also on the requirements of the business and how it wants to process or maintain the data. Different corporations within the same industry are not bound to store or maintain the data in the same way and have different ways of approaching their customer base. In some regulated industries, historical data is maintained according to a set of rules, and a journalizing is also sometimes required. In these industries, historical data becomes even more difficult to handle, because the underlying data has to be maintained for a historical period and the journal's changes must also be maintained separately for the same period.

Physical Design

Certain liberties have to be taken with the various types of physical structuring for historical data for the sake of space. Using today's emerging tendencies, it must be assumed that there is no forced difference in the structuring of the data due to differences in online and batch processing. Furthermore, it is also assumed that maximum data availability is also a goal. Therefore, there are no real differences in data structuring by processing types, but instead a general approach to physical structuring based on general principles. The data must be structured in either a vertical stack or a horizontal plane. It may have to be partitioned, either by the means available in DB2 or by user partitioning.

In most systems, the data has to be partitioned. This partitioning is generally driven by either the small window for utility maintenance or a simple means of removing data at a prescribed point in time. The removal of data is the first example we discussed. The requirement is to drop a period of historical data at a certain age. The physical problem is how to drop this data without having to drop and recreate the underlying physical structure. Since most historical data is stored in date sequence, the clustering index is by date and ID. Here we are talking about ID in the generic sense. The ID might be a single attribute or a composite attribute (multiple columns). The classic example is the storage of data on a 13-month cycle, where the oldest month is dropped as a new month is begun (figure 8.5). Assuming that there is a large amount of data, it is simply not efficient to drop the structure, remove the old data, and recreate the table based on partitioning by a new date range. The proper method to use here is to define another table that effectively maps the ranges in the partitioned table. This higher-level table can be thought of as a user-maintained index mapped into a table structure, which will then have a DBMS index added for the actual accessing of the data. This simple method requires a control table that contains the date ranges in each of the partitions, requiring the addition of a partition ID to the historical data in the partitions. When it comes time to drop a period of data, the partition that holds that data can be offloaded to archival storage and then replaced, maybe using the load replace utility, with rows for the new period added. The control table is modified to reflect the change, and the process is complete. This is the best method to control the fixed cycle of historical data. This type of storage can accommodate a fixed period or date ranges, although date ranges do give rise to more difficult query access (figure 8.6).

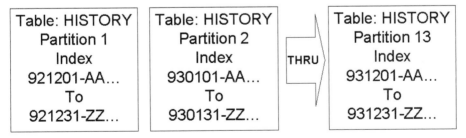

Normal Partitioned Tablespace
Clustered on: Timestamp and 'ID'

Table: HISTORY	Table: HISTORY		Table: HISTORY
Partition 1	Partition 2		Partition 13
Index	Index	THRU	Index
921201-AA…	930101-AA…		931201-AA…
To	To		To
921231-ZZ…	930131-ZZ…		931231-ZZ…

In order to archive or delete the oldest month, drop and recreate the tablespace (problem!). Therefore define a mapping on control or 'logical index' table, as a director to the data in the partitioned table. This adds a column to the partitioned table called PARTITION NUMBER, used in the mapping table.

Figure 8.5 Partition Control Table Usage

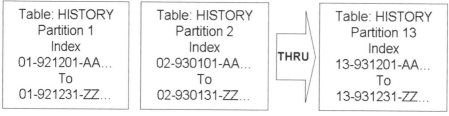

Normal Partitioned Tablespace
Clustered on: Partition ID Number, Timestamp and 'ID'

Table: HISTORY	Table: HISTORY		Table: HISTORY
Partition 1	Partition 2		Partition 13
Index	Index		Index
01-921201-AA...	02-930101-AA...	THRU	13-931201-AA...
To	To		To
01-921231-ZZ...	02-930131-ZZ...		13-931231-ZZ...

There are many examples of SQL that could be used, but for example, assume
we wanted to find all the historical transactions for a particular account during
the month of November, 1993, then the following would be used.

Table: MAPPING	`SELECT REQUIRED COLUMNS`
PARTITION ID NUMBER	`FROM HISTORY, MAPPING`
And TIMESTAMP	`WHERE MAPPING.DATE = 931101`
01|921201|AA...	`AND MAPPING.PARTITION_ID=HISTORY.PARTITION_ID`
To	`AND MAPPING.DATE>=HISTORY.DATE`
01|921231|ZZ...	`AND HISTORY.ID=:host-variable`

Figure 8.6   Partition Control Table Usage, Cont.

The partitioning scheme used in these examples can be one of at least two types: DB2-defined partitioning or user-defined partitioning. DB2-defined partitioning is obviously the easiest to build and maintain, but user-defined partitioning has unique benefits. In user-defined partitions, the base physical unit (DB2 table space) benefits from features perhaps not available in the partitioned scheme. This method simply uses individual tables to hold the data for a particular period. Using the same 13-month example as before, the tables here could be TABLE01 through TABLE13. This generally alleviates the need for a control mapping table but often gives rise to the perceived requirement for dynamic SQL. While dynamic SQL can be used where the number of individual period tables is small, it is generally not a good idea. It is better to name each of the individual tables using an alias or a synonym. In the 13-month example, the tables might be named physically as TABLE01 through TABLE13, but in the programs that access the data or in query tools, the tables might be logically named MONTH1 through MONTH13; CURRENT, PREVIOUS, PREVIOUS2, and so on; or any naming convention that is appropriate. In this structure, the periods with the highest activity can have different index and data structuring, which might be absolutely necessary for performance. The maintenance for this system requires the redefinition of the logical names mapped to the physical names when a period is removed from the historical structure. Although it is possible to scan through periods with this structuring, the obvious problem is that only individual periods can be scanned. If scans across date periods are required, extensive SQL UNIONing could be used. It all comes down to ease of mainte- nance vs. processing capabilities based on the service-level agreements required by the busi- ness. You can see an example of the two different partitioning schemes in figures 8.7 and 8.8.

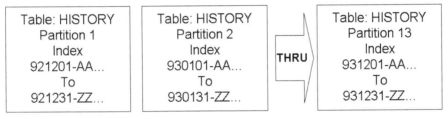

Normal Partitioned Tablespace
Clustered on: Timestamp and 'ID'

Define separate tables for the above partitioned table. Separate tables have both advantages and disadvantages. The choice should be modeled and implemented with care.

Figure 8.7   User Defined Logical Partitioning

Normal Partitioned Tablespace Clustered on:
anything required - can be different on different tables

Synonym/Alias Names

Synonyms will allow the tables to be referenced in STATIC SQL – using STATIC SQL we can find in a program all the activity for a particular account spread over two time periods from the 15th day.

```
SELECT REQUIRED COLUMNS
FROM CURRENT
WHERE CURRENT.DATA BETWEEN :first-of-month AND :middle-of-month
AND HISTORY.ID=:host-variable
UNION ALL
SELECT REQUIRED COLUMNS
FROM PREVIOUS
WHERE CURRENT.DATA BETWEEN :middle-of-month AND :end-of-month
AND HISTORY.ID=:host-variable
```

Figure 8.8   User Defined Logical Partitioning, Cont.

Some applications require access to historical data always within a period, and some require access to individual components of a period. Depending on the requirements, the horizontal distribution of historical data can produce much better performance. This type of structuring allows all data for a particular ID to be stored in repeating columns within a date range. This is formally called *denormalization* but can actually be thought of as normalized if each component of a period is viewed as a single attribute. In many financial systems, access to financial data is only within a fiscal period, and in these cases, the data can be structured across a row instead of in individual rows. Systems that roll up financial data for a period can achieve a great performance boost if the data can be stored horizontally within a fiscal period. If the data is extremely large, the horizontal groups can further be partitioned by ranges within the ID, although this is not necessarily an easy task, as it is commonly very difficult to predict data sizing for an ID grouping. However, by horizontal structuring, the amount of I/O can be significantly less, and disk storage requirements are generally lower, since the ID is not repeated for the data within each period (figures 8.9, 8.10, and 8.11). A primary guideline to be followed whenever this type of structuring is considered is to model one method of design against the other to prove the worthiness of denormalization.

Table: HISTORY (48 Partitions by year and month)				
Partition 1				
GL CODE	SUB CODE	ACCT	YYMM DATE	EXPENSED
AA1300	1211	101318940	990101	47849.90
AA1300	1211	101314903	990101	8949.90
AA1300	2211	147389240	990101	8459.90
AA1310	0211	105890240	990101	90819.90

Normal Partitioned Tablespace:
Partitioned by Year And Month with 48 partitions
Representing the 4 fiscal Years needed to be retained.
 Clustered on: YYMMDATE, GLCODE, SUBCODE and ACCOUNT

Using horizontal data structuring over normalized vertical structuring to
Improve performance. Assume that 4 years of accounting history summaries
Need to be retained and accessed within a fiscal year

Figure 8.9   Vertical Structuring

Table: HISTORY					
GL CODE	SUB CODE	ACCT	FISCAL-1 JAN	FISCAL-1 ... FEB ...	FISCAL-4 DEC
AA1300	1211	101318940	47849.90	47849.90	47849.90
AA1300	1211	101314903	8949.90	7659.90	5869.10
AA1300	2211	147389240	8459.90	46831.30	98549.50
AA1310	0211	105890240	190819.90	39489.90	43459.50

```
SELECT *
FROM HISTORY
WHERE HISTORY.GLCODE BETWEEN :host01 AND :host02
AND HISTORY.ACCT = :host-variable
GROUP BY GLCODE, SUBCODE
ORDER BY GLCODE, SUBCODE
```

Figure 8.10 Horizontal Structuring

Table: HISTORY Partition 1							
YEAR	GL CODE	SUB CODE	ACCT	JAN	FEB	...	DEC
1999	AA1300	1211	101318940	47849.90	47849.90		47849.90
1999	AA1300	1211	101314903	8949.90	7659.90		5869.10
1999	AA1300	2211	147389240	8459.90	46831.30		98549.50
1999	AA1310	0211	105890240	190819.90	39489.90		43459.50

Horizontal structured data can also be partitioned to further enhance performance and access. If the horizontal data was only accessed within a fiscal year then the data could be partitioned by fiscal year.

Table: HISTORY Partition 2							
YEAR	GL CODE	SUB CODE	ACCT	JAN	FEB	...	DEC
2000	AA1300	1211	101318940	47849.90	47849.90		47849.90
2000	AA1300	1211	101314903	8949.90	7659.90		5869.10
2000	AA1300	2211	147389240	8459.90	46831.30		98549.50
2000	AA1310	0211	105890240	190819.90	39489.90		43459.50

NOTE: this structuring can be further enhanced by applying the logical partitioning scheme, using individual tables for each partition, naming them CURRENT, PREVIOUS-1, PREVIOUS-2, and PREVIOUS-3. If necessary, within each of the fiscal years, physical partitioning with a mapping table could also be used to break the structure by the distribution of the data (GLCODEs and SUBCODEs in these examples)

Figure 8.11 Horizontal and Partitioned

There are several other methods of mapping historical data, generally composites of one or more of the preceding examples with some deviations, but they tend to fall into the extreme groups. These other cases occur mostly where the distribution of data does not allow easy DB2 partitioning, but where DB2 partitioning is a requirement. These types of systems are not considered part of a general solution to storing and accessing historical data and are not further examined here.

SQL Access

The dominant SQL processing for the preceding examples is listed in the explanatory figures. However, some general guidelines to be used when processing date-effective data are crucial to performance. A common DB2 myth states that you must always use SQL BETWEEN instead of >= and <=. In the following example, a table has columns called COLUMN_BEGIN_DATE and COLUMN_END_DATE, and the index includes both columns.

Applying the rule of thumb gives this selection:

```
WHERE COLUMN_DATE BETWEEN :hostdate1 and :hostdate2
```

This leads to the incorrect application:

```
WHERE :hostdate BETWEEN COLUMN_BEGIN_DATE AND
COLUMN_END_DATE
```

This is the correct application:

```
WHERE :hostdate >= COLUMN_BEGIN_DATE AND :hostdate <=
COLUMN_END_DATE
```

The BETWEEN is a single predicate, while >= and <= are two predicates. DB2 can make more effective use of the indexes with the last choice. In other words, blind application of prior SQL rules and guidelines can make date-effective systems perform worse, potentially severely worse, than they should.

Date-effective processing, required by most systems that record and store historical data, is at best very difficult to define properly for all access. Because data is date- and perhaps time-sensitive and can change over time, as in the personnel systems, there are two dominant access needs: the need to change the data while retaining the old data and the ability to reconstruct what the data looked like at any point in time. The issue becomes more complex where a parent table is bounded by effective dates and changes must be made to a child table that is also bounded by effective dates. Since data integrity must also be maintained and since a change can be made to a child between the dates in the parent, the defined RI in DB2 cannot be used, and the RI that is defined via DBMS rules becomes not only more complex, but has performance implications as well. You can see some SQL examples in figures 8.12 and 8.13.

Restoring Archived Data

A final problem is the ability to restore archived data to respond to queries or business needs. There are two major problems to be addressed. The first is, Where do we restore the data to? The second is, What format is the data in, meaning, Is the archived structure of the table the same as the current structure of the table? These issues are often overlooked until the time comes to answer the query. There is no simple answer to these questions, but the most often used approach is to restore the data from the archive, by the period

Sample History and Date Effective SQL

Before Picture of the Data

CUSTOMER#	POSTED DATE	EFFECTIVE DATE	EXPIRY DATE	CUSTOMER NAME
121314	09/09/99	03/09/99	12/09/00	Smith
145324	04/10/99	02/21/99	05/09/00	Jones

After Picture of the Data

CUSTOMER#	POSTED DATE	EFFECTIVE DATE	EXPIRY DATE	CUSTOMER NAME
121314	09/09/99	03/09/99	12/09/00	Smith
145324	04/10/99	02/21/99	05/09/00	Jones
149028	04/30/99	02/20/99	05/12/00	Cartwright

Figure 8.12 Date-Effective Problems

```
SELECT CUSTOMER_NO, ....
FROM CUSTOMER
WHERE CUSTOMER_NO =:host-variable
AND EXPIRY_DATE = (SELECT MAX(EXPIRY_DATE) FROM CUSTOMER
                        WHERE CUSTOMER _NO=:host-variable)
```

This is an example of locating the row to update. Then UPDATEing
That row and INSERTing a new row in the same unit of work.

```
SELECT CUSTOMER_NO, ....
FROM CUSTOMER
WHERE CUSTOMER_NO =:cust_num
AND :effect_date >= EFFECTIVE_DATE
AND :effect_date <= EXPIRY_DATE
```

Points at the correct row, but RI defined constraints cannot reach this row through comparison of data in a primary key/foreign key comparison, as it would fail as there is no direct match

This assume that all insert/update processing prevents invalid, over lapping, or missing ranges for effective and expiration dates. This is also the approach that must be taken for RI constraints that must be checked against Data effective data. It is not 'does a parent row exist', but rather 'does a parent row exist for A particular row for a particular point-in-time'. DDL defined RI cannot handle this so Application programmed RI must be used.

Figure 8.13   Date-Effective SQL Problems

required, into a separate data structure that is named logically so that programs can process it, if required, without change. If the structure of the data archived is different from the current structure, then either a translation program is required to extract from the archive into the corrected format, or the data has to be returned to the same structure and dynamic SQL used to extract from it the queried data. There are obviously many other methods that can be used. The primary point here is that not only is the data itself archived, but the underlying structure of the data has to be archived also, with a potential mapping that must be maintained throughout the life cycle of the archived data, mapping it to whatever the data structure is today.

Historical data will grow and grow in size, far beyond the scope of the initial design. A comprehensive design at the very beginning must address structuring the data, archiving the data, archiving associated or related data, archiving the data structures, tracking the archived data by period and storage medium, and restoring the data for a short period. If these issues are not addressed at the very beginning of the design, difficult and sometimes insurmountable problems will occur later. It is a classic case of paying the piper now or paying for the piper's new castle later!

Methods of Archiving Historical Data

There are many methods of archiving historical data, and most are written based upon the application's needs. Archive methods often are complex and sometimes never get written, but a few options in DB2 can help.

One method of archiving data is the use of either of two options of the REORG utility (figure 8.14). One option is REORG UNLOAD EXTERNAL, which allows you to perform a fast unload of your data to a data set. REORG UNLOAD EXTERNAL works with records that have been decompressed, EDITPROC decoded, FIELDPROC decoded, and padded to maximum length. SMALLINT, INTEGER, FLOAT, and DECIMAL types are converted to a DB2 internal format. EBCDIC and ASCII are unloaded in the same format. This feature is supported only for REORG SHRLEVEL NONE.

The other option is REORG DISCARD, which allows data to be discarded or discarded to a data set. REORG DISCARD is supported for SHRLEVEL NONE or SHRLEVEL REFERENCE, but not CHANGE. It is also supported only for UNLOAD CONTINUE or PAUSE, but not ONLY or EXTERNAL.

The WHEN clause that is used by both options can use AND and OR conditions for column and value comparisons; however, currently no column-to-column comparisons are allowed. For archiving, you could use the WHEN clause to specify a date range by which to move data (UNLOAD or DISCARD) from the primary table to the archive.

Another relatively new method for archiving data is IBM's DB2 Row Archive Manager utility.

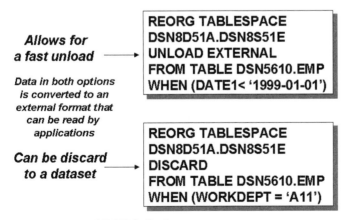

Figure 8.14 REORG Options

## CHAPTER 9

Roles in Database Implementation

The Changing Role of Data Administrators

Ignored, praised, misunderstood, and often just a token position, the role of the data administrator (DA) and data administration has become critical in the emerging world of client/server, the Internet, distributed data, e-commerce, and business intelligence. Recognition of the importance of the DA, common in the beginning of the relational trend, is unfortunately diminishing. In actuality, the role of the DA is more critical for a far larger number of reasons today than in the mainframe-centric environments of yore. What is more damaging is that the division between the DA's role and the database administrator's (DBA's) role is often unknown. Some organizations combine both functions into one (logically and physically), then blame the resulting problems on the DBMS of choice to prove that the overhead of data administration is truly not needed.

Data Administrators versus Database Administrators

To understand the implications of misunderstanding the role of the DA, you must understand the differences between the basic functions of the DA and the DBA. A simplified list of functions is in figure 9.1.

DATA ADMINISTRATION AND THE DA	DATABASE ADMINISTRATION AND THE DBA
Data Analysis Data Modeling Logical Data Definition Logical Design	Physical Data Definition Physical Design Physical Data Management DBMS Care and Feeding

Figure 9.1   Roles of the DA vs. the DBA

By former definition, the DA should not know or need to know the volume of data or the physical destination of the database. That definition died the day we reinvented the terms client-server, distributed database, object relational, e-stuff, b-stuff, and c-stuff. One of the primary tools in the DA's arsenal is the data dictionary, and based on some simple sampling, fewer than 10% of DBMS environments even have one. Data models are the domain of the DA, but a common trend is to have pseudo-data models in a mainframe case tool, some built into the application generator, some built on workstation software, and most built piecemeal by the application technicians as the perceived need for a specific table with specific columns arises when implementing enhanced functions for users. Market-driven, time-constrained design (MDTC design) is the number one nightmare for the DA and the DBA today and the most common design method currently in use!

Process-Driven Legacy

Process-driven design has been in force since the beginning of automation, and it is very difficult to change design methodology, because the risk and cost analysis do not seem to justify it—until too late. But if you look closely at the trend today, processing is being split between servers and clients, data storage is being split between servers and client, and data is being replicated in full, in part, and in fragments (e.g., some of the rows and some of the columns for the purposes of performance, integrity checking, and query use). Who and what are supposed to keep track of just where the account number is stored? If there is no DA and no data dictionary, it is common to find the account number masquerading in various formats and names, replicated without controls or integrity. The lack of even this small responsibility of the DA is damaging in today's environment.

Logical Modeling

The logical data model has farther-reaching impact than ever before, even to the performance of the system, because the logical model overrides the physical database design. If there is no logical data model, heavy I/O and massive data replication creep into the database system. In some cases where there is no DA, the task of creating the logical data model falls to the DBA, who generally is buried under day-to-day problems and in addition is almost never given credit for the ability to recognize problems in a design put forth by the applications arena ("Those DAs and DBAs don't know my system or my users"). In addition to the logical data model, the logical access paths to build the information that the business needs are part of the result of the DA's work, and these directly relate to the physical data model, potentially the indexes built for the data, and the validation of the SQL used in the processes. Without the access path analysis and its documentation, the developers generally use simple navigation methods, which lead to poor performance. In the distributed world, constant use of navigation instead of defined-set processing via documented access paths can destroy any benefit likely to be gained by splitting the function between client and server. Imagine an SQL query that performs navigation across multiple networks to put together different pieces of data in the program to formulate the result, slap it into an HTML page, and ship it over the Internet for the end user. Rather than simply burying the I/O services in the mainframe as was done before in legacy systems, the networks and their servers now become bogged down in passing all the unnecessary data to the process. Without the access path analysis, no one has the information necessary to determine the best way to store the data. In addition, the access path analysis must now include the techniques being in the client-server implementation, which is a new direction in design and documentation.

Here is an example of failure of a new access technique. The developer of a process for a client, application, or web server decides to use a pull-down pick list that is defined over a table that exists only on the server (common on web pages). During the testing, with only 10 rows on the server, the process is valid and quick, and neither the DA nor the DBA is aware of the potential problem. However, when the referenced table grows to 10,000 rows in production, and the 10,000 rows are now required on the net for the client to implement the pick list, a major performance and personnel problem occurs. Phase 1 of the correction of this problem is to blame the network, phase 2 is to blame the DBMS, phase 3 is to blame the DBA, and the final phase is to blame or dismiss the DA, but never to blame the oversight of failing to implement proper design methods.

The implications of ignoring the DA approach to design is even more damaging when the goal is to implement distributed databases. It is not that the DA should be aware of the distributed database or perform the logical design based on this knowledge, but rather that the lack of logical design can destroy the integrity and performance of the distributed database. The data dictionary also has to show the locations of the data and even the processes that work on the data in the distributed database. The data dictionary should provide further detail about the individual server components, when true server components exist at any node within the distributed environment (e.g., discrete application servers, web servers, database servers, routing servers, mart servers).

Life-Cycle Development

Should system development life cycle (SDLC) be homegrown or official? It is not necessary to put together a team for a year to determine which SDLC method is correct. Just put something in place that standardizes an approach based on accepted principles, then fine-tune it later if necessary.

Building today's distributed and integrated systems and implementing a data warehouse require a solid SDLC, including all the data-driven process steps. Success is defined as implementation that is completed on time, easily modified, and well documented; acceptable performance with data integrity; and correct results. The two major goals are correct data and flexibility for easy changes and enhancements. If data integrity is built into the system and the system is correctly defined for the relational model, any performance problems can be easily addressed. But if the DA's role is ignored or if his or her only involvement is clerical or for after-the-fact diagram drawing, then there will be no data integrity and no flexibility, and performance issues will be very difficult, if not impossible, to correct without a redesign at the logical level at incredible cost.

Database Administrators

There are many flavors of DBAs in the industry and many interpretations of their role. The most common tend to fall into a few categories:

- System DBAs—mainly responsible for installing DB2, applying maintenance, installing new products, and defining and sizing global subsystem parameters
- Database DBAs—mainly responsible for designing the database, working with the DAs, defining objects, running utilities to maintain data, conducting design reviews, and reviewing SQL
- Application DBAs—same as database DBAs, but dedicated solely to a particular application
- Hybrid DBAs by default—any combination of the preceding types, often in smaller shops with a shortage of staff
- Hybrid DBAs by choice—hybrids in organizations that realize there is very little distinction needed between the categories to achieve high levels of performance

Most DBAs fall into one of these categories, with some variances. A common problem is too few DBAs, because then too many tasks rest on the shoulders of too few individuals. On the other side of the coin, usually more detrimental, is when a separation of duties occurs and a wall is put up between DBAs. For example, often the system DBA responsibilities are given to a system programmer who is not wholly involved with DB2. Often control is lost, and necessary changes are very difficult to execute, mostly due to the politics of task ownership. Other problems occur as SQL and other functionality become more complex. It is hard enough for DBAs to keep up their normal duties without having to learn the intricacies of the SQL language and such things as UDFs, triggers, and stored procedures. Why is that an issue? Because in the past it was the responsibility of the DBA to review the SQL for all applications. We describe in the next section a new breed of DBA—really more of a programmer with some DBA knowledge to help with the important effort of tuning.

DBA Ratio

Many organizations have a very low ratio of DBAs to application programmers. Some guidelines are based upon the organizational structures of some of the highest-performing organizations. The ratio affects the amount of work assigned to the DBAs. For example, an ideal high-performance DB2 department usually has around one DBA and one DA for every five application developers. But more often than not, this ratio is somewhere in the area of one DBA to 20 application developers.

Impacts of Warehouses

The design of a warehouse and its data analysis is more difficult than that of a normal OLTP or batch system. Performance analysis and design are more difficult, and the model and database are always changing. This has a big impact on the DAs and especially the DBAs. The life of the DBA has become more complex because of the high demand for delivery.

Impacts of E-Business

E-business has affected all of us, but the impact is especially felt by the DBA. In addition to normal processing requirements, DBAs have to worry about the availability of the data, because the web doesn't sleep. Web applications are spawning off several thousands of transactions that query data faster than we could have ever imagined. The DBA now has to give a lot of consideration to all the aspects of continuous availability. Utility windows are a luxury of a time long past.

Database Procedural Programmers

Recently, there has been a push for a position called the procedural DBA. But this suggestion really doesn't go far enough, and it focuses on the wrong people, partly because the concept of a procedural DBA is too simplistic and too narrow for the level of talent required.

Today's enterprise database systems require more modularization as they support multiple multi-tiered applications across broad networks (figure 9.2). Features such as stored procedures, user-defined functions, and triggers are necessary to ensure that critical functional code resides in one place where it can be used by any process, anywhere in the network. In addition, complex and compound SQL is finally becoming more common-place, especially within triggers and stored procedures. The bottom line is this: specialists are needed who will be responsible for guru-level SQL support and tuning analysis and who have the ability to write complex SQL for triggers that invoke stored procedures and user-defined functions. Programming talent in Java, C, C++, COBOL, and ASM is another requirement, since stored procedures and user-defined functions are written in these high-level languages; these languages are often used as interfaces to legacy software such as

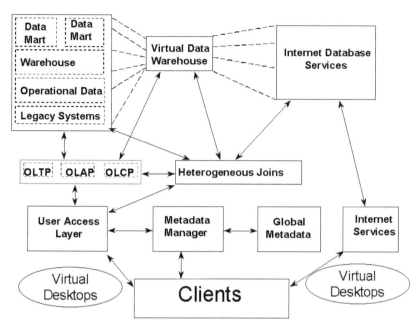

Figure 9.2   Programmers Do Not Just Write Code

IDMS, Natural databases, and VSAM and BDAM file storage. This is not basic-level programming, but fairly complex coding.

Another area of heavy responsibility for such specialists is to map the hierarchy of these functions in support of the business objective. It is quite common to have a trigger invoke a user-defined function or a stored procedure. Either process could cause other triggers to be fired or could call a remote stored procedure. A client process could initiate a DB2 DataJoiner heterogeneous join process, which might initiate a hierarchy of functions. This is not the normal environment of applications, nor is it the normal environment of the DBA. The additional responsibility for check constraints and declarative referential integrity is a natural extension of the role of these specialists, since nondeclarative referential integrity is generally supported by triggers.

It is agreed that the requirements prove the need for SQL gurus who can write complex code in Java, C, C++, or COBOL (and others). These are not DBAs but a new group within the organization. Both application and subsystem DBAs have enough responsibility and are already overloaded. In addition, today's DBAs generally did not come up through the programming ranks and are never faced with the need to write complex SQL.

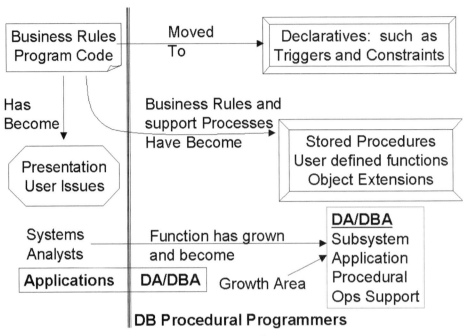

Figure 9.3 Changing Roles and Responsibilities

Many DBAs complain to us that they have difficulty trying to analyze the complex SQL being written in the application areas. Some companies are already building a special staff to address the verifying, teaching, tuning, and analysis of complex SQL. The responsibilities of this group need to be expanded to include triggers, stored procedures, and user-defined functions as well as check constraints and declarative referential integrity. This group, the database procedural programming (DPP) staff, should become commonplace in every organization (figure 9.3).

Application Design and Tuning

General Application Design

Version 6 Late Additions and Version 7

Program Design and Processing

Locking and Concurrency

Temporary Tables

Enterprise Resource Planning

## CHAPTER 10

General Application Design

D o not accept that a thing cannot be done or made to perform at the level required; rather, be like Arthur Jones. There are many different types of guidelines for writing applications for DB2, depending on the type of processing required. In this chapter we look at just some general guidelines regarding program logic, commit strategies, SQL, and binding for performance. In Chapter 12, we look at performance issues surrounding some of the different types of programs (i.e., batch and OLTP).

Program Structure

Putting the Logic in the SQL

The more IF logic you perform after an SQL statement, the more tests you are missing in your SQL statement. Move the program-functionality work into the SQL. For example, if the following program tests appear after fetches from a cursor, then every row from the table is being returned to the program for the calculations:

```
IF RCODE = 'B'
THEN AMOUNT = AMOUNT + B-AMOUNT
```

```
ELSE IF RCODE = 'C'
THEN AMOUNT = AMOUNT + C-AMOUNT
ELSE IF RCODE = 'D'
THEN AMOUNT = AMOUNT + D-AMOUNT
```

The preceding logic (fetches and calculations) can be transferred to the following SELECT clause:

```
SELECT SUM(CASE WHEN RCODE = 'B' THEN AMOUNT)
     , SUM(CASE WHEN RCODE = 'C' THEN AMOUNT)
     , SUM(CASE WHEN RCODE = 'D' THEN AMOUNT)
FROM TABLE
INTO :b-amount, :c-amount, :d-amount
```

Now since there is only one row that can be returned, both response time and code quality are greatly improved. In many cases, logic in the program needs to be moved to the SQL. It should be the assumption in any program that the business process for the resultant data can be done in one SQL statement. Then if it requires more SQL statements, fine. We need to emphasize that SQL is not just a row retriever. If the final business process can be visualized as a spreadsheet, then we need an SQL statement that simply builds the spreadsheet.

Retrieving Only What Is Needed

From a performance point of view, fetching into a structure is better than fetching into a field. Every field that DB2 has to service involves a separate movement from DB2 to the program, because DB2 moves one column at a time from the DB2 address space to the program storage using a cross-memory process. When fetching into a structure, generally only one data transfer is required, since the data in the structure matches the column order in the selected rows. This is also the reason that you should limit yourself to selecting only the columns needed by the application program. However, from a coding point of view, fetching into fields makes your programs more readable and maintainable. SELECT in frequently executed programs should always be reviewed and optimized by using structures.

I/O Modules

Extensive use of I/O modules in relational database applications usually causes performance degradation. This is because an I/O module that performs a simple "get next row from table" function generally contains a simple SELECT statement. This SELECT is not part of any relational join or any other complex function that can be performed by the relational engine.

Specific SELECT statements should be formed to push as much work as possible into the relational engine. These more complicated statements can also be combined with program logic to perform logical business functions, such as "enroll new employee." This type of I/O module is preferred in today's relational database applications—logical functions are reused instead of logical database reads being issued.

Another area of concern that might disguise this I/O layer problem is object-oriented (OO) programming. There is absolutely nothing wrong with OO methods, and we strongly support them. But we have seen cases where the OO paradigm is pushed to the extreme, so that every access to a database must become a class (method) unto itself. On paper and according to high-level OO design methods, this looks wonderful, but it is rather an absolute rule that does not belong in the implemented world. Processing can be embedded in any of the following objects:

- Programs
- Triggers
- Stored procedures (local and remote)
- User-defined scalar functions
- User-defined table functions
- Declarative referential integrity (DDL)
- Declarative check constraints (DDL)
- APPC targets (CICS transactions, for example)

The code needs to be put in the best place, and encapsulating a business process in SQL is fine. Mapping to an OO strategy does not mean that the whole purpose of SQL is just to feed data into a Java class, for example. There is nothing wrong with the Java class being returned as an "object" that is the entire resultant process, a result set table, from the SQL. There is nothing wrong with using the SQL statement `SELECT` `udf(AX(parm1,parm2,parms)...` to invoke a rather large process AX, which in turn issues `EXEC SQL CALL SP1(...)` to invoke a stored procedure SP1. The processes AX and SP1 are external programs, written to exact specifications, to perform some specific, reusable function. In addition, stored procedures can be used in conjunction with the RRS attachment facility to use EXCI to invoke a CICS transaction.

Cursors

A cursor must be used when a SELECT statement will manipulate more than one row from a multirow result set. The exception is when no data is required; however, a test for 0, 1, or more rows is needed for proper existence checking. Following is an example of a singleton SELECT used for existence checking when there is a unique or nearly unique index used for the access path:

```
SELECT '1'
    INTO :hv1
FROM TABLE
WHERE COLX = :inputx

IF SQLCODE = 0
    -- 1 row found
IF SQLCODE = 100
    -- 0 rows found
IF SQLCODE =-811
    -- more than 1 row was found
```

More often than not, only one way for existence checking is used in applications. But there is no "always do it this way" when it comes to SQL and performance. Unlike the preceding case, if there is no unique or nearly unique index for the access path, the SQL should be written using a cursor optimized for a one-row clause as follows:

```
DECLARE CS1 CURSOR FOR
    SELECT '1'
    FROM TABLE
    WHERE COLX = :inputx
```

```
    OPTIMIZE FOR 1 ROW
    WITH UR;

OPEN CS1;
    FETCH CS1 INTO :hostv;
CLOSE CS1;
```

Older methods of existence checking with a correlated subquery actually have very little use today and tend to be the slowest of this type of existence check. Here are examples of this and other methods that should be avoided:

```
SELECT count(*)
INTO :hostvar
FROM PRODUCTION_TABLE
WHERE "some matching condition"

SELECT count(*)
INTO :hostvar
FROM SYSIBM.SYSDUMMY1
WHERE "some subquery condition"

SELECT 1
INTO :hostvar
FROM SYSIBM.SYSDUMMY1
WHERE "some subquery condition";

SELECT 1 FROM SYSIBM.SYSDUMMY1
INTO :hostvar
WHERE EXISTS
    (SELECT 1 FROM PRODUCTION_TABLE
    WHERE ACCT_NO = :hostvar);

SELECT 1 FROM SYSIBM.SYSDUMMY1
INTO :hostvar
WHERE EXISTS
    (SELECT 1 FROM PRODUCTION_TABLE
    WHERE ACCT_NO = :hostvar
    AND SYSIBM.SYSDUMM1.IBMREQD  ' ');
```

None of these examples, as a general rule, whether or not they are put into cursors or use as singleton SELECTS, will ever outperform the earlier recommended choices. The whole point is that a cursor can have a benefit even when a single result is the answer, since we cannot use OPTIMIZE FOR 1 ROW with a singleton SELECT. The singleton SELECT chooses the same access path as a cursor definition, but only within a cursor definition can we use the OPTIMIZE FOR 1 construct.

As a general rule, use a single SELECT when one and only one row will be returned in a program; otherwise, use a cursor. There is more on the single SELECT later in this chapter.

Ambiguous Cursors

When DB2 does not know whether or not you will use the cursor for updating or deleting, it prepares for a worst-case scenario (that you will perform an update). In this case, the cursor is called *ambiguous,* and the access path chosen by the optimizer is not necessarily the best for the function being performed. The way to avoid ambiguous cursors is to use a FOR UPDATE OF clause when the cursor will be used in an UPDATE WHERE CURRENT OF statement, or to use a FOR FETCH ONLY or FOR READ ONLY when the cursor is going to be used only to retrieve data.

It is best never to leave anything to a default or assumption. Every cursor should have one of the preceding phrases specified. Whether the cursor is used for updates or reads only, state so explicitly.

Singleton SELECT

A singleton SELECT is an SQL SELECT statement that expects only one row to be returned (e.g., retrieving by the primary key). You can avoid the overhead of declaring a cursor by coding the INTO section in the SELECT statement. The overhead of the statement processing is the same, whether you use singleton SELECT or cursor for one row. The difference is that the cursor requires three calls to DB2, whereas the singleton SELECT requires one call to DB2.

A singleton SELECT should be used in a program whenever exactly one row is returned. There are two ways to ensure that exactly one row is returned. The first way is to request the result of a built-in function, as follows:

```
SELECT SUM(SALARY), AVG(SALARY)
FROM EMP
```

```
INTO :totalsal, :avgsal
WHERE WORKDEPT = :workdept
```

The second way is to provide a WHERE clause that uniquely identifies a row, as follows:

```
SELECT LASTNAME, ADDRESS, BIRTHDAY
FROM EMP
INTO :lastname, :address, :birthday
WHERE EMPNO = :EMPNO
```

If you code a singleton SELECT and DB2 has more than one row after execution of the statement, an SQLCODE of –811 is returned.

> *Note: A problem is often overlooked here. When a SQLCODE of –811 is returned, the integrity of the data is not guaranteed. The host variables are filled with the data from the first row returned as long as there is only one row found and an SQLCODE of 0 is returned.*

CURSOR WITH HOLD

Some considerations for using CURSOR WITH HOLD run counter to the guidelines for normal cursor use. CURSOR WITH HOLD provides an important function but does so at a cost for availability and partition independence. A cursor defined with HOLD retains a CLAIM on tables referenced in the cursor. This prevents a DRAIN from being satisfied, but once the DRAIN LOCK is issued, all other processes using the tables are prevented from reacquiring the object once they issue a COMMIT. At this point, any other work now waiting behind the DRAIN could start to time out, and eventually the work issuing the DRAIN LOCK could time out. For the period of time that the DRAIN is waiting, everything could be stopped, except the process that issued the CURSOR WITH HOLD.

The critical process that could issue a DRAIN LOCK is a utility, and the most important utility is perhaps the online REORG for a partition of a table space.

Cursors in Cursors

You should not open a cursor several times; instead use an inner or outer join, a subselect with an EXISTS, or perhaps an IN LIST. This process can take from minutes to hours, depending on the amount of data processed. Cursors in cursors generally indicate a relationship, either mandated or optional, and therefore should be written as a single statement.

Repetitive Cursors

If you are going to process more than 25% of the table, open a cursor and read through the data using a table-space scan. After all, if DB2 is using an index and qualifies more than 25% of the RIDs, it will abort the index processing and return to do a table-space scan. Twenty-five percent is the breakpoint where scanning all the data with sequential prefetch outperforms any kind of index processing (at least currently).

Often a cursor is opened to process data, say perhaps 2% of the data, based on some input activity and then closed. Another input process drives the cursor to process another set of data from the same table, say 9%, then another process and another do the same. After all is done, over 25% of the table has been touched. As in the previous situation, a single cursor and sequential prefetch should have been used, processing the input over the whole table. Of course, all the input would have to be there, sorted in the clustering sequence, but the savings of this type of processing can be dramatic.

Application-Enforced Referential Integrity

DB2-defined referential integrity (RI), correctly called declarative RI because it is declared using DDL definition, is always preferred over using and maintaining application-enforced RI for several reasons. Application-enforced relationships must be documented and accounted for when running utilities that require related tables be included in the table-space set for integrity purposes. Each application program has to account for the same relationships between related tables in their program logic, which becomes difficult to ensure and maintain. When programs are modified or enhanced, application-enforced RI is often overlooked, allowing unrelated data into the system and potentially causing serious data integrity problems. DB2-defined RI is kept in the DB2 catalog, can be easily reported with an SQL query, and is accounted for by the DB2 Report utility. Declarative RI also has a performance benefit in most cases, because the access path used to check the existence of relationships is done by DB2 with less overhead than that incurred when application-enforced RI is used.

However, there are always cases where application-controlled RI must be used. In all cases of mandatory RI application checks, triggers should be considered as the viable alternative. Since triggers cannot be bypassed, the integrity is always maintained, just as with declarative RI.

Plans and Packages

It is extremely difficult to justify the use of one plan containing all the packages for an installation or even for just all CICS transactions or batch jobs. A misrepresentation of this strategy in the past has led to the continuing myth of putting all packages into one plan. Plans need to be granular, the same as all other definitions. Large, cumbersome plans cause performance degradation, buffer pool problems, and EDM pool problems. The number of packages put into a single plan needs to be based on functionality, such as all the packages supporting a particular function of an online application. Generally, each batch job should have a separate plan, which should be as specific as possible.

With one plan for all packages, you give up an easy way to monitor and tune. If you get an SMF record for every transaction in CICS (TOKENI or TOKENE), you might be able to manage using only one plan, but the task is much harder. If you are getting the rollup, accounting data is not useful.

Also, if you are losing the ability to find long-running units of work that may be causing problems in the system, such as not committing, potentially causing contention, and precluding lock avoidance, refer to Chapter 13 for more on lock avoidance. If you have a unique plan for each transaction program, you can use the DSN035I message that is displayed when a threshold is hit, when a unit of recovery exists after a certain number of system checkpoints have occurred. This parameter is the DSNZPARM called URCHKTH. You can set it based on how often your system takes checkpoints and how often your applications should commit.

You can take up more storage in the EDM pool if using only one plan. If you specify RELEASE(DEALLOCATE) for a plan with a large number of packages, the space in the EDM pool is expanded greatly and could take away storage from other potential uses. Increases in EDM pool storage may force you to use RELEASE(COMMIT) where you would otherwise use RELEASE(DEALLOCATE) for better performance.

It also takes more CPU processing to manage the storage and longer chains.

With only one plan and one set of parameters, some tuning options are precluded. It is best to have one plan for each batch program and to have plans containing packages for online applications grouped by some common function or process.

When to Rebind Packages

Packages should be considered for rebinding when any of the following are true, based on current statistics from the catalog:

- Changes > 20% (NLEAF, NPAGES, NACTIVE)
- CLUSTERRATIO < 80%, NLEVELS increases > 2
- HIGH2KEY and LOW2KEY range changes > 10%
- Cardinality and row count changes > 20%

Dynamic SQL

Dynamic SQL should be used when necessary, which is when the data involved in the query can cause a different access path to be selected. Normally, this is when there are outliers, heavily skewed data, or major differences in the correlation between any set of columns. More than one choice should be available for the optimizer to take. That generally should not be problem, since the basic difference in access paths for these situations is either a table-space scan or index access.

A problem occurs when dynamic SQL uses host variables. In this case, the dynamic SQL does not get a different access path based on the value of the data, unless reoptimization occurs at run time.

While dynamic SQL itself is not a problem, repetitive use of the same statement can be. Dynamic SQL construction can vary, with different performance impacts. When it is used with host variables, it appears to be the same statement every time, and the dynamic SQL cache can be beneficial. But when the dynamic SQL is built using real values, it appears different each time, and the cache does not have a benefit. But dynamic SQL with real values may get a different access path on each PREPARE, whereas dynamic SQL with host variables will not. Trade-offs and design decisions abound.

Dynamic SQL Cache

The dynamic SQL cache is a primary source of performance benefits for ERP applications (for more information on ERP systems, refer to Chapter 15) or any application that uses repetitive dynamic SQL. When caching dynamic SQL statements, DB2 first checks the cache when a dynamic SQL statement is issued. If found, the statement can be reused without incurring the overhead of a redundant PREPARE. With dynamic SQL caching, some ERP queries can experience up to 80% CPU reduction.

To allow dynamic SQL caching in your DB2 subsystem, you must turn it on through a DSNZPARM. By specifying YES for CACHEDYN, you enable all dynamic SQL in the subsystem to use the dynamic SQL cache. You should be careful, because while some applications truly benefit from the cache (e.g., ERP applications), all other dynamic SQL has the potential to flood the cache and force out statements that need to be there for other applications.

When you use SQL caching, the EDM pool needs to be adjusted to allow reuse. Because the cache uses an LRU algorithm, pages on the bottom of the queue can be stolen to make room for new skeleton packages before they can be reused. When this happens, the statements in the local caches are not affected. The global cache for dynamic statements is not backed up on DASD as the normal EDM pool entries are; when the same SQL statement is issued again, it has to be prepared again.

Dynamic SQL caching has had many performance improvements since it was released in version 4, including the ability to flush the cache when RUNSTATS is executed on a table or index affected by the utility execution (figure 10.1). By flushing the cache, you allow the statement to be reprepare and pick up new statistics to use for optimization. However, RUNSTATS on a *new* index does not invalidate the cached statements; it needs to be run on the table space. An UPDATE(NONE) option of the

Figure 10.1   Flushing the Dynamic SQL Cache

RUNSTATS utility allows you to flush the cache without affecting the catalog. This allows statements to be invalidated without changing catalog statistics.

KEEPDYNAMIC and MAXKEEPD

The KEEPDYNAMIC(YES) bind parameter allows you to keep dynamic statements through a commit point. With this parameter, an application needs to issue a PREPARE only once for a statement and can execute that statement several times.

You also need to carefully set the MAXKEEPD DSNZPARM. This specifies the number of prepared dynamic SQL statements to save past a commit point. This does not affect the storage used by the EDM pool for caching the dynamic statements. It applies to the copies of the SQL in DBM1 storage. If you set MAXKEEPD to 0, you disable keeping cached statements past a commit.

If the dynamic SQL cache is not used, you can still use KEEPDYNAMIC(YES) to keep the statement string for a prepared dynamic statement through a commit. Thus, after a commit is issued, the dynamic statement can be executed again without an explicit PREPARE; DB2 does an implicit PREPARE for the statement. If dynamic SQL caching is active, a copy of the prepared statement, as well as the statement string, is kept. The prepared statement is locally cached (in a chunk of memory in DBM1) for the application thread, and it may also be cached globally (in the EDM pool) for the benefit of other applications.

The local (in-thread) cache holds the prepared dynamic statement in DBM1 storage until the application ends, a rollback occurs, another PREPARE is issued for the same named statement, or the statement is removed because the MAXKEEPD was reached. If the MAXKEEPD is exceeded, the statement is thrown out of the local cache. This does not affect the skeleton dynamic statements in the EDM pool. If the same statement needs to be reprepared, an implicit PREPARE takes place. MAXKEEPD needs to be set high enough to avoid this but not too high to cause storage problems.

REOPT(VARS) and Parameter Markers

There is one caveat to using caching and bind variables: if literals were used previously and the data is skewed or contains outliers, the same access path is chosen, regardless of the filtering when bind variables are used. In such cases, you should change the code to move the offending SQL statement into a separate package and bind that package with REOPT(VARS), which restores the benefit of potentially different access paths at execution time.

Monitoring the Dynamic SQL

New instrumentation has been added to DB2 to facilitate monitoring and tuning the cache by providing EDM pool statistics for pages used for cached statements, statement cache searches, and cache statements inserted.

Statistics are available for successful and unsuccessful cache searches in both the accounting report and the statistics report (figure 10.2). There are also statistics for the efficiency of PREPARES when using KEEPDYNAMIC(YES).

In addition, IFCIDs can be used to show statistics for all statements in the cache (sorted by highest values), the number of executions, total CPU time, and much more. IFCIDs 316, 317, and 318 can help detect and diagnose performance problems with dynamic SQL statements that use the cache. IFCID 316 provides information about what is in the cache. It pro-

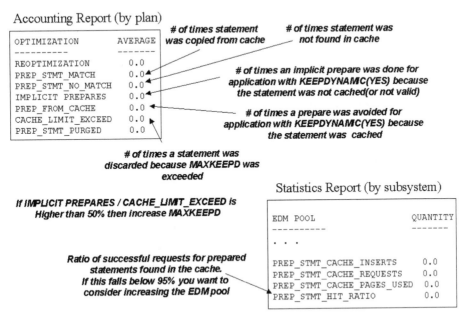

Figure 10.2 Dynamic SQL Monitoring

vides the statement name and ID, performance statistics (if 318 is also active), and the first 60 bytes of the statement. IFCID 317 returns the complete SQL text for the statement in the dynamic cache. You can use the ID obtained from the output of 316 to identify the statement. Capturing these IFCIDs can be costly, so use them sparingly and only when necessary.

Program Functionality

Retry Logic

A –911 SQL return code means that a deadlock or a time-out occurred and DB2 has issued a successful rollback to the last commit point. If the rollback was not successful, the application receives a –913 SQL return code, signifying that a rollback was not performed. The –912 SQL return code occurs when the maximum number of lock requests has been reached for the database (because insufficient memory was allocated to the lock list). With a –912 or a –913 return code, the application needs to issue a COMMIT or ROLLBACK statement before proceeding with any other SQL.

When a –911 occurs, the choice of whether or not to use retry logic depends on the individual application. If a large amount of work has been rolled back and if there are other non-DB2 files present, it may be difficult to reposition everything and retry the unit of work. With most –911 situations, a restart process (vendor supplied or user written) is generally easier than a programmatic reposition and retry. If a small amount of work was lost, a simple retry can be performed some fixed number of times. It is important not to retry with a breakpoint, since the source of the problem that caused the negative codes might still exist.

With the –913 SQL return code, the single statement can be retried, and if it is successful, the program can simply continue. However, if repeated retries fail, the application probably needs to be rolled back.

There are situations where a –904 SQL return code can best be handled by retry logic. A –904 means some required resource is unavailable, but many condition codes further describe the type of resource. Some of the resource types become unavailable only for short periods, such as in data sharing when a component has failed but is in a fail-over state that might last only a few seconds. In cases such as this, it is better to wait for a period and then retry the failing SQL statement than to abort the entire process, which could cause worse problems.

Commit Strategies

There are two good reasons to commit: to improve concurrency and to prevent massive, long-running rollbacks when abnormal terminations occur. Even programs that have no concurrency problems should do a commit at least every 10 minutes as a general rule.

If you design a good batch program, commit processing is part of it. If you use commit processing, you have to identify the unit of work in your program and also design the batch program so that it is restartable. This is why some programmers claim that commit processing would complicate their logic and was not part of the original design. Many of their programs must be redesigned when they begin to cause concurrency problems. The best thing is to design the program properly the first time.

When concurrency is an issue, you probably want a commit frequency somewhere between 2 and 20 seconds. A very good practice is to make sure the commit frequency can be influenced from the outside. Identify a logical unit of work in your program and execute this x number of times before committing. The magic number x can come from a control card to your program or from a heuristic control table. This way, programs that cause concurrency problems can be tuned, and you can also have separate settings for different times of day. It is a good idea to have the same design in all of your programs. Software solutions available from independent software vendors (ISVs) can take care of all commit–restart problems.

It is not good practice to do intermittent committing in online transactions rather than committing at the end of the transaction. You should design long-running (background) transactions (e.g., printing) so that they reschedule themselves and then terminate (doing an implicit commit). Thus, all resources are released, and the transaction server can shut down in an orderly way when needed.

Heuristic Control Tables

Heuristic control tables are used to allow great flexibility in controlling concurrency and restartability. Simply put, these are tables that have rows unique to each process to assist in controlling the commit scope (number of database updates or time between commits). They can also have an indicator to tell an application that it is time to stop. Each application or batch job has its own unique entries.

These tables are accessed each time an application commits. The normal process is for an application to read from the table at the very beginning of the process to get the dynamic parameters and commit time to be used. The table stores information about the frequency of commits as well as any other dynamic information that is pertinent to the application process, such as the unavailability of some particular resource for a period of time. Once the program is running, it both updates and reads from the control table at commit time. Information about the status of all processing at the time of the commit is generally stored in the table so that a restart can occur at that point if required.

For more information on heuristic control tables refer to Chapter 8.

Binding Programs and Commit Considerations

Some consideration should be given to the way you bind your programs for best performance, especially for application programs with heavy insert and update activity. When you bind with RELEASE(COMMIT) you could be unintentionally adding overhead to your programs, and not just because of reacquiring locks. Refer to Chapter 13 for more information regarding locks and the effects of RELEASE(COMMIT). Objects get destroyed at commit time only when you bind with RELEASE(COMMIT). These objects are all described in the following paragraphs.

IPROCs, UPROCs, and SPROCs

DB2 monitors inserts, and after the third insert it builds an executable procedure to repeat the inserts so that it does not have to rebuild the code. This is referred to as an IPROC (insert procedure). After the fifth insert, DB2's use of the IPROC reduces CPU overhead and improves insert performance. There is a similar construct for updates, called UPROC, and one for SELECTs, called SPROC.

When you use RELEASE(COMMIT) in conjunction with a frequently committing program, the IPROCs and UPROCs are built and then destroyed before much benefit can be gained from their existence. Another problem is that you have incurred all the overhead to build them.

Other items that get destroyed at commit when programs are bound with RELEASE(COMMIT) are the cache used for sequential detection to determine when to turn on dynamic prefetch and the cache used for index look-aside operations to avoid index probes. Losing these caches continually can cause performance degradation, because your program is unable to take advantage of these data access facilities.

With RELEASE(DEALLOCATE), the DB2-built UPROCs, IPROCS, and caches remained after commits are taken, until the end of the program.

Rollbacks

DB2 creates undo log records for rollbacks and redo log records for recovery for every row that is changed. DB2 also logs these change records to all affected indexes. So the general rule is that it will take twice as long to roll back application changes as it took to make them.

However, there are always exceptions to the rule. We have seen situations where update batch jobs that were running for 10 or more hours (but shouldn't have been) were allowed to continue because the DBA feared a 20-hour rollback (this particular program had no commits). But what if the application has a problem? Do you really want it to keep running, not knowing when (or if) it is going to end?

In this particular instance, the application program was in a loop that was causing the updates to occur on the same small-number pages. This was detected by looking at the online monitor thread activity detail, where we could see that over 89,000 updates had

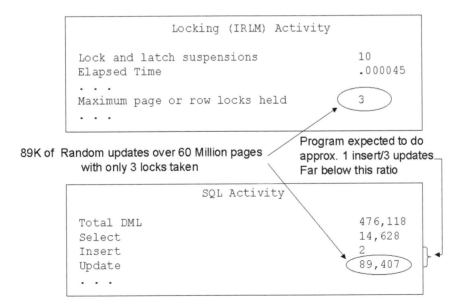

Figure 10.3   Determining If a Program Is in Trouble

occurred, but only a handful of locks were taken, and the buffer pool hit ratio was 100% (figure 10.3). This program was supposed to be doing random updates and inserts over a table with billions of rows, with a target average of one insert for every three updates. Only two inserts were done for the 89,000 updates, and only three locks were taken, showing that not a lot of different pages were affected. The job was cancelled, and in a couple of hours it was rolled back.

The moral of the story? Before making a decision to let a process run to completion or to roll back, carefully look at the thread detail statistics. Do not let the rules and consequences of standard guidelines be the sole decision basis. Altering the buffer pools and thresholds can speed up the normal termination, at perhaps the sacrifice of other processes' performance.

Savepoints

A savepoint enables milestones within a transaction or unit of recovery to be "bookmarked." An external savepoint represents the state of data and schema at a particular point in time. After the savepoint is set, changes made to data and schemas by the transaction can then roll back to the savepoint, as application logic requires, without affecting the overall outcome of the transaction.

If there are outstanding savepoints, access to a remote database management system (via DRDA or private protocol using aliases or three-part names) is not permitted, because the scope of a savepoint is the database management system on which it was set. DRDA access using a CONNECT statement is allowed; however, the savepoints are local to their site. DB2 does not restrict the use of aliases and three-part names to connect to a remote site when there are outstanding savepoints at the remote site, but this practice is not recommended.

There is no limit to the number of savepoints that can be set.

Establishing a Savepoint

To set a savepoint, you use the SAVEPOINT statement. You can choose a meaningful name for the savepoint if you wish. Application logic determines whether the savepoint name will need to be reused as the application progresses or used to denote a unique milestone. You can specify the UNIQUE option in the SAVEPOINT statement if you do not intend for the name to be reused. This prevents an invoked procedure from unintentionally reusing the name. If a savepoint is coded in a loop, however, there is no choice; do not use UNIQUE.

If the name identifies a savepoint that already exists within the unit of recovery and the savepoint was not created with the UNIQUE option, that savepoint is destroyed and a new savepoint is created. Destroying a savepoint by reusing its name for another savepoint is not the same as releasing the savepoint. Reusing a savepoint name destroys only one savepoint. Releasing a savepoint releases the named savepoint and all savepoints that were subsequently set (releasing savepoints is described later).

The following statement shows an example of setting a unique savepoint named START_AGAIN. After executing this statement, the application program needs to check the SQL return code to verify that the savepoint was set.

```
SAVEPOINT START_AGAIN UNIQUE ON ROLLBACK RETAIN CURSORS
```

The SAVEPOINT statement sets a savepoint within a unit of recovery. This statement, like the ROLLBACK and RELEASE statements, can be embedded in an application program, external user-defined function, stored procedure (i.e., defined as MODIFIES SQL DATA), or issued interactively. It cannot be issued from the body of a trigger. It is an executable statement that can be dynamically prepared only if DYNAMICRULES run behavior is implicitly or explicitly in effect. The syntax is as follows.

```
SAVEPOINT svptname
        UNIQUE
   ON ROLLBACK RETAIN CURSORS
      ON ROLLBACK RETAIN LOCKS
```

Here is a brief description of each part of the SAVEPOINT syntax:

svptname	Savepoint identifier that names the savepoint.
UNIQUE	Specifies that the application program cannot reuse this savepoint name within the unit of recovery. An error occurs if a savepoint with the same name as *svptname* already exists within the unit of recovery. If you do not use UNIQUE, the application can reuse this savepoint name within the unit of recovery.

ON ROLLBACK RETAIN CURSORS	Specifies that any cursors opened after the savepoint is set are not tracked and thus are not closed upon rollback to the savepoint. Even though these cursors remain open after rollback to the savepoint, they may not be usable.
ON ROLLBACK RETAIN LOCKS	Specifies that any locks that are acquired after the savepoint is set are not tracked and therefore are not released upon rollback to the savepoint.

Restoring to a Savepoint

To restore to a savepoint, the ROLLBACK statement is used with the new TO SAVEPOINT clause. The following example shows pseudocode for an application that sets and restores to a savepoint. The example application (supplied by IBM) makes airline reservations on a preferred date and then makes hotel reservations. If the hotel is unavailable, the application then rolls back the airline reservations and repeats the process for a next-best date. Up to three dates are tried.

```
EXEC SQL SAVEPOINT START_AGAIN UNIQUE
         ON ROLLBACK RETAIN CURSORS;
   Check SQL code;
   Do i = 1 to 3 UNTIL got_reservation;
      Book_Air (dates(i),ok);
      If ok then
         Book_Hotel(dates(i),ok);
      If ok then
         got_reservations
      Else
         EXEC SQL ROLLBACK TO START_AGAIN;
      End loop;
EXEC SQL RELEASE SAVEPOINT START_AGAIN;
```

The ROLLBACK statement with the TO SAVEPOINT option backs out data and schema changes that were made after a savepoint. This can be embedded. The skeleton syntax is as follows.

```
ROLLBACK WORK
TO SAVEPOINT svptname
```

Here is a description of the preceding syntax:

ROLLBACK WORK	This statement rolls back the entire unit of recovery. All savepoints that were set within the unit of recovery are released.
TO SAVEPOINT	This option specifies that the rollback of the unit of recovery occurs only to the specified savepoint. If no savepoint name is specified, rollback is to the last active savepoint.
svptname	Name of the savepoint to roll back to.

In the following example, the ROLLBACK TO SAVEPOINT statement causes the rollback to savepoint TWO, which causes the second and third sets of application code to be rolled back.

```
SAVEPOINT ONE ON ROLLBACK RETAIN CURSORS;
    First application code set . . .
    SAVEPOINT TWO ON ROLLBACK RETAIN CURSORS;
    Second application code set . . .
    SAVEPOINT THREE ON ROLLBACK RETAIN CURSORS;
    Third application code set . . .
    RELEASE SAVEPOINT THREE;
    ROLLBACK TO SAVEPOINT;
```

If the named savepoint does not exist, an error occurs. Data and schema changes made after the savepoint was set are backed out. Because changes made to global temporary tables are not logged, they are not backed out, but a warning is issued. A warning is also issued if a global temporary table is changed and there is an active savepoint. None of the following items are backed out: opening or closing of cursors, changes in cursor positioning, acquisition and release of locks, and the caching of the rolled back statements.

Savepoints that are set after the one to which rollback is performed are released. The savepoint to which rollback is performed is not released. For example, in the following scenario, the ROLLBACK TO SAVEPOINT TWO statement causes savepoint THREE to be released, but not savepoint TWO.

```
SAVEPOINT ONE ON ROLLBACK RETAIN CURSORS;
First application code set . . .
SAVEPOINT TWO ON ROLLBACK RETAIN CURSORS;
Second application code set . . .
SAVEPOINT THREE ON ROLLBACK RETAIN CURSORS;
Third application code set . . .
ROLLBACK TO SAVEPOINT TWO;
```

Releasing a Savepoint

Releasing a savepoint involves the RELEASE SAVEPOINT statement. You cannot roll back to a savepoint after it is released. There is just a small amount of overhead to maintain a savepoint, but it is important to release them because any outstanding savepoints block any system-directed connections to remote locations. After a savepoint is no longer required for an application rollback, you should release it. The following example releases a savepoint named START_AGAIN and all the savepoints that were subsequently set by the transaction.

```
RELEASE SAVEPOINT START_AGAIN;
```

The RELEASE SAVEPOINT statement releases the named savepoint and any subsequently established savepoints. Once a savepoint has been released, it is no longer maintained, and rollback to the savepoint is no longer possible. The syntax is as follows:

```
RELEASE
    TO
SAVEPOINT svptname
```

The *svptname* is the savepoint identifier that identifies the savepoint to be released. If there is no named savepoint, an error occurs. The named savepoint and all the savepoints that were subsequently established by the transaction are released.

Isolation Levels

There are four levels of program isolation from which to choose when binding a plan or package. You should not mindlessly take the default of RR (repeatable read), because, of all defaults in DB2, that is the one that can most hurt performance. You need to choose a program isolation level based upon how you are processing your data. Following are descriptions of the isolation levels available.

Cursor stability (CS) is the level of program isolation that holds a lock on the row or page (depending on the lock size defined) only if the cursor is actually positioned on that row or page. The lock is released when the cursor moves to a new row or page, but the lock is held until a commit is issued if changes are being made to the data. This option allows the maximum concurrency for applications that are accessing the same data that cannot allow uncommitted reads.

Repeatable read (RR) is the option that holds a lock on all rows or pages touched by an application program since the last commit was issued, whether or not all those rows or pages satisfied the query. It holds these locks until the next commit point, which ensures that if the application needs to read the data again, the values will be the same (no other process can update the locked data). This option is the most restrictive in terms of concurrency of applications.

Read stability (RS) is the option that holds locks on all rows or pages qualified by stage 1 predicates for the application until the commit is issued. Unqualified rows or pages, even though touched, are not locked, as they are with the RR option. Uncommitted changes of other applications cannot be read, but if an application issues the same query again, any data changed or inserted by other applications is read, since RS allows other applications to insert new rows or update rows that can fall within the range of the query. This option is less restrictive but similar in function to RR.

Uncommitted read (UR) is the option that allows the maximum concurrency between applications, and it is highly recommended for applications that do not need to have absolutely current information. It improves performance because applications do not have to wait for locks to be released and deadlocks will not occur. UR allows you to read through a lock to see the data, even if it is not committed (for more on UR, refer to Chapter 13).

Logging

Every system has some component that eventually becomes the final bottleneck. Logging is not to be overlooked when you are trying to get one more transaction through the system in a high-performance environment. Logging can be tuned and refined, but the synchronous I/O will always take place. We control logging and response time in various ways, depending on the issue we are trying to address. Logging is affected by several areas. Following is a list of the key people who are responsible for the various aspects of the logging process.

1. The table designer determines the size of the records written to the log via table and column design.
2. The data designer determines the size of the records written to the log.
3. The applications programmer determines the size of the records written to the log.
4. The application designer determines the commit frequency.
5. The DBA determines the size and number of log buffers.

It appears that the greatest percentage of logging overhead is in the applications developer's hands. For information on how to tune table design, refer to Chapter 5 and to Chapter 1 for tuning the log buffers.

What Gets Logged

There is always a great debate on exactly what gets logged during the different DML statements. The following list shows what occurs during each statement type:

- INSERT: After the image of the entire row is logged
- DELETE: Before the image of the entire row is logged
- UPDATE: Both before and after the image is logged
  - Fixed-length row: The first byte updated through the last byte updated
  - Variable-length row: The first byte updated in the row through the end of the row

A proper commit strategy is critical for logging performance, and it must occur at the proper frequency. The frequency of commits can affect the number of log records written and can increase the number of log checkpoints. Refer to the section "Commit Strategies" in this chapter for more information.

## CHAPTER 11

Version 6 Late Additions
and Version 7

Contained in this chapter is the most complete list of important version 7 enhancements that we could uncover at the time of writing. We plan on adding to this list and keeping the list posted on our web site. When we wrote this, version 7 was still a fantasy but we knew it would be reality when the book was published, so we got a sneak peak. For more details on this exciting version and for our views of what these enhancements mean for performance, go to www.ylassoc.com.

Note: The information on version 7 features is subject to dramatic change. Since version 7 will not be generally available for quite some time, some of the features might not be implemented or might be implemented differently than described here.

Version 6 Late Additions

External Savepoints

Savepoints enable milestones within a transaction (unit of recovery) to be marked. An external savepoint represents the state of data and schema at a particular point in time. Data and schema changes made by the transaction after the savepoint is set can then roll back to the savepoint, as application logic requires, without affecting the overall outcome of the transaction.

```
SAVEPOINT name ABC (other options)
ROLLBACK TO SAVEPOINT name
```

You can use ROLLBACK to restore to a savepoint. This is useful when you need to back out to a certain point during a unit of work without rolling back the entire unit of work. You can name the individual savepoints and then roll back to the point required by the application. You can also skip over individual savepoints. For information on how to use external savepoints, refer to Chapter 10.

Star Join

A star schema is a logical database design used primarily in decision support and ware-house applications (refer to Chapter 6 for additional information). Star schemas are composed of a central fact table and one or many connecting dimension tables. The fact table, which is normally much larger than the dimension tables, can be pictured in the center with dimension tables around it, an arrangement resembling a star. This schema also benefits some nonwarehouse applications that have a large main table surrounded by many smaller tables that are often joined together.

The enhancement permits more tables to participate in the star join process and identification in EXPLAIN that a star join is being used. Additional enhancements pertaining to how star joins are processed, especially in the area of improved performance, are planned for star joins.

Declared Temporary Tables

Support for declared temporary tables, which provide a new way to temporarily hold or sort data, was introduced in the refresh of version 6.

The DECLARE GLOBAL TEMPORARY TABLE statement defines a temporary table for the current session, not just for a unit of work. The table description does not appear in the system catalog. It is not persistent and cannot be shared.

This statement can be embedded in an application program or issued through the use of dynamic SQL statements. It is an executable statement that can also be dynamically prepared. Each thread that defines a declared global temporary table of the same name has its own unique instantiation of the temporary table. When the thread terminates, the rows of the table are deleted, and the temporary table is dropped. With declared temporary tables, some of the locking, DB2 catalog updates, and DB2 restart forward and backward log recovery that is associated with persistent base tables is avoided. No authority is required to issue the DECLARE GLOBAL TEMPORARY TABLE statement, but authority is required to use the new work table space where the table will be materialized.

Declared temporary tables can be useful for applications that need to extract data from various sources and use it in SQL joins or for data that needs to be used repetitively or kept separate from other OLTP processes. They can also be used as staging areas to make data that comes from various sources (e.g., VSAM or IMS) available.

For detailed information about the use of declared temporary tables, refer to Chapter 14. Following are a couple of examples of the syntax for declared temporary tables.

```
DECLARE GLOBAL TEMPORARY TABLE SESSION.ACCOUNT
  LIKE CLAIMS.ACCOUNT
INSERT INTO SESSION.ACCOUNT
  SELECT * FROM CLAIMS.ACCOUNT
  WHERE ACCOUNT_NUMBERS > :host_var

DECLARE GLOBAL TEMPORARY TABLE SESSION.ACCOUNT
  AS
  SELECT * FROM CLAIMS.ACCOUNT
  WHERE ACCOUNT_NUMBERS > :host_var
```

Identity Columns

The version 6 refresh included support for the use of identity columns. In Chapters 5, 8, 12, and 13, we talk about where these columns can be used. Identity columns provide a way to have DB2 automatically generate unique, sequential, and recoverable values for each row in a table.

This new identity column is defined with the AS IDENTITY attribute in column definition.

```
CREATE TABLE MY_TABLE
(ACCOUNT_NO INTEGER NOT NULL
   GENERATED ALWAYS AS IDENTITY
```

```
START WITH 100000
INCREMENT BY 100,
.  .  .
CACHE 20
```

Each table can have only one identity column defined to it. Identity columns are ideally suited for the task of generating unique primary key values, such as employee number, order number, item number, or account number. The columns must be of a data type that is arithmetic and exact, which means that SMALLINT, INTEGER, BIGINT, or DECIMAL with a scale of zero can be used. It is also possible to use a distinct type based on one of these types. Single- and double-precision floating-point data types are not listed, since they are considered to be approximate numeric data types, not exact.

Identity columns can also be used to alleviate concurrency problems caused by application-generated sequence numbers (refer to Chapter 12 for more information).

LOG SUSPEND and RESUME

The new SUSPEND and RESUME options give you the ability to temporarily freeze updates to a DB2 subsystem while the logs and database are copied. This might be necessary for those who use IBM's Enterprise Storage Server FlashCopy or RVA SnapShot to produce copies for remote site recovery. The copies can then be sent to a remote standby system (using PPRC, for example). The remote site could then be restarted quickly in the event of a disaster at the primary site, and DB2 restart would roll back any in-flight units of recovery at the time the copies were made, bringing the subsystem to a point of consistency.

The ability to freeze updates in a DB2 subsystem allows the recovery of the DB2 subsystem to a particular point in time without an extended recovery outage and without having to stop or quiesce the primary system.

New options have been added to the -SET LOG command to enable SUSPEND and RESUME logging for a DB2 subsystem. When a SUSPEND request is issued, a system checkpoint is taken (in a non-data sharing environment), any unwritten log buffers are written to DASD, the BSDS is updated with the high-written RBA, and the log-write latch is obtained to prevent any further log records from being created. Further updates to the database are not permitted until update activity is resumed. The latch is held until a -SET LOG RESUME or a -STOP DB2 command is issued. The SUSPEND option is not allowed when a system quiesce is active by either the -ARCHIVE LOG or -STOP DB2 command. The RESUME option allows the logging and update activity for the current DB2 subsystem to be resumed.

The scope for these commands is a single subsystem. In a data sharing environment, you have to enter the commands on each member. A highlighted message shows that logging has been suspended, and the message is deleted when logging is resumed. If you enter a -DISPLAY LOG command after a -SET LOG SUSPEND command has been issued, you can see that logging is suspended. Provided that there is no other resource contention, read-only activity should be able to continue while update activity is suspended.

The SUSPEND option should not be issued during periods of high activity, nor should it be used for extended periods of time. Suspending update activity can cause timing-related problems, such as lock time-outs or DB2 and IRLM diagnostic dumps when delays are detected. Also, avoid using this function while long-running units of recovery are active. DB2 restart time is lengthened by long-running updates.

The command syntax is as follows:

```
SET LOG LOGLOAD(xxx) SUSPEND
or
SET LOG LOGLOAD(xxx) RESUME
```

Defer Definition

In many cases when organizations install large software packages (such as ERP packages) almost two thirds of the data sets provided with the product remain empty. In the past, all data sets had to be defined because all the tables and indexes had to be defined, even though many would not be used. Now you can defer the definition of these data sets to provide faster installs and make data set management much simpler.

IFI Consolidation

Prior to the version 6 refresh, DB2 did not have a global trace facility. Therefore, if you were trying to diagnose a problem involving several DB2 members in a data sharing environment before this enhancement, you had to start the trace on each member, then use the sysplex timer value in the header to put records in time sequence, and use the member names supplied in the traces to help identify where the problem lay.

Now there is a new option SCOPE (GROUP) on the START TRACE command. This allows you to specify that the trace is to be group wide and will collect detailed information from each member, so combining the records for analysis is not as difficult. This new SCOPE (GROUP) option can also be used on the -START PROCEDURE and -START FUNCTION commands.

DDF SUSPEND and RESUME

DDF SUSPEND and RESUME support for DDL adds new function to the DDF STOP command to allow a customer to quiesce DDF processing and release all locks held by DDF server threads. This new option allows you to *suspend* DDF server processing without termination. Prior to this enhancement, DDF DRDA server threads could hold locks that prevented database maintenance, especially when running the new DDF pool threading. The syntax for the new command is as follows:

```
-STOP DDF MODE(SUSPEND)
```

Update with Subselect

Now you can have an UPDATE with a subselect to perform an update based on criteria from another table, for example:

```
UPDATE RECEIVABLE RC
    SET AMOUNT_PAID =
        (SELECT AMOUNT
         FROM INCOME IC
         WHERE IC.ACCT_NO = RC.ACCT_NO
         AND IC.INV_NO = RC.INVOICE_NO)
```

REXX Language Support and Stored Procedures

You can write SQL application programs in the REXX programming language that can communicate directly to DB2. Dynamic SQL can be issued from REXX with no precompiling or link-editing. REXX is an interpreted language that has been around a long time and can be used to build quick and easy scripts.

REXX is an interpreted language with no precompiler, compiler, or linker and can contain SQL. The SQLCA is automatically included. All parameters are passed as strings, and integers are passed as numeric strings. Only one OUT parameter is allowed. The simple syntax identifies an SQL string and allows retrieval, storing, and processing of DB2 data. For more information on REXX, refer to Chapter 20.

```
CREATE PROCEDURE XYZ (IN p_name CHAR(20),
      OUT p_address CHAR(64),
      OUT p_retcode INT)
      LANGUAGE(REXX)

    END;
```

Up to 225 Tables

Increasing the 15-table limit for a single SQL statement has become more necessary recently for some ERP products and for processing in some of the larger warehouses. Now DB2 allows more than 15 tables. If the resources are available, it is possible to use up to 225 tables in an SQL statement. Theoretically, it is possible to use up to 225 tables in a single join. This allows you to write more complex SQL and is a specific requirement of PeopleSoft, in which more than 15 tables often need to be joined together to produce reports. In truth, many applications need more than 15 tables in a single SQL statement due to a large number of subqueries that validate codes and references and multiple-relationship existence checks.

The greater-than-15-table join is supported only in version 7 and only for star joins. We understand that the intent is to extend this capability in the future to more join types.

Version 7

Applications

Scrollable Cursors

Scrolling in applications has always presented problems both for the application programmer and for good performance. Scrolling forward can be performed by walking an index or walking through a result set, but scrolling backward is a more difficult situation.

The only truly effective way to implement forward scrolling from a performance perspective is to use an ascending index. Scrolling in reverse requires either some sophisticated programming or another (descending) index.

With the introduction of a scrollable cursor, you will be able to move more of the work for this operation into SQL (fetch the next row, fetch the previous row). You will be able to move the cursor forward or backward a given number of rows. In addition, this positioning can be either relative or absolute in the result set. This feature will truly benefit distributed processing, as there will be an ODBC interface for scrolling as well as the standard SQL interfaces. The following example shows the logical construct of this fetch enhancement, which can be written using either SQL or ODBC/CLI.

```
FETCH NEXT
     Same as normal fetch, fetch the next row
     in the result set
FETCH PRIOR
     Returns the row before the
     current one in the result set
FETCH RELATIVE 100
     Fetch the row 100 rows ahead, relative to
     the start of current row in the result set
FETCH RELATIVE -20
     Fetch prior 20 rows, relative to the start of the current row
FETCH ABSOLUTE 120
     Fetch the 120th row in the result set
FETCH LAST
     Fetch the last row of the result set
FETCH BOOKMARK 12
     Fetch the 12th row after
     the row that is contained in
     a bookmark pointer variable
```

In the near future, only one index will be required because another new type of index will be introduced; the bidirectional index. This index will give you the ability to efficiently scroll both forward and backward using one index instead of two. We understand that initially a temporary table will be used instead of a bidirectional index to support the new enhancements to the SQL language and the new functions implemented in ODBC/CLI.

Precompiler Coprocessor

The previous method of precompiling and then passing the output to the compiler will be eliminated. The precompiler services are going to be able to precompile and compile in one step. This will allow improved integration for host language support, more consistent rules, easier portability, and greater flexibility.

Unicode Data Storage and Manipulation

Unicode support is another very important enhancement. Support for Unicode will help with multinational applications. Unicode is an encoding scheme that allows the representation of code points and characters of several different geographic locations and languages. Unicode is a fixed-length, character-encoding scheme that includes characters from most of the world's languages. Unicode characters are usually shown as U+*xxxx*, where *xxxx* is the hexadecimal code of the character. Each character is 16 bits wide, allowing 65,000 characters. The normal support that will probably be provided is the UCS-2/UTF-8 standard. With UCS-2, or Unicode encoding, ASCII and control characters are also two bytes long, and the lead byte is zero. Since extraneous NULLs may appear anywhere in the string, this could be a problem for ASCII. UTF-8 is a transformation algorithm that is used to avoid this problem for programs that rely on ASCII code. UTF-8 transforms fixed-length UCS characters into variable-length byte strings. ASCII characters are represented by single-byte codes, but non-ASCII characters are two or three bytes long. UTF-8 transforms UCS-2 characters to a multibyte code set.

The UCS-2 code page is registered as code page 1200. When new characters are added to a code page, the code page number does not change. Code page 1200 always refers to the current version of Unicode/UCS-2 and has been used for UCS-2 support in DB2 on many of the other platforms. UTF-8 is registered as CCSID 1208 (code page 1208), the multibyte code page number for UCS-2/UTF-8 support.

DB2 supports UCS-2 as a new multibyte code page. CHAR, VARCHAR, LONG VARCHAR, and CLOB data are stored in UTF-8, and GRAPHIC, VARGRAPHIC, LONG VARGRAPHIC, and DBCLOB data are stored in UCS-2.

Databases are created in the code page of the application creating them as a default. Alternatively, UTF-8 can be specified as the CODESET name using any valid two-letter TERRITORY code.

```
CREATE DATABASE dbname USING CODESET UTF-8 TERRITORY US
```

A UCS-2 database allows connection from every single-byte and multibyte code page supported. Code-page character conversions between the client's code page and UTF-8 are automatically performed by DB2. Data in graphic string types is always in UCS-2 and does not go through code-page conversions. While some client workstations use a limited subset of UCS-2 characters, the database allows the entire repertoire of UCS-2 characters.

All supported data types are also supported in a UCS-2 database. In a UCS-2 database, all identifiers are in multibyte UTF-8. Therefore, it is possible to use any UCS-2 character in identifiers where the use of a character in the extended character set is allowed by DB2. This feature will also allow UCS-2 literals to be specified either in graphic string-constant format using the G'. . .', or N'. . .' format or as a UCS-2 hexadecimal string using the UX'. . .' or GX'. . .' format.

Fetch for Limited Rows

The ability to tell DB2 to only fetch the first or top *n* rows has been a much-anticipated requirement for a long time. There are ways to do this in SQL and the application program; however; they are not exactly efficient. With this new clause, DB2 will add the functionality with improved performance, as the clause sets a maximum number of rows that can be retrieved through a cursor. The application will have a way to tell the database that it does not want to retrieve more than some number of rows, regardless of how many rows there might be in the result table when this clause is not specified. A program that tries to fetch beyond the specified number of rows will get the normal end-of-data SQL return code.

```
DECLARE EXAMPLE CURSOR FOR
    SELECT columns
    FROM table
    FETCH FIRST ROW ONLY

DECLARE EXAMPLE CURSOR FOR
    SELECT columns
    FROM table
    FETCH FIRST 15 ROWS ONLY
```

It appears at this time that the values for FETCH FIRST and OPTIMIZE FOR clauses will be considered independently by the optimizer. For example, an application might want to fetch the first 200 rows but know that the majority of the time only one or few rows will be retrieved. If the OPTIMIZE FOR *x* ROWS is set to 1 or a small number, it will be used for costing the best access path for that number of rows. If the application wants to go beyond that amount, it will be able to retrieve up to the number specified in the FETCH FIRST clause.

Row Expressions

Row expressions are an extension to predicates to allow more than one set of comparisons in a single predicate using a subquery that returns more than one column and even more than one row. Row expressions will give you the ability to use the following syntax:

```
SELECT * FROM TABLE
WHERE (col1, col2, col3) IN (SELECT cola, colb, colc from TABLE)
```

This predicate will be true when all three columns on the left equal the three values in any single row returned in the result set from the subquery. Row expressions will also allow the use of quantified predicates. The following examples show how these might be used.

```
SELECT * FROM TABLEA
   WHERE (COL1, COL2) = SOME (SELECT COLA, COLB FROM TABLE1)

SELECT * FROM TABLEA
   WHERE (COL1, COL2) = ANY (SELECT COLA, COLB FROM TABLE1)

SELECT * FROM TABLEA
   WHERE (COL1, COL2) = ALL (SELECT COLA, COLB FROM TABLE1)
```

UNION and UNION ALL Operators

The ability to define UNION statements in views has been a desired feature. It has been available in DB2 on the other platforms for several versions and will now become a feature on the OS/390. Over the last several years, the need for UNION statements has diminished somewhat with the addition of outer joins and the CASE expression. But some other features that will be added in the future will require not only UNION statements, but also UNION statements defined in views.

So as of version 7, the first step in that direction has been taken. You will be able to use the UNION or UNION ALL clause within a view, nested table expression, or subquery predicate. This is a significant enhancement, especially for UNION statements, since they are much more difficult to optimize than UNION ALL.

```
CREATE VIEW BOOK_EXAMPLE (EMP_NUMBER, FOUND_WHERE)
AS SELECT EMPNO, 'EMP'
FROM EMPLOYEE
WHERE WORKDEPT LIKE 'E%'
UNION
SELECT EMPNO, 'EMP_ACT'
FROM EMP_ACT
WHERE PROJNO IN ('MA2100', 'MA2110', 'MA2112')
```

The best use of UNION ALL will be with host variables embedded in table expressions and especially in subqueries. This has been a long-standing need for many types of SQL constructs for existence checking.

Self-Referencing Subselect on UPDATE or DELETE

In previous releases, a searched UPDATE or DELETE could not contain a WHERE clause referring to the same table. This restriction has been removed for searched UPDATEs and DELETEs but does not apply to positional UPDATEs and DELETEs.

Scalability

Unload Utility

There has been much discussion over the unload utility. A new high-performance unload utility will allow you to unload from table space, partition, image copy, or incrementals with field selection, ordering, and formatting options. This utility will also allow sampling or unloading a limited number of rows. Both SHRLEVEL CHANGE and SHRLEVEL REFERENCE are supported. In addition, parallel processing will be enabled for partitioned table spaces.

Improved Optimization and Parallelism

Utility Parallelism   The copy and recover utilities will be enhanced again with more parallelism. They will be given the ability to parallel load with multiple inputs. These loads will be able to execute in a single step rather than multiple jobs.

Indexable Correlated Subqueries   Another area that will have significant performance impact will be the ability for correlated subqueries to use indexes, making them stage 1 predicates.

Parallel Processing for In-List   Restrictions will be removed for parallel processing with in-list access.

Sort Improvements   Improvements will be made to have more sort avoidance with ORDER BYs.

Availability

Online Utility Improvements

There will be improvements to the online utilities. The first is the ability to do an online REORG without data set renaming, a significant enhancement. This is a very important enhancement, because when the data sets are renamed during the switch phase (as they are prior to version 7), overhead is added to the online REORG. With this new enhancement, test measurements have shown a performance improvement in the elapsed time of the online REORG by a factor of 10 to 15. The online LOAD resume will allow you to use the LOAD utility instead of SQL INSERTs without disrupting other access to the table.

Online DSNZPARMs

The ability to dynamically change some of the system parameters (DSNZPARMs), another one of the more requested enhancements, will start to appear with version 7. This will prevent having to stop and restart the DB2 subsystem to make certain configuration changes. This will give you better opportunities for performance tuning without sacrificing availability. We are told to expect more and more parameters to be added to the list of dynamic DSNZPARMs.

Restart and Thread Cancellation

Thread restarting will be improved to be more consistent by allowing the ability to cancel the thread and recover without having to wait for rollbacks of long-running jobs to complete.

Management

Several improvements will be made for easier manageability of objects and processes in the DB2 environment. It is important that managing DB2 be easy; else performance and availability can suffer.

Utility Improvements

There will be support for utility wild cards and dynamic allocation. Utilities will be easier to invoke, and DB2 will also have the ability to perform dynamic allocation instead of using JCL. In addition, you will be able to define a list of table spaces for use multiple times, specify a pattern for table-space matching, or specify a parameter for all table spaces in a database.

Faster Restart in Data Sharing

Data sharing will see some more improvements in the area of faster restart. With "restart light," to restart work faster, DB2 will reduce the memory and time to free retained locks during a member failure. (For information on retained locks, refer to Chapter 27.)

Statistics Reporting

Enhancements will be made to elapsed time reporting and statistics. You will have the ability to keep a history of statistics for better performance analysis. This kind of history will better enable proactive performance tuning. These statistics will be stored in the catalog and will come with a utility to purge older, unneeded historical statistics.

Index Advisor

You will soon have use of the Index Advisor, which is a tool to assist you in choosing an optimal set of indexes for your table data. This tool was introduced to the other DB2 family members in version 6.1. However, at this moment it appears this may not make the first release of V7 on OS/390, but will be here soon. One of the ways to use this tool will be through the Control Center.

The Index Advisor (which perhaps will be renamed the Index Wizard) reduces the need to design and define suitable indexes for your data but certainly does not do away with all index design strategies. It will certainly help to find the best indexes for a problem query and for a particular set of queries. It will be a real help for testing an index on a workload without having to create the index.

This utility will be able to work on a set of SQL statements that have to be processed over a given period of time and will handle SELECT, INSERT, UPDATE, and DELETE statements. In addition, it will use statistics from the system and user input to evaluate strategies for given workloads. It will also be able to scan the catalog tables holding SQL from bound applications to make determinations and suggestions.

Control Center

Many of the enhancements for version 7 have been added to the Control Center. IBM has stated many times that the Control Center will be a single point of entry for controlling DB2 family members. Following are some of the major features that have been added for the OS/390.

- Integrated SQL assistance for OS/390
- Generating DDL from existing objects
- Restart for OS/390 utilities
- Utility interface to warehouse center for OS/390
- User-defined utility ID support for OS/390
- Management of data sets produced by utilities
- Utility support for LIST and TEMPLATE

Some of these features are explained in more detail in the following sections.

Integrated SQL Assistance for OS/390

There will be some additional help for adding SQL statements for triggers and views. The SQL Assist helps you to build SQL statements and is available in the Create Trigger and Create View windows. This assistant helps build an SQL SELECT statement that is needed in the AS clause of the CREATE VIEW statement. The SQL statement is then inserted into the text area of the dialog after it is created.

There is a button in the Create Trigger window on the Triggered Action tab to invoke the SQL Assist. By using this button, you get help building an SQL statement to use as the triggered action. The assistant can be invoked multiple times to build multiple triggered SQL statements.

There is a similar button to invoke the SQL Assist in the Create View window.

Generating DDL from Existing Objects

Almost every DBA has some procedure in place for generating DDL from information stored in the catalog. Some of these procedures are programs, while others are sophisticated SQL streams. In Chapter 4, we discussed such an SQL query stream, which is also available on our web site, www.ylassoc.com. Many other DBAs use various proprietary products to re-engineer the physical database definitions back into a tool that can regenerate the DDL. That capability will soon be added to the Control Center as the "generate DDL" function. This function will allow users to selectively generate the DDL statements used for a database. As an example, a user can request that the DDL be generated for a table and all dependent objects, which includes all the table's indexes and all views based on the table. This function will be accomplished by a back-end stored procedure that runs on the named OS/390. The generated statements can be saved on any platform addressable by the database or the local workstation.

Restart for OS/390 Utilities

A function will be added to the Command Center to be able to restart utilities. Utilities that have been stopped need the ability to be restarted. The display utility command will show the status of any utility that is active or stopped. You will be able to restart utilities only if the status is stopped, and you will be able to restart from the Command Center only utilities that were initially started from the Command Center. The utilities can be restarted from either the last committed point or the last committed phase.

This function will be available through the restart command on the pop-up menu for the selected utility line in the Display Utility dialog. Restart cascades to two commands:

> Current—to restart from the last committed point
>
> Phase—to restart from the last committed phase

Utility Interface to Warehouse Center for OS/390

Other enhancements in the utility interface will allow you to do the following:

- Input load parameters that may invoke the CC390 load table dialog
- Input RUNSTATS parameters for a table

These parameters are stored in a Java class. This class can be used later to invoke the utility on the visual warehouse center table.

User-Defined Utility ID Support for OS/390

Whenever a utility is executed, you need the ability to specify utility IDs. A new enhancement will allow you to specify a default utility ID on a new OS/390 tab of the DB2 Control Center Tools Settings window. This tab will allow you to modify the CC390-generated utility ID each time a utility is run.

An "Edit Utility ID each time" check box and a utility ID template specification area will be provided through the Utility ID specification part of the DB2 Control Center Tools Settings window. A combination of characters or symbolic variables can be used to specify a utility ID expression. The Change Utility ID Template window will help you build the Utility ID expression. It will be displayed when you select the Change button and is also shared with the "Change Data Set Name Template" function.

The Control Center will generate a default utility ID from the date and time stamp if you do not specify a default utility ID template. Checking the "Edit Utility ID" check box will display a Change Utility ID window each time a user runs a utility. The Change Utility ID window will also display the default utility ID and allow you to specify a different utility ID. The Control Center will substitute all utility ID expression variables prior to running the utility.

Access

Remote Access

Many improvements will be made for DB2 Connect, JDBC, and ODBC. Support will be added for ODBC 3.0 and initial JDBC 2.0. Kerberos security for Windows 2000 will also be supported.

Stored Procedure COMMIT and ROLLBACK

In the first implementation of stored procedures, there was no COMMIT at all. Then came the ability to COMMIT ON RETURN to reduce the network traffic. Soon the ability to commit or roll back in a stored procedure will be added. This will have implications only for new stored procedures and for careful enhancements to existing stored procedures. This ability is not something that will be needed in the majority of existing stored procedures, since they were written with the knowledge that a stored procedure was just a continuation of an existing thread. But with more movement to object-oriented programming that uses stored procedures as one way of introducing classes and methods, this feature will have more use.

Content Management

An XML extender will be added to the DB2 extenders. This will allow marking the meaning of the data so that it can be more easily used. XML is an acronym for Extensible Markup Language. It is extensible in that it is a meta-language that allows you to create your own language based on the needs of your enterprise.

You will be able to combine structured XML information with traditional relational data. You will be able to choose whether to store entire XML documents in DB2 as a non-traditional user-defined data type or to map the XML content as traditional data in relational tables. The XML extender will add powerful searching of rich data types of XML elements or attribute values, even for nontraditional XML data types.

You will be able to decompose incoming XML documents from traditional SQL data and to use traditional SQL data to compose outgoing XML documents. Mapping methods will enable the transformation between XML documents and relational data. This will allow decomposing an XML document into one or more pieces for storing in tables. You will be able to use data in existing relational tables to compose XML documents.

By using the XML extender and its set of defined UDTs, an application will be able to store entire XML documents as column data in an application table. The UDTs will also provide the composition or decomposition of the contents of XML documents from or into an XML collection. These XML collections can be made up of one or more regular DB2 tables. These provided user-defined functions will supply a long list of capabilities.

Resources for Latest DB2 Information from IBM

IBM
    www.ibm.com

IBM Software
    www.software.ibm.com

IBM Data Management: white papers, products
    www.software.ibm.com/data

DB2 Family
    www.software.ibm.com/data/db2

DB2 for OS/390

    www.software.ibm.com/data/db2/os390

    www.software.ibm.com/data/net.data

    www.ibm.com/software/db2o3390/u6apav .html

DB2 Family Performance

    www.software.ibm.com/data/db2/performance

DB2 Solutions Directory Applications and Tool Search

    www.ibmlink.ibm.com/cgi-bin/s390sasw

    www.software.ibm.com/solutions/isv

"Red Books"

    www.redbooks.ibm.com/redbooks

DB2 Magazine

    www.db2mag.com

CHAPTER 1 2

Program Design and Processing

$\mathbf{P}$rograms often simply get written, not designed
and written. Individual processes are often just arrived at by trial and error rather than
designed. This works, and we have often done it, as has any programmer, but when it
comes to high performance and cutting every last unneeded instruction out of the code
path, you can feel as though you are gaping into a bottomless abyss. So many little things
can be done for performance improvement, but they are so easy to overlook during normal programming.

Yesterday, it was write the program for either batch processing or online transaction
processing. Today, there are batch processing, online processing, presentation, servlets,
applets, reusable procedures, user-defined functions, and triggers, just to name a few. But
in reality, when interacting with the database, there are still only two styles: batch-style
processes and transaction-style processes. With some exceptions, the majority of batch
processing is sequential in nature, and the majority of transaction processing is random.
Throughout this chapter, we approach batch performance as the proper application of rules
for sequential processing and, of course, random rules for transactions.

Batch Processing Issues

There are many best practices for designing and executing batch programs. We look at
some techniques for designing batch programs for particular types of processes. In general,
for best performance, batch programs need to take advantage of asynchronous processes

299

(i.e., deferred write, sequential prefetch, dynamic prefetch, and list prefetch) and parallelism while avoiding any operations that are single-threaded and processes that are synchronous. One of the biggest detriments to the performance of batch applications is processing the data sequentially where the table was designed with meaningless random surrogate keys. This is often called "death by random I/O," and we have seen cases where processes were reduced from over 50 hours to less than 1 hour by redesigning the system, removing the surrogates, and using either a natural sequential key or a meaningful sequential clustering surrogate. This strategy generally works, since the general process is random on the OLTP or transaction side. If there was a problem with this physical design on the online side, we have generally been able to find an access solution that provides the same mission-critical performance.

Cursors and Parallelism

Batch programs can benefit from parallelism, provided that the resources are set up correctly to support it (refer to Chapter 21 for more information). One way to help out batch processes with parallelism is to separate the data into batches that identically match the partition key ranges. If this strategy is followed, the benefit arises from the ability to process partitions in parallel in different batch jobs. But, as always, there is a caution: non-partitioning indexes (NPIs) can play havoc with this strategy.

Generally, if it is possible to process in batches with different jobs, then by proper application of the SQL, the same result can be accomplished much more easily with DB2 driving parallelism, which does not suffer the problems of NPI contention. The method used is to construct cursors that use an IN list or several OR conditions on the first matching columns of the partitioning or clustering index. While this is never a good practice in normal situations, since this would prevent decent indexing, it is a successful strategy when using SQL to drive page-range scans by matching the data to the key ranges. In this way, the query can be rewritten to benefit from CPU parallelism over the partitions defined by the key ranges.

Sequential Numbering

We consider sequential numbering to be both a physical design issue and a logical design issue. Behind sequential numbering today is something called surrogate keys. When sequential numbering won't go away, there are a few techniques you can use.

Before we get into the various recommended options, there is one technique that should never be used, at least not in any situation where there are multiple simultaneous insertion processes. The technique is to use a descending index and control the next number by adding 1 to the current maximum number assigned. There are a couple of different methods used for this technique, but quite simply, this technique should never be used. The normal strategy is to use the descending index so that the MAX function requires only what is called I1 index access. Even when selecting MAX + 1 with uncommitted-read isolation, this technique is still funneling of all processes through a single gate, and that destroys concurrency. If there is no concurrency, a program can quite simply self-increment without the need for any control table.

There is a variation that does not use a control table, but the table itself. The result, however, is the same: the single gate. There is a theory that if multiple inserts use the same table, get the maximum key already assigned, and use the isolation level of uncommitted read, the bottleneck to concurrency can be limited. This is true as long as the level of concurrency does not exceed the clock time required to get the next number. But there are so many other ways of controlling sequencing that this method should simply not be used. The following example is about as good as this technique can get, but it still has concurrency problems. This example uses a control table, called INUMTAB, to hold one row with the ascending sequence number.

```
SELECT MAX(NUMBER)+1 AS ACCTSEQ
FROM INUMTAB
WITH UR;

INSERT ACCTSEQ INTO INUMTAB;
```

If you commit as soon as practical, the ACCTSEQ could be used then for the next INSERT in the primary table. It is critical in this example that the commit be done immediately after the INSERT back into the control table, INUMTAB.

Then there is the issue of using the current time stamp as an ascending sequencing column. It is often stated that the time stamp retrieved by using the DB2 CURRENT TIMESTAMP feature is guaranteed to be unique. Well, it is not. It would be unique only if there were never a situation where two requesters asked for the time stamp in under a microsecond, since the precision of the time stamp is only a microsecond (six decimal digits). On today's faster CPUs, it is highly unlikely but possible for multiple requesters to get the same time stamp, as has occurred at some high-volume-insert installations. It would be best to simply retry and go on, but for some reason retrying is always avoided. It shouldn't be, because any other method of processing on an insertion failure due to a duplicate would take more processing effort and more application coding than simply retrying with the time stamp.

While the time stamp and the system clock are kept only to the microsecond, the bits in the system clock after the microsecond are almost purely random, based on the CPU speed. Since there can be only one process accessing the hardware clock due to CPU cycling speed, those random bits after bit 51 in the double word that houses the clock achieve uniqueness if they are used as an extension of the system clock. This technique is presented in more detail in a later section.

Major–Minor Technique

There are many different major–minor techniques for sequential numbering. Although the following method is certainly not the best way to do sequential numbering today, it can be used when a control number needs to be used and DB2 is not at the level that supports the identity column.

The concept is simple and can be implemented many ways. Several major keys can be used for the high-order digits of the control-number key, and individual table entries control the lower digits. For example, certain types of batch processes or transactions are each assigned to a group (perhaps a control table), dramatically limiting dependency on a control number. Then similar mechanisms are used for the lower digits. There are so many variations of this strategy in use that it is not beneficial to recommend any single one. The issue here is to avoid at all cost a single table's controlling an ascending sequence number. By assigning different ranges to different sets of data for the high digits, concurrency without a lot of lock wait time is achieved. In the simplest method, each set gets the next sequential key when the lower digits wrap, and separate control tables are used for the lower digits.

Seed Ahead

Once upon a time seed ahead was necessary, especially due to the older type 1 indexes. With type 2 indexes, there is generally not a problem. However, in a couple of cases, this technique is still required. Assume, for example, that a critical system uses inserts heavily during the online day but is batch intensive otherwise. Also assume that many indexes are required on the critical account (master) table, enough to cause slower-than-required responsiveness during the online day with the insert load.

The method to handle this is to insert ahead during the batch cycles and allow the inserts during the day to be just updates. This requires a significant amount of planning and is truly only a stop-gap measure, but in one instance where there were over 10 indexes on a critical table, it was the only solution. Normally, if a significant number of indexes are required, we immediately look to see whether there has been overdenormalization of the data to solve some other problem. If this is the case, a physical redesign is a much better alternative.

Store Clock

Here is another way of obtaining either the ascending time stamp, which is not unique, or a truly unique ascending value. The store clock is the generic name for the STCK instruction at the machine level. The granularity of the double-word result of the STCK instruction refers to bits 0–51 of the STCK value. However, bits 52–63 give you additional granularity, depending on the CPU speed, and represent an almost random value due to the cycling speed of the CPU. The maximum precision of this clock is 244 picoseconds, 2^{-12} microseconds, which is also called a clock unit. A CURRENT TIME-STAMP value could therefore be a valid identifier in the internal form used by DB2 but is not be unique, since two processes can execute the instruction in under a microsecond on today's machines. But if you do not use bits 0–51 but instead bits 0–63, you can acquire a truly random, sequentially ascending number. Using the STCK instruction instead of the CURRENT TIMESTAMP can potentially be much cheaper.

Actually, the only method used for obtaining time-of-day clock values in a sysplex environment is through use of the STCKSYNC macro, not the STCK instruction. In fact, STCK SYNC should always be used in place of the STCK instruction, since this macro invokes the service routine IEATSTCK and returns a double-word STCK value obtained from a sysplex timer, if there is one, or the local CPU STCK value.

STCK can also be used to generate an almost random surrogate key (assuming that there is no natural key to use). The following code, which is missing some entry and exit code, serves as an example of how to use bits 52–63 as the high-order bits in the field and therefore in the index.

```
Standard entry code then
        STCK  CLOCK               CLOCK IN BYTES 0-7
        LM    R6,R7,CLOCK         LOAD CLOCK INTO R6 AND R7
        SRDL  R6,12               MICROSEC TO LOW BIT OF R7
        SLDL  R6,32               LOW 32 BITS OF CLOCK R6
        SRDL  R6,3                MOVE 3 BITS TO TOP, REST ZERO
        SRL   R7,1                AVOID SIGN BY SHIFTING RIGHT 1
```

```
        ST     R7,RANDOM            SAVE IT
        XR     R7,R7               CLEAR R7
        SRDL   R6,4                NEXT 4 LOW BITS TO R7
        SRL    R7,4                SHIFT TO SECOND HALF OF TOP BYTE
        STCM   R6,1,RANDOM+1       STORE NEXT 3 BYTES OF TIME IN
        STCM   R6,2,RANDOM+2       REVERSE ORDER IN RND
        STCM   R6,4,RANDOM+3
        O      R7,RANDOM               OR WITH R7
standard exit code and return value code

        L      R2,0(0,R1)          PARAMETER ADDRESS
        ST     R7,0(0,R2)          SAVE SCRAMBLED VALUE
        XR     R15,R15             ZERO RETURN CODE
        PR                         PULL FROM STACK AND PGM RETURN
X       DSECT
RANDOM  DS     F      * 1 FULL WORD
CLOCK   DS     2F     * 2 FULL WORDS
        END
```

This type of method can actually create another key as well, if the system ID must be known. The following code retrieves the SID (current system identifier) from the MVS physical configuration communication area (PCCA):

```
        L      R15,16              CVT
        L      R15,764(,R15)       PCCAVT
        LA     R1,16               Number processors to check
TOP     DS     0H
        ICM    R2,15,0(R15)        If PCCA
        BNZ    B                   Yes use it
        LA     R15,4(,R15)         No try again
        BCT    R1,TOP              Loop for each processor
        B      ERROR               Oops
BOTTOM  DS     0H
        MVC    CPUID(10),6(R15)    Get 10-byte CPU ID
```

The returned value contains the character representation of the CPU ID and CPU model number. This value could be either the front end or the back end of the clock retrieved from the system, or it could be used as the back end when bits 52–63 are used on the front to simulate a random number.

INSERT Stored Procedures

Prior to the implementation of triggers, any process could benefit from using functional stored procedures to control the input sequencing of data. This method does have potential for problems with concurrency since it can force a single toll-gate bottleneck if not carefully designed. It is suggested only where WLM is in place to maintain the level of service required. In a single stored procedure address space not under WLM control with high concurrency, this would probably not work unless combined with something like the major–minor technique. There is also the drawback that stored procedures can be bypassed, and to prevent the bypassing, manual check controls need to be put in place. But this method is a nice precursor to moving to a version of DB2 that supports triggers.

INSERT Trigger

Triggers cannot be bypassed, generally have a short code length, and are therefore excellent for setting sequence columns for inserts. They can be programmatically controlled by using one of the other strategies for sequence number control, but are best implemented using the identity column introduced in DB2 Version 6 (explained shortly). If the identify column is not available, the time stamp is the next logical choice, followed by the store clock method.

FIELDPROC

FIELDPROC is one of the exits that have existed in DB2 since the beginning. One use was to control different collating sequences for certain types of alphabets, and others were for some types of security mechanisms. However, it needs to be coded in assembly language, and the coding is not simple. FIELDPROC is archaic; quite simply, avoid using it.

Identity Columns

The version 6 refresh included support for identity columns. Identity columns allow DB2 to automatically generate unique, sequential, and recoverable values for each row in a table.

An identity column is defined with the AS IDENTITY attribute in the column definition. Each table can have only one identity column defined to it. Identity columns are ideally suited for the task of generating unique primary key values, such as employee number, order number, item number, or account number. Identity columns can also be used to alleviate concurrency problems caused by application-generated sequence numbers.

The identity column value can be generated by DB2 or by the application. DB2 always generates the column value and guarantees its uniqueness for identity columns defined as GENERATED ALWAYS. Applications cannot provide an explicit value for a column defined this way. If an identity column is defined as GENERATED BY DEFAULT, an application can provide an explicit value for the column, but if it is absent, DB2 will generate a value. DB2 guarantees the uniqueness of the value only if it is always generated by DB2. The use of GENERATED BY DEFAULT is intended for data propagation (copying the contents of an existing table or unloading and reloading a table).

Identity column counters are increased or decreased independently of the transaction. There may be gaps between numbers that are generated, because several transactions may concurrently increment the same identity counter by inserting rows into the same table. Exclusive locks should be taken on the tables that contain identity columns if an application must have a consecutive range of numbers. Gaps in the generated identity column numbers can also occur if a transaction that generated a value for the identity column is rolled back or if a DB2 subsystem that has a range-of-values cache terminates abnormally. As a general rule, gaps in identity values should not cause a great deal of concern (unless you are still using preprinted forms).

Additional properties of identity column values include the following:

- Values must have a numeric data type (SMALLINT, INTEGER, or DECIMAL) with a scale of zero (or a distinct type based on one of these types).
- You can specify the difference between consecutive values.
- The counter value for the identity column is recoverable from the DB2 log.
- Identity column values are incremented across multiple members in a data-sharing group.
- Identity column values can be cached for better performance.

The CREATE TABLE, ALTER TABLE, INSERT, and UPDATE statements have all been enhanced to support identity columns. The next sections give a brief description of these changes, as well as some examples.

CREATE and ALTER TABLE

The AS IDENTITY attribute can be specified as part of the table definition in the CREATE TABLE statement or when adding a column with the ALTER TABLE statement to create an identity column. In addition, when a table is being created like another table that contains an identity column, a new option on the LIKE clause can be used to specify whether the identity column attributes are inherited. A skeleton example (not the exact syntax) of the new syntax is as follows.

```
COLUMN-DEFINITION:
 column-name  data-type  column-options
```

```
COLUMN-OPTIONS:
      NOT NULL
      UNIQUE
      PRIMARY KEY
      FIELDPROC
      references clause
      check constraint
      generated column spec
```

```
GENERATED COLUMN SPEC:
WITH
                DEFAULT default clause
GENERATED ALWAYS
                BY DEFAULT identity spec
```

```
IDENTITY SPEC:
AS IDENTITY
                START WITH 1|n
                INCREMENT BY 1|n
CACHE n
NO CACHE
LIKE-clause (CREATE TABLE)
 LIKE  table-name
       view-name
INCLUDING IDENTITY column attributes
```

These are the elements of the identity column definition:

GENERATED   DB2 generates values for the column. This column
                             must specify GENERATED if the column is to be
                             considered an identity column (or if the data type is a

	ROWID or a distinct type that is based on a ROWID).
ALWAYS	DB2 always generates a value for the column when a row is inserted into the table.
BY DEFAULT	DB2 generates a value for the column when a row is inserted into the table unless a value is specified. This is recommended only when using data propagation.
AS IDENTITY	Specifies that the column is an identity column for the table. A table can have only one identity column. AS IDENTITY can be specified only if the data type for the column is an exact numeric type (SMALL-INT, INTEGER, or DECIMAL or a distinct type based on one of these types) with a scale of zero. An identity column is implicitly NOT NULL.
START WITH *n*	The numeric constant *n* provides the first value for the identity column. The value can be a positive or negative value. Nonzero digits are not allowed to the right of the decimal point. The default is 1.
INCREMENT BY *n*	The numeric constant *n* provides the interval between consecutive values of the identity column. This value can be any positive or negative nonzero value, and the default is 1. With a positive value, the sequence of values for the identity column will ascend. If it is negative, the sequence of identity column values will descend.
CACHE/NO CACHE	Whether or not preallocated values are kept in memory. This improves performance for inserting rows into a table that has an identity column.
CACHE *n*	The number of values of the identity column sequence that DB2 preallocates and keeps in memory. The default is 20. If a system fails, no cached identity column values are ever used. Thus, the value speci-

	fied for CACHE also represents the maximum number of values for the identity column that may be lost during a system failure. In a data sharing environment, each member has its own range of consecutive values to use. For instance, CACHE 30 means that DB2T may get values 1–30 and DB2U may use values 31–60. The values might not be assigned in the order in which they are requested if transactions from different members generate values for the same identity column.
NO CACHE	Caching is not to be used. Use NO CACHE if you need to guarantee that the identity values are generated in the order in which they are requested for non-affinity transactions in a data sharing environment.
LIKE-clause	Create the table like (columns/attributes) another table. For an identity column, the newly created table inherits only the data type of the identity column. No other column attributes are inherited unless the INCLUDING IDENTITY clause is used.
INCLUDING IDENTITY COLUMN ATTRIBUTES	
	Allows the new table (created by LIKE) to inherit all of the column attributes of the identity column.

There are some restrictions on identity columns. They cannot be specified on a table for which an edit procedure is defined. An identity column cannot be defined with the FIELDPROC clause or the WITH DEFAULT clause. You cannot update the value of an identity column that is defined as GENERATED ALWAYS. If you are doing an ALTER TABLE to add an identity column to a table that is not empty, the table space that contains the table is placed in the REORG pending state. When the REORG utility is executed, DB2 generates the values of the identity column for all existing rows, and the REORG pending status is removed. The values are guaranteed to be unique, and their order is determined by the system.

A quick creation of a table with an identity column is as follows:

```
CREATE TABLE ACCOUNT_TRANS
     (ACCOUNT_NO    INTEGER GENERATED ALWAYS AS IDENTITY,
      TYPE          CHAR(4),
      LAST_NAME     CHAR(40),
      BALANCE       DECIMAL(8,2)
      DATE          DATE)
IN ACCTDB.ACCTTS
```

This creates an ACCOUNT_TRANS table with an identity column named ACCOUNT_NO. The identity column is defined so that DB2 always generates the values for the column. It uses the default (1) for the first value to be assigned and for the incremental difference between the subsequently generated consecutive numbers.

INSERTs and UPDATEs

The DEFAULT keyword can be used in the VALUES clause for identity columns. This allows DB2 to generate the value to be inserted into the column.

```
INSERT INTO ACCOUNT_TRANS (ACCOUNT_NO, TYPE, LAST_NAME)
     VALUES (DEFAULT, :type, :lname)
```

DB2 always generates the value for an identity column that is defined as GENER-ATED ALWAYS. If you specify a value to insert, DB2 either issues an error or ignores the value. DB2 ignores the value and generates a value for insertion if the OVERRIDING USER VALUE clause is used. Because this clause is not used in the following statement it will produce an error.

```
INSERT INTO ACCOUNT_TRANS (ACCOUNT_NO, TYPE, LAST_NAME)
 VALUES (:account, :type, :lname)
```

DB2 uses a specified value if the identity column is defined as GENERATED BY DEFAULT. But DB2 does not verify the uniqueness of the value, which might be a duplicate of another value in the column if you do not have a unique index defined on the column.

The rules for an INSERT with a subselect are similar to those for an INSERT with a VALUES clause. If you want the value implicitly specified in the column list to be inserted into a table's identity column, the column of the table from which the data is selected must be defined as GENERATED BY DEFAULT. If you want DB2 to ignore the value and insert a generated value, the identity column of the table from which data is selected must be defined as GENERATED ALWAYS, and the INSERT statement must include the OVERRIDING USER VALUE clause. Following is an example of this clause.

```
INSERT INTO ACCOUNT_TRANS OVERRIDING USER VALUE
SELECT * FROM ACCOUNT_UPDT;
```

Updates are allowed on the value in an identity column, but only if the identity column is defined as GENERATED BY DEFAULT. DB2 does not guarantee the value's uniqueness during the update. You cannot make updates to identity columns defined with GENERATED ALWAYS.

Mass Inserts

Mass insert processes need to be defined carefully. Sometimes a program should be used, and other times a utility should be used. We have encountered organizations that do not allow system utilities to be used in a production job stream but instead spend an inordinate amount of time doing programmatic inserts. Quite simply, which of the two processes produces the best result needs to be determined, and that process used in production. For mass insert, quite often the utility is the best choice. There are repercussions either way, but part of designing a quality system is to perform the analysis and make a solid judgment based on the results of modeling, including elapsed time modeling.

Often batch processes perform a large number of updates, deletes, inserts, and archives. A large number in this case is the 25% barrier. When 25% of the data contained in the table is going to be processed, you need to determine whether it would be better to unload the data; process all the inserts, updates, deletes, and archives; and then sort and reload the data with a utility. This generally does away with the need for a reorganization utility and in many cases provides other benefits as well. This decision again needs to be the result of a modeling effort to prove its case.

There are batch processes that use 9%, then 5%, then 12% of the data, and so on. This is another situation where modeling is useful, since if you add up all the batches, more than 25% of the table is processed. Most often these batches require repetitive use of something like list prefetch. But when that 25% barrier is reached again, it is generally better to sort the input batches in the clustering sequence and use a table-space scan to do the processing.

Watch out for CURSOR HOLD

The feature CURSOR HOLD has its good points and its bad. It allows position to be maintained in a result set over a commit, but it also prevents any utility process from acquiring a DRAIN lock. However, once the DRAIN LOCK is issued by the utility, all the claimers will stop processing at the next commit, except for the one with the CURSOR HOLD option. This can prevent or upset the schedule for any utility that processes partitions. For example, it can stop an online REORG from running. If this feature is planned, it needs to be planned based on what the process is running against, not only on the benefit to the individual program. Many other future features could be hurt by using CURSOR HOLD. CURSOR HOLD should be used only for short-running processes, if used at all.

Checkpoint/Restart

When a batch process needs to standardize on using a checkpoint/restart process, the first thing to do is to determine the cost of the routine in comparison to the time it will actually save over a year of use. It might be absolutely necessary to add the overhead of the feature to save time, but the savings need to be proven. After all, 20 years ago systems were not as stable as they are today, and weekly failures of batch processes were commonplace. That is simply not the case today, so you need to determine whether it is truly necessary to pay for this feature.

Star Joins

A star schema is a logical database design used in decision support and warehouse applications that was enhanced in the version 6 refresh. Star schemas are composed of a central fact table and one or many connecting dimension tables. The fact table, which normally is much larger than the dimension tables, can be pictured as being in the center with dimension tables around it, like a star.

For example, a star schema could be composed of a fact table for sales with dimension tables around it for time, products, and geographic locations. The time table could have an ID for each month, the quarter, and the year. The product table could have an ID for each product item and its class and inventory. The geographic location table could have an ID for each location (maybe a city, state, and country). The sales table would contain the IDs from each dimension table in columns for time, product, and location, instead containing three columns for time, three columns for products, and three columns for location. Thus, the size of the fact table is greatly reduced. In addition, if an item needs to be changed, it can be changed once in a dimension table instead of several times for each instance of the item in the fact table. Even more complex star schemas can be created by breaking dimension tables into multiple tables. Join predicates are used to join a fact table to its dimension tables. The following conditions must be met for DB2 to use the star join technique:

- The query must reference at least two dimensions.
- All join predicates are between the fact table and the dimension tables, or within tables of the same dimension.
- All join predicates between the fact table and dimension tables must be equi-join predicates.
- All join predicates between the fact table and dimension tables must be Boolean term predicates.
- No correlated subqueries may cross dimensions.
- A single fact table column cannot be joined to columns of different-dimension tables in join predicates. For example, fact table column F1 cannot be joined to both column D1 of dimension table T1 and column D2 of dimension table T2.
- After DB2 simplifies join operations, no outer join operations can exist.
- The data type and length of both sides of a join predicate must be the same.
- The fact table contains at least 25 times the number of rows in the largest dimension table.

For example, suppose you want to join the following tables:

- A fact table for SALES (S)
- A dimension table for TIME (T) with columns for an ID, month, quarter, and year
- A dimension table for geographic LOCATION (L) with columns for an ID, city, region, and country
- A dimension table for PRODUCT (P) with columns for an ID, product item, class, and inventory

You could write the following query to join the tables:

```
SELECT *
  FROM SALES S, TIME T, PRODUCT P, LOCATION L
  WHERE S.TIME = T.ID    AND
  S.PRODUCT = P.ID      AND
```

```
S.LOCATION = L.ID      AND
T.YEAR = 1999          AND
P.CLASS =  'AUDIO'     AND
L.CITY = 'SAN JOSE';
```

You could use the following index:

```
CREATE INDEX  XSALES_TPL ON SALES (TIME, PRODUCT, LOCATION)
```

Your EXPLAIN output would look like the following table. The EXPLAIN table has been enhanced to support more join information, including star joins (F = FULL OUTER JOIN, L = LEFT OUTER JOIN, S = STAR JOIN, blank = INNER JOIN or no join):

QUERYNO	QUERYBLOCKNO	METHOD	TNAME	JOIN TYPE	SORTN JOIN
1	1	0	TIME	S	
1	1	1	PRODUCT	S	
1	1	1	LOCATION	S	
1	1	1	SALES	S	

For a second example, suppose you wanted to use the same SALES (S), TIME (T), PRODUCT (P), and LOCATION (L) tables for a similar query and index, though the index does not include the TIME dimension. A query doesn't have to involve all dimensions. In this example, the star join is performed on one query block at stage 1, and another star join is performed on another query block at stage 2.

```
SELECT *
    FROM SALES S, TIME T,  PRODUCT P,  LOCATION L
    WHERE S.TIME = T.ID    AND
    S.PRODUCT = P.ID       AND
    S.LOCATION = L.ID      AND
    T.YEAR = 1999          AND
    P.CLASS = 'AUDIO';
```

You could use the following index:

```
CREATE INDEX XSALES_PL ON SALES (PRODUCT, LOCATION)
```

Your EXPLAIN output would look like the following table:

QUERYNO	QUERYBLOCKNO	METHOD	TNAME	JOIN TYPE	SORTN JOIN
1	1	0	TIME	S	
1	1	2	DSN_DIM_ TBL(02)	S(Note 1)	Y
1	2	0	PRODUCT	S(Note 2)	
1	2	1	LOCATION	S(Note 2)	
1	2	1	SALES	S(Note 2)	

Notes: (1) This star join is handled at stage 2, as evidenced by the query being joined with a merge-scan join (METHOD = 2). (2) This star join is handled at stage 1, as evidenced by the query block being joined with a nested loop join (METHOD = 1).

Note: For star joins, a missing key predicate does not cause termination of matching columns to be used on the fact table index.

Transaction Processing Issues

General Index Design

A good rule to follow when designing indexes, especially for high-volume transactional systems, is that you should generally add all the indexes necessary until performance starts to degrade and then back one off. While this is not a truly scientific method, it works. Index design is involved in all aspects of putting a system into production, from physical design (when you might add additional columns to the table just for indexing) up until production load is reached (when you might find situations that require additional indexes for performance). The only general guideline is to create all the necessary indexes, try to give them as many matching columns as required, maintain correlated statistics on dependent columns, and adjust as necessary throughout the production cycle.

Browsing Data

Browsing data has always been problematic. We design application programs that seem to meet all possible conditions for searching but then find out that whenever they want to browse for last name, they enter only one column, which hurts. When building browsing applications, you should never allow all conditions to be equal. You can maintain a table of frequent values, application or system controlled, and then the program can query that take to see whether or not it should ask the user for more specific data or at least some additional letters. You should never allow browsing far in excess of what will be required. Enhancements will be made in DB2 Version 7 (described in Chapter 11), and more in later releases, to improve browsing. But until that time, you should not allow unlimited browsing. It is just too difficult to achieve good performance, not for the process doing the browsing perhaps, but for the other critical processes that are fighting for the resources.

Cursor Repositioning

When you scroll through screens of data, you need an efficient browsing technique—a way to search tables with only partial search criteria. Also, a batch application that cannot use CURSOR WITH HOLD must use a browsing technique to navigate a DB2 table when frequent commits or restartability is required.

Although the ORDER BY clause is critical for browsing, you should focus on the WHERE clause, which uses an index to browse DB2 tables.

There are two types of cursor statements used for browsing tables. One is based on a single-column index; the other is based on a multiple-column index. The single-column-index browsing technique is quite simple. Using the table BRWZUM (table 12.1), assume that COL1 is a unique index for the table. Also assume that a sample online screen can hold a total of five rows of data. The first time the cursor is opened, you would like to start fetching at the beginning of the table. To do this, set the host variable for COL1, :COL1-LAST, to a low value, zero, or default data (e.g., 0001-01-01), depending on the data type, and then open the following cursor:

```
DECLARE   C_BRWZUM1 CURSOR FOR
SELECT   COL1, COL2, COL3, COL4, COL5
FROM   BRWZUM
WHERE   COL1> :COL1-LAST
ORDER BY COL1
```

The screen is filled with the first five rows fetched, and the cursor is closed.

Table 12.1   BRWZUM TABLE

COL1	COL2	COL3	COL4	COL5
A	1	TT	99	data
A	1	UU	77	data
A	4	SS	66	data
B	2	RR	66	data
B	3	RR	77	data
B	3	RR	88	data
B	3	SS	66	data
B	4	SS	99	data
B	4	UU	88	data
C	1	SS	66	data
C	1	SS	77	data

The second time the cursor is opened, you want to start fetching at the sixth row. The value of COL1 from the last line on the screen, saved in a protected work area, is placed in the host variable :COL1-LAST. When the cursor is opened for the second screen, you'll start fetching at the sixth row.

This process continues until SQLCODE = 100, which means there is no more data to be returned. It is recommended that you fetch one more row than you need for each screen in order to detect when the end of the results corresponds to the last line on the screen. This also saves an additional OPEN, FETCH, and CLOSE execution. Beware that fetching from a perfectly clustered, read-only table does not guarantee the sequence in which rows are retrieved. The ORDER BY clause is what guarantees that this browsing process is accurate.

The following cursor allows an inclusive range for COL1, which changes the WHERE clause only slightly:

```
DECLARE   C_BRWZUM1 CURSOR FOR
SELECT    COL1, COL2, COL3, COL4, COL5
FROM      BRWZUM
WHERE     COL1 BETWEEN :COL1-LOW AND :COL1-HI
ORDER BY  COL1
```

Now you have two values to store: the initial COL1-HI value and the last COL1 value on the screen, which is placed in :COL1-LOW prior to each OPEN CURSOR. To scroll backward with either cursor, all you need to do is store the last value of COL1 from the two previous pages: the :COL1-LAST or the :COL1-LOW value of the C-BRWZUM1 cursor, used by the OPEN CURSOR statements for scrolling forward. No descending index is required. The only drawback to this method of scrolling backward is that inserted rows will change the screen contents as you scroll forward again. If you have heavy insertion activity, you may want to restrict the number of screens that the user can scroll backward.

A second type of cursor statement used for browsing is much more complex because it is based on a multiple-column index and data in the high-order column, COL1, may change between screens, so you cannot just open WHERE COL1 > :COL1-LAST.

You could get around this by using C-BRWZUM1 and always opening and closing the cursor when COL1 does change. This works for a few batch programs that have a consistent number of COL1 values and where the total number of common values (the number of rows between commits) closely reflects the commit scope required (the time between commits). Since many batch programs have changing commit scopes, this workaround is probably not an option.

Instead, you need a cursor that works without special knowledge of the data. There are two common techniques for accomplishing multicolumn index browsing. The first technique uses Boolean logic to browse. Assume that the unique index on the BRWZUM table is now a composite of COL1, COL2, COL3, and COL4. The following cursor has four logical sections (one for each column in the index) and a fixed pattern of operators and parentheses and is easily memorable:

```
DECLARE   C_BRWZUM3 CURSOR FOR
   SELECT   COL1, COL2, COL3, COL4, COL5
   FROM    BRWZUM
   WHERE    ((COL1 = :COL1-LAST
      AND    COL2 = :COL2-LAST
      AND    COL3 = :COL3-LAST
      AND    COL4 > :COL4-LAST )
   OR
            (COL1 = :COL1-LAST
      AND    COL2 = :COL2-LAST
      AND    COL3 > :COL3-LAST )
      OR
            (COL1 = :COL1-LAST
```

```
    AND    COL2 > :COL2-LAST )
    OR
          (COL1 > :COL1-LAST))
  ORDER BY COL1,COL2,COL3,COL4
```

The host variable values are initially set to low values, zero, or a default date, just like C-BRWZUM. Upon the first OPEN, the first five rows are fetched, and the last values of COL1 through COL4 are stored. The second OPEN is where the repositioning begins. The first three lines of the following WHERE statement look for the same values for COL1, COL2, and COL3, and the comparison for COL4 has to be a greater-than comparison in order to start at the next value above 77.

```
WHERE    ((COL1 = 'B'
   AND    COL2 = 3
   AND    COL3 = 'RR'
   AND    COL4 > 77 )
```

The rows that qualify by matching the first three comparisons are concatenated with all the remaining section's results. The second section, which follows, looks for the same values for COL1 and COL2; however, COL3 has to be greater than its previous value. (COL4 can be any value because it is not mentioned.)

```
OR
     (COL1 = 'B'
AND    COL2 = 3
   AND    COL3 > 'RR' )
```

The third section looks for the same value of COL1 and a greater value for COL2; COL3 and COL4 can be any value:

```
OR
          (COL1 = 'B'
   AND    COL2 > 3 )
```

The fourth section only looks for a greater value for COL1.

```
OR
          (COL1 > 'B'))
```

The combination of the results qualifies rows that have not previously been retrieved from the C-BRWZUM3 cursor. Like the single-column cursor, this cursor can also be used to browse backward by saving the bottom values from the two previous screens; use the hidden index values from the two previous screens to scroll back one screen, the values from the three previous screens to scroll back two screens, and so on. Once you memorize the pattern of the AND, OR, >, and = elements, you can create a browsing cursor for a 10-column index in minutes. Like the single-column index cursor, an ORDER BY statement is required to guarantee the results.

Another cursor technique that retrieves rows based on a multicolumn index uses negative logic to browse. Assume the same unique index on the BRWZUM table of COL1, COL2, COL3, and COL4. The following cursor has four logical sections (one for each column in the index) and a fixed pattern of operators and parentheses but is not as easily memorable as the first one:

```
DECLARE   C_BRWZUM4 CURSOR FOR
    SELECT   COL1, COL2, COL3, COL4, COL5
    FROM    BRWZUM
    WHERE   COL1 >= :COL1-LAST
                AND NOT
            (COL1 = :COL1-LAST
       AND   COL2 < :COL2-LAST )
            AND NOT
            (COL1 = :COL1-LAST
       AND   COL2  = :COL2-LAST
       AND   COL3  < :COL3-LAST )
            AND NOT
            (COL1 = :COL1-LAST
       AND   COL2 = :COL2-LAST
       AND   COL3 = :COL3-LAST
       AND   COL4 <= :COL4-LAST)
    ORDER BY COL1,COL2,COL3,COL4
```

Upon the first OPEN, the first five rows are fetched, and the last values of COL1 through COL4 are stored. The second OPEN is where the repositioning begins. The first section of the WHERE looks for every row that has a COL1 value greater than or equal to the last COL1 value. The rest of the sections exclude rows from this long list by using AND NOT, which is why this is sometimes called the exclusion cursor.

```
WHERE    COL1 >= 'B'
```

The second section excludes rows (using NOT) that have the same value for COL1 and a smaller value for COL2:

```
AND NOT
          (COL1 = 'B'
   AND    COL2 < 3 )
```

The third section excludes rows that have the same value for COL1 and COL2 and a smaller value for COL3:

```
AND NOT
          (COL1 = 'B'
   AND    COL2  = 3
   AND    COL3  < 'RR' )
```

The fourth section excludes rows that have the same value for COL1, COL2, and COL3 and an equal or smaller value for COL4:

```
AND NOT
         COL1 = 'B'
   AND COL2 = 3
   AND COL3 = 'RR'
   AND COL4 <= 77)
```

The rows left after all the exclusions are the remaining combinations of COL2, COL3, and COL4, together with rows that have a greater value for COL1. This cursor also requires an ORDER BY clause to guarantee results.

While the options for browsing a table are diverse, the real solution is consistency. Choose one of the multicolumn-index browsing techniques for each site and publish it in an application-coding standards document. Each technique can be extended to handle ranges (using BETWEEN or LIKE) for any of the columns in the index.

An improvement for browsing cursors is a new extension to the SELECT clause: FETCH FIRST 20 ROWS. This clause from the SQL3 standard is available for DB2 UDB Version 5.2 and will be available on Version 7 for OS/390. This clause limits the number of rows returned in a result set; however, to point the cursor to the correct 20 rows, you still need to use one of the aforementioned browsing techniques.

Transaction Design Issues

There are two primary rules for transaction design:

1. All non-SELECT SQL (INSERTs, UPDATEs, AND DELETEs) should be at the end of the commit scope.
2. All non-SELECT objects should be processed in a predefined order, alphabetically for example.

These two rules can significantly improve performance. If all the DML SQL is at the end of the transaction, it does not affect the logic but does reduce lock wait time for other processes. Because the amount of lock wait time accumulates in systems with a high number of concurrent users, you should do everything possible to reduce lock wait time.

The second rule is important, especially in systems that are built with modular concepts. This rule prevents "designed" deadlocks, which are about 99% of all deadlocks. Deadlocks almost never "just happen." They have to be "designed" in. If all processes were to process tables with DML in alphabetic order, there would never be an application-triggered deadlock.

CICS Considerations

Resource Control Table

The information in the resource control table (RCT) defines the connection between CICS and DB2. CICS uses only one RCT at a time, even though you may have several defined. The RCT describes the relationship between CICS and DB2 resources. You can define different types of threads (connections) in the RCT, and there are specific options to define for each. Many of these parameters can be tuned for optimal access to DB2.

In the example RCT, the INIT thread allows a maximum of 40 threads at a time for the connection from CICS to this DB2 (THRDMAX = 40). The entry threads—transaction threads—define the application plan to a CICS thread. THRDA gives the maximum number of active threads allowed for that plan. The sum of all THRDA values on all threads plus 3 should be the number for THRDMAX. When the number provided in THRDMAX minus 2 is reached, CICS terminates currently active subtasks if more subtasks are still being requested. TWAIT provides the option for what to do when a thread is no longer available for an SQL request. In this example, the entry threads use a pool thread if all the entry threads are used.

```
DSNCRCT TYPE=INIT,SUFFIX=Z,TOKENI=YES,DPMODI=EQ,
    SIGNID=CICSS, SUBID=DB2P,SNAP=T,THRDMAX=40
DSNCRCT TYPE=COMD,TWAIT=POOL,AUTH=(USERID,TERM),DPMODE=HIGH,
    ROLBE=NO,THRDM=1,THRDA=1,THRDS=1,TXID=DSNC
DSNCRCT TYPE=POOL,TWAIT=YES,AUTH=(USERID,TERM,TXID),
    THRDM=3,THRDA=3
*   Transaction Threads
DSNCRCT TYPE=ENTRY, TXID=DBT1,AUTH=(USERID,TERM,TXID),
    THRDM=1,THRDA=1, TWAIT=POOL,PLAN=DB2PLN2
DSNCRCT TYPE=ENTRY, TXID=DBT2, AUTH=(USERID,TERM,TXID),
    THRDM=1,THRDA=1, TWAIT=POOL,PLAN=DB2PLN3
```

Two main types of threads are defined in the RCT: pool threads (TYPE = POOL) and dedicated threads (TYPE = ENTRY). There are two types of dedicated threads: protected threads and unprotected threads. Protected threads are the most exclusive type of CICS thread. They are recommended for high-volume transactions of any type or terminal-oriented transactions with several commits. These threads allow thread reuse for the same plan only, although any transaction bound to that plan can use the thread. It is possible for threads to remain active for about 45 seconds, allowing other transactions with the same TXID to reuse the thread. At the end of the plan execution, the thread is kept for a predetermined amount of time defined in PURGREC or two consecutive 30-second periods. Protected threads are defined as TYPE = ENTRY with THRDS and THRDA greater than zero.

Creation of the RCT entries requires a person who is knowledgeable in CICS, the RCT itself, and DB2. Performance should be monitored during the initial rollout of the system so that additional tuning can be done if necessary. There are several parameters in the RCT that you can tune for optimal performance of your CICS/DB2 applications. Here are a few recommendations for tuning the RCT.

- Explicitly code POOL and COMD threads.
- The sum of all the THRDA values for all thread types (COMD, POOL, and ENTRY) needs to be less than the value for THRDMAX –2.
- Carefully choose ENTRY threads.

- The THRDA for pool threads should initially be set at the sum of all threads expected to be in the pool. Following are the threads that utilize the pool:
  - All plans and transactions defined in the RCT with TYPE = POOL
  - Plans and transactions defined as TYPE = ENTRY, THRDA = 0, and TWAIT = POOL (which are forced into the pool)
- Keep in mind that plans that were defined with protected threads may overflow to the pool if there are no more protected threads available for use (i.e., if the THRDA value is exceeded).
- If queuing is acceptable for high-volume transactions using protected threads (TYPE = ENTRY, THRDA and THRDS greater than 0), then define TWAIT = YES, or allow the overflow to utilize the pool. You should avoid using too many of these.
- Define a plan as TYPE = ENTRY with THRDA greater than 0, THRDS = 0, and TWAIT = YES in order to control the number of concurrent transactions, force serialization, and avoid too many plans utilizing pool threads. These threads are known as high-priority, unprotected entry threads.
- For tuning purposes, THRDA and THRDM should have at least one thread difference between them.
- You can code ROLBE = YES to have DB2 back out changes rather than counting on the application program to perform this function. However, ROLBE = NO may be useful to maintain placement in a job and allow retry logic in case a deadlock occurs in a CICS transaction. ROLBE = NO is common in high-performance systems to avoid losing work that the transaction has previously performed.
- To help with performance tuning and debugging efforts, code TOKENI as YES to ensure that all threads produce multiple accounting records.

The number of threads attached to your application program depends on how you define the entries in your RCT and is not based on either the open cursor or the number of tables being used through cursor fetching.

The value in THRDS defines the number of protected threads. When the attachment is started, the number of threads available for each RCT entry is the value specified in THRDS. The value in THRDA defines the maximum number of active threads and can be dynamically increased or decreased. THRDM defines the maximum value to which THRDA can be set. Other types of threads include command threads and pool threads.

You can monitor the CICS threads by using attachment facility commands. The DSN DISP STAT command provides statistics on each of the entries defined in the RCT. In the output from that command, the column HIGH represents the maximum number of threads required by transactions associated with the entry at any time since the connection was started. This number includes transactions that were forced to wait on a thread or that were diverted to the pool. The column W/P is the number of times that all available threads for this entry were busy and the transaction had to wait or was diverted to the pool. The W/P value compared with the total number of transactions using this entry shows whether enough threads are defined for this entry.

Thread Reuse

A thread may get some amount of reuse even if it is not defined as protected. If a nonprotected thread is reused within 45 seconds, it does not have to be reallocated.

By observing the thread deallocations per commit in the accounting detail reports and doing some quick calculations, you can determine the amount of thread reuse that you are achieving. Take the number of NEW USER terminations plus the number of RESIGNONs, and divide this by the total number of terminations (NEW USER + DEALLOCATION + RESIGNON). This gives you the percentage of threads that are being reused. For example, if NEW USER = 0, RESIGNON = 10,894, and DEALLOCATION = 150, (0 + 10894)/ (0 + 150 + 10894) = 98.6%. If you are not getting much thread reuse, you may want to look into defining some protected threads in CICS.

There are a number of techniques in CICS that you can use to improve transaction throughput when using DB2. Even though some of these recommendations apply to both entry and pool thread use, entry thread use generally achieves better effects, primarily for high-volume transaction processing.

Reverse-Order Retrieval

If a ROWID column is defined in your table, you can use it to retrieve rows in reverse order very quickly without the overhead of the older methods of backward scrolling, such as using two indexes (one ascending, one descending). You can do this by storing the ROWID value from the SELECT in working storage or in a global temporary table or a declared global temporary table). Then retrieve the values in reverse order by executing a SELECT statement with a WHERE clause that compares the value in the ROWID column to the stored value of the ROWID. You can use this technique even if you do not have an index on the table.

Dependent Table Cascade

Declarative referential integrity has different rules for child tables when deleting a parent row. When you use declarative referential integrity, the deletion of a row in a parent table cascades to the dependents in the order in which they were defined. To determine this order, you can query the SYSIBM.SYSRELS catalog table using the creation time stamp column. Many times this order needs to be examined to deal with performance and concurrency concerns. It is necessary in some cases to programmatically delete rows in a child table considering the number of locks and commit strategies. Then the parent row can be removed and the deletion cascaded to the other tables if necessary.

## CHAPTER 13

Locking and Concurrency

D$_{B2}$ performance and integrity with a less sophisticated locking manager would be like living in a house without a lock on the door, fearing the knocks. It is important to design your application to provide maximum concurrency for best performance and to prevent intruders at the same time, which is no small feat. This design includes how you structure your program, what bind option you choose, and how well-behaved other applications in your subsystem are.

Programming for Concurrency

Hot pages or hot rows are those that are locked for more than 10% of the time. This can happen in a high-volume environment with concurrent programs constantly accessing the same data and can cause concurrency problems. Often, programs are designed to follow a logical flow of processing, but in a high-performance situation, you may consider moving the SQL to the end of the process (transaction, subroutine, etc.) to lessen the amount of time the locks are held. This technique may seem a little bizarre and a lot of work and may not be feasible for all programs, but you should consider it for the 10% of transactions or programs that run 90% of the time and consume a high percentage of the resources. If you can use this technique to shave some time off of any heavy used transaction it will add up.

By moving all physical changes to the end of the transaction, not where they "logically" occur, and applying DML to tables in a predetermined sequence (say in table name alphabetical order), you can avoid lock contention and deadlocks (figure 13.1).

Row-Level Locking

DB2 supports row-level locking. If applications are experiencing a lot of concurrency problems, it might be a consideration. However, it should not be used as a fix for what could be a physical design issue (refer to Chapter 5) or an application design issue (refer to Chapter 12). It should be used when a page of data is simultaneously needed by multiple applications, and each user's interest is in different rows. If the interest is in the same row, row-level locking buys you nothing. Use row-level locking only if the increased cost (concurrency and wait-time overhead) of locking is tolerable and you can definitely justify the benefit.

The IRLM uses the same resources in memory and the same CPU usage for row locking as for page locking. It costs just as much to lock a single row as it does to lock a single page. If a program is updating several rows in the same page, it could suffer if you change from page locking to row locking. The more rows per page, the higher the cost. For example, in figure 13.2 you can see how much CPU overhead is involved in row-level

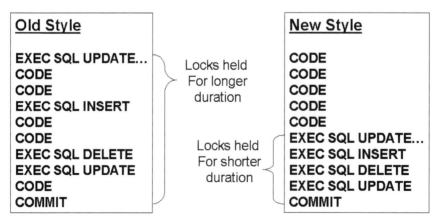

Figure 13.1   Lock Duration/Transaction Re-design

LOCKSIZE	ELAPSED CLASS 2	CPU CLASS 2 LOCK	LOCK REQUESTS	MAX.LOCKS HELD
Table	13.37	1.98	2	25
Page	12.89	2.08	660	607
Row	21.68	3.27	23,983	23,826

Elapsed Time Executing DB2 Calls   *Max Number of Locks Held by Program*

CPU Time Executing DB2 Calls

Source: IBM SG24-4725-00 Locking in a DB2 MVS Environment

Figure 13.2 Elapsed Time and CPU Time for Locking Levels

locking versus page-level locking. In this example, a single dynamic SQL update state-ment updates 28,326 rows (on a 50-MIPS processor). The overhead of table locking, page locking, and row locking is measured. The chart shows that it takes more elapsed time and CPU time to execute the same SQL statement when using row-level locking. Also by dividing the difference in CPU time by the difference in lock requests, you can see the CPU cost for locking.

$$(3.27 - 2.08)/(23,983 \text{ locks} - 660 \text{ locks}) = 51 \text{ } \mu/\text{lock request}$$

This shows the CPU averaging about 51 microseconds for the total lock operation (lock, change, unlock), or about 17 seconds for each individual operation. This can accumulate significantly if you are updating several rows in the program.

Row-level locking can also potentially *increase* contention and deadlocks. This can happen if two applications perform updates on the same rows of a page in a different sequence. If you use page-level locks, the second application has to wait to access the page (it may time out waiting, but if the commit scope is properly set, that can be avoided). If you use row-level locking, the applications access the same page at the same time and may deadlock while attempting to access the same rows (figure 13.3). In this example, two programs (PRG1 and PRG2) access the data in two different sequences (PRG1 is more sequential, and PRG2 is more random). This example shows what could happen if you use row-level locking. PRG1 wants to make sequential updates to rows 1, 5, and 7, in this order, and then it will commit. PRG2 wants to make random updates to

PRG1 needs to update ROW 1,5,7 (in this order) then commits
PRG2 needs to update ROW 7,5,3 (in this order) then commits

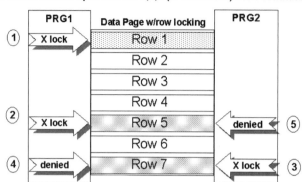

Now have deadlock between
the PRG1 and PRG2 on rows 5 and 7

Figure 13.3   Row Level Locking and Deadlocks

rows 7, 5, and 3, in this order, and then commit. If these program start at about the same time, PRG1 gets its X lock on rows 1 and 5, and then PRG2 gets its X lock on row 7. These programs will then deadlock as PRG1 tries to get an X lock on row 7 and PRG2 tries to get an X lock on row 5.

In figure 13.4 you can see what would happen with page-level locking in this scenario. PRG1 gets the X lock on the page, makes its updates, and then commits. PRG2 waits until PRG1 has committed, gets the X lock on the page, and then makes its updates. PRG2 may or may not time out, depending on the commit scope and the length of time specified for the system time-out period (DSNZPARM IRLMRWT, discussed later in this chapter).

You may say that you eliminated time-outs by going with row-level locking, but you may have increased your chances for deadlocks (depending on how the data is accessed), not to mention that you also increased the CPU overhead for the applications. If there seems to be no happy medium, revisit your application processes and your physical design. You should consider row-level locking only for random processes, not sequential ones, because for sequential processes, row-level locking is just more overhead without any benefit and could be more troublesome if the data is out of sequence (unclustered).

PRG1 needs to update ROW 1,5,7 (in this order)
PRG2 needs to update ROW 7,5,3 (in this order)

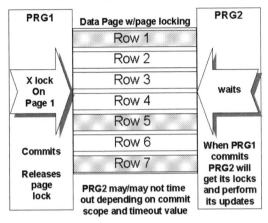

Figure 13.4   Row Level Locking and Deadlocks cont.

Unique Generated Numbers and Identity Columns

Applications can use identity columns to avoid the concurrency and performance problems that can result when an application generates its own unique counter outside the database. Refer to Chapter 12 for more information on identity columns and sequential key
generation.

Releasing Locks

It is time to forget once and for all the rule that the default for the isolation bind parameter should be RELEASE(COMMIT). Using the RELEASE(COMMIT) option on the
bind package statement releases table and table-space intent locks (IS, IX) at each commit point. Intent locks do not interfere with each other, and there is really no reason for
their release at commit points. However, reacquiring them after a commit is expensive
for your application. In a data sharing environment, reacquiring the locks also requires
repropagating them to the coupling facility which can add significant overhead. The
DEALLOCATE option holds intent locks through to the end of the program, but this does

not cause any concurrency problems, because page locks and row locks are still released when a commit is performed.

The RELEASE(COMMIT) parameter also destroys information required to help reduce some labor-intensive processes as well as information needed to help performance (refer to Chapter 10 for more details).

Since RELEASE(COMMIT) is the default, several organizations have the majority of their programs bound with this option. When choosing to bind programs with RELEASE(DEALLOCATE), be careful and approach this wisely. If CICS thread reuse is used and you rebind the heavily used transactions with RELEASE(DEALLOCATE), you will require more memory in the EDM pool, so this resource needs to be monitored. Do not just perform a mass rebind using RELEASE(DEALLOCATE). Instead, initiate a process that will follow an 80/20 rule for program rebinds (80% of the processing is normally done by only 20% of the programs or transactions).

Using RELEASE(DEALLOCATE) does not release any locks acquired by the LOCK TABLE statement.

DSNZPARMs of Interest

IRLMRWT

IRLMRWT is the number of seconds that a transaction will wait for a lock before a time-out is detected. The IRLM uses this value for time-out and deadlock detection. Most shops take the default of 60 seconds, but more and more high-performance situations where detection should occur sooner (so the applications do not incur excessive lock wait times), it is set lower. It is set to 5 or 10 seconds at several high-performance sites. If this threshold is exceeded the application often is reviewed and tuned. The simple philosophy in practice here is that in a high-performance application, those that do 10,000 to 20,000 SQL statements per second, waiting more than 5 seconds for a lock signals that something really wrong has occurred.

When this parameter is set to 60 seconds, it is quite possible that no deadlocks or time-outs are occurring. However, everything may wait for almost 60 seconds, consuming vast amounts of lock wait time due to some design flaw. Many businesses have achieved significant throughput increases by performing analyzing lock wait times.

RECURHL

The use of the DSNZPARM RECURHL (release cursor hold) can help with concurrency. When RECURHL is set to YES, it allows DB2 to release the locks that are held by a cursor defined WITH HOLD but still to maintain the position of the open cursor.

XLKUPDLT

The DSNZPARM XLKUPDLT is new with version 6. It allows you to specify the locking method to use when a searched update or delete is performed. The default is NO, which is the best for concurrency. When it is set to NO, DB2 uses an S or U lock when scanning qualifying rows and then upgrades to an X lock when a qualifying row is found. The value of YES is useful in a data sharing environment when the searches involve an index, because it takes an X lock on qualifying rows or pages. During the scan of the index, no data rows are touched, but when a qualifying row is found, an immediate request for an X lock is issued, thus assuring that the update or delete completes rapidly when the lock is acquired and that the transaction does not have to get involved in lock negotiation.

NUMLKTS

NUMLKTS represents the maximum number of locks on an object. If you turn off lock escalation (LOCKMAX 0 on the table space), you need to increase this number. If you use LOCKMAX SYSTEM on any individual table space, the value defined here in NUMLKTS is the value for SYSTEM.

NUMLKUS

NUMLKUS is the maximum number of page or row locks that a single application can hold concurrently on all table spaces. This includes data pages, index pages, index subpages (if you still use those old type 1 indexes), and rows. If you specify 0, there is no limit on the number of locks. You should be careful with 0, because if you turn off lock escalation and do not commit frequently enough, you could run into storage problems (DB2 uses approximately 250 bytes for each lock). These storage problems can completely consume all available storage and potentially shut down the system.

LOCK TABLE Statement

You can save the overhead of multiple lock acquisitions for locking table data by using the LOCK TABLE statement. This statement allows you to lock an entire table in either share mode or exclusive mode. This lock is held until the end of the transaction. Although using the exclusive mode does not allow concurrent transactions to either read or update the table, the transaction that issued the LOCKTABLE statement may finish more quickly because it will not have to wait on locks or find that data is unavailable due to locks held by other transactions.

If you need to lock and cannot frequently commit, consider the use of SQL LOCK TABLE statements. After successful execution, your process will have an S or X lock on the table, so you will not have the problem of page or row locks escalating to table locks automatically, potentially causing unforeseen problems with lock contention. This solves the problem of failing batches caused by the lock not being granted, and you also save a lot of resources.

The isolation level uncommitted read (UR) has many uses in the application development life cycle. The first and most practical use of UR is retrieving read-only data—the more, the better. Any table that is read-only *at the time the data is selected* should have WITH UR included in the SELECT. Up to 30% of CPU time can be saved from long-running queries.

Although UR is nicknamed the "dirty read," a more appropriate name is the "high-performing read." This speed is the reason that UR has more practical uses than just selecting read-only data. Another use for UR is estimating, as when summary information is needed but the answer does not have to be exact. An example of estimating is running a query to calculate an average over a large number of rows that are constantly being updated, inserted, or deleted.

Browsing rows of data is another good use of UR, for example, in an online application that displays a list of rows with all last names beginning with YEV%. It usually is not necessary to list the precise, up-to-the-second names for selection. This is especially true when the list can change within a matter of seconds. After the estimated list is displayed and one of the names is selected, a second screen can retrieve the detail using a stricter isolation to enforce proper locking.

Deadlocks and Retry Logic

Ensure that retry logic is coded for applications requiring high availability. For SQL used in applications requiring high concurrency, the SQL/process should sometimes be retried if an SQL code of –911, –912, –913, or –904 (data sharing) is received before ABENDing the program. Five retries is a good starting point.

This type of error abort process really needs to be examined with the new implementation of savepoints in version 6. When a rollback is forced, savepoints have no place in the transaction. But in other cases where you have a rollback but do not need the complete transaction rolled back, savepoints are a performance design strategy. (See Chapters 10 and 11 for more information on savepoints.)

Lock Escalation

Lock escalation can occur when the value for LOCKMAX is reached. At this time, DB2 releases all the locks held in favor of taking a more comprehensive lock (i.e., it releases several page locks to escalate to a table lock). DB2 tries to balance the number of locks on objects based upon the amount of concurrent access. Lock escalation can occur for objects defined with LOCKSIZE ANY, PAGE, or ROW. LOCKSIZE ANY allows DB2 the choice of lock to take only initially. The LOCKMAX option further determines when and if escalation occurs.

The value of LOCKMAX is set in the CREATE TABLESPACE statement to define how many locks can be held simultaneously on an object. Locks are escalated when this number is reached. You can specifically set this value to a number. If you leave it at the default of SYSTEM and you use LOCKSIZE ANY, it uses the number set by the NUMLKTS DSNZPARM. Otherwise, the default of 0 is used for specific object lock sizes, such as page, row, table, or table space.

It is possible to turn off individual lock escalation on a table space by using the LOCKMAX = 0 parameter in the CREATE TABLESPACE statement. If you choose to turn off lock escalation, be sure that your applications that access those objects are committing frequently and that you have adjusted the DSNZPARM NUMLKTS to allow more locks to be taken, else you run the risk of hitting negative SQL codes when you reach the maximum number of locks (without escalation you could hold more smaller locks). Lock escalation is there to prevent using excessive system resources, so if you turn it off, you need to control the number of locks or it needs to be static and known. If you are CPU bound, it may not be a good idea to turn off lock escalation, because DB2 will take longer to traverse long chains of locks and IRLM latch activity will take more CPU time.

Monitoring Lock Escalation

A new message in version 6 is produced when lock escalation occurs (figure 13.5). This shows you when lock escalation occurs and may help you determine whether you have the potential for concurrency problems. If an object that is used by many processes is continually escalating its locks, you may run the risk of greater contention.

Selective Partition Locking

Selective partition locking (SPL) gives you the ability to tell DB2 to acquire locks only at a partition level and not to escalate locks to the table-space level. This avoids some propagation of locks to the coupling facility and allows better concurrency for applications that access data in various partitions. This can be especially useful if usage against the partitions is spread over multiple data-sharing members using affinity routing. Performance trace class 6 (IFCID 0020) shows whether you are truly using SPL on your table-space partitions, or you can use the -DISPLAY DATABASE(LOCKS) command to display information about SPL.

However, SPL helps in a non-data sharing environment only if an agent actually escalates. If you are not having escalation problems, you may not want to use SPL. Without SPL, the parent intent lock is taken on the last partition, regardless of which ones are accessed. These locks are almost always intent locks and therefore almost never cause a problem. With SPL, the parent intent lock is taken on whichever partition is accessed. If escalation occurs with SPL, it occurs just for the partition (or partitions) on which too many locks are held. Without SPL since the parent lock is on only the last partition, the entire page set is escalated, and access is prevented to all partitions.

```
DSNI031I - csect - LOCK ESCALATION HAS OCCURRED FOR
RESOURCE NAME                        = name
LOCK STATE                           = state
PLAN NAME : PACKAGE NAME             = id1 : id2
STATEMENT NUMBER                     = id3
CORRELATION-ID                       = id4
CONNECTION-ID                        = id5
LUW-ID                               = id6
THREAD-INFO                          = id7 : id8 : id9 : id1
```

Figure 13.5 Lock Escalation

Monitoring Locking

Monitoring Time-outs and Deadlocks

Deadlocks and time-outs need to be monitored on a continual basis, especially when new programs or additional users are added to the existing workload mix. These can be monitored in the statistics and accounting reports. If you experience a high number of deadlocks or time-outs, you can get a closer look at who the culprits are by looking at IFCID 172 for deadlocks and IFCID 196 for time-outs. DB2PM also provides a deadlock report and a timeout trace report that show every occurrence of a deadlock or time-out in a given time period and the resources involved.

Lock Wait Time

Probably one of the most common mistakes is thinking that you do not have issues or problems with locking just because you never see time-outs or deadlocks or have very few per day. Although you may not encounter those conditions, that is a very reactive form of performance monitoring. While deadlocks and time-outs are indicators of probable locking problems, there is another statistic that should be monitored: lock wait time.

Usually a lock time-out period is 60 seconds (the default value). So what if your application is waiting 30 seconds, 40 seconds, or 59 seconds for a lock? You will never see a time-out, but you probably have a performance problem. Monitor the lock wait time to estimate how much time your application is waiting for locks (figure 13.6) in addition to doing reactive monitoring when you actually experience a time-out or deadlock.

How much time is too much? Probably anything over one second if you are trying to achieve high performance (okay, this might be extreme). You can also set the time-out value (IRLMRWT DSNZPARM, discussed earlier in this chapter) to 5 seconds instead of the default of 60 to immediately deal with problems in a highly tuned environment when you cannot afford to have applications waiting on locks. This allows you to identify applications that are waiting on locks for a long period of time, and from there you can do further analysis to find the problem. You could also use a DB2PM exception report and set a specific lock wait time for applications. The hard part is finding the "problem children" who are causing the excessive lock waits. You have to identify the programs that were running at the same time as the excessive wait time occurred and what resources they were accessing. This, of course, can be done through traces and additional monitor reports, but

Accounting Report (by plan)

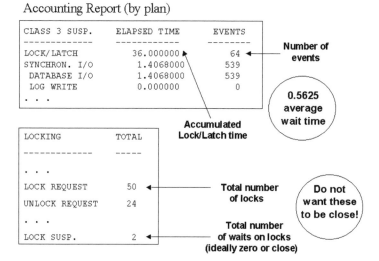

Figure 13.6   Lock Wait Time

these come at a cost. But if you could shave maybe 40 seconds off a transaction that executes a couple of thousand times a day just by reducing the contention for resources, isn't the upfront cost worth it? Another problem with leaving the lock wait time at 60 seconds, especially when it comes to deadlocks, is that deadlocks have a ripple effect. Other threads contend for locks held by the deadlocked threads, thus magnifying the outage far beyond one minute for effected threads (e.g. time-outs, rollbacks). So it becomes more and more important to adjust the default time. Often it will require two adjustments: one for pure OLTP during the high-volume times, perhaps 10 seconds, and another for the off times, probably between 30 seconds and the default of 60 seconds.

DB2PM provides a lock suspension report that displays the resource, its total number of suspends, average elapsed time, and more. This report gives you a more granular picture of your lock wait time. However, this report requires a performance trace started on class 7.

Recommendations for Lock Performance

Periodic monitoring of locking issues, such as suspensions and time-outs, can help you determine whether you have potential locking problems. Here are some guidelines:

- If the lock suspension time for all DB2 programs is greater than 1% of total elapsed execution time for the programs, you are waiting too long for locks. You need to get down to the individual program level to determine the cause.
- If the number of transactions with greater than five seconds of suspension time is greater than 0.01% of total transactions, you have a lock wait time problem.
- If the number of TSO/batch programs with greater than 60 seconds of lock suspension times is more than 0.01% of the total number of TSO/batch programs, you need to investigate who is holding the locks and why.

You can get these numbers from an accounting or statistics report and from the lock suspension report in DB2PM.

DISPLAY DATABASE LOCKS

The DISPLAY DATABASE LOCKS command can help to monitor locks online during normal processing. With this command, you can see what locks are held by applications, on what resources, and for what duration (figure 13.7). Use it to find potential abusers.

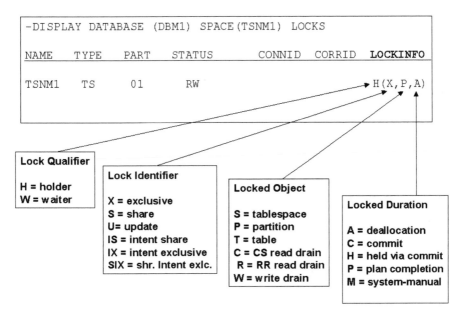

Figure 13.7 –DISPLAY DATABASE Locks

Lock Avoidance

Lock avoidance was introduced in DB2 to reduce the overhead of always locking everything. DB2 checks to be sure that a lock is probably necessary for data integrity before acquiring a lock. Lock avoidance is critical for performance. Its effectiveness is controlled by application commits. Lock avoidance is also generally used with both isolation levels CS and RR for referential integrity constraint checks. For a plan or package bound with RR, a page lock is required for the dependent page if a dependent row is found. This is held to guarantee repeatability of the error on checks for updating primary keys when deleting is restricted.

Bind Option

We need to bind our programs with CURRENTDATA(NO) and ISOLATION(CS) for lock avoidance. This must be specified. The default is CURRENTDATA(YES), which turns off lock avoidance and is only needed in a few rare situations. Ambiguous cursors are considered read-only as well, and there could be a need for a YES specification in that remote possibility also.

The real implication of using CURRENTDATA(NO) is that if a program uses an SQL cursor to move through a table and then uses singleton updates, there is a possibility that the rows have changed between the time the fetch was issued and the update occurred. This situation does not occur in too many places, but if it does, the solution is to use the better SQL practice of UPDATE . . . WHERE CURRENT OF or to make checks in the WHERE clause of the UPDATE to guarantee that the rows have not changed. This requires saving many columns to verify the check. These columns are not required otherwise, an unnecessary increase in CPU overhead, which is why the cursor use is best.

Lock avoidance also needs frequent commits so that other processes do not have to acquire locks on updated pages. Frequent commits also allow for page reorganization to occur to clear the PUNC bits. Frequent commits allow the CLSN to be updated more often, since it is dependent on the Begin_UR record on the log, the oldest Begin unit of recovery required (Figures 13.8 and 13.9).

Using Uncommitted Read

The best way to have lock avoidance is to avoid the lock altogether. A lock takes over 1,000 instructions and a cross-memory call to the IRLM, and lock avoidance requires

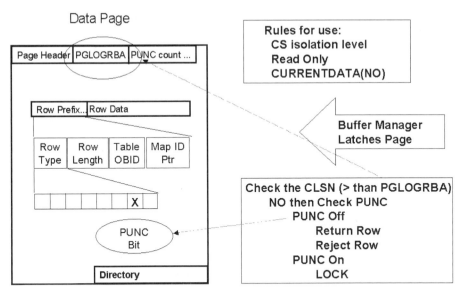

Figure 13.8   Lock Avoidance

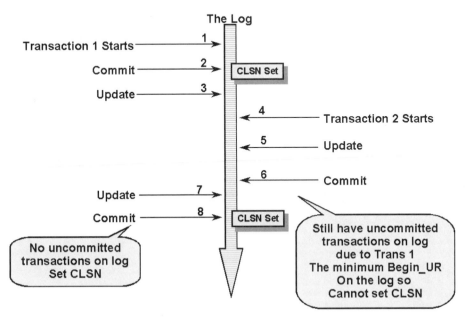

Figure 13.9   Setting the CLSN

approximately 60 instructions to determine if a lock is required or not and then take a latch. You can avoid that entire overhead by making use of uncommitted read (UR) wherever possible, because it eliminates data locking entirely. UR almost never interferes with programs updating the database. If bound with ISOLATION (UR), mass deleters cannot run concurrently with UR programs, and UR programs are held up for mass deleters. A good example of UR use is scrolling, as when looking forward or backward for the right account so the update process can continue. UR should be used as a single SQL statement:

```
EXEC SQL SELECT … WITH ISOLATION UR
```

Determining Whether Lock Avoidance Is Used

To determine whether your application is getting lock avoidance, you can run the performance trace class 6 or accounting class 1 IFCID 214 and look at the lock summary trace. This provides information about whether or not lock avoidance was used for a particular page set in a unit of work. A Y or N in field QW0218PC indicates whether lock avoidance was used. IFCID 223 in trace class 7 includes more detailed information about the usage of lock avoidance on a particular resource. You can monitor this during peak periods and determine whether lock avoidance use is degrading for any reason. This information can also be tracked with accounting or monitor class 3. When lock avoidance degrades, CPU usage increases and throughput is lessened, which is exactly what we are trying to avoid.

Temporary Tables

Temporary storage became a daily requirement with business data processing about the same time as the "temporary" music of the Beatles arrived. In both cases, there was nothing temporary. Today, with large systems and more complex transactions, we need both quick and dirty individual temporary tables in a unit of work and large scratch-pad temporary tables in a given process. We have both in DB2 with global temporary tables and declared global temporary tables. Although they both have global in their names, they are completely different and serve different purposes.

Global Temporary Tables

Global temporary tables can help improve performance in many different ways. Any time repetitive SQL is used to return a result set, producing exactly the same result each time, a global temporary table might provide benefit. A subquery that is used more than once is a prime example. It is better to issue the subquery once, store the result-set rows in the global temporary table, and use the table in subsequent subqueries. Another use is to retrieve and hold data from non-DB2 sources and then to join or otherwise use this data in SQL statements.

The biggest advantage of global temporary tables is that no logging is done, since no recovery is possible. However, no indexing is done either, so a table-space scan is always used as the access path. Also, no modifications can be made to the data in the global temporary table by either an SQL update or delete. Only inserts are allowed. The global temporary table exists for the duration of the unit of work and is automatically deleted when a commit is issued, unless the table is used in a cursor definition using CURSOR WITH HOLD.

Global temporary tables can be used like regular tables, except that they are not logged, not recoverable, and have no indexes. One difference from a normal table is that only inserts can be performed; updates and deletes are not allowed. Global temporary tables are very useful for stored procedures. For example, they can be used as a holding area for nonrelational or non-DB2 data, such as data extracted from VSAM files. The data is held for the duration of the unit of work and can be referenced in SQL statements. This is particularly valuable when a left or full outer join is required using one DB2 table and one non-DB2 table (for example, using VSAM data). An INSERT statement can load the global temporary table with the VSAM data, and then the following SQL statement can perform the outer join:

```
SELECT *
FROM T1 LEFT JOIN global-temp-name
ON join predicates
```

This technique logically fits in a stored procedure, so any other process that needs the result specifically for its thread can just execute the stored procedure and use a result set. The benefit is that the DB2 join algorithms are used to perform the outer join instead of a homegrown program.

Another major benefit of global temporary tables is when a materialized set is present for a result set, a view, or a table expression and the materialized set needs to be used more than once.

Sometimes it is necessary to use a work-around in SQL due to the 15-table limit for an SQL statement in DB2 prior to version 6. Global temporary tables can be used to hold the results of some of the tables, then a later statement can combine the global temporary tables to the remaining tables. Version 6 raised the limit from 15 tables in an SQL statement to a maximum of 225 tables, with more than 15 allowed in a join.

The only access path available against a global temporary table is a table-space scan, so keep the size of the scan in mind when analyzing performance. When a global temporary table is used in a join, the access path is generally a merge scan join, which might require sorting the global temporary table.

A global temporary table can be held longer than a unit of work when it is used inside a cursor definition that is defined WITH HOLD.

Creating a Global Temporary Table

A global temporary table is created in the same manner as a normal table, through DDL, except that it is not physically created in a table space. These tables cannot be created with default values, and unique, referential, or check constraints cannot be defined for them. The following example shows the creation of a global temporary table that will hold rows containing an amount and a date.

```
CREATE GLOBAL TEMPORARY TABLE SUMMARY
(AMOUNT_SOLD DECIMAL(5,2) NOT NULL,
(SOLD_DATE DATE NOT NULL)
```

An empty instance of the table is created when the first implicit or explicit reference is made to it in an SQL statement. In normal use, an INSERT is the first statement issued.

Determining How Often Global Temporary Tables Are Materialized

Global temporary tables are materialized in DSNDB07. If multiple global temporary tables are being continually materialized, you can run into a problem with the performance of all processes using DSNDB07 work files (e.g., sorting). To keep control over DSNDB07, you can monitor this materialization through DB2 traces.

Performance trace class 8, IFCID 311, contains information about global temporary table materialization and cursor processing. Field QW0311CI shows whether an instance of a temporary table was created in a work file. You can also see whether a cursor was opened or closed. This information gives you an idea of the amount of work occurring against the work-file table space for temporary tables.

If you find a lot of activity and feel that it may be causing problems, you can also use the trace fields to determine what queries or programs are causing the materialization:

```
0017 QW0017TT    'TT'=TEMPORARY TABLE SCAN.
```

Declared Temporary Tables

Declared temporary tables complement the features of global temporary tables. These are some of the features of declared temporary tables:

- Not recorded in the DB2 catalog
- Not sharable
- Declared in program code
- Not predefined
- Can be updated
- Can have indexes created on them
- New SQL for declaring in a program

An example of how to define and use a declared temporary table is in figure 14.1.

    Declared temporary tables provide a new way to temporarily hold or sort data. With declared temporary tables, some of the locking DB2 catalog updates, and DB2 restart forward and backward log recovery that are associated with persistent base tables are avoided. Somewhat similar to created temporary tables, which are defined with the CREATE GLOBAL TEMPORARY TABLE statement, declared temporary tables have some of the same characteristics but also have some new attributes, which are described in the following sections.

```
DECLARE GLOBAL TEMPORARY TABLE SESSION.ACCOUNT
      LIKE CLAIMS.ACCOUNT
INSERT INTO SESSION.ACCOUNT
      SELECT * FROM CLAIMS.ACCOUNT
      WHERE ACCOUNT_NUMBERS > :host_var
```

```
DECLARE GLOBAL TEMPORARY TABLE SESSION.ACCOUNT
      AS
      SELECT * FROM CLAIMS.ACCOUNT
      WHERE ACCOUNT_NUMBERS > :host_var
```

Figure 14.1   Declared Temporary Tables

Defining

The description of a declared temporary table is not persistent and is not stored in the DB2 catalog tables. Therefore, a declared temporary table cannot be shared across application processes, and each application process that uses the table can define the table with the same table name but with a unique description. A declared temporary table can have indexes and can be modified by the positioned as well as the searched form of the DELETE and UPDATE statements. Rows of a declared temporary table can be rolled back to the last commit or savepoint. DB2 uses UNDO log records to accomplish this. A declared temporary table does not require an associated cursor declared WITH HOLD to keep its rows across a commit operation. Changes were made to SQL statements, DB2 commands, utilities, and SQL return codes to accommodate these new tables.

Changes to SQL to support declared temporary tables include the new DECLARE GLOBAL TEMPORARY TABLE statement, syntax changes to the CREATE DATABASE, and the ability to reference declared temporary tables in many existing SQL statements.

The DECLARE GLOBAL TEMPORARY TABLE statement defines a temporary table for the current application process and instantiates an empty table for the process.

A database that is defined AS TEMP (a TEMP database) and a table space within that database must be created before a declared temporary table can be defined. Maintenance and structure are similar to using DSNDB07.

The DECLARE GLOBAL TEMPORARY TABLE statement is an executable statement that can be embedded in an application program or issued interactively. It can also be dynamically prepared. It must specify the name of the temporary table. It has an implicit qualifier, SESSION, that can also be specified explicitly.

Referencing

To reference a declared temporary table in any SQL statement other than DECLARE GLOBAL TEMPORARY TABLE, you must qualify the table name with SESSION. You can either specify SESSION explicitly in the table-name reference in SQL statements or use the QUALIFIER bind option to specify SESSION as the qualifier for all SQL statements in the plan or package. (The requirement to use SESSION as the qualifier for declared temporary tables can introduce a release-to-release incompatibility if existing tables are qualified with SESSION.) If SESSION is not the qualifier for the table, DB2 assumes that you are not referring to a declared temporary table. If you use SESSION as the qualifier for a table name but the application process does not include a DECLARE GLOBAL TEMPORARY TABLE statement for the table name, DB2 assumes that you are not referring to a declared temporary table. DB2 resolves such table references to a table whose definition is persistent and appears in the DB2 catalog tables. Any static SQL statement that references a declared temporary table is incrementally bound at run time, because the definition of the declared temporary table does not exist until the DECLARE GLOBAL TEMPORARY TABLE statement is executed in the application process that contains the SQL statements and the definition does not persist after the application process finishes running.

A table space must be created in the TEMP database before a DECLARE GLOBAL TEMPORARY TABLE statement can be issued. DB2 will not implicitly create the table space, so it must be created with the CREATE TABLESPACE statement.

Usage

Let P denote an application process, and let T be a declared temporary table in an application program in P:

- When the program in P issues a DECLARE GLOBAL TEMPORARY TABLE statement, an empty instance of T is created.
- Any program in P can reference T, and any of these references is to that same instance of T. (If a DECLARE GLOBAL TEMPORARY TABLE statement is specified within the SQL procedure language compound statement BEGIN-END, the scope of the declared temporary table is the application process and not the compound statement.) Where remote servers are involved, the reference to T must use the same server connection that was used to declare T, and that server connection must never have been terminated after T was declared there.
- When the connection to the application server where T was declared terminates, T is dropped and its instantiated rows are destroyed.

The following example defines a declared temporary table with column definitions for a consultant ID, rate, rate type, number, and amount.

```
DECLARE GLOBAL TEMPORARY TABLE SESSION.TCONSULT
   (CONSULT_ID  CHAR(6)   NOT NULL,
```

```
RATE        DECIMAL(9, 2),
RATE_TYPE   DECIMAL(9, 2),
NUMBER      DECIMAL(9, 2),
AMOUNT      DECIMAL(9, 2)  )
CCSID EBCDIC
ON COMMIT PRESERVE ROWS;
```

For the next example, assume that base table YLA.CONSTAB exists and that it contains three columns, one of which is an identity column. The following statement declares a temporary table that has the same column names and attributes (including identity attributes) as the base table.

```
DECLARE GLOBAL TEMPORARY TABLE TEMPCONS
    LIKE YLA.CONSTAB
    INCLUDING IDENTITY
    ON COMMIT PRESERVE ROWS;
```

In this example, DB2 uses SESSION as the implicit qualifier for TEMPCONS.

The CREATE DATABASE statement is enhanced to support TEMP as an additional keyword on the AS clause to allow the database to be defined for declared temporary tables only.

```
CREATE DATABASE
. . .
AS WORKFILE
        TEMP FOR member
AS TEMP
```

This syntax indicates that the database is for declared temporary tables only. The AS TEMP syntax must be specified to create a database for declared temporary tables, otherwise the database will not be used for declared temporary tables.

A DB2 subsystem or data sharing member can have only one database defined AS TEMP, the same as with DSNDB07. A TEMP database cannot be shared between DB2 subsystems or data sharing members. A FOR *member-name* syntax specifies the DB2 member for which the database is to be used. If FOR *member-name* is not specified, the database is created for the DB2 subsystem or DB2 member on which the CREATE DATABASE statement is executed.

CHAPTER 15

Enterprise Resource Planning

Y ou may have heard that enterprise resource planning (ERP) applications such as SAP R/3 and PeopleSoft do not perform well on DB2, but you shouldn't believe everything you hear. ERP applications are nothing more than large, complex applications that store their data in a database. It's difficult for any application—especially packaged applications like ERP applications—to perform well on a database without being properly tuned for that environment. For example, although DB2 has a very sophisticated SQL optimizer, it can't solve every SQL access problem or rewrite every query. You also have to adjust both the application and DB2 parameters to take advantage of DB2's service engine and sophisticated caching facilities.

Even organizations that put an effort into tuning ERP applications can sometimes be their own worst enemies. ERP installations' not performing well often results from both difficulties in the delivered application code and inappropriate tuning methods or a lack of tuning altogether. ERP packages come with a fixed set of application modules adjusted by the vendors; problems tend to arise in the customized, user-generated modules that make the application unique to the customer.

Many of the topics and recommendations in this chapter appear elsewhere in more detail in this book but are repeated here for easy reference. References are made to the appropriate chapters so more details can be found if needed.

ERP/DB2 Usage Overview

What is so different about ERP packages that makes them a performance challenge when using DB2 as the database server? From a tuning perspective, there are really only three areas of uniqueness:

1. The number of database objects that an installation comprises
2. The dynamic SQL required to process the data
3. The two and three-tier architecture

In this chapter we look at the challenges and solutions for each area.

Separate DB2 Subsystem

To allow proper horizontal memory expansion in the DB2 subsystem and best support for large ERP applications, it is best to isolate the application in a separate DB2 subsystem.

First of all, just the contention for storage is a good reason for isolation. In DB2 versions earlier than 6, you are limited to 2 GB of virtual memory for the DBM1 address space. ERP applications tend to have a large number of database descriptors that are required to be open at any given time, and this can have a large impact on the usage of the EDM pool and other areas of memory. The EDM pool also has to support the memory required for the dynamic SQL cache. Keep in mind that the dynamic SQL cache is used by all applications for the entire subsystem, so if you are using it for necessary support of ERP applications, other transactions (even those with static SQL) could suffer or have performance problems due to the usage of this area.

The catalog is another shared resource of contention if it is shared with other applications. ERP applications put several thousand objects into the catalog, which can potentially cause problems with other applications, not to mention manageability issues.

ERP applications often require specific DSNZPARMs. These are set at a subsystem level and could have negative effects on other applications. A vast number of tuning issues need to be addressed at the subsystem level, and for that reason it is best to establish ERP applications in their own subsystem. Many of these tuning issues are addressed in more detail in this chapter.

Database Objects

It is not uncommon for a SAP installation to comprise 18,000 objects or more. PeopleSoft Version 7.5 normally comes with five databases. In version 7.0, the HR module alone installs with one database containing 19 table spaces for more than 1,700 tables and 2,700 indexes, and one table space contains more than 400 tables. SAP R/3 comes with more than 100 table spaces in about 100 databases, with each containing more than 100 tables plus associated indexes. Therefore, proper sizing and packaging of these objects are critical for performance, availability, and manageability.

In DB2, a single database does not mean the entire object set but a logical subgrouping of a small number of objects (normally not more than 10 to 20 table spaces per database and, optimally, one database per table space for ultimate flexibility and availability). PeopleSoft recommends using multiple databases, especially for the tables used by the process scheduler; however, you cannot issue any DDL (data definition language) changes to objects in the database while the process scheduler is executing. DBD (database descriptor) locking occurs at the database level, and a single reader of a single table would prevent the changes. The entire DBD is written to the log when any updater makes changes, which can cause significant delays when the log is processed. The size of each DBD is an issue, because the DBD must always be resident in contiguous memory in the EDM pool (until version 6, where it is loaded in 32K pieces). With ERP applications, you should allow one table space per database, which has no negative impact as long as a good naming convention exists. This recommendation assumes that you can tailor the ERP vendor's installation process for table and table-space configurations, which is not always allowed.

Tables and Table Spaces

With more than 13,000 tables to manage, you have to separate them into the correct groups. Each ERP installation's use of data can be different; the logical grouping for one may not be appropriate for the other, and both can differ from the way the package was delivered. Multiple-table table spaces were beginning to disappear from general use but have come back with a vengeance; they require special considerations for tuning, I/O strategies, and manageability. Although multiple-table table spaces are not difficult to implement, there are some guidelines to follow for using them.

Number of pages	Table-space design
> 10,000	Consider partitioning
> 1,000	One-table segmented table space
> 128 but < 1,000	Multiple-table segmented table spaces
< 128	Multiple-table segmented table spaces

About 100 tables should be the maximum in a shared, segmented table space. It is extremely important to make sure that the segment sizes are appropriate for the table grouping. For segment sizing, use the following guidelines:

Number of pages	SEGSIZE
≤ 28	4 to 28, similar to number of pages
> 28 but < 128	32
≥ 128	64

Define segmented groupings carefully, making sure all the tables have the same basic characteristics. PeopleSoft's temporary and work tables have very different characteristics and definitely need to be in their own table spaces, as they generally have from zero to very many rows. You have to manually update catalog statistics for these tables. These statistics should be representative of the data normally contained in the tables, based on the access paths for set retrieval. Many work tables hold data that is transmitted to clients; thus, they tend to be a normal size. The segmented table spaces should be reorganized frequently so that all segments of each table are together. One or more of the segmented table spaces should hold just code, reference, and lookup tables. These tables usually contain a small number of rows and should be placed in a buffer pool together; however, the total number of the pages in the segmented table space should be less than 1,000 to minimize the prefetch activity that occurs on these tables, even when they are not needed. Some users prefer to have one or more buffer pools containing 999 pages or fewer to hold only these tables, minimizing the prefetch to 16 pages. However, the preferred way is to make sure that the buffer pool holds all the pages of these tables by setting VPSEQT to 0 to turn off the prefetch activity and then setting the queuing method to FIFO in version 6 to turn off the overhead for latch management.

Indexes

Then there are the indexes. As delivered, many of the indexes defined in the customized ERP application code in need to be tuned. For example, some indexes don't have all the appropriate columns for the best possible access path selection, and some have columns in the wrong order. You always have to add indexes, matching the way the data is used for a specific installation. Sometimes finding missing indexes takes a serious effort—a problem most ERP purchasers don't expect. Another major area of concern arises when users define reporting processes by using generation features. Often, there are no indexes to drive the access path over complex joins, which results in many Cartesian joins. Solving this problem requires working with end users and making sure the appropriate indexes have been defined.

Primary and Clustering Index

You should never change the primary index for ERP tables. ERP packages do not use DB2-enforced RI (declarative RI), and changing the index could affect the integrity and uniqueness of the data, since the primary index is usually the unique index providing entity integrity.

The clustering index also needs to be carefully evaluated. Often the clustering index is the primary index as shipped. However, this may not be the most efficient choice of a clustering index. The packages are kept somewhat generic for multiple DBMSs and the different DBMSs have different definitions of how data gets clustered. You want your clustering index to be an index to support such operations as range retrieval. By being selective about which indexes are defined as the clustering index, many ERP users have seen significant reductions in I/O and elapsed time for batch processes.

Index-Only Access of VARCHAR Columns

Because of the heavy usage of VARCHAR columns by ERP applications, DB2 added support (late in version 5) for index-only access of variable-length columns, which was not previously possible because the index manager does not include the length of the columns in the index key for VARCHAR columns. Earlier versions of DB2 therefore needed to go to a data page to fetch the actual size. Now there is a new subsystem parameter to return data from the index and pad it with the blanks to the maximum column length. This allows DB2 to return data using only the index. This new DSNZPARM is RETVLCFK=YES. If you choose to turn this on, you must rebind your programs. Also, keep in mind that host variables have original data and are padded with blanks to the maximum length.

Deferring Object Definition

A new feature came out with the refresh of version 6 to allow the deferral of data set creation for table spaces and indexes. In large software packages such as SAP or People-Soft, almost two thirds of the data sets provided with the product often remain empty. In the past, all data sets had to be defined, because all the tables and indexes had to be defined, even though many would not be used. Now we have the ability to defer the definition of these data sets to provide faster installs and make data set management much simpler.

Dynamic SQL

ERP brings with it another problem: dynamic SQL. In fact, most ERP tuning deals with SQL problems; unfortunately, these problems are different for each ERP system. Because ERP systems can be defined with different sets of processing strategies and business rules, much of the SQL (delivered and generated as dynamic SQL) is different from installation to installation. While dynamic SQL itself is not a problem, repetitive use of the same statement can be. Dynamic SQL construction can vary, with different performance impacts. Following are some suggestions for improvements.

Dynamic SQL Cache

The use of the dynamic SQL cache is a primary source of ERP performance benefits. When caching dynamic SQL statements, DB2 first checks the cache when the next dynamic SQL statement is issued. If found, the statement can be reused without the application incurring the overhead of a redundant PREPARE. By using dynamic SQL caching, SAP queries can experience up to 80% CPU reduction. Caching works more thoroughly for SAP than for PeopleSoft, because SAP uses bind variables substituted at execution time, whereas PeopleSoft uses both literals (in most online modules) and bind variables (in batch processes). When using different literals in the same SQL statement coming from different application modules, the match fails, and the statement has to be prepared again. PeopleSoft is addressing this issue: in version 7.5, most generated code will use bind variables, resulting in an estimated 30% to 50% CPU reduction in online modules.

When using SQL caching, the EDM pool needs to be adjusted to allow reuse. Because the cache uses an LRU algorithm, pages on the bottom of the queue can be stolen to make room for new skeleton packages before they can be reused. The cache for dynamic statements is not backed up on DASD as the normal EDM pool entries are; when the same SQL statement is issued again, it has to be prepared again. New instrumentation has been added to DB2 to facilitate the monitoring and tuning of the cache by providing EDM pool statistics for pages used for cached statements, statement cache searches, and cache statements inserted.

Statistics are available for successful and unsuccessful cache searches. In addition, two IFCIDs show statistics for all statements in the cache (sorted by highest values): the number of executions, total CPU time, and much more. It is possible to tune the cache effectively no matter which ERP application you use.

There is one caveat to using caching and bind variables: if literals were used previously and the data is skewed or contains outliers, the same access paths are chosen, regardless of the filtering when bind variables are used. In PeopleSoft 7.5, if literals were used previously, different access paths could be chosen, but not when bind variables are reused. In such cases, you should change the code to move the offending SQL statement into a separate package and bind that package with REOPT(VARS), which restores the benefit of potentially different access paths at execution time. Many performance improvements were made to dynamic SQL caching, including the ability to flush the cache when RUNSTATS is executed.

SQL and Optimization

Tuning SQL queries may require adding or changing indexes, adjusting the column sizes in some of the tables, and rewriting the queries. Queries that were part of the customized code, generated queries, and user-written queries often need serious tuning. In many cases in which programs are generated onsite, joins are produced without join columns, causing Cartesian joins. These queries have to be changed to add the appropriate columns. If queries are generated that exceed the allowable number of tables in an SQL statement, you have to manually change these by using intermediate global temporary tables to hold the results of part of the statements and combine those global temporary tables to get under the limit. Sometimes generated queries, especially in the reporting areas, generate table joins of more than 15 tables, the limit in DB2 through version 5. In the version 6 refresh, you can have up to 225 tables in an SQL statement and more than 15 tables in a join.

Often, SQL queries in ERP applications end up having join columns of unequal lengths—for example, joining a CHAR (5) column in one table with a CHAR (8) column in another—especially in the facilities that generate report processes. Since the column lengths are unequal, DB2 cannot use indexes to drive the join processing and must use expensive table-space scans and inappropriate join methods (sorting and merging large amounts of data). When columns are used in this fashion (common in PeopleSoft), these column definitions should be changed. However, when new releases are installed, the definitions have to be redone. To alleviate this problem DB2 version 6 supports indexes for joins of unequal lengths.

The CASE expression is seldom seen in delivered code and never seen in generated SQL in ERP modules. More common, especially in customized and user-generated ERP code, are UNION statements that can be rewritten using the CASE expression. If a five-block UNION statement can be collapsed into a single-block statement using CASE, the reduction in elapsed and CPU time is around 80%. You should examine all UNION statements to determine whether they can be replaced by a CASE expression or outer joins. Performance enhancements for outer joins in the supplemental releases of DB2 Version 5 and in the base product of Version 6 show an improvement of up to 17 times in both CPU and elapsed time. Following is a multiple-block UNION statement that is improved by rewriting as a CASE statement (figure 15.1).

```
SELECT SUM(AMOUNT) AS TOT1 , 0, 0, 0, 0
    FROM TABLE_1 T1, TABLE_2 T2,
         TABLE_3 T3, TABLE_4 T4
WHERE T1.COL1 = T2.COL2
  AND T1.COL1 = T3.COL3
  AND T1.COL2 = T4.COL4
  AND T1.COLX IN ('X', 'Y', 'Z')
UNION ALL
SELECT 0, SUM(AMOUNT) AS TOT2 , 0, 0, 0
    FROM TABLE_1 T1, TABLE_2 T2,
         TABLE_3 T3, TABLE_4 T4
WHERE T1.COL1 = T2.COL2
  AND T1.COL1 = T3.COL3
```

```
   AND T1.COL2 = T4.COL4
   AND T1.COLX IN ('A', 'B', 'C')
UNION ALL
SELECT 0, 0, SUM(AMOUNT) AS TOT3,  0, 0
   FROM TABLE_1 T1, TABLE_2 T2,
        TABLE_3 T3, TABLE_4 T4
WHERE T1.COL1 = T2.COL2
  AND T1.COL1 = T3.COL3
  AND T1.COL2 = T4.COL4
  AND T1.COLX IN ('E', 'F', 'G')
UNION ALL
SELECT 0, 0, 0, SUM(AMOUNT) AS TOT4,  0
   FROM TABLE_1 T1, TABLE_2 T2,
        TABLE_3 T3, TABLE_4 T4
WHERE T1.COL1 = T2.COL2
  AND T1.COL1 = T3.COL3
  AND T1.COL2 = T4.COL4
  AND T1.COLX IN  ('Q', 'R', 'S')
UNION ALL
SELECT  0, 0, 0, 0, SUM(AMOUNT) AS TOT5
   FROM TABLE_1 T1, TABLE_2 T2,
        TABLE_3 T3, TABLE_4 T4
WHERE T1.COL1 = T2.COL2
  AND T1.COL1 = T3.COL3
  AND T1.COL2 = T4.COL4
  AND T1.COLX IN ('T', 'U', 'V')
ORDER BY 2, 4, 3
```

Here is the same task rewritten as a more efficient CASE statement:

```
SELECT
   SUM(CASE WHEN T1.COLX='X' OR T1.COLX='Y'...)
      THEN AMOUNT END)
  ,SUM(CASE WHEN T1.COLX='A' OR T1.COLX='B'...)
      THEN AMOUNT END)
  ,SUM(CASE WHEN T1.COLX='E' OR T1.COLX='F'...)
      THEN AMOUNT END)
  ,SUM(CASE WHEN T1.COLX='Q' OR T1.COLX='R'...)
      THEN AMOUNT END)
```

```
  ,SUM(CASE WHEN T1.COLX='T' OR T1.COLX='U'...)
       THEN AMOUNT END)
    FROM TABLE_1 T1, TABLE_2 T2,
        TABLE_3 T3, TABLE_4 T4
WHERE T1.COL1 = T2.COL2
  AND T1.COL1 = T3.COL3
  AND T1.COL2 = T4.COL4
  AND T1.COLX IN ('A', 'B', 'C','E', 'F', 'G',
    'Q', 'R', 'S','T', 'U', 'V','X', 'Y', 'Z')
ORDER BY 2, 4, 3
```

Key Correlation Statistics

Version 5 introduced key correlation statistics to provide the DB2 the ability to gather statistics when one column's value is related to the value of another column. Previous releases offered only limited information on the FIRSTKEYCARD and FULLKEYCARD columns, and the correlation was on columns for FULLKEYCARD only. This provided no second- or third-key cardinality, and multikey cardinality was considered independently, often leading to inaccurate estimation of filter factors, join size, join sequencing, and join methods and inefficient access path selection.

The new key correlation statistics are collected by RUNSTATS with minimal additional overhead and can provide big CPU and elapsed time reductions through improved cost and resource estimations. These key correlation statistics play a major role in access path selection by providing the optimizer with new columns with information on multicolumn cardinalities and multicolumn frequent values. The new KEYCARD parameter indicates that cardinalities for each column, concatenated with all previous key columns, are to be collected. This gives you the option to build the frequency values for critical concatenated key columns, such as the first, second, and third columns.

Using this parameter is a big help for ERP, because it helps provide the optimizer with better statistics where the cardinality of the first column of the key is rather low. Many organizations have seen better join methods and access paths chosen by the optimizer, overall elapsed time reduced by almost a third, and a significant reduction in both I/O wait time and CPU time.

List Prefetch

Because there is extensive use of list prefetch in the access paths behind ERP SQL, you can improve performance by applying index screening for list prefetch, an enhancement in version 5. You should examine access paths where list prefetch is selected and there is a gap in the number of index columns in the SQL WHERE clause. For example, consider the situation where an index is made up of four columns and only columns 1, 3, and 4 are supplied. Before this enhancement was available, only column 1 was used to select the RIDs for the list prefetch process. With the enhancement, columns 3 and 4 are also checked to eliminate the RIDs prior to the list prefetch process, reducing the load on the RID pool that could cause RID pool failures and other problems and dramatically reducing the overhead of retrieving all those additional rows only to have them filtered out. One little area of concern here that needs to be watched in online applications is when list prefetch is selected due to the significantly reduced number of rows.

Uncommitted Read

Whenever possible, add the isolation level of uncommitted read (UR). Isolation-level UR lets ERP applications avoid unnecessary lock overhead. The most practical use of UR is to retrieve read-only data: the more, the better. Any table that is read-only *at the time the data is selected* should have WITH UR included in the SELECT. Some clients have saved up to 30% of CPU time on long-running queries.

PREPARE and EXECUTE Messages

Implementing two- and three-tier architectures brings about another set of problems. DB2 Connect is used more often now than third-party middleware due to the performance gains realized, for example, less overhead and faster network throughput. However, as with any product, parameters should be adjusted when working with ERP applications.

To collapse PREPARE and EXECUTE messages on the network, and thus reduce network conversations, set the parameter DeferredPrepare to 1 (the default in DB2

Connect Version 5). For additional information on how to reduce network traffic, refer to Chapter 24.

Releasing Locks

In multi-tier environments, locks end up being held by idle active threads or by inactive threads after a commit. In DB2 Connect, you can set the parameter Cursorhold to 0 (not the default), which releases locks at a commit point. Also check the Autocommit parameter, which can vary, depending on the ERP package used. Some ERP packages set Autocommit to 0 to suppress commits between each SQL statement because all commits are explicitly written into the application. In other cases, you need the Autocommit (such as when using the Tuxedo product).

Batch Workload Location

The batch job location can be adjusted for client or server execution. Specifying server execution boosts performance because it eliminates the overhead of communicating across the network with a client.

Row-Level Locks

Avoid row-level locking if possible. Although required in SAP, row-level locking is often used in PeopleSoft to solve what appear to be concurrency problems. However, this approach generally causes more problems than it solves, especially because it can result in an increase in deadlocks by allowing more processes on a single page. For much more information about row-level locking and other locking options, refer to Chapter 13.

Lock Escalation

For many table spaces, it's probably advisable to turn off lock escalation. SAP's cluster table interface can read cluster tables without causing a problem with lock escalation;

however, with other ERP applications, lock escalation is one of the biggest contributors to poor performance. DB2 lets you turn lock escalation off at the table-space level by ALTERing the table-space parameter LOCKMAX to 0 (you also have to be sure that LOCKSIZE is set to PAGE or ROW). This tells DB2 not to escalate a lock to one of higher restriction. Keep in mind, however, that more locks will be held because they will not be given up for a single larger one. You need to monitor the number of locks held on objects and may have to adjust NUMLKTS (locks per table space) accordingly, or else programs will abnormally terminate. Also, you should make use of selective partition locking (SPL). You enable SPL by using the LOCKPART YES parameter in the ALTER or CREATE TABLESPACE statement for a partitioned table space. Doing so allows only the partitions being accessed to be locked instead of all the partitions in the table space. However, in order for SPL to work, certain conditions must be met. For instance, partition-level locking does not work if any of the following conditions are true:

- A type 1 index is used in the access path.
- The plan is bound with ACQUIRE (ALLOCATE).
- The table space was created with LOCKSIZE TABLESPACE.
- LOCK TABLE IN EXCLUSIVE MODE is used without the PART keyword. You can alter this by using the ALTER TABLESPACE parameter. The entire table space must be stopped using the -STOP DATABASE command.

LOGLOAD Monitoring

One DSNZPARM that needs to be evaluated is LOGLOAD, which has to be increased in most cases. By increasing the LOGLOAD parameter, you increase the number of log records written between checkpoints. Make sure that your DB2 subsystem is taking checkpoints every 1 to 30 minutes and that reasonable deferred write thresholds are set on the buffer pools to write out the updated pages and minimize write activity on the checkpoint process buffer. This should remove any performance bottlenecks, which sometimes occur while an application waits for DB2 to take a checkpoint. Even though it's not usually a time-consuming process, the time spent taking checkpoints can add up. The LOGLOAD parameter can be set online, which is especially handy when it is necessary to dynamically change the DB2 checkpoint interval time.

Buffer Pool Tuning

Volumes have been written on buffer pool tuning, and it has never been more important to get it right than with ERP applications (for additional information about buffer pool tuning, refer to Chapter 3, "Memory"). Because ERP applications involve a heavy mix of table spaces that are never used and table spaces that are heavily used, some with random access and others with always sequential access, you should use small, multiple buffer pools to isolate table spaces based on usage types. The basic rules still apply:

1. BP0 for DB2 only
2. BPx for DSNDB07 only, backed up by several large work table spaces
3. BPx+(s) for code, reference, and lookup pools

You should define several buffer pools based solely on object type and object use. Isolate indexes from table spaces and heavy readers from heavy writers. Isolate randomly accessed objects from sequential objects, then adjust all thresholds appropriately. Pay particular attention to the horizontal and vertical deferred-write thresholds. The horizontal threshold should generally be changed from 50% and set precisely at a percentage point representing a number of pages, generally lower for minimal reference of updated pages and higher for frequent reference of updated pages. The same rule applies to the vertical threshold, except that it should be set at 0 when there are fewer than 10 pages written per I/O and in the 5% range in most other cases. These suggestions are guidelines for starting the buffer pool strategy; you should always monitor and adjust these thresholds as the functions go into full production with full system loads.

Keep the DB2 Catalog Clean

With the large number of objects associated with ERP packages, you should maintain the DB2 catalog and keep it clean and orderly. Keep unused objects out, and keep the catalog reorganized. Some SAP and PeopleSoft shops have seen between 10% and 12% reduction in I/O times and 11% to 14% reduction in elapsed time for transactions just by reorganizing the DB2 catalog. In some cases where the catalog was very fragmented, there was a 50% reduction in I/O to the catalog after a reorganization.

DB2 as an ASCII Server

DB2 can be used as a server for ASCII data. Normally, everything in OS/390 is designed to be in EBCDIC format. However, enhancements were made to DB2 to support ASCII so that DB2 could be used as a server for large ERP packages, such as SAP, PeopleSoft, and Baan.

The ASCII support was specially designed so that translation does not need to be performed when the data is transported into an ASCII environment, such as UNIX. When DB2 is used by a UNIX application server (such as the SAP implementation), no DB2 connect is involved. DB2 on OS/390 has to be regarded as a database server for the UNIX application, and translation to EBCDIC would be pointless.

Be aware that ASCII and EBCDIC data cannot be used together in the same SQL statement. If joins are required between an ASCII support table and both ASCII tables and EBCDIC tables, two copies must be maintained. This is necessary with some code, control, and reference tables.

Conclusion

In essence, tuning ERP applications for optimal performance is no different from DB2 tuning as usual. However, it is more critical with these complex applications that tuning be done and be done correctly. Many new options in DB2 maximize ERP performance. (For the latest in the refresh of version 6 and a look at version 7, refer to Chapter 11.) It is important to stay current on maintenance and apply any supplemental enhancements to the base product, because many enhancements are made specifically for ERP product performance and manageability.

SQL and Advanced Function Tuning

SQL

Triggers and User-Defined Functions

LOBs and Extenders

Stored Procedures

REXX, Java, and SQL Procedure Language

Parallelism

Predictive Analysis, governing and Tuning

Influencing the Optimizer

E-Business, the Web, and Networks

## CHAPTER 16

SQL

A good portion of Chapter 2, "CPU," discussed several situations that would lead to reductions in resource usage. A large portion of the discussion was of the serious CPU consumption by SQL when used inappropriately. Numerous issues regarding SQL fall into basically two areas. One situation is where SQL is not performing up to the levels required. The second situation is very simply the failure to do the work in DB2 and instead just using DB2 as a service layer to pass data unnecessarily back to the program. Even as this book went to publication, we just heard the statement made by a group setting standards at a client site that "DB2 just can't do joins efficiently," which is a 15-year-old myth.

We have seen standards that say to keep the SQL simple so it is easy to understand. Well, no one really does this with program code, not if they want very high performance, and the same is true of SQL. There are only a few major constructs that can be used in SQL, which represent the building blocks for larger SQL statements. We have been teaching basic SQL, advanced and complex SQL, and SQL tuning seminars for years and have learned one very important thing. SQL can be written just like any other language, if the individual pieces are seen as building blocks and if the statement is built from the bottom up. Also, after this technique has been learned, anyone can see and understand what any other SQL statement is doing, even when they know nothing about the objects and the data. The bottom line is that if we can do the work inside DB2, if we ask DB2 to return just the data we want, transformed or otherwise, DB2 can generally do it faster and better than program code.

This chapter should assist in clearing up some of the SQL inconsistencies we see in practice and set some good guidelines for better use. We also show you some techniques for writing SQL that you may not have seen before: processes that DB2 can do with SQL that, unless you have seen them, you would not believe could be done with SQL. DB2 many times also rewrites the SQL to make it perform better.

The generally accepted guideline is to make sure that the SQL query is coded as simply and efficiently as possible. However, that does not mean to write simple SQL, but rather to code the SQL as efficiently as possible. There is a big difference. SQL is not just another way to issue unit-record I/O. However, it is often not only written that way, but hidden inside I/O layers to "remove the complexity of SQL" from the programmers. Myths and more myths permeate the area of SQL performance.

> *Note: Please be aware that the actual SQL techniques, and all supporting information in this chapter are subject to change by a new version of DB2, a new release, or normal maintenance. Also, not everything works the same way in every situation.*

Other chapters further enhance the information discussed here. Chapter 21 on parallelism has information on parallel access path selection. The section in Chapter 22 on EXPLAIN digs deeply into the knowledge required for and how to use EXPLAIN and the information it provides to tune SQL. Chapter 23 is on the optimizer and how you can influence access path direction through techniques in SQL and catalog statistics.

DB2 SQL Engine Review

In figure 16.1, we have simplified the internal processing of SQL by DB2. All the names should be familiar, except that sometimes there is a misunderstanding about sargable (stage 1) and non-sargable (stage 2) predicates and processing, which we will examine. The flow of the diagram shows that a program retrieves its access path decisions (bound and optimized in advance), requiring access to the directory and the catalog. The executing program issues SQL, and this is the major performance consideration in this section. All the processing on behalf of the SQL occurs in either the stage 1 or stage 2 areas. The query actually coming from the process first passes through the stage 2 area, where many things occur that are well documented and fairly static but have nothing to do at this time with what is called stage 2 predicate processing. Any performance improvements here

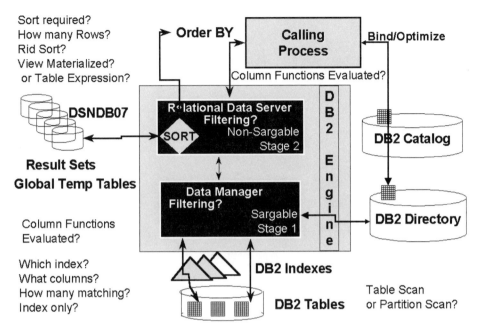

Figure 16.1   DB2 SQL Engine

would be from the construction of the SQL components for the access paths, access to the directory, and the building of the skeleton plan and packages section in the EDM pool, for example. The path from here proceeds to stage 1, where what occurs needs to be very precise and directed. In Chapter 2 on CPU tuning, we discussed all the negatives of asking for too much data not only to be brought into the buffers, but to be passed back through the system cross-memory to the application program.

The sargable stage 1 is also called the data manager, since really no relational set processing happens at this time, just raw data access and filtering. Data has been brought into the buffer pool from either the table spaces or index spaces, so that table data and index data are in the pool as required. The important application tuning question is, How exactly was the data brought in to the engine's buffers? The critical questions are noted on the figure:

- Were indexes used?
- Was list prefetch used?
- Were all the columns in the index correct?
- How many of the columns were matched?

- If fewer than all the columns were matched, did we have cardinality statistics on the subset?
- Was index-only access used, or should it have been used?
- Were column functions evaluated in stage 1 or stage 2 or otherwise? Could they have been evaluated during data retrieval?
- Is an ORDER BY being matched by an index, or does it require a sort?
- How many rows are being passed to stage 2 from stage 1?
- Is a view used and materialized?
- Is a table expression used and materialized?
- Is everything possible done to the data before returning it to the program?

This all comes down to a very simple guideline: you should be as selective as possible, via index access, to stage only the data that might actually contain rows needed by the application. If you are as specific as possible, the best access path will most likely be chosen by the optimizer's algorithms. A simple example is where the SQL very specifically identifies a successive series of random rows, but always sequentially forward in ascending sequence. DB2 in its evaluation of the random access path saw that by turning on dynamic sequential prefetch, it could actually improve performance by staging more data than would be used but retrieving this data in a way to minimize the I/O overhead.

After index or data has been retrieved, you should filter the data as much as possible through the application of stage 1 predicates. This is an area of some difficulty, since more predicates are pushed down to stage 1 with each release of DB2, but just because a predicate is potentially indexable in stage 1 does not mean that it is always going to be processed at stage 1. This analysis must be done and is discussed at length in Chapter 22, "Predictive Analysis, Governing and Tuning."

Any filtering that cannot be done in stage 1 is performed in stage 2, the relational data server layer. Stage 2 evaluates all predicates not evaluated in stage 1, such as scalar functions, aggregates, sorting, and others. Here we are concerned with the rest of the filtering and the final building of the results to be sent to the program. Quite often, a lot of the processing done in stage 2, the stage 2 predicate processing, could have been done in stage 1 if the SQL were coded differently. More often, no processing is done in stage 2, and all the data is sent to the program.

In figure 16.2, we have again simplified the internal processing of SQL by DB2, but this figure should demonstrate a few more items. Quite often the circles of inadequate pro-

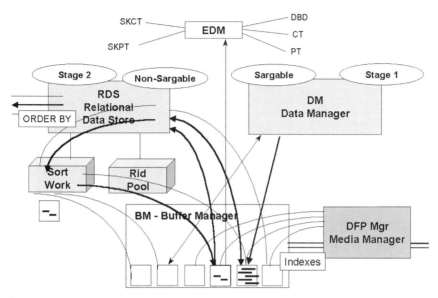

Figure 16.2   Program Execution

cessing never get demonstrated. But let's assume for a minute that there is a simple ORDER BY in the SQL, and for any number of reasons it has to be processed as a SORT. The flow in figure 16.2 shows that it is quite possible for the data to move from the buffer pool to stage 2, where a sort is initiated. But again, for any number of reasons, there is simply not enough room in the sort work area for the sort to complete. So the sort runs (see Chapter 3, "Memory") overflow into the buffer pool designated for DSNDB07. But this is not the end of the story. DSNDB07's buffer pool is very active and threshold dependent, and some of these pages that hold the sort runs are externalized to disk and stolen for other activity. As the sort progresses, there have to be sort mergers, which require data in sort runs that are no longer in memory in the buffer pool. So additional I/O is required to retrieve those pages from the work table spaces and bring the rows being sorted back to the sort pool for the mergers. A fine balancing act always has to be managed between all the resources in DB2. Here we are faced with memory definitions for the sort pool and the buffer pools, the thresholds in the buffer pools, the number of columns in the ORDER BY, and the number of columns in the SELECT list. Tuning all these areas is necessary for a balanced system and high performance.

General Recommendations

Genericness is counter to performance.
Specificity and granularity yield performance.

The following guidelines for the construction of SQL queries always apply when performance is a consideration. The list is by no means complete but does set the tone and method for tuning SQL. The list can be summarized as bringing only the absolute minimum amount of data into the DB2 engine, filtering out all the nonqualifying data, and returning only the absolute minimum amount of data to the application. Do the processing in the fewest number of specific functional SQL statements, and do as much of the processing as possible in the SQL statement, not the program code. These guidelines allow the SQL to complete with the least amount of resource consumption:

- Retrieve the fewest number of rows
- Retrieve only the columns needed by the program
- Reduce the number of SQL statements
- Code predicates based on selectivity
- Use stage 1 predicates
- Never use generic SQL statements
- Avoid unnecessary sorts
- Sort only truly necessary columns
- Use the ON clause for all join predicates
- Avoid UNIONs
- Use joins instead of subqueries
- Code the most selective predicates first
- Use the proper method for existence checking
- Avoid unnecessary materialization

Retrieve the Fewest Rows

The only rows of data returned to the application should be those actually needed for the process and nothing else. We should never find a data-filtering statement in a program, as DB2 should handle all filtering of rows. Whenever a process needs to be performed on the data and where the process is done, in the program or in DB2, must be decided, leave it in DB2. There will always be that rare situation when all the data needs to be brought to the application, filtered, transformed, and processed. However, this is generally due to an inadequacy somewhere else in the design, normally a shortcoming in the physical design, missing indexes, or some other implementation problem. During many application performance audits, we have found the problem not to be the SQL itself, but the guidelines and often the myths in practice. Two very simple examples (figures 16.3 and 16.4) show this problem of program code versus DB2 SQL dramatically. These are both examples where an existing system was reengineered in DB2. Similarly flawed code is not uncommon from code generators also.

Retrieve Only the Columns Needed

At some point, most of us have seen the following type of SQL statement:

```
SELECT ACCT_NO, NAME, BALANCE
FROM CUSTOMERS
WHERE ACCT_NO = :hv
```

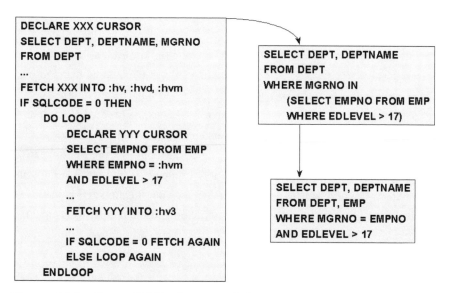

Figure 16.3   Cursor Within Cursor to Subquery to Join

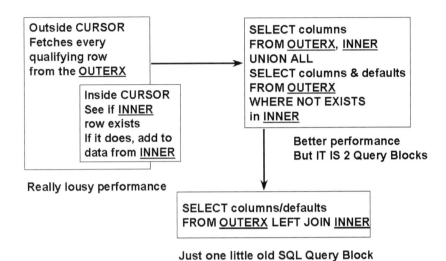

Figure 16.4   Cursor Within Cursor to UNION to OUTER Join

which should have been

```
SELECT NAME, BALANCE
FROM CUSTOMERS
WHERE ACCT_NO = :hv
```

There is simply no reason to retrieve the ACCT_NO, since it is known. The access path is based on the predicates. Retrieving the extra column results in the column being moved from the page in the buffer pool to a user work area, passed to stage 2, and returned cross-memory to the program's work area. That is an unnecessary expenditure of CPU. In this case, it is only one row probably, right? But how many transactions and how many times a day? As with all SQL, the damage is not the single statement, but the multiplicative effect. If this type of extra column selection occurs in statements that retrieve multiple rows, as in the case of a child table to a customer table, then the situation gets worse.

Often it is stated that the result set must be ordered and the column is needed for selection of the proper indexes. The following SQL statement shows how a simple statement and indexes can lead to different solutions:

```
SELECT AC.ACCT_NO, AR.INV_NO, IV.INV_AMOUNT, IT.ITEM_NO,
  IT.ITEM_DESC, IT.ITEM_COST
```

```
FROM
   ACCOUNTS AC, RECEIVABLES AR, INVOICES IV, ITEMS IT
WHERE AC.ACCT_NO = :value
AND AC.ACCT_NO = AR.ACCT_NO
AND AR.INV_NO = IV.INV_NO
AND IV.ITEM_NO = IT.ITEM_NO
ORDER BY
   AC.ACCT_NO, AR.INV_NO, IV.ITEM_NO
```

There is no single interpretation of what can happen, but many interpretations. The query is isolated to a single account number, so it is possible that the ACCT_NO in the select line is not needed and that the ACCT_NO in the ORDER BY is causing sort problems. This is a four-table join, so the chance that the ACCT_NO in the ORDER BY is required for proper selection of indexes to avoid sorting is extremely unlikely. The query might be coded better as follows:

```
SELECT AR.ACCT_NO, AR.INV_NO, IV.INV_AMOUNT, IT.ITEM_NO,
   IT.ITEM_DESC, IT.ITEM_COST
FROM
   RECEIVABLES AR, INVOICES IV, ITEMS IT
WHERE AR.ACCT_NO = :value
AND AR.INV_NO = IV.INV_NO
AND IV.ITEM_NO = IT.ITEM_NO
ORDER BY
   AR.ACCT_NO, AR.INV_NO, IT.ITEM_NO
```

The result set is the same as the first query, but it is coded entirely differently. The accounts table is not even used, and the relationship from the account table to the item table is not run, unlike the code a couple of commonly used code generators might have generated. We have a three-table join instead of a four-table join. There are simply too many variables to try to figure out all possibilities, but it is possible that the following query might work even better.

```
SELECT IV.INV_NO, IV.INV_AMOUNT, IT.ITEM_NO,
   IT.ITEM_DESC, IT.ITEM_COST
FROM
   RECEIVABLES AR, INVOICES IV, ITEMS IT
WHERE AR.ACCT_NO = :value
```

```
AND AR.INV_NO = IV.INV_NO
AND IV.ITEM_NO = IT.ITEM_NO
ORDER BY
  IV.INV_NO, IV.ITEM_NO
```

Here the account number has been removed from the SELECT, since we already have the value in the host variable. Many rows will definitely be returned, so removing the account number reduces substantially the overhead for the query. Also, there are only two columns now in the sort key instead of three, and only five columns instead of six in the sort row. That definitely reduces the sort memory requirements and quite probably the buffer pool requirements and potential I/O behind the buffer pool. It might also let the sort complete in the sort pool alone, whereas the first example might not. A single row in the receivables table could have multiple invoices associated to it in this particular example, so the number of rows returned could be significant. Here we have taken a very simple query, made it simpler, and removed a large portion of the overhead of the statement, returning only what is absolutely necessary and retrieving only the rows from the necessary tables. In trying to reduce overhead by applying the rule to retrieve only the necessary columns, we have totally rewritten the statement. This same approach needs to be taken with any SQL statement.

Reduce the Number of SQL Statements

Each SQL statement is a programmatic call to the DB2 subsystem that incurs fixed overhead for each call. The amount of overhead is related to the type of SQL statement; the following table is based on figures published by Akira Shibamiya of IBM and research done by Michael Hannan from Australia:

SQL type	SQL cost	Additional CICS cost	Other factors
OPEN and CLOSE together	0.33 ms	Task switch +0.4 ms	
FETCH	0.12 ms	Task switch +0.2 ms	Plus column overheads, class 2 accounting, and more
Singleton SELECT	0.11 ms plus all the same overhead as for FETCH	Task switch +0.2 ms	

These costs were based on a model of a 3090-180J and need to be adjusted for your particular environment. The issue is not the milliseconds but the fact that redundant or unnecessary SQL accumulates overhead.

The two most prominent wasteful scenarios are issuing repetitive, unnecessary SQL statements and issuing the same SQL statement repetitively.

The first case is the "Have you seen Jones?" scenario, where repetitive SQL statements are issued for the same row but different columns each time. Correcting this is not as simple as it might seem. Let's use a pseudocode example:

```
SELECT Jones's name and address
Do some work
If we are done with Jones, then leave
Else SELECT Jones's phones, birthday
Do some work
If we are done with Jones, then leave
Else SELECT Jones's nickname, alias, email id
If we are done with Jones, then leave
Else . . .
```

The quick and dirty solution is too simple and is not the correct approach either:

```
SELECT Jones's name, address, phones, birthday, nickname, alias,
email id, etc.
```

The real problem belongs with the percentage of processing at each level. For example, if the fall-through to the second SELECT occurs only 10% of the time, then all those columns are retrieved for no reason 90% of the time. If the query is issued only once per performance time period, that would be acceptable. However, if it is a frequently occurring transaction, you have a problem.

If the normal process falls through all the functions most of the time, the SQL needs to be collapsed into one call that retrieves all the columns. This strategy illustrates the point that genericness is counter to performance, whereas specificity and granularity yield performance.

Sometimes it is not intuitively obvious where the redundancy is occurring. The following example was uncovered during a performance review. There is absolutely nothing wrong with the SQL, but it is a classic case of what we call "cut and paste" SQL, which generally leads to disaster somewhere down the line. In this case, there were three cursors in the program, each one built from a "cut and paste" of the original. Each cursor was built to return a different result set based on a different rule set. The SQL from these three cursors has been collapsed and modified into individual SQL SELECT statements to make it easier to demonstrate. In each one of the following, notice that there are two things that change in each statement: the rule set in the WHERE clause and the host variable that receives the answer.

SELECT Statement 1

```
SELECT SUM(CUMQT) INTO :WS-CAT-ONE
FROM LEDGER
WHERE ITEM_TYPE = :WS-ITEM-TYPE
AND ITEM_AMOUNT_CLASS = :WS-AMOUNT_CLASS
AND GROUP_NUM = :WS-GROUP-NUM
AND ITEM_YEAR = :WS-ITEM-YEAR
AND TRAN_CODE IN (208,400,434,441)

AND TRANSACTION_DATE  =
     (SELECT MAX(TRANSACTION_DATE)
      FROM LEDGER)
```

SELECT Statement 2

```
SELECT SUM(CUMQT) INTO :WS-CAT-TWO
FROM LEDGER
WHERE ITEM_TYPE = :WS-ITEM-TYPE
AND ITEM_AMOUNT_CLASS =:WS-AMOUNT_CLASS
AND GROUP_NUM =:WS-GROUP-NUM
AND ITEM_YEAR =:WS-ITEM-YEAR
AND TRAN_CODE IN (210,211,221,223,224,225)
AND TRANSACTION_DATE  =
     (SELECT MAX(TRANSACTION_DATE)
      FROM LEDGER)
```

SELECT Statement 3

```
SELECT SUM(CUMQT) INTO :WS-CAT-THREE
FROM LEDGER
WHERE ITEM_TYPE = :WS-ITEM-TYPE
AND ITEM_AMOUNT_CLASS = :WS-AMOUNT_CLASS
```

```
AND GROUP_NUM = :WS-GROUP-NUM
AND ITEM_YEAR = :WS-ITEM-YEAR
AND TRAN_CODE IN (034,100,104,105,106,332,334,341)
AND TRANSACTION_DATE  =
    (SELECT MAX(TRANSACTION_DATE)
    FROM LEDGER)
```

The improvement in performance comes from collapsing the repetitive SQL statements into a single statement (cursor), thus collapsing three passes of a table into a single pass of the table. The following SQL is the result of the collapse.

Three SELECT Statements Collapsed

```
SELECT SUM(CASE WHEN TRAN_CODE = 034 OR ... = 341
           THEN CUMQT END)
     , SUM(CASE WHEN TRAN_CODE = 208 OR ... = 441
           THEN CUMQT END)
     , SUM(CASE WHEN TRAN_CODE = 210 OR ... = 225
           THEN CUMQT END)
INTO :WS-CAT-ONE, :WS-CAT-TWO, :WS-CAT-THREE
FROM LEDGER
WHERE ITEM_TYPE = :WS-ITEM_TYPE
AND ITEM_AMOUNT_CLASS = :WS-AMOUNT-CLASS
AND GROUP_NUM = :WS-GROUP_NUM
AND ITEM_YEAR = :WS-ITEM-YEAR
AND TRAN_CODE IN (208,400,434,441,210,211,221,
                  223,224,225,034,100,104,
                  105,106,332,334,341)
AND TRANSACTION_DATE =
    (SELECT  MAX(TRANSACTION_DATE)
   FROM LEDGER)
```

Repetitive SQL statements are not just too many SQL statements or redundant SQL statements within a process, but the same statement issued repetitively simply because the process is issued repetitively. Take, for example, frequently occurring OLTP transactions that run in a daily system. The first thing the transactions do is to issue SQL statements to get the current date, two million times a day. Imagine the CPU savings if two million calls can be removed each online day. This performance pressure point can return substantial resources to the application to enable it to do more work. Even if this is a 24 × 7 system, there are ways to control the repetitive nature of this type of SQL. The basic rules need to be followed when writing any kind of code, including SQL:

- Make it work.
- Make it work right.
- Make it work fast.

Standards in place at some companies never allow singleton SQL statements and insist that everything be done with cursors. From the table at the beginning of this section, you can just add up the costs of using a cursor when only 0 or 1 row is possible for a rule set. For example,

```
OPEN CURSOR x;
FETCH FROM x;
CLOSE CURSOR x;
```

versus

```
SELECT FROM table;
```

In both cases, a cursor is used, but in the second, the cursor is built, opened, and closed inside DB2 without the costs of the cross-memory call and the associated entry and exit code length. Whenever only 0 or 1 row can be returned from the SQL, it should never be coded in a cursor unless it violates one of the other rules. In an OLTP transaction that is frequently executed, the unnecessary overhead becomes very significant. Quite often, all these SQL statements are simply looked at as "no big deal," but it is not the statement, but the number of times it is executed, that can be problematic.

A singleton SQL statement should be used when

- 0 or 1 row is normally returned,
- there is no possibility of an SQLCODE of –811, and
- there is no unnecessary overhead (prefetch staging, etc.).

One other frequently occurring case needs to be mentioned here. If an OLTP transaction contains many SQL statements, it incurs task switch overhead for every one of these calls. It is better for improved performance to put all the work in a DB2 stored procedure, incur the task switch overhead just once, and let the stored procedure handle all the work. Always look for a method of reducing the overhead and consolidating the work.

Quite often some OLTP transactions that have many SQL statements can be combined in a join, inner or outer, which not only works inside DB2 with less overhead, but also reduces the task switch and SQL statement overhead in the transaction.

Code Predicates Based on Selectivity

Many times we have seen the guideline to just write the SQL and let DB2 worry about it. This basically ignores the performance design of the SQL. When you are concerned with high performance, you must design performance into the SQL statement. Take, for example, the three statements in figure 16.5, which all return the same answer. The subqueries and the joins determine the selectivity of the rows for the answer. While this is an extreme example, it points out the difficult of SQL coding when it comes to performance. First, most of the time there is one attempt at the SQL, which follows the philosophy of "get it through the precompiler, and if it returns data, move it to production." Project time lines often dictate this kind of philosophical coding method. But if you look hard at those three

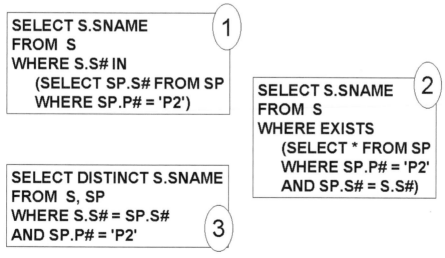

```
SELECT S.SNAME          1
FROM  S
WHERE S.S# IN
    (SELECT SP.S# FROM SP
    WHERE SP.P# = 'P2')
```

```
SELECT S.SNAME          2
FROM  S
WHERE EXISTS
    (SELECT * FROM SP
    WHERE SP.P# = 'P2'
    AND SP.S# = S.S#)
```

```
SELECT DISTINCT S.SNAME
FROM  S, SP
WHERE S.S# = SP.S#
AND SP.P# = 'P2'        3
```

Figure 16.5 Same simple query written 3 ways

examples in figure 16.5, it is incredibly difficult to tell which one will do the best filtering with the least overhead. If you stick to one single release of DB2 and fully analyze these examples as described in Chapter 22, maybe you would end up with the best-performing statement. But within those three statements, the optimizer's techniques have changed a significant number of times over the last few releases and versions of DB2. We cannot say which one would work best, since we don't know what indexes are in place, we don't know the cardinality of the data, we don't know the optimization techniques that will be invoked, and in fact, we don't know anything other than that the answer would be the same in each case, and that is not enough.

As a gentle proof of what we are saying, major new optimization techniques (for possibly processing the noncorrelated IN subquery more or less the same way as an IN list) introduced in DB2 Version 6 could apply to statement 1. In fact, if DB2 could perform this optimization, then the subquery would be executed at cursor OPEN time, and matching the outer query block would be delayed until the FETCH was performed. DB2 almost rewrites this as if it were a partially delayed type of nested loop join. In statement 2, if the proper indexes were in place, rather than comparing the data from the outermost query block to the subquery, a simple existence check could be performed against the subquery, returning a quick true or false. In statement 3, we are using a join, which generally outperforms all other types of processing, but it would depend on the selectivity of the filtering and the cardinality of the data. So which one works best? We truly don't know, and that is why we need to write all SQL many ways, analyzing it by the data content and business rules.

What we can never afford to do is to grab the data and then filter it further in the application code. In the SQL, we need to apply every possible filtering technique at the lowest level of optimization. Most of the other guidelines are enhancements of this general philosophy. It would be wise at this juncture to explain exactly how DB2 processes predicates. There are two sets of rules used to determine the order of predicate evaluation.

How DB2 Applies SQL Predicates

    I. Indexable predicates are applied first.

        A. Matching predicates on index key columns are evaluated when the index is accessed.

            1. All equal predicates and IN list of one value

2. All range predicates and column IS NOT NULL

3. All other predicate types

B. Index screening is performed.

1. All equal predicates and IN list of one value

2. All range predicates and column IS NOT NULL

3. All other predicate types

II. Other stage 1 data predicates are applied next, evaluated after data page access.

A. All equal predicates and IN list of one value

B. All range predicates and column IS NOT NULL

C. All other predicate types

III. The stage 2 predicates are applied on the returned data rows.

A. All equal predicates and IN list of one value

B. All range predicates and column IS NOT NULL

C. All other predicate types

IV. All remaining predicates are evaluated in the order in which they appear in the query.

Use Stage 1 Predicates

The best performance for filtering occurs when stage 1 predicates are used. A chart in all the IBM manuals shows what simple predicates are classified as stage 1 and indexable. But just because a predicate is listed in this chart does not mean that it will be either used for an index or processed in stage 1, as many other factors must also be in place. The first thing that determines whether a predicate is stage 1 is the syntax of the predicate, and the second thing is the type and length of constants used in the predicate. If the predicate, even though it could be classified as a stage 1 predicate, is evaluated after a join operation, it is a stage 2 predicate. All indexable predicates are stage 1, but not all stage 1 predicates are indexable.

Never Use Generic SQL Statements

It bears repeating here that genericness is counter to performance, and specificity and granularity yield performance. Generic SQL means that in every case, something is retrieved that is not needed. Generic SQL usually appears in those incredibly poor-performing I/O layers that seem to regularly surface in this arena. SQL is already the "I/O layer." We have seen I/O layers with names and SQL like the following:

Module name: `GET_CUSTOMER(ws-acct-number, structure)`

Code: `SQL SELECT * FROM CUSTOMER`
                `WHERE  ACCT_NUM = :ws-acct-number`
                `INTO :structure`

Program code: `GET-CUSTOMER.`
                `    CALL GET_CUSTOMER(acctnum, customer-rec)`
                `    IF CUSTOMER_CODE NOT EQUAL x`
                `    THEN GOTO GET-CUSTOMER`

This violates almost every rule we have discussed so far regarding SQL performance. Generic SQL generally has logic that retrieves only some specific data or data relationship and leaves the entire business-rule processing in the application. Generic SQL and generic I/O layers do not belong in high-performing systems.

Avoid Unnecessary Sorting

Avoiding unnecessary sorting is a requirement in any application but is more important in any high performance environment, especially with a database involved. Generally, if ordering is always necessary, there should probably be indexes to support the ordering. Sorting can be caused by GROUP BY, ORDER BY, DISTINCT, and join processing. If ordering is required for a join process, it generally is a clear indication that an index is missing. If ordering is necessary after a join process, hopefully the result set is small. The worst possible scenario is where a sort is performed as the result of the SQL in a cursor, and the application processes only a subset of the data. In most such cases, the sort overhead needs to be removed. This is common sense: if the SQL has to sort 100 rows but only 10 are processed by the application, probably there is no problem, as long as the data is retrieved with the best possible predicate filtering. There can be no rule for how much data is too much when sorting is involved, as "too much" depends on many subsystem parameters and environment settings, but there is a point when sorting should be considered as an external action or implemented in other ways. The rule is very simple in this case: use full volume testing to determine the best solution.

Sort Only Necessary Columns

When DB2 sorts data, the columns used to determine the sort order actually appear twice in the sort rows. Consider the following SQL statement:

```
SELECT LASTNAME, CITY, STATE, COUNTRY, PLANET
FROM DEMOGRAPHICS
WHERE PLANET = :planet
AND COUNTRY = :country
ORDER BY PLANET, COUNTRY, STATE, CITY, LASTNAME
```

Assume that there is no index on this table in order to make this discussion more meaningful. Here it is relatively simple to see that there is a problem, in that planet and country are already known. If the five columns in the ORDER BY were indexed, the columns would still not be required. The query can be rewritten:

```
SELECT LASTNAME, CITY, STATE
FROM DEMOGRAPHICS
WHERE PLANET = :planet
AND COUNTRY = :country
ORDER BY STATE, CITY, LASTNAME
```

The benefit here is eliminating unnecessary data retrieval. But with this construct, we could easily be forced to sort the last names of every individual in the country selected. If we used the original query and an index was used for data retrieval, no sort would have been required. In the first case, the data would have immediately been available to the application inside a cursor. In the second example, the query and the sort would have to complete before the first row could be returned. Here is a third alternative (as of Version 6):

```
SELECT LASTNAME, CITY, STATE
FROM DEMOGRAPHICS
WHERE PLANET = :planet
AND COUNTRY = :country
ORDER BY PLANET, COUNTRY, STATE, CITY, LASTNAME
```

This time the sort could have been avoided, as the five-column index could be used to retrieve the data in order, and we would not incur the overhead of the two additional columns being returned to the program.

But what if these solutions are not available to the process? There is another way of looking at certain queries, when absolute sorting is required and too many columns are involved. Here is an example of a query that requires a GROUP BY, which requires a sort. However, unnecessary columns are involved in the sort. We can use nested table expressions in situations like this to remove the unnecessary sorting. This query needs grouping by department.

```
SELECT DEPTNO, DEPTNAME, ADMRDEPT, COUNT(*)
FROM DEPT, EMP
WHERE WORKDEPT = DEPTNO
GROUP BY DEPTNO, DEPTNAME, ADMRDEPT
```

The columns for department name and administrative department are unique for each department, so they really do not need to be included in the GROUP BY. We can use a table expression to do the grouping ahead of time, sorting on less data, or maybe even grouping by index access then using the results with the other data.

```
SELECT DEPTNO, DEPTNAME, ADMRDEPT, COUNTEMP
FROM DEPT,
     (SELECT WORKDEPT AS COUNTDEPT,
      COUNT(*) AS COUNTEMP
      FROM EMP
      GROUP BY WORKDEPT) AS TEMP
WHERE DEPTNO = COUNTDEPT
```

If a sort was required in both cases, this is the difference in the sort row.

Query 1: DEPTNO, DEPTNAME, and ADMRDEPT as the sort key and
        DEPTNO, DEPTNAME, ADMRDEPT, and COUNT(*) as the data
        portion

Query 2: WORKDEPT as the sort key and WORKDEPT and COUNT(*) as the
        data portion

The chances for query 2 to complete sorting inside the sort pool in memory are much better than for query 1. The key columns for the sort have to appear separately in front of the row for sorting (most of the time, although in some cases a tag sort is required where the data to be sorted gets to be too large, as discussed in Chapter 3, "Memory").

Use the ON Clause for All Join Predicates

There are two formats for inner joins. One format is the comma notation, and the other is the ON clause. There is really no reason to use the comma notation any longer, and there are many new benefits to using the ON clause and the INNER JOIN syntax. One of the best reasons to use the ON clause is not the optimization techniques that were added in version 6, but the documentation and ensuring that join predicates are in the query. Take, for example, the following simple queries:

```
SELECT STATE, REGION, T1.EMPNO, TOTAL
FROM SALES T1, EMPLOYEES T2
WHERE T1.EMPNO = T2.EMPNO
AND T1.STATE = :hostvar

SELECT STATE, REGION, T1.EMPNO, TOTAL
FROM SALES T1 INNER JOIN EMPLOYEES T2
ON T1.EMPNO = T2.EMPNO
WHERE T1.STATE = :hostvar
```

In the second query, it is difficult to forget the join predicate. The join predicate is documented in other queries. The enhancements in version 6 for the ON clause were extensive, and many directly affect performance. Predicate transitive closure between the ON clauses and the WHERE predicates was nice but not as important to performance as the ability to include join predicates in the ON clause, so that filtering occurs during the join process, not before or after. All predicates can be included in an ON clause, with the exception of a subquery.

Avoid UNIONs

UNIONs are simply expensive, especially where each union block processes the same table. In addition, many union statements are written with the UNION ALL syntax, which forces DB2 to remove duplicates from the result, which in the majority of cases might not be there anyway. Outer joins removed the requirement for UNIONs in many SQL statements (but most code generators still do not generate the outer join syntax). The introduction of the CASE expression also removes many other requirements for the UNION syntax. UNIONs are very difficult for the optimizer to optimize or rewrite. Where the UNION syntax is still required, quite often a UNION is coded instead of a UNION ALL, although an analysis of the statement shows that no duplicates could ever occur. This is most common where literals have been included on the SELECT to tag the data. So in effect, we have DB2 invoking a sort and passing the entire result set to remove duplicates that cannot be there. Even if a sort is required for ordering the data, the distinct removal code does not need to be invoked. This is another performance pressure point.

The following query, which is a four-table join with a GROUP BY in four UNION blocks, is reduced to a single four-table join with a GROUP BY in one block for an approximately 75% reduction in resource consumption.

This is the query with the four UNION blocks:

```
SELECT SE.TYPE, CJ.CODE ,CJ.GROUP, CJ.TDATE,
     DM.CLASS ,SUM(CJ.AMOUNT),0,0,0
FROM CJ, SE, DM, TC
WHERE CJ.CLASS = DM.CLASS
AND  CJ.CODE = TC.CODE
AND  CJ.TYPE = SE.TYPE
AND  TC.BASE_CODE = 'I'
AND  CJ.TDATE = (SELECT MAX(CJ2.TDATE)
     FROM CJ AS CJ2
     WHERE correlated predicates)
GROUP BY SE.TYPE, CJ.CODE, CJ.GROUP,
     CJ.TDATE, DM.CLASS
UNION ALL
SELECT SE.TYPE, CJ.CODE ,CJ.GROUP, CJ.TDATE,
     DM.CLASS , 0, SUM(CJ.AMOUNT),0,0
FROM CJ, SE, DM, TC
WHERE CJ.CLASS = DM.CLASS
AND  CJ.CODE = TC.CODE
AND  CJ.TYPE = SE.TYPE
AND  TC.BASE_CODE = 'DE'
AND  CJ.TDATE = (SELECT MAX(CJ2.TDATE)
     FROM CJ AS CJ2
     WHERE correlated predicates)
GROUP BY SE.TYPE, CJ.CODE, CJ.GROUP,
     CJ.TDATE, DM.CLASS
UNION ALL
SELECT SE.TYPE, CJ.CODE ,CJ.GROUP, CJ.TDATE,
     DM.CLASS ,0, 0, SUM(CJ.AMOUNT),0
```

```
FROM CJ, SE, DM, TC
WHERE CJ.CLASS = DM.CLASS
AND   CJ.CODE = TC.CODE
AND   CJ.TYPE = SE.TYPE
AND   TC.SEC_CODE = 'I'
AND   CJ.TDATE = (SELECT MAX(CJ2.TDATE)
      FROM CJ AS CJ2
      WHERE correlated predicates)
GROUP BY SE.TYPE, CJ.CODE, CJ.GROUP,
      CJ.TDATE, DM.CLASS
UNION ALL
SELECT SE.TYPE, CJ.CODE ,CJ.GROUP, CJ.TDATE,
      DM.CLASS, 0, 0, 0, SUM(CJ.AMOUNT)
FROM CJ, SE, DM, TC
WHERE CJ.CLASS = DM.CLASS
AND   CJ.CODE = TC.CODE
AND   CJ.TYPE = SE.TYPE
AND   TC.SEC_CODE = 'DE'
AND   CJ.TDATE = (SELECT MAX(CJ2.TDATE)
      FROM CJ AS CJ2
      WHERE correlated predicates)
GROUP BY SE.TYPE, CJ.CODE, CJ.GROUP,
      CJ.TDATE, DM.CLASS
ORDER BY 2, 3, 4
```

This is the query using CASE and one query block:

```
SELECT SE.TYPE, CJ.CODE, CJ.GROUP, CJ.TDATE,
      DM.CLASS
, SUM(CASE WHEN TC.BASE_CODE = 'I' THEN CJ.AMOUNT END)
, SUM(CASE WHEN TC.BASE_CODE = 'DE' THEN CJ.AMOUNT END)
, SUM(CASE WHEN TC.SEC_CODE = 'I' THEN CJ.AMOUNT END)
, SUM(CASE WHEN TC.SEC_CODE = 'DE' THEN CJ.AMOUNT END)
FROM CJ, SE, DM, TC
WHERE CJ.CLASS = DM.CLASS
AND   CJ.CODE = TC.CODE
AND   CJ.TYPE = SE.TYPE
AND (TC.BASE_CODE IN ('I', 'DE')
      OR TC.SEC_CODE IN ('I', 'DE'))
```

```
AND   CJ.TDATE = (SELECT MAX(CJ2.TDATE)
      FROM CJ AS CJ2
      WHERE correlated predicates)
GROUP BY SE.TYPE, CJ.CODE, CJ.GROUP,
      CJ.TDATE, DM.CLASS
ORDER BY 2, 3, 4
```

Use Joins Instead of Subqueries

This has held true since the beginning of DB2 and is still true today: joins generally outperform subqueries. It is relatively easy to see why if you think about what is occurring
and how it occurs. There are more access path alternatives for joins, and it is possible to
walk through two tables simultaneously. Almost all subqueries can be converted to joins,
and in many cases DB2 performs the rewrite. So why then do we find so many subqueries
in applications instead of joins? Joins are commonly avoided due to either urban folklore
about DB2 join performance or in-house standards requiring joins to be avoided.

There are two types of subqueries, correlated and noncorrelated. Noncorrelated subselects are the simplest to understand. They execute in a bottom-up pattern, one time only
for each level. Following is an example of a noncorrelated subselect using NOT EXISTS:

```
SELECT TA.COL1, TA.COL2
FROM TA
WHERE NOT EXISTS
  (SELECT 1
  FROM TB
  WHERE TB.COL1 = :hv1 )
```

A correlated subselect is when the subquery (bottom SELECT) refers to a column in
the top SELECT. Single correlated subselects execute in a top-bottom-top pattern, once
for each qualifying row in the top SELECT. Following is an example of a single correlated
subselect:

```
SELECT TA.COL1, TA.COL2
FROM TA
WHERE TA.COL3 = 'ABC'
  AND NOT EXISTS
```

```
(SELECT 1
 FROM TB
 WHERE TB.COL2 = TA.COL2)
```

There are cases when a correlated subquery can outperform a join due to a look-aside cache assist. The cache holds the results of a subquery, and if the same values are fed to the subquery again, the query can retrieve the same correct answer from the cache.

In general, we should try to code the join and resort to subqueries only if they yield a better access path. It is not always obvious, but both NOT EXIST and NOT IN subqueries can generally be converted to joins. Sometimes DB2 converts noncorrelated IN subqueries to a join, but prior to version 6 optimizations, this was not always better. It is possible to disable the query rewrite by adding to the subquery without changing what it returns, such as by using a GROUP BY on noncorrelated subqueries.

Stage 2 processing is normally used for EXIST predicates with correlated subqueries and with IN predicates with noncorrelated subqueries. If these are converted to joins, the inner table can use the predicates at stage 1. The rule then is quite simple. You should always try to use joins before subqueries if performance is a concern.

Code the Most Selective Predicates First

Many times in recent years we have heard the statement made that worrying about predicate ordering is a waste of time and money. However, this is simply not true. Earlier in this chapter we listed the order of predicate evaluation. In normal application SQL, most often many predicates are chosen at the same level, and the process does flow from top to bottom. The earlier a predicate is evaluated, the better. We have shown that stage 1 predicates are better than stage 2 predicates because they qualify rows earlier and reduce the amount of stage 2 processing. All SQL queries should be written to evaluate the most restrictive predicates first and thus filter unnecessary rows earlier, reducing processing cost at a later stage.

Use the Proper Method for Existence Checking

The proper method for existence checking is often an emotional topic, as analysts have so many different opinions on this issue. However, much research has been done on this topic; some of the most detailed is by Michael Hannan in Australia. There are many issues here, and we need to be very specific about them. We need to distinguish responsiveness to the query from processes that may go on inside DB2 on behalf of the query but with no effect on the query, for example, sequential prefetch enablement.

Most often, the following SQL is best, assuming that KEYCOL is the first column in at least one index on the table.

```
SELECT '1' INTO :hostvar1
FROM TABLE
WHERE KEYCOL = :hostvar2
IF SQLCODE = 0 OR SQLCODE = -811 THEN
     WE HAVE EXISTENCE
IF SQLCODE = +100 THEN
     WE HAVE NO EXISTENCE
```

It is not safe to test the value of :hostvar1 because, by definition, on an −811 condition, the contents are not guaranteed (this is true with any negative SQLCODE in DB2). If the access path chosen was a list prefetch, we have a problem, since the list prefetch must be completed before we get our answer, which is not only unresponsive but also wasteful of resources.

But what about sequential prefetch? Is this really a problem? We have a different perspective on this than most people. Sequential prefetch is not a single event but consists of a set of I/O operations, the first of which is synchronous and returns the answer to the single SQL query immediately. The problem here is why anyone would ever want a tablespace scan to do existence checking. It comes down to what you are checking the existence of. If the SQL is looking into a small code table, 100 rows on a single page in DB2, then the sequential prefetch is okay, as long as there is no index that could have supplied the answer. Yes, this is an extreme case, but it often occurs. It is difficult to make solid rules and guidelines, as each case might be different. But as a general rule, you should not use sequential prefetch, dynamic prefetch, list prefetch, any materializing, any sorts, or hybrid or merge scan joins for existence checking, since they simply require too much overhead for the answer and significantly hurt responsiveness.

There is a way to handle queries for existence checking when the access path chosen is not adequate; simply put the query into a cursor and use the OPTIMIZE FOR 1 ROW clause, usually with uncommitted read isolation. This works in every case, but it does require three calls to DB2 instead of one, and that is the extra code that we are trying to eliminate for high performance.

One other query is often recommended but only is valid in very rare cases:

```
SELECT '1'
INTO :hostvar1
FROM SYSIBM.SYSDUMMY AS A
WHERE EXISTS
     (SELECT '1'
      FROM TABLE
      WHERE A.IBMREQG >= ' '
      AND filter/matching predicates)
WITH UR
```

This query generally is outperformed by the singleton SELECT. Even though the subquery ends on the first match and we do not get an –811 SQLCODE, there is the overhead of the second query block, additional GETPAGEs, and unobvious coding. Using the cursor with the OPTIMIZE clause should not be recommended, because there are cases where even this method will not outperform due to the length of nonmatching index scans that are sometimes necessary. The guideline is to try the singleton SELECT but make sure there are no access problems. If there are, find out which of the other solutions will give you the best with the least.

Although the sample code above should not be recommended, there are cases where even using a cursor with the optimize clause with the same code above will not outperform a singleton SELECT due to the length of nonmatching index scans that are sometimes necessary.

One other point is don't repeat this process for the same check. We reduced a batch insert process significantly where a client decided to use application RI. This was not the normal, large, multiple insert in a child table for a single parent. Multiple queues submitted data to the insert process with only one existence check query, so when repeated items came from a queue, the unnecessary existence check was repeated. The solution was obvious and simple but, as with many complex strategies, was overlooked in testing. A separate existence check was put on each queue and checked to see if the next entry on the queue had the same parent as the last entry. Many performance SQL tricks end up being necessary once the real volume is the data pool.

Avoid Anything Unnecessary

Avoiding the unnecessary is the last guideline for high performance. For example, consider materialization of large result sets when only 10 rows are needed in an OLTP. While this might not even appear to be a problem until you look at a trace, it needs to be avoided. For example, when list prefetch is triggered for 100 rows but only 10 rows are used on the screen 90% of the time, this is such a small amount that responsiveness or performance does not appear to be a concern. But that overhead takes resources away from some other transaction, and removing it might allow one more transaction per period. The online cursor should have an OPTIMIZE FOR 10 ROWS on it. The access path might be the same, but most of the time it is turned into something more beneficial for 10 rows, not 100.

> Note: List prefetch is often considered bad. It can be good or bad, just like any other item. Even in OLTP, it can be quite beneficial. It just depends on the amount of usage and the size of the result set.

Special Techniques

This section shows just how far you can go with SQL to push the logic inside the DB2 engine, where it can be done faster and more cleanly. The goal is to have DB2 return just the data absolutely needed for some process. In figure 16.6 is a high-level formula for creating the type of SQL statements we discuss here. We do not present the whole statement in all these examples, but just the part that you need to see what can be done where performance is an issue.

CASE in Predicates

Most guidelines tell you of the horrors of using a CASE expression in predicates in an SQL statement, and they are correct to a degree. CASE used in a WHERE clause is stage 2 overhead, and it can be significant. But if it does the work and provides the answer, this is good.

Following is an amalgamation of a couple of SQL statements for an online screen that allows the user to scan data by any or all of several ranges. Rather than writing multiple queries or using dynamic SQL, another selection can be used if other predicates filter the data prior to this.

1. Put the work in the SQL
2. Let DB2 OPTIMIZE it
3. Allow the engine to:

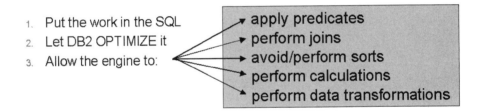

- apply predicates
- perform joins
- avoid/perform sorts
- perform calculations
- perform data transformations

Method to Build Complex SQL	Method to Build Complex SQL

Gather requirements
List tables needed for:
    Data to be displayed
    Data to be filtered
    Data required for joins
Create join predicates
Create local predicates
Create look-up subqueries
	Add data transformations in SELECT
	Add GROUP BY / HAVING if required
	Add FULL/LEFT join if required
	Add Table Expressions if required
	Roll components together
	Test
	EXPLAIN -- Tune (if necessary)

Figure 16.6 "Push Down" Work with Complex SQL

All :ws host variables used for comparisons are set to blanks or other defaults before the query to enable the filtering.

```
-- SELECT ACCOUNT NUMBER RANGE
AND (CASE WHEN :WS-ACCT-NUMBER-RANGE  = 'Y'
     THEN ACCT_NUMBER ELSE '           ' END)
     BETWEEN :WS-ACCT-LOW AND :WS-ACCT-HIGH
-- SELECT GROUP NUMBER RANGE
AND (CASE WHEN :WS-GROUP-NUMBER-RANGE = 'Y'
     THEN (GRP_NBR_ID CONCAT
           SUBGRP_NBR_ID CONCAT
           DIGITS(GRP_NBR_SEQ)) ELSE '          ' END)
     BETWEEN :WS-GROUP-LOW AND :WS-GROUP-HIGH
-- SELECT SERIAL NUMBER SEARCH
AND (CASE WHEN :WS-SERIAL-SEARCH = 'Y'
     THEN SERIAL_CODE ELSE ' ' END)
     = :WS-SERIAL-CODE
AND (CASE WHEN :WS-SERIAL-SEARCH = 'Y'
     THEN DOMAIN ELSE '     ' END)
     = :WS-DOMAIN
```

```
AND (CASE WHEN :WS-SERIAL-SEARCH = 'Y'
     THEN SERIAL_NUMBER ELSE 0000000000 END)
     BETWEEN :WS-SERIAL-LOW AND :WS-SERIAL-HIGH
```

GROUP BY to Allow Single Pass

Quite often it is necessary to get counts of different items in a table based on business rules, which generally results in successive passes or in the returning of all rows to an application program that then does the counting. Either of these two possible solutions are full of overhead and diametrically opposed to good performance.

The solution can best be demonstrated by the following example of counting and percentage calculations done in a single pass of the data. One count is done of all the rows to get the basis for the percentage calculations. The summarization of the individual fields is done in the table expression, and then the percentages are calculated in the outer query block. Only the necessary information from the real query is presented here.

```
SELECT MAJOR, MINOR, ITEM_COUNT * 100, WITH_SUB_ITEMS * 100
  ,(WITH_SUB_ITEMS * 100.0)/ITEM_COUNT AS SUB_ITEM_PCT
  ,(ITEM_SIZE_8_12 * 100.0/WITH_SUB_ITEMS) AS SIZE_8_12_PCT
  ,(ITEM_SIZE_13_18* 100.0/WITH_SUB_ITEMS) AS SIZE_13_18_PCT
  ,(MALE_ITEMS * 100.0/WITH_SUB_ITEMS) AS MALE_ITEMS_PCT
  ,(FEMALE_ITEMS * 100.0/WITH_SUB_ITEMS) AS FEMALE_ITEMS_PCT
FROM (SELECT MAJOR, MINOR
      ,SUM(CASE SUB_ITEM_IND WHEN 'Y' THEN 1 ELSE 0 END)
          AS WITH_SUB_ITEMS
      ,SUM(CASE SUB_ITEM_IND WHEN 'N' THEN 1 ELSE 0 END)
          AS NO_SUB_ITEMS
      ,SUM(CASE ITEM_SIZE_8_12 WHEN ' ' THEN 0 ELSE 1 END)
          AS ITEM_SIZE_8_12
      ,SUM(CASE ITEM_SIZE_13_18 WHEN ' ' THEN 0 ELSE 1 END)
          AS ITEM_SIZE_13_18
      ,SUM(CASE WHEN ITEM_SIZE_0_3 = 'M'
          OR ITEM_SIZE_4_7 = 'M'
          OR ITEM_SIZE_8_12 = 'M'
          OR ITEM_SIZE_13_18 = 'M'
          THEN 1 ELSE 0 END) AS MALE_ITEMS
      ,SUM(CASE WHEN ITEM_SIZE_0_3 = 'F'
          OR ITEM_SIZE_4_7 = 'F'
```

```
    OR ITEM_SIZE_8_12 = 'F'
    OR ITEM_SIZE_13_18 = 'F'
    THEN 1 ELSE 0 END) AS FEMALE_ITEMS
,COUNT(*) AS ITEM_COUNT
FROM   some tables
WHERE  some conditions
GROUP BY MAJOR, MINOR) as X;
```

GROUP BY to Work Both Sides

We just read an SQL guideline that you should try to avoid the HAVING clause in SQL. Why we are not exactly sure, since the explanation was confusing at best. In fact, HAVING can be confusing at best, although it is normally just shown as a filtering for GROUP BY partitions of the data. That is basically a waste of an incredible resource. The capability that we are after is to load DB2 with all the information to do the processing and return to us just an answer. Since the GROUP BY produces logical partition sets of data, or what might be considered an "intermediate table," we can use HAVING to do some work on the right side to balance out the work done on the left side during the creation of the data partition or table. Figure 16.7 is a good, simple example. Here we use GROUP BY to partition the data

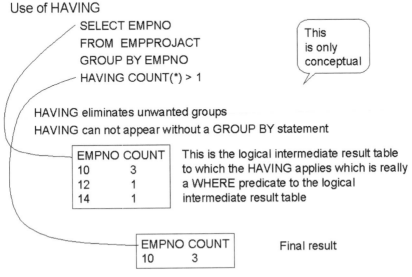

Figure 16.7 GROUP BY & HAVING

into a new intermediate table and then filter those rows with HAVING. The rows in the intermediate table are determined by reference in the SELECT and in the GROUP BY. This so far is not anything new or exciting, until we take it a step further by changing what we use in the GROUP BY and the HAVING. In figure 16.8, we change the HAVING to use a host variable for the comparison and an SQL subselect, or subquery, for the right side, with one little twist. We have now correlated the subselect/subquery to a "row" in the intermediate table that was built by the GROUP BY. The intermediate table would logically contain the following columns:

A.STATE	A.CITY	:value
TEXAS	AUSTIN	0
CALIFORNIA	SAN DIEGO	0

We are going to select cities and states where some particular calculation returns the answer 0 but the calculation is anchored only to the data pertaining to the state, which is used to additionally correlate the calculation, which uses data from a join of two other tables. This is actually not an uncommon business function, but it normally appears in multiple application processes with multiple SQL statements.

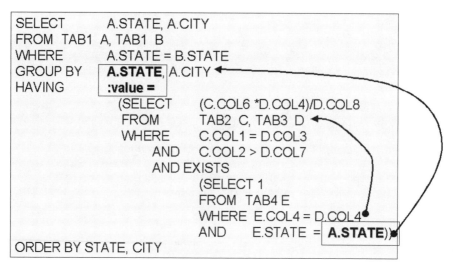

Figure 16.8 GROUP BY & HAVING

Perhaps it is better to give a real example and embed it into another query block that returns to the user only the simple answer.

```
SELECT   1                            -- returns no data however
FROM DUMMY1                           -- answers the question:
WHERE EXISTS                          -- Are they  balanced ?
(SELECT 1  FROM TAB1, TAB2
   WHERE TAB1.D = TAB2.Z              -- join predicate
      AND TAB1.A = :hv                -- local filter
   GROUP BY A, B, C, D                -- summarize
   HAVING SUM(TAB1.E)                 -- compare
       (SELECT SUM(TAB3.G)            -- summarize
        FROM TAB3
        WHERE TAB3.Z = TAB1.D))       -- correlate
```

An SQLCODE equal to 0 means that the system is "not in balance," whereas an SQLCODE equal to 100 means that the system is "in balance."

If the question can be asked, SQL can (probably) get the answer.

Triggers and User-Defined Functions

D B2's support for triggers and user-defined functions (UDFs) brings users a vast capability to invent many new ways of enhancing applications, limited only by their imagination. But with any extension of user code into a database, many considerations for achieving good performance are required. User code embedded using these facilities can completely obliterate any service-level agreement. This chapter covers the performance and implementation issues surrounding these features.

Triggers

The trigger implementation in DB2 is called *active triggers,* which means triggers supported on changes to data, or data activity. Triggers are attached to tables and are invoked by updates, deletions, and insertions, either before or after the event occurs (figure 17.1). Auditing changes to data and complex referential integrity (RI), for example, updating an audit table whenever financial information changes in another table, can be handled easily with triggers.

Triggers have been criticized since they can contain only SQL, but SQL can invoke stored procedures and UDFs (figure 17.2), so an underlying process can be written to satisfy many types of business requirements. The stored procedures can update other tables, causing other triggers to be fired.

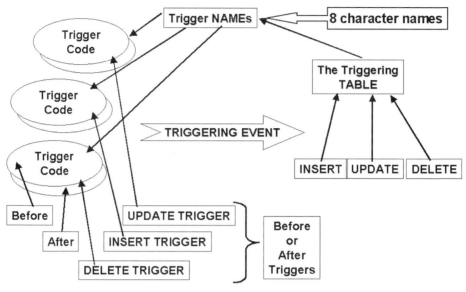

Figure 17.1 Triggers

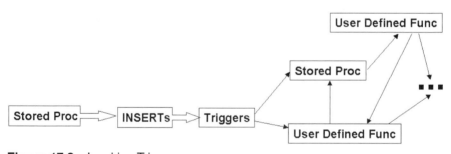

Figure 17.2 Invoking Triggers

We can use triggers to enforce business rules, create new column values, edit column values, validate all input data, or maintain summary tables or cross-reference tables. Triggers provide enhanced enterprise and business functionality, faster application development, and global enforcement of business rules:

• Rapid application development. Triggers are stored in the database, and the trigger actions do not need to be coded in each application.

- Code reusability. A trigger can be defined once on a given table and then used by any application that can access that table.
- Easier maintenance. When business rules change, simply modify the trigger without having to change the applications.

Limited only by your imagination, the trigger is just a way of getting control to do anything whenever a table's data is modified. A single trigger invoked by an update on a financial table could invoke a UDF or call a stored procedure to invoke another external action, which could trigger an e-mail to a pager to notify the DBA of a serious condition. Far-fetched? No, it is already being done.

Triggers can cause other triggers to be invoked and through the SQL can call stored procedures. These stored procedures could issue SQL updates that invoke other triggers. This allows great flexibility.

There is currently a safe limit on the cascading of triggers, stored procedures, and UDFs: an execution-time nesting depth of 16. This prevents the endless cascading that would otherwise be possible. There is a *big* performance concern here, because if the 17th nested level is reached, an SQLCODE of –724 is set, but all 16 levels are backed out. That could be a significant problem: processes that are executed outside the control of DB2 are not be backed out, and it might be very difficult to determine what was changed. There are limitations in the calling sequences; for example, stored procedures that are WLM managed cannot call stored procedures that are DB2 managed. More about the nested calling of stored procedures appears in Chapter 19.

Trigger Definitions

Triggers are like stored procedures in that they create a package, except the package is created when a CREATE TRIGGER statement is executed. There are two types of triggers: BEFORE triggers and AFTER triggers.

BEFORE Triggers

Use BEFORE triggers to set column values with SQL such as a CASE. BEFORE triggers are always row triggers that apply a FIX or CONDITION data before a row is entered. A BEFORE trigger is used to validate or modify input values, modify or set column values, or prevent invalid update operations. It can be used for SELECT, VALUES,

SIGNAL, CALL, or SET but not for UPDATE, INSERT, or DELETE. In other words, it cannot manipulate the database. The following example shows a BEFORE trigger.

```
CREATE TRIGGER Update_TS
    NO CASCADE BEFORE INSERT ON Accounts
    REFERENCING NEW AS New_TS
    FOR EACH ROW
    MODE DB2SQL
SET New_TS.UPDATE_TIMESTAMP = CURRENT_TIMESTAMP
```

A popular use of a BEFORE trigger is to clean and condition data before moving it into a data warehouse.

AFTER Triggers

Use the AFTER triggers to update audit or column tables. A possible use of AFTER triggers is to update warehouse summary tables.

AFTER triggers are evaluated totally after the triggering event. They can be row triggers or statement triggers. AFTER triggers can be used to initiate actions outside the database (stored procedures or UDFs) to do normal application logic that would otherwise be done by any program or transaction that updates the database. AFTER triggers can operate on any table in the database using any of the following statements: SELECT, VALUES, SIGNAL, CALL, INSERT, DELETE, or UPDATE. An example of an AFTER trigger is shown here:

```
CREATE TRIGGER UPDATE_IDMS
    AFTER INSERT ON Financials
    FOR EACH STATEMENT
    MODE DB2SQL
CALL PGM_TO_UPDATE_IDMS;
```

Trigger Actions

There are two parts of a triggered action. First, there is the action condition, which is an optional section to decide whether to execute the process in the trigger or not. It contains the WHEN clause, similar to a WHERE clause, which executes the triggered SQL statements only when true. Second, there is the triggered SQL statements section, where one or more SQL statements can be executed if the WHEN tests true. There is a BEGIN ATOMIC . . . END group for multiple SQL statements, which can include stored procedure calls or user-defined functions (figure 17.3).

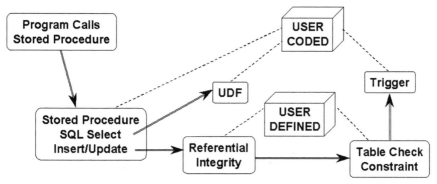

Figure 17.3 Triggers, Stored Procedures, and UDFs

Transition Variables and Tables

Transition variables allow row triggers to access row data. They provide a way to see row data as it existed before and as it exists after the triggering operation. These transition variables are implemented by a REFERENCING clause in the trigger definition, for example:

```
REFERENCING OLD AS OLD_ACCOUNTS
            NEW AS NEW_ACCOUNTS
```

Transition tables allow AFTER triggers to access the set of affected rows as they were before or as they are after the triggering operation. These tables are implemented by a REFERENCING clause in the trigger definition, for example:

```
REFERENCING OLD_TABLE AS OLD_ACCT_TABLE
            NEW_TABLE AS NEW_ACCT_TABLE
```

A new VALUES statement, shown in figure 17.4, is used to invoke UDFs as well as normal SQL.

Trigger Packages

DB2 creates a trigger package when you create a trigger. The qualifier of the trigger name determines the package collection, which for static SQL is the authorization ID of the QUALIFIER bind option and for dynamic SQL is the CURRENT SQLID.

Trigger packages are different from regular packages. They can be rebound locally, but you cannot bind them. They are rebound only with the REBIND TRIGGER

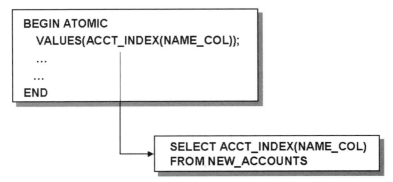

Figure 17.4 VALUES Statement to Invoke UDF from Trigger

PACKAGE command. You might want to rebind to change default bind options such as CURRENTDATA, EXPLAIN, FLAG, ISOLATION, RELEASE, which are useful for picking up new access paths and achieving better performance. Trigger packages cannot be freed or dropped. To delete a trigger package, use the DROP TRIGGER statement. Trigger packages cannot be copied, so while they might act like a normal process, they are entirely different. UDFs and stored procedures have many similarities, but triggers are a completely different entity.

Creating and Adding Triggers

Triggers are defined using the CREATE TRIGGER statement, which contains many options. The primary options are whether it is a BEFORE or AFTER trigger, whether it is a row TRIGGER or statement trigger, and the language of the trigger. The language currently can be only SQL, but that will probably change in the future. There is a rumor that the SQL procedure language is a candidate for triggers. The phrase MODE DB2SQL is the execution mode of the trigger. This phrase is required for each trigger to ensure that an existing application will not be negatively affected if alternative execution modes for triggers are added to DB2 in the future.

You can have up to 12 types of triggers on a single table. The triggers are invoked in the order they were created! A time stamp is recorded when the trigger is created (and recreated). A DROP and RECREATE of a trigger can completely mess up a process by changing the order in which triggers are executed. Be careful!

Rows that are in violation of a newly added trigger are not rejected. When a trigger is added to a table that already has existing rows, it does not cause any triggered actions to be activated. If the trigger is designed to enforce some type of integrity constraint on the data rows in the table, those constraints may not be enforced for the rows that existed in the table before the trigger was added.

If an update trigger without an explicit column list is created, packages with an update usage on the target table are invalidated. If an update trigger with a column list is created, packages with an update usage on the target table are invalidated only if they also have an update usage on at least one column in the column-name list of the CREATE TRIGGER statement. If an insert trigger is created, packages that have an insert usage on the target table are invalidated. If a delete trigger is created, packages that have a delete usage on the target table are invalidated.

A lot of functions can be used within a trigger. For example, a CASE expression can be used in a trigger, but it needs to be nested inside a VALUES statement, as shown here:

```
BEGIN ATOMIC
    VALUES CASE
        WHEN condition
            THEN something
        WHEN other condition
            THEN something else
    END
END;
```

Triggers versus Table Check Constraints

If a trigger and a table check constraint can enforce the same rule, it is better to use a table check constraint. Use triggers only when a constraint is not enough to enforce a business rule. Constraints and declarative RI are more useful when you have only one state to enforce in a business rule. Although triggers are more powerful than table check constraints and can be more extensive in terms of rule enforcement, constraints can be better optimized by DB2. (Additional information about table check constraints is in Chapter 5).

Table check constraints are enforced for all existing data at the time of creation, and for all statements affecting the data. A table check constraint is defined on a populated table using the ALTER TABLE statement, and the value of the CURRENT RULES special register is DB2. Constraints offer a few other advantages over triggers—such as that they are written in a less procedural way than triggers, are better optimized, and protect data against being placed into an invalid state by any kind of statement—whereas a trigger applies only to a specific kind of statement, such as an UPDATE or DELETE.

Triggers are more powerful than check constraints because they can enforce several rules that constraints cannot. You can use triggers to capture rules that involve different states of data, such as when you need to know the state of the data before and after a calculation.

Triggers and Declarative RI

Trigger operations may result from changes brought about by DB2-enforced referential constraints. For example, if you delete a row from the EMPLOYEE table that propagates DELETEs to the PAYROLL table through referential constraints, the delete triggers defined on the PAYROLL table are subsequently executed. The delete triggers are activated as a result of the referential constraint defined on the EMPLOYEE table.

Trigger Invalidations

Invalid updates can be detected and stopped by triggers in a couple of ways. You can use SIGNAL SQLSTATE or RAISE_ERROR.

SIGNAL SQLSTATE

SIGNAL SQLSTATE is a new SQL statement that is used to return an error code with a SQLSTATE and a specific message to the application and to stop processing. This statement can be used only as a triggered SQL statement within a trigger and can be controlled with a WHEN clause. The following example shows the use of the SIGNAL statement.

```
WHEN NEW_ACCT.AMOUNT < (OLD_ACCT.AMOUNT)
   SIGNAL SQLSTATE '99001' ('Bad amount field')
```

RAISE_ERROR

RAISE_ERROR is not a statement but a built-in function that causes the statement that includes it to return an error with a specific SQLSTATE, SQLCODE –438, and a message. It does basically the same thing as the SIGNAL statement and can be used wherever an expression can be used. The RAISE_ERROR function always returns NULL with an undefined data type. RAISE_ERROR is most useful in CASE expressions, especially when the CASE expression is used in a stored procedure. The following example shows a CASE expression with the RAISE_ERROR function.

```
VALUES (CASE
    WHEN NEW_ACCT.AMOUNT < OLD_ACCT.AMOUNT
    THEN RAISE_ERROR('99001', 'Bad amount field')
```

Forcing a Rollback

If you use the SIGNAL statement to raise an error condition, a rollback is also performed to back out the changes made both by the SQL statement and by the trigger, such as cascading effects from a referential relationship. SIGNAL can be used in either BEFORE or AFTER triggers. Other statements in the program can be either committed or rolled back.

Performing Actions outside a Database

Triggers can contain only SQL, but stored procedures and user-defined functions can be invoked through SQL. Since stored procedures and user-defined functions are user-written code, almost any activity can be performed from a triggered event. For example, the trigger can send a message via e-mail. A BEFORE trigger might be written to handle complex referential integrity checks, which could involve checking whether data exists in another non-DB2 storage container. Through the use of stored procedures and user-defined functions, the power of a trigger is almost unlimited.

Performance Issues

Recursive triggers are updates applied by trigger that cause the same trigger to fire off. These can easily lead to loops and can be very complex statements. However, they may be required by some applications for related rows. You need code to stop the trigger.

Ordering multiple triggers can be an issue because triggers on the same table are activated in the order they were created (identified in the creation time stamp). The interaction among triggers and referential constraints can also be an issue because the order of processing can significantly affect the results produced.

Invoking stored procedures and UDFs from triggers presents some performance and manageability concerns. Triggers can include only SQL but can call stored procedures and UDFs that are user written and therefore have many implications for integrity and performance. Transition tables can be passed to stored procedures and UDFs also.

Trigger cascading is when a trigger modifies the triggering table or another table. Triggers can be activated at the same level or different levels, and when AFTER triggers are activated at different levels, cascading occurs. Cascading can occur for UDFs, stored procedures, and triggers. To determine how many levels you are cascading, refer to figure 17.5, which shows an example of this information from a statistic report.

Monitoring and Controlling Triggers

Monitoring Triggers

There are various ways to monitor the various actions of triggers. The DB2PM statistics and accounting reports include these statistics:

- The number of times a trigger was activated
- The number of times a row trigger was activated
- The number of times an SQL error occurred during the execution of a triggered action

Other details can be found in the traces. For example, in IFCID 16 you can find information about the materialization of a work file in support of a transition table, where TR indicates transition table for triggers. Other information in IFCID 16 includes the

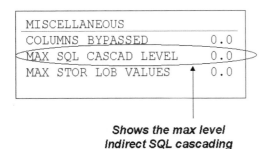

*Shows the max level
Indirect SQL cascading*

Figure 17.5   Monitoring Cascading SQL

depth level of the trigger (0–16), where 0 indicates that there are no triggers. You can also find the type of SQL that invoked the trigger: I = INSERT, U = INSERT into a transition table because of an update, D = INSERT into a transition table because of a delete. The type of referential integrity that caused an insert into a transition table for a trigger is also indicated with an S for SET NULL (which can occur when the SQL type is U) or C for CASCADE DELETE (which can occur when the SQL type is D).

If a transition table needs to be scanned for a trigger, IFCID 17 is TR (transition table scan for a trigger).

Catalog Information

The SYSIBM.SYSTRIGGERS catalog table contains information about the triggers defined in your databases. To find all the triggers defined on a particular table, the characteristics of each trigger, and the order in which they are executed, you can issue the following query:

```
SELECT DISTINCT SCHEMA, NAME, TRIGTIME, TRIGEVENT,
       GRANULARITY, CREATEDTS
FROM SYSIBM.SYSTRIGGERS
WHERE TBNAME = table-name
  AND TBOWNER = table-owner
ORDER BY CREATEDTS
```

You can get the actual text of the trigger with the following statement:

```
SELECT TEXT, SEQNO
FROM SYSIBM.SYSTRIGGERS
WHERE SCHEMA = schema_name
  AND NAME = trigger_name
ORDER BY SEQNO
```

User-Defined Functions

User-defined functions (UDFs) allow users and developers to extend the function of the DBMS by applying function definitions provided by users to the database engine itself. This provides more synergy between application and database and helps with the development cycle because it is more object oriented and can be used for application improvements in many areas. This ability leads to a new breed of developers: the database procedural programmers (see Chapter 9 for more details).

UDFs are functions that are created by the user through DDL using the CREATE FUNCTION statement. This statement can be issued in an interactive query interface or in an application program. UDFs can be simple or complex, inside data or outside data. They can provide application-specific functions or business-specific functions that cross applications. They provide a performance advantage because they execute on the server, not client. Also, they are stored in one location, so change control issues need to be revisited but are less problematic.

Use UDFs with LOBs (large objects) for both searching and analysis and with UDTs (user-defined data types) for object processing unique to your business and application needs. These functions can provide simple data transformations, financial calculations, complex calculations and various types of data analysis. UDFs are limited only by your imagination and good performance guidelines (discussed later in the chapter).

UDFs are created with the CREATE FUNCTION statement and are used in SQL just like built-in functions. They define the behavior of a user-defined data type as a method and encapsulation.

There are three types of UDFs: sourced functions, external scalar functions, and external table functions. Basically, sourced functions are based on existing built-in functions, while external functions are written in a host language.

- *Sourced functions* mimic other functions. They can be column functions that work on a collection of values and return a single value (e.g., MAX, SUM, AVG), or scalar functions that work on individual values and return a single value (CHAR, CONCAT), or operator functions such as >, <, or =.
- *External scalar functions* are written in a programming language, such as C, C++, or Java, and return a scalar value. External scalar functions cannot contain SQL, cannot be column functions, cannot access or modify the database, and can perform calculations only on parameters.
- *External table functions* can return a table and can be written in C or Java. These work on scalar values that may be of different data types with different meanings and return a table. For example:

```
CREATE FUNCTION EXM()
RETURNS TABLE (COL1 DATE . . . . ))
```

Just like user-defined data types, UDFs, which are user-created SQL functions, play a role in both normal data types and object types.

Sourced Scalar Functions

Scalar functions return a single-value answer each time they are called, and table functions simply return a table. Table functions as a rule are not distributed as part of the extenders, but large libraries of scalar functions are included. Extenders include user-defined functions required for each of the distinct data types supported (more on the use of extenders appears in Chapter 18). These UDFs perform operations unique to image, audio, video, XML, and spatial objects. Any developer can create additional UDFs for the objects supported by the extenders as well as for any other reason. UDFs are created with the SQL CREATE FUNCTION statement. The parameter list is rather large but easily understood. In the following example, a UDF is created that specifies the data type to which the UDF can be applied, and it performs a financial calculation on the data.

```
CREATE FUNCTION something_financial (EURO_DOLLAR)
     RETURNS EURO_DOLLAR
     EXTERNAL NAME "SOME_FIN"
     LANGUAGE C
     PARAMETER STYLE DB2SQL
     NO SQL
     DETERMINISTIC
     NO EXTERNAL ACTION
```

The previous statement defines the data type of the parameter and the data type of the returned information, both as UDTs. It also states that it is an external function, written in the C language, and contains no SQL. UDFs can be used in SQL statements the same way as built-in functions. For example:

```
SELECT something_financial (OZ_ANNUAL)
FROM places
WHERE location= :whatever
```

UDFs open up a world of options for highly specialized processing for a wide variety of applications. UDFs are basically subroutines that can be invoked through SQL statements and can range from simple SQL statements to large COBOL programs. We could create a UDF called EURO_TO_DOLLAR and use as a parameter EURO amounts or columns, with the result as a dollar amount. The UDF could get conversion data in real time from another source, but the UDF has to be written only once and can be used everywhere. UDFs can search and index LOB data, while others define the behavior of a UDT.

There are about 100 built-in functions, some of which are supplied as examples of UDFs. Casting functions are helpful when dealing with UDTs. Other very important built-in functions are ROUND, JULIAN_DAY, LOCATE, LTRIM, RTRIM, RAISE_ERROR, TRIM, and TRUNCATE. The list is long, but these functions help keep more of that program-code processing inside the engine via SQL, where it belongs and is better optimized. Among the sample UDFs is ALTDATE, which can return the current date in any of 34 possible formats, DAYNAME for weekday name, and MONTHNAME for the name of the month. Watch for many others coming from IBM and elsewhere.

External Functions

Scalar Functions

External scalar function provide additional functionality written in an application program. They are user written in a host language and are defined to DB2 with a reference to an MVS load module, which contains the object code of the function. The module is loaded when the function is invoked. The following example shows how to create and invoke an external scalar function:

```
--Creating an external scalar
CREATE FUNCTION ADD_IT(INTEGER,INTEGER)
     RETURNS INTEGER
     EXTERNAL NAME 'ADDIT'
     LANGUAGE COBOL;


--Invoking an external scalar
UPDATE INVENTORY
     SET ITEM_COUNT = ADD_IT(INSTOCK, ON_ORDER);
```

Table Functions

A table function takes as parameters individual scalar values and returns a table to the SQL statement. This type of function can be specified only within the FROM clause of a SELECT. Table functions are external functions and are used, for example, to retrieve data from a non-DB2 source, pass it to the SQL statement, and perhaps participate in a join. This is a way to build a table from non-DB2 data and can be used in a table expression containing a SELECT that is a subquery of an INSERT statement.

These are some characteristics of table functions:

- They are written in normal programming languages.
- They can perform operating system calls.
- They can read data from files.
- They can read data across a network.
- They use SQL to process any kind of data from anywhere.
- They can join the data from the table function to another table.
- They are like scalar functions (which return one value), except they return rows of columns.

Following is an example of how a table function might be used.

```
SELECT MONTH(people.birthdate) AS MONTH, EMP.LASTNAME
FROM EMPLOYEE AS EMP, TABLE(people(CURRENT DATE)) as people
ORDER BY MONTH, EMP.LASTNAME
```

Basically, this example invokes a UDF that gets data from somewhere else and returns it as columns and rows to the SQL statement. There are many implications, such as how the optimizer can determine which table is the inner and which is the outer for the join process.

Examples of UDFs That Come with DB2

Following are some of the UDFs that come with DB2. Some are written in C and some in C++.

- ALTDATE 1 converts the current date to a user-specified format.
- ALTDATE 2 converts a date from one format to another.
- ALTTIME 3 converts the current time to a user-specified format.
- ALTTIME 4 converts a time from one format to another.

- DAYNAME returns the day of the week for a user-specified date.
- MONTHNAME returns the month for a user-specified date.
- CURRENCY formats a floating-point number as a currency value.
- TABLE_NAME returns the unqualified table name for a table, view, or alias.
- TABLE_QUALIF returns the qualifier for a table, view, or alias.
- TABLE_LOCATION returns the location for a table, view, or alias.
- WEATHER returns a table of weather information from an EBCDIC data set.

UDF in a Trigger

You can use a user-defined function in a trigger, which can help to centralize rules to ensure that they are enforced in the same manner in current and future applications. To invoke a UDF in a trigger, the VALUES clause has to be used. In the following example, PAGE_DBA is a user-written program, perhaps in C or Java, that formulates a message and triggers a process that sends a message to a pager. It is possible for a trigger using these kinds of UDFs to perform any kind of task and not be limited to just SQL.

```
BEGIN ATOMIC
   VALUES(PAGE_DBA('Tablespaces:' CONCAT TS.NAME,
      'needs to be reorged   NOW!'));
END
```

UDF Restrictions

The implementation and use of user-defined functions have a few restrictions. DB2 uses the Recoverable Resource Manager Services attachment facility (RRSAF) as its interface with your user-defined function. You cannot include RRSAF calls in your UDF; DB2 will reject any RRSAF calls that it finds. If the UDF is not defined with SCRATCHPAD or EXTERNAL ACTION, it is not guaranteed to execute under the same task each time it is invoked. You cannot execute COMMIT or ROLLBACK statements in your UDF, and you must close all open cursors in a UDF scalar function. DB2 returns an SQL error if cursors are not closed before it completes.

The number of parameters that can be passed to a routine is restricted in each language. User-defined table functions in particular can require large numbers of parameters.

UDF Performance Considerations

UDFs have the same basic set of performance considerations that stored procedures have. These considerations are basically common sense, such as how much work is done, where is the work done, and how long does it take. A UDF needs to have a very specific function and to do that one thing well.

Monitoring and Controlling UDFs

You can invoke user-defined functions in an SQL statement wherever you can use expressions or built-in functions. User-defined functions, like stored procedures, run in WLM-established address spaces. DB2 user-defined functions are controlled by the following commands.

The START FUNCTION SPECIFIC command activates an external function that has been stopped. You cannot start built-in functions or user-defined functions that are sourced on another function. You can use the START FUNCTION SPECIFIC command to activate all or a specific set of stopped external functions.

To activate an external function that is stopped, issue the following command:

```
START FUNCTION SPECIFIC (function-name)
```

The new SCOPE (GROUP) option can also be used on the -START PROCEDURE command to allow you to start a UDF on all subsystems in a data sharing group (refer to Chapter 11 for more information).

The DB2 command DISPLAY FUNCTION SPECIFIC displays statistics about external user-defined functions that are accessed by DB2 applications. This command displays an output line for each function that a DB2 application has accessed. The information that is returned by this command reflects a dynamic status for a point in time that may change before another DISPLAY is issued. This command does not display information about built-in functions or user-defined functions that are sourced on another function.

To display statistics about an external user-defined function accessed by DB2 applications, issue the following command:

```
DISPLAY FUNCTION SPECIFIC (function-name)
```

Stopping UDFs

The DB2 command STOP FUNCTION SPECIFIC prevents DB2 from accepting SQL statements with invocations of the specified functions. This command does not prevent SQL statements with invocations of the functions from running if they have already been queued or scheduled by DB2. Built-in functions or user-defined functions that are sourced on another function cannot be explicitly stopped. While the STOP FUNCTION SPECIFIC command is in effect, any attempt to execute the stopped functions are queued. You can use the STOP FUNCTION SPECIFIC command to stop access to all or a specific set of external functions.

Use the START FUNCTION SPECIFIC command to activate all or a specific set of stopped external functions.

To prevent DB2 from accepting SQL statements with invocations of the specified functions, issue the following statement:

```
STOP FUNCTION SPECIFIC (function-name)
```

UDF Statistics

The optimizer uses statistics if available for estimating the costs for access paths where UDFs are used. The statistics that the optimizer needs can be updated by using the SYSSTAT.FUNCTIONS catalog view.

A field in the statistics report shows the maximum level of indirect SQL cascading, which includes cascading due to triggers, UDFs, or stored procedures (figure 17.5).

Cost Information

User-defined table functions add additional access cost to the execution of an SQL statement. DB2 must determine the total cost of user-defined table functions when selecting the best access path for an SQL statement. This cost is determined by three components:

- Initialization cost that results from the first call processing
- Cost associated with acquiring a single row
- Final cost of the call that performs the clean-up processing

For more details on how to assist DB2 in determining these costs, refer to Chapter 23.

To determine the elapsed and CPU time spent for UDF operations, you can view an accounting report (figure 17.6).

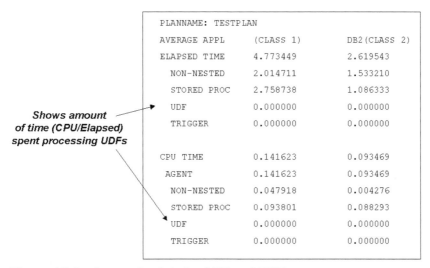

```
            PLANNAME: TESTPLAN

            AVERAGE APPL      (CLASS 1)        DB2(CLASS 2)

            ELAPSED TIME      4.773449         2.619543

              NON-NESTED      2.014711         1.533210

              STORED PROC     2.758738         1.086333

              UDF             0.000000         0.000000

              TRIGGER         0.000000         0.000000


            CPU TIME          0.141623         0.093469

              AGENT           0.141623         0.093469

              NON-NESTED      0.047918         0.004276

              STORED PROC     0.093801         0.088293

              UDF             0.000000         0.000000

              TRIGGER         0.000000         0.000000
```

Shows amount of time (CPU/Elapsed) spent processing UDFs

Figure 17.6 Accounting Info for CPU and UDFs

Catalog Information

The SYSIBM.SYSROUTINES catalog table describes user-defined functions. To retrieve information about UDFs, you can use the following query:

```
SELECT SCHEME, NAME, FUNCTION_TYPE, PARM_COUNT
FROM SYSIBM.SYSROUTINES
WHERE ROUTINETYPE='F'
```

## CHAPTER 18

LOBs and Extenders

Extenders

Extenders for DB2 help in the use of large objects (LOBs), the base storage for the object relational environment. Extenders are a complete package that defines distinct data types and special functions for many types of large objects, including image, audio, video, text, XML, and spatial objects. Extenders eliminate the worry over defining these data types and functions in applications. You can use SQL to manipulate these data types and functions. LOBs can range in size from relatively small to extremely large and can be cumbersome to deal with. Typical sizes of different object types are shown in figure 18.1.

LOB and Extender Usage

When using an extender for a particular LOB type, additional options allow the data to be stored in its native format in a separate file, such as a picture that is a single JPEG file. The hierarchical path name is stored in support tables that allow the extender to use the indirect reference to process the actual data. The different extenders also require varying administrative support tables. These tables are also referred to as metadata tables, as their content enables the extenders to appropriately handle user requests, such as inserting audio, displaying images, and so on. These tables identify base tables and

Object	Size
Check Image	45K
Text	30- 40 K/ page
Small Image	30- 40K
Large Image	200K- 3M
Color Image	20- 40M
Radiology Image 4	0- 60M
Video	1G/ Hour
High Res Video	3G/ Hour
High Definition TV	200M/ sec

Figure 18.1   Example Object Sizes

columns that are enabled for the extender and reference other support tables used to hold attribute information about LOB columns. Triggers supplied by the extenders are used to update many of these support tables when underlying LOB data is inserted, updated, or deleted. At the present time, six extenders are available in the DB2 family: image, audio, video, text, XML, and spatial. Many others are planned, and vendors also supply extender packages.

Applications generally use SQL to retrieve pointers to the data, and UDFs are used to assist with more complex and unique operations. Extender APIs are more commonly used, because all the coding for dealing with the LOBs is supplied. The extender for image data comes with 18 user-defined functions (UDFs), audio has another 27 UDFs, video has 18 UDFs, and the QBIC API (query by image content) has another 24 UDFs. For application programmers, the supplied UDFs are a considerable advantage, because they eliminate having to program them yourself and ease the pain of the learning curve. For example, the image extenders support several different formats. The common ones (BMP, EPS, GIF, JPG, TIF) are provided, of course, along with over 15 other formats. This means that if you were browsing through a series of pictures, each LOB picture could be of a different format, but the program would not have to be aware of this, because the extender would take care of the format. The same is true of the text extender. A user could browse through a series of text documents, one in Microsoft Word format, another in WordPerfect format, and so on. But it is not the browsing of documents, the playing of video, or the streaming of audio that represents the LOB extenders' greatest power. It is their searching ability. For example, the text extender can search by soundex, synonym, thesaurus, proximity, linguistic content, and several others. With images, the QBIC API allows searching by image content; it is a very extensive and powerful API.

Application programming for objects generally requires the use of the extenders. Without their use, little can be done without extensive user programming. The power of objects comes with the user-defined functions and API libraries that are packaged with the extenders. They allow an application to easily store, access, and manipulate any of the supported object types. Although only the six extenders previously mentioned are currently supplied, many others are in development and will be released as they are completed. The application programmer can use UDFs in the SQL to position the necessary LOB and then use an API to manipulate it, as when displaying a picture on the screen, so there are really two completely different libraries to strategize from. Without forcing a match to any particular programming language, the following simple example represents first storing a picture in a LOB and then displaying it on the screen.

First insert the data into the LOB by using the DB2IMAGE extender:

```
EXEC SQL BEGIN DECLARE SECTION;
   storage_type;
EXEC SQL END DECLARE SECTION;

SET storage_type = MMDB_STORAGE_TYPE_INTERNAL

EXEC SQL INSERT INTO MY_PERSONAL_DIGITAL_PICTURES
   VALUES ('OZ TRIP 2',
     'Sydney Opera House',
     DB2IMAGE (
       CURRENT SERVER,
       'c:/My Pictures/1999/Australia/OpraHse.jpg',
       'ASIS',
       :storage_type));
```

Second, retrieve and display the data on the screen using the API DBiBROWSE:

```
EXEC SQL BEGIN DECLARE SECTION;
  image_handler;
EXEC SQL END DECLARE SECTION;

EXEC SQL SELECT PICTURE INTO :image_handler
  WHERE NAME = 'Sydney Opera House';

Set return_code to DBiBROWSE("ib %s,
  MMDB_PLAY_HANDLE,
  image_handler,
  MMDB_PLAY_BI_WAIT);
```

From the pseudocode, it is easy to see that the extenders offer significant power and enable applications to be written quickly. In addition, most of the work is going on at the server, and the client is simply the recipient of all that power. When implementing extenders, you need to keep in mind that the program needs enough memory available, because the LOBs are going to be used on GUI clients.

Enabling Extenders

A software developers kit (SDK) and client and server run-time environment are provided with the DB2 extenders' installation package. DB2 extender applications can be executed on a server machine that has the extender client run-time code and server run-time code (automatically installed when the server run-time code is installed). Extender applications can also be run on a client machine with the client run-time code, and you will need to ensure that a connection can be made to the server.

Extenders are available in DB2 Version 6 client-server environment. OS/390 is the supported server, and clients can use Windows NT, Windows 98, Solaris, AIX, or OS/390.

You do not store image, audio, video, or text objects in the user table; rather, you store an extender-created character string referred to as a handle, which represents the objects, in the user table. The object is actually stored in an administrative support table (or file identifier if the content is a file). The attributes and handles are also stored in these administrative tables. The extender then links the handle in the user table to the object and its attributes in the administrative tables.

Text Extenders

Text extenders bring full text retrieval to SQL queries for searching large text documents intelligently. Text extenders can search several thousand large text documents very quickly. They can also search by word variations and synonyms. Documents to be searched can be stored directly in the database or in a separate file.

Files such as native word processing documents can be searched by keywords, wildcards, phrases, and proximity. IBM has built into these text extenders a high-performance linguistic search technology, giving you multiple options for searching and retrieving documents. These text searches can be integrated with your normal SQL queries. This gives you the ability to integrate attribute and full-text searches into your SELECT statements very easily.

The following example shows how you can perform this integration. In this example, a SELECT from a table also performs a search on a specified document using a text extender called DB2TX.CONTAINS. We are searching the legal cases document to see if the words "malpractice" and "won" appear in the same paragraph for cases occurring after 1990-01-01. LEGCSE_HANDLE refers to the column LEGCSE that contains the text document.

```
SELECT DOC_NUM, DOC_DATE
FROM LEGAL_CLAIMS
WHERE DOC_DATE > '1990-01-01'
AND DB2TX.CONTAINS
  (LEGCSE_HANDLE,
  "malpractice"
  IN SAME PARAGRAPH AS "won") = 1
```

Text extenders *will* allow applications to

- search documents in several languages and formats,
- perform wildcard searching using masks,
- search for words that sound like the search input,

- perform fuzzy searches for similar words (with various spellings),
- search for specific text, synonyms, phrases, or proximity, and
- perform free-text searches where the input is a natural language.

Indexing Text Extenders

Scans are just as undesirable in text documents as they are in DB2 tables. You need to create indexes so that sequential scans of documents are not necessary. A text index can speed up the searches performed on these documents.

A text index contains important words. There is a list of words known as stop words, such as *and* or *the,* which are prevented from being in a text index. You can modify this list, but you should do it only once at installation time.

When a request is made, the index is searched to determine which documents contain the specified terms.

To set up these indexes, you first record the text documents that need to be indexed in a log table. This indexing process occurs when a DB2 trigger is fired off during an insert, update, or delete of a text document column. When the terms are inserted or updated in the text document, they are added to the index. They are also deleted from the index if they are deleted from the text document.

There are four types of indexes, and the type must be established before you implement columns that use text extenders. The reason is that not all search options are available to all index types, so make sure the index suits your search criteria. The four types of indexes are as follows:

- Linguistic. In this type of index, linguistic processing is performed during the analysis of the text when creating an index. Before a word is inserted into the index, it is reduced to its base form. Queries also use linguistic processing when searching against this index. This index requires the least amount of space, but searching may take longer than against a precise index.
- Precise. In this index, the search terms appear exactly as they are in the text document and are case sensitive. The same processing is used for the query search terms, so they must match exactly. The search can be broadened by using masks. This index provides a more precise search, and the retrieval and indexing is fast, but more space is required for its storage.
- Dual. Dual indexes are combinations of linguistic and precise indexes. They allow the user to decide which type of search to use. This index requires the most

disk space. It is slower for searching and indexing than the linguistic index and is not recommended for a large number of text documents.

- Ngram. The Ngram index is used primarily for indexing DBCS documents and analyzes text by parsing sets of characters. This index type also supports fuzzy searches.

When creating tables that support the ability to search text using extenders, you must consider a few design options. You can create one text index for all text columns in the table, or you can have several different text indexes, one for each text column. A separate index for each text column offers you the most flexibility. It also gives you other options, such as how frequently the index is updated and where it is stored. One common index is easier to maintain but less flexible. If your indexes are large, you should consider storing them on separate disks, especially if you expect to have concurrent access to the indexes.

You can also have multiple indexes on a single text column. You may want to do this if you need to allow different types of searches on a text column.

Just like other DB2 indexes, text indexes need to be reorganized. The text extender automatically reorganizes text indexes in the background. Despite this feature, you still may have to reorganize an index manually every so often, depending on its volatility. If a text column is continually updated, you need to reorganize it. The REORGANIZE INDEX command does this, and you can see when you need to use this command by issuing the GET INDEX STATUS command.

Frequency of Index Updates

When text documents are added, deleted, or changed, their content must be synchronized with the index. This information is automatically stored by triggers in a log table, and the documents are indexed the next time an index update is executed.

The indexes can be immediately updated via the UPDATE INDEX command, but it is easier to have this performed automatically on a periodic basis. The index update frequency is kept in an environment variable called DB2TXUPDATEFREQ. This variable provides default settings, but these can be changed during the ENABLE TEXT COLUMN, ENABLE TEXT TABLE, or (for an existing index) CHANGE INDEX SETTINGS command.

The variable for determining when indexing should occur is based on the minimum number of queued text documents in the log table. When this minimum is reached the index is updated. Because updating indexes is a resource-intensive and time-consuming task, this frequency should be set carefully.

Catalog View for Text Extenders

A catalog view is created for each subsystem when you run the ENABLE SERVER. This view is DB2TX.TEXTINDEXES. It has information about the tables and the columns that have been enabled for the text extender. The entries are made during table, column, or external file enablement. If they are disabled, the row is removed. You can view the entries in the catalog view via SQL.

In this view you can see information such as how often the indexes are scheduled for updates, whether or not you have a multiple-index table, and the type of index.

Image, Audio, and Video Extenders

The DB2 video extender can store as many as three representative frames per shot. Displaying the frames offers a quick yet effective view of a video's content. The DB2 video extender provides sample programs that demonstrate how to build and display a video storyboard.

Video storyboards let you preview videos before you download and view them. This can save you time and reduce video traffic on the network.

When image data is inserted into a table using the DB2IMAGE user-defined functions, many processes are performed for the application automatically. The following code demonstrates using this function.

```
EXEC SQL INSERT INTO CONSULTANTS VALUES(
   :cons_id,
   :cons_name,
   DB2IMAGE(
      CURRENT SERVER,
      '/YLA/images/current.bmp'
      'ASIS',
      MMDB_STORAGE_TYPE_INTERNAL,
      :cons_picture_tag);
```

In this particular example, the DB2IMAGE reads all the attributes about the image (height, width, colors, layers, pixels, and more) from the source image file header, in this case current.bmp. All the input is of a standard supported format, and all graphic files contain header information about the structure of the content. The function then creates a unique handle for the image and records all the information in the support table for administrative control of the image. This table would contain these items:

- The handle for the image
- A time stamp
- The image size in bytes
- The comment contained in :cons_picture_tag
- The content of the image

The content of the image source file is inserted into the LOB table as a BLOB. No conversion is done, and the image is stored in its native format. A record in the administrative table contains all the image-specific attributes, such as the number of colors in the image, as well as a thumbnail-sized version of the image.

This example uses the storage-type constants. We used MMDB_STORAGE_ TYPE_INTERNAL to store the image into a database table as a BLOB. By using the extenders, we could have stored it elsewhere. If you want to store the object and have its content remain in the original file on the server, you can specify the constant MMDB_STORAGE_TYPE_EXTERNAL. Just because you are using LOBs does not mean that they have to be in DB2-managed tables. The administrative support table for image extenders tells where the LOB is actually stored. Supporting externally stored LOBs requires Open Edition support services on the S/390.

There are many performance considerations about where the LOB is stored, how it is used, where it is materialized, and so on. These details are covered in Chapters 3 and 7.

XML Extenders

XML has been added to the available extenders. For next-generation B2B e-commerce solutions, XML is the standard for data interchange. With the XML extender for DB2, you can put your critical business information into DB2 databases and engage in B2B solutions using XML-based interchange formats.

You can use XML documents stored in DB2 in a single column or as a collection of data items in multiple columns and tables. The XML text extender in DB2 supports structured XML documents. The powerful search functions can be applied to a section or a list of sections within a set of XML documents, which significantly improves the effectiveness of the search. Additionally, specific XML elements or attributes can be automatically extracted into traditional SQL data types to take advantage of DB2's sophisticated indexing and SQL query capabilities.

The DB2 XML extender supplies a visual administration tool for easy definition and mapping of elements and attributes from an XML document into columns and tables.

Stored Procedures

Stored procedures are implemented on all of the DB2 family platforms, including OS/390. But it is OS/390 that keeps receiving extensive changes that allow more and more use of stored procedures, not just for performance improvements but for other reasons as well. Stored procedures have changed remarkably since they were introduced and now can be used almost without limits.

> *Note: Of the two address spaces that work with stored procedures, it is the Work Load Manager (WLM) address spaces that will continue to be enhanced. It is time to start migrating away from DB2-managed stored procedure address spaces (SPAS).*

Stored Procedures

Stored procedures are application programs executed by DB2 for OS/390 in response to a single SQL CALL statement. A stored procedure can contain SQL statements and can be written in many languages. You can invoke a stored procedure and process result sets from many client applications using ODBC, JDBC, and SQLJ standards. In addition, result sets can be processed by local applications running on the OS/390 using static SQL. Stored procedures can be local or remote and can be called by programs running on the same server or by programs running remotely. There are many different reasons for using stored procedures.

One situation in which stored procedures are useful is when a client-server application must issue several remote SQL statements. The network overhead involved in sending multiple SQL commands and receiving result sets is quite significant. Using stored procedures lessens the traffic across the network and reduces the application overhead (figure 19.1).

You can also use stored procedures to access information on the host server that is required to be secure. This information remains more secure because you can use result sets to return the required data to the client and the client needs to have authority only to execute the stored procedure, not to access the DB2 tables.

Stored procedures should also be used to encapsulate business functions that can be programmed once and executed by any and all processes—OLTP, local, remote, warehouse, ad hoc, or others. Such a functional process might add or update a purchase order. Both of these transactions are long and involve accessing and updating many tables. They are processes that are invoked both in OLTP and batch environments. Therefore, writing the process as a stored procedure allows the function to exist in only one place and yet to be used anywhere in the system, by any type of process. If for some reason the business

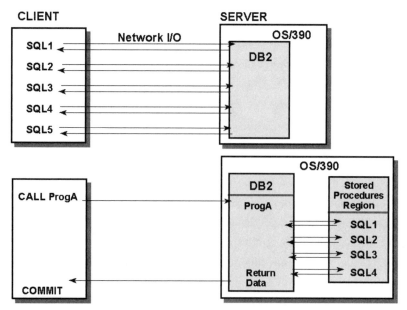

Figure 19.1 Network Improvement

needs to change the way this function is implemented, only one program needs to be changed. Similarly, if the database structure changes, only that one program needs to be updated.

Another possibility is to code complex processes in a stored procedure that can then be invoked by any process in the network. This can be especially useful where applications require the use of non-DB2 data. For instance, when data needs to be retrieved from a VSAM or IMS data store and used by a DB2 client, a stored procedure can retrieve the data into a global temporary table, and then the application can use SQL and result-set logic for row retrieval of this data, alone or combined through joins with other DB2 data.

Language Support

A stored procedure for DB2 OS/390 up to the initial release of version 5 can only be written in COBOL, S/390 Assembler, C, C++, or PL/I. Stored procedures for the other DB2 family members can be written in any languages that conform to the parameter-passing and linkage conventions defined by either C or Java. The C calling and linkage convention is defined by the standard ANSI C prototype. To conform to the Java language convention, the database manager must call the stored procedure as a method in a Java class.

Starting with DB2 OS/390 Version 5 enhancements and beyond, you can write stored procedures in Java, procedural SQL, or REXX. Java stored procedures can use SQLJ (static SQL for Java) and JDBC (dynamic SQL for Java). Java stored procedures are written the same way as in the other languages, have the benefit on OS/390 of a high-performance Java compiler, and late in 2000 will benefit from a very powerful JVM.

REXX can also be used as a DB2 stored procedure language, but it is interpreted, not compiled (it has no precompiler, compiler, or linker). REXX is able to contain SQL but is limited to only one output parameter. Also, all parameters passed to REXX have to be strings; integers are passed as numeric strings. The SQLCA is automatically included. REXX stored procedures allow retrieval, storing, and processing of DB2 data.

To achieve a higher level of portability and assist in migrations to DB2, the SQL language has been extended with procedural syntax, which at one time was called SQL Procedures. This is the IBM subset of PSM (persistent stored modules), which is an SQL3 syntax standard. SQL stored procedure syntax requires the stored procedure to be defined in the

CREATE PROCEDURE statement, rather than written in a compiled or interpreted language. An example of an SQL stored procedure follows:

```
CREATE PROCEDURE YLASSOC (IN x_acct CHAR(5),
      OUT x_name CHAR(20),
      OUT x_address CHAR(80),
      OUT x_code INT
   LANGUAGE(SQL)
   BEGIN;
      SET x_code = 0;
      SELECT x_name, x_address
         FROM YLASSOC_ACCTS
         WHERE ACCT = x_acct;
      IF SQLCODE < 0 THEN
         x_code = SQLCODE;
   END;
```

This code is actually prepared as a procedure by a DB2-supplied REXX stored procedure. More information about DB2 support of REXX and SQL stored procedures is in Chapter 20, and a larger example in figure 19.2 was built using the Stored Procedure Builder tool.

Performance Considerations

Numerous options are available for improving the performance of stored procedures when the procedures are defined or created. Procedures can be coded as main programs (MAIN) or subroutines (SUB). SUB allows a shorter code path for entry and exit logic but is much more difficult to write, since all initializations, entry and exit logic, allocating and freeing of storage, and other environmental issues have to be handled. This option is only for very knowledgeable programmers and very special situations where that last bit of code length reduction is required. It also can be used only in a WLM-established environment. Using the residency features to keep the program in memory once loaded and making the code reentrant to handle multiple requests are other performance techniques. Using the WLM-established address space option of OS/390 is another way to improve performance, as it establishes additional address spaces when the need arises due to increased workload.

```
CREATE PROCEDURE DW.SQLProc1 ( IN gender char(6) )
    SPECIFIC DW.Genders
    RESULT SETS 1
    LANGUAGE SQL
P1: BEGIN
    DECLARE gender_value CHAR(1);
    DECLARE bad_gender CONDITION FOR SQLSTATE '99001';
    CASE gender
       WHEN 'MALE' THEN
          SET gender_value = 'M';
       WHEN 'FEMALE' THEN
          SET gender_value = 'F';
       ELSE
          SIGNAL bad_gender;
    END CASE;
    -- Declare cursor
    DECLARE cursor1 CURSOR WITH RETURN FOR
       SELECT E.EMPNO, E.LASTNAME, E.HIREDATE, D.DEPTNO, D.DEPTNAME
       FROM DW.DEPARTMENT D, DW.EMPLOYEE E
       WHERE E.WORKDEPT = D.DEPTNO
         AND E.SEX = :gender_value
       ORDER BY E.WORKDEPT;
    -- Cursor left open for client application
    OPEN cursor1;
END P1
```

Figure 19.2 SQL Procedures

Reentrant Code

Stored procedures should be coded as reentrant for performance reasons. First, if the stored procedure is coded as reentrant, it does not have to be loaded into storage each time it is called. Second, several threads can share a single copy of a reentrant stored procedure, thus requiring less virtual storage. You should use the "stay resident" option with the reentrant programs. For any program that is not reentrant, you need to absolutely negate the "stay resident" option.

Fenced and Nonfenced Procedures

A fenced stored procedure executes in a separate process from the database agent. Nonfenced stored procedures execute in the same process as the database agent and can increase application performance because less overhead is needed for communication between the application and the DB2 coordinating agent. However, nonfenced stored procedures can overwrite the DB2 control blocks. A stored procedure that is not fenced is generally one that is considered safe to run in the process or address of the database manager's operating environment.

On DB2 for OS/390, all stored procedures are fenced. On the other platforms, they can be fenced or nonfenced.

Limiting Resources Used

Stored procedures are designed for high-volume online transactions. You can limit the resources used by stored procedures by setting a processor limit for each stored procedure. You can do this by updating the ASUTIME column in SYSIBM.SYSROUTINES (as of version 6) to allow DB2 to cancel stored procedures that are in a loop. ASUTIME is designed for runaway stored procedures. The routine to check for overages on ASUTIME runs only once per minute of clock time, so it does not provide very strict control of how much CPU time a stored procedure can use. You should use the priorities and service goals of the Workload Manager (WLM) to tightly control system resource usage. Using both ASUTIME and WLM provides total control.

You can also specify a limit for the number of times procedures can abnormally terminate. On the installation panel DSNTIPX, a field called MAX ABEND COUNT allows you to specify a value to prevent a stored procedure from overloading the subsystem with ABEND dumps.

Workload Manager

A simple performance guideline is to use WLM in goal mode if you use stored procedures.

WLM-established address spaces provide multiple isolated environments for stored procedures so that failures do not affect other stored procedures. WLM-established address spaces also reduce demand for storage below the 16MB line, removing the limitation on the number of stored procedures that can run concurrently. These address spaces also inherit the dispatching priority of the DB2 thread that issues the CALL statement. Inheriting the dispatching priority of the thread allows high-priority work to have its stored procedures execute ahead of lower-priority work and its stored procedures. In a DB2-established address space, you cannot prioritize stored procedures and are limited by storage in the address space. There is no separation of the work by dispatching priorities, and high-priority work gets penalized. The real benefits to stored procedures using WLM are static priority assignment and dynamic workload balancing. Stored procedures designated as high priority to WLM achieve very consistent response times. WLM provides dynamic workload balancing and distribution by routing incoming requests to the stored procedure address space that is the least busy or by starting new address spaces if required. This is fully automatic and does not require monitoring and tuning.

CICS EXCI

CICS EXCI is an interface that allows an OS/390 application program executing in an OS/390 address space to link to a CICS program running in a CICS address space. DB2 stored procedures run in OS/390 address spaces. By using the EXCI commands, you can call a program that is running in a CICS region from a client (non-CICS) program. Thus, you can run client programs from the same OS/390, multiple OS/390 images, or another platform and execute a CICS program for any number of client programs.

The CICS transactions, programs, and connections in the CICS regions can be called by stored procedures and must be defined for you to implement the stored procedures with EXCI. The DB2 address spaces need to have the CICS load library in their concatenation and to have proper access to the CICS regions.

Using EXCI gives the CICS program the ability to both run as an online transaction in CICS and as a program called via the stored procedure by a client application. In figure 19.3, multiple clients are invoking stored procedures through the WLM-managed queues, with the stored procedures executing in the WLM-managed address spaces. From those address spaces, additional processes such as CICS can be used through the EXCI-APPC connection as described previously. Stored procedures are really unbounded when it comes to integrating with existing systems. One of those clients could be a web transaction that drives to the back-end CICS applications through DB2 stored procedures and WLM.

Programming Considerations

LE/370 Required

The LE/370 product libraries are used to load and execute the stored procedures in the stored procedures address space. When you create a stored procedure, either by the INSERT process in version 5 or by CREATE DDL in version 6, you pass run-time information for

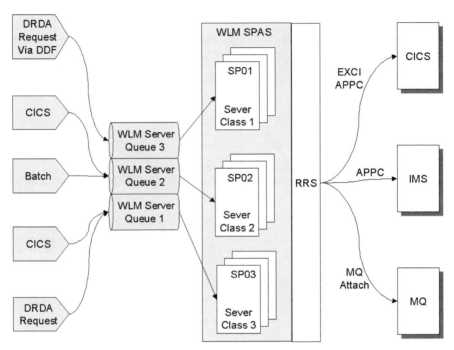

Figure 19.3   WLM Managed Servers with RRS

LE/370 when the stored procedure is executed. LE/370 is used because it establishes a common run-time environment for the many different languages used for stored procedures. It provides a consistent set of interfaces for essential run-time services. When using LE/370, you do not have to specify the language-specific libraries in the JCL procedure of the stored procedures address space.

There are several functions performed for DB2 by LE/370.

- Cloaks the differences among the programming languages
- Permits a stored procedure to be resident in the SPAS
- Provides you the option to debug stored procedures at run time by allowing you to invoke the CODE/370 debugger or VisualDebugger.

COMMIT ON RETURN

The COMMIT ON RETURN option for stored procedures reduces network traffic and allows predictable locking in a stored procedure. Without COMMIT ON RETURN, the locks would be held until the connected application issued the COMMIT, and an interchange would require many more network messages during which the locks were held. With the COMMIT ON RETURN option, the locks are freed as soon as the stored procedure ends.

However, there are always trade-offs. COMMIT ON RETURN cannot be used in nested stored procedures and is ignored if specified in them. The design of nested stored procedures as of version 6 requires some delicate planning. There is more on the nesting of stored procedures later in this chapter.

Return of Columns

The default in DB2 is to not return column names for stored procedures. However, updating a DSNZPARM parameter can change this default. If the SELECT statements inside the stored procedure are static, you must set the DESCSTAT parameter to YES on the host DB2 where the procedure was compiled in order to retrieve column names from your stored procedure result sets. Then you need to rebind the stored procedure's application packages. If the SELECT statements inside the stored procedure are dynamic, the result-set column names should be returned automatically.

Result Sets

As of DB2 Version 5, stored procedures can return result sets to the client, allowing data to be retrieved more efficiently and improving application security by requiring a client to have only execution authority on a stored procedure, not access to the referenced tables. Result sets from DB2 or nonrelational sources can be returned from either base tables or temporary tables to clients on any DB2 server. For a stored procedure to return multiple result sets to clients, the following conditions must be present:

- Cursors must be opened using the WITH RETURN clause.
- The procedure needs to be defined for returning result sets. This is specified differently in version 5 and version 6.
- The DRDA client needs to support level 3 result sets.

To prepare a distributed application to receive result sets, you need to use a CLI application or an ODBC or CLI application tool able to receive result sets, such as Visual

Age, PowerBuilder, or Visual Basic. New additions to the static SQL language support running the application code on the same OS/390 server as the stored procedure. Following is a skeleton example of code to receive a stored procedure result set when the application program is running on the same OS/390 server as the stored procedure.

```
EXEC SQL
    BEGIN DECLARE SECTION;
EXEC SQL
    RESULT_SET_LOCATOR VARYING locater1;
EXEC SQL
    END DECLARE SECTION;

EXEC SQL
    CALL SP1(:parm1, :parm2, . . .);

EXEC SQL
    ASSOCIATE LOCATOR (:locater1) WITH PROCEDURE SP1;
EXEC SQL
    ALLOCATE CSR1 CURSOR FOR RESULT SET :locater1;
EXEC SQL
    FETCH CSR1 INTO :acctno, ;billingno;
```

To allow result sets to be returned from the stored procedure on the server, the WITH RETURN clause must be used in the cursor definition in the stored procedure, and the cursors cannot be closed before the program ends. DB2 returns the rows in the result set from the opened cursors to the application program when the stored procedure ends. The following example shows the stored procedure code necessary to return the result set to the application shown in the previous example.

```
EXEC SQL
    DECLARE SP_CSR1 CURSOR
        WITH RETURN FOR
            SELECT ACCT_NO, BILLING_NO
            FROM  ORDER_TABLE
            WHERE ITEM = :parm1;

EXEC SQL
```

```
OPEN SP_CSR1;
```

```
RETURN;
```

From a design standpoint, most result sets are of this variety. But there is a very powerful way to build totally dynamic stored procedures and still interface with client processes. This can be very significant for web-enabled applications that provide dynamic pages to a client.

The DESCRIBE PROCEDURE can be used to retrieve all the information about a procedure's result set. It is not required if result sets are predefined, and it cannot be dynamically prepared. It returns information that a "dynamic" client needs to use the result sets. SQLDA contains the number of result sets, with one SQLVAR entry for each result set in the stored procedure. SQLDATA(x) contains the result-set locator value, and SQLNAME(x) contains the server application's cursor name. The procedure is invoked by using either of the following commands:

```
DESCRIBE PROCEDURE SP1 INTO sqlda
```

```
DESCRIBE PROCEDURE :hv INTO sqlda
```

DESCRIBE CURSOR can be used to retrieve all the information about a cursor left open inside a stored procedure to return a result set. This command works for any allocated cursor but is not needed if result sets are predefined. It also cannot be dynamically prepared. This feature returns information needed by "dynamic" clients, such as the name, length, and type of columns contained in a result set. The output SQLDA is very similar to that produced by the DESCRIBE of a SELECT. This cursor is invoked by using either of the following commands:

```
DESCRIBE CURSOR SPC1 INTO sqlda
```

```
DESCRIBE CURSOR :hv INTO sqlda
```

Figure 19.4 shows how a program might be coded to invoke the client-side DESCRIBE processes, and figure 19.5 shows what is in a stored procedure using dynamic SQL. It is this capability for dynamic SQL that makes the client dependent on the DESCRIBE features before actually retrieving any result-set rows.

```
exec sql
   BEGIN DECLARE SECTION;
exec sql
   static volatile SQL TYPE IS
         RESULT_SET_LOCATOR VARYING locater1;
exec sql
   END DECLARE SECTION;
exec sql
   CALL SP1(:parm1, :parm2, ...);
exec sql
   DESCRIBE PROCEDURE SP1 INTO :sqlda;
exec sql
   ASSOCIATE LOCATOR (:locater1) WITH PROCEDURE SP1;
exec sql
   ALLOCATE CSR1 CURSOR FOR RESULT SET :locater1;
exec sql
   DESCRIBE CURSOR CSR1 FOR RESULT SET :locater1;
exec sql
   FETCH CSR1 INTO :sqlda;
```

> Determine the number of result sets

> Determine the number of columns

Figure 19.4   DESCRIBE Example: Client Application

```
EXEC SQL
   DECLARE SP_CSR1 CURSOR
      WITH RETURN FOR
            S1;

EXEC SQL
   PREPARE S1 FROM
         'SELECT ACCT_NO, BILLING_NO
         FROM  ORDER_TABLE
         WHERE ITEM = ?';

EXEC SQL
   OPEN SP_CSR1 USING :parm1;

return;
```

Figure 19.5   Stored Procedure with Dynamic SQL

Again, there are trade-offs. Query result sets are returned to the previous level only when they occur in nested stored procedures. There is more on the nesting of stored procedures in the next section.

Nesting

A scary DB2 enhancement allows stored procedures to invoke UDFs and subsequently call other stored procedures (local or remote), any of which could also invoke triggers. The triggers could call additional stored procedures and invoke UDFs. This could go on forever; despite an initial defined limit of 16 nesting levels in version 6, careful planning is required to prevent endless looping. With this enhancement, N-tier client-server applications can be built using SQL and stored procedure RPCs (remote procedure calls) to communicate between servers. In addition, IBM's DataJoiner has DRDA server capability; this means that a DB2 requester can issue a SELECT to DataJoiner. It also means that a client in this N-tier application can be presented with data via a stored procedure result set that came from multiple servers in the network, DB2, and any other DBMS servers.

Nesting has obvious impacts on resource consumption and the scope of registers. When stored procedures are nested, the following list of DB2 special registers is saved when pushing deeper and restored when popping back up:

- CURRENT DATE
- CURRENT DEGREE
- CURRENT PACKAGESET
- CURRENT PATH
- CURRENT RULES
- CURRENT SERVER
- CURRENT SQLID
- CURRENT TIME
- CURRENT TIMESTAMP
- CURRENT TIMEZONE
- CURRENT USER

There are some very important limitations of nesting stored procedures:

1. Nesting between DB2-managed and WLM-managed address spaces is not allowed (another reason to move away from DB2-managed address spaces).
2. No COMMIT ON RETURN is executed when nested.
3. Query result sets are returned to the previous nesting level.

Building a simple stored procedure to facilitate reusable code or to write a process only once is easy. But deciding to integrate it in an N-tier environment obviously takes some very careful planning. Accidents can happen, since any updating of a table can cause a trigger to be invoked. The implementation of that trigger depends on everything using the table, since it would be possible for the trigger to call a stored procedure. The same holds true for user-defined functions. There needs to be a well-defined storyboard of all the dependencies of stored procedures and user-defined functions that can update processes or call other processes at the same or deeper levels.

Good coordination and planning are needed among the application programmers, database procedural programmers, system programmers, and DBAs to make sure that unnecessary levels, trigger cascading, and looping cannot occur.

Stored Procedure Builder

The Stored Procedure Builder (figure 19.6) is a Windows-based graphical application that runs on Windows NT, 95, or 98 and supports the rapid development of DB2 stored procedures written in either Java or the SQL procedural language. It can work as a Microsoft Visual Studio plug-in, with Microsoft Visual Basic or IBM VisualAge for Java, or as a

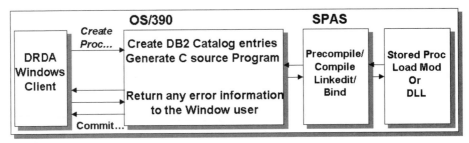

Figure 19.6 DB2 Stored Procedure Builder

Stored Procedure Builder **447**

stand-alone. It is used to generate a C program that DB2 will precompile, compile, linkedit, and bind without requiring you to log on to TSO. The Stored Procedure Builder supports the entire DB2 family from a single development environment. We examine each of the many options.

Using the Stored Procedure Builder, you can perform the following tasks:

- Create new stored procedures
- Build stored procedures on local and remote DB2 servers
- Modify and rebuild existing stored procedures
- Run installed stored procedures to test their execution

The Stored Procedure Builder is implemented with Java, and all database connections are managed by using JDBC, so you can connect to any local DB2 alias or any other database for which you can specify a host name, port, and database name.

The stored procedure SmartGuide and SQL Assistant help you develop stored procedures using the Stored Procedure Builder. You launch the stored procedure SmartGuide from the Project window of the Stored Procedure Builder. The most important feature is that you can create stored procedures in Java and SQL. Java and SQL stored procedures are highly portable. You can use the code editor to modify the stored procedure to use highly sophisticated logic.

Note: Using the Stored Procedure Builder with Java is also a nice way to rapidly develop a C program that can then be maintained and developed further simply as C source code.

When creating a stored procedure, you can choose to return a single result set, multiple result sets, or output parameters only. You can use the stored procedure SmartGuide to define input and output parameters for a stored procedure so that it receives values for host variables from the client application. When you finish building a stored procedure on a target database, the Stored Procedure Builder drives the CREATE PROCEDURE process in DB2, so there is nothing more to do.

The Stored Procedure Builder allows you to modify, rebuild, run, or test existing stored procedures. When you open a stored procedure, the source code is displayed in the editor pane on the right side. The editor pane has a language-sensitive editor for stored procedures written in Java. You cannot see the color of the display in figure 19.7, but it distinguishes user code, syntax, reserved words, and so on.

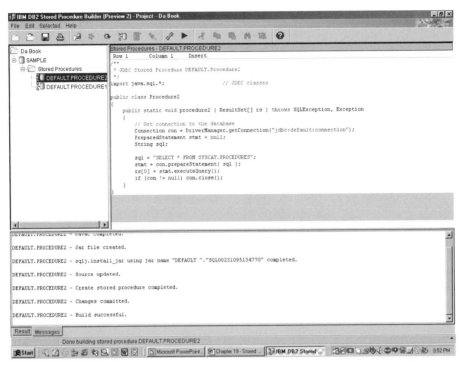

Figure 19.7   Stored Procedure Builder

To test a stored procedure using this tool, you can run it from within the Stored Procedure Builder to make sure that a stored procedure is correctly installed. Testing stored
procedures this way makes programming a lot easier, and you know that the stored procedure is correctly installed on the DB2 database server. You can also delete a stored
procedure or copy it to another database connection from within the Stored Procedure
Builder.

SQL Procedures and the Stored Procedure Builder

Although the Stored Procedure Builder can be used to build stored procedures using the
SQL procedural language, there are other ways to build stored procedures using the SQL
language. You can prepare and run SQL procedures using just JCL. The SQL Procedures
Processor can prepare SQL procedures for execution without JCL.

Java and the Stored Procedure Builder

In the example in figure 19.7, you can see the results of about 10 seconds of work simply defining an SQL statement (which could have been built with the SmartGuide) and then telling the Stored Procedure Builder to build the procedure. On the bottom of that display, you can see the immediate steps that were completed, in very rapid succession in this case:

- Built the stored procedure
- Invoked the javac Java compiler
- Created the jar file
- Installed the jar
- Updated the source
- Issued the DDL
- Committed the process

This might not look like what you see on the OS/390. This example was run on Windows NT using version 6.1 for that platform. If we had an S/390 connection, the Stored Procedure Builder would have performed most of the process on the OS/390, converted the code into C, run it through the preprocessor, compiled and linkedited it, bound the package, and issued the DDL. By the time this book is in print, that process might have changed. In general on the OS/390, you will probably see Java stored procedures and Java code simply compiled if there is no JVM available for that particular type of address space. A new JVM may soon be available to allow the normal Java process. There are many options, and this environment is changing weekly.

We are relatively certain that in the future, there will be no need for a native OS/390 compiler and there will be no need to convert the Java into C. Rather, an industrial-strength JVM will allow Java byte code to be executed with the same throughput that we have seen for years in high-volume COBOL systems.

DB2-Delivered Stored Procedures

Some additional stored procedures that come with DB2 are not documented. They were included starting with version 5. It is possible that some are no longer included.

DSNUTILS, however, was initially not documented but later was announced as a major feature.

- DSNWZP returns all the values of the normal and hidden DSNZPARMs and the version 6 DSNHDECP values.
- DSNWSPM retrieves many performance statistics, such as SQL CPU.
- DSNACCMG formats SQLCA as DSNTIAR did.
- DSNACCAV gives partition information for table spaces and index spaces to show which need REORG, RUNSTATS, or image copy utilities executed.
- DSNUTILS executes DB2 utilities from any process that can issue an SQL call statement.

DSNWZP

DSNWZP is the stored procedure that sits behind Visual Explain to return information to the client about the values of the DSNZPARMs (and the DECP values, as of version 6). There is no published documentation on this stored procedure. This process uses a READS call to IFI and returns the results to the client, either local or remote. IFI returns record 106, which contains all the DSNPARMs. DSNWZP adds additional information to the data that is in the 106 records and returns all of this to the client in a single long VARCHAR (8,600 in version 5, 12,000 in version 6).

The values that are returned for each DSNZPARM or DECP value are

- Internal parameter name
- Macro name
- External parameter name
- Install panel name
- Install panel number
- Install panel field name
- Current value

While DSNWZP does not require WLM and, as we have stated many times, it is time to stop using normal DB2-managed stored procedure address spaces, DSNWZP can run in such an address space.

If you really want to make use of this procedure, it is better to use the Visual Explain interface, since everything regarding the presentation of the output is taken care. However, DSNWZP is directly available through the normal SQL call statement. You can invoke it by issuing

```
EXEC SQL CALL DSNWZP (output parameter)
   The output parameter needs to be defined as:
      Version 5 -- VARCHAR(8600)
      Version 6 -- VARCHAR(12000)
```

The data in the output parameter is separated by an X'25' value, and the individual values are separated by a /, so you could call it from COBOL, Java, or REXX to build your own particular interface. The actual definition used in version 6 to register the stored procedure is

```
CREATE PROCEDURE SYSPROC.DSNWZP
   (OUT P10 VARCHAR (12000) CCSID EBCDIC)
    PROGRAM TYPE MAIN
    EXTERNAL NAME DSNWZP
    COLLID DSNWZP
    LANGUAGE ASSEMBLE
    RUN OPTIONS 'TRAP(ON), TERMTHDAC(UADUMP)'
    PARAMETER STYLE GENERAL
    NO WLM ENVIRONMENT
    COMMIT ON RETURN NO
```

DSNWSPM

We believe that DSNWSPM is still undocumented but may be documented in the future. DSNWSPM supports the Stored Procedure Builder but was originally used for testing. It returns performance information for the thread on which it is running. This has real potential, since any process can invoke this stored procedure and return data about what resources it is consuming. This is nice for performance tuning, as the call can be made as the final code in any process, returning detailed information about the resources used, such as CPU time, lock wait time, number of GETPAGES and number of I/O's.

DSNWSPM is directly available through the normal SQL call statement. You can invoke it by issuing

```
CALL DSNWSPM (TWACDBL1, TWACDBL2, TWACAJST,
              TWACAWTL, TBINAJST, TBINAWTL,
              TBACGET, TBACIMW, TBACIMW)
```

The parameters used in the stored procedure call are

- TWACDBL1 CHAR(8) FOR BIT DATA INOUT: Call type or begin CPU time
- TWACDBL2 CHAR(8) FOR BIT DATA INOUT: Begin lock/latch time
- TWACAJST CHAR(15) OUT CPU: Time in external format
- TWACAWTL CHAR(15) OUT: Latch/lock contention wait time, external format
- TBINAJST INTEGER OUT CPU: Time as an integer in hundredths of a second
- TBINAWTL INTEGER OUT: Latch/lock contention wait time, integer
- TBACGET INTEGER OUT: Number of GETPAGES, integer
- TBACRIO INTEGER OUT: Number of read I/O operations, integer
- TBACIMW INTEGER OUT: Number of write I/O operations, integer

To use DSNWSPM accurately, you should call it as the first part of the process and then again at the end of the process. If you call it this way, you get the additional accumulated data from the thread creation. If the thread is in reuse, you could get quite erroneous data.

You should call DSNWSPM first to get the beginning CPU time and the beginning lock and latch contention wait time. To do this, you need to send a double word of x'FF's (high values) in the first parameter. This tells the procedure to return the beginning times in STCK (store clock) format in the parameters of TWACAJST and TWACAWTL in the first double words.

At the end, call ESPM again, passing it the begin times that were returned to you in the first call. As a result of the second call, the output parameters will contain either net changes or cumulative values as follows:

- Returned as the net change between the starting call and the ending call: TWACAJST, TWACAWTL, TBINAJST, TBINAWTL
- Returned as the cumulative values for the process: TBACGET, TBACRIO, TBACIMW

The other method of using DSNWSPM is to call it just once, but the information returned is not as useful as the data that is returned when it is called at the beginning and at the end. To call it just once, call it at the end of the process being monitored. The first input parameter needs to be set to low values (x'00'). The data returned is the raw beginning CPU and wait times for the thread and an ending CPU time. The beginning CPU time does not change until you end your connection to DB2.

For installation information, you need to check whether or not DSNWSPM is already installed at the precise point when you want to use it. There were PTFs for versions 5 and 6, but we understand that since most people use the Stored Procedure Builder, it will be installed as part of that process. Updated information is available on our web site, www.ylassoc.com.

While DSNWSPM does not require WLM and it is time to stop using normal DB2-managed stored procedure address spaces, DSNWSPM can run in such an address space.

DSNACCMG

Another stored procedure, DSNACCMG, was developed as a plug-in for the Control Center, to assist in formatting an SQLCA. It uses the established DSNTIAR process to convert the SQLCA into a text message. It initializes an SQLCA data structure as an output message area. The SQLCA is passed to the stored procedure as a set of parameters, any of which can contain valid SQLCA data or null values for anything not required. The fully formatted SQLCA will be returned as a single parameter.

The actual definition used in version 6 to register the stored procedure is

```
CREATE PROCEDURE SYSPROC. DSNACCMG
   (IN SQLCODE INTEGER,
     IN SQLERRML SMALLINT,
     IN SQLERRMC VARCHAR(70) CCSID EBCDIC,
     IN SQLERRP VARCHAR(8) CCSID EBCDIC,
     IN SQLERRD0 INTEGER,
     IN SQLERRD1 INTEGER,
     IN SQLERRD2 INTEGER,
     IN SQLERRD3 INTEGER,
     IN SQLERRD4 INTEGER,
     IN SQLERRD5 INTEGER,
     IN SQLWARN VARCHAR(11) CCSID EBCDIC,
```

```
    IN SQLSTATE VARCHAR(5) CCSID EBCDIC,
    OUT MSGTEXT VARCHAR(1210) CCSID EBCDIC)
PROGRAM TYPE MAIN
MODIFIES SQL DATA
EXTERNAL NAME DSNACCMG
COLLID DSNACC
LANGUAGE C
RUN OPTIONS 'TRAP(OFF), STACK(,,ANY,) '
ASUTIME NO LIMIT
STAY RESIDENT NO
NO WLM ENVIRONMENT
COMMIT ON RETURN NO
PARAMETER STYLE GENERAL WITH NULLS
RESULT SETS 0
```

It is directly available through the normal SQL call statement. You can invoke it by issuing

```
CALL DSNACCMG (SQLCODE, SQLERRML, SQLERRMC, SQLERRP,
               SQLERRD0, SQLERRD1, SQLERRD2, SQLERRD3,
               SQLERRD4, SQLERRD5, SQLWARN, SQLSTATE,
               MESSAGE_TEXT)
```

These are its parameters:

- SQLCODE INTEGER IN
- SQLERRML SMALLINT IN
- SQLERRMC VARCHAR(70) IN
- SQLERRP VARCHAR(8) IN
- SQLERRD0-5 INTEGER IN
- SQLWARN VARCHAR(11) IN
- SQLSTATE VARCHAR(5) IN
- MESSAGE_TEXT VARCHAR(1210) OUT

The output parameter MESSAGE_TEXT contains between one and ten, 121-byte lines that are terminated by a normal new-line character.

DSNACCAV

DSNACCAV is another stored procedure that was written in support of the Control Center. There is documentation for this in the *DB2 Utility Guide and Reference*. This stored procedure provides the following information about partitions in your table spaces and indexes:

- Partitions that need to be image copied
- Partitions that are in a restricted state
- Partitions on which RUNSTATS needs to be run
- Partitions on which REORG needs to be run
- Partitions that exceed a user-specified number of extents

The information that is returned comes from queries about the following objects:

- SYSIBM.SYSCOPY
- SYSIBM.SYSINDEXES
- SYSIBM.SYSINDEXPART
- SYSIBM.SYSTABLEPART
- SYSIBM.SYSTABLES
- SYSIBM.SYSTABLESPACE

The actual definition used in version 6 to register the stored procedure is

```
CREATE PROCEDURE SYSPROC.DSNACCAV
    (IN QUERY_TYPE VARCHAR(20) CCSID EBCDIC,
        IN CRITERIA VARCHAR(4096) CCSID EBCDIC,
        IN DAYS INTEGER,
        IN IC_TYPE VARCHAR(1) CCSID EBCDIC,
        IN EXTENTS INTEGER,
        OUT RETURN_CODE INTEGER,
        OUT LAST_STATEMENT VARCHAR(8012) CCSID EBCDIC,
        OUT IFCA_RET INTEGER,
        OUT IFCA_RES INTEGER,
        OUT XS_BYTES INTEGER,
        OUT ERROR_MSG VARCHAR(1331) CCSID EBCDIC)
```

```
PROGRAM TYPE MAIN
MODIFIES SQL DATA
EXTERNAL NAME DSNACCAV COLLID DSNACC
LANGUAGE C
RUN OPTIONS 'TRAP(OFF), STACK(,,ANY,)'
ASUTIME NO LIMIT
```

It is directly available through the normal SQL call statement. You can invoke it by issuing

```
CALL DSNACCAV (query-type,
               search-condition/NULL,
               maximum-days/NULL,
               image-copy-type/NULL,
               maximum-extents/NULL,
               return-code,
               error-statement,
               ifi-return-code,
               ifi-reason-code,
               ifi-excess-bytes,
               message-text)
```

The parameters for the call statements are defined as follows:

- *query-type* specifies the type of information that you want to obtain. This is an input parameter of type VARCHAR(20). The contents must be one of the following values:
- COPY TABLESPACE: Returns table-space partitions that need to be image copied.
- RESTRICT TABLESPACE: Lists table-space partitions that are in a restricted status.
- RESTRICT INDEX: Lists index partitions that are in a restricted status.
- RUNSTATS TABLESPACE: Returns table-space partitions on which RUNSTATS needs to be run.
- RUNSTATS INDEX: Obtains information about index partitions on which RUNSTATS needs to be run.

- REORG TABLESPACE: Returns table-space partitions on which REORG needs to be run.
- REORG INDEX: Obtains information about index partitions on which REORG needs to be run.
- EXTENTS TABLESPACE: Lists table-space partitions that have used more than a user-specified number of extents.
- EXTENTS INDEX: Lists index partitions that have used more than a user-specified number of extents.
- *search-condition* narrows the search for objects that match *query-type*. This is an input parameter of type VARCHAR(4096). The format of this parameter is the same as the format of *search-condition* in an SQL WHERE clause. The parameter *search-condition* is described in Chapter 5 of *SQL Reference*. If the call is executed to obtain table-space information, *search-condition* can include any column in SYSIBM.SYSTABLESPACE. If the call is executed to get index information, *search-condition* can include any column in SYSIBM.SYSINDEXES. Each column name must be preceded by the string "A." For example, to obtain information about table spaces with creator ADMF001, specify this value for *search-condition:* `A. CREATOR= 'ADMF001'.`
- *maximum-days* is an input INTEGER that specifies the maximum number of days that should elapse between executions of the REORG, RUNSTATS, or COPY utility. DSNACCAV uses this value as the criterion for determining which table-space or index partitions need to have the utility that you specified in *query-type* run on them. This value can be specified if *query-type* has one of the following values:
  - COPY TABLESPACE
  - RUNSTATS TABLESPACE
  - RUNSTATS INDEX
  - REORG TABLESPACE
  - REORG INDEX
- *image-copy-type* specifies the types of image copies about which DSNACCAV should give you information. This value can be specified if *query-type* is COPY TABLESPACE. *image-copy-type* is an input parameter of type CHAR(1). The contents must be one of the following values:

- B: Specifies partitions for which the most recent image copy was either a full or an incremental image copy
- F: Specifies partitions for which the most recent image copy was a full image copy
- I: Specifies partitions for which the most recent image copy was an incremental image copy
- *maximum-extents* is an INTEGER that specifies the maximum number of extents that a table space or index partition should use. This value can be specified if *query-type* is one of the following values:

  - REORG TABLESPACE
  - REORG INDEX
  - EXTENTS TABLESPACE
  - EXTENTS INDEX

- *return-code* is an output INTEGER that specifies the return code from the DSNACCAV call. *return-code* is one of the following values:

  - 0: DSNCCAV executed successfully.
  - 12: An error occurred during DSNACCAV execution.

- *error-statement* specifies the SQL statement or DB2 command that DB2 was executing when the error occurred if *return-code* is not 0. *error-statement* is an output parameter of type VARCHAR(8012).
- *ifi-return-code* specifies the return code from the IFI call that submitted a DISPLAY DATABASE command to obtain information about restricted objects, when *query-type* is RESTRICT TABLESPACE, RESTRICT INDEX, COPY TABLESPACE, or REORG TABLESPACE. *ifi-return-code* is an output parameter of type INTEGER.
- *ifi-reason-code* specifies the reason code from the IFI call that submitted a DISPLAY DATABASE command to obtain information about restricted objects, when *query-type* is RESTRICT TABLESPACE, RESTRICT INDEX, COPY TABLESPACE, or REORG TABLESPACE. *ifi-reason-code* is an output parameter of type INTEGER.
- *ifi-excess-bytes* specifies the number of bytes that did not fit in the return area for the IFI call that submitted a DISPLAY DATABASE command to obtain information about restricted objects, when *query-type* is RESTRICT TABLESPACE,

RESTRICT INDEX, COPY TABLESPACE, or REORG TABLESPACE. *ifi-excess-bytes* is an output parameter of type INTEGER.

- *message-text* contains information, including the formatted SQLCA, about the SQL error if one occurs while DSNACCAV executes. The message text consists of one to ten lines, each with a length of 121 bytes. The last byte of each line is a new-line character. *message-text* is an output parameter of type VARCHAR(1210).

DSNACCAV does not require WLM but can run in a normal DB2-managed stored procedure address space.

DSNUTILS

DB2 provides a stored procedure called DSNUTILS that acts as a wrapper around DSNUTILB, enabling the execution of DB2 utilities from an application, local or remote, using an SQL CALL. The results from the utility, the SYSPRINT data, is stored in a temporary table and returned in a result set. This procedure can help with managing DB2 remotely.

The stored procedure supports all JCL management aspects, such as dynamic data set allocation, building and filling SYSIN data sets, invoking the DSNUTILB program, capturing SYSPRINT output, and returning SYSPRINT output to the calling program.

This stored procedure must run in a WLM environment to enable multiple address spaces. This is becoming a requirement for many features in DB2, so it is time to start moving away from DB2-managed address spaces.

The client application calls the DSNUTILS stored procedure with appropriate parameters. DSNUTILS then analyzes the parameters to create a SYSIN input stream and allocate all necessary data sets. After the data sets are allocated, DSNUTILS calls DSNUTILB, which then executes the appropriate utility (figure 19.8). The utility statements are then processed, and DSNUTILS retrieves the execution results from the SYSPRINT file and stores the data in the SYSIBM.SYSPRINT temporary table. It then opens a cursor on the table and passes control back to the client application. The client application then fetches all rows from the result set.

Although the primary objective of DSNUTILS was as a plug-in for the Control Center, it has other uses as well. It is possible for the calling program to build or update a status table that has a trigger on it. The trigger could watch for critical exception conditions

SELECT SEQNO, TEXT FORM SYSIBM.SYSPRINT ORDER BY SEQNO

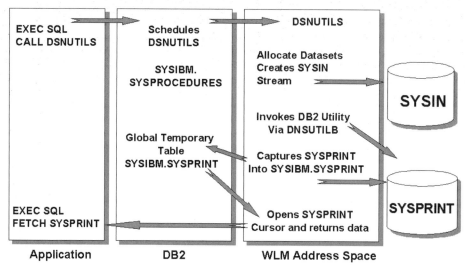

Figure 19.8   Utilities as Stored Procedures

```
PLANNAME: TESTPLAN
AVERAGE APPL      (CLASS 1)          DB2(CLASS 2)
ELAPSED TIME      4.773449           2.619543
  NON-NESTED      2.014711           1.533210
  STORED PROC     2.758738           1.086333
  UDF             0.000000           0.000000
  TRIGGER         0.000000           0.000000

CPU TIME          0.141623           0.093469
  AGENT           0.141623           0.093469
  NON-NESTED      0.047918           0.004276
  STORED PROC     0.093801           0.088293
  UDF             0.000000           0.000000
  TRIGGER         0.000000           0.000000
```

Shows amount of time (CPU/Elapsed) spent processing Stored Procedures

Figure 19.9   Accounting Info for Stored Procs

and use some kind of external notification, such as e-mail, pager notification, or cell phone, with an automated message. What we always needed was more ways to rouse a DBA out of bed at 4 A.M. on a Sunday morning to fight yet another work emergency that could probably have been handled another way!

Commands and Monitoring

Stored procedures are fairly unlimited in what they can do. You can issue a DB2 command from a stored procedure by using IFI (Instrumentation Facility Interface) calls on OS/390.

Normal accounting and statistics traces produce most of the necessary information you need to monitor and tune a stored procedure. You can monitor stored procedures from the accounting and statistics reports (figure 19.9). There is additional information from accounting classes 7 and 8 on stored procedure packages.

REXX, Java, and SQL Procedure Language

This chapter covers the issues surrounding DB2's support for REXX, Java, and SQL procedure language. Amidst all the hoopla when DB2 Version 6 came out, a lot of enhancements were not in the original announcement or release guide for version 6. Some of the enhancements added to DB2 at that time were SQL Procedures (PSM), the Stored Procedure Builder, and direct DB2 support for REXX. The SQL procedures function makes it possible to write complete SQL stored procedures that conform to the ISO SQL/PSM standard. The Stored Procedure Builder tool can build SQL and Java stored procedures for the DB2 family of products in a simple and consistent manner. And there is another piece that many of us have waited for: the ability to use the REXX language with DB2 as a normal supported language.

The Stored Procedure Builder supports Java stored procedures. The direction of Java and DB2 is our concern, and that concern comes down to performance. As this book goes to print, the world of OS/390, Java, and DB2 is in the midst of major change. The driving reason is that Java is being pursued heavily as an enterprise language and needs the same characteristics that have been achieved with COBOL, DB2, and transactional systems. In addition, it must fully support web-based applications and the new style of transactions that are being driven by the web and business-to-business Internet applications. Therefore, much is changing in all the areas that this chapter focuses on.

Note: Even at this moment, Java implementations are changing, and enhancements are being added. It is quite possible that some of the items discussed in this chapter might not exist in the future, having been replaced by newer processes.

The overriding strategy at IBM at this time is called "Java Everywhere." Most of the new functionality produced through this strategy will be delivered in pieces during the year 2000.

REXX

The OS/390 REXX language now offers an interface to DB2 so that REXX programs can use SQL DML. Even though REXX is an interpreted language, DB2 provides the same capabilities as for other languages: a REXX program can run in any OS/390 address space, and REXX programs can run as stored procedures. In fact, a stored procedure written in REXX was delivered with this feature as one of the many components of the SQL Procedures implementation.

You can write SQL application programs in the REXX programming language, and dynamic SQL is issued from REXX with no precompiling or linkedit. REXX is an interpreted language that has been around a long time. It is loved by technical experts and system programmers, and can build quick and easy scripts. The REXX language can be used for DB2 stored procedures and is supported across the DB2 family.

REXX stored procedures are interpreted and require no precompiler, compiler, or linker. They can contain SQL, and the SQLCA is automatically included. All parameters are passed as strings, and integers are passed as numeric strings. Only one OUT parameter is allowed. This simple syntax identifies an SQL string to REXX, allowing retrieval, storing, and processing of DB2 data (figure 20.1).

We used to need freeware or vendor utilities to execute REXX. REXX now allows dynamic SQL execution. We can now put programs or queries for DBA functions (such as REORGs) into a REXX stored procedure and execute them remotely.

REXX is not helpful for performance so much as for function. Even though there is no real concern with dynamic SQL performance (remember SAP and PeopleSoft are two systems based on dynamic SQL), the interpretive nature of REXX is suited for ease of use and power, not performance.

```
CREATE PROCEDURE XYZ (IN p_name CHAR(20),
                      OUT p_address CHAR(64),
                      OUT p_retcode INT)
                 LANGUAGE(REXX)
......
    END;
```

Figure 20.1 REXX Example

Java and DB2

Java is changing forever the way business applications are written. Java now fully utilizes DB2, which is good, since most of the business world uses DB2 for relational business systems. DB2 is also the industry leader in large-scale enterprise database systems on OS/390, and Java is gaining a strong foothold on that platform, as it is on all others. Java provides more freedom in developing code and more platform independence than any language developed. Java allows programmers to focus more on the business problems and less on the technology, especially by using the building block approach made possible by the reusability of Java code. There are now three ways to exploit DB2 and the Java programming language on the OS/390. You can program in Java using JDBC, program in Java using SQLJ, and develop stored procedures written in Java. SQLJ performance strategies on the OS/390 are undergoing a lot of change. The initial implementation of Java and SQLJ or JDBC when much of the implementation was still in beta, left much to be desired in terms of performance and ease of use. But by the end of the year 2000, it is hoped that the JVM (Java virtual machine) will allow performance similar to that of COBOL.

JDBC and SQLJ

JDBC is a method for using dynamic SQL with the Java programming language. It is based on the call-level SQL interface model and operates basically the same way, through a large API. JDBC conforms to the X/Open SQL call-level interface specification and requires a minimal SQL conformance to the SQL92 entry-level standard.

SQLJ, however, is an implementation of static SQL for use with Java. It was designed by IBM, Oracle, and Sun to eliminate the weaknesses of JDBC, which is for dynamic SQL. SQLJ was released with version 6 of DB2 for OS/390 and is available for some previous versions.

The static SQL syntax for Java is easier than JDBC, and its performance is much better than that of JDBC. Figures 20.2 and 20.3 show the amount of difference in coding between JDBC and SQLJ.

SQLJ supports binary portability of static SQL and stored procedures across DBMS vendors' products. There is a potential for wide DBMS vendor acceptance. SQLJ has been submitted to ANSI/ISO for inclusion in the SQL-related standards.

SQLJ supports INSERT, UPDATE, DELETE, singleton SELECT, cursor SELECT, calling stored procedures that include result sets, COMMIT, ROLLBACK, and methods for CONNECT and DISCONNECT. Dynamic SQL is supported only through JDBC. When using both SQLJ and JDBC in a single process, you must share the connection handles and connect state.

Java applications with SQLJ clauses (figure 20.4) are translated by a Java precompiler (the SQLJ translator, invoked with the command `sqlj`) and produce modified Java

```
JDBC:
  java.sql.PreparedStatement ps = con.prepareStatement(
      "SELECT SOMETHING
       FROM MYTABLE WHERE ACCT=?");
  ps.setString(1, acct);
  java.sql.ResultSet things = ps.executeQuery();
  things.next();
  something = things.getString(1);
  things.close();
```

```
SQLJ:
  #sql (con) { SELECT SOMETHING
               INTO :somewhere
               FROM MYTABLE
               WHERE ACCT = :acct };
```

Figure 20.2   Retrieve a Single Row

```
JDBC:
  CallableStatement insert1 = con.prepareCall(
      "INSERT INTO MYTABLE VALUES(?,?,?,?)");
   insert1.setString(1,var1);
   insert1.setString(2,var2);
   insert1.setInt(3,var3);
   insert1.setString(4,var4);
   insert1.executeUpdate();
```

```
SQLJ:
  #sql (con) {INSERT INTO MYTABLE
                VALUES( :var1, :var2, :var3, :var4) };
```

Figure 20.3   INSERT One Row

```
#sql iterator MyClients (String name, float grade);
MyClients client;
#sql (recs) client =
   (SELECT CLIENT AS "company", ACCT AS "account"
      FROM MY_CLIENTS
      WHERE INVOICE >= :dollar_limit
      AND DUE >= CURENT_DATE - :term_days
      AND TERMS = :normal
      ORDER BY ACCT);
while (client next()) {
   System.out println(client.company() + " " + client.acct()
   + " Invoices Over Due Big Time! " );
}
```

Identifies SQL within JAVA

Figure 20.4   Java SQLJ Example

code with standard JDBC calls and a profile. The profiles are platform-independent descriptions of the SQLJ clauses. The modified code is compiled with the command `javac`, producing one or more class files containing the Java byte codes. The profile is then customized with the command `db2profc` and produces a DB2 for OS/390–dependent DBRM that is bound into a package or plan. The application is executed via the OS/390 JVM. The profiles are portable across platforms. A profile generated on Oracle and compiled on Windows NT against Oracle8 can be moved to DB2 for OS/390 and then customized and bound into a DB2 package or plan without modification of any source code. SQLJ applications have all the benefits of JDBC plus the advantages of the static-model SQLJ compilation, shown in figure 20.5.

These are the major differences between JDBC and SQLJ:

- SQLJ follows the static SQL model, while JDBC follows the dynamic SQL model.
- SQLJ source programs are smaller, since all the JDBC code is generated by the SQLJ translator and does not have to be coded in the source.

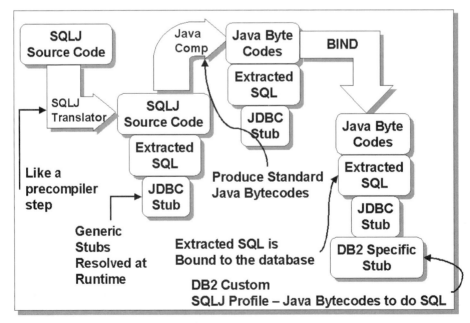

Figure 20.5 SQLJ and Compilation

- SQLJ, even though it becomes JDBC, does all the DB2 data type checking during the preparation process and performs strong typing with Java host expressions. JDBC does not encounter data type errors until execution.

- With SQLJ, Java host expressions are embedded in the statement, whereas with JDBC, additional call statements must be written for each bind variable and need to use positional notation, which makes changes error prone.

- With SQLJ, you get normal DB2 authorization checking, driven by the authorization ID of the package or plan owner, and privileges are checked at bind time. With JDBC, no authorization checking of privileges occurs until run time.

Java

To achieve the performance required by high-volume transactional business, Java needed some help. The interpretive nature of Java, along with the whole concept of what Java is and how it is implemented and operates, tends to create longer code paths, so high-performance systems have difficulty. Much progress has been made in this direction. With the advent of Java stored procedures, however, the JVM could not be used, since it is an unsupported attachment of started-task address spaces. At some point in the future, Java stored procedures will execute through a new attachment, currently referred to as Java 2, Wave 2 JVM. Until that time, there is a high-performance compiler, called VisualAge for Java Enterprise Toolkit for OS/390, or simply ET/390. It is a byte-code binder, a special static compiler, that takes Java byte codes as input and produces an S/390 load module (figure 20.6). There is no reliance on JVM and its interpretive overhead when using ET/390, but we expect it to go away except for those rare situations in which the new and improved JVM cannot be used. Other changes coming to WebSphere, MQ, and basically

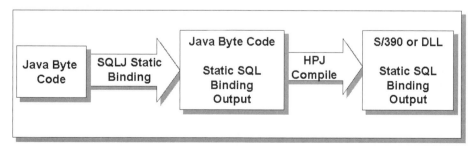

Figure 20.6 OS/390 VisualAge for Java Enterprise Edition

everything else running on OS/390 with the movement toward web-based transactional systems will affect the Java/DB2 arena.

SQL Procedure Language

SQL/PSM is an ISO standard, and the SQL/PSM for DB2 OS/390, which is called SQL procedure language, is a subset of this standard. SQL procedure language initially was designed only for writing stored procedures, although we expect to see it used for triggers as well some day. Its major benefit is that users can create stored procedures very quickly using a simple, easily understood language, without the headaches of precompilers, compilers, link editors, binding, and special authorizations. Stored procedures written using SQL procedure language are managed mostly by DB2; this automates the process and allows programmers and users to simply write the logic and pass it off to DB2. The language itself is primarily SQL (DML and DDL) with local variables, cursors, assignment statements, flow control, and signal-resignal conditions (normally used for error handling). Here are the primary language statements, which show the strength of this approach:

- IF
- CASE
- LEAVE
- LOOP
- REPEAT
- WHILE
- FOR
- CALL
- RETURN
- GET DIAGNOSTICS
- SIGNAL
- RESIGNAL

The real difference of SQL procedures is how they become stored procedures: all you do is write a DDL statement that reads "CREATE PROCEDURE . . LANGUAGE SQL . . . name: BEGIN . . . END name." All the code is in the body of the CREATE statement. You might think that this would be similar to dynamic SQL within an interpreted language, but that simply would not have the performance characteristics needed. What really happens is that the SQL procedure code is processed by a dynamically invoked PSM compiler, which turns the code into a C language program. The code is then precompiled, compiled, linkedited, and bound either under the control of an OS/390 SQL Procedure Processor or manually. After the process is successful, certain catalog tables are filled with the necessary information about the stored procedure. Of course, a user might be a connected client rather than a user on the OS/390 server. The Stored Procedure Builder, which runs on Windows and UNIX platforms, can be used in this case. This client tool takes the user's language input and interfaces with the OS/390 SQL Procedure Processor. Thus there are three ways that an SQL-based stored procedure can be built:

- Code and use the Stored Procedure Builder on a connected client.
- Code and pass to the OS/390 Procedure Processor directly. The Procedure Processor is called DSNTPSMP and is a REXX stored procedure (and a good way to examine REXX and DB2).
- Code and use normal prepare, compile, linkedit, and bind processes.

The Procedure Processor is written in REXX and runs as a stored procedure. But the Stored Procedure Builder is perhaps more interesting, since the initial target is Microsoft Visual Studio or IBM VisualAge plug-ins that accept the PSM syntax and the Java syntax. The Stored Procedure Builder creates a C program that DB2 precompiles, compiles, linkedits, and binds. The Stored Procedure Builder on the client frees the end user from everything but writing the SQL procedure in either PSM SQL3 syntax or Java syntax. The user writes the code and pushes a button, and the compiled stored procedure is ready to be invoked.

An example of an SQL procedure (PSM) module demonstrates the power of this approach. Using any of the automated approaches, the following selection is all you have to use to create a stored procedure called YLASSOC.

```
CREATE PROCEDURE YLASSOC (IN switch CHAR(1),
                          IN x_acct CHAR(5),
                          OUT x_name CHAR(20),
                          OUT x_phone CHAR(30),
                          OUT x_code INT,
                          OUT x_message CHAR(50)
                LANGUAGE(SQL)
```

```
BEGIN;
    SELECT x_name,
        coalesce('Work Phone ' CONCAT x_work_phone,
                 'Home Phone ' CONCAT x_home_phone,
                 'Cell Phone ' CONCAT x_cell_phone,
                 'No Phone') AS x_phone
    FROM YLASSOC_ACCTS
    WHERE ACCT = x_acct;
    DO;
        X_code = SQLCODE;
        IF SQLCODE < 0 THEN
            Leave;
        ELSE
        CASE switch
            WHEN '1' then
                X_message = 'Ya-ba-da-ba-do'
            WHEN '2' then
                X_message = 'Ya-da-ya-da-ya-da'
            ELSE
                X_message = 'Oh Pshaw';
    END;
END;
```

SQL procedures support multiple parameters (input, output, and input/output) and multiple output result sets for clients. SQL procedures are defined in the DB2 catalog (SYSIBM.SYSPSM). An SQL procedure can access local or remote tables across the DB2 family of products.

For many years, we have been waiting for a method to develop and port stored procedures across the entire DB2 family. SQL procedure language makes this more straightforward. Now that DB2 supports SQL procedures, we can also begin migrating applications written using Informix SPL, Oracle PL/SQL, and Sybase Transact SQL systems to DB2.

## CHAPTER 21

Parallelism

Τhis chapter covers how DB2 uses parallelism for queries. In order to reduce elapsed time for a query, DB2 can provide a query with parallel resources, such as several I/O paths or processors. By taking advantage of these resources, queries can run in a shorter period of time, allowing more work to be pushed through the system. However, like all other features in DB2, parallelism must be controlled and managed; otherwise, the benefits will not be realized and unnecessary resources could be expended.

Until version 6, parallelism was achieved only with partitioned table spaces, but the rules changed, and simple and segmented table spaces can now be processed using parallelism. Parallelism can help improve the performance of I/O- and CPU-bound read-only queries. It can help queries that are reading large amounts of data, regardless of the filtration.

Some CPU overhead is associated with the use of parallelism. DB2 scales processor-intensive work across all available processors. However, in an OLTP environment, you do not want it utilizing all of the available resources, as response time of other processes could suffer as transactions begin to queue, waiting on the CPU. Parallelism can average less than 1% for long-running queries and less than 10% for short-running queries.

Query Parallelism

DB2 can utilize two different methods for achieving query parallelism: I/O or CPU. With I/O parallelism, the goal is to split data access into equal sequential prefetch streams to bring I/O time down to estimated CPU time. If CPU time is estimated as 1 second and I/O as 3 seconds, three I/O parallel streams of approximately equal size that should each cost about 1 second are started. They are implemented with a round-robin type of GET paging, where pages are removed from the front of each queue instead of reading down the whole queue. However, I/O parallelism is not very effective, because some streams take a long time to finish, and therefore there is little or no benefit in terms of reduced elapsed time. With current releases of DB2, I/O parallelism is very infrequently chosen. Instead, the preferred method generally is CPU parallelism.

The goal of CPU parallelism is to split queries into equal, multiple, smaller queries and process those queries in multiple execution units, or as parallel tasks. CPU parallelism uses the MRU (most recently used; figure 21.1), not LRU (least recently used), algorithm for pages in the buffer pool to support the queries.

At execution time, DB2 takes into consideration the number of processors available. If there are not enough processors to support the degree of parallelism initially chosen by the optimizer, the degree is degraded. There are a couple of reasons that CPU parallelism may not be chosen. If the optimizer estimates that the ratio of I/O work to CPU work is 1:1, additional processors are not necessary. The second reason is that there may only be one processor configured to the subsystem or instance for the query.

When Parallelism Is Chosen

DB2 parallelism is decided both at the time of the bind and at run time. If parallelism is not chosen at bind time, there is no possibility of it being chosen at run time. Even if parallelism is chosen at bind time, it may not be used at run time due to several factors. If

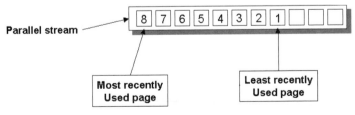

Figure 21.1 MRU Bufferpool Queuing

there is not enough space in the virtual buffer pool to support the requested degree of parallelism, the degree can be reduced from that chosen at bind time, or parallelism can be turned off altogether. Host variables in the SQL query can prevent DB2 from determining which partitions qualify in a query; therefore, the degree of parallelism will be decided at run time. If the machine on which DB2 is running does not have the hardware sort feature at run time, parallelism is disabled. If DB2 determines that a cursor is ambiguous and can be updated, parallelism is disabled. If parallelism is disabled, the query does not fail; DB2 simply uses the normal access path for the data. Both the parallel and the normal access path are present in the package or plan.

During BIND or PREPARE, DB2 chooses the access path best suited for the query. It then performs a postoptimization step where it identifies the sections of the access path that will benefit most from parallelism. If any are found, it identifies the part of the actual query that can be executed in parallel and determines the degree of parallelism to use.

Degree of Parallelism

Parallelism is measured by the number of concurrent parallel processes, which is known as the degree of parallelism. This degree is determined in a multiphase optimization at bind time.

The degree cannot exceed total number of partitions for query I/O parallelism. However, for CPU parallelism, the degree can be larger than the number of processors available, and we will examine this issue shortly. Host variables and buffer pool size are not taken into consideration during the bind process.

When determining the degree of parallelism, DB2 is a little more sophisticated than many DBMSs because it takes into account the possibility of the data being skewed across the partitions and whether or not the data process is I/O or CPU intensive. Most other DBMSs simply assign a degree based solely on the number of partitions or a manually entered parameter. With DB2, you can achieve maximum benefits from parallelism even if the data becomes skewed over time.

To obtain an optimal degree of parallelism, DB2 must take into account the number of partitions, the estimated I/O cost of the largest partition, the processing costs and complexity of the query, and the speed and number of available processors. The actual degree of parallelism is decided at bind time, when DB2 takes the total number of active pages in the entire table and divides it by the total number of active pages in the largest partition of the table. This is the degree that shows up in PLAN_TABLE after EXPLAIN is executed and may not always be the degree achieved at run time. At run time, if the appropriate resources are not available, degradation of the degree of parallelism can occur.

If you are experiencing a great deal of degradation in your parallelism, you may want to consider not using it at all, by binding your programs with DEGREE(1) or not allowing any space in the buffer pool for parallel activities (VPPSEQT = 0). There is also an option, available with updates to version 5, to control the actual degree of parallelism for everything in the entire subsystem. The maximum degree can be controlled by the DSNZPARM PARAMDEG on install panel DSNTIP4 in the MAX DEGREE field.

The degree of DB2 parallelism is influenced by the largest partition. DB2 divides a table space into logical pieces (work ranges) based on the size of the largest physical partition of the table. For example, a table with 10K pages and 10 partitions, with 5K pages in the largest partition, would have degree 2. For a large table with a total of 60,612,084 active pages and a maximum partition size of 691,050 active pages, the degree is calculated as follows:

$$60{,}612{,}084 \text{ active pages} / 691{,}050 \text{ maximum partition active pages} = 87.710$$
$$\text{Degree} = 88$$

Queries Best Suited for Parallelism

Queries with the following characteristics can take advantage of parallelism:

- Long-running, read-only queries, in both static and dynamic SQL, from both local and remote sites, that use either private or DRDA protocols
- Table-space scans and index scans
- Joins
  - Nested loops
  - Merge scans
  - Hybrid joins without sorting on new tables
- Sorts
- Aggregate functions

As of version 6, there are only a few places where parallelism is not considered:

- Queries that materialize views
- Queries that perform materialization because of nested table expressions
- Queries that perform a merge-scan join of more than one column
- Queries that use direct row access

Only Sysplex parallelism is not considered in these queries:

- Queries with list prefetch and mutliple-index access
- Queries accessing LOB data

Parallelism generally should not be used if a system is already CPU constrained, because parallelism would only add to the problem in most (but not all) situations. Sometimes getting that long-running hog query out faster returns CPU resources back to the critical tasks faster. It just depends!

CPU parallelism cannot be used when a cursor is defined WITH HOLD, since this cursor's use is potentially interrupted by a commit, which causes processing to stop. Parallelism would cause many resources to be held ineffectively if it were allowed.

Keep in mind that adding parallelism to poorly tuned queries is simply wasting resources, and you will probably not see any benefit from parallelism. Short-running queries, queries that complete in less than a second, usually do not benefit from parallelism. But how are long-running queries separated from short-running queries? If you are trying to get the benefits of parallelism without unnecessary overhead where it does not belong, this separation is necessary. For example, you could separate the long-running queries into a separate package, bind it with DEGREE(ANY) in a different collection, and then use the SET CURRENTPACKAGE statement to switch between it and a program bound with DEGREE(1) for shorter queries that are better allowed to run sequentially.

Achieving Parallelism for Nonpartitioned Table Spaces

Prior to version 6, you had to design for parallel operations, because statistics were not collected on nonpartitioned table spaces, which are necessary for parallelism. For nonpartitioned table spaces, you could still have parallelism by designing a table space with one partition. This provided a performance benefit, especially if the table was used in join process, as it could be processed in parallel. DB2 split the query into multiple queries and ran them in parallel.

As of version 6, the appropriate statistics are collected even for nonpartitioned tables, so now all tables can participate in parallel operations.

Parallelism on Nonpartitioning Indexes

In order to have parallelism for SQL operations against nonpartitioning indexes, you need to take advantage of the PIECESIZE feature, introduced in DB2 Version 5. Pieces allow you to break a nonpartitioning index into multiple data sets, or pieces. Operations can then be performed on the pieces in parallel. Pieces also help to eliminate bottlenecks caused by insert and update processes.

Parallelism Impacts on Buffer Pools

The buffer pool resources influence DB2's decision of whether or not to use parallelism at bind time. If the resources are not adequate at run time, you can experience quite a bit of degradation, or fallback, during execution time.

The buffer pool threshold VPPSEQT = 0 means *all* parallelism is turned off and cannot be supported by the buffer pool. One of the most difficult aspects of tuning a buffer pool for parallelism is that VPPSEQT is a percentage of VPSEQT, which determines the sequential portion of the buffer pool. So ideally, you want the sequential area to be as large as possible, but what if most of your processing is random? If you want to take advantage of parallelism, you may want to start at around 25% and monitor how effectively parallelism is being used, if at all, or if there is a lot of fallback. If fallback occurs, you should revert to the best nonparallel access plan.

You can view the buffer pool settings for parallelism through the DISPLAY BUFFERPOOL command. This shows you the threshold setting for the buffer pool (VPPSEQT), and DISPLAY BUFFERPOOL DETAIL (figure 21.2) shows whether fallback is occurring.

When DB2 determines that it can take advantage of parallelism, it must negotiate with the buffer manager to obtain resources in the buffer pools to support the degree of

```
-DISPLAY BUFFERPOOL(BP1) DETAIL

DSNB401I - BUFFERPOOL NAME BP1, BUFFERPOOL ID 1, USE COUNT 2
DSNB402I - VIRTUAL BUFFERPOOL SIZE = 2000 BUFFERS
              ALLOCATED       = 2000  TO BE DELETED = 0
              IN-USE/UPDATED  =  300
DSNB403I - HIPERPOOL SIZE 4000 BUFFERS, CASTOUT = YES
              ALLOCATED       = 4000  TO BE DELETED = 0
              BACKED BY ES    = 2890
DSNB404I - THRESHOLDS -
              VP SEQUENTIAL    = 80       HP SEQUENTIAL = 80
              DEFERRED WRITE = 50         VERTICAL DEFERRED WRT = 10
              PARALLEL SEQUENTIAL = 50  ASSISTING PARALLEL SEQT = 0
..........

DSNB440 - PARALLEL ACTIVITY -
              PARALL REQUEST =    0   DEGRADED PARALL        = 0
```

Figure 21.2   Use of DIS BP for Parallelism

parallelism required to run the parallel group. The buffer manager calculates one prefetch I/O stream for each parallel degree for each table space, index, and work file. One I/O stream is required per parallel task per object. The assumption is that 32 buffers are required for each I/O stream and that this is the amount of space needed in the buffer pool(s) to execute the parallel group. Even for sort work files, DB2 uses 32 buffers for its calculation, even though work files prefetch eight pages at a time, because there is additional work going on in the sort and merge phases.

If a parallel degree of 20 is requested for a query where an index is used for table access and a sort is required, the buffers required can be calculated. This is when buffer pool separation of objects becomes important for determining how many buffers are required for each process and whether or not the buffer pool can support them. For our example, we will assume that the buffer pool layout is as follows:

BP1—Table space (VPSIZE 5000, VPSEQT 80, VPPSEQT 50). 2,000 buffers are available for parallelism.

BP2—Index space (VPSIZE 2000, VPSEQT 50, VPPSEQT 50). 500 buffers are available for parallelism.

BP3—DSNDB07 (VPPSIZE 5000, VPSEQT 95, VPPSEQT 50). 2,375 buffers are available for parallelism.

So, if each prefetch stream takes 32 buffers and the degree is 20, for the table space BP1 we need a total of 640 buffers in the buffer pool to support the parallel operations. For the index space and sort work space, we also need x buffers.

If it is determined that a buffer pool cannot support the requested degree of parallelism, the degree is reduced or parallelism is not used at all; therefore, the query executes sequentially. You can tell when this happens by monitoring the statistics report (figure 21.3). When degradation of the degree occurs, DB2 is also forced to adjust the work ranges for every parallel task, because it has fewer parallel streams to use.

There is a way to estimate the number of buffers needed for the parallel tasks (degree). From a statistics report, use the PREF.DISABLED NO BUFFER field, which gives you the number of prefetch I/O streams denied due to a buffer pool shortage. Then compare this to field PARALL.QUERY REQ.REDUCTION, which gives you the number of times there were not enough pages in the buffer pool for the planned degree to be executed (figure 21.4). Take that value times the number of buffers needed per prefetch I/O stream (32). DB2 uses one prefetch I/O stream per parallel task per object in the buffer pool. This result is the additional number of buffers you need to support the required degree.

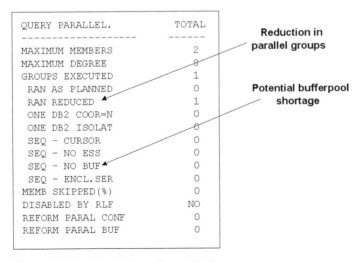

Figure 21.3   Parallelism Degradation

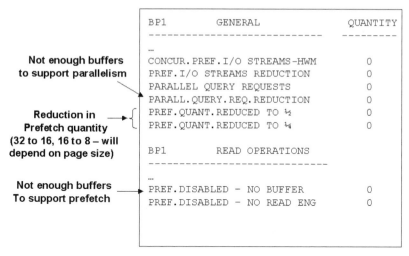

```
BP1          GENERAL                    QUANTITY
-----------------------------           ---------
...
CONCUR.PREF.I/O STREAMS-HWM               0
PREF.I/O STREAMS REDUCTION                0
PARALLEL QUERY REQUESTS                   0
PARALL.QUERY.REQ.REDUCTION                0
PREF.QUANT.REDUCED TO ½                   0
PREF.QUANT.REDUCED TO ¼                   0

BP1          READ OPERATIONS
-----------------------------
...
PREF.DISABLED - NO BUFFER                 0
PREF.DISABLED - NO READ ENG               0
```

Not enough buffers to support parallelism

Reduction in Prefetch quantity (32 to 16, 16 to 8 – will depend on page size)

Not enough buffers To support prefetch

Figure 21.4 Determining Buffers Needed

You can give more buffers to the parallel tasks by increasing the size of the buffer pool:

> BP1—VPSIZE 5000, VPSEQT 80, VPPSEQT 50. 2,000 buffers are available for parallelism.

```
ALTER BUFFERPOOL(BP1) VPSIZE (7000)
-- BP1 now has 2800 buffers available for parallelism
```

Or you can gain more room for parallelism by increasing the number of buffers allocated for parallel tasks:

```
ALTER BUFFERPOOL(BP1) VPPSEQT(100)
-- BP1 now has 4000 buffers available for parallelism
```

Or you can increase both the size and threshold:

```
ALTER BUFFERPOOL(BP1) VPSIZE(7000) VPPSEQT(100)
-- BP1 now has 5600 buffers available for parallelism
```

Because VPPSEQT is a percentage of VPSEQT, this can be a hard number to increase to get enough buffers, especially if the objects in this pool are processed randomly (therefore VPSEQT is low). This may force you to overinflate the buffer pool size just to get enough buffers to support the parallel tasks. Overallocation of buffer pool is not a good thing and can lead to paging problems if there is not enough memory to support it (refer to Chapter 3 for more information). Just another one of those DB2 trade-offs! You have to determine whether the parallelism benefits of reducing elapsed time can be realistically achieved and whether it is worth the risk of causing a performance problem somewhere else.

When DB2 executes parallel groups, the buffer manager dynamically adjusts prefetch quantities in the buffer pool. To keep the buffer pool from thrashing, the buffer manager may reduce prefetch quantities by half (from 32 pages per prefetch I/O stream to 16 or even to 8). Note that the pages per prefetch I/O stream depend on the page size in the buffer pool. After the parallel tasks are completed, the prefetch quantity will be increased. You can see whether the prefetch quantities are being reduced in the PREF.QUANT.REDUCED field(s) in the statistics report (figure 21.4).

Parallelism and Hiperpools

Prior to version 5, hiperpools were not used for parallelism. But after a version 5 APAR, if the buffer pool plus the hiperpool is large enough to contain the entire table space or index space, a hiperpool is used for parallelism.

Parallelism and I/O

Because the MVS serializes I/O operations at the volume level, to get the most out of parallelism, you should place the partitions for the table space, the index spaces, and the NPI pieces on separate volumes. If you have the luxury of several volumes, it is ideal to have one partition per volume. If that is not possible, you should define them across a set of given volumes in a round-robin fashion (figure 21.5). With RAID volumes, you should separate the partitions onto different logical volumes, even though the data is spread across physical volumes.

You also should not have too many partitions behind one controller, because the excessive queuing can cause performance problems with parallelism.

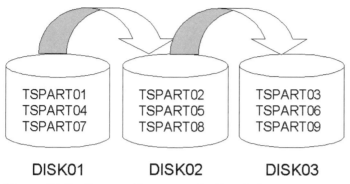

DISK01   DISK02   DISK03

Figure 21.5   Dataset Placement for Parallelism

Trace Records for Parallelism

Statistics trace records may be necessary to troubleshoot problems with parallelism. Some information you can get only from a trace, such as the actual degree of parallelism at execution time and buffer pool resources at execution time. Some of the following IFCIDs can help with monitoring parallelism problems:

- Statistics trace record
  - IFCID 2   System statistics
  - IFCID 202   Buffer pool attributes
- Accounting trace record
  - IFCID 3   Accounting trace
- Performance trace record
  - IFCID 201   Buffer pool alter before and after values
  - IFCID 221   Parallel group execution trace
  - IFCID 222   Parallel group elapsed time trace
  - IFCID 231   Parallel operations
  - IFCID 237   SET CURRENT DEGREE trace

You may want to monitor the buffer pool attributes during execution (IFCID 202) to ensure that the size and thresholds are the appropriate settings you were anticipating and were not altered (IFCID 201). You should also monitor the actual degree at run time and see how that compares with the degree determined at bind time. IFCID 221 is the only way to view the actual degree used at run time. This IFCID also contains the QUERYNO of the query, which matches the QUERYNO in the PLAN_TABLE. If you build a table to hold the trace data from this IFCID, you can join it on the QUERYNO column of the PLAN_TABLE to create a nice report comparing the degree chosen at bind time with the degree chosen at run time. You can even compose a query joining those two tables to the DSN_STATEMNT_TABLE to verify the accuracy of the data. Other useful information in this IFCID includes why a particular degree was chosen or, more important, why the degree was degraded:

- 0 = degree at run time was the same as at bind time
- 1 = host variables
- 2 = no ESA sort support
- 3 = cursor used for update or delete
- 4 = parallel group is empty
- 5 = MVS/ESA enclave services not available
- 6 = SPRMMDEG value was applied

The parallel group elapsed time (IFCID 222) helps evaluate whether you are getting the response time improvements you were hoping to achieve with parallelism.

EXPLAINing Parallelism

In the PLAN_TABLE you can see how a query is making use of parallelism. Parallelism is not chosen for access paths where it would simply incur more overhead without benefit.

When reading the PLAN_TABLE, you should pay attention to the ACCESS_DEGREE and JOIN_DEGREE columns to determine whether parallelism has been chosen for the query. Then you can look at the parallel groups, which represent the portion of work done by a set of parallel tasks. Several parallel groups can operate in a query, and each one can be individually identified. Figure 21.6 gives you a quick look at these columns in the PLAN_TABLE.

Figure 21.7 shows the EXPLAIN output for access to a single table with a table space scan that uses parallelism. The ACCESS_DEGREE shows that DB2 will access the table with two parallel processes in one parallel group. The other EXPLAIN in this figure shows the output for a query with a nested loop join. It shows that both the inner table and the

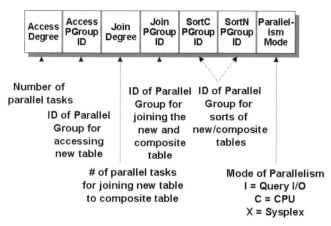

Figure 21.6   EXPLAIN Columns for Parallelism

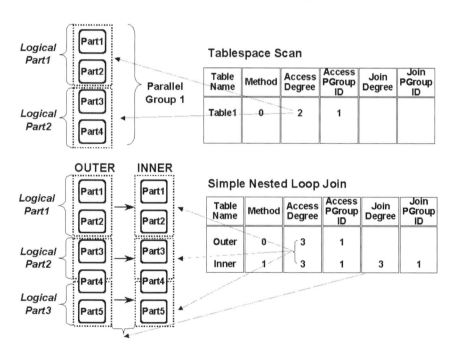

Figure 21.7   EXPLAIN—Table Scan and Nested Loop Join

outer table were accessed using three parallel streams. For a nested loop join, all retrievals are within the same parallel group. The parallel group is a set of consecutive operations that are executed in parallel and contain the same number of parallel tasks. You can see that the new and composite tables were joined together with three parallel tasks (JOIN_DEGREE).

Figure 21.8 shows how a sort affects the EXPLAIN of a nested loop join when parallelism is involved. In this example, the outer table is accessed with two parallel tasks in parallel group 1 and then is sorted. In parallel group 2, the sorted outer table and the inner table are joined together in three parallel tasks. Figure 21.9 is an example of a merge-scan join using parallelism. The query performs a merge-scan join of a table with four partitions and a table with six partitions. The data is accessed and sorted in two parallel groups and then merged together in a third.

Sysplex Query Parallelism

Sysplex query parallelism works in much the same multitasking way as CPU parallelism. In addition, it gives you the ability to take a complex query and run it across multiple

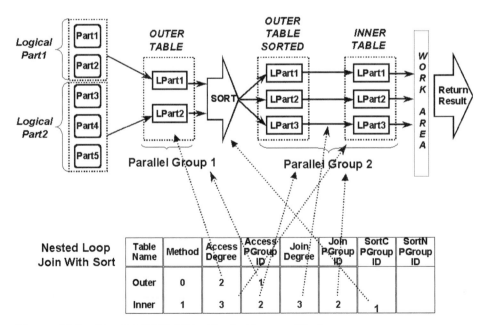

Figure 21.8 Parallel EXPLAIN—Nested Loop w/Sort

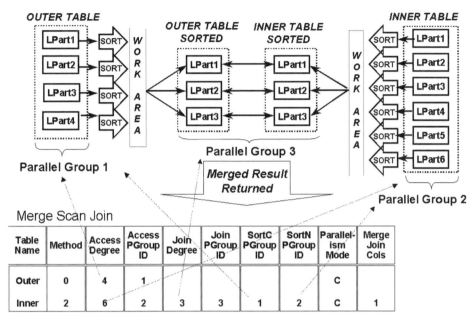

Figure 21.9   Parallel EXPLAIN for a Merge Scan Join

members in a data sharing group (figure 21.10). Good candidate queries for sysplex query parallelism are long-running, read-only queries; static and dynamic queries; local and remote queries; queries using private and DRDA protocols; table-space scans and index scans; joins (nested loop, merge scan, hybrid without sort on new table); and sorts. Sysplex query parallelism is best used with isolation-level UR (uncommitted read) to avoid excess lock propagation.

A query is issued by a coordinator, which sends the query to the assistant members in the group. The data is then processed and returned to the coordinator. The coordinator reads each of the assistants' work files or uses XCF links when a work file is not necessary.

Controlling Sysplex Query Parallelism

It might be better for a highly tuned member, a member using affinity processing on a particular subsystem for performance, or a member with constrained resources not to participate in a sysplex query operation. One way to prevent a query from running on a member is to set VPXPSEQT to 0 for the appropriate buffer pools. This prevents a query from

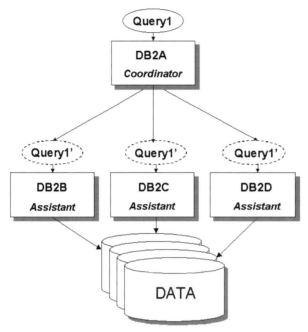

Figure 21.10   Sysplex Query Parallelism

using sysplex query parallelism for any objects assigned to those buffer pools on the member, thus preventing it from running on that member (figure 21.11). It does not use work files on that member either. This technique gives you control at the buffer pool level.

You can also control participation at the member level through installation options. These installation parameters are set in the COORDINATOR and ASSISTANT fields on the DSNTIPK install panel (figure 21.12). A member must be defined as a coordinator (COORDINATOR = YES) in order to issue a query that can take advantage of sysplex query parallelism, otherwise, the query can only run on one DB2 member. When a noncoordinator DB2 issues a query that has a parallel access path but is not a coordinator, it is accounted for in the SINGLE DB2-C.PARM = N field in the statistics report. If a DB2 member is set up to be an assistant (ASSISTANT = YES), when any coordinator issues a query, it can run on any of the assistant DB2s, provided that the buffer pool resources are available, of course. If you have a member in the sysplex that you do not want to participate in parallelism for any queries, you can turn off this ability by setting the ASSISTANT parameter to NO. You should have only one DB2 acting as an assistant per CEC. If you

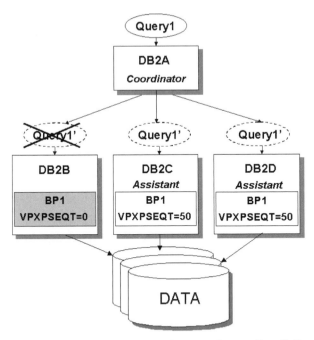

Figure 21.11 Disallowing Sysplex Query Parallelism

```
DSNTIPK          INSTALL DB2 - DEFINE GROUP OR MEMBER
==>

Check parameters and reenter to change:

1  GROUP NAME    ==> DSNDB0G   Name of the DB2 group
2  MEMBER NAME   ==> DB2G      Name of DB2 member in group
3  WORK FILE DB  ==> WRKDB2G   Work file database name for this member
4  GROUP ATTCH   ==> DB0G      Group Attach name for TSO and batch
5  COORDINATOR   ==> YES       NO or YES. Allow this member to coordinate
   parallel processing on other members
6  ASSISTANT     ==> YES       NO or YES. Allow this member to assist
                               with parallel processing.



PRESS:    ENTER to continue   RETURN to exit  HELP for more information
```

Figure 21.12 Install Panel DSNTIPK

have more than one DB2 subsystem defined to a CEC, you will not get any additional benefit by allowing both to be assistants for a query.

When a sysplex query is executed, you can view who the coordinator is and who all the assistants are by issuing a DISPLAY GROUP DETAIL command (figure 21.13). If your query is not getting the response you anticipated, you may want to issue this command to ensure that all the DB2 members that you expected to participate are actually participating. They may not be defined as assistants, or they may not be active.

Buffer Pool and Work File Impacts

In order to implement sysplex query parallelism, you have to adjust the buffer pool threshold VPXPSEQT. The parameter defaults to 50%, and it represents the amount of VPPSEQT to use for inbound queries. This is another parameter that is tricky to set, because it is a percentage of buffers allocated for normal query parallelism (VPPSEQT), which is a percentage of buffers allocated for sequential processing (VPSEQT; figure 21.14).

There are impacts to any member that participates in the query. Each assistant writes to its own work file (whatever is representing the functionality of DSNDB07), and then the coordinator can read the results from each one. If no work file is necessary, XCF is used.

```
-DB2P  DISPLAY GROUP DETAIL

DB2                              SYSTEM     IRLM
MEMBER ID SUBSYS CMDPREF STATUS NAME  LVL SUBSYS IRLMPROC
----------------------------------------------------------------
DB2P    1  DB2P   -DB2P    ACTIVE   MVSA 610 ZRLM  ZRLMPROC
DB2R    1  DB2R   -DB2R    ACTIVE   MVSB 610 RRLM  RRLMPROC
----------------------------------------------------------------
DB2       PARALLEL       PARALLEL
MEMBER  COORDINATOR    ASSISTANT
----------------------------------------------
DB2P          YES           YES
DB2R          NO            YES
----------------------------------------------------------------
SCA  STRUCTURE SIZE:      1024 KB,  STATUS= AC, SCA IN USE: 11%
LOCK1 STRUCTURE SIZE:     1536 KB,          LOCK1 IN USE: < 1%
NUMBER LOCK ENTRIES:      262144,     LOCK ENTRIES  IN USE: 33
NUMBER LIST ENTRIES:      4390,        LIST ENTRIES IN USE: 20
```

Figure 21.13 DISPLAY GROUP Command

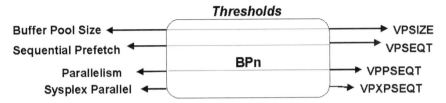

Figure 21.14   Buffer Pool Thresholds and Parallelism

IRLM Storage Impact

IRLM notification messaging is used by sysplex query parallelism for communication and data passing between the coordinator and the assistants. These messages need to use space in the IRLM, so there needs to be enough ECSA storage to handle them. This space needs to be evaluated for the IRLM of each member that is an assistant in sysplex query parallelism. It is relatively simple to estimate this storage requirement by estimating the number of parallel tasks that can run concurrently on that DB2 (the number of parallel tasks can be estimated from the EXPLAIN output for queries that will use sysplex query parallelism). Divide this by the number of participating members, and multiply this result by 32 MB. A coordinator needs around 200 K of IRLM ECSA storage.

Monitoring Sysplex Query Parallelism

You can display information about sysplex query parallelism, the coordinator, and all the assistants with the DISPLAY THREAD command on any assisting DB2.

DB2 determines the parallel degree and mode at bind time and assumes that the same number of members will be available at run time. To determine if sysplex query parallelism will be used, you can view the PARALLELISM_MODE column in EXPLAIN output. It shows an X for SQP.

Depending on the buffer resources of a given member, the parallel degree can be different at run time. To determine actual degree, use IFCID 0221, 0222 and 0231. These IFCIDs show you how many members were used in parallel group execution, whether a member's buffer pool was constrained, the names for participating members in the parallel group, and whether a member can be skipped if the buffer pool resources are not enough.

Use performance class 8 (0221, 0222, 0231), QXREDGRP, or QXDEGBUF in the statistics trace record to find shortages. The shortages could be due to a size problem or the threshold settings of the buffer pools.

You can also use DB2PM to monitor the effectiveness of the parallelism and the assisting buffer pools. In figure 21.15, a shortage of buffer pool resources is shown in the RAN REDUCED field and the SEQ - NO BUF field. The traces mentioned earlier can help you to determine which buffer pools are causing the problem. You can also see from this report whether DB2 had to reformulate the parallel degree because of buffer pool shortages by viewing the field REFORM PAR-BUF. A member that was unable to perform its duties for the parallel query is indicated in the MEMB SKIPPED(%) field.

Utilities and Parallelism

With version 6 and beyond, everything seems to be going parallel. The DB2 utilities have the ability to run several tasks in parallel, but you must also be careful with this feature. Just like query parallelism, you must control the parallelism invoked by the utilities so that it does not consume resources needed by other processes. But taking advantage of this built-in parallelism can greatly reduce batch windows by reducing the elapsed time and speeding up necessary utility processing.

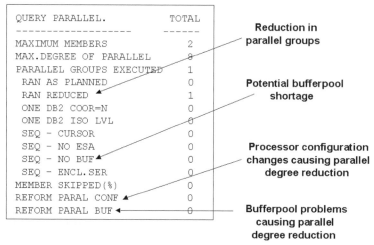

Figure 21.15   Sysplex Query Parallelism DB2PM

The LOAD, REORG TABLESPACE, and REBUILD INDEX utilities all have the ability to perform parallel index builds (beginning with version 6). The keys are sorted and the indexes built in parallel with the use of the SORTKEYS keyword. Sort work options (SORTDEVT and SORTNUM keywords) can allow dynamic allocation of sort work data sets.

Inline statistics (RUNSTATS) can also be executed in parallel for a LOAD (REPLACE, RESUME NO) or a REORG. The REBUILD INDEX utility can also gather inline statistics. This requires the use of the STATISTICS keyword. A subtask collects statistics during reload and build phases (figure 21.16).

The parallel COPY and RECOVER utilities can be used for table spaces or indexes with version 6 (with the COPY YES attribute defined in the DDL definition or changed through ALTER).

Note: Keep in mind that you do not want (or need) the ability to image copy all indexes because of the additional logging overhead. You should copy critical or large indexes only where normal REBUILD is a problem.

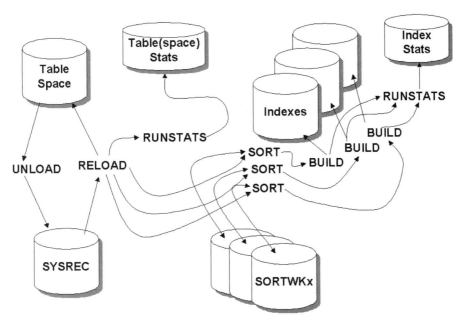

Figure 21.16   REORG—Parallel Index Build/In-line Runstats

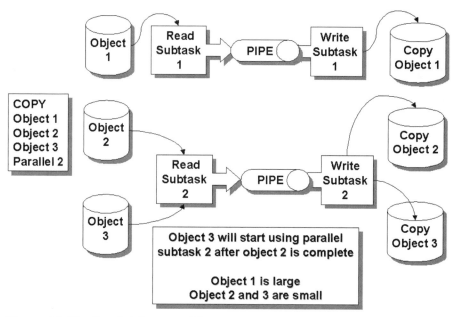

Figure 21.17   Parallel Copy and Recover

With the PARALLEL keyword you can make a full or incremental copy of objects in parallel (figure 21.17). You can tell DB2 how many parallel tasks to execute at one time so that your utility does not consume all the available resources.

You can also recover these objects in parallel. Recovering table spaces and indexes can be done with one pass of the log using FAST LOG APPLY. The records are read and applied in parallel.

Note: To recover in parallel, the copies must be on disk, not tape.

## CHAPTER 22

Predictive Analysis, Governing and Tuning

To stay ahead of performance problems, you need to perform predictive analysis on various aspects of your applications and the DB2 subsystem. DB2 provides some tools to perform this task, and we discuss how to use these tools throughout this book. In this chapter, we take a deeper look at these tools and some strategies to determine when performance may be suffering.

EXPLAIN

This section covers the issues about how to use DB2's EXPLAIN facility to best determine the performance of your queries. While it may seem that EXPLAIN is pretty straightforward, it actually is not. A large amount of analysis must be done with the information provided by EXPLAIN, and this analysis must use statistics representing the data and an understanding of the process. We look at EXPLAIN output where, when the standard rules of thumb are applied, what appears to be a good access path is actually a deadly one—worst-case performance.

We also provide an example of how one organization developed a system to analyze queries and to hunt out potential problem queries.

EXPLAIN Explained

DB2 EXPLAIN has been described as a crystal ball that application developers and DBAs use to help them predict the access path that the optimizer will choose at execution time. The proper definition is that EXPLAIN is a tool to assist in determining the plan that the DB2 optimizer picks for the single SQL statement that *might be executed.* It is important to understand what EXPLAIN tells us and what it does not tell us.

The crystal ball, through mystic powers, gives its owner a glimpse into the future. How DB2's EXPLAIN predicts the access path of an SQL call is not as mysterious. DB2 basically takes the SQL statement being explained, goes through the DYNAMIC SQL PREPARE process, but instead of storing the result for execution, returns the information to us. The EXPLAIN statement can be invoked against a single SQL statement from within an application program, interactively in SPUFI or QMF, or from dynamically prepared statements. You can EXPLAIN a plan or package with a BIND or REBIND statement as long as you have the EXPLAIN parameter set to YES, you have the required access to the tables in the SQL statement, and there is a *plan table* that you can use. EXPLAIN inserts one row into the plan table (USERID.PLAN_TABLE) for each step used in executing the SQL statement. Optionally, there can be a *statement table* (USERID.DSN_STATEMNT_TABLE) and a *function table* (USERID.FUNCTION_TABLE). The statement table can be populated with information about the estimated cost of executing the SQL statement, and the function table can be populated with information about how user-defined functions that are referred to in the SQL statement are resolved.

If you are doing distributed processing, you can explain your remote queries and packages with the remote unit of work. There must be a plan table under your ID on the remote DB2 subsystem, and you must have access to the tables in the query. Once the query is explained, the plan table is accessed using a distributed unit of work.

Several things affect the output of the EXPLAIN statement, a lot more than just the catalog statistics. The number of rows, the number of distinct values in the columns of the index, the cluster ratio, the type of indexes, the number of levels of the index tree, the buffer pool size, the sort pool size, the RID pool size, the CPU speed, and whether RUNSTATS has been run are some of the factors. Because of these factors, you need the testing subsystem to look as much like the production system as possible. To accomplish this, you have two alternatives. One is to define your test system exactly like the production system. This includes having a production-size data volume on the test system and setting the DSNZPARM values the same. A better alternative is to load a representative sampling of production data into the tables, define the buffer pools and other memory areas the same, have identical indexes, and update the DB2 catalog with statistics from production (discussed in Chapters 4 and 23).

There are some queries that everyone should be able to execute or that should be run for all objects and produced in a reference report. This information is needed in conjunction with the EXPLAIN output to determine whether the indexes selected by the optimizer are really being fully utilized, and if not, why not, and if never, why the extra columns are carried and maintained.

The plan table provides an application programmer or DBA with information on which indexes are being used. (The catalog tables SYSPLANDEP and SYSPACKDEP also show some of this information.) The plan table also shows the type of locks that will be held on tables and table spaces at execution time for the single SQL statement (generally a meaningless indicator). It lets you know whether only index access is required, what kind of sorts (if any) are being used, and whether prefetch may be invoked. The EXPLAIN output does not show any additional tables required to satisfy an SQL statement that is enforcing referential constraints.

The Plan Table

The first thing you need to do before executing EXPLAIN statements in testing is to set up a plan table. The best way to manage plan tables in testing is to create a "developer database" for each application programmer who wants to create a plan table. The database name and table space name are the same as the user ID. If a developer needs to create a plan table in more than one subsystem, a naming convention should be used to uniquely identify the databases across subsystems (unless you have only one subsystem per logical system). The database is defined with a small amount of DASD space, and DBADM authority to the database can be granted to the developer. When you are ready to create the plan table, it must have your user ID as the owner of the table. The table definition in IBM's *SQL Reference Manual* can be used to create your plan table. Another way to create a plan table is to have the DBAs create a plan table with public SELECT access or have a close friend give you select authority against his or her plan table. Then anyone who wants a plan table can use the CREATE LIKE feature of the CREATE TABLE statement, for example:

```
CREATE TABLE MYID.PLAN_TABLE
   LIKE DBA.PLAN_TABLE
   IN MYID.MYID ;
```

There is also sample DDL in the DSNTESC member of the DB2 sample library, if you have access to it. Take care to keep that plan table manageable in size, and keep only what you really need. EXPLAIN only when you need to in testing. There is no point in using up resources to do an EXPLAIN every time you BIND. A description of the plan table is shown in figures 22.1 through 22.5.

The Statement Table

The statement table contains processor consumption information to assist in the analysis of SQL statements prior to execution for static SQL and in conjunction with the RLST for dynamic SQL. This is discussed in more detail in the section later in this chapter on predictive governing. A description of the statement table is shown in figure 22.6.

QUERYNO	field allows you to distinguish among EXPLAIN statements by assigning a value; or assigned by DB2; or from a hint
QBLOCKNO	a number indicating a query or subquery for the row, generally showing the query's order in the SQL statement
APPLNAME	name of application plan for static SQL
PROGNAME	name of the program that contains the statement
PLANNO	number of the step in the plan where QBLOCKNO is processed; each new table accessed has a new step in the plan; this shows the order in which the steps of the plan were executed
METHOD 0 1 2 3 4	number showing the join method used in the plan the first table accessed - no join nested loop join - for each row of the present composite table, matching rows of the new table are joined merge scan join - composite table and another table are scanned in order of the join column, and joined when matched additional sorts for ORDER BY, GROUP BY, SELECT DISTINCT, or quantified predicates hybrid join

Figure 22.1   EXPLAIN's [userid.PLAN_TABLE]

CREATOR	creator of the table accessed in the plan step
TNAME	name of table, temp table, materialized view, table expression Or intermediate result table for outer join
TABNO	IBM internal use only – no externalized meaning
ACCESSTYPE I I1 N R M MX MI MU " "	how to access the table by an index one-fetch index scan Index scan for a where clause with an IN by sequential scan (tablespace scan) by a multiple index scan always followed by MX or MI or MU multiple index scan on referenced index intersection of multiple indexes union of multiple indexes Not applicable to the current row
MATCHCOLS	number of matched columns in the INDEX key where ACCESSTYPE is I, I1, N, or MX, else 0
ACCESSCREATOR	creator of index if ACCESSTYPE is I, I1, N, or MX
ACCESSNAME	name of index if ACCESSTYPE is I, I1, N, MX
INDEXONLY	Y/N for index access with NO DATA REFERENCE

Figure 22.2   EXPLAIN's [userid.PLAN_TABLE]

SORTN_UNIQ	sort on new table to remove duplicates
SORTN_JOIN	sort inner table for Merge Scan or Rid list & Int. table for Hybrid
SORTN_ORDERBY	sort on new table for an ORDER BY
SORTN_GROUPBY	sort on new table for a GROUP BY
SORTC_UNIQ	sort on composite table to remove duplicates
SORTC_JOIN	sort on composite table for a Method 2 Merge Scan Join
SORTC_ORDERBY	sort on composite table for an ORDER BY or a quantified predicate
SORTC_GROUPBY	sort on composite table for a GROUP BY
TSLOCKMODE	show the tablespace lock mode LOCK is IS, IX, S, X, SIX, U, N at bind time; NS, NIS, NSS, SS at run time when no bind determination
TIMESTAMP	when the row was processed, Incremented by .01 sec for uniqueness for same query
REMARKS	a field for users to insert up toe 254 characters

Figure 22.3   EXPLAIN's [userid.PLAN_TABLE]

PREFETCH S L " "	shows when Prefetch is used pure sequential prefetch list prefetch no prefetch or unknown
COLUMN_FN_EVAL R S " "	shows when an SQL column function was evaluated at data retrieval time at sort time at data manipulation or unknown
MIXOPSEQ	shows the sequence of steps in multiple index access
VERSION	version identifier of a package - in embedded SQL
COLLID	collection id for a package - embedded SQL
ACCESS_DEGREE	Degree of parallelism for accessing new table
ACCESS_PGROUP_ID	Parallel group identifier for accessing the new table
JOIN_DEGREE	Degree of parallelism for joining the composite table with the new table
JOIN_PGROUP_ID	Parallel group identifier for joining the composite table with the new table

Figure 22.4   EXPLAIN's [userid.PLAN_TABLE]

V4	SORTC_PGROUP_ID	Sort outer or composite table in parallel
	SORTN_GROUP_ID	Sort inner or new table in parallel
	PARALLELISM_MODE	C = CPU Parallelism, I = I/O Parallelism, X = Sysplex
	MERGE_JOIN_COLS	Number of columns used to do the join
	CORRELATION_NAME	Name of table or view for the statement
	PAGE_RANGE	Y = a partition scan is used
	JOIN_TYPE	F = Full outer join, L = Left outer join
	GROUP_MEMBER	Member that execution explain
V5	IBM_SERVICE_DATA	Reserved
	WHEN_OPTIMIZE	When access path was chosen, B=bind, R=run
	QBLOCK_TYPE	The type of SQL operation performed
	BIND_TIME	Time package or plan, statement or query block was bound
V6	OPTHINT	Identifies this row as an optimization hint
	HINT_USED	Identifier for the hint used
	PRIMARY_ACCESSTYPE	Whether direct row access will be attempted

Figure 22.5   EXPLAIN's [userid.PLAN_TABLE]

QUERYNO	field allows you to distinguish among EXPLAIN statements by assigning a value; or assigned by DB2; or from a hint
APPLNAME	name of application plan for static SQL
PROGNAME	name of the program that contains the statement
COLLID	collection id for a package - embedded SQL
GROUP_MEMBER	Member that execution explain
EXPLAIN_TIME	Time package/plan statement/query block was bound
STMT_TYPE	Type of statement that is being explained: SELECT, INSERT, UPDATE, DELETE, SELUPD, DELCUR, UPDCUR
COST_CATEGORY	If estimates were made using defaults; A=ok, B=defaults were used and the reason is in REASON below
PROCMS	Estimated processor cost in milliseconds
PROCSU	Estimated processor cost in service units
REASON	When B in COST_CATEGORY: HOST VARIABLES, TABLE CARDINALITY, UDF, TRIGGERS, REFERENTIAL CONSTRAINTS (CASCADE or SET NULL Exist on target table of DELETE statement)

Figure 22.6 EXPLAIN's [userid.DSN_STATEMNT_TABLE]

The Function Table

The function table contains user-defined function information to assist in the analysis of SQL statements. This is discussed in more detail in the section later in this chapter on predictive governing. A description of the function table is shown in figure 22.7. There is much more on user-defined functions and the function table in Chapter 17.

Effective Use of EXPLAIN's Output

SQL and the EXPLAIN output should be reviewed before the application goes into production. If staffing or time does not permit review of all SQL, limit the review to six categories:

- Joins
- Unions
- Subselects

QUERYNO	field allows you to distinguish among EXPLAIN statements by assigning a value; or assigned by DB2; or from a hint
APPLNAME	name of application plan for static SQL
PROGNAME	name of the program that contains the statement
COLLID	collection id for a package - embedded SQL
GROUP_MEMBER	Member that execution explain
EXPLAIN_TIME	Time package/plan statement/query block was bound
SCHEMA_NAME	The schema name of the function invoked
FUNCTION_NAME	The name of the function invoked
SPEC_FUNC_ID	The specific name of the function invoked
FUNCTION_TYPE	S = scalar function; T = table function
VIEW_CREATOR	If FUNCTION_NAME was used in a view, the view creator
VIEW_NAME	If FUNCTION_NAME was used in a view, the view name
PATH	Value of the SQL path used to find the schema name
FUNCTION_TEXT	The function name and parameters

Figure 22.7   EXPLAIN's [userid.DSN_FUNCTION_TABLE]

- Selects, deletes, or updates (when the WHERE clause doesn't utilize existing indexes and the table is larger than 10 pages)
- Selects that have ORDER BY or GROUP BY clauses, when the table is larger than 10 pages
- Any SQL using UDFs

Note: This does not mean that application programmers should only code simple SELECTs in order to bypass the review process. If an application has only simple SELECTs, then a code review is a must! Chances are it will not perform to expectations, as simple SQL statements are a strong indication that unit-record methodology is being emulated with SQL (i.e., using SQL as simply a read/write replacement—a disaster).

As a general guideline, for the production environment, RUNSTATS followed by rebinds based on established thresholds should be run regularly, and there should be a centralized plan table for each subsystem. The ID of the owner of the plan table needs to be the ID under which binds are done. SELECT access should be PUBLIC. All plans should have EXPLAIN set to YES. When a program is transferred into production, the bind process causes an EXPLAIN to run. (Rebinds also produce the same result.) Like testing, production requires a periodic purge to keep the size of the plan table manageable. You don't want to purge all EXPLAIN information for a plan. Some history is needed for performance analysis purposes. Here is sample SQL to perform this process:

```
EXEC SQL
   SELECT MIN(SUBSTR(TIMESTAMP,1,8))
   INTO :PURGE-DATE
   FROM PRODID.PLAN_TABLE
END-EXEC.
```

This retrieves one row: the oldest date on the plan table.

```
EXEC SQL
DELETE FROM PRODID.PLAN_TABLE
   WHERE SUBSTR(TIMESTAMP,1,8) = :PURGE-DATE
   END-EXEC.
```

This deletes all rows from the plan table that contain the oldest date.

> *Note: Soon new enhancements will allow you to code the SELECT as a subquery in the DELETE.*

It is recommended that you check for any changes in the access path after you perform an EXPLAIN either through a BIND or REBIND. Here is a sample query to perform this checking (assuming the same DB2 version and release and that no maintenance has occurred between the REBINDs):

```
SELECT <all columns from both tables>
FROM PRODID.PLAN_TABLE A, PRODID.PLAN_TABLE B
WHERE A.PROGNAME = B.PROGNAME    -- same program
  AND A.QUERYNO = B.QUERYNO      -- same source line number
  AND A.QBLOCKNO = B.QBLOCKNO    -- same block number
  AND A.TABNO = B.TABNO          -- match table references
  AND A.TIMESTAMP =              -- isolate to current
    (SELECT MAX(C.TIMESTAMP)
     FROM PRODID.PLAN_TABLE C
```

```
      WHERE A.PROGNAME = C.PROGNAME
        AND A.QUERYNO = C.QUERYNO
        AND A.TABNO = C.TABNO
        AND A.QBLOCKNO = C.QBLOCKNO)
  AND B.TIMESTAMP < A.TIMESTAMP --  join current to previous
  AND NOT B.METHOD = A.METHOD    -- and look for differences
  AND NOT B.ACCESSTYPE = A.ACCESSTYPE
  AND NOT B.MATCHCOLS = A.MATCHCOLS
  AND NOT B.ACCESSNAME = A.ACCESSNAME
  AND NOT B.INDEXONLY = A.INDEXONLY
  AND NOT B.PREFETCH = A.PREFETCH
  AND NOT B.SORTN_UNIQ = A.SORTN_UNIQ
  AND NOT B.SORTN_JOIN = A.SORTN_JOIN
  AND NOT B.SORTN_ORDERBY = A.SORTN_ORDERBY
  AND NOT B.SORTN_GROUPBY = A.SORTN_GROUPBY

. . . okay add all the other columns of the table here

  AND NOT B.MIXOPSEQ = A.MIXOPSEQ
ORDER BY A.PROGNAME, A.QUERYNO, A.QBLOCKNO,
        A.PLANNO,A.MIXOPSEQ;
```

There is a fine subtlety here: the join is by program, program line number (QUERYNO), block number within the SQL statement, and table reference within the SQL statement. Notice that PLANNO, the step sequence within the block, is not used, nor is MIXOPSEQ. What is important is to join the lines on the table references, that is, table reference 2 from the old with table reference 2 from the new, and then look for any changes. It might now be a different table. If it is the same table, access type or index names may have changed. This same comparison continues through the process.

This technique will not work across versions or releases or even between DB2 maintenance sessions, because optimizer rules change and more complicated types of comparison are required, involving full outer joins and row-count comparisons by statement, among other things. But it does give you the general idea for creating queries to analyze the plan table.

As stated earlier, there are several ways to execute an EXPLAIN on a plan in testing. The first is through SPUFI, which is accessible through the DB2I panels. It is recommended that programmers develop and test the SQL they're going to need for their application prior to writing one line of COBOL code. The SQL can be placed in a PDS for easy access and for explaining in SPUFI. The syntax for EXPLAIN is

```
EXPLAIN PLAN SET QUERYNO = nnn FOR
   SQL code
           . . .
```

If the EXPLAIN is successful, your SQL statement and the following messages are displayed:

```
DSNE616I STATEMENT EXECUTION WAS SUCCESSFUL, SQLCODE IS 0
DSNE617I COMMIT PERFORMED, SQLCODE IS 0
```

The syntax is the same for explaining a QMF query, but the message is slightly different. If it is successful, you see this message on the screen:

```
OK, running your query changed the database
```

There are two ways to EXPLAIN a plan when binding. The first is through the BIND/REBIND/FREE option on the DB2I panel. Be sure that EXPLAIN PATH SELECTION is equal to YES. The other option is in batch when you are compiling, linkediting, and binding the program or plan. The default for EXPLAIN is NO. To insert access path information into the plan table, add EXPLAIN(YES) to your bind statement.

In production, since you have a centralized plan table, it is probably not qualified with your ID. This means a BIND or REBIND must be executed in batch mode. The syntax is the same for a BIND in production as it is in testing. REBINDs don't require any syntax changes, since EXPLAIN is always set to YES.

After gathering EXPLAIN information in your plan table, you will undoubtedly want to report it. Many people have developed their own QMF queries and forms for reporting access path information. Here is an example for reporting just the important columns for query performance analysis on a specific program:

```
SELECT QUERYNO, QBLOCKNO, APPLNAME
     , PROGNAME, PLANNO, METHOD, CREATOR
     , TNAME, TABNO, ACCESSTYPE, MATCHCOLS
     , ACCESSCREATOR, ACCESSNAME
```

```
        , INDEXONLY, SORTN_UNIQ, SORTN_JOIN
        , SORTN_ORDERBY, SORTN_GROUPBY
        , SORTC_UNIQ, SORTC_JOIN
        , SORTC_ORDERBY, SORTC_GROUPBY
        , TSLOCKMODE, TIMESTAMP, REMARKS
        , PREFETCH, COLUMN_FN_EVAL, MIXOPSEQ
        , JOIN_TYPE, PAGE_RANGE
        , CORRELATION_NAME, QBLOCK_TYPE
        , ACCESS_DEGREE, JOIN_DEGREE
FROM DBA.PLAN_TABLE
WHERE PROGNAME = :program_name
ORDER BY PROGNAME, TIMESTAMP, QUERYNO,
         QBLOCKNO, PLANNO, MIXOPSEQ
```

If you do not have time to analyze even the six categories listed, build a set of queries that can be run against the plan table to find exceptional conditions (a user-developed system to do this is discussed later in this chapter).

One of the more important queries for companies that use views is a query to look for table materializations, such as from views, table expressions, or join composite tables. Materialization is shown in the plan table as either a view name in the table-name column or as a generated work-file name when DB2 has to materialize something into a result table before executing an SQL step. Materialization can be bad or good, but it is important to find all its occurrences. For example, to look for view materialization, use the following SQL query, which extracts the table name from the plan table and looks it up in the SYSIBM.SYSTABLES, where the TYPE column is also a V. Then analyze any SQL statement where materialization occurs.

```
SELECT QUERYNO, QBLOCKNO, PROGNAME, PLANNO
FROM PLAN_TABLE
WHERE EXISTS
    (SELECT 1 FROM SYSIBM.SYSTABLES
     WHERE NAME = PLAN_TABLE.TNAME
     AND   TYPE = 'V')
```

Analyzing the output of EXPLAIN in any fashion requires a good understanding of what EXPLAIN is telling us. While most EXPLAIN output is straightforward, referencing the NEW and COMPOSITE tables for sort purposes during any of the join types can be confusing. In all the joins, the names refer to specific occurrences of tables as follows:

- Composite table: the first table accessed in the first step of the join and the latest composite table or interim table in any of the later steps. It is the outer table of any join step.
- New table: the inner table of any join step, whose rows are joined to the rows from the composite table to form a new composite table or the final result table.

One row in the EXPLAIN table for joins always identifies the join process by listing a code in the METHOD column. This is the row for the table that was selected as the inner table. If more than two tables are joined, the composite table built from the first join is the outer table in the next join step. The results might appear as follows:

| BLOCK | METHOD | TABLE | ACCESS | SORT NEW | | | | SORT COMP | | | |
	PLAN	NAME	TYPE	U	J	O	G	U	J	O	G
10	1	0	ACCT	I	N	N	N	N	N	N	N	N
10	2	1	INVOICE	I	N	N	N	N	N	N	N	N
10	3	2	ITEMS	R	N	Y	N	N	N	Y	N	N
10	4	3			N	N	Y	N	N	N	N	N

Here, the ACCT table is the outer table to the INVOICE table during a nested loop join. The result of this join step is the composite table that is the outer table to the ITEMS table during a merge-scan join. The composite table from the first join step is sorted (SORT COMP J = Y) and the ITEMS table is also sorted (SORT NEW J = Y).

Then a final sort is done on the final result table to satisfy an ORDER BY (SORT NEW O = Y). This is obviously going to be a poor-performing SQL statement, one that qualities for further analysis.

There are many fine subtleties in the output of an EXPLAIN. EXPLAIN results can only tell us so much, and except for simple SQL statements, most of what EXPLAIN is telling us has to be analyzed and inferred by an analysis of the data, the structure of the tables and indexes, and even some guess work. Even with the automation of EXPLAIN analysis tools, there are some things that cannot be directly handled without additional analysis and information. A primary example of this is the order of predicate processing (WHERE clauses).

The order of predicate processing can be determined only by an analysis of the SQL statement after the results of the EXPLAIN have been applied. Remove from the WHERE clauses the ones that were used for the index(es) listed in EXPLAIN, and then apply the preceding rules to the remaining clauses. It is very difficult at times to determine whether a clause can be processed in stage 1 or stage 2 (which is why Visual Explain is so much better). This is especially true with compound predicates, such as

```
WHERE ((A > B or C > D) and E = F) or G IN (list)
```

Also, because DB2 rewrites SQL and adds clauses for predicate transitive closure (PTC, adding redundant WHERE clauses only during access path selection), analysis can become difficult. It is very easy to miss predicate closure changes unless each block in the plan table for a query is strictly analyzed. This is even more critical in version 6, as PTC can close predicates between ON predicates and WHERE predicates.

Many times an SQL statement as written appears to show a subquery being executed many times that in reality is executed only once. EXPLAIN only tells us the access path to be used whenever the subquery is executed and tells us nothing about how many times it is executed. One of the most troublesome EXPLAIN outputs, which constantly raises questions, occurs when both the SORTC_UNIQ and the SORTC_ORDERBY columns are Y. This seems to imply that a sort is being performed for uniqueness and that the result table is being reordered to satisfy an ORDER BY. Normally, this occurs only when a non-correlated subquery is used and sorted for performance reasons.

Many SQL statements can be written either as a join, a correlated subquery, or a noncorrelated subquery. In theory, based on the indexes available and the size of the data matches over the join, any one of these forms might outperform any other at any time. But in reality, with production statistics in the catalog and proper indexes, only one will perform the best. This is why all SQL should be written and explained several ways, because it is almost always impossible to write the best-performing SQL statement the first time.

Important Information Not in EXPLAIN

INSERT Indexes

One bit of information that is not available from EXPLAIN output is the index that is used for inserts. Normally, a clustering index is defined on every table, and this index is used for insert purposes as well as for utilities. When a clustering index is not defined on a table, how do you determine which index is used for inserts? (Of course, no sensible person would create a table without a clustering index. For more on clustering indexes, refer to Chapter 5.)

When a clustering index is not defined, DB2 inserts the row using the index at the top of the index chain in the DBD for the table. Since the lowest OBID is not a surefire way of determining which index is the oldest, the DIAGNOSE utility should be run. The JCL to execute this utility is

```
//STEP001   EXEC  DSNUPROC,SYSTEM=subsystemid,
//                UID=utilityid,UTPROC=''
//STEPLIB   DD    DSN=DSN.DSNLOAD,DISP=SHR
//SYSIN     DD    *
  DIAGNOSE DISPLAY OBD database.tablespace ALL
```

The output from this utility is a hexidecimal dump. In the listing, look for the first occurrence of OBD TYPE = INSERT. The OBD TYPE is on the lines that begin with DSNU8641. The OBID of the object is between the DBID and OBD TYPE. The first index in the dump is the index DB2 is using to cluster the data.

To further verify in which sequence the data is clustered, DSN1PRNT can be run against the table-space data set. The drawback to this is that the table space cannot be allocated to DB2. The STOP DATABASE command must be executed for the utility to run successfully. (You have the option of running it against an image copy.) The JCL to execute the DSN1PRNT utility is

```
//STEP001   EXEC PGM=DSN1PRNT,PARM='PRINT,FORMAT'
//STEPLIB   DD DSN=DSN.DSNLOAD,DISP=SHR
//SYSPRINT  DD SYSOUT=*
//SYSUT1    DD
DSN=hilevel.DSNDBC.database.tablespace.I0001.A001,
//             DISP=SHR
```

If there is a large quantity of data in the table, consider limiting the number of data pages that are printed. A lot of trees have to be sacrificed to print all the pages of a million-row table! To limit the number of pages printed, specify the page range in hexadecimal format, one to six characters in length. The syntax to accomplish this is

```
//STEP001   EXEC
PGM=DSN1PRNT,PARM='PRINT(00000C,00002A),FORMAT'
```

In this example, all data pages are printed, beginning with page X'00000C' and stopping at page X'00002A'. If FORMAT is not specified, page control fields are not specified, and individual records are not printed, which makes the report prettier and easier to read.

Indexes for Referential Integrity

You will not see indexes that are used to support referential integrity in EXPLAIN output because these indexes are picked at run time. You need to be careful when trying to eliminate indexes that are not used, because just looking at the catalog or EXPLAIN does not let you know whether an index may be used for RI processing.

Sequence of Query Block Execution

Many rows can be placed in the plan table, but they tell us nothing about the order of query block execution. They do show the order of tables within an individual query block, but even that does not tell us how the query block will execute. SQL statement analysis is needed to make this determination. Even then, many people reach an erroneous conclusion. The SQL could show a noncorrelated IN subquery. Analysis would assume that the subquery was performed first and only once, building an IN list result set, and that the outer query block then executed, comparing something to the data in the IN list built in the first step. But in reality, the IN list result set could become the outer table, probing via an index into the table that was the outer table but is now the inner table.

If a query involves several tables, if they are all joined via a nested loop method, and if no sorts are involved, DB2 "walks" through all the indexes linearly and returns the order that matches across all indexes. There is no way that EXPLAIN can show you that, since it shows a nested loop join from one table to the next for several rows, making you think that each is a step. So much for what EXPLAIN can tell you about execution: it tells you basically nothing. It is your own knowledge of the SQL statement, the data volumes, and how the current release of DB2 works. Knowing all that, you have a chance of describing the processing of the SQL statement. Yes, you could perform a detailed trace and actually see the exact process, but that should be left for when you know you have a problem to address.

Predicate Evaluation Sequence

A table showing how DB2 applies SQL predicates is in Chapter 16. There we stress how important it is to try to know where the predicates are applied. It would be nice if EXPLAIN showed us exactly where all the predicates were applied, but it does not. We have to figure that out for ourselves.

Columns Sorted

Sort is invoked at several places with SQL, and in some cases it would be nice to know how many columns were actually sorted and what keys were used. The number of sort columns in a sort key can be less than you might logically expect. But again, you are told of the sort, not how many columns compose the key.

Estimated CPU, I/O, and Sort Cost

With the new statement table, you can get an estimate of processor cost and an indication in some cases of just how good or bad the processing will be for a given SQL statement. But you are not given the actual internal estimates for CPU, I/O, and sort costs.

Estimate of Qualifying Rows

You are not told how many rows were estimated for materializations, results sets, intermediate composite tables, and if there was any packaging of rows during the process. This estimate would be nice, since an obscenely large number would jump off the page and you would know to adjust the SQL. However, you are not given this opportunity.

Filter Factors Used

You are not told what filter factors were used or which were calculated rather than defaulted. Again, this information would be nice, since a large number would be noticeable.

Statistics Used

All of the statistics used in the evaluation of the access path are not externalized in any way. It would be nice to have this information, especially since it might show where our catalog statistics are out of whack.

Assumptions Made

Yeah, right! Do we really want to get hints about the assumptions made? Well, we would if they were wrong, which would give us an indication that something in the SQL statement is generating the wrong information. Few of us want the optimizer to be externalized, nor do we want to know all the assumptions and calculations made, but sometimes when the optimizer is "unsure," it would be nice to assist it.

Stage 1 and Stage 2 Predicate Evaluation

There is no indication whether a predicate is considered stage 1 or stage 2. This is one area where Visual Explain should be used in conjunction with EXPLAIN and the plan table data.

RID List Sort

DB2 tells you that it is using list prefetch, but list prefetch does not always require a RID list sort. It would be nice to know whether a RID list sort was bypassed or used.

Other Indicators

We have a much longer list of missing information, but it starts to really nitpick. It is enough to know that other information is missing, which makes analysis of the various tables populated by EXPLAIN somewhat difficult.

Developing a Methodology

Anyone who is responsible for query performance of a mixed workload application that includes large tables needs to get organized. He or she needs a method for tuning SQL queries and finding problem queries. One of our clients developed such a method, and we would like to share it with you as an example of how to analyze performance in an environment with several thousand OTLP and DSS queries and large amounts of data. (This client's system contained a six-billion-row core table. There was no room for poor-performing queries.)

This system was designed and built primarily by Rick States at the U.S. Department of Treasury, Bureau of Public Debt. It was driven by ISPF panels, which organized all the performance-related tasks necessary for SQL tuning. These were the goals of the performance analysis efforts:

- Update the test subsystem statistics. This step is required for effective performance analysis and often must be performed manually by copying statistics from a current production environment to the test environment. This effort started with the top 10 fields each at 5%, used DB2 default statistics for any tables between 2,000 and 40,000 rows with low first key cardinality, used CLUSTERRATIO = 40 for most nonclustering indexes, and asked business analysts to verify FULLKEYCARDs. A spreadsheet was also created to list all tables, their estimated total number of rows, and catalog statistic columns.
- Review the global plan table (which stored every program's EXPLAIN output). Although access path analysis was performed on the top-priority applications individually, other performance problems needed to be identified prior to implementation.

- EXPLAIN individual programs.
- Review current catalog statistics. It is also essential to have this information for program reviews. If catalog statistics are altered, these reports need to be current.
- Identify potential problems. Individual queries that identified potential performance problems in the global plan table were organized. Reports that showed any access against the VLTB were also executed so that they could be immediately identified for any index or table-space scanning.

SQL Performance Analysis Reporting System

We now look at some screen snapshots and some of the queries that composed the system and describe the purpose of the reports produced.

The first screen (figure 22.8) shows the main menu, "SaBRe SQL Performance Analysis," which provides the choice of either collecting statistics from the catalog, performing analysis against the global plan table, performing EXPLAIN against individual queries or programs, or executing canned queries against the catalog. Usually, during a performance review or detailed analysis, several of these options are used to produce several reports with all necessary information for the analysis.

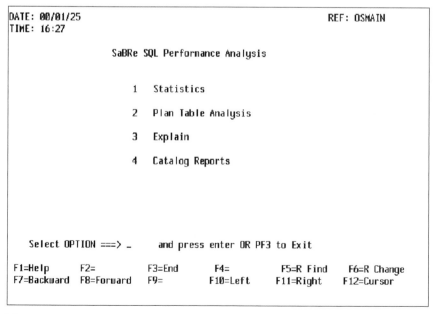

Figure 22.8 Performance Analysis Screen

Option 1: Statistics   Choosing the statistics option takes you to another menu (figure 22.9) with choices for executing queries against the catalog tables in order to obtain statistics about the objects used in the queries, such as tables, table spaces, indexes, and columns. In the next several sections, we look at some of these queries.

Option 1.1: Tables   The tables option executes a query for selecting information about the table spaces where the selected tables reside. This information includes the number of pages in the tables, the length of the row, the cardinality, and the buffer pool it is using.

```
SELECT T1.NAME, T1.TSNAME, T1.COLCOUNT
   , T1.NPAGES, T1.PCTPAGES, T1.RECLENGTH, T1.STATUS
   , T1.AUDITING, T1.STATSTIME, T1.CARDF, T2.BPOOL
FROM   SYSIBM.SYSTABLES T1
   , SYSIBM.SYSTABLESPACE T2
WHERE T1.DBNAME    = T2.DBNAME
  AND T1.TSNAME    = T2.NAME
  AND T1.CREATOR   = :creator
  AND T1.DBNAME    = :dbname
ORDER BY T1.NAME
```

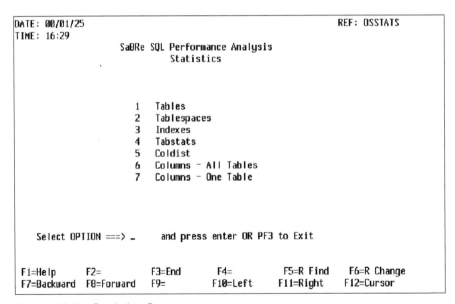

```
DATE: 00/01/25                                             REF: OSSTATS
TIME: 16:29
                       SaBRe SQL Performance Analysis
                              Statistics


                    1    Tables
                    2    Tablespaces
                    3    Indexes
                    4    Tabstats
                    5    Coldist
                    6    Columns - All Tables
                    7    Columns - One Table



     Select OPTION ===> _    and press enter OR PF3 to Exit


 F1=Help      F2=        F3=End      F4=        F5=R Find    F6=R Change
 F7=Backward  F8=Forward F9=         F10=Left   F11=Right    F12=Cursor
```

Figure 22.9   Statistics Screen

Option 1.2: Tablespaces   The tablespace option executes a query that returns the specifics about the tablespace.

```
SELECT NAME, CREATOR
    , BPPOL, PARTITIONS, LOCKRULE
    , PGSIZE, NACTIVE, CLOSERULE
    , SEGSIZE, CREATEDBY, STATSTIME
    , LOCKMAX, TYPE, MAXROWS
FROM SYSIBM.SYSTABLESPACE
WHERE DBNAME = :dbname
ORDER BY NAME
```

Option 1.3: Indexes   The indexes option provides index statistics.

```
SELECT NAME, TBNAME
    , UNIQUERULE, COLCOUNT, CLUSTERING
    , CLUSTERED, DBNAME, NLEAF
    , NLEVELS, BPOOL, CLOSERULE
    , INDEXTYPE, FIRSTKEYCARDF, FULLKEYCARDF
FROM SYSIBM.SYSINDEXES
WHERE DBNAME = :dbname
ORDER BY TBNAME, NAME
```

Option 1.4: Tabstats   The tabstats option provides statistics, such as cardinality, about each partition in the table.

```
SELECT CARD, NPAGES, PCTPAGES, NACTIVE
    , PCTROWCOMP, STATSTIME
    , TSNAME, PARTITION, OWEVER
    , NAME
FROM SYSIBM.SYSTABSTATS
WHERE DBNAME = :dbname
ORDER BY NAME, PARTITION
```

Option 1.5: Coldist   The coldist option provides column distribution statistics.

```
SELECT FREQUENCY, STATSTIME, TBOWNER
    , TBNAME, NAME, HEX(COLVALUE), TYPE
    , CARDF, COLGROUPCOLNO, NUMCOLUMNS
    , FREQUENCYF
FROM SYSIBM.SYSCOLDIST
```

```
WHERE TBOWNER = :creator
ORDER BY TBNAME, NAME, FREQUENCYF DESC
```

Option 1.6: Columns—All Tables   The columns—all tables option provides a list
of all columns in all tables of a given database.

```
SELECT T1.NAME, T1.TBNAME, T1.CREATOR, T1.COLNO
    , COLTYPE, LENGTH, SCALE, NULLS
    , COLCARD, HEX(HIGH2KEY), HEX(LOW2KEY), UPDATES
    , T1.REMARKS, DEFAULT, KEYSEQ, FOREIGNKEY
    , FLDPROC, T1.LABEL, T1.STATSTIME,
    , DEFAULTVALUE, COLCARDF
FROM SYSIBM.SYSCOLUMNS T1, SYSIBM.SYSTABLES T2
WHERE T1.TBCREATOR = :creator
  AND T1.TBNAME = T2.NAME
  AND T2.CREATOR = :creator
  AND T2.DBNAME  = :dbname
ORDER BY T1.DBNAME, T1.COLNO
```

Option 2: Plan Table Analysis   Option 2 from main screen gives a list of "hunt-
ing" queries for analysis of queries in the global plan table (figure 22.10).

Figure 22.10 Plan Table Analysis

Option 2.1: Column Function Evaluation (Stage 2) The first query looks for programs that contain queries that process in stage 2.

```
SELECT QUERYNO, QBLOCKNO, APPLNAME
     , PROGNAME, PLANNO, METHOD, CREATOR
     , TNAME, TABNO, ACCESSTYPE, MATCHCOLS
     , ACCESSCREATOR, ACCESSNAME
     , INDEXONLY, SORTN_UNIQ, SORTN_JOIN
     , SORTN_ORDERBY, SORTN_GROUPBY
     , SORTC_UNIQ, SORTC_JOIN
     , SORTC_ORDERBY, SORTC_GROUPBY
     , TSLOCKMODE, REMARKS
     , PREFETCH, COLUMN_FN_EVAL, MIXOPSEQ
     , JOIN_TYPE, PAGE_RANGE
     , CORRELATION_NAME, QBLOCK_TYPE
FROM PLAN_TABLE
WHERE COLUMN_FN_EVAL = 'S'
ORDER BY TIMESTAMP, QUERYNO, QBLOCKNO, PLANNO, MIXOPSEQ
```

In addition to these queries, IBM's Visual Explain was used to identify stage 2 predicates located in any query.

Option 2.2: Hybrid Join Method The next query shows queries that use hybrid joins.

```
SELECT QUERYNO, PROGNAME, METHOD, TNAME
     , ACCESSTYPE, MATCHCOLS, ACCESSNAME
     , SORTN_UNIQ, SORTN_JOIN, SORTN_ORDERBY
     , SORTN_GROUPBY, SORTC_UNIQ, SORTC_JOIN
     , SORTC_ORDERBY, SORTC_GROUPBY, PREFETCH
FROM OS.PLAN_TABLE
WHERE METHOD = 4
  AND SORTC_JOIN = 'Y'
 ORDER BY PROGNAME, QUERYNO
```

Option 2.3: Indexes Not Used Option 3 identifies indexes that are not being used. It compares the indexes in the global plan table used by the queries.

```
SELECT NAME
     , CREATOR
     , TBNAME
```

```
FROM SYSIBM.SYSINDEXES   T1
WHERE T1.DBNAME = :dbname
AND NOT EXISTS
    (SELECT 1
     FROM PLAN_TABLE
     WHERE ACCESSNAME = T1.NAME)
```

Option 2.4: Indexes Matching on Fewer Columns   Option 4 looks for indexes that are matching on fewer columns than expected. It gets as input the number of actual columns in the index.

```
SELECT QUERYNO
     , PROGNAME
     , :index_name
     , MATCHCOLS
     , :number
FROM PLAN_TABLE
WHERE ACCESSNAME = :index_name
  AND MATCHCOLS <= :number
```

Option 2.5: List Prefetch   Option 5 identifies queries that use list prefetch.

```
SELECT QUERYNO
     , PROGNAME
     , TNAME
     , ACCESSNAME
     , PREFETCH
FROM OS.PLAN_TABLE
WHERE PREFETCH = 'L'
ORDER BY PROGNAME, QUERYNO
```

Option 2.6: List Prefetch with Sorting   Option 6 shows whether sorting occurs on a new table or the composite table.

```
SELECT QUERYNO
     , PROGNAME
     , TNAME
     , ACCESSNAME
     , PREFETCH
     , SORTN_JOIN
     , SORTC_JOIN
```

```
FROM OS.PLAN_TABLE
WHERE PREFETCH = 'L'
  AND (SORTN_JOIN = 'Y' OR
       SORTC_JOIN = 'Y')
ORDER BY PROGNAME, QUERYNO
```

Option 2.7: Multiple Index Scans Option 7 is a report to identify SQL queries that are accessed by multiple indexes.

```
SELECT QUERYNO
     , PROGNAME
     , TNAME
     , ACCESSTYPE
FROM PLAN_TABLE
WHERE ACCESSTYPE LIKE 'M%'
  AND CREATOR = :creator
ORDER BY PROGNAME, QUERYNO
```

Option 2.8: Index Access—No Matching Columns The next option identifies queries that use index access but do not match any columns in the index.

```
SELECT QUERYNO
     , PROGNAME
     , TNAME
     , ACCESSNAME
     , INDEXONLY
FROM OS.PLAN_TABLE
WHERE ACCESSTYPE = 'I'
  AND MATCHCOLS = 0
ORDER BY PROGNAME, QUERYNO
```

Option 2.9: Percentage of Columns Matching Option 9 ranks the queries from least columns matching to most.

```
SELECT IX.CREATOR, IX.NAME
    , IX.COLCOUNT, PT.MATCHCOLS
    , (FLOAT(PT.MATCHCOLS) / FLOAT(IX.COLCOUNT) * 100)
    , 1
FROM SYSIBM.SYSINDEXES IX, PLAN_TABLE PT
WHERE IX.CREATOR    = PT.ACCESSCREATOR
  AND IX.NAME       = PT.ACCESSNAME
```

```
  AND PT.MATCHCOLS > 1
ORDER BY 1, 2, 5
```

Option 2.10: Sorting—New and/or Composite Tables   Option 10 gives a list of the queries that perform sorts on new or composite tables.

```
SELECT QUERYNO, QBLOCKNO, APPLNAME
     , PROGNAME, PLANNO, METHOD, CREATOR
     , TNAME, TABNO, ACCESSTYPE, MATCHCOL
     , ACCESSCREATOR, ACCESSNAME
     , INDEXONLY, SORTN_UNIQ, SORTN_JOIN
     , SORTN_ORDERBY, SORTN_GROUPBY
     , SORTC_UNIQ, SORTC_JOIN
     , SORTC_ORDERBY, SORTC_GROUPBY
     , TSLOCKMODE, TIMESTAMP, REMARKS
     , PREFETCH, COLUMN_FN_EVAL, MIXOPSEQ
     , JOIN_TYPE, PAGE_RANGE
     , CORRELATION_NAME, QBLOCK_TYPE
  FROM OS.PLAN_TABLE
WHERE SORTN_UNIQ     = 'Y'
   OR SORTN_JOIN     = 'Y'
   OR SORTN_ORDERBY  = 'Y'
   OR SORTN_GROUPBY  = 'Y'
   OR SORTC_UNIQ     = 'Y'
   OR SORTC_JOIN     = 'Y'
   OR SORTC_ORDERBY  = 'Y'
   OR SORTC_GROUPBY  = 'Y'
ORDER BY TIMESTAMP, QUERYNO, QBLOCKNO, PLANNO, MIXOPSEQ
```

Option 2.11: Access by Tablespace Scan   Option 11 identifies tables being accessed by a table-space scan. This query filters out the small tables where table-space scans are not a concern.

```
SELECT QUERYNO
     , PROGNAME
     , TNAME
FROM PLAN_TABLE
WHERE ACCESSTYPE = 'R'
  AND CREATOR    = :creator
```

```
AND TNAME NOT IN (list of really small tables)
ORDER BY PROGNAME, QUERYNO
```

Option 2.12: Index Usage by Table   The last report joins the global plan table to
the SYSIBM.SYSINDEXES catalog table. It shows the percentage of columns chosen by
the optimizer that match, and these can be measured and sorted. The results of this query
identify which programs to address first (those with 100% matching are filtered out).

```
SELECT T1.ACCESSNAME, T1.QUERNO, T1.PROGNAME
   ,T1.MATCHCOLS,T2.TBNAME
FROM OS.PLAN_TABLE T1, SYSIBM.SYSINDEXES T2
WHERE T1.ACCESSNAME = T2.NAME
  AND T2. CREATOR = :creator
  AND T2.TBNAME = :table
  AND T2.NAME LIKE :table_prefix
ORDER BY 1,2,3,4
```

Option 3: EXPLAIN   The screen in figure 22.11 is displayed when option 3 is
selected from the main screen. This screen offers options to run a report from the plan
table for either all programs or just one.

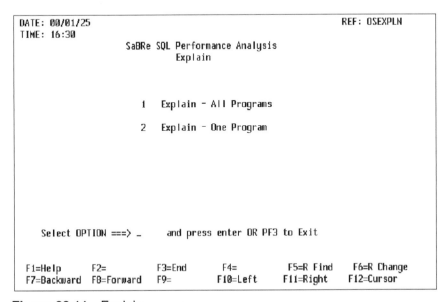

Figure 22.11 Explain

Option 3.2: EXPLAIN—One Program   Option 2 is a query to select the columns
of the EXPLAIN table important to query performance analysis for one program.

```
SELECT QUERYNO, QBLOCKNO, APPLNAME
    , PROGNAME, PLANNO, METHOD, CREATOR
    , TNAME, TABNO, ACCESSTYPE, MATCHCOLS
    , ACCESSCREATOR, ACCESSNAME
    , INDEXONLY, SORTN_UNIQ, SORTN_JOIN
    , SORTN_ORDERBY, SORTN_GROUPBY
    , SORTC_UNIQ, SORTC_JOIN
    , SORTC_ORDERBY, SORTC_GROUPBY
    , TSLOCKMODE, TIMESTAMP, REMARKS
    , PREFETCH, COLUMN_FN_EVAL, MIXOPSEQ
    , JOIN_TYPE, PAGE_RANGE
    , CORRELATION_NAME, QBLOCK_TYPE
    , ACCESS_DEGREE, JOIN_DEGREE
FROM OS.PLAN_TABLE
WHERE PROGNAME = :program_name
ORDER BY PROGNAME, TIMESTAMP, QUERYNO, QBLOCKNO,
PLANNO, MIXOPSEQ
```

Option 4: Catalog Reports   The last option from the main menu (figure 22.12)
executes reports on the DB2 catalog that can be used with the EXPLAIN reports to help
with analysis.

A few of the queries possible from this menu follow. (For more queries that you can
use against the DB2 catalog to retrieve helpful information, refer to Chapter 4, "Catalog
and Directory.")

Option 4.1: All Tables
```
SELECT T1.DBNAME, T1.CREATOR, T1.NAME, T1.TSNAME
FROM SYSIBM.SYSTABLES T1
WHERE T1.DBNAME = :dbname
  AND T1.CREATOR = :creator
  AND T1.TYPE = 'T'
ORDER BY DBNAME, NAME
```

Option 4.2: All Table with All Columns
```
SELECT C.TBNAME, C.NAME, C.COLNO,
,C.COLTYPE, C.LENGTH, C.SCALE
FROM SYSIBM.SYSCOLUMNS C, SYSIBM.SYSTABLES T
```

```
DATE: 00/01/25                                          REF: OSCATRPT
TIME: 16:31
                         SaBRe SQL Performance Analysis
                              Catalog Reports

                    1    All Tables
                    2    All Tables with Columns
                    3    Specific Table with Columns
                    4    All Tables with Specific Column
                    5    All Indexes
                    6    All Indexes for Specific Table
                    7    Referential Integrity for All Tables
                    8    SaBRe DB2 Objects by Bufferpool
                    9    SaBRe Plan Components List
                    10   Plans Bound with Restart
                    11   SaBRe Tables Used - by Program
                    12   SaBRe Programs by DB2 Tables
                    13   Tables with Row Level Locking

        Select OPTION ===> _    and press enter OR PF3 to Exit

   F1=Help      F2=       F3=End     F4=        F5=R Find    F6=R Change
   F7=Backward  F8=Forward F9=       F10=Left   F11=Right    F12=Cursor
```

Figure 22.12 Catalog Reports

```
WHERE T.DBNAME    = :dbname
  AND T.CREATOR   = :creator
  AND T.NAME      = C.TBNAME
  AND T.CREATOR   = C.TBCREATOR
ORDER BY TBNAME, C.COLNO
```

Option 4.3: Specific Tables with Specific Columns
```
SELECT T.NAME, C.NAME, T.CREATOR
FROM SYSIBM.SYSTABLES T, SYSIBM.SYSCOLUMNS C
WHERE T.NAME      = C.NAME
  AND T.CREATOR   = C.TBCREATOR
  AND T.DBNAME    = :dbname
  AND T.CREATOR   = :creator
  AND C.NAME      = :column_name
```

Option 4.9: Plan Component List
```
SELECT A.PLANNAME, A.NAME, 'PACKAGE'
FROM SYSIBM.SYSPACKLIST A
WHERE A.PLANNAME LIKE :planname_prefix
UNION ALL
```

```
SELECT B.PLNAME, B.NAME, 'DBRM     '
FROM SYSIBM.SYSDBRM B
WHERE A.PLNAME LIKE :planname_prefix
ORDER BY 1,2
```

Option 4.13: Tables with Row-Level Locking   This query finds tables that are accessed by row-level locking, either by being defined as LOCKRULE ROW or through simulation by allowing only one row per page (MAXROWS 1).

```
SELECT T1.DBNAME, T1.NAME, T2.NAME
   , T1.LOCKRULE, T1.MAXROWS
FROM SYSIBM.SYSTABLESPACE T1
   , SYSIBM.SYSTABLES T2
WHERE T1.DBNAME    = T2.DBNAME
  AND T1.NAME      = T2.TSNAME
  AND T1.DBNAME    = :dbname
  AND (T1.LOCKRULE = 'R' CONCAT '  '
   OR T1.MAXROWS = 1)
ORDER BY T1.NAME
```

Exception Reporting

One of the easiest ways to prevent a performance problem is to ensure that RUNSTATS has been run on all the tables in the shop. If RUNSTATS has not been run, the DB2 optimizer will choose default values for the columns when choosing the access path of an SQL statement. Here is an example of a query to locate such tables and the dependent plans:

```
SELECT A.NAME, A.CREATOR, A.TSNAME, A.DBNAME, B.DNAME
FROM SYSIBM.SYSTABLES A,
     SYSIBM.SYSPLANDEP B
WHERE TYPE = 'T'          -- T is for tables
  AND CARD = -1           -- -1 if no runstats
  AND BTYPE = 'T'         -- dependent object of table
  AND A.NAME = B.BNAME
ORDER BY A.DBNAME, A.TSNAME, A.NAME, B.DNAME;
```

After executing RUNSTATS on the tables listed in the report produced by this SQL statement, be sure to rebind all plans that are dependent on those tables. To determine which packages (instead of plans) are dependent on the tables, substitute SYSPLANDEP with SYSPACKDEP. The column names remain the same.

EXPLAIN Interpretation

We now present some examples of interpreting EXPLAIN output that show that there is more to this analysis than meets the eye. The rows inserted into the plan table by analyzing an SQL statement with EXPLAIN do not really tell us whether the statement is good or bad, how it will run, or anything other than raw data that must be analyzed. Most tools that analyze the plan table also do not go far enough. Take, for example, the three queries in figure 22.13, which all provide the same answer for a problem. The large table is divided by the small table to find all the accounts in the PARTS table that have at least all the IDs identified in the QUE table. This is a typical query used in applications where the number of items in the smaller table can vary from one request to another, such as "find all the customers that have call waiting, call forwarding, or caller ID so that we can offer them a better package that includes more features" or "find a supplier from whom we can get at least all those items we used to get from deadbeat supplier." The three examples are all very different to test of our analysis strategy.

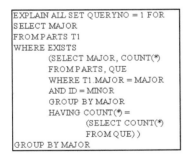

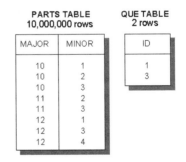

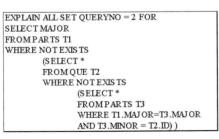

Figure 22.13 Explain Example 1 All Options

First of all, this is the only way to analyze a query. We have the plan table data, the SQL query itself, the table structure, and the cardinality of the tables (very critical). It is impossible to determine from looking at the queries which would work best. Figure 22.14 shows the raw output of EXPLAIN for these queries with no indexes defined. Obviously, this data is very difficult to read, much less to use to determine what is happening. So we decided to add the appropriate indexes to the tables as shown in figure 22.15. Again, the data is very difficult to read and cannot be used to derive any kind of intelligible answer to how the three queries will work.

So we move to figure 22.16, which truly shows how to analyze an SQL statement. We have all the details in front of us. The first, most important thing to do is to determine which lines in the plan table refer to which parts of the query. If we look at the query closely, a join stands out in query block 2, so we can tag that. There is a column function evaluation on the QUE table, so that is easy to tag as path 2, and we now know which query block pertains to which part of the SQL statement. But what else do we know? When we look at the AT (access type) column, we see all index access except for the QUE table, which will never have more than a few rows anyway. Also, we see that index-only access is used for three accesses, and two of those are matching the index. Without going further, all rules and all automated plan table tools would say the same thing: wonderful

| Qry | Blk | Pl | Mt | Table | | | | INDEX | | SORTN | | | | SORTC | | | | TS | P | C | M |
No	No	No	hd	Name	TN	AT	MCOL	XNM	XONLY	U	J	O	G	U	J	O	G	LOCK	F	F	X
1	1	1	0	P ARTS	1	R	0		N	N	N	N	N	N	N	N	N	IS	S		0
1	1	2	3		0		0		N	N	N	N	N	N	N	N	Y				0
1	2	1	0	P ARTS	2	R	0		N	N	N	N	N	N	N	N	N	IS	S		0
1	2	2	1	QUE	3	R	0		N	N	N	N	N	N	N	N	N	IS	S		0
1	2	3	3		0		0		N	N	N	N	N	N	N	N	Y			S	0
1	3	1	0	QUE	4	R	0		N	N	N	N	N	N	N	N	N	IS	S	R	0
2	1	1	0	P ARTS	1	R	0		N	N	N	N	N	N	N	N	N	IS	S		0
2	2	1	0	QUE	2	R	0		N	N	N	N	N	N	N	N	N	IS	S		0
2	3	1	0	P ARTS	3	R	0		N	N	N	N	N	N	N	N	N	IS	S		0
3	1	1	0	P ARTS	1	R	0		N	N	N	N	N	N	N	N	N	IS	S		0
3	1	2	3		0		0		N	N	N	N	N	N	N	N	Y				0
3	2	1	0	QUE	2	R	0		N	N	N	N	N	N	N	N	N	IS	S		0
3	3	1	0	P ARTS	3	R	0		N	N	N	N	N	N	N	N	N	IS	S		0
3	3	2	3		0		0		N	N	N	N	Y	N	Y	N				0

No INDEXES on either PARTS or QUE

Figure 22.14   Explain Example 1 W/Out Indexes

Qry No	Blk No	P1 No	Mt hd	Table Name	TN	AT	MCOL	INDEX XNM	XONLY	SORTN U	J	O	G	SORTC U	J	O	G	TS LOCK	P F	C F	M X
1	1	1	0	PARTS	1	I	0	PTX	Y	N	N	N	N	N	N	N	N	IS	S		0
1	2	1	0	PARTS	2	I	1	PTX	Y	N	N	N	N	N	N	N	N	IS			0
1	2	2	1	QUE	3	I	1	QEX	Y	N	N	N	N	N	N	N	N	IS			0
1	3	1	0	QUE	4	R	0		N	N	N	N	N	N	N	N	N	IS	S	R	0
2	1	1	0	PARTS	1	R	0		N	N	N	N	N	N	N	N	N	IS	S		0
2	2	1	0	QUE	2	R	0		N	N	N	N	N	N	N	N	N	IS	S		0
2	3	1	0	PARTS	3	I	2	PTX	Y	N	N	N	N	N	N	N	N	IS			0
3	1	1	0	PARTS	1	I	0	PTX	Y	N	N	N	N	N	N	N	N	IS	S		0
3	2	1	0	QUE	2	R	0		N	N	N	N	N	N	N	N	N	IS	S		0
3	3	1	0	PARTS	3	I	1	PTX	Y	N	N	N	N	N	N	N	N	IS			0
3	3	2	3		0		0		N	N	N	N	Y	N	Y	N					0

Index on PARTS on (MAJOR,MINOR)

Index on QUE on (ID)

Figure 22.15 Explain Example 1 W/Out Indexes

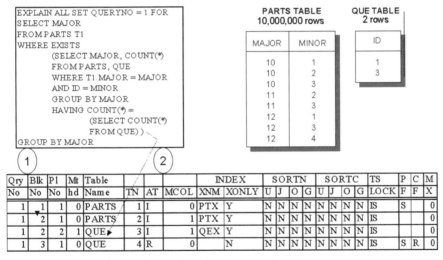

Qry No	Blk No	P1 No	Mt hd	Table Name	TN	AT	MCOL	INDEX XNM	XONLY	SORTN U	J	O	G	SORTC U	J	O	G	TS LOCK	P F	C F	M X
1	1	1	0	PARTS	1	I	0	PTX	Y	N	N	N	N	N	N	N	N	IS	S		0
1	2	1	0	PARTS	2	I	1	PTX	Y	N	N	N	N	N	N	N	N	IS			0
1	2	2	1	QUE	3	I	1	QEX	Y	N	N	N	N	N	N	N	N	IS			0
1	3	1	0	QUE	4	R	0		N	N	N	N	N	N	N	N	N	IS	S	R	0

Figure 22.16 Explain Example 1 Queryno = 1

query. But it ain't so! There is a correlated subquery with a nested loop join that will be executed 10 million times. Right answers, worst possible solution.

Let's move now to figure 22.17, which presents all the same data but with a different solution. Here we have the classic double-not-exists relational query. We follow the same analysis to identify which rows pertain to which parts of the query, and we start here

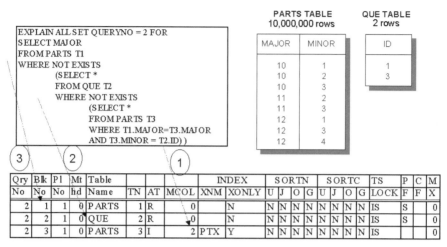

```
EXPLAIN ALL SET QUERYNO = 2 FOR
SELECT MAJOR
FROM PARTS T1
WHERE NOT EXISTS
        (SELECT *
        FROM QUE T2
        WHERE NOT EXISTS
                (SELECT *
                FROM PARTS T3
                WHERE T1.MAJOR=T3.MAJOR
                AND T3.MINOR = T2.ID) )
```

PARTS TABLE
10,000,000 rows

MAJOR	MINOR
10	1
10	2
10	3
11	2
11	3
12	1
12	3
12	4

QUE TABLE
2 rows

ID
1
3

Qry No	Blk No	Pl No	Mt hd	Table Name	TN	AT	MCOL	INDEX XNM	XONLY	SORTN U	J	O	G	SORTC U	J	O	G	TS LOCK	P F	C F	M X
2	1	1	0	PARTS	1	R	0		N	N	N	N	N	N	N	N	N	IS	S		0
2	2	1	0	QUE	2	R	0		N	N	N	N	N	N	N	N	N	IS	S		0
2	3	1	0	PARTS	3	I	2	PTX	Y	N	N	N	N	N	N	N	N	IS			0

Figure 22.17   Explain Example 1 Queryno = 2

with the two matching columns, which quickly point to query block 3. Query block 2 is the only one referencing the QUE table, so that is an easy identification. We have two table-space scans out of three accesses, bad. Query block 3 is correlated to both query blocks 1 and 2, which means that for every row in the top query block, query block 1, we have to execute query block 2, a loop, and for each item in query block 2, we have to execute query block 3. All rules and all analyzers flag this as a disaster. Wrong again! The nature of the query says we have to scan all the rows in query block 1, so that is okay. The not-exists predicates are a true-false probe, which simply gets us to ignore all the bad rows, rapidly returning the result set as fast as we can sequentially prefetch through the table. Not a bad query at all.

Move to figure 22.18 now. Perform the same line analysis. Use the matching index lookup on one column to identify the correct block; then the analysis is easy because the QUE table appears only once. Following all the rules for plan table data for access paths, it does not look too bad at all, sort of like the first example. But the GROUP BY on the top query will leave over a million rows, maybe as many as five million. For each row in the GROUP BY, we have to execute the correlated subquery on the right side, which has to count the number of rows matching in the QUE table every time and do the lookup in the bottom block. Plan table says okay, but the query is the second-worst performer.

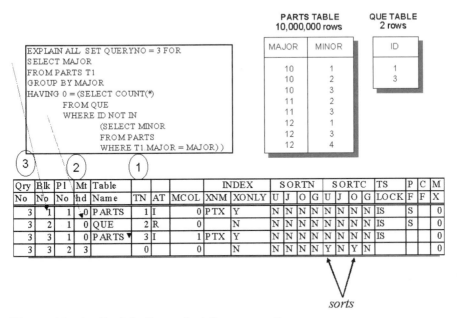

```
EXPLAIN ALL SET QUERYNO = 3 FOR
SELECT MAJOR
FROM PARTS T1
GROUP BY MAJOR
HAVING 0 = (SELECT COUNT(*)
        FROM QUE
        WHERE ID NOT IN
            (SELECT MINOR
            FROM PARTS
            WHERE T1.MAJOR = MAJOR))
```

PARTS TABLE — 10,000,000 rows

MAJOR	MINOR
10	1
10	2
10	3
11	2
11	3
12	1
12	3
12	4

QUE TABLE — 2 rows

ID
1
3

Qry No	Blk No	Pl No	Mt hd	Table Name	TN	AT	MCOL	XNM	XONLY	U	J	O	G	U	J	O	G	TS LOCK	P F	C F	M X
3	1	1	0	PARTS	1	I	0	PTX	Y	N	N	N	N	N	N	N	N	IS	S		0
3	2	1	0	QUE	2	R	0		N	N	N	N	N	N	N	N	N	IS	S		0
3	3	1	0	PARTS	3	I	1	PTX	Y	N	N	N	N	N	N	N	N	IS			0
3	3	2	3		0		0		N	N	N	N	Y	N	Y	N					0

sorts

Figure 22.18   Explain Example 1 Queryno = 3

```
EXPLAIN ALL SET QUERYNO= 1 FOR
SELECT AAA.LOCA_NO, AAA.RXNO, AAA.REFILLNO, AA.MAJOR_CAT , AAA.MINOR_CAT,
    AAA.TYPE , AAA.ITEM_NO, AAA.QUANTITY, AAA.SUPPLY, AAA.DEPT, AAA.FACTOR
    , AAA.TRANS_DATE , AAA.FAMILY_ID , BBB.RELATIONSHIP_ID
FROM AAA00 AAA, BBB01 BBB
WHERE AAA.TRANS_DATE BETWEEN ? and ?
 AND AAA.STATUS = '*'
 AND AAA.MAJOR_CAT BETWEEN ? and ?
 AND (BBB.RELATIONSHIP_ID BETWEEN ? AND ? OR 0 = 1)
 AND BBB.MAJOR_CAT = AAA.MAJOR_CAT
 AND BBB.MINOR_CAT = AAA.MINOR_CAT
 AND EXISTS (SELECT 1 FROM CCC00 CCC
        WHERE CCC.REPORT_ID = ?
        AND CCC.FAMILY_ID = AAA.FAMILY_ID
        AND CCC.TYPE = AAA.TYPE)
```

Q NO	B NO	P NO	T H	TABLE NAME	A	M COL	ACCESSNAME	I O	SSSS NNNN UJOG	SSSS CCCC UJOG	P	C F N	MX
1	1	1	0	XXXBBB01	R	0		N	NNNN	NNNN	S		0
1	1	2	2	XXXAAA	I	1	XXXAAA02	N	NYNN	NYNN			0
1	2	1	0	XXXCCC	I	3	XXXCCC01	Y	NNNN	NNNN			0
1	3	1	0	XXXBBB	R	0		N	NNNN	NNNN	S		0
1	3	2	3			0		N	NNNN	YNNN			0

Figure 22.19   Explain Example 2 Query 1

Now move to figure 22.19, an entirely different situation. If you analyze the query as we did before, using the plan table output, it is obvious that this query is not going to work very well. It might be difficult to see quickly but a view is used, and it needs to be materialized. Figure 22.20 does some tweaking to make the access look better, at least according to the data in the plan table. But the materialization issue is still here. Figures 22.21 and 22.22 show the query broken down into two separate queries, with one used as an outer cursor (figure 22.22) and the other used as an inner cursor (figure 22.21). The access paths both look great now according to the data in the plan tables, and there is no view materialization. Many organizations try to break queries apart into multiple cursors just like this, but in reality, this is a disaster! If you think about it long enough, you will be able to see why. We explain throughout this book all the reasons that this solution would not work. Figure 22.20 is the solution that works best in this case. A final listing of all the plan table output for this particular analysis which shows dramatically just how different reality and plan table data are, is given in (figure 22.23).

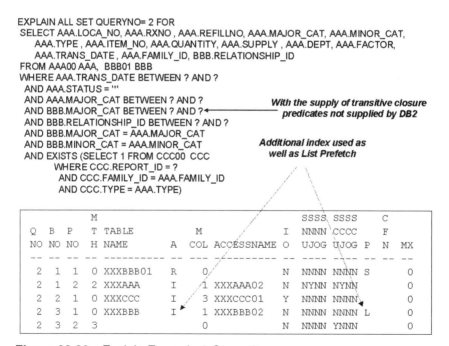

Figure 22.20   Explain Example 2 Query 2

```
EXPLAIN ALL SET QUERYNO= 3 FOR
SELECT AAA.LOCA_NO, AAA.RXNO
    , AAA.REFILLNO, AAA.MAJOR_CAT
    , AAA.MINOR_CAT, AAA.TYPE
    , AAA.ITEM_NO, AAA.QUANTITY
    , AAA.SUPPLY, AAA.DEPT, AAA.FACTOR
    , AAA.TRANS_DATE, AAA.FAMILY_ID
FROM AAA00 AAA
WHERE AAA.TRANS_DATE BETWEEN ? AND ?       -- INPUT PARMS
  AND AAA.STATUS = '*'                     -- FIXED (???)
  AND AAA.MAJOR_CAT = ?                    -- FROM SGP OUTER
  AND AAA.MINOR_CAT = ?                    -- FROM SGP OUTER
  AND EXISTS (SELECT 1 FROM CCC00 CCC
          WHERE CCC.REPORT_ID = ?          -- INPUT PARMS
            AND CCC.FAMILY_ID = AAA.FAMILY_ID
            AND CCC.TYPE = AAA.TYPE)
ORDER BY AAA.TRANS_DATE                    -- "FORCE INDEX"
```

This becomes the inner cursor

```
          M                             SSSS SSSS   C
  Q   B  P  T  TABLE        M         I  NNNN CCCC   F
 NO  NO NO  H  NAME      A  COL ACCESSNAME O  UJOG UJOG  P  N  MX
 --- -- -- -- ---------- -- --- ---------- -- ---- ---- -- -- --
  3   1  1  0  XXXAAA    I   1  XXXAAA02   N  NNNN NNNN        0
  3   2  1  0  XXXCCC    I   3  XXXCCC01   Y  NNNN NNNN        0
```

Figure 22.21   Explain Example 2 Query 3

This becomes the outer cursor

```
EXPLAIN ALL SET QUERYNO= 4 FOR
SELECT BBB.MAJOR_CAT
    , BBB.MINOR_CAT
    , BBB.RELATIONSHIP_ID
FROM BBB01 BBB
WHERE BBB.MAJOR_CAT BETWEEN ? AND ?             -- INPUT PARMS
  AND BBB.RELATIONSHIP_ID BETWEEN ? AND ?       -- INPUT PARMS
```

```
          M                             SSSS SSSS   C
  Q   B  P  T  TABLE        M         I  NNNN CCCC   F
 NO  NO NO  H  NAME      A  COL ACCESSNAME O  UJOG UJOG  P  N  MX
 --- -- -- -- ---------- -- --- ---------- -- ---- ---- -- -- --
  4   1  1  0  XXXBBB    I   1  XXXBBB02   N  NNNN NNNN  L     0
  4   1  2  3             0                N  NNNN YNNN        0
```

Figure 22.22   Explain Example 2 Query 4

Q NO	B NO	P NO	M T H	TABLE NAME	A	M COL	ACCESSNAME	I O	SSSS NNNN UJOG	SSSS CCCC UJOG	C F P	N	MX
1	1	1	0	XXXBBB01	R	0		N	NNNN	NNNN	S		0
1	1	2	2	XXXAAA	I	1	XXXAAA02	N	NYNN	NYNN			0
1	2	1	0	XXXCCC	I	3	XXXCCC01	Y	NNNN	NNNN			0
1	3	1	0	XXXBBB	R	0		N	NNNN	NNNN	S		0
1	3	2	3			0		N	NNNN	YNNN			0
2	1	1	0	XXXBBB01	R	0		N	NNNN	NNNN	S		0
2	1	2	2	XXXAAA	I	1	XXXAAA02	N	NYNN	NYNN			0
2	2	1	0	XXXCCC	I	3	XXXCCC01	Y	NNNN	NNNN			0
2	3	1	0	XXXBBB	I	1	XXXBBB02	N	NNNN	NNNN	L		0
2	3	2	3			0		N	NNNN	YNNN			0
3	1	1	0	XXXAAA	I	1	XXXAAA02	N	NNNN	NNNN			0
3	2	1	0	XXXCCC	I	3	XXXCCC01	Y	NNNN	NNNN			0
4	1	1	0	XXXBBB	I	1	XXXBBB02	N	NNNN	NNNN	L		0
4	1	2	3			0		N	NNNN	YNNN			0

Figure 22.23   Explain Example 2 All Queries

Predictive Governing

Predictive governing is simply a prediction of CPU time as part of the BIND or PREPARE process for an SQL statement. It can be used with the new RLF (resource limit facility) to prevent dynamic SQL queries that exceed user limits. This information can be helpful when using EXPLAIN data to analyze access path selection. The SQL path selection may look fine, but the estimate can show that some changes are required.

We can generate a cost value for a statement and then act upon it. This works only if the statistics in the catalog are correct; otherwise, you may stop a query that truly was okay. RLF gives you the ability to trap a runaway query before it starts, which is more effective than letting a query run and consume resources for a period of time before it is stopped. You must have good statistics to take advantage of this feature.

RLST

The RLST (resource-limit specification tables) is used for predictive governing (figure 22.24). It gives governing information to DB2. The RLST lets you set warning and error

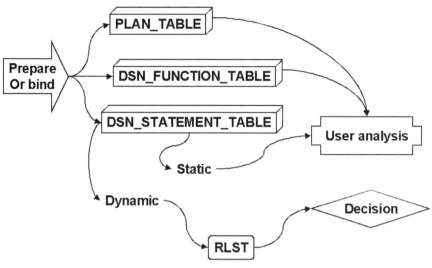

Figure 22.24   Predictive Governing

thresholds. The governor can inform users that a certain processing limit might be exceeded for a particular dynamic SELECT, INSERT, UPDATE, or DELETE statement. This information is communicated via application programs.

For incoming client requests, the requester must be at DRDA level 4 and must use DB2 for OS/390 Version 6 with DB2 Connect Version 5.2.

For dynamic SQL DML, you can govern the dynamic statements before execution. Actions are determined by the information in the new DSN_STATEMNT_TABLE and the RLST. These actions may be to run the statement, warn the user, or not run the statement. Static SQL DML uses the new EXPLAIN output to advise of resource consumption and allows you to analyze program SQL before moving to production.

DSN_STATEMNT_TABLE

The DSN_STATEMNT_TABLE is populated (if it exists) when EXPLAIN is run. Some of the columns are similar to those in the plan table, and some are new and only related to the statement cost. The columns are listed in figure 22.6, and an example of the DDL for the DSN_STATEMNT_TABLE is in figure 22.25.

```
CREATE TABLE <userid>. DSN_ STATEMNT_ TABLE
   (QUERYNO              INTEGER NOT NULL,
   APPLNAME              CHAR( 8) NOT NULL,
   PROGNAME              CHAR( 8) NOT NULL,
   COLLID                CHAR( 18) NOT NULL,
   GROUP_MEMBER          CHAR( 8) NOT NULL,
   EXPLAIN_TIME          TIMESTAMP NOT NULL,
   STMT_TYPE             CHAR( 6) NOT NULL,
   COST_CATEGORY         CHAR( 1) NOT NULL,
   PROCMS                INTEGER NOT NULL,
   PROCSU                INTEGER NOT NULL,
   REASON                VARCHAR( 254) NOT NULL )
      IN <database- name>.< table- space- name>;
```

Figure 22.25   DSN_STATEMNT_TABLE

The data in the statement table provides cost estimates, in service units and in milliseconds, for SELECT, INSERT, UPDATE, and DELETE statements, both static and dynamic. The estimates do not take several factors into account, including cost adjustments that are caused by parallel processing and the use of triggers or user-defined functions.

Two cost categories are used for cost estimates. Category A is used for estimates for which DB2 has adequate information to make a better estimate than those that are reported in category B. Category A is considered to be very accurate, but not 100% accurate. Category B is used when DB2 simply does not have enough information to accurately estimate the cost, primarily when it is forced to use default values. Category B may be required when no statistics are available or because host variables are used in a query.

Do not spend time tuning a query based on estimates that are returned in cost category B. It is perhaps better to understand why the cost category was B and see whether the results of the estimate might be accurate if the reason for category B is removed. Host variables cause cost category B, so ignore those, but situations such as triggers and UDFs should generally have a fixed cost that can be estimated.

When using the RLST and the statement table to govern dynamic SQL, you probably should go easy on category B costs and focus your attention on category A, but not always, of course. The RLST and the plan table can be joined to provide more specific information about a query, and this query could then be joined to the catalog statement tables for a listing of the actual SQL statement. The QUERYNO, APPLNAME, PROGNAME, COLLID, and EXPLAIN_TIME columns contain the same values as the corresponding columns of the plan table for a given plan. These columns can be used to join the statement table to the plan table:

```
SELECT PT.*, ST.PROCMS, ST.COST_CATEGORY
FROM PLAN_TABLE PT,
     DSN_STATEMNT_TABLE ST
WHERE PT.APPLNAME = 'YLA'
  AND PT.APPLNAME = ST.APPLNAME
  AND PT.PROGNAME = ST.PROGNAME
  AND PT.COLLID  = ST.COLLID
  AND PT.BIND_TIME = ST.EXPLAIN_TIME
ORDER BY PT.QUERYNO, PT.QBLOCKNO, PT.PLANNO, PT.MIXOPSEQ;
```

Cost category B appears when any of the following conditions are present:

- The SQL uses UDFs.
- Triggers are defined on the target table.
- An INSERT statement and insert triggers exist on the table.
- An UPDATE statement and update triggers exist on the table.
- A DELETE statement and delete triggers exist on the table.
- A DELETE statement with RI defined on it exists on the parent table, and the DELETE rules are either CASCADE or SET NULL.
- A WHERE clause has one of the following:
  - COL [>, >=, <, <=, LIKE, or NOT LIKE] *literal* or COL BETWEEN *literal* AND *literal*, where *literal* is a host variable, a parameter marker, or a special register.
  - LIKE with an escape clause that contains a host variable
- Cardinality statistics are missing for one or more tables that are used in the statement.

Monitoring and Tracing

DB2 Tracing

It is important to have the appropriate classes always gathering information about your DB2 subsystem and its activity. It is generally recommended that you select SMF account class 1, 2, and 3 and SMF statistics class 1, 3, and 4 (1 and 3 at a minimum) during normal execution. These are specified on the DSNTIPN install panel (figure 22.26) and can be changed in the DSNZPARMs SMFACCT and SMFSTAT. The classes have a small amount of overhead but are not usually an issue and are used by the majority of DB2 shops. Any other trace classes should not run at all times, because they cause excessive overhead if run for long periods of time.

When you execute other traces, it is wise to run the trace with only the IFCIDs necessary for the appropriate performance analysis or problem diagnosis. These traces also should be run only for short periods of time. The following example shows limiting a trace.

```
-start trace(perftrc1) class(8) ifcid(0221) planname(yourplan)
```

This example limits a performance trace to class 8 with IFCID 221, which is used to view the actual degree of parallelism at run time.

```
DSNTIPN                    DB2-TRACING
===>
Enter data below:

1 AUDIT TRACE       ===> NO          Audit classes to start.NO,YES,List

2 TRACE AUTO START ===> NO          Global classes to start. YES,NO,List
3 TRACE SIZE        ===> 65536       Trace table size in bytes. 4K-396K

4 SMF ACCOUNTING    ===> 1,2,3       Accounting classes to start. NO,YES,List
5 SMF STATISTICS    ===> 1,3,4       Statistics classes to start. NO,YES,List
6 STATISTICS TIME   ===> 30          Time interval in minutes. 1-1440

7 MONITOR TRACE     ===> NO          Monitor classes to start. NO,YES,List
8 MONITOR SIZE      ===> 8192        Default monitor buffer size. 8K-1M

9 CHECKPOINT FREQ   ===> 10000       Number of log records per checkpoint
```

Figure 22.26   Trace Classes

There are five different types of DB2 traces: accounting, statistics, monitoring, auditing, and performance.

DB2PM

There are several DB2 monitors on the market by various vendors and all have features for performance monitoring and tuning. In this book, we use IBM's DB2PM for performance reporting and monitoring for consistency of reference. Almost every DBMS comes with its own monitor, and there is a good reason for that. Who else other than the DBMS vendor knows where the real information is stored and how it is used?

The statistics reports provide an excellent source of information, such as buffer pools, EDM pools, RID processing, and logging, all at a subsystem level. The accounting reports provide information about applications for specific time periods. Those are the most popular and most useful reports for ongoing analysis, trend analysis, and predictive monitoring. There are also some more specific reports, such as the lock detail analysis report for monitoring locking problems. The more detailed reports require some additional traces to be turned on and should be used only for problem analysis, not run continually.

User-tailored reports (UTRs) allow you to tailor reports for more precise analysis.

In DB2 version 6, the online portion of the DB2PM product has a very user-friendly GUI interface. Figure 22.27 shows the main screen of the DB2PM GUI interface. It has a look and feel similar to the DB2 Control Center. From here you can monitor all your DB2 subsystems and your data-sharing environment. Figure 22.28 gives you a look at a detail screen.

IFCID and Trace Field Descriptions

Ever wonder what all those IFCIDs and trace fields mean? The best source of information comes right with the DB2 product. In the SDSNSAMP library provided by IBM, a member called DSNWMSGS gives you a lot of detailed information about IFCIDs and field descriptions. It also comes with DDL to create tables to hold this information and the load card statements to load the data from the file into these DB2 tables. From there,

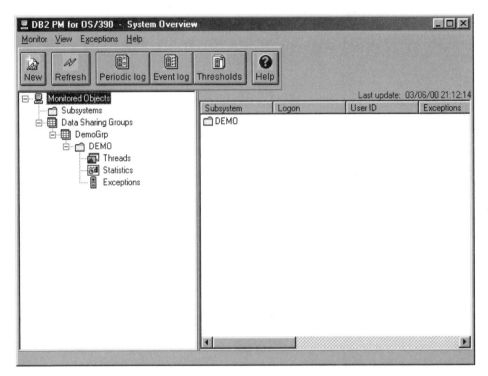

Figure 22.27　DB2PM GUI

very simple systems can be developed to query these tables to gain valuable information during performance analysis and problem diagnosis.

Following is the DDL for the tables.

```
CREATE TABLE DBDB001.TRACE_DESCRIPTIONS
   (IFCID       INTEGER   NOT NULL,
    NAME        CHAR(8)   NOT NULL,
    DESCRIPTION CHAR(60)  NOT NULL,
    SEQ         INTEGER   NOT NULL)
    IN DATABS1.TRACETS;

CREATE TABLE DBDB001.TRACE_TYPES
   (TYPE      CHAR(17) NOT NULL,
    CLASS     INTEGER  NOT NULL,
```

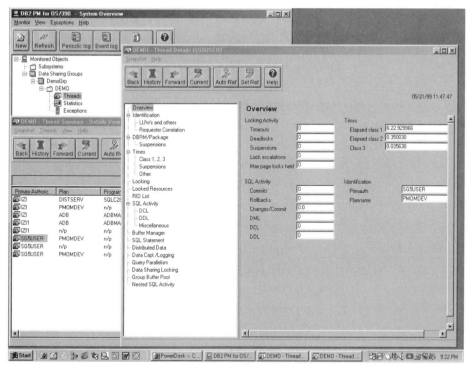

Figure 22.28   DB2PM GUILocking Detail

```
IFCID     INTEGER  NOT NULL,
COMMENTS CHAR(35) NOT NULL WITH DEFAULT)
IN DATABS1.TRACETS;
```

An example of a very simple query system to include queries driven from the menu was developed as a CLIST to drive QMF queries behind the scenes (figure 22.29).

Following are the queries behind the panel options. Many of these queries are derived from those supplied with the DSNWMSGS member.

Option 1: All Trace Field Descriptions
```
SELECT DISTINCT *
   FROM DBDB001.TRACE_DESCRIPTIONS
   ORDER BY NAME, SEQ;
```

```
DATE: 01/15/00
TIME: 04:09:00



                    TRACE AND IFCID INFORMATION REPORTING


        1 - ALL TRACE FIELD DESCRIPTIONS
        2 - ALL TRACE FIELD DESCRIPTIONS AND IFCIDS
        3 - FIELD DESCRIPTIONS FOR TRACE RECORD FOR A PARTICULAR IFCID
        4 - FIELD DESCRIPTIONS FOR A PARTICULAR FIELD
        5 - FIELD DESCRIPTIONS FOR AUDIT TRACE RECORDS
        6 - FIELD DESCRIPTIONS FOR MONITOR TRACE RECORDS
        7 - FIELD DESCRIPTIONS FOR PERFORMANCE TRACE RECORDS
        8 - FIELD DESCRIPTIONS FOR PERFORMANCE TRACE RECORDS FOR PARTICULAR CLASSES




    SELECT OPTION ===> _      PRESS ENTER OR PF3 TO EXIT
```

Figure 22.29   Trace and IFCID Reporting

Option 2: All Trace Field Descriptions and IFCIDs

```
SELECT TYPE, CLASS, A.IFCID, DESCRIPTION, SEQ
    FROM DBDB001.TRACE_TYPES A,
    DBDB001.TRACE_DESCRIPTIONS B
    WHERE A.IFCID = B.IFCID
    ORDER BY TYPE, CLASS, SEQ;
```

Option 3: Field Descriptions for Trace Record for a Particular IFCID

```
SELECT DISTINCT *
    FROM DBDB001.TRACE_DESCRIPTIONS
    WHERE IFCID = 21
    ORDER BY SEQ;
```

Option 4: Field Descriptions for a Particular Field

```
SELECT DISTINCT *
    FROM DBDB001.TRACE_DESCRIPTIONS
    WHERE NAME = 'QWACRINV'
    ORDER BY SEQ;
```

Option 5: Field Descriptions for Audit Trace Records

```
SELECT DISTINCT NAME, DESCRIPTION, A.IFCID, SEQ
    FROM DBDB001.TRACE_DESCRIPTIONS A,
    DBDB001.TRACE_TYPES B
    WHERE A.IFCID = B.IFCID
    AND TYPE = 'AUDIT'
    ORDER BY SEQ;
```

Option 6: Field Descriptions for Monitor Trace Records

```
SELECT DISTINCT A.NAME, A.DESCRIPTION,
    A.IFCID, A.SEQ
    FROM DBDB001.TRACE_DESCRIPTIONS A,
    DBDB001.TRACE_TYPES B
    WHERE A.IFCID = B.IFCID
    AND TYPE = 'MONITOR'
    ORDER BY SEQ;
```

Option 7: Field Descriptions for Performance Trace Records

```
SELECT DISTINCT NAME, DESCRIPTION, A.IFCID, SEQ
    FROM CTCDBU01.TRACE_DESCRIPTIONS A,
    DBDB001.TRACE_TYPES B
    WHERE A.IFCID = B.IFCID AND
    TYPE = 'PERFORMANCE'
    ORDER BY SEQ;
```

Option 8: Field Descriptions for Performance Trace Records for Particular Classes

```
SELECT DISTINCT NAME, CLASS, DESCRIPTION, A.IFCID, SEQ
    FROM CTCDBU01.TRACE_DESCRIPTIONS A,
    DBDB001.TRACE_TYPES B
    WHERE A.IFCID = B.IFCID AND
    (TYPE = 'PERFORMANCE' AND
    CLASS IN (1,2,3,4,5,6,7)
    ORDER BY SEQ;
```

This is probably one of the most useful traces for performance tuning. Many of the IFCIDs used in this book are included in the IFCIDs in the performance trace. Figure 22.30 is a very small example of the data you get from this query (with a little creative QMF formatting).

```
                        PERFORMANCE TRACE CLASS REPORT

CLASS IFCID NAME        DESCRIPTION
----- ----- ---------   -------------------------------------------------------------
  6    20   QW0020PL    TABLE SPACE HELD BY THE THREAD.
             QW0020PC    THIS FIELD IS FOR SEGEMENTED TABLE SPACES AND FOR
                        PARTITIONED TABLE SPACES THAT USE SELECTIVE PARTITION
                        LOCKING. FOR SEGMENTED TABLE SPACES, THIS NUMBER IS THE
                        TOTAL NUMBER OF TABLE WITHIN THE TABLE SPACE FOR
                        WHICH LOCKS ESCALATED. FOR PARTITIONED TABLE SPACES
                        THAT USE SELECTIVE PARTITION LOCKING, THIS NUMBER IS
                        THE TOTAL NUMBER OF PARTITIONS FOR WHICH LOCKS
                        ESCALATED.
             QWOO20PS    THIS FIELD IS FOR NONSEGMENTED TABLESPACE, EXCEPT
                        FOR PARITIONED TABLE SPACES THAT USE SELECTIVE
                        PARTITIONED LOCKING.
                        HIGHEST PAGE SET (TABLE SPACE) LOCK STATE:
             QW0020S1      X'01' = (RESERVED)
             QW0020S2      X'02' = INTENT SHARE (IS LOCK)
. . .
```

Figure 22.30   Performance Trace Class Report

A query information system such as this could also be easily developed in a tool such as IBM's VisualAge for Java. The system can be used by the DBAs and application staff who are responsible for performance and could be deployed on the company intranet.

Influencing the Optimizer

E merson's quotation has perhaps more meaning for query optimization than any other area of DB2, SQL, and performance. Any consistency of approach in this area is foolish, such as "always use OPTIMIZE FOR 1 ROW since it always get the best index," "never let DB2 do the sorting," "always only rebind right after a reorganization," and others not worth even mentioning. This discussion of optimization is needed because you always know more about the structure and organization of the data than the optimizer does. Even if the optimizer could always choose the right path to the data, it would still depend on the statistics that you provided, the time of their collection, and the time of the path selection process to get enough information to choose correctly when it must use defaults due to the use of host variables in the SQL and to have enough possible paths to choose from.

Today, many performance problems arise with access path selection because users have told the optimizer-that massive structure of complex code and logic—to choose from the worst choices by providing only one index when both random processing by one key and sequential processing by another key are required. Even physical design issues cause problems with optimization, such as always providing surrogate keys that have no natural relationships and kill attempts at optimization for sequential access. Modern logical, warehouse, dimensional, and object-oriented designers are always claiming that "every table should have a single-column surrogate key." Certainly, some DBMSs can achieve much better performance when designers have followed that philosophy, but DB2 handles multicolumn natural keys just wonderfully, if we provide it with choices and statistics and timing.

Optimization of access paths is a fine art, but in DB2, it generally is done correctly over 93% of the time by the optimizer itself, if the designers and coders have done their jobs well. That percentage comes from years of analysis of massive amounts of SQL code. Using one of the other most popular DBMSs, we find that about 60% of the time we need to "assist" optimization, compared with the 7% for DB2—and those are hard facts based on the real world, not overhead projector marketing. We work on performance tuning with all the vendors' DBMSs, but it is often a fruitless process with the other products, since optimization guidance, pushing, and hinting can be ignored for no reason and there is little information to go on when trying to optimize. In DB2, we are given extensive tools to monitor what is happening, to adjust, and to figure out whether what we did was correct or a disaster.

In this chapter, we discuss influencing the optimizer with methods and strategies that work in the real world. With the exception of adding additional indexes, most of the issues discussed here assume that a decent logical and physical relational design has been used. Design issues are addressed elsewhere in this book. We deal here with the issue of making the final product work to the best of its ability, and we destroy more myths in the process.

The DB2 Optimizer

The best way to describe the optimizer's goal is to use the IBM definition, which is that the key objective of query optimization is to build the best query plan to achieve the optimal performance for a given query. That lofty goal is generally achieved.

The actual process is quite complicated. The precompiler extracts SQL from an application program and passes it to the optimizer, or the optimizer receives it directly as dynamic SQL. The SQL is parsed for syntax, the catalog is accessed to check out database objects used, and the optimizer looks at the catalog statistics and much more. Often overlooked is the fact that optimization of access paths also requires information contained in the DSNZPARMS as well as the definitions of the RID and sort pools, the buffer pool, and hiperpool. The optimizer then finds which of the available access paths can be used. It does not tell us which access path should be there, but the Index Wizard will be released soon (see Chapter 11).

Access Path Selection Statistics

The optimizer is not always right. It can only make assumptions based on the data that you provide it. How often you update the catalog statistics with RUNSTATS and user updates, how often you bind or rebind, and whether you are using features such as user-defined functions and global temporary tables dramatically affect the outcome of the optimizer. RDS performs the details of optimization by evaluating the estimated CPU and I/O costs based on the items in the following list:

I. Catalog statistics from the following tables (used for access path selection as of version 6)
   A. Columns from SYSTABLES
      1. CARDF
         a) Total number of rows in the table
         b) Total number of LOBs in an auxiliary table
      2. EDPROC
         a) Tells whether an edit exit routine is used
      3. NPAGES
         a) Total number of pages that hold rows
      4. PCTROWCOMP
         a) Percentage of rows compressed
   B. Columns from SYSTABLESPACE
      1. NACTIVEF
         a) Number of active pages in the table space
   C. Columns from SYSCOLUMNS
      1. COLCARDF
         a) Estimated number of distinct values in the column
      2. HIGH2KEY
         a) First 8 bytes of the second-highest column value
      3. LOW2KEY
         a) First 8 bytes of the second-lowest column value
   D. Columns from SYSINDEXES
      1. CLUSTERING
         a) For indexes created with CLUSTER keyword

2. CLUSTERRATIOF

   a) Percentage of rows in clustering order

3. FIRSTKEYCARDF

   a) Number of distinct values of the first key column

4. FULLKEYCARDF

   a) Number of distinct values of the full key

5. NLEAF

   a) Number of active leaf pages in the index

6. NLEVELS

   a) Number of levels in the index tree

E. Columns from SYSCOLDIST

1. COLVALUE

   a) Frequently occurring key distribution value

2. FREQUENCYF

   a) The percentage of rows that contain the value of COLVALUE

3. TYPE

   a) Cardinality or frequent value statistics

4. CARDF

   a) Number of distinct values for the column group

5. COLGROUPCOLNO

   a) Set of columns associated with the statistics

6. NUMCOLUMNS

   a) Number of columns associated with the statistics

F. Columns from SYSTABSTATS

1. CARDF

   a) Total number of rows in the partition

2. NPAGES

   a) Total number of pages on which rows of the partition appear

G. Columns from SYSINDEXPART

1. LIMITKEY

   a) The limit key of the partition in an internal format

H. Columns from SYSROUTINES

1. IOS_PER_INVOC

   a) Estimated number of IO operations per invocation

2. INSTS_PER_INVOC
   a) Estimated number of instructions per invocation
3. INITIAL_IOS
   a) Estimated number of IO operations performed the first and last time the function is invoked
4. INITIAL_INSTS
   a) Estimated number of instructions executed the first and last time the function is invoked
5. CARDINALITY
   a) The predicted cardinality of a table function
   Note: Catalog statistics from SYSCOLSTATS are used for degree of parallelism *only*

I. Columns from SYSCOLSTATS
   1. COLCARD
      a) The number of distinct values in the partition
   2. HIGHKEY
      a) First 8 bytes of the highest value of the column within the partition
   3. LOWKEY
      a) First 8 bytes of the lowest value of the column within the partition
   4. HIGH2KEY
      a) First 8 bytes of the second-highest value of the column within the partition
   5. LOW2KEY
      a) First 8 bytes of the second-lowest value of the column within the partition

II. Number of processors
   A. The number of available processors is used to assist in degree of parallelism and also for sysplex query parallelism for data sharing.

III. CPU processing speed
   A. The rating of the processors. This is critical in data sharing also when different class machines are used with sysplex query parallelism.

IV. Buffer pool size
   A. Both virtual pool size and hiperpool size are taken into consideration for various decisions such as in inner and outer tables for joins and for parallelism.

    V. RID pool size

       A. The RID pool size is critical for any process, since DB2 assumes that a user query can use only 50% of the pool, and that amount needs to be double that needed to hold the RIDs. If the pool is not large enough, the processes that need list prefetch cannot be chosen.

    IV. Sort pool size

       A. Sorting and I/O and CPU cost of sorting are critical for the selection process, and these costs are dramatically affected by the sort pool size.

   VII. SQL statement contents

       A. SQL statement content and construction are obviously of critical importance to access path selection and are the one area that you can easily correct.

After the optimizer looks at these items, optimization is within the hands of the SQL coder and some other subtle twists. There are no hard and fast rules, just guidelines, tips, tricks, hints, and perhaps a little guesswork. Optimization can be a case of trial and error until the right result is achieved. It is important to remember that first you must give the optimizer the best information to work with, and then make your adjustments according to accepted practice.

Global Temporary Table Statistics

Note: A technique similar to the one that follows is required for declared temporary tables as well.

When DB2 needs to determine an access path that uses a global temporary table, it can use either statistics that it has accumulated as the table was built or statistics from the catalog that you have updated. No statistics are kept until the table exists, since that is the only time that DB2 can remember anything about the table. RUNSTATS cannot be used on a global temporary table to gather accurate statistics. In addition, each user gets his or her own copy of the table and his or her own statistics when data is inserted into the table. During the loading of data into the global temporary table, DB2 tracks statistics for the number of rows (CARDF) and the number of pages (NPAGES) containing rows. Since these statistics are kept only during the data loading of the table, only dynamic SQL can really benefit.

If these tables need to have more accurate access paths involving static SQL, there is only one option, and that is to update the catalog with default data to be used instead of the normal default of 1 for both CARDF and NPAGES. It might be quite difficult to do the estimation, since every user of the table might need a dramatically different set of statistics. However, it is better to make some type of accurate estimate based on the average normal amount to use instead of the one-row and one-page statistics for static SQL. You need to estimate the normal row count and number of pages and update the values in the CARDF and NPAGES columns of the SYSTABLES row for each global temporary table defined.

As with many things involving the optimizer, there are some consequences. Any change in these statistics is not used for dynamic SQL when dynamic SQL statement caching is used. The access path selected for dynamic SQL with caching enabled is whatever actual counts existed at the time of the PREPARE, not the count in SYSTABLES, regardless of the state of the global temporary table.

As a general guideline, any dynamic SQL statement should be prepared after loading the data into the temporary table, if possible. If static SQL is used, the catalog row for the global temporary table should be updated with accurate estimates.

User-Defined Table Function Statistics

One type of user-defined function is the table function, and the optimizer must be provided with some statistics for this table in order to estimate the cost of using it in various operations, such as joins. Any user-defined table function adds additional resource cost to the execution of the SQL statement. The optimizer needs to determine the total cost of the user-defined table function exactly, and without user input, it cannot do this. Join ordering is extremely dependent on this information and also predictive governing. There are three pieces of information that the optimizer needs to be able to predict the cost of the user-defined table function:

- The overhead of the first call that initialized the table
- The cost for accessing one single row
- The cost for the clean-up processing

As data is loaded into the user-defined table, some of the I/O cost can be calculated, but the costs of the preceding three items are unknown, and therefore the access path determination might not be correct. To make sure that the optimizer makes the best possible decision, fields in the catalog table SYSROUTINES can be updated with cost data for the optimizer to use:

- IOS_PER_INVOC: Estimated number of I/O operations per row
- INSTS_PER_INVOC: Estimated number of instructions
- INITIAL_IOS: Estimated number of I/O operations performed the first and last time the function is invoked
- INITIAL_INSTS: Estimated number of instructions the first and last time the function is invoked

The number of rows in the table and these four items are what the optimizer uses to determine the cost of the statement and thus the best access path. You need to estimate the number of I/O operations by either examining the code or using extensive tracing or monitors, a difficult but necessary task involving very precise estimates. The instruction estimate can be made for high-level languages by counting the instructions and multiplying by 20. Once you have calculated the numbers of I/O operations and instructions, update SYSROUTINES. Following is an example of updating SYSROUTINES with more accurate information:

```
UPDATE SYSIBM.SYSROUTINES
  SET IOS_PER_INVOC   = 1800,
      INSTS_PER_INVOC = 35000,
      INITIAL_IOS = 20.0
      INITIAL_INSTS   = 8000,
      CARDINALITY = 70000
  WHERE SCHEMA = 'SYSADM'
      AND SPECIFICNAME = 'GETIDMS'
      AND ROUTINETYPE = 'F'
```

Key Correlation Statistics

Key correlation statistics are statistics about how one column's value relates to the value of another column. Releases before version 5 offered only cardinalities on the first key of the index (FIRSTKEYCARD) and the full key of the index (FULLKEYCARD) with limited information about the values and their frequency, and correlation was only on the columns for FULLKEYCARD. For example, this provided no second- or third-key cardinality information in a five-column index. Multikey cardinality was considered independently by using only individual column cardinality, which often led to inaccurate estimation of filter factors, join size, join sequencing, and join methods and thus inefficient access path selection.

The key correlation statistics are collected by RUNSTATS with minimal additional overhead and can provide big CPU time and elapsed time reductions through improved cost and resource estimations. These key correlation statistics play a major role in access path selection by providing the optimizer with information on multicolumn cardinalities and multicolumn frequent values. These are the values used in the catalog table and columns SYSCOLDIST and SYSCOLDISTATS:

- TYPE
  CHAR(1) NOT NULL DEFAULT `F'
  Type of statistic (cardinality or frequent value)
- CARDF
  FLOAT NOT NULL DEFAULT −1
  Number of distinct values for column group
- COLGROUPCOLNO
  VARCHAR(254) NOT NULL W/DEFAULT
  Identifies the set of columns
- NUMCOLUMNS
  SMALLINT NOT NULL DEFAULT 1
  The number of columns in the group

The option to collect key correlation statistics gives you the ability to specify the number of columns on which to collect statistics (NUMCOLS) and to specify the number of values (COUNT). These keywords are used in the RUNSTATS utility. The KEYCARD parameter indicates that cardinalities for each column, concatenated with all previous key columns, are to be collected. Figure 23.1 shows the syntax. Using this RUNSTATS feature gives us the option to build the frequency values for critical concatenated key columns, such as the first, second, and third columns.

For example, consider the following two queries, assuming an index of state, city, and last name. Without gathering the additional correlation statistics, only the first key cardinality and full key cardinality are stored in the index, and the ratio of values between

Key Correlation Statistics – Figure 23.1

Figure 23.1   Key Correlation Statistics

people and cities in New York State is not linear. There are many more New Yorkers in New York State than there are people from Herkimer. With the three-column index, the cardinality does not exist on only the first two columns. With the key correlation statistics, the first query would probably result in a table-space scan, possibly using page-range scanning, and the second query would probably result in index access. Without key correlation statistics, all DB2 can do is use the FIRSTKEYCARD or FULLKEYCARD column statistics, and it would probably use index access for both queries, even though the first would be better as a table-space scan because more rows would qualify.

```
SELECT *
FROM USA
WHERE STATE = :hv-state    -- value'NY'
AND CITY = :hv-city        -- value 'NEW YORK'

SELECT *
FROM USA
WHERE STATE = :hv-state    -- value 'NY'
AND CITY = :hv-city        -- value 'HERKIMER'
```

DSTATS

Skewed data can have a major impact on access path selection and can result in the optimizer choosing an incorrect access path that can lead to poor performance. The optimizer could choose an incorrect access path because of an incorrect estimation of the number of matching row for a qualified predicate.

DB2 maintains distribution in the catalog table SYSIBM.SYSCOLDIST. Using these statistics along with the cardinality statistics in SYSIBM.SYSCOLUMNS during access path selection can possibly improve query response times. This optimization can be improved by holding frequency and cardinality statistics not just for single columns but also for skewed combinations of columns.

RUNSTATS collects utility distribution statistics, but only for such columns as those that form an index, and only for the most frequently occurring values. Performance can be further improved by providing distribution statistics for nonindexed columns also, especially for significantly skewed predicates.

Performance tests indicate that there are benefits to be gained from collecting frequency statistics for all columns likely to be used in local predicates. This includes low-cardinality columns (e.g., status codes, company codes). Keep in mind that NULLs are treated the same as any other value by the optimizer, and a high proportion of NULLs in a column could distort your access paths.

The product DSTATS, developed at IBM in Hursely, provides an easy method for collecting distribution statistics for any column or combination of columns in a database. It requires DB2 for OS/390 Version 5 or later and is provided in the form of a load library and a DBRM library in unloaded format. The input to DSTATS is a list of provided columns. The output contains a report displaying the highest values (and optionally the lowest) by frequency and corresponding rows stored in a user-defined table called TEST.SYSCOLDIST. The contents of this table can be copied to the DB2 SYSIBM.SYSCOLDIST table using an SQL INSERT statement. These statistics can be collected for single columns or up to three correlated columns.

It is not recommended to run DSTATS on tables containing more than two billion rows. DSTATS also depends on the catalog statistics being complete and current and the RUNSTATS utility being executed in advance with the COLUMN(ALL) option for all tables involved.

Figure 23.2 is an example of the execution JCL from the IBM installation instructions of the DSTATS product. You specify the creator, the table name, and each column on which you want to gather the statistics. If you specify one column, you get the distribution statistics for that column. You can also collect distribution statistics for correlated columns (up to three). If you specify * for the columns, you collect distribution statistics for all columns (excluding indexed columns and data types that would not be used in local predicates).

The VALUES statement has a default value of 5,5, which collects the 5 most frequent values and the 5 least frequent values. CARDINALITY has three options. These are used to determine whether or not cardinality statistics are collected for requests with multiple columns. The option IFLOW, which is the default, collects cardinality statistics only

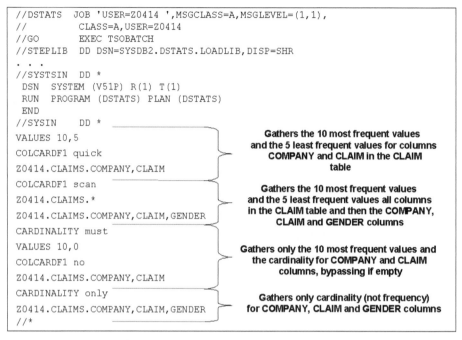

```
//DSTATS   JOB 'USER=Z0414 ',MSGCLASS=A,MSGLEVEL=(1,1),
//         CLASS=A,USER=Z0414
//GO       EXEC TSOBATCH
//STEPLIB  DD DSN=SYSDB2.DSTATS.LOADLIB,DISP=SHR
. . .
//SYSTSIN  DD *
 DSN  SYSTEM (V51P) R(1) T(1)
 RUN  PROGRAM (DSTATS) PLAN (DSTATS)
 END
//SYSIN    DD *
 VALUES 10,5

 COLCARDF1 quick

 Z0414.CLAIMS.COMPANY,CLAIM

 COLCARDF1 scan

 Z0414.CLAIMS.*

 Z0414.CLAIMS.COMPANY,CLAIM,GENDER

 CARDINALITY must

 VALUES 10,0

 COLCARDF1 no

 Z0414.CLAIMS.COMPANY,CLAIM

 CARDINALITY only

 Z0414.CLAIMS.COMPANY,CLAIM,GENDER
 //*
```

Gathers the 10 most frequent values and the 5 least frequent values for columns COMPANY and CLAIM in the CLAIM table

Gathers the 10 most frequent values and the 5 least frequent values all columns in the CLAIM table and then the COMPANY, CLAIM and GENDER columns

Gathers only the 10 most frequent values and the cardinality for COMPANY and CLAIM columns, bypassing if empty

Gathers only cardinality (not frequency) for COMPANY, CLAIM and GENDER columns

Figure 23.2   DSTATS JCL

if the frequencies are collected for low-frequency values. A value of MUST always collects cardinality statistics. A value of ONLY collects just cardinality statistics (not frequency, which also overrides the values in the VALUE clause).

The other parameter—COLCARDF1—has three values to determine what to do when a column has a cardinality of 1. SCAN is the default, and it scans the column and creates a value for SYSCOLDIST. The option QUICK reads only the first row. The other option is NO, which bypasses the column.

Several columns can be scanned in a single job. The following data types are supported (unsupported data types cause an error and bypass the statement):

- CHAR up to 64 bytes
- VARCHAR up to 62 bytes (single columns only)
- INTEGER and SMALLINT
- DECIMAL up to 15 digits
- DATE and TIME

The frequency and cardinality records are written to the TEST.SYSCOLDIST table that was created. They overwrite any previous values in the table and can then be propagated into SYSIBM.SYSCOLDIST using the following statement (provided that you have SYSADM authority):

```
INSERT INTO SYSIBM.SYSCOLDIST
SELECT * FROM TEST.SYSCOLDIST
  WHERE TBOWNER = 'creator'
    AND TBNAME = 'table'
    AND NAME = 'column'
```

If the data distribution changes and you need to execute the statistics collection, you need to delete the existing rows in the SYSIBM.SYSCOLDIST table. You can easily identify these rows because the rows created by DSTATS are identified by time stamp equal to CURRENT TIMESTAMP + 1,000 years. If you need back out changes, you can use the following statement:

```
DELETE FROM SYSIBM.SYSCOLDIST
  WHERE STATSTIME > CURRENT_TIMESTAMP + 999 YEARS
```

. . .

Here is a sample report.

```
                    DSTATS COLUMN VALUE DISTRIBUTION REPORT
                       HIGH/LOW VALUES BY FREQUENCY


PARAMETER:          Z0414.CLAIMS.COMPANY.CLAIMS

CREATOR:            Z0414
TABLE:              CLAIMS
STATS:              1999-01-15
ROWS:               130,905

COLNO:              6
COLUMN:             COMPANY
TYPE:               CHAR
CARDINALITY:        540
FILTER FACTOR:      .362319%
```

```
    FREQUENCY        ACCT_CLOSE_DATE
  -----------       ----------------

  86.006998%            -- null --
     .421616%        1998-08-01
     .197945%        1998-09-01
     .159277%        1998-06-30
     .113511%        1997-11-26
     .111300%        1998-04-30
     .094471%        1997-09-06
     .087048%        1998-05-27
     .086452%        1997-09-24
     .078678%        1998-04-01
```

Updating Catalog Statistics

You can update catalog statistics to help influence the access paths chosen by the DB2 optimizer. We truly hate to even mention this as an alternative anymore, since it affects all accesses that use the given object, not just the one you are trying to adjust. One of the more common statistics changed is the cluster ratio on nonclustering indexes. In the past, this had a big influence on some, but not all, access paths.

Basically, changing catalog statistics is lying to DB2, except when you adjust the statistics to paint a picture of an average, normal state of highly volatile tables. The general rule is to try everything else first. Remember that if you change statistics, you need to keep on changing them after version and release migrations, after RUNSTATS, and so on.

We should state some simple guidelines for manipulating catalog statistics. You should never update catalog statistics on columns that are updated by RUNSTATS, unless extremely necessary. Exceptions are the cluster ratio on nonclustering indexes when all accesses to the underlying object need it and columns for nonuniform statistics and for user-entered correlation statistics for user updates.

Influencing Access Path Selection

There are many ways to talk to the DB2 optimizer to persuade it to choose one access path over another. Over the years and releases, the DB2 optimizer has become more and more sophisticated; some old techniques are no longer valid, and some have a very specific use that needs to be investigated before applying them. For example, OPTIMIZE FOR *n* ROWS often is applied incorrectly and can hurt performance. The older options of OR 0 = 1 and 0 <> 0 have given way to better, more meaningful methods:

- OPTIMIZE FOR *n* ROWS clause
- Adding +/– 0 to a numeric stage 1 predicate
- Add CONCAT ' ' to a character stage 1 predicate
- Use NOT logic to remove indexability of predicates, including stage 1
- Add a stage 1, nonindexable, "impossible" predicate
- Force materialization to access the detail table first in a join
- Force the detail table first in a join by using additional predicates on the detail
- Use columns from the preferred index in an ORDER BY

There are many other examples, but they should be used only when all else fails, and they should be documented, preferably with comments in the SQL.

OPTIMIZE FOR *n* ROWS

Local Applications

The OPTIMIZE FOR *n* ROWS clause on an SQL statement is used to ensure nested loop joins, to alter table join order, or to discourage list prefetch (and hybrid joins and multiple-index access), sequential prefetch (and dynamic prefetch), table-space scans, and other heroism. It should *never* be applied as an across-the-board standard for all queries. It should be used when there would be a large result set and only a small percentage of the rows are really needed.

OPTIMIZE FOR 1 ROW has special meaning for the optimizer and truly means to optimize for one row. It almost always turns off access path enhancers such as list prefetch and uses an access path that qualifies a single row. This normally results in an access path that uses the best index to get one row the fastest way possible. Of course, this does not mean that you cannot fetch more rows from the cursor. It just means that the rest of the rows might not use the optimal access path.

Basically, with this parameter you are specifying the final filter factor for the query. The same holds true if you add OPTIMIZE FOR 15 ROWS where you need 15 rows of a large result set to display quickly. When you use any value other than 1, the optimizer picks the access path based on cost, so when you specify even two rows, you could get a sort. With one row, you never get a sort.

If there is truly no way to limit the size of the result set, you can use FOR 1 ROW to effectively "walk the index." It all depends on the way the result set is built and how many rows would compose the result set. With OPTIMIZE, you are optimizing for something less than the full result set. If you need 80% of the result set, you should not use this clause.

Sometimes we find queries where the OPTIMIZE clause has no meaning or effect but is used anyway with the assumption that it affects the result. If the entire result set has to be materialized before the first row is returned, the OPTIMIZE clause is ignored. When a query uses DISTINCT, GROUP BY, or ORDER BY without a supporting index, UNION, or a column function without a GROUP BY, the OPTIMIZE clause is ignored since the entire result set must be materialized before the first row can be returned.

Remote Applications

The OPTIMIZE FOR *n* ROWS clause in a DRDA network transmission takes on a slightly different meaning. It basically limits the number of rows that the server returns for a single DRDA network transmission, as long as the OPTIMIZE clause specifies a number that does not exceed the DRDA single-query block size. A couple of critical areas of the OPTIMIZE clause can positively or negatively affect performance in a networking situation.

One way to use OPTIMIZE is very similar to the preceding description for the locally attached user. When a remote user needs a small percentage of the data from a full result set, he or she can use the OPTIMIZE clause to limit the amount of data staged in a DRDA packet. For example, if the result set qualifies 1,000 rows and you are going to display a screen of data at a time, you could limit the transmitted packet to 10 rows by using OPTIMIZE FOR 10 ROWS. Even if you decide to continue the processing, the packets of 10 rows are all that is needed to refresh each browse screen. There are many dependencies here on DRDA block size versus the block size based on the OPTIMIZE clause, client configuration settings, and DRDA level. But, in general, setting the OPTIMIZE clause precisely as needed aids performance. If the OPTIMIZE size is actually smaller than the DRDA default block size, performance can be improved, since rows not needed are not transferred. Conversely, if the number of rows specified is greater than the number of rows allowed in the DRDA block, multiple DRDA blocks can be sent, improving the elapsed time of the process.

There are some potential problems with specifying a number for the OPTIMIZE clause that is greater then the DRDA block size. If the application needs to issue another

SQL statement before all the blocks containing rows have been retrieved, it has to wait until the transmission is complete, for example, when a client fetching rows from the cursor needs to issue an update or an insert. Another case of performance degradation occurs when not all of the blocks to fit the OPTIMIZE size have been retrieved, but the process needs to stop fetching. If the application closes the cursor before the block is done, it has to wait for the transmission blocks to finish, delaying the process from continuing.

When performance is the driving factor, some guidelines need to be followed when using the OPTIMIZE clause to specify a row block larger than the DRDA block. These guidelines are primarily common sense: make sure that all rows specified are retrieved and that there are no intervening DML statements, and there should be only one open cursor with the OPTIMIZE clause specified.

Manipulating Index Selection

Tricks have been used in the past to "fool" the optimizer, but with every new release (or even maintenance tape), these rules can become useless or even contrary to performance. Be careful when implementing any tricks to fool the optimizer, and be sure to document them in the SQL so that others know why the predicate is there.

Some tricks are very specific and are recommended in the IBM manuals. These "allowable" tricks include the use of CONCAT ' ' (concatenate with null string), /1 (divide by 1), *1 (multiply by 1), and +/– 0 (plus or minus 0) to get the optimizer to ignore a predicate when choosing an index or to possibly alter the table ordering in a join. These tricks are preferred over the older methods of using compound predicates such as (*predicate* OR 0 = 1) or (*predicate* OR 0 <> 0). Another method is to use additional bogus predicates to tighten the filtering calculations, which changes the access path. In some cases, this tightening of the filter factor may be applicable, especially to switch the join order of tables. In all cases, it takes a good understanding of the process and the data involved to be sure that the manipulation being considered is valid.

A couple of examples can explain how to use these types of manipulations and show what happens. Let's assume that we have a table called TABLE. This table comprises columns A through Z. It also has the following three indexes:

Index A on columns A, B, and C

Index B on column B

Index C on column C

We are going to use the same basic SQL statement as we walk through several scenarios. The following statement without any manipulation could use any or all of the preceding indexes. We are not going to worry about uniqueness or duplicates in this situation.

```
DECLARE MYCSR CURSOR FOR
SELECT A, B, C
FROM TABLE
WHERE A = :hostvar1
  AND B = :hostvar2
  AND C BETWEEN :hostvar3 AND :hostvar4
```

Let's assume, right or wrong, possible or not, that DB2 picks multiple index access and index C is not desired because the percentage of rows qualified by the BETWEEN is significantly larger than the default filter factor (which is less than 10%). We could use the following statement to remove index C from the possible choices.

```
DECLARE MYCSR CURSOR FOR
SELECT A, B, C
FROM TABLE
WHERE A = :hostvar1
  AND B = :hostvar2
  AND C BETWEEN :hostvar3 + 0 AND :hostvar4
```

Now let's assume that, based on our knowledge of the data, we don't want index B. We could use OPTIMIZE FOR 1 ROW to use the single best index for retrieving the first row the fastest. But what if DB2's choice is index B? For example:

```
DECLARE MYCSR CURSOR FOR
SELECT A, B, C
FROM TABLE
WHERE A = :hostvar1
  AND B = :hostvar2
  AND C BETWEEN :hostvar3 AND :hostvar4
OPTIMIZE FOR 1 ROW
```

We can combine two tricks and drop the optimize clause to get the following:

```
DECLARE MYCSR CURSOR FOR
SELECT A, B, C
```

```
FROM TABLE
WHERE A = :hostvar1
  AND B = :hostvar2 CONCAT ''
  AND C BETWEEN :hostvar3 + 0 AND :hostvar4
```

Now we have forced the optimizer to consider only index A. Now suppose that we have come to realize that over 25% of the table is actually going to be qualified for the query, so we really want to force a relational scan (also called a table-space scan, but that is not as precise a term since you could be scanning just a partition, not a table space). Now we use the allowable method of taking away all the choices from the optimizer but still leaving all the predicates as potentially stage 1. In addition, we have added the clause FOR FETCH ONLY to make sure that DB2 understands that the cursor is not ambiguous and is read-only.

```
DECLARE MYCSR CURSOR FOR
SELECT A, B, C
FROM TABLE
WHERE A = :hostvar1 CONCAT ''
  AND B = :hostvar2 CONCAT ''
  AND C BETWEEN :hostvar3 + 0 AND :hostvar4
FOR FETCH ONLY
```

We thus can trick the optimizer into choosing what we think is the correct access path from a limited selection of possibilities. But in other situations, the access path selected is sort of correct for a join, but the tables are in the wrong order. We have seen several situations like this, where the outer table in a nested loop join was a small table and the inner table was very large, which caused severe problems. The next example is based on a real situation where two tables, each with fewer than 100 rows were joined to a billion-row table. The two tables were joined using an early Cartesian join then were used in a nested loop join against the large table. In other words, the large table was scanned over 280 times.

We have two small tables, SMALL1 T1 and SMALL2 T2, and one large table, LARGE T3, with indexes as follows:

LARGE T3: Index on A, B, and C

SMALL2 T2: Index on B

```
DECLARE MYCSR CURSOR FOR
SELECT T3.A, T3.C, T2.D, T1.Z
FROM SMALL1 T1, SMALL2 T2, LARGE T3
WHERE  T1.A = T2.B
  AND T1.A = T3.A
  AND T2.B BETWEEN :hostvar2 AND :hostvar4
  AND T3.A = :hostvar3
```

The preceding cursor definition results in a join of the two small tables first, before the join of the large table. While we might also have to use one of the techniques described earlier to play games with index selection, additional filtering predicates are needed to force the large table first.

The following statement solves the problem.

```
DECLARE MYCSR CURSOR FOR
SELECT T3.A, T3.C, T2.D, T1.Z
FROM SMALL1 T1, SMALL2 T2, LARGE T3
WHERE  T1.A = T2.B
  AND T1.A = T3.A
  AND T2.B BETWEEN :hostvar2 AND :hostvar4
  AND T3.A = :hostvar3
  AND T3.B > ' '           -- additional filtering
  AND T3.C > 0             -- additional filtering
```

These additional predicates do not filter any rows out but tighten the filtering so that the optimizer chooses the large table first, solving the performance problem.

Once you update DB2 to version 6, it might be better to use access path hints, although they might actually require more controls and manual labor than the preceding methods. It is very important, however, to make sure that this kind of manipulation does not adversely affect performance in the future. Tricks tend to become problems if they are not constantly monitored to make sure they are accomplishing what they were intended to do.

Forcing Partition-Range Scanning

Partition-range scanning (page-range scanning) was first introduced in version 4, enhanced in version 5, and further improved in version 6 (figure 23.3). It defines an access path that allows DB2 to scan a series of noncontiguous partitions for data

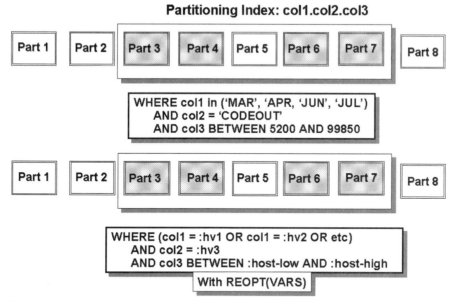

Partitioning Index: col1.col2.col3

WHERE col1 in ('MAR', 'APR', 'JUN', 'JUL')
AND col2 = 'CODEOUT'
AND col3 BETWEEN 5200 AND 99850

WHERE (col1 = :hv1 OR col1 = :hv2 OR etc)
AND col2 = :hv3
AND col3 BETWEEN :host-low AND :host-high
With REOPT(VARS)

Figure 23.3 Limited Partition Scan

retrieval. In figure 23.4, assume that there is a clustering index on COLUMN1 and a nonpartitioning index on COLUMN32. Key ranges are by 10 thousands, so the predicates state that partitions 2, 4, and 7 are scanned. In fact, these partitions could be scanned in parallel and perhaps over different physical machines using sysplex query parallelism. Besides using the clustering index for access, nonpartitioning indexes can be used for access into each of the qualifying partitions with a page-range scan. This can

Clustering index: COLUMN1
NPI: COLUMN32

```
                 SELECT COLUMNS, ...
                 FROM PARTITIONED_TABLE
Part 2  ───▶     WHERE (COLUMN1 BETWEEN 20000 AND 29999
Part 4  ───▶     OR COLUMN1 BETWEEN 40000 AND 49999
Part 7  ───▶     OR COLUMN1 BETWEEN 70000 AND 79999)
NPI     ───▶     AND COLUMN32 BETWEEN '1997-01-01' AND '1997-05-12'
```

Figure 23.4 Limited Partition Scan

be a significant performance improvement, but in some cases the SQL needs a little push to get a page-range scan to be invoked. Notice that in each of the queries in figure 23.4, there is an OR or IN list predicate on the first columns of the partitioning index, something that is not normally considered a good practice. However, that is what drives page-range scans.

Partition-range scanning can take advantage of query parallelism by rewriting the query into multiple statements to scan only particular partitions. The limit keys have been checked using COLUMN1, driving the query rewrite for the individual partitions, and the NPI on COLUMN32 is used for index access. Only qualified data pages are now accessed by NPI (figure 23.5).

However, in some past cases the data characteristics were not what the optimizer assumed, and in addition only one partition was selected for page-range scanning. The access path always used the clustering index for the individual partition. Now, this might have changed with advances in optimization, but it is worth noting. To get DB2 to scan one partition of a partitioned table space, an additional predicate has to be added. An OR'ed predicate on the first column of the clustering index forces a page-range scan, but since there is only one partition, in the example in figure 23.6 we just repeated the predicate. Other predicates can then be used to obtain access through the NPI.

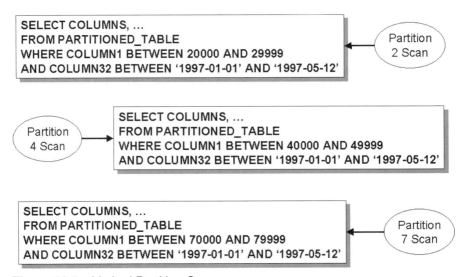

Figure 23.5 Limited Partition Scan

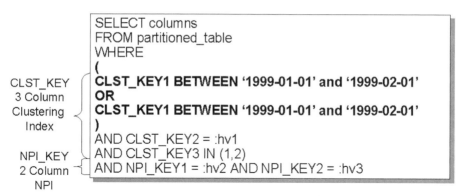

Figure 23.6   Forcing Partition-Range Scanning for One Partition

Direct Row Access

Direct row access uses the data type ROWID. Any row containing a column defined as ROWID gets a unique value generated by DB2. You cannot generate your own values for ROWID, nor can you update the ROWID. A column in the plan table called PRIMARY_ACCESSTYPE has a value of D when direct row access has been selected as the primary access path. With direct row access, no index or table-space scan is required.

Although there are cases where using the ROWID to directly access the data might not work, they are extremely rare. In the case of a failure with direct row access using the ROWID, DB2 uses the alternate access path. When a query that uses direct row access is bound, a normal access path is also picked for backup; in effect, the DBRM has two access paths, similar to parallel access paths. This secondary access path is the access path that is used in case of failure of direct row access.

If direct row access fails at run time, DB2 uses the access type defined in the ACCESSTYPE column of the plan table, the alternate access path put in the DBRM at bind time. It is recommended that you have an index on the ROWID column so that you do not fall back to a table-space scan. If there are other predicates, there probably is a backup access path. This is the case when the ROWID is added to existing queries, but when you develop new queries, you can potentially overlook adding the predicates to establish a backup access path.

Parallelism and list prefetch are mutually exclusive to direct row access. Although if using the ROWID for direct row access is not normally a problem, this will disallow parallelism for that query. If a query qualifies for direct row access and parallelism, direct row access is used. If direct row access would fail, the fallback is not to parallelism but to the optional access path selected at bind time.

There are some WHERE clause restrictions when using ROWID access:

- ROWID can be used with simple Boolean term predicates, such as COL = noncolumn expression, where COL is ROWID and the noncolumn expression contains a row ID,
- ROWID can be used with a simple Boolean term predicate COL IN (*list*), where the COL is ROWID, the in-list values are row IDs, and an index exists on COL.
- ROWID can be used with a compound Boolean term combining simple predicates using the AND operator when one of the simple term predicates fits one of the preceding rules.

When direct row access fails and the other predicates are not indexable, a tablespace scan is chosen as the backup access path. Therefore, it is critically important to make sure that an index exists on ROWID column as a backup strategy. The other alternative is to make sure that another predicate uses an index on the table, but as mentioned previously, this might be difficult to enforce and only creates more burdens on an SQL review staff. Reports from performance monitors can show how many times direct row access failed and what backup access paths were used. Figure 23.7 shows the number of attempts and the number and type of failures.

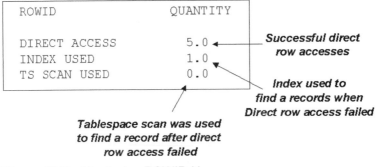

Figure 23.7 Monitoring ROWID Usage

The following example is a complete picture of using ROWID for direct row access. The table is created with the ROWID column:

```
CREATE TABLE BRIEF_TAB
(LTT_ID ROWID . . .
```

Then a host variable is defined

```
BRIEFID VARCHAR(40)
```

We can use this host variable to store the ROWID selected for some particular row:

```
SELECT LTT_ID
INTO :briefid
FROM LEGAL_TEXT_TAB
WHERE . . .
```

We can now use the ROWID to retrieve the row, bypassing all index access:

```
SELECT CASE, SUBSTR(BRIEF,1,500)
INTO :case_name, :brief_text_substr
FROM LEGAL_TEXT_TAB
WHERE LTT_ID = :briefed
```

Once the ROWID has been stored in the pointer host variable, it can be used for any DML, such as:

```
UPDATE LEGAL_TEXT_TAB
SET CASE = 'some corrected data'
WHERE LTT_ID = :briefid
```

In each of these cases, we omitted access to all the levels of the index, which can be very significant. If a browse cursor returned the ROWID as it walked the rows, looking for a row to update, think of the overhead it would save, as such transactions tend to occur thousands of times a day, if not more frequently. While direct row access can be beneficial on any access path, multilevel indexes on large tables benefit the most, since it is almost impossible to get a decent hit ratio on such objects in the buffer pool.

For example, in one case the index had five levels as follows:

Level	Number of pages
Root	1
2nd level	3
3rd level	377
4th level	57,209
5th level	8,695,653

With an index structure like this, we would need all the memory allowed for all buffer pools and data spaces just to hold the index pages for the critical index, which is absurd. Even just holding the four levels in memory to minimize I/O would require almost 58,000 pages, again absurd. So for any access, we can comfortably assume that there would be physical, probably synchronous, I/O. Using the ROWID with this object would bypass the five GETPAGEs on the index and any physical I/O. That would be quite a significant improvement, especially in an OLTP system. For example, in this particular case, a table-space scan of the table that this index supports required 7.5 days. (We know that because it happened.) This is a prime example of where you would want the backup index, even though it is quite large. In many cases, it could be used as a surrogate key index when direct row access is not used.

For an update transaction on this table that occurs only once a second, or 64,800 times in 18 hours (which is very little in today's OS/390 OLTP systems), the savings would be

- $64,800 \times 5$ GETPAGEs = 324,000 GETPAGEs
- $64,800 \times 3$ I/O operations = 194,400 I/O operations

Also, the amount of buffer pool usage no longer required could be given to other needed processes.

Access Path Hints

DB2 Version 6 introduced a feature called access path hints, a direct way of suggesting to the optimizer what access path to use. This feature should be used only in extreme cases, as with any trickery. When the optimizer cannot pick a correct access path (and this is rare), the hint feature can be considered if all other techniques of SQL manipulation fail. A more appropriate place to use access path hints is when a good access path has changed due to some change in the system. Many access paths have been tuned extensively and use an access path appropriate to the current release. Then along comes a new release with optimizer enhancements, and the access path suddenly changes. This occurred many times with the movement from version 3 to version 4, when list prefetch was chosen more often, and again with the movement from version 5 to version 6. In such cases, where an access path that had been tuned is changed to list prefetch, the path might no longer be the most desirable.

Access path hints give you a way to assist the optimizer in choosing an access path. Hints can be used to fall back to an already tuned access path or to alter an access path for performance. Use this feature only after trying normal optimization or the usual tuning techniques (i.e., SQL coding manipulation or statistics manipulating).

The hints are implemented using the plan table as input to the optimizer. The information contained in one or more rows is considered as a potential choice during the normal access path selection. Some very specific rules regarding what the optimizer chooses are listed in figure 23.8.

METHOD	Must be 0, 1, 2, 3, or 4
CREATOR and TNAME	Must name a table or view in the query
CORRELATION_NAME	If specified, it will be used as an additional qualifier to TNAME
TABNO	It is only used when the fields, CREATOR, TNAME and CORRELATION_NAME do not uniquely identify the table
ACCESSTYPE	Must be either 'R', 'I', 'I1', 'N', or 'M'
ACCESSCREATOR and ACCESSNAME	If ACCESSTYPE is 'R' or 'M' then these fields are ignored. If the ACCESSTYPE is 'I', 'I1', or 'N' then these fields must identify an index on the specified table
SORTN_JOIN and SORTC_JOIN	Must be 'Y', 'N' or blank
PREFETCH	Must be 'S', 'L' or blank
PAGE_RANGE	Must be 'Y', 'N' or blank
PARALLELISM_MODE	If the query is to be run in parallel, then this field must be either 'I', 'C', 'X' or null.
ACCESS_DEGREE and JOIN_DEGREE	If PARALLELISM_MODE is specified, then the degree of parallelism can also be specified. If the degree isn't specified then the optimizer will determine the degree of parallelism. If PARALLELISM_MODE is not specified, then ACCESS_DEGREE and JOIN_DEGREE are ignored.

Figure 23.8   Access Paths Hints: Plan Table Validation

But is a hint really a *hint?* Actually, it is more a FORCE than a hint! First, you must set the OPTHINTS DSNZPARM on the subsystem level to allow this option in the subsystem (the default is NO). Then you need to bind or rebind your packages with the option OPTHINT, which is sort of like a high-level qualifier for all the individual hints in the package, and a column in the plan table is populated during EXPLAIN to reflect this. There is also a new special register for dynamic SQL.

```
SET CURRENT OPTIMIZATION HINT = 'hint01'
```

Also, additions to any SQL statement are required using the QUERYNO <integer> clause. This is used in the actual SELECT statement, as in

```
EXEC SQL SELECT . . . QUERYNO <integer>
```

A hint thus requires a well-thought-out plan. The QUERYNO <integer> is used as the query number for access path selection. It is assigned to the QUERYNO column of the plan table for SELECT, INSERT, UPDATE, DELETE, and SELECT . . . INTO statements. This relates an access path in the plan table to the statement (figure 23.9). The opti-

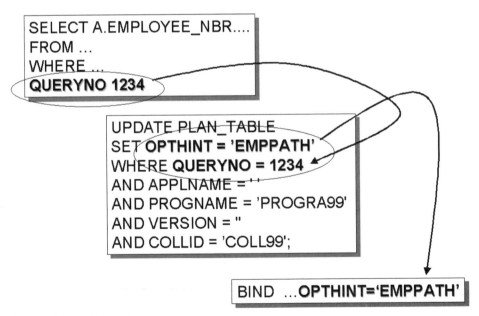

Figure 23.9   SQL Hints

mizer searches authid.PLAN_TABLE by QUERYNO, APPLNAME, PROGNAME, VERSION, COLLID, and OPTHINT.

Note: You need to create an index on these fields if using hints for better performance.

The rows are ordered by QBLOCKNO, PLANNO, MIXOPSEQ, just the set of rows that qualify for the hint. If multiple rows exist, the optimizer uses the most current one based on the time stamp.

The QUERYNO gets the text of the static SQL statement and then obtains the access path in the plan table. The QUERYNO column of the plan table is joined with the STMTNO column of SYSIBM.SYSSTMT. This column contains the query number from QUERYNO in the SQL statement. A bind detects duplicate QUERYNO values and issues

```
SQLCODE +20105 STATEMENTS stmtno-1 AND stmtno-2 IN
PROGRAM program-name HAVE DUPLICATE QUERYNO queryno
```

Special columns in the plan table support access path hints. OPTHINT is an eight-character column updated to identify the hint, and HINT_USED is an eight-character column to indicate and identify the hint used. A blank value indicates that the access path was determined by the optimizer, and a nonblank value indicates the OPTHINT column value.

The plan table columns used by the optimizer when hints are supplied are as follows:

- METHOD
- CREATOR
- TNAME
- TABNO
- CORRELATION_NAME
- ACCESSTYPE
- ACCESSCREATOR
- ACCESSNAME
- SORTN_JOIN
- SORTC_JOIN
- PREFETCH
- PAGE_RANGE
- PARALLELISM_MODE

- ACCESS_DEGREE
- ACCESS_PGROUP_ID
- JOIN_DEGREE
- JOIN_PGROUP_ID

Anything not listed here is ignored by the optimizer, and the values are determined by the optimizer based on the information provided in the fields listed.

The hints provide statement-level optimization. If the REOPT(VARS) bind option is specified and the statement qualifies for reoptimization, the WHEN_OPTIMIZE column can be used to disable reoptimization for that statement. A B or blank indicates no reoptimization, and an R indicates that reoptimization will occur even if valid hints are provided.

The OPTHINT column is in SYSPLAN and SYSPACKAGE to indicate the value of the OPTHINT bind option. The ACCESSPATH column is in SYSSTMT and SYSPACKSTMT and indicates whether access path hints were used or not. A blank indicates that access path hints were not used, and an H indicates that they were used.

Application Programming Change with Hints

You need to use the QUERYNO clause for statements to reduce the maintenance involved in keeping the application and the authid.PLAN_TABLE in sync and to keep the PLAN_TABLE in sync with the hints used. Existing applications that currently only check for a nonzero return code may need to be changed to handle the return codes from hint failures:

- +394 (access path hints were used)
- +395 (access path hints are invalid)

Modifying an application may invalidate old access path hints in the authid.PLAN_TABLE. Applications must be EXPLAINed in order to save their associated access paths in case they are needed during a future rebind.

Monitoring and Diagnosing Access Path Hints

You should make use of this feature *only where needed.* Access path hints may cause performance problems and could be inefficient. Missing the critical index on the plan table could cause bind performance problems, and execution times for dynamic statements could degrade.

Check the columns in the catalog tables SYSPLAN, SYSPACKAGE, SYSPACK-STMT, and SYSSTMT for information about access path hint usage. You can also check the HINT_USED column in the authid.PLAN_TABLE. For diagnosing problems, you can use IFCIDs 22, 106, 108, 112, 113, and 177 to indicate whether hints were used.

Reoptimization at Run Time

In DB2 OS/390 only, the REOPT(VARS) bind option is justifiable when the host variable contents are volatile and the application can withstand an increased response time of 0.1 to 0.5 seconds. The reoptimization time depends on the complexity of the query: the more columns, tables, and predicates, the greater the increase in reoptimization time.

Reoptimization at run time should always be considered before trying to manipulate the optimizer to pick an access path, because reoptimization allows the optimizer to use real values for host variables, parameter markers, and special registers. This process works for both static SQL and dynamic SQL that uses host variables. It makes more sense to let the optimizer evaluate the real data and make a solid access path selection than try to force a selection through tricks and hints. This is not to say that you won't end up manipulating something to force an access path, but you should just do that last. Reoptimization can be monitored to determine whether it is working or not. If monitoring proves that reoptimization is not beneficial, then you can resort to something else.

When you use host variables with either static or dynamic SQL, the optimizer must use default filter factors to estimate the number of rows to eliminate for each predicate. It cannot make full use of many catalog statistics, such as the frequency statistics in SYSCOLDIST. For example, the contents of a variable may determine which partition range of a partitioned table to scan.

A good example of justifiable REOPT(VARS) is a long-running batch program with four queries that contain host variables and access several partitioned tables. These queries cannot qualify for a partition scan because of their host variable use. Instead, the queries do index and table-space scanning. Significant reductions in run time (from 30% to 70%) are attainable by rebinding the program with REOPT(VARS) and incurring an extra 2.0 seconds (a worst case of 0.5 seconds per query) of reoptimization at execution time. This is easy to accept when a query is reduced from a 100% table-space scan to a 34% partition scan. The optimizer can carve a precise path to the data within a partitioned table when the host variable's contents are known.

Version and Release Upgrades

Version and release changes can sometimes catch business off guard and cause ugly performance problems. For example, when businesses moved from version 4 to version 5 access paths often changed something well tuned to list prefetch. Such problems can be prevented or at least handled.

Normally you should always have a copy, or plan table entries, of all production access paths before moving into a new version or release. When running on the new release, you should run REORG and RUNSTATS and then rebind, perhaps even to dummy plans with EXPLAIN YES. Then you need to compare access paths for changes. This technique is explained in Chapter 22. This is a critical migration task, as many optimizer changes occur with each new version or release.

E-Business, the Web, and Networks

At the rate of change in the industry today, the title of this chapter will probably die of old age within three months and be replaced by something else. You must remember e-commerce and all the i-stuff in very recent history. Further back, it was either networking within a business to connect to a mainframe, distributed processing, or distributed databases. Old buzzwords all had to do with the type of architecture used, whereas today acronyms like B2B (business-to-business), describe what is provided, not how it is done.

We know that trends will change soon. Way back in history, there was this thing called client-server, generally within an organization. We moved from fat clients with servers everywhere, to thin clients with servers everywhere, to thin clients and one large server (mainframe, UNIX, Sun, whatever). Now businesses step outside of themselves and connect to other businesses over the Internet. Web-based transactions have dramatically changed the way business is conducted. But for how long? WAP (Wireless Application Protocol) and pervasive platforms on the horizon will change business again. What IBM is currently planning with its web technology strategies will have serious impact on all large enterprises.

This chapter covers some the issues surrounding DB2's support for e-business, including interaction with the web. We also look at issues surrounding performance in distributed and networked environments, since they still exist. If you listen to the press, you might get the impression that the entire world is now using Java, the web, and e-business, when in actuality, these technologies are small players today, though they will grow more rapidly than anything we have ever witnessed in the computer industry. In the not too distant future, all interchanges between businesses will be by connected, federated systems. This new advanced technology is adding on to our existing legacy systems, more so than it is replacing them.

E-Business and the Web

Today's e-businesses need to take advantage of DB2's capabilities and make it perform beyond its limits. They have to begin to look at their core systems in a new way. Many core systems involve a web server and the ability to provide services over the Internet. Some of these systems will be built from the ground up, but more often than not businesses are going to have to open traditional OLTP systems up to the world by providing Internet access. These new systems must be up 24 hours a day, seven days a week, and must support more concurrent users with lighting speed. They cannot afford to be unavailable and are very exposed. No longer are you dealing with just your in-house users. Your new users may not be so understanding when response time is slow or the system is unavailable. The competition on the web gets aggressive, and if you cannot provide your good or service because your system is down or unresponsive, it is very easy for customers to simply hop over to your competitor's web site.

DB2 supports some of the most critical, high-volume systems in OLTP environments, and it is very well suited to handling the new requirements of e-business, provided that you are ready. Many success stories prove that DB2 can handle these requirements. DB2 can provide the performance necessary to meet the needs of e-business, including support for popular web development environments and tools such as WebSphere, Java, JDBC, SQLJ, and others. DB2 offers you a choice of both dynamic and static SQL support in Java (refer to Chapter 20 for more on JDBC, SQLJ, and Java).

DB2 provides many components necessary for the support of e-business. Some of the newer features specifically geared toward e-business include

- Java support
- JDBC and SQLJ support
- Manageability and scalability to move existing applications to e-business
- XML support

- Large object (LOB, CLOB, BLOB) support
- Connectivity
- Connection pooling
- Multiple-platform Stored Procedure Builder
- Workload Manager

It is important to remember that DB2 is just one of the components of a successful e-commerce, e-business, or business-to-business site. While DB2 performance is affected by mostly the DB2 database server component, other items (figure 24.1) play a major role in end-to-end performance:

- Client
- Internet
- Web servers
- Load directors

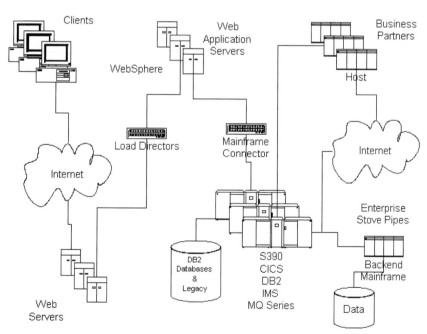

Figure 24.1   The Web and E-Commerce, End to End

- Web application servers
- Mainframe connection
- S390
- CICS
- MQ series
- Back-end information systems
- Business partners
- External services

In addition, various workload patterns and different site classifications each present their own set of issues. There are five basic, distinct workload patterns and web site classifications:

- Publish and subscribe services (e.g., news, sporting events)
  - Provide users with information
  - Minimal security
  - Low data volatility
  - Fewest transactions
  - Almost no legacy connections
- Online shopping (e.g., book or computer stores)
  - Users browse and buy
  - Significant security issues
  - Privacy concerns
  - Burst-mode transactions
  - Some connection to legacy systems
- Customer self-service (e.g., online banking)
  - Users help themselves to services
  - High security concerns for some
  - Low traffic, but will increase
- Trading sites (stocks, auction)
  - Users buy and sell
  - High security
  - Privacy concerns
  - Burst-mode and volatile transactions
  - Extremely high-volume, complex transactions

- Tightly connect to back-end systems, including high-volume CICS systems and heavy use of MQ series
- Business-to-business (e.g., purchasing departments)
  - Legacy data driven
  - Multiple back-end system connections
  - Data consistency issues
  - Heavy and significant security concerns
  - Complex transactions
  - Multiple connections to multiple businesses
  - Medium to heavy transaction volume

DB2 Web Application Performance

There is no single set of guidelines for DB2 performance except one: do as much work in DB2 as possible. There is no need to constantly move unnecessary data across the networks or to make unnecessary calls. However, that is what we often find, especially with object-oriented approaches to design and programming (C++, Java). The problem is not with the object-oriented approach, but rather with the hard-core rules mandated, which generally end up with all the work in the object-oriented modules and with DB2 as an I/O service layer, dealing with meaningless surrogate keys and driving web disaster by random I/O. Code can be encapsulated in triggers, stored procedures, UDFs, and declarative rules without violating object-oriented principles, but that often requires some loud and boisterous meetings that often lead to the wrong conclusion. When the system is built and the web cannot handle the load, the finger always is pointed at the database first. Proper design for performance does not go away, just because new paradigms are driving development methods.

Java

It came, it saw, and it is conquering. According to many published reports, by the end of December 1999, Java was being used in over 35% of the major enterprise businesses. Its growth for web work, initially as applets and then as servlets, is well documented. But it was its reusability feature and its object orientation that brought it to the attention of general applications development. In addition, schools are teaching Java, so there is a workforce graduating in data processing and information systems with knowledge of a language that is actually being used; they have jobs waiting for them. The lack of staff who know general programming languages has been a problem for some time.

The web and interactive web sites have grown beyond simply serving up HTML text and running small applets. Web sites are becoming the new transaction managers, interfacing to all the back-end and legacy data stores. To get better performance, scripts had to give way to coded programs, and Java fulfilled the need for a robust, object-oriented language. Java could execute on a web server, running processes that we now call servlets. Java could run on the client, within browsers, or on by anything capable of interacting with a Java virtual machine (JVM). Java could also be embedded in HTML text, providing Java server pages.

The pressing need now is for Java to work with all back-end systems, mostly database systems. JDBC, the ODBC interface for Java, has simply too much overhead for high-performance systems. Static SQL for Java was developed to assist in that area, and SQLJ was the result (see Chapter 20). DB2 supports both dynamic SQL (JDBC) and static SQL (SQLJ) from Java, which could be called dynamic Java, since it is still interpretive. Java, compiled through a JIT (just-in-time) compiler, exists on the OS/390, but it is intended only for those places where the JVM cannot be invoked. But we need to focus on the fact that SQLJ really is JDBC. DB2 does provide statement caching to help with all this dynamic SQL that is frequently called and executes in a very short time; it provides almost static performance. It allows the reuse of the dynamically prepared access plan, reducing dynamic PREPARE overhead.

IBM's focus today is on improving the performance of Java and DB2 access by reducing the code length. These are a few web sites anyone interested in Java and DB2 should visit regularly:

- www.software.ibm.com/data/db2/java
- www.ibm.com/s390/corner
- www.software.ibm.com/data/db2/os390/jdbc.html
- www.software.ibm.com/data/db2/os390/sqlj.html
- www.ibm.com/s390/java

Net.Data

There are easy and slow ways and hard and fast ways to allow web servers or applets to get to DB2 data. Regardless of which method you use, you can use tools to get to the data that exists, rather than building a separate data sorter for the data or some complex system to provide this feature.

Net.Data, available as part of DB2 starting with version 5, is one solution to quickly get to DB2 data and other types of data in the back-end systems. Net.Data is a macro language, an interpreter, an HTML generator, and an SQL generator. Net.Data runs where the web server is running. DB2 Connect is also needed to connect to DB2 on OS/390 when the web server is not on the OS/390. Moving the web server to OS/390 is becoming more commonplace with the improvements to WebSphere. These improvements are nice, since setting up DB2 Connect and IP addressing on OS/390 can sometimes be difficult due to standards, block point changes, and "don't mess with my production environment" rules. But it is an easy setup, and Net.Data itself is easy. Using the macro language, you just describe your web pages, generate some normal GUI elements such as buttons and pull-downs, and perform all the other tasks typical on a page.

The trade-off here is performance, as you are trading simplicity and speed of development for speed of execution. But pages developed with Net.Data can be used as prototypes or as the startup before the system becomes heavily used. With WebSphere, performance comes with the price of more complex application development.

Workload Management

Scalability and performance become two very important issues for larger enterprise web sites, especially the buy-sell and business-to-business kind. As soon as the web or application servers must connect to existing DB2 data on OS/390 systems, performance degrades. The major movement today on larger web commerce systems is to consolidate on the OS/390 server. If the web server and the legacy systems are on the same machine, then the time to pass data through memory can be in the nanosecond range versus the network approach, with times in the millisecond range. The major online catalog and brokerage businesses cannot survive with response times in milliseconds, so they use more and more integration on the OS/390 production application server.

The Workload Manager (WLM) is a requirement for these types of systems and any system where differing workloads coexist. More of the data in enterprise systems needs to be shared by disparate processes operating with different service-level agreements. WLM does a great job of managing that kind of environment. Besides, if you use DB2 stored procedures and DB2 user-defined functions, you need WLM for performance and dependency reasons. WLM can run either in compatibility mode or in goal mode, but there is really only one choice; goal mode allows WLM to manage everything it can based on specific priorities.

XML

HTML, the first language for the development of web pages, has evolved into a graphical and object-oriented extended language called XML. XML provides for the management of text and graphical objects beyond alphanumeric data. Now that DB2 supports LOBs, it is a natural extension to support LOBs containing XML markers. The big impact of XML is its potential as an enabler of the data interchange necessary for business-to-business e-commerce. Data interchange formats with XML are very flexible. When XML is the message format, the two applications on either end of the business-to-business connection can dynamically interpret the message format using an XML parser. XML message formats are very extensible, which means that the same application that created the XML document could simply add a data element to support another application. XML as a data interchange format also allows individual companies to define specific XML grammars for their internal use. XML is probably the future for all document interchange, since it describes only data; since relational databases store data, XML integration is key.

DB2 supports XML through an XML extender. DB2 can act as a repository of XML documents for web publishing and content management, and it facilitates business-to-business e-commerce and application integration using XML documents as an interchange format for business data. The DB2 XML extender includes a visual tool for mapping the extracted elements from the XML document to the columns and tables where they are stored. This mapping, called document access definition (DAD), and the DTD describing the XML document are stored in tables managed by the XML extender. There is no need for individual applications to access the document and keep track of the DADs and DTDs. Once the documents are all stored in or managed by DB2, they can be made available over the Internet. You can use IBM's Net.Data, which supports XML, to quickly build applications to deliver the XML documents to an XML web browser that can display the documents. WebSphere Application Server can be used to deliver XML documents by interfacing with applications built as Java servlets.

With DB2's entrance through extensions into XML, there are going to be more performance considerations. There are no guidelines yet, but rather a warning to pay close attention to developments in this big arena.

Connection Performance Issues

The connection to DB2 is obviously another pressure point for performance and design. When a web server is not on OS/390 but on another server machine, it must connect to DB2 on OS/390. Each connection to OS/390 incurs overhead, since starting, stopping, and removing threads consumes resources and can be expensive (which is good, as that is where a lot of the benefit of OS/390 comes from). A new task needs to be started whenever a new connection is opened from a web server via middleware such as DB2 Connect to DB2 on OS/390. When the connection is stopped, the task must be removed. This process is very inefficient in DB2 for OS/390 unless connection pooling is used, which was not available until version 6.

DB2 connection pooling allows a preallocation of a set number of DB2 connections or threads, even if very few or no connections are established. With connection pooling, connections can be established very quickly between DB2 and a non-OS/390 web server. DB2 connection pooling supports large numbers of TCP/IP or SNA connections. These can range into the thousands and use much less storage than was required in previous releases before connection pooling was enabled.

E-business for large sites requires connection pooling. It allows applications connected via DB2 Connect to reuse threads to DB2 on the mainframe, thus substantially increasing performance for peak application usage.

Stored Procedures, User-Defined Functions, and Triggers

We have mentioned many times the benefits of program code encapsulation through stored procedures, triggers, user-defined functions, and declarative rules. Encapsulation techniques are even more important with the movement to e-commerce, since they work on the database server and reduce the need for network traffic, which is slow in comparison. These techniques are discussed in many chapters, but refer specifically to Chapter 17 on triggers and UDFs and Chapter 19 on stored procedures.

Data Sharing Design and Tuning

Overview and Processing Costs

Hardware Considerations

Locking

Group Bufferpools

Migration

Application Tuning

Physical Design

Problem Diagnosing

Long Term Monitoring

CHAPTER 2 5

Data Sharing Overview
and Processing Costs

D B2 has been operating in organizations for over
15 years now, and just when you think you have a handle on performance, along comes a
new feature known as data sharing. This section covers the authors' experiences over the
years working with DB2 data sharing customers on issues ranging from application selection and migration to problem diagnosing and tuning for overall system performance. It
includes how to migrate effectively to the data sharing environment, tuning the current
DB2 environment in preparation for data sharing migration, and troubleshooting after the
migration. There are also several reporting examples to demonstrate how to monitor and
diagnose problems in this new environment. The intention of this chapter is not to introduce
you to all of the components and concepts of data sharing, but rather to discuss performance issues in a data sharing environment. A base knowledge of data sharing is assumed.

Data Sharing Benefits

The many advantages of using DB2 data sharing include:
- Improved price and performance by using S/390 microprocessor technology
- Increased capacity with more power and a higher degree of intertransaction paral-
  lelism available
- Continuous availability through the ability to hide unplanned and planned outages
  (e.g., rolling maintenance) to keep the system processing even if a member is lost
- Incremental growth (horizontal growth) by adding processors without any
  disruption

587

- Configuration flexibility with the ability to start and stop members as required and separate subsystems by function (such as batch, ad hoc, and OLTP)
- Ability to split large queries across all CPCs with sysplex query parallelism (covered in detail in Chapter 21, "Parallelism")
- Flexibility for scheduling existing workloads by cloning CICS regions on another MVS and removing the restriction of a CICS application being able to run on only one MVS
- Running applications concurrently on several subsystems to increase throughput
- Reduced need for distributed processing, because applications do not have to use DRDA to share data, which eliminates the overhead of DRDA for this purpose
- Affinity and nonaffinity workloads in the same group, running workloads of different processors or a specific workload on a particular processor, because data is shared
- Shared data architecture (SDA) based on coupling technology, which allows high-speed coupling facility channels, reduced system-to-system communication (message passing), multiple paths to the data for higher availability, and dynamic workload routing based on capacity, not location.
- No need for data partitioning for growth and it does not rely on node-to-node communication for resources

Performance

What is new about DB2 performance when you add data sharing? Data sharing has thrown a whole new spin on DB2 performance and tuning. From application selection to post-implementation troubleshooting, there are several new places to look for problems. Old performance problems that were acceptable or tolerable in the past are magnified in the data sharing environment. New skills are needed in diverse areas to monitor and tune for overall performance.

A data sharing environment introduces new hardware and new rules. Contrary to popular belief, data sharing is not just an install option! The introduction of the coupling facility in the parallel sysplex data sharing architecture accounts for a whole new set of factors to be concerned with in terms of performance. The coupling facility, an S/390 exclusive feature, provides data sharing with many performance benefits (high-performance data sharing protocols) over other sharing architectures used in other environments, but it must also be cared for. You need to be concerned with activity involving the coupling facility, including DB2 LOCK and UNLOCK requests, physical directory reads, cache updates, and reads of buffer invalidated data to maintain the consistency and coherency of the shared data.

In an ideal world with more processors in the complex, the transaction rate achieved by a single DB2 would be multiplied by the number of available processors, but get real! Due to the requirement of additional buffer management and global locking capability, DB2 and IRLM processing costs increase and as a result can decrease the overall transaction rate attainable. Typical overhead for data sharing is around 5% to 15% after a second member is defined for data sharing. As each member is added, overhead is generally low but is very dependent on the amount of sharing among the members.

For estimating data sharing performance, you must understand the overhead involved and appreciate the tuning efforts required to minimize the impact of this overhead. First of all, you must set realistic goals, define performance objects, and, most important, tune your current environment. Keep in mind that bad performers will become worse and new problems will surface. The key to a successful implementation is education of those involved in the migration and support of the data sharing environment. This makes the monitoring, tuning, and troubleshooting much less painful. The majority of DB2 performance problems in a data sharing environment are concentrated in two areas—locking and buffer pools (figure 25.1)—and are often related to poor application design.

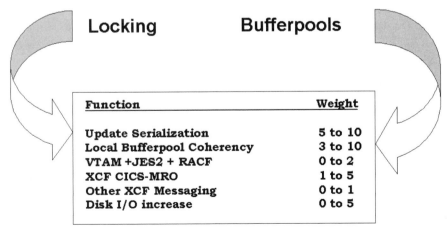

Figure 25.1   Best Buy for Your Tuning Dollars

Processing Costs

Processing costs for data sharing vary, depending on the degree of data sharing, locking factors, workload characteristics, hardware and software configurations, application design, physical design, and various application options. The processing costs can be controlled to some degree by application and system tuning. Data sharing costs are a function of the processing required, in addition to the normal processing for concurrency control and inter-DB2 interest and data coherency. Hardware and software costs can include the speed of the processors, the level of the CFCC (coupling facility control code), coupling facility structure sizes, coupling facility link configurations, level of hardware, software maintenance, and the number of members in the data sharing group. The hardware-related items are discussed briefly in Chapter 26, "Hardware and Configuration Considerations." Workload characteristics can include real, false, and XES contention (cross-system extended services, a set of MVS services allowing multiple instances of an application or subsystem to utilize data sharing features through the use of the coupling facility); disk contention; workload dynamics; thread reuse; and the application's use of lock avoidance.

You can expect to incur the following costs for these reasons:

- CPU time for DB2 applications will increase due to . . .
  - Accessing shared data in read-write mode across the group
- CPU time of allied tasks will increase due to . . .
  - XES lock requests
  - Group Buffer pool read and register requests
- MSTR SRB time will increase due to . . .
  - Synchronous group buffer pool write requests
  - XES unlock requests
- DBM1 SRB time will increase due to . . .
  - Castout activity to write changed pages to disk
  - Asynchronous group buffer pool write requests
  - Group buffer pool read and register requests
- IRLM SRB time will increase due to . . .
  - Global lock contention resolution
  - Deadlock processing

Movement to Data Sharing

The movement to a DB2 data sharing environment can generally be done in two different ways. A new install of DB2 gives you the opportunity to start with a clean subsystem in which to move applications. This also makes monitoring initial data sharing performance easier, and at this time new naming standards could be implemented. While a new install is less painful, it is not often practical. The other option is to migrate existing subsystems by first enabling a DB2 subsystem as a data sharing subsystem and then adding members to the group. This is much easier for the movement of very large applications, and it has less of an impact on distributed processing. It is also the more common method for moving to a data sharing environment. The complications come with the catalog merge process and the measure of application performance as the migration occurs. Whether you decide to do a new install or a migration of existing subsystems, you need to effectively measure the performance of data sharing and the impact it is having on your system. Keep in mind that not all applications belong in a data sharing environment. Some applications still benefit from isolation. For more information on migration, refer to Chapter 29, "Migration."

Application Analysis

Application analysis, or selection, is the process of evaluating which applications will benefit from data sharing and belong in a data sharing environment. You need to determine the application objectives for data sharing in order to set performance objectives. Ask such questions as

1. What is the overall goal of implementing data sharing?
2. Are we looking to offload CPU cycles?
3. Will we benefit from transaction-routing capabilities?
4. Is 24X7 availability the driving requirement?

These are just a few of several questions that should be addressed to implement data sharing with maximum performance in mind.

Migration Considerations

When you make the move to the data sharing, one way to keep on top of performance problems is to monitor the movement or migrations. This can be done by generating statistics and accounting reports before the migration to one-way data sharing (one member enabled) (using your monitoring tool of choice) and then comparing them to the same reports after one-way is turned is enabled. Then repeat this for the two-way migration (2 members enabled in the data sharing group) and so forth. Items to monitor in these reports are locking rates, buffer pool activity, and CPU times per address space. If problems exist after the movement to one-way, investigate and tune as much as possible before making the decision to fall back from one-way. This fallback has implications, and it is extremely rare. It is wise to avoid fallback at all costs, because once you initiate data sharing for a DB2 subsystem, some underlying constructs change, and fallback cannot reverse everything.

Current Environment Evaluation

Evaluate your current DB2 system and applications before moving to data sharing. Even movement to one-way can expose overlooked performance problems (although few, because interaction with the coupling facility is minimal), and two-way can further magnify them. The time to fix known application or system performance issues is prior to any movement into the data sharing environment. Of course, these same items still need to be investigated as workload and other factors change in the new data sharing environment. Such items to evaluate are locking activity, application commit frequency, bind parameters, use of standard rule-of-thumb recommendations, ZPARMS, maintenance schedule and hiper application, buffer pools, and recovery and restart procedures. The next chapter covers these areas in more detail as we discuss application and system tuning and items to monitor in your environment for achieving the best possible long-term performance in data sharing.

Hardware and Configuration Considerations

T his chapter covers some of the different consid-
erations for achieving best performance and availability in a data sharing environment. We
talk about the coupling facility and its configuration options, such as ICMF and ICFs. We
also take a look at the implementation of geographically dispersed parallel sysplex
(GDPS) for availability.

Coupling Facility

Data sharing overhead is directly related to the interaction with structures that reside in
the coupling facility, which can be a separate piece of hardware or an internal coupling
facility (ICF) in its own LPAR. It is worth the time and effort to be sure that the coupling facility is configured correctly and optimally for best performance.

Dedicated Coupling Facility versus ICMF

It is a known fact and recommended practice that you should have at least two coupling
facilities for each data sharing group, mainly for availability and capacity reasons. It is
also ideal to have at least one of these coupling facilities be a dedicated 9674 processor
that runs only the coupling facility control code. This is recommended for both availability and performance. You can use an integrated coupling migration facility (ICMF), where
the coupling facility control code runs in an LPAR on a CMOS bipolar machine, but this

is not recommended for a production environment. It is fine for a test environment or a disaster recovery site.

An S/390 9674 is a dedicated microprocessor that is used as a dedicated coupling facility. It is a CPC that runs only as a coupling facility in a logical partition with dedicated processor resources. This is the optimal configuration, because a failure of a coupling facility and a connected MVS image (which is more likely when they are both on the same CPC) can lead to extended recovery times. You also get better performance and better connectivity to the coupling facility by using dedicated hardware.

Storage

The coupling facility storage is often significantly undersized. At least 1 GB on each coupling facility is recommended to start. Attempting to support a data sharing group with anything less can be very difficult, if not impossible.

You need enough storage to hold all the necessary structures and enough empty room to hold the structures from the other coupling facility in the group to be able to rebuild all the necessary structures from a failing coupling facility (figure 26.1) or a coupling facility that has been taken offline for maintenance.

Links

You must not forget to consider the speed and number of links to the coupling facility. Performance and availability can both be affected by having an inappropriate number of links

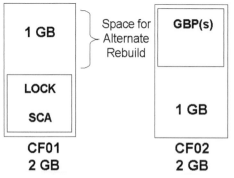

Figure 26.1   Coupling Facility Configuration

from the coupling facility to the processors running on the operating system. Two links from each coupling facility to each MVS are recommended. One link would give you a single path to buffers and lock structures and for communications, not to mention a single point of failure.

You should keep your links around 40% busy and not overload them, or performance will degrade. For information on monitoring link usage refer to Chapter 33 "Long-Term Monitoring." Each coupling facility link has two subchannels and two link buffers. If the links are overloaded, MVS will wait and retry operations until the link is cleared. This results in excess overhead for operations using the coupling facility and can degrade application response time and overall performance. There are three types of links: ICBs (integrated cluster buses) supporting data transfer rates up to 280 MB per second over a 10-m copper cable, multimode fiber (50/125 micron) links supporting distances up to 1 km, and single-mode fiber (9/125 or 10/125 micron) links supporting distances up to 3 km.

Cycles

Just having enough coupling facilities and enough coupling facility links is not enough. Having enough coupling facility engines is just as critical. A shortage of coupling facility processing cycles backs up work in the complex. One physical machine can have more than one logical coupling facility, but each logical coupling facility needs to have dedicated processors. There should be no sharing of processors, because sharing processors degrades coupling facility service time to members. There is a simple rule to follow: do *not* assign a single processor to more than one logical coupling facility. Logical coupling facilities cannot outnumber processors. If you have only one processor, you should have only one logical coupling facility. However, you can have more processors than logical coupling facilities. The speed of the processors varies by the model number of the coupling facility. For example, a 9674-C04 takes about 30 microseconds to handle a lock request.

Coupling facility utilization should be monitored and should not be allowed to exceed 40%. Keep in mind that the overhead for lock requests is not linear. Once performance goes, it's gone! There is no curve of decreasing performance; you just die. For more information, refer to Chapter 33, "Long-Term Monitoring."

Internal Coupling Facilities

Internal coupling facilities (ICFs) are a relatively new option for coupling facility configuration. An IBM 9672 machine can be configured with an ICF. The ICF can use one or more engines, depending on the generation of the machine. ICFs are an attractive alternative to the dedicated 9674, mainly because they cost less. A small performance advantage can be observed in an ICF communications path because it is internal and has a transfer rate of about 700 MB per second. ICFs can also be configured across CPCs. However, this is useful only if the DB2 subsystem resides on the same 9672 as the ICF; no other members in the data sharing group get this benefit. However, in a high-performance situation, you may want to place a DB2 subsystem on this machine to take advantage of this reduced data sharing overhead for that particular subsystem.

There are some additional considerations for ICFs. You should still have at least one external coupling facility for high availability. If you have a DB2 subsystem on the same machine as the ICF, you could experience what is known as a double failure because if you lost the machine, you would lose both the ICF and the DB2 subsystem. This creates some additional issues regarding placement of coupling facility structures (lock, group buffer pools, and shared communication area [SCA]).

If your SCA and your lock structures are on the same 9672 as your ICF and you lose the 9672, you lose both the DB2 subsystem and the ICF. This means that you must perform a group restart, because to rebuild the structures, the member must be available. If your group buffer pools are defined in the ICF on the same machine as a DB2 member and you lost the 9672 but you were using group buffer pool duplexing (more on this in Chapter 28, "Group Buffer Pools"), you could switch to the secondary group buffer pool and continue processing without any datasets becoming GRECP (group buffer pool recover pending). Figure 26.2 shows the best configuration. If you were not using duplexing and this scenario occurred, you may have some GRECP data sets and may fail to recover them because of retained locks held by the failed member. For information on retained locks, refer to Chapter 27, "Locking."

These are some recommendations for ICFs:

- Have at least one external ICF.
- Place group buffer pools in the ICF, and use group buffer pool duplexing.
- Place the lock and SCA structures in the external coupling facility.

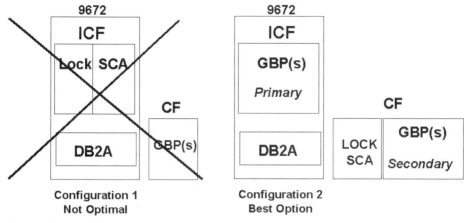

Figure 26.2   ICF Configuration

Geographically Dispersed Parallel Sysplex

While data sharing adds another dimension to large-system processing, one piece is missing, and that is the ability to integrate multiple sites, especially for the purposes of disaster recovery. IBM introduced geographically dispersed parallel sysplex (GDPS) as a way of managing systems across multiple sites for maximum availability and disaster recovery (see figure 26.3). GDPS is a very automated environment with enhanced system management functions, including disk configuration management and peer-to-peer dynamic device switching through extended use of remote copy software. The GDPS technology builds upon the existing parallel sysplex technology and remote copy technology and exploits DB2 for OS/390. Planned and unplanned outages become less painful and less risky since GDPS provides data redundancy and site redundancy. With GDPS, two copies of data at two sites provide another level of redundancy over single-site redundancy for greater application availability.

Continuous operation and support for all enterprise-wide computing are also critical requirements. Most organizations cannot afford to lose more than a couple of days of processing after a site disaster (some of our clients would be out of business if not back online within 24 hours). Depending on the plans for business-segment processing after a disaster, full recovery may never be possible. The financial impact depends on the line of business but has been known to approach $6 million per hour.

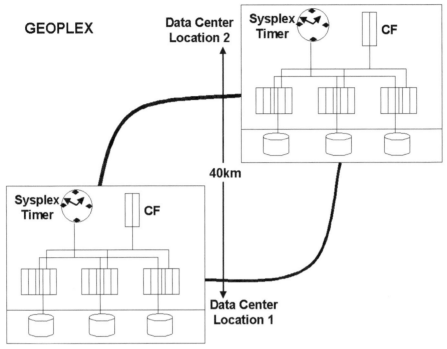

Figure 26.3   GDPS

Cross-Site Reconfiguration

A site can be automatically reconfigured with GDPS with very little disruption to the
application for both planned and unplanned outages across multiple sites or within one
site. Planned cross-site and single-site reconfigurations can be automated and controlled
by predefined customer policies. The system is actually removed, temporarily or permanently, from the GDPS. A switch is then performed, and after a restart, the workload is
reconfigured, and the primary disk and secondary disk are swapped. This process allows
the new environment to mimic the original environment. Whether the reconfigurations are
for planned outages, such as maintenance or testing, or for traditionally long, manual, and
error-prone unplanned outages, the multisite capability of GDPS provides a faster, more
reliable recovery method. The single-site capabilities of GDPS handles outages such as
loss of image, loss of processor, or other failures.

While planned reconfigurations are beneficial for activities such as maintenance,
unplanned cross-site reconfiguration was the main driving force behind the development

of GDPS. In the event that the primary site fails, operations are moved to the surviving site. This too is based on predefined customer policies and provides fast, automated fail-over while maintaining consistency and integrity of data across affected volumes. With unplanned reconfigurations, you have the option to preserve committed data or to continue on a new image of data in the secondary system with some data loss. Options are also available to analyze problems at a single site without switching sites. This method expedites and helps to automate disaster recovery. With a GDPS, it is easier to implement disaster recovery procedures. Using GDPS technology for this process may also soon eliminate the need for a disaster recovery site subscription. At the present time, its applicability is limited to enterprises with two sites within 40 km of one another.

GDPS Configuration Options

The GDPS may be configured in a variety of ways. The first option is to have one complete parallel sysplex at a given site, with a controlling system at the other site that is a member of the sysplex. This controlling site member can monitor the primary site and can possibly have an expendable workload at its site. The data is primary on one parallel sysplex and secondary on the remote site. With this configuration, if there is a loss or disaster at one site, a switch will occur. The disk switch from primary to secondary occurs with minimal disruption or intervention, and then processing continues as normal. The benefits of this option include little or no data loss (depending on customer policies) and minimal disruption of business processes. This option is supported for both planned and unplanned site reconfigurations.

The second option is to divide only one parallel sysplex between two sites sharing the workload. Each site can monitor the other site and have some potentially expendable work on the other site. All data is divided between the two sites; all primary data is located at one site, with the secondary data at the other. The site takeover supports both planned and unplanned outages with the same requirements as the first option and with minimal or no data loss or process disruption.

GDPS Implementation

There are costs associated with implementing a GDPS. The parallel sysplex environment has to be replicated at both sites. The hardware in both environments must include at least one coupling facility, a sysplex timer, processor(s), and a disk with remote mirroring.

There are many prerequisites for establishing a site, including an operation system, disk subsystem support, communications, system automation software, and a disk subsystem with FREEZE/RUN support. The data required for restart needs to be disk resident and mirrored. With all these requirements, it is easy to see that the implementation of a GDPS is not an easy, or inexpensive, task.

The GDPS is a reality today. One customer who has successfully implemented GDPS technology for unplanned site reconfigurations has seen a reduction in the recovery window from 12 hours to 22 minutes. Other customers' results vary, depending upon their respective workloads. One way to estimate the reduction in recovery time is to determine the restart time after a system failure. This time can be reduced by 10 to 15 minutes if stand-by, IPL'ed, minimal OS/390 images are ready. Customers testing GDPS have also experienced the elimination of data loss during reconfiguration with minimal operation intervention.

Currently, the distance between GDPS sites is limited. The possible distance constantly increases with new technology and could well exceed the older 40-km limit for synchronous protocols. For unlimited distances, there is discussion about the possibility of providing a similar function using asynchronous protocols based on XRC technology. Eventually, advanced technology will probably provide support for all disk vendors and better support for continuous availability during reconfigurations.

GDPS Impacts on DB2 Data Sharing

DB2 data sharing supports some of the largest businesses and their most mission-critical systems. Disaster recovery for data sharing requires complex planning, and it is difficult to stage a backup site recovery. Many varied strategies to handle a potential loss of systems require much effort and talent, not to mention down time. GDPS eliminates the difficulty of disaster recovery, providing the level of safe security that most firms are seeking today.

Locking

Overview of Locking in a Data Sharing Environment

Consistency of data among the members in a data sharing group is protected in two ways:

- Concurrency controls
- Coherency controls

To provide concurrency control among the DB2 members in the data sharing group, a new locking structure is used. Since tuning locking is extremely critical to performance in a data sharing environment, it is important to understand how it works.

Explicit Hierarchical Locking

Data sharing locking is not quite like locking in a single subsystem environment. Data sharing introduces explicit hierarchical locking (EHL). Prior to data sharing, you used implicit hierarchical locking. The only difference is that with EHL, a token is kept that identifies parent-child relationships. A parent lock is a table-space or partition lock, and a child lock is a page or row lock (figure 27.1). The benefit of EHL is that only the most restrictive lock moves to the coupling facility, reducing the number calls to the coupling facility to control concurrency, which can create a great deal of overhead. Lock avoidance still works with EHL, and type 2 indexes work best. This does not alter the recommendation that uncommitted read (UR) be used wherever possible.

With EHL, only the most restrictive parent lock is propagated until it is necessary for the child to be propagated (recorded in the coupling facility), thus lessening the amount of lock activity.

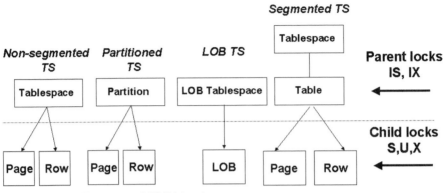

Figure 27.1   Parent and Child Locks

Here is an example of how EHL works: if parent lock is on a table space in IX (intent exclusive) mode, then a child lock in S (share) mode on a page does not have to be propagated to the coupling facility lock structure because the lock on the parent is more restrictive, unless there is inter-DB2 read/write interest on the parent, which causes the child lock to be propagated.

You should lock only what is necessary and negotiate locks in the coupling facility if there is conflict. Child locks are propagated only if the parent locks are in conflict.

Lock Management

There is a lot of new terminology for data sharing locking. In the following sections, we take a brief look at each of these.

- Local lock manager (LLM)
- Global lock manager (GLM)
- Global locks
- P-locks (subsystem or physical locks)
- L-locks (transaction or logical locks)
- Modified locks
- Retained locks

Local Lock Manager

The local lock manager (LLM) is basically each IRLM in the data sharing group. The LLM provides all the intra-DB2 locking and local lock functions that it always has. Each IRLM, or LLM, can communicate via XES (Cross System Extended Services) to the coupling facility for global locking functions.

Global Lock Manager

The global lock manager (GLM) is the responsibility of XES and the coupling facility that tracks resources locked at each LLM. At the GLM, the locks are still owned by each LLM; at the LLM, locks are owned by the transactions. If the GLM detects lock conflicts between LLMs, it uses the XCF (cross-system coupling facility) to communicate between them to resolve the lock.

To resolve contention, an XES is assigned as the GLM. This responsibility is assigned to the first XES to declare an X-lock on a particular hash class (the first to take the lock).

It is important to understand lock contention in terms of performance. In normal lock-request functions, XES communicates the request to the coupling facility to get the lock. This communication between the IRLM, XES, and coupling facility takes about 100 microseconds (down to about 20 microseconds for ICBs and the latest coupling facility hardware). If there is a contention problem that cannot be resolved in the coupling facility, the IRLM must use the XCF to pass messages between the DB2 members to resolve the lock contention. This type of messaging can get expensive and time-consuming because it takes about 20 milliseconds and precludes some of the benefit of using a coupling facility in a shared data architecture. If this type of messaging occurs often, performance of the application will suffer.

Local Locks

Local locks are the same locks that we have always known and loved in non-data sharing environments. These locks are requested on local subsystem and provide only intra-DB2 concurrency control.

Global Locks

Global locks are the locks that a DB2 subsystem needs to make known to the group through the coupling facility. These locks are propagated to the coupling facility and provide intra-DB2 and inter-DB2 concurrency control. In a data sharing environment, almost all locks are global.

Whether a lock becomes global depends on whether the lock request is logical (L-lock) or physical (P-lock). P-locks, or physical locks, are owned by a DB2 member and are negotiable. Unlike normal transaction locks, these locks are not used for concurrency but rather for coherency. There are two types of P-locks: page set and page.

P-Locks

Page-set P-locks are used to track intersystem interest among DB2 members and determine when a page set becomes dependent on a global buffer pool (GBP). These locks have different modes, depending on the level of read or write interest on the page set among the DB2 members. A P-lock cannot be negotiated if it is retained. It is released when page set or partitioned data set is closed. Few P-locks are taken, and they are usually held for long periods of time.

Page P-locks are used to ensure the physical consistency of a page when it is modified; they work at the subpage level and are used in the same manner as latches in a non-data sharing environment. P-locks are also used when changes are made to a GBP-dependent space-map page.

Page-set P-lock negotiation takes place when P-locks are noted as being incompatible. The two members with the incompatible locks negotiate the lock so that both can still use the object. Since the P-lock is used for coherency, not concurrency, this negotiation does not sacrifice any data integrity. An example of page-set P-lock negotiation is shown in figure 27.2.

Page-set P-locks provide the mechanism for dynamic inter-DB2 read/write interest tracking. The inter-DB2 interest on the P-lock dictates to DB2 whether or not the GBP needs to be used and, if so, in what capacity. This also reduces the number of locks that are propagated to the coupling facility. When there is inter-DB2 read/write interest, P-lock negotiation is needed. The most restrictive P-lock is taken first and then, if necessary, negotiated so that another process can have access to the page set. Page-set P-locks are used to track interest in a page set and determine when it is necessary to propagate child locks because of the level of interest in the page set by the DB2 members. P-lock negotiation can be thought of as "I need to know what you are doing. Here is what I am doing. Let's find a way to work together, or do we have to take turns?"

If a good deal of sharing goes on among the members, be careful, because you can run out of engines available for P-lock negotiation, thus causing waits in the applications. This is rather rare with 500 available engines.

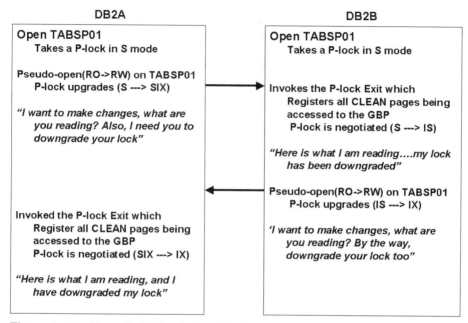

Figure 27.2   Page-Set P-Lock Negotiation

L-Locks

L-locks, or logical locks, occur in both data sharing (local or global locks) and non-data sharing subsystems. These locks are transaction or program owned. They are non-negotiable locks and work like the normal locks in a single-subsystem environment to serialize access to objects. L-locks are controlled by the IRLM of a member and are held from update to commit. There are two types:

- Parent L-lock on table space or partition (page set): Almost always propagated to find whether conflict exists with another member.
- Child L-lock on table, data page, or row: Based on parent L-lock conflict. If no conflict, they are not propagated.

Modified Locks

Modified and retained locks are two more types of locks introduced in data sharing. Modified locks are used to identify a lock on a resource that is being shared (updated). An active X-type (X, IX, SIX) P-lock or L-lock is kept in a modified resource list in the lock structure of the coupling facility and is kept regardless of the group buffer pool dependency of the object. These locks are used to create retained locks if the DB2 member holding the modified lock fails.

Retained Locks

Retained locks are modified locks that are converted when a member of the group fails. You can think of a retained lock as the captain going down with the ship. Retained locks are necessary to preserve data integrity in the event of a failure. A retained lock is held when a DB2 subsystem fails. The locks belongs to the failing member and must be resolved before access to the locked object by other members is allowed.

Retained locks can create an availability bottleneck if proper procedures are not in place for recovering a failed DB2 member. These locks are held at the GLM level and are owned by the LLM, not a transaction. This means that only the DB2 member that had the lock can resolve it, so the subsystem must come up to resolve the lock. Regardless of where a transaction may resume (i.e., in another subsystem), the locks are still retained, and the data is still not accessible by any process (although readers using uncommitted read can still view the data). The DB2 subsystem can be restarted on the same MVS or on another one in the same group; it does not matter, as long as it comes up. This is why the ARM (automatic restart manager) is so important. For information on ARM, refer to Chapter 29, "Migration."

Each local IRLM keeps a local copy of retained locks for fast reference, so retained locks can survive a coupling facility failure.

Late in version 5 (via an APAR), we were given the ability to purge retained locks. If you are at all concerned with data integrity, *do not use this function!* It should be used carefully only in a test or development environment, *never* in production.

To find out whether you are experiencing retained locks, you can issue the commands in figure 27.3. They tell you what member is holding the locks.

Lock Avoidance and Data Sharing

Lock avoidance still works with data sharing and is very beneficial, but it works only if you design your application correctly. Let's revisit a figure similar to one in Chapter 13, Locking and Concurrency, Figure 13.9 (figure 27.4). We know that the CLSN (commit log

-DISPLAY DATABASE(db) SPACE(sp) LOCKS

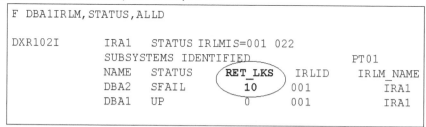

```
-DISPLAY DATABASE (DBM1) SPACE (TSNM1) LOCKS

NAME     TYPE    PART    STATUS          CONNID   CORRID   LOCKINFO

TSNM1    TS      01      RW                                R(X,P)
                         MEMBER NAME DB21
```

MODIFY IRLMPROC, STATUS, ALLD

```
F DBA1IRLM,STATUS,ALLD

DXR102I        IRA1   STATUS IRLMIS=001 022
               SUBSYSTEMS IDENTIFIED               PT01
               NAME    STATUS   RET_LKS   IRLID   IRLM_NAME
               DBA2    SFAIL      10       001      IRA1
               DBA1    UP          0       001      IRA1
```

Figure 27.3 Viewing Retaining Locks

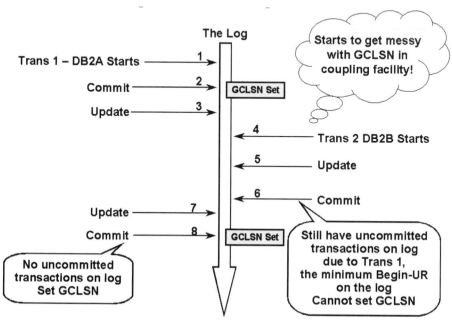

Figure 27.4 Setting the GCLSN

sequence number) gets set only when the process with the oldest BEGIN-UR commits, since the CLSN represents the minimum BEGIN-UR log record of all the processes that hold a write claim. If an application is not committing, it is not possible for the CLSN to be reset, and as a result the PGLOGRBA on the page is never less than the CLSN, the PUNC bit, if set, causes locking, and lock avoidance is not used. Therefore you are sending more locks to the coupling facility than necessary.

You may ask why lock avoidance is more of an issue than it is in a single-subsystem environment. Well, think about this: If you have several members in the same data sharing group manipulating the same data, you could run into trouble if someone decides not to play nice. Suppose you have a highly tuned application that commits frequently, as it should. But little do you know that a renegade application in the group has decided that it does not feel like committing. In a data sharing environment, the CLSN is global: GCLSN (global commit log sequence number). There is one GCLSN for the entire group, and the oldest unit of work wins! This means that if an application is not committing and therefore not setting the GCLSN for a particular page set, that application can directly impair performance, because you will never get lock avoidance and it drives unnecessary locks to the coupling facility. What to do? Have strict standards for commit strategies, especially in a nonaffinity data sharing environment.

There are more application tuning tips for locking in a data sharing environment in Chapter 30, "Application Tuning."

Global Locking Considerations

A parent lock is acquired by a DB2 transaction. The first lock acquired on the parent for a specific DB2 is propagated by IRLM to XES. Once the parent lock is propagated, only a more restrictive lock on the parent will be propagated. Locks are secured on the parent first, then locks are obtained on children. Typically, intent locks are granted on parents for best concurrency. Gross locks (S, SIX, X) can be obtained on parents when any of the following occur:

- LOCKSIZE TABLESPACE is defined on the table-space CREATE.
- Lock escalation has occurred.
- A LOCK TABLE clause is used in the application.
- Data definition language (DDL) is used.

- Repeatable read scans occur.
- The STOP DATABASE command is issued.

When DB2 first detects inter-DB2 read or write interest on a parent, all new child lock requests for that parent must be propagated to the coupling facility as well. All existing children for the parent must be propagated. This is done asynchronously to any transactions, and the requestor of the parent lock causing new inter-DB2 interest is suspended and then released only when all children are propagated. When inter-DB2 read or write interest on a parent disappears, new child lock requests for the parent are not propagated, but the existing children stay recorded in XES and the coupling facility.

Lock Structure

The lock structure is the structure in the coupling facility that controls concurrency between the DB2 members by keeping track of the locks. The IRLM connects to the lock structure during DB2 startup. The lock structure is made up of a logical grouping of two coupling facility list structures:

- Lock table: Used for quick intersystem lock-conflict detection. Its size is critical to transaction performance.
- Modified record list: Used to hold modify locks and retained locks. Its size is critical for faster recovery after system failure.

There is a one-to-one distribution of storage between the lock table and the record list (if the lock structure is defined as a power of 2). For information on how to size the lock structure, refer to Chapter 29, "Migration."

The lock table is a large hash table with millions of entries, usually two bytes each. It is always sized in a power of 2. The initial width of each entry depends on the MAXUSRS parameter in the startup procedure. This parameter is the maximum number of IRLMs in this group. You should specify this parameter exactly because it determines the size of the hash entry in the lock table. This number is the number of members in your data sharing group. If the number in MAXUSRS is less than 7, the entries will be two bytes each. If it is greater than 7 and less than 16, entries will be four bytes; if it is greater than 16, entries will be six bytes.

Each entry in lock table consists of

- A global byte used to declare the member's exclusive interest in the hash class
- Share bits used to declare the member's share interest in the hash class

The lock resource name maps to the hash class passed by DB2 via a hash algorithm.

Locking Support by Various Data Sharing Components

Locking in a data sharing environment can be rather complex because different components support different levels of locking and each has different responsibilities. When tuning locking in this environment, you need to know where your problem is and what component to tune. Figure 27.5 shows which components in the environment support what types of locking. There are three layers of locking components. Each understands a different aspect of the locking process, and each has a different function. The coupling facility lock structure is used for quick detection of potential inter-DB2 contention, and

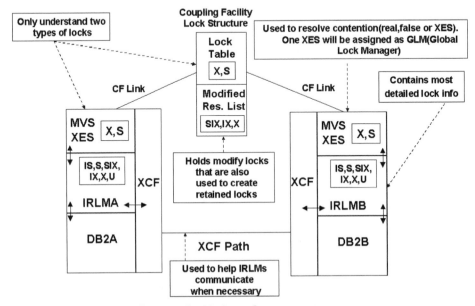

Figure 27.5 Locking Support by Various Components

this determination is rather quick because it uses the hash table. XES is used to manage inter-DB2 resource concurrency, and it understands only two types of locks: X and S. This can cause problems with XES contention if appropriate tuning steps are not followed (discussed in Chapter 30, "Application Tuning"). The IRLM, of course, manages intertransaction resource concurrency, and it understands all of the different types of locks.

Locking Contention

Three types of locking contention can occur in a data sharing environment:

- Global lock contention (IRLM, or real) occurs when there is real contention against one resource by two or more members (figure 27.6).
- False lock contention occurs when two locks hash to the same entry in the lock table but the actual locks are not in contention (figure 27.7).
- XES contention occurs because XES interprets locks only as X or S. Therefore, some locks that are in contention are actually compatible because they are really intent locks (figure 27.8).

To determine whether you are experiencing too much contention and how to resolve or lessen it, refer to Chapter 33, "Long-Term Monitoring."

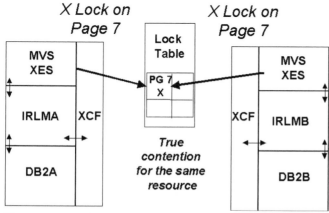

Figure 27.6   Global Contention

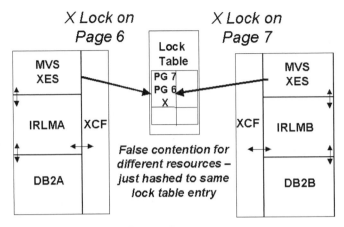

Figure 27.7   False Contention

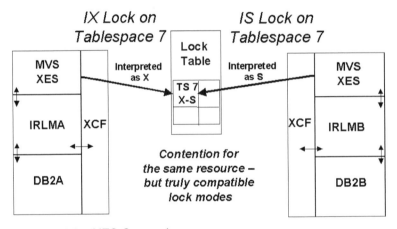

Figure 27.8   XES Contention

Deadlock Considerations

Resolving deadlocks in a data sharing environment can be rather expensive in terms of time, even though the CPU overhead of deadlock detection is negligible. The GLM with the lowest ID takes responsibility for doing deadlock resolution. In a highly tuned environment, you may want to consider the DB2 that is the originating member (if it also has the IRLM with the lowest ID). Is this a fast machine with lots of CPU? Or is it the least busy? Of course, you are probably not concerned with this, since you will not be having any deadlocks because you have an optimal database design and proper workload distribution in the data sharing group—right? However, this best way to ensure fast and efficient deadlock detection is to be sure that the DEADLOK parameter in the IRLMPROC is set to (5,1). You can specify lower numbers for quicker detection if necessary. Higher numbers will be ignored.

What is important to understand about deadlock contention and resolution in a data sharing environment is the cost to your application performance. To resolve deadlocks, a lot of message passing must occur outside the coupling facility, which is time-consuming and expensive. Deadlock detection cycles can also take longer in a data sharing environment than in a single-subsystem environment. The process of detection and resolution can also be further delayed if there are XCF signaling delays, a large number of global waits, or IRLM latch contention. You should take all measures to avoid deadlocks in your applications and physical design.

Group Buffer Pools

$\mathbf{G}$roup buffer pools (GBPs) are structures in the coupling facility in a data sharing environment. They allow the sharing of data among multiple subsystems. In a data sharing environment, one key performance issue is how well you control the caching and writing of data. We look at some of the issues of designing and tuning group buffer pools.

Page Registration

Page directory entries are used to check the existence of a page copy in the group buffer pool. They are also used to determine which members need to be sent XI (cross-invalidation) signals. Only one directory entry is needed for a page, regardless of how many virtual buffer pools it is cached in.

Registration

Interest in a page is registered in the page directory when a page is read by a member from disk into the local buffer pool or the group buffer pool (for a group buffer pool–dependent page set). With CFLEVEL 2 or above, DB2 prefetch can register up to 32 pages with a single coupling facility interaction; otherwise, registering is done on a page-by-page basis. When a page set or partition becomes GBP dependent, all changed pages in the local buffer pool are moved synchronously into the GBP. All these pages, both clean and changed, are registered in the directory in the GBP (figure 28.1).

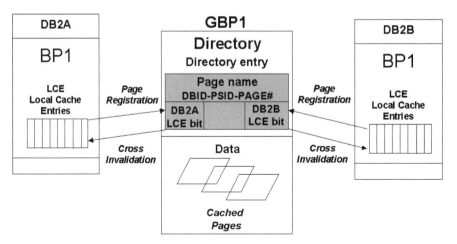

Figure 28.1   GBP Directory and Data Entries

Deregistration

A few situations can cause the deregistration of a page. If buffers are stolen from the local buffer pool of a GBP-dependent page set, the page is deregistered. If the new page belongs to a GBP-dependent object, the registration of the new page and the deregistration of the old page are handled with one request to the coupling facility. However, this buffer stealing could indicate a problem with either the size or threshold of the virtual buffer pool, because the pages are falling off the LRU queue. This is not a problem if the page is not re-referenced, but if it is needed and has to be read back into the virtual buffer pool, it must also be re-registered.

If an existing directory entry that still has registered interest must be reclaimed for new work, the reclaim sends XIs for the old page, marking it invalid before deregistering it and assigning the directory entry to the new page. If the original page is re-referenced, it has to be reread from disk. This can happen if the group buffer pool is too small or its ratio is incorrect. For information on how to monitor this, refer to Chapter 33, "Long-Term Monitoring." If inter-DB2 read or write interest is gone and the page is no longer GBP dependent, the page is deregistered, and the dirty pages are cast out to disk and purged from the GBP.

Sizing

Sizing group buffer pools is not like sizing normal virtual buffer pools. The group buffer pools are defined as structures in the coupling facility. They are given an initial size when they are defined in the CFRM policy and for performance and availability reasons should be created in a coupling facility separate from the coupling facility that holds the lock and SCA (shared communication area) structures. It must also have enough room for fail-over in the other coupling facility in the event of a failure (figure 28.2). However, implementation of group buffer pool duplexing (discussed later in this chapter) changes the required size somewhat.

For the best sizing of group buffer pools, you have to understand the amount of sharing of the objects in the group buffer pool that will occur. In other words, you are going to have to worry about object separation in virtual buffer pools even more when implementing group buffer pools; otherwise, your initial size estimates will be rather difficult.

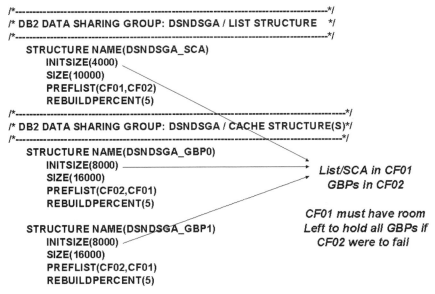

```
/*-------------------------------------------------------------------*/
/* DB2 DATA SHARING GROUP: DSNDSGA / LIST STRUCTURE   */
/*-------------------------------------------------------------------*/
     STRUCTURE NAME(DSNDSGA_SCA)
          INITSIZE(4000)
          SIZE(10000)
          PREFLIST(CF01,CF02)
          REBUILDPERCENT(5)
/*-------------------------------------------------------------------*/
/* DB2 DATA SHARING GROUP: DSNDSGA / CACHE STRUCTURE(S)*/
/*-------------------------------------------------------------------*/
     STRUCTURE NAME(DSNDSGA_GBP0)
          INITSIZE(8000)
          SIZE(16000)
          PREFLIST(CF02,CF01)
          REBUILDPERCENT(5)

     STRUCTURE NAME(DSNDSGA_GBP1)
          INITSIZE(8000)
          SIZE(16000)
          PREFLIST(CF02,CF01)
          REBUILDPERCENT(5)
```

List/SCA in CF01
GBPs in CF02

CF01 must have room
Left to hold all GBPs if
CF02 were to fail

Figure 28.2 Sample CFRM

Generic Guidelines and Rules of Thumb

Some guidelines have been published for sizing group buffer pools, but they are all so generic that they can be considered only a starting point. You have to consider so many aspects of objects in the group buffer pools that any generic "one-size-fits-all" formula is almost useless. You have to consider such questions as these:

1. How many members currently in the data sharing group share the data in the group buffer pool, and how many members are going to be added in the future?
2. Is there use for affinity processing in the group? If some subsystems are not going to use the data in the group buffer pool but still have a virtual pool that is backed by a group buffer pool, why include their virtual pool size in the sizing formula?
3. Were existing subsystems merged into the group, or were they new, clean installs? If subsystems were merged, it is doubtful that all virtual buffer pools are using the same separation strategies.
4. What about GBPCACHE(NONE) and GBPCACHE(SYSTEM)?
5. Is the group buffer pool going to use GBPCACHE(NO)?
6. Are the virtual buffer pools sized correctly?
7. What is the size of the pages in the virtual pools (4K, 8K, 6K, 32K)?

Listed below are the general rules of thumb for sizing group buffer pools. As you can see, a lot of assumptions are made here, so be careful if you choose to use these formulas, and be sure to monitor the group buffer pools and adjust their sizes accordingly.

- For objects defined with GBPCACHE(CHANGED), take the total allocation of all members' virtual pools and hiperpools and multiply by 10% (for light sharing with little updating), 20% (for medium sharing with moderate updating), or 40% (for much sharing and lots of updating).
- For objects defined with GBPCACHE(ALL), take the total allocation of all members' virtual pools *only* and multiply by 50% (for few data sets), 75% (for half the data sets), or 100% (when almost everything is shared).

Keep in mind that oversizing local buffer pools is not of any benefit in a data sharing environment and that if you use GBPCACHE(ALL), hiperpools are not used.

GBP Sizing for Cached and Changed, Noncached, and LOB Data

Recently some more specific formulas have been published for specific types of data (see *IBM Data Sharing Planning and Administration,* SC26-9007-00). These take into account whether or not the data is cached and LOB usage. For sizing a group buffer pool where all data is cached, the rules of thumb mentioned earlier can provide some guidelines.

Caching Changed Data

For group buffer pools that cache changed data, first calculate the estimated number of data entries by using a variable to represent the estimated degree of data sharing (U in the following formula). For U, use one of these values:

1—high degree of data sharing and high update activity

0.7—moderate sharing and moderate update activity

0.5—low amount of sharing and low update activity

$$\text{Data entries} = \text{Degree of data sharing } (U) \times \text{Pages written to disk per second for all members } (D) \times \text{Page residency time in GBP in seconds } (R)$$

This gives an estimate of the number of data entries needed to store cache pages for a period of time suitable for the necessary re-referencing of the pages. Next, take this number times the page size (P) of the pages in the group buffer pool (4, 8, 16, or 32K) to determine the size of the actual data entry, and divide this by 1,024 (1K) to get the size in megabytes required for the data entries.

Next, you need to determine the number of directory entries required. Add up the number of data pages required for all the hiperpools (HP) for all members plus the total number of data pages for virtual buffer pools (VP) across all members. Take this result times the estimated degree of data sharing determined earlier (U). Add this result to the data entries. This provides an estimated number of pages that will need to be registered in the directory. But you still need to determine their size, so take this result times 1.1 (which is additional storage required for the coupling facility control structures) and then times 0.2K (the size of a directory entry). Divide this by 1,024 (1K) to get the size in megabytes needed for the directory entries.

Now you need to size the group buffer pool and determine the directory/data entry ratio. Add together the amounts determined for the data entries and the directory entries. The result is the total megabytes required for your group buffer pool. You can then divide the directory entries by the data entries to get the estimated ratio.

In summary, these are the calculations for sizing a GBP that caches changed data:

$$U \times D \times R = \text{Number of data entries}$$

$$\text{Data entries} \times P/1{,}024 = \text{Data entries (MB)}$$

$$\text{Data entries} + [U \times (VP + HP)] = \text{Number of directory entries}$$

$$1.1 \times \text{Directory entries} \times 0.2/1{,}024 = \text{Directory entries (MB)}$$

$$\text{Data entries (MB)} + \text{Directory entries (MB)} = \text{Group buffer pool (MB)}$$

$$\text{Directory entries/Data entries} = \text{Ratio}$$

Caching No Data

For group buffer pools that do not cache data, first calculate the estimated number of directory entries by using a variable to represent the estimated degree of data sharing (U). For U, use one of these values:

1—high degree of data sharing and high update activity

0.7—moderate sharing and moderate update activity

0.5—low amount of sharing and low update activity

Directory entries = Degree of data sharing (U) × (Total number of pages in all virtual pools (VP) + Total number of pages in all hiperpools (HP))

Multiply the degree of data sharing by the total number of pages in the virtual and hiperpools for all members. This gives the total number of pages that will need to be registered in the directory. Remember, even if you do not cache data, it still must be registered for cross-invalidation purposes. You still need to determine the size, so take this result times 1.1 (additional storage required for the coupling facility control structures) and then times 0.2K (size of a directory entry). Divide this by 1,024 (1K) to get the size in megabytes needed for the directory entries. Remember, the ratio is not needed here because it will be ignored.

In summary, these are the calculations for sizing a GBP that does not cache data:

$$U \times (VP + HP) = \text{Data entries}$$

$$1.1 \times \text{Directory entries} \times 0.2/1{,}024 = \text{Directory entries (MB)}$$

$$\text{Directory entries (MB)} = \text{Group buffer pool (MB)}$$

Caching LOB Space Maps

If you plan to have a group buffer pool for LOB and it is defined as GBPCACHE (SYSTEM) to cache only the space map pages, there is an another formula to consider.

First calculate the estimated number of data entries by using a variable to represent the estimated degree of data sharing (U). Use one of these values for U:

1—high degree of data sharing and high update activity

0.7—moderate sharing and moderate update activity

0.5—low amount of sharing and low update activity

$$\text{Data entries} = (\text{Degree of data sharing } (U) \times \text{Pages written to disk per second}$$
$$\text{for all members } (D)/10) \times \text{Page residency time in GBP in seconds } (R)$$

When determining the pages written to disk per second, you need a count of pages per member. You can get this count from the PAGES WRITTEN field in the statistics report. Divide this count by 10 for an estimate of the LOB system pages written per LOB data page, and then take this times the degree of data sharing (U), and then multiply by the residency time (R). This gives you an estimate of the number of data entries needed to store space map pages for a period of time suitable for any necessary re-referencing. Next, take this number times the page size (P) of the pages in the group buffer pool (4, 8, 16, or 32K) to determine the size of the actual data entry, and divide this by 1,024 (1K) to get the size in megabytes required for the data entries.

Next, to determine the number of directory entries required, add up the number of data pages required for all the hiperpools (HP) for all members plus the total number of data pages for virtual buffer pools (VP) across all members. Take this result times the estimated degree of data sharing determined earlier (U). Add this result to the data entries. This provides an estimated number of pages that will need to be registered in the directory. But you still need to determine the size, so take this result times 1.1 (additional storage required for the coupling facility control structures) and then times 0.2K (the size of a directory entry). Divide all of this by 1,024 (1K) to get the size in megabytes needed for the directory entries.

Now you need to size the group buffer pool and determine the directory/data entry ratio, which is a little different for LOBs. Add together the amounts determined for the data entries and directory entries. The result is the total megabytes required for your group buffer pool. You can then divide the directory entries by the data entries to get the estimated ratio. For the LOB space map pages, if the ratio you calculate is greater than 255, use 255 as the ratio. The maximum is 255 because this is the largest numerical value that can be stored in a byte. (This maximum will probably change in the future to support the correct ratio for LOBs using GBPCACHE (SYSTEM).)

In summary, these are the calculations for sizing a GBP that caches LOB space maps:

$$(U \times D/10) \times R = \text{Number of data entries}$$

$$\text{Data entries} \times P/1{,}024 = \text{Data entries (MB)}$$

$$[U \times (VP + HP)] + \text{Data entries} = \text{Number of directory entries}$$

$$1.1 \times \text{Directory entries} \times 0.2/1{,}024 = \text{Directory entries (MB)}$$

$$\text{Data entries (MB)} + \text{Directory entries (MB)} = \text{Group buffer pool (MB)}$$

$$\text{MIN (Directory entries/Data entries, 255)} = \text{Ratio}$$

These formulas provide a much more accurate way of calculating the group buffer pool size and ratio. Keep in mind that these do still add up all pages in all the members' virtual buffer pools and hiperpools. If you are using affinity processing, you may not want to include all of the members' pools in the calculation. Also, do not forget that when new members join the group, you may have to resize.

As you see, to size a group buffer pool appropriately, you need to start by placing objects in separate buffer pools first, based on whether they are shared or not, and then further separate them by whether all the pages for these objects, just the changed pages, or no pages need to be cached. Also, be sure that the buffer pool usage is the same on every subsystem in the data-sharing group.

The bottom line here is that there really is no one formula for sizing group buffer pools. *Adherence to generic formulas means generic performance.* Choose your formula wisely, monitor, and be sure to leave room in your coupling facility structure definitions for growth.

Tuning

First of all, if you are not implementing good local (virtual) buffer pool standards, good luck tuning your GBPs, because the same rules apply! You need to have a clear separation of buffer pools by the type and the use of the data, because tuning the size and the parameters of the GBPs depends on these factors, just as sizing and tuning virtual buffer pools do. It is recommended that virtual buffer pools on all subsystems in the data sharing group have the same size and thresholds (figure 28.3). For more guidelines for buffer pool breakouts and settings, refer to Chapter 3, "Memory."

Ratio

The ratio of the number of directory entries to the number of data entries is a setting on the group buffer pool. If you do not have enough directory entries (one entry for each page read on any DB2 member, only one page registered regardless of the number of members with interest), then when a new page needs to be registered, a directory entry is reclaimed to register a new page. This causes the process requiring the page to have to go to disk to reread and register the page. Depending on the number of times this occurs, it can add up to significant overhead. Use the -DISPLAY GROUPBUFFERPOOL command to determine how

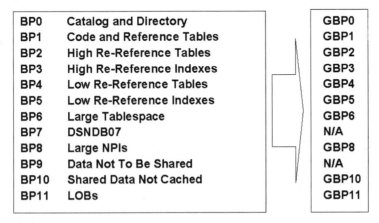

BP0	Catalog and Directory	GBP0
BP1	Code and Reference Tables	GBP1
BP2	High Re-Reference Tables	GBP2
BP3	High Re-Reference Indexes	GBP3
BP4	Low Re-Reference Tables	GBP4
BP5	Low Re-Reference Indexes	GBP5
BP6	Large Tablespace	GBP6
BP7	DSNDB07	N/A
BP8	Large NPIs	GBP8
BP9	Data Not To Be Shared	N/A
BP10	Shared Data Not Cached	GBP10
BP11	LOBs	GBP11

Ideally the virtual bufferpools should be sized the same on all subsystems with appropriate thresholds

Figure 28.3 Virtual Pools and Group Buffer Pools

many times this occurs. IFCID 0255 can also be used to determine the number of occurrences of a buffer refresh caused by cross-invalidation of a data page in the GBP to give
you an idea of the number of reads and updates occurring among the members.

Castout and Checkpoint

Since there is no connection between the coupling facility and disk, DB2 must have a way
to move changed pages out to disk. It does this through a process called castout. The
castout process (performed by castout engines) moves the changed pages from the group
buffer pool through a private area in the DBM1 address space (*not* a virtual buffer pool) to
disk (Figure 28.4).

The castout process is triggered when the number of changed pages exceeds the
CLASST threshold, when the number of changed pages exceeds the GBPOOLT threshold,
when a pseudo-close or physical close is performed on a data set by the last updating
member. Think of the CLASST threshold the same as the VDWQT threshold on local
buffer pools, and the GBPOOLT threshold as the DWQT threshold.

CLASST

The CLASST threshold is monitored by the castout owner for a particular page set
that is assigned to a particular changed class queue (figure 28.5). Pages are assigned to
class queues and are generally kept together by table space and index space. There are
1,024 changed class queues used, and they are managed in LRU order. When the number

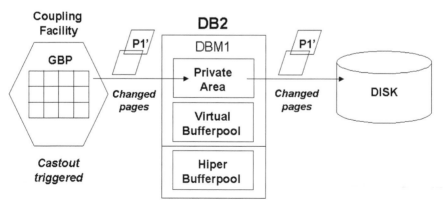

Figure 28.4 GBP Castout Process

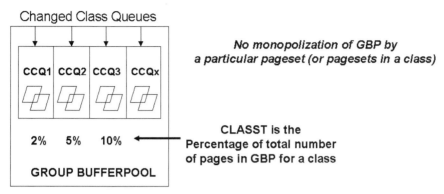

Figure 28.5 CLASST Threshold

of changed pages in a class reaches the CLASST threshold (the percentage of changed pages in the group buffer pool), the pages are cast out to disk (figure 28.6). The default for CLASST is 10%. You should drive your castout processes by this threshold as much as possible to keep the writes constant. When the threshold is hit, the castout owner begins to cast out the pages. The purpose of this threshold is to keep a particular page set from monopolizing the group buffer pool.

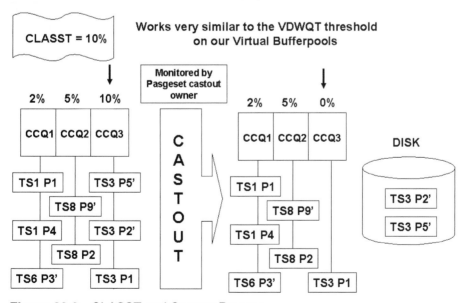

Figure 28.6 CLASST and Castout Process

GBPOOLT

The GBPOOLT threshold is monitored by the structure owner for the GBP, and when this threshold is reached, the pages are cast out until a reverse threshold of 10% is reached (figure 28.7). The default for the GBPOOLT is 50% (figure 28.8). The default for the CLASST threshold may not be bad in most cases, but a default of 50% for the GBPOOLT threshold is probably not suitable unless the objects in that buffer pool have a lot of re-referencing. If you allow the GBPOOLT threshold to control all writes, you may run out of write engines. You can use IFCID 0262 to get summary statistics each time the GBPOOLT is reached. Use this to monitor how efficiently the threshold is handling work. Use IFCID 0263 to get summary statistics for the castouts done by the page set and partition castout owners.

GBPCHECKPOINT

The group buffer pool checkpoint is the time in which all changed pages are cast out to disk and an LRSN (log record sequence number) is recorded in the log. When a checkpoint is reached, it is the responsibility of the castout owners to begin to cast pages out to disk. The default for this is eight minutes, but it needs to be adjusted for each group buffer pool, depending on the usage and re-reference of the data in the group buffer pool. Remember, you have to adjust this value in conjunction with the CLASST and GBPOOLT parameters, which also drive the castout process. You can use IFCID 0261 to obtain additional information about GBP checkpoints.

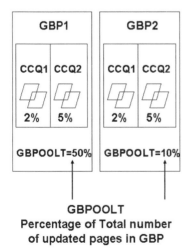

Figure 28.7 Castout and GBPOOLT Threshold

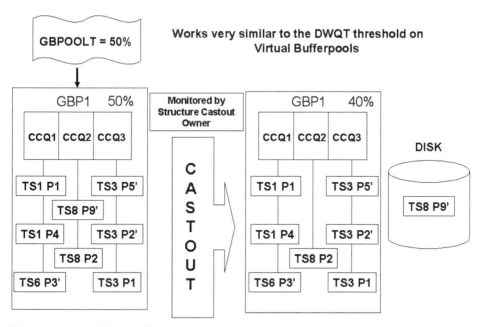

Figure 28.8   GBPOOLT and Castout Process

If checkpoints are not advancing the LRSN fast enough, you should decrease the interval. You can determine how fast the checkpoint is advancing by issuing the -DIS GROUPBUFFERPOOL command. This shows the LRSN of the last checkpoint taken (figure 28.9). The best interval is one that achieves balance between the performance impact of frequent group buffer pool checkpoints and the impact on recovery. The lower the checkpoint interval, the higher the resource consumption due to more frequent checkpoints. The higher the checkpoint interval, the slower the recovery from a group buffer pool failure due to the extended time between checkpoints.

Tuning castout thresholds and the group buffer pool checkpoint interval is similar to tuning virtual buffer pools. Tuning these thresholds depends on the referencing rates of the

```
-DISPLAY GROUPBUFFERPOOL(GBP1)

-DB2P LAST GROUP BUFFERPOOL CHECKPOINT 16:20:01 APRIL 1, 1999
        GBP CHECKPOINT RECOVERY LRSN          = ABFE83C11EF30
        STRUCTURE OWNER                       = DB2P
```

Figure 28.9   Viewing the Checkpoint LRSN

data by the application. In figure 28.10, you can see an example of how you could set the thresholds and the checkpoint interval for highly re-referenced data and rarely re-referenced data.

Forcing Castout Ownership

Here is a quick thought on controlling castout performance. In high-performance situations, if you do a good deal of affinity processing (not using WLM), you may be able to control which DB2 is responsible for the castout process, thus forcing a less active member to become castout owner. You may want to drive castout through a subsystem that has less I/O activity to get better castout performance. Remember, the castout process drives the changed pages through the DBM1 address space on their way to disk, so you may not want castout to occur on a subsystem where the DBM1 address space is already constrained. It is best to try to control by forcing the structure owner. You should force ownership to a member by having the member first allocate and then use the group buffer pools. Then use this member to drive I/O to disk. This is not an easy task to accomplish, and it does not always guarantee success, so be careful.

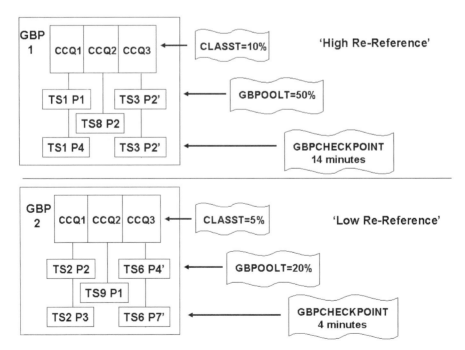

Figure 28.10   Castout Threshold and Checkpoint

GBPCACHE Option

GBPCACHE (ALL) can be used to cache all pages in the group buffer pool, even if they are not changed. The primary time to do this is when some very 'hot' pages would benefit from remaining in the GBP. Also, if you use 3390 disk cache, it is possible for there to be less overhead for reading pages from the cache than from the GBP. For example, reading 32 pages from a GBP incurs more CPU overhead than scheduling a single request to read 32 contiguous pages from disk (cache); therefore, this would out perform GBPCACHE (ALL) and would not require as large a GBP. In general, however, if you use the latest and greatest model of coupling facility, the coupling facility reads are almost always cheaper than disk reads, even with the enhanced cached disks.

There are a couple of other reasons to use GBPCACHE (ALL), but they need to be evaluated carefully. One is to cache pages for very large table spaces that are infrequently used and for very large indexes. This allows you to free up the pages that were defined to hold these objects in the individual members' virtual buffer pools, leaving the pages in the group buffer pool for access. Another reason is to cache entire objects that are small and infrequently referenced, such as seldom used code and reference tables.

GBPCACHE (CHANGED) is the default, suitable for most situations. This option caches only the changed pages in the GBP; however, clean pages are still registered in the GBP for cross-invalidation purposes (figure 28.11). (You will have directory entries, but no data entries.)

DB2 Version 6 now offers a few new options for GBP caching. GBPCACHE (NONE) allows you to use the GBP only for cross-invalidation purposes, with no data pages cached and all changes written directly to disk. This is rarely needed but is very useful in a high-insert, low-re-reference environment where it is not necessary to keep the updated pages in the GBP. The other new option, GBPCACHE (SYSTEM), allows only the space map pages to be GBP dependent, and all other pages are written directly to disk. This option is applicable only to LOBs (introduced in version 6), to prevent these extremely large objects from using the coupling facility. Both of these options help performance in the coupling facility, but the trade-off is the overhead associated with the immediate writes and reads to and from disk versus to and from the group buffer pool. However, GBPCACHE (NONE) is not recommended for availability purposes. A better option for availability is to use group buffer pool duplexing. The dynamic intersystem interest tracking has been recently enhanced to help lessen the need for this option for heavy insert and low re-reference.

You can also change GBPCACHE option through ALTER at the group buffer pool level. The GBPCACHE(YES) option on the group buffer pool means that the buffer pool

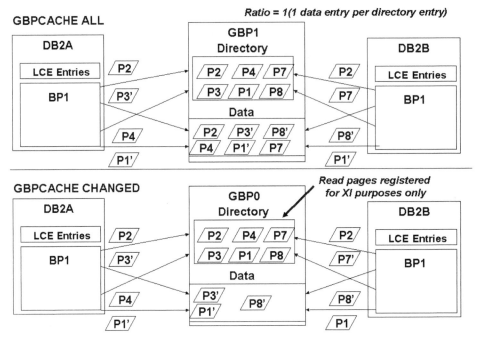

Figure 28.11   GBPCACHE ALL versus GBPCACHE CHANGED

is used as usual and the value specified in the page set or partition GBPCACHE option is used for caching. If the group buffer pool is defined as GBPCACHE(NO), all changed pages are written to disk, not to the group buffer pool. Damage assessment is avoided, and no data is needed during a recovery. It is less disruptive to change this setting than to change the page set attribute. It takes precedence over the GBPCACHE option on the page set. You can use different types of processing at different times of the day, because there may be times when caching is not necessary. It is recommended that you put objects that do not require caching into a group buffer pool defined with GBPCACHE(NO) and do not mix page sets with different caching options—say, some with GBPCACHE (CHANGED) and some with GBPCACHE (NONE)—because this makes appropriate sizing very difficult and inaccurate. If a group buffer pool is defined with GBPCACHE(NO), the ratio is ignored because there is no storage of data.

The question to be answered is when to cache. There is no need to cache an updated page that is rarely re-referenced, for example, a batch job sequentially updating a large table. Not caching offers a performance benefit for the application in these cases: the cost of transferring data to and casting out from GBP is saved, which in turn saves the cost of synchronous I/O to disk during a commit. Additional overhead reduction can also be achieved by reducing the amount of synchronous disk I/O at commit by lowering the DWQT threshold on the virtual buffer pool so that DB2 writes more page asynchronously prior to the commit. To help you determine whether you should be caching at all, you can look at group buffer pool statistics. If the ratio of READS, DATA RETURNED/PAGES WRITTEN is less than 1%, you may benefit from using GBPCACHE(NONE) or maybe GBPCACHE (NO) at the GBP level.

Group Buffer Pool Dependency

Group buffer pool dependency of a data set occurs if a data set is open for read access by one or more DB2 members and open for read/write access by another member. Dependency can also occur if there are changed pages in the group buffer pool that have not been cast out. The reason you need to be concerned with group buffer pool dependency is that it affects data sharing overhead. The amount of activity in the group buffer pool is driven by the number of data sets that are GBP dependent. This dependency can also drive additional lock propagation to the coupling facility.

You can issue the -DISPLAY BUFFERPOOL command to show whether a page set is GBP dependent (version 6 only). You can issue a -DISPLAY DATABSE LOCKS command to show whether P-locks are being held. For a look at the output of each these commands, refer to Chapter 33, "Long-Term Monitoring."

PCLOSEN and PCLOSET

When a data set moves from read only to read/write or from read/write to read only, it moves in and out of the group buffer pool (which affects whether or not the data set is GBP dependent). This movement is performed during a pseudo-open or pseudo-close.

- Pseudo-open occurs when a page set is first physically updated, after it was already opened in a read-only state.
- Pseudo-close occurs when a page set has not been updated for a period of time (determined by PCLOSEN and PCLOSET). Interest goes from read/write to read only.

This process narrows the range of log records necessary for recovery of a page set and is partially controlled by the PCLOSEN and PCLOSET DSNZPARMs. You do not want these parameters so low that they continually drive data sets in and out of the group buffer pool. It is recommended that you set the PCLOSEN ZPARM (number of checkpoints between write activities before a data set is closed) very high to virtually disable it, thus allowing you to control data set closure through the PCLOSET ZPARM (amount of time between write activities before the data set is closed). You can set PCLOSET at 15 or 20 minutes and then monitor the number of data set closures, which can cause excessive overhead. Improvements were made in version 6 to help reduce elapsed time for open and close activity for data sets (approximately 20% according to initial testing by IBM, reported in SG24-5351-00). This came about with DFSMS/MVS 1.5 enhanced catalog sharing, which allows MVS catalog information to be stored in the coupling facility so that it can be shared among the members in the sysplex.

Group Buffer Pool Duplexing

Eliminating unplanned outages is always a goal, both in systems and within the DBMS component. A group buffer pool recovery can take a significant amount of time, since DB2 has to recover data from the logs. To eliminate this single point of failure in data sharing,

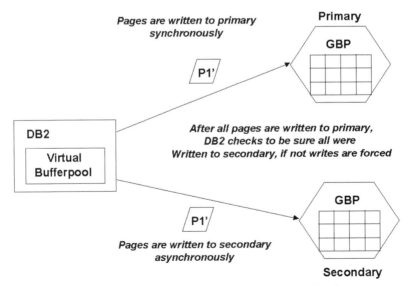

Figure 28.12   Writing to the Duplexed Group Buffer Pool

group buffer pools can now be duplexed, implementing the strategy of a hot backup. This feature allows the same buffer pool to reside in two different coupling facilities. Any changes made to the primary group buffer pool are reflected in the backup, and the backup can take over as the primary if the primary fails, without causing an outage. The backup group buffer pool receives only changed pages that are written to the primary. Thus, read operations are not affected by duplexing. When a page is updated, it is written asynchronously to the backup and synchronously to the primary (figure 28.12). Thus, the writes are overlapped for better performance. Also, when castouts occur, they are only written to disk from the primary group buffer pool. After the castout is complete, the pages are simply deleted from the backup.

Migration

T he purpose of this short chapter is not to walk you through the process of migrating to a data sharing environment, but rather to provide you with some tips and recommendations to help ease the pain of migration. In many ways, the commitment to move to data sharing is just that—a commitment, and a rather permanent one. The better prepared you are through proper planning and design, the easier it will be and the better overall performance will be.

Sharing of Data

Not all data must be shared just because the DB2 subsystem is a member in a data sharing group. As a matter of fact, there may be some data that should not be shared for security or other reasons. Objects can still be dedicated to one DB2 subsystem. Since the only way to share data among the members is to define a group buffer pool to back the virtual buffer pool in which an object is defined and to define that object on shared disk, the way to prevent particular data from being shared is to isolate it in its own virtual buffer pool with no group buffer pool. Figure 29.1 shows both shared and nonshared data in the data sharing group. The nonshared data in this case is the historical and archive data, which is processed only by DB2B, which is responsible for batch processing.

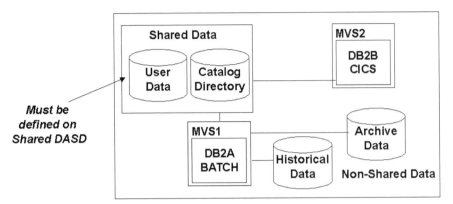

Figure 29.1 To Share or Not to Share

Policies and Structures

CFRM

When you define the policies to the coupling facilities, it is important to remember a few things. First, when you define the CFRM (coupling facility resource management) policy, make sure to leave room for growth of the structures. Be sure that you can dynamically increase a structure with a SETXCF command rather than having to change the CFRM and do a rebuild. The way to ensure this is to set the SIZE parameter larger that the INIT-SIZE parameter. SIZE really is the maximum to which you can increase a structure dynamically, and INITSIZE is the initial size of the structure. Of course, you should care-fully plan what the SIZE should be according to the space available in your coupling facil-ity and also account for fail-over conditions. A SIZE larger than the INITSIZE is generally recommended, but keep it around two to three times the INITSIZE for the SCA and lock structures. SIZE should be no more than four times the size of the group buffer pool struc-tures. In figure 29.2, you can see an example of the CFRM policy.

SFM

Be sure that you are aware of the settings in the SFM (sysplex failure management) policy, because it holds information about the importance of each system in the sysplex. During a

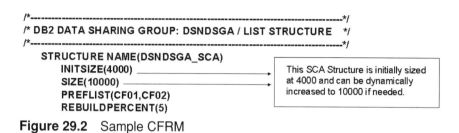

```
/*--------------------------------------------------------------------*/
/* DB2 DATA SHARING GROUP: DSNDSGA / LIST STRUCTURE   */
/*--------------------------------------------------------------------*/
     STRUCTURE NAME(DSNDSGA_SCA)
          INITSIZE(4000)
          SIZE(10000)
          PREFLIST(CF01,CF02)
          REBUILDPERCENT(5)
```

> This SCA Structure is initially sized at 4000 and can be dynamically increased to 10000 if needed.

Figure 29.2 Sample CFRM

coupling facility failure and subsequent structure rebuilds, the REBUILDPERCENT in the CFRM is compared to the WEIGHT in the SFM policy to determine whether or not to rebuild a structure (figure 29.3).

ARM

Using ARM (automatic restart manager) is optional but highly recommended. It is ARM's job to keep specific work running in the event of a failure. The more quickly you can get DB2 restarted in the event of a hardware failure or ABEND, the better. It is important for availability that all retained locks be resolved quickly. The only way to do this is to restart the failing member, and this is where ARM is critical.

```
DATA TYPE(SFM)
DEFINE POLICY NAME(POLICY1) CONNFAIL(NO) REPLACE(YES)
     SYSTEM NAME(*)
          ISOLATETIME(0)
DEFINE POLICY NAME(POLICY2) CONNFAIL(YES) REPLACE(YES)
     SYSTEM NAME(*)
          ISOLATETIME(0)
          WEIGHT(5)
     SYSTEMNAME(SYS1)
          PROMPT
          WEIGHT(25)
```

> WEIGHT given to an MVS and compared to REBUILDPERCENT in CFRM during a CF failure

Figure 29.3 Sample SFM

Lock, SCA, and GBP Structures

Here are a few guidelines for establishing the structures in the coupling facility necessary to support DB2 data sharing. The lock and SCA structures are pretty simple to size. While there are calculations you can follow in the IBM manuals, there are also easier methods that have been proven effective in many shops.

The SCA structure is the easiest: size it at 32 MB. That's it. The lock structure is fairly straightforward as well. Most organizations size this structure at 32 MB also. If you have a very busy shop with more than 5,000 lock and unlock requests a second, you may consider a 64MB structure. The only other thing to keep in mind about the lock and SCA structures is that you should have enough space in the alternate coupling facility to be able to rebuild them during a failure, because without them your data sharing group is powerless.

That leaves the group buffer pool structure. Unfortunately, sizing the group buffer pool structure is a little more complex, and a few more factors need to be considered. Please refer to Chapter 28, "Group Buffer Pools."

Naming Conventions

The establishment of a flexible naming convention is the most important planning event in the process of migrating to a data sharing environment. When done properly, it reduces confusion and operational and administration errors and allows easy extension of the sysplex. Plan names carefully, because some cannot be changed at all, and changes are difficult and often error prone.

The names need to be unique within the sysplex, and several categories of names need to be decided, such as group-level names, DB2 member-level names, IRLM group and member Names, subsystem data sets (DB2), and ICF catalog names. Many organizations have to change from their current naming convention (which may give your standards people a heart attack). Of course, this depends on migration options, in particular, whether you are starting a data sharing group from scratch or migrating existing systems into the group.

Figure 29.4 shows some of the objects you will need to name for the data sharing group. This figure shows a two-way data sharing group, and you can see how the group name established the naming convention for the group. The DB0G in the group name was used in some high-level objects (such as the coupling facility structures and the data set high-level qualifier), and each subsystem and its objects use DBxG, where x is a number

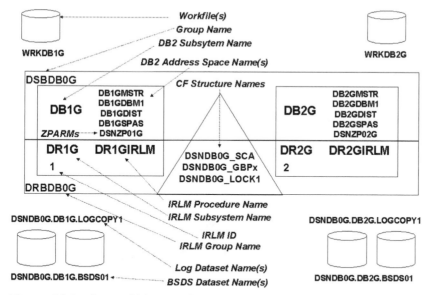

Figure 29.4   Some Objects to Name

to identify the subsystem. This is a very high level example. Depending on how many members you have in a subsystem and how the migration occurs, naming can be a time-consuming task, but a very important one. In figure 29.5 is a sample spreadsheet that can help you begin to lay out your naming convention. Start with your existing subsystem, and then develop a naming standard beginning with the group definition and the first member (new or existing). Then use this as a worksheet for applying the naming standard through-out all the objects in the group. The worksheet serves as a nice reference in the future.

Here are some recommendations for naming conventions and descriptions that may help explain the previous figures. For more information, refer to the IBM *Data Sharing Planning and Administration Guide* (SC26-9007-00). Following are a few points on the names in a data sharing environment:

I. Group-level names (owned by group, one per group)
   A. DB2 group name
      1. Defines the data sharing group to the operating system
      2. Seen when displaying via D XCF,GROUP
      3. Do not use A or I as first character, which can cause confusion with XCF group names

	Prior to Datasharing	Data Sharing Group	Originating Member	Member 'x'
Group Names				
DB2 Group		DSBDB0G		
Catalog Alias	DB0G	DB0G		
DB2 Group Attach		DB0G		
Location	DB0G			
Generic LU	DB0G01			
IRLM Group		DRBDB0G		
CF Structure Names				
Lock		DSBDB0G_LOCK		
SCA		DSBDB0G_SCA		
GBP		DSBDB0G_GBPx		
DB2 Member Names				
Member	DB0G		DB0G	DB1G
Subsystem	DB0G		DB0G	DB1G
LU	DB0G01		DB0G01	DB0G01
Command Prefix		"-"	DB0G	DB1G
Workfiles	DSNDB07		WRKDB0G	WRKDB1G
Address Spaces	DB0GMSTR,DB0GDBM1		DB0GMSTR,DB0GDBM1	DB1GMSTR,DB1GDBM1
DSNZPARMs	DB0GPARM		DB0GPARM	DB1GPARM
BSDS	DB0G.BSDS01		DB0G.BSDS01	DB1G.BSDS01
Active Log Datasets	DB0G.LOGCOPY.DS01		DB0G.LOGCOPY.DS01	DB1G.LOGCOPY.DS01
Archive Log Datasets	DB0G.ARCHLOG1.xxxx		DB0G.ARCHLOG1.xxxx	DB1G.ARCHLOG1.xxxx
DB2 Target Libraries	DB0G.REF.SDSNxxxx		DB0G.REF.SDSNxxxx	DB1G.REF.SDSNxxxx
IRLM Member Names				
IRLM Subsystem	DR0G		DR0G	DR1G
Procedure	DR0GIRLM		DR0GIRLM	DR1GIRLM

Figure 29.5   Sample Worksheet for Naming Conventions

B. IRLM group name

   1. Defines the IRLM data sharing group

C. Location name

   1. Each DSG has one DDF location name

   2. Make group name and location name the same

D. Group attach name

   1. Generic 4-byte name used by applications from TSO of CAF

   2. Allows attachment to any member running on that MVS

E. DRDA port

   1. DRDA port number for group if using TCP/IP

   2. 446 is recommended

F. Sysplex domain name

   1. Location.sysplexname

   2. Used for workload balancing with TCP/IP

   3. Must be registered in domain name server

    G. ICF catalog names (alias names)

        1. Recommendation: same as group name

II. Member-level names (owned by each member in the group, one per member)

    A. DB2 member name

        1. Name that DB2 passes to MVS to join its DSG

    B. Subsystem name

        1. Name used by all attachment interfaces

        2. Prefix for startup procedures

        3. Recommendation: same as member name

    C. Command prefix

        1. Default is concatenation of '-' with subsystem name

        2. Default recommended

    D. Work-file DB name

        1. DSNDB07 can no longer be used, as it is unique to a member

        2. Each member has its own work-file database

        3. Base the name on the member name, e.g., DB2A is member and subsystem and WRKDB2A is workfile

    E. ZPARM load module name

        1. Each member has its own ZPARM load module

        2. Base the name on the member name

        3. Can have several since version 4, specified as a parameter in the DB2 startup procedure

    F. IRLM subsystem name

        1. Name that defines the IRLM subsystem

    G. IRLM procedure name

        1. Name of the IRLM startup procedure

    H. IRLM member ID

        1. Unique number assigned to each IRLM in the group

    I. LU name

        1. Logical unit name

        2. Unique within the group and the network

    J. Member domain name

        1. Luname.location.sysplexname.domainname

        2. Allows DB2 to handle in-doubt TCP/IP threads

Workload Distribution Planning

How the workload is distributed across the data sharing group affects the sizing of coupling facility structures and certain aspects of hardware configurations. You really need to know how you plan to use the data sharing environment before you jump into it. It is important to configure the group adequately and not have any surprises.

Data sharing allows you to move parts of a DB2 application workload across processors in the sysplex. All processors in the sysplex have efficient and direct access to the same DB2 data. It is up to you to decide how that workload utilizes its resources.

Here are some ways you can distribute your workload:

- Execute batch jobs on separate processors
- Move CICS regions between processors
- Execute utilities on different processors

Data sharing allows you to move processing from away from processors with capacity constraints. This is probably one of the best and quickest benefits that can be realized by a system that is constrained and having problems completing its workload because it has simply outgrown its processor.

The way you configure your group buffer pools and the requests to them affects how you distribute the workload. All members can concurrently access data, or just one member can access data. The number of members accessing data directly affects the amount of data sharing overhead you experience and the hardware you need to support your workload.

CICS Workload Distribution

There are two ways to distribute your CICS workload: static and dynamic.

Static

Static workload distribution (also referred to as affinity processing) allows the workload to run on previously defined processors. This can help to reduce overhead of data sharing (no inter-DB2 interest) but also does not take advantage of data sharing. To implement static workload distribution, you can simply force affinity routing and route all CICS transactions accessing certain data through one particular region.

Dynamic

Dynamic workload distribution can run the work anywhere, based on defined criteria (i.e., capacity or availability). A CICS transaction can run on any processor in the sysplex. This removes application dependency on certain hardware or software. With dynamic workload distribution, you gain higher availability and improved processor usage, but your trade-off is higher data sharing overhead due to the potentially high amount of inter-DB2 read/write interest among the same page sets. You cannot use dynamic workload routing if you have existing affinities on the CICS transactions, if the required software does not exist on all processors in the sysplex, or if the necessary hardware components are not available.

With dynamic workload routing, the CICS sessions can be balanced across the sysplex dynamically using VTAM generic resources. VTAM interacts with the WLM to ensure that the processor usage is considered when choosing a TOR (terminal owning region) to establish a session with. The WLM defines performance goals for CICS transactions and can raise the priority of transactions during execution. The WLM works at the CICS region level to satisfy the performance goals defined for a CICS transaction. If a CICS transaction has a performance goal of less than 2 seconds 75% of the time and the goal is not being met, the WLM tries to meet the required goal by raising the priority of the CICS region in which the transaction is executing. Therefore, it is recommended to have CICS transactions that belong to high-priority applications run in different CICSPlexes, separate from the transactions that are associated with less important applications.

With CICSPlex SM Dynamic Transaction Routing, the workload can be routed among AORs (application owning regions) that are determined by availability and activity. You can route work away from busy or failing regions, which improves availability and conceals problems.

When trying to determine how to distribute your workload, keep in mind that the data sharing overhead is directly related to the amount of communication necessary among the members and the amount of access to the coupling facility structures. The more dynamic and flexible the workload, the higher the overhead. If a high level of flexibility is necessary, physical design and application tuning become more critical.

Distributed Workload

The DB2 data sharing group configuration is transparent to SQL users and programs. Connected users and programs have no awareness that a DB2 sysplex exists, and the system selects which DB2 member processes the SQL request. There are a few methods for supporting this selection.

Group Generic Method

By using VTAM generic resources (group generic method), the client requester connects to a generic LU name representing all members. Then VTAM controls which DB2 member's LU is selected. The workload is balanced at the client level (figure 29.6).

Member-Specific Method

The member-specific method uses the DDF sysplex support for distributed workload distribution. A client requester can connect to one or more real DB2 LU names, and then the MVS Workload Manager tells the client which DB2 LU names should be used. This method balances the workload at the thread level and can be stopped or started on an individual-member basis (figure 29.7).

Hard-Coded Method

In the hard-coded method, the client connects to a single DB2 member LU name. Thus, the client controls which DB2 member is selected, and the workload is balanced at the client level.

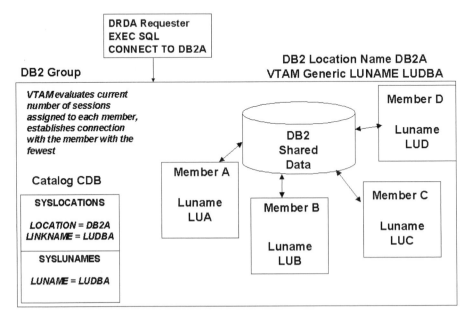

Figure 29.6   Group Generic Method

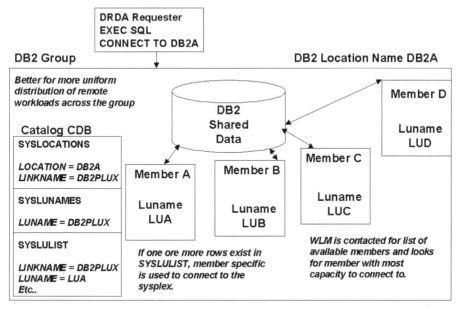

Figure 29.7   Member-Specific Method

Migration Considerations

When you move to data sharing, one all-important question must be answered up front. Do you start with a brand-new DB2 subsystem or merge existing subsystems? A new install makes monitoring the impact of data sharing easier. It gives you the freedom to introduce new naming standards and selectively move only necessary applications and objects to data sharing. It eases the initial pain. However it is not usually the option available to most shops.

Install or Merge

Most shops merge existing subsystems. There are some pros and cons of merging. The pros include easier movement of large applications and fewer distributed-processing implications. However, the cons include complications with catalog merge process because there is no automated tool to help with this process. Depending on number of objects and method, the catalog merge can be a laborious and error-prone process. Naming conventions for several objects are more complex because you have existing names to deal with. Recovery and availability of applications need to be revisited because each sub-system's applications have potentially different requirements.

You should not merge subsystems that do not need shared data, and you definitely should not merge test subsystems with production subsystems. You should merge subsystems if they are split out only because of capacity constraints, if they need common data, or if they currently rely on distributed connections or replication to satisfy needs that could be resolved by data sharing. When merging subsystems, be sure to evaluate the security schemas for all subsystems and ensure that the same level of security will be in place after they are merged.

Originating Member

When migrating existing systems, you also need to decide which DB2 subsystem will become the originating member. When you are installing or updating a DB2 subsystem using the GROUP keyword on DSNTIPA1, you are essentially defining a new data sharing group (figure 29.8). The member being installed or updated becomes the originating member of the group. This originating member is basically the house where the party is taking place; when people come over, it is BYOB (or rather BYOD—bring your own data), and the glasses (catalog and directory) are provided. The catalog and directory of the originating member becomes the new, centralized catalog for all members in the group. Choose this member wisely! Base your decision on the number of objects in this member and the number of objects in other members. All the objects in every joining member have to be moved to the catalog and directory of the originating member (figure 29.9).

```
DSNTIPA1        INSTALL, UPDATE, MIGRATE DB2 - MAIN PANEL
==>

Check parameters and reenter to change:

1   INSTALL TYPE              ==> INSTALL      Install,Update,or Migrate
2   DATA SHARING FUNCTION     ==> GROUP        None,Group,Member,or Enable

Enter the following value for migration only
3   DATA SET NAME(MEMBER)     ==>

...
```

Figure 29.8 Install Panel Example

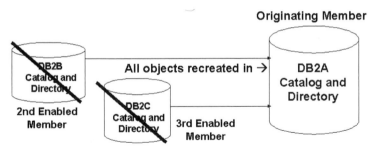

Figure 29.9 The Originating Member

Migration of Catalog and User Data

The actual migration of the catalog is not too bad (compared with the migration of the data, that is). You first decide to which catalog to migrate all other objects, taking into consideration the items previously mentioned. Query the catalog to determine which databases, table spaces, and indexes must be defined in the target system. Then define the objects in the target catalog using DDL. Depending on the number of objects for which you need to create DDL, this can be a cumbersome process, but we all save all our DDL, right? If not, you may need the help of a third-party tool to reverse engineer this DDL out of the catalog.

The migration of the user data is a bear. First, the user data needs to be moved to shared DASD, and the DBID, PSID, and OBIDs must be converted. There are a few options for doing the actual movement:

- Run a REORG with the ONLOAD ONLY option on sources
  - Use LOAD on target
  - Not recommended for large tables or large numbers of tables
- Perform a DSN1COPY using OBDIXLAT, RESET
  - Better for large tables and large numbers of tables
  - Can be risky
- Perform a REPAIR on the object
  - Better for large tables and large numbers of tables
  - Can also be risky: be sure not to mistype any IDs!
- Find someone who has developed an in-house process and borrow it!

When you perform a migration, it is ideal to first do this in a test environment for practice. You should have a test data sharing group totally separate from the production group.

Measuring the Migration

During the migration, you should measure statistics on the amount of overhead each member adds to the group. You should, of course, have baseline statistics before you perform any migration. Collect both accounting and statistics reports for your subsystems and critical applications. Then, after the first member is enabled as data sharing, take these measurements again. You will see some increases in overhead, particularly in class 2 TCB time, even for one-way data sharing, because all of the enablement pieces for connectivity to the coupling facility have to be in place and working, even though there is no inter-DB2 read/write interest. P-locks are still taken, even in one-way data sharing. The overhead increase should be about 2% to 3%. After the second member is added, take these measurements again.

CHAPTER 3 0

Application Tuning

Some applications can move to a data sharing environment rapidly without significant changes, some applications require significant changes, and some applications should not move. Ideally, you should see an improvement in application performance due to the additional CPU cycles and parallelism (logging and connections are spread out over members).

However, the reality is that application performance may degrade. If controlled and tuned, data sharing adds minimal overhead to applications while adding resources, availability, and flexibility. But if you go blindly into a data sharing environment without using some standard tuning recommendations, you may find some real performance problems.

Let's review the list of application tuning recommendations: use type 2 indexes, minimize or eliminate row-level locking, use uncommitted read as much as possible, use RELEASE (DEALLOCATE), design for CICS thread reuse, bind plans with CURRENT-DATA (NO), and be objective with physical design and object placement. Although this list is in every DB2 book and presentation, more often than not these recommendations still do not make it into the production data sharing environment, which often causes post-migration performance problems. It is important that you know why each of these items is important to data sharing performance.

Lock Avoidance

The acquisition of a DB2 lock requires around 1,460 instructions (plus a cross-memory call), and avoidance of a lock requires around 60 instructions. However, 60 unnecessary

instructions can add up. Unnecessary locks can become additional overhead in a data sharing environment if lock avoidance cannot be achieved. Lock avoidance works the same in
a data sharing environment as in a single-system environment with a few new "gotchas."
When two members update the same table, the GCLSN (global commit log sequence
number) is not set until the process with the oldest BEGIN-UR in the data sharing group
finally commits. Therefore, if any one of the update processing members is not committing, the GCLSN does not get set and is never greater than the PGLOGRBA on the page,
so lock avoidance will be hindered. This is why it is very important that commit scopes be
evaluated for applications in a data sharing environment. You should also make use of the
CURRENTDATA (NO) bind parameter for lock avoidance.

The issue with lock avoidance is *avoiding* the overhead of lock avoidance by using
uncommitted read. The isolation level of uncommitted read can be used in most cases and
should be evaluated for each statement.

Bind Parameters

In a data sharing environment, it is important to be aware of how your plans and packages
are bound and what bind parameters are in effect. There are a few bind parameters that can
have a large impact on data sharing performance. In the following sections, each is
described in terms of its relevance to data sharing performance. For additional information
about these parameters, refer to Section 3, "Application Design and Tuning."

RELEASE

Using RELEASE (DEALLOCATE) and CICS-protected threads can help to reduce XES
contention and global and false lock contention. The number of locks taken will go down
because the transactions now hold onto only the parent locks, and the number of locks
propagated to XES will decline as parent locks are maintained. You should see a decrease
in the class 2 CPU time as well. However, do not go overboard with using RELEASE
(DEALLOCATE). Use the 80-20 rule for deciding which transaction threads can benefit
most, do a few at a time, and measure the results.

Combine the use of RELEASE (DEALLOCATE) with thread reuse for optimal performance. By observing the thread deallocations per commit in the accounting detail reports and doing some quick calculations, you can get an idea of the amount of thread reuse currently being achieved (figure 30.1). Add the number of NEW USER terminations and the number of RESIGNONs, and divide this by the total number of terminations (NEW USER + DEALLOCATION + RESIGNON). This gives you the percentage of threads that are being reused. If you are not getting a good deal of thread reuse you may want to look into defining some protected threads in CICS.

Overusing this parameter could cause your EDM pool to grow if the transactions are heavily accessed. The EDM pool feels the impact of RELEASE (DEALLOCATE) and protected threads because plans and packages are held longer in the EDM pool. However, the EDM pool is in virtual memory, so concerns over expansion have less of an impact than you might think. Keep in mind that the EDM pool is not backed in the coupling facility in the data sharing environment because of its low activity, but it is cross-invalidated through the SCA for such things as newly rebound packages or DBD changes, so sizing is still done on an individual subsystem level.

CURRENTDATA

Using the CURRENTDATA (NO) option on the bind is recommended even in non-data sharing environments; however, in a data sharing environment lock avoidance, when achieved, can help reduce global locking. For more information on lock avoidance in data sharing, refer to Chapter 27, "Locking."

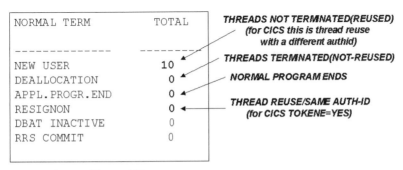

Figure 30.1 Thread Reuse

ISOLATION

Isolation-level UR (uncommitted read) should be considered for programs and statements that do not require up-to-the-minute data for processing and for any application that can tolerate seeing uncommitted data. This helps reduce the number of locks propagated to the coupling facility. Reducing the level of data sharing results in less concurrent access between members on particular DB2 objects. This may appear to somewhat defeat the purpose of being able to share objects and route workloads, but it is all a matter of appropriate application selection and tuning.

IMMEDWRITE

A row-not-found condition can occur in certain situations in a data sharing environment. This can happen if a transaction updates DB2 data and then, before it commits, spawns another transaction that depends on updates made by the first transaction. You should use the IMMEDWRITE (YES) option on the BIND or REBIND statement for any plan or package that spawns dependent transactions that may run in other DB2 members in the group. With this option, DB2 immediately writes any updated buffers for pages belonging to GBP-dependent objects so that the other transactions know about them (instead of waiting for the force-at-commit process to write the data to the group buffer pool). However, you should *not* use this option if you do not have row-not-found problems because the IMMEDWRITE (YES) feature forces synchronous I/O to occur, thus causing waits to your application.

Physical Design

Partitioning

The use of table-space partitioning can yield several benefits in a data sharing environment. For instance, you can partition a table space and, through affinity routing, control members' access to the partitions to avoid the overhead of lock propagation and group buffer pool dependency for partitions that otherwise would have read/write interest from several members. You can also use partitions to help with utility processing, such as LOAD or REORG. If you split a table into 10 partitions, you can run five concurrent LOAD utilities on two members (figure 31.1); however, keep in mind that any NPIs defined on the table become GBP dependent during this process. If these are large NPIs, this could be a problem. It would be best to drop the NPIs before the LOAD and re-create them afterward.

Selective Partition Locking

Selective partition locking (SPL) gives you the ability to tell DB2 to acquire locks only at a partition level and not to escalate locks to the table-space level. This reduces propagation of locks to the coupling facility and allows better concurrency for applications that access data in various partitions. This can be especially useful if partition access is spread over multiple members using affinity routing. Performance trace class 6 (IFCID 0020) shows whether you are truly using SPL on your table-space partitions. You can also use the -DISPLAY DATABASE (LOCKS) command to display information about SPL.

653

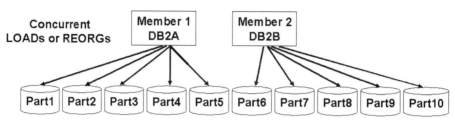

Figure 31.1   Using Table-Space Partitioning

However, SPL helps in a non-data sharing environment only if an agent actually escalates. If you are not having escalation problems, you may not want to use SPL. Without SPL, the parent intent lock is taken on the last partition, regardless of which ones are accessed. These locks are almost always intent locks and therefore almost never cause a problem. With SPL, the parent intent lock is taken on whichever part is accessed. If escalation occurs, with SPL the lock escalation occurs just for the part or parts with too many locks. Without SPL, since the parent lock is taken only on the last one, the entire page set is escalated, and access is prevented to all partitions.

Be careful with SPL. It can increase the amount XES contention if you don't have true partition independence because it locks all parts accessed (instead of just the last one). Therefore, an agent that accesses multiple parts holds more parent locks than without SPL, and if other agents are doing the same, the chance of XES contention is greater. That is one of the reasons not to use SPL unless you are sure that partitions are accessed only by one application or one member.

If you have affinities per partition, SPL can buy you independence if one of the applications escalates, since the escalation happens at the part level with SPL instead of the table-space level without SPL. If using SPL, you can avoid GBP dependency on the additional table-space partitions and lessen coupling facility overhead.

Type 2 Indexes

Type 2 indexes should be used regardless of whether or not you use data sharing with version 4 and later. Locking rates have been reduced by an average of 50%—from 25%

for version 4 or 5 and data sharing environments with low read/write activity, to 75% in some data sharing environments with high read/write activity.

Row-Level Locking versus MAXROWS = 1

People often wonder about the effect of row-level locking on the coupling facility. Row-level locking does have a greater negative effect on the coupling facility than page-level locking. While it may appear that you would be taking the same number of locks, in a data sharing environment the number of locks is a bit different. The locks most people think of are L-locks, the ones used in a non-data sharing environment, but the problems arise in data sharing and coupling facility overhead with excessive P-locks (physical locks used to control page coherency, not transaction concurrency).

Here is a quick example. If you are locking a row (RID 111) on page 7 in member DB2A, a P-lock is taken on the page. Then member DB2B wants a row lock on RID 112 (which is on the same page). DB2B also wants a P-lock on the page. This causes the members to perform P-lock negotiation, which is expensive and drives additional requests through the coupling facility. If you do a lot of row-level locking, the overhead associated with taking P-locks on the page and then negotiating these P-locks so that both members can have interest in the page kills any benefit of row-level locking. The coupling facility works at a page level, not a row level (figure 31.2).

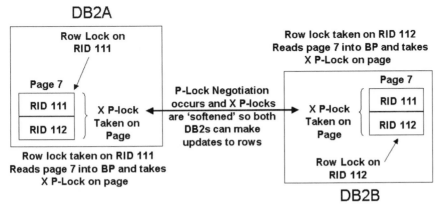

Figure 31.2   Row-Level Locking and P-Locks

With MAXROWS = 1, you work at the page level, and you can get a lock on two different rows from two different members without having to go through P-lock negotiation. You also get the concurrency benefits you are looking for.

Multiple Page Sizes

Two new page sizes, 8 K and 16 K, are available in DB2 Version 6. Appropriate use of these sizes can improve data sharing performance, since an 8 K page requires only one page lock instead of the two required for 4 K pages. This reduces coupling facility overhead, since locking is effectively cut in half. These larger page sizes also help for those wide rows required to support of certain types of warehouse applications, specifically those very wide fact tables used in some enterprise warehouses. Only 4 K and 32 K pages are still used for the work files, however, which should not be a concern.

Member Clustering

Space map contention is another performance problem as more and larger data sharing installations move into production. Hot spots are often caused by the current space management techniques for optimum space utilization, which cause high update activity in the associated space map pages. This often results in a significant increase in P-lock negotiations, due to the attempt to cluster data by using the clustering index or the default index. To provide relief for these situations, a new page set type called MEMBER CLUSTER (PQ02897) allows inserts to choose the insert location to avoid lock and latch contention. This is done by allowing each member in the data sharing group to identify and use a separate space map page so that insert space management can avoid acquiring page P-locks unconditionally. This option is defined by using a new MEMBER CLUSTER keyword on the CREATE TABLESPACE statement. As with many performance tuning features, there is a down side. Inserts do not cluster the data; instead, DB2 chooses an insert location that minimizes lock and latch contention. Space maps must be changed to cover only 199 data pages instead of the normal 10,000 pages for table spaces that use the MEMBER CLUSTER option. Each member then gets a different space map page so that they insert into different areas of the table space (figure 31.3).

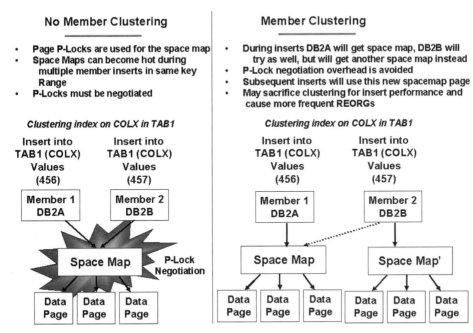

Figure 31.3 Member Clustering

Space Map Page Tracking

When DB2 maintains information in the space map pages in a page set, to help optimize the performance of incremental image copies, it may be prone to causing hot spots. Hot spots occur frequently in data sharing environments when multiple processes from more than one member update the same space map pages. These updates usually cause logical contention on the space map page as well as additional page P-locking. DB2 Version 6 provides another new option for dealing with contention on space map pages. This new feature is called TRACKMOD YES/NO and is defined on the CREATE or ALTER TABLESPACE statement. You can now specify whether or not to have DB2 track the data page changes in the space map, which identifies the pages that have changed. TRACK-MOD YES generally causes incremental copies to run more slowly, since they are now required to scan the page set to identify which pages have changed. However, TRACK-MOD YES can provide faster application performance due to less contention on the space map pages.

Nonpartitioning Indexes

Even if you spread your work across multiple partitions and use SPL, you are still inserting into one NPI, which is GBP dependent. There is not a great deal you can do about the NPI and GBP dependency. Page P-locks are taken on the index leaf pages, and although a page P-lock is not expensive, the process of P-lock negotiation is when two processes must negotiate locks for data on the same index page. You help to reduce the negotiation by not allowing access to the same data.

Problem Diagnosing

Once the initial tuning has been performed at both the application and system levels and data sharing has been enabled, the real fun begins! Diagnosis of performance problems and overall system availability problems in the data sharing environment comes with a few extra caveats. However, there are also additional features in DB2 to help with the diagnosis.

Diagnosing problems in a data sharing environment is a very similar to that in a single-system DB2 environment. Data sharing problems generally involve system or application hangs, deadlocks, time-outs, inconsistency, or incoherency.

In a data sharing environment, hangs can occur on a single system, or they can involve the entire data sharing group. A single-system hang can occur when there is contention for the same resource on a single DB2 subsystem. A group-wide hang can occur when there is contention for the same resource on different DB2 subsystems. To properly diagnose problems resulting from a single-system hang, a console dump of the offending DB2 is needed. However, with a group hang, a console dump of multiple DB2s is needed. If a data sharing DB2 subsystem is hung, the console dump may be required of not only the MSTR, DBM1, and IRLM address spaces, but also the XES.

System Hangs

Single-system hangs can occur in non-data sharing environments. When they happen in a data sharing environment, they can be diagnosed in relatively the same manner as they are in a single system environment. Group hangs involve evaluating activity on all members through the use of the -DISPLAY GROUP command (figure 32.1) . You can use the -DISPLAY GROUP command to get status of each member (active, quiesced, failed). To diagnose a hang situation in a data sharing environment requires a console dump of several DB2 subsystems and their associated IRLMs.

If a DB2 is not coming down and you cannot get into it to display thread activity, you can go to another DB2 in the data sharing group and display the threads in the failing DB2 (or route the commands through the console). You may be able to find the culprit and cancel it without having to further force down DB2.

Application Hangs

Application hangs generally are caused by a problem with the local DB2 subsystem or local IRLM, a peer member DB2 subsystem or its IRLM, or the XES component of MVS. Application lock or resource contention can occur among various application processes within the same DB2 or between DB2 subsystems. If an application is hung on one subsystem, it can hold resources required by another application in another subsystem. An application can experience a hang while XES is determining P-lock negotiation; however, this is a very minimal disruption because of the speed of P-lock negotiation. The -DISPLAY DATA-BASE LOCKS command can help determine whether an application hang is caused by lock contention or retained locks (figure 32.2). An R in the LOCKINFO column indicates that a retained lock is being held and by which member.

```
-DB2P DISPLAY GROUP DETAIL

DB2                              SYSTEM     IRLM
MEMBER ID SUBSYS CMDPREF STATUS NAME  LVL SUBSYS IRLMPROC


DB2P    1  DB2P  -DB2P    ACTIVE   MVSA 510 ZRLM  ZRLMPROC
-------------------------------------------------------------------
SCA  STRUCTURE SIZE:        1024 KB,  STATUS= AC, SCA IN USE: 11%
LOCK1 STRUCTURE SIZE:       1536 KB,            LOCK1 IN USE: < 1%
NUMBER LOCK ENTRIES:         262144,      LOCK ENTRIES IN USE: 33
NUMBER LIST ENTRIES:           7353,      LIST ENTRIES  IN USE:  0
```

Figure 32.1   -DISPLAY GROUP Command

```
-DISPLAY DATABASE (DBM1) SPACE(TSNM1) LOCKS

NAME    TYPE   PART   STATUS          CONNID   CORRID   LOCKINFO

TSNM1   TS     01     RW                                R(X,P)
                             MEMBER NAME DB21
```

Figure 32.2   -DISPLAY DATABASE LOCKS

Data sharing environment hangs can occur for a variety of reasons, such as global locking contention, P-lock negotiation, unavailability of a coupling facility structure, thread hangs (DB2, CICS), or IRLM notification messaging. Global locking—depending on whether it is real or false contention-can cause delays. Real contention hangs (i.e., –911s) are dealt with much the same as in a single-system environment, except the resource could be held by another subsystem. P-lock negotiation occurs through XES and may or may not cause a delay in the application process, depending on the whether or not false or real contention is detected. Coupling facility structures (lock, SCA, GBP) can become unavailable for various reasons, cause a failure in the data sharing group, and need to be rebuilt. If an entire coupling facility is unavailable, the structures are rebuilt in another coupling facility, depending on how the SFM and CFRM policies are defined.

If you are using group buffer pool duplexing, you experience a delay if there is a switch between duplex and simplex mode, and vice versa. This can happen if the SETXCF DUPLEX ENABLED or DISABLE command is issued.

Thread hangs can be caused for a number of different reasons. It is important to identify the thread (-DISPLAY THREAD), the holder, and the implications of canceling the thread. DB2 uses IRLM notification to send notification messages among members in a DB2 data sharing group. A hang can result if a sender is held up while waiting for a response (however, this notification messaging is used by other services as well). You can diagnose delays in the IRLM by using the MODIFY irlmproc, DIAG, DELAY command. Delays in the IRLM can also occur if child locks cannot be propagated to the coupling facility due to a member failure or structure connectivity failure. To see whether a structure is allocated or not, use the D XCF, STR command to view the status or the D XCF, STR STRNAME = xx command to view additional information about a structure (figure 32.3).

```
D XCF, STR

IXC359I 12.10.34       DISPLAY XCF 975

STRNAME         ALLOCATION TIME        STATUS

DSNDBG1_GBP0  01/01/98   12:01:00  ALLOCATED

DSNDBG1_GBP1  01/01/98   12:01:00  ALLOCATED

DSNDBG1_LOCK1 01/01/98   12:01:00  ALLOCATED

DSNDBG1_SCA   01/01/98   12:01:00  ALLOCATED
─────────────────────────────────────────────
D XCF, STR, STRNAME=DSNDBG1_LOCK1
IXC360I 12.10.34       DISPLAY XCF 137
STRNAME: DSNDBG1_LOCK1
 STATUS: ALLOCATED
 POLICY SIZE    :64000K
 POLICY INITSIZE: 32000K
 REBUILD PERCENT: 5
 PREFERENCE LIST: CF02 CF01
 EXCLUSION LIST IS EMPTY
```

Figure 32.3 Structure Display

Deadlocks and Time-Outs

Deadlocks and time-outs are more fun to diagnosis in a data sharing environment and can be caused by any group member, not just the local subsystem. There are new accompanying messages to help identify the members on which a deadlock or time-out has occurred.

- DSNT375I—plan deadlock (IFCID 172 trace record also holds information regarding all participants in a deadlock)
- DSNT376I—plan timeout
- DSNT377I—plan conflict with in-doubt threads (the lock could not be acquired because the resource required was undergoing recovery)

To detect deadlocks or time-outs, use the –DISPLAY DATABASE command with the LOCKS keyword. This displays the lock status on DB2 objects across all the members of the group. The CLAIMERS keyword displays all the claimers of DB2 objects on the participating members. The LOCKS keyword on this command at one time caused excessive overhead to the IRLM; however, version 5 APARs PQ15854 (IRLM) and

PQ14274/PQ19277 (DB2) minimize the disruptions of this command. To obtain more detailed information on locks in a data sharing environment, the following trace classes and IFCIDs can be examined:

- CLASS 3 (statistics) trace contains information regarding deadlocks, time-outs, connect and disconnects from GBPs, and long-running URs in IFCIDs 172, 196, 250, 261, 262, and 213.
- CLASS 6 (performance) trace contains summary lock information with details in IFCIDs 20, 44, 45, 105, 106, 107, 172, 192, 213, 214, and 218.
- CLASS 7 (performance) trace contains detail lock information in IFCIDs 21, 105, 106, 107, and 223.

The -START TRACE command can be issued on the problem member, and depending on the trace used, DB2 can collect data from the group (for group buffer pools or global locking) or from each member. The refresh of DB2 Version 6 introduced the SCOPE(GROUP) option on START TRACE command to support global traces. If you are trying to diagnose a locking contention problem involving several members using an older version, you have to start the trace on each member, then use the sysplex time value in the header to put records in time sequence, and use the member names that are supplied in the traces to identify where the problem lies. Just a reminder: always limit your traces by specifying the IFCIDs necessary for identifying the problem to avoid excessive overhead when running traces.

Inconsistency and Incoherency

The traditional causes of inconsistency and incoherency problems still apply (ever had a C90101?). These traditional causes include broken pages, inconsistent pages between the data and the index, and down level data set detection (level ID). These problems are resolved using the same methods you used before data sharing.

The new causes that data sharing provides include buffer pool incoherency, data incoherency, and communication failures between the DB2 members in the data sharing group. Buffer pool coherency involves XI (cross-invalidation) signaling among the buffer pools of the data sharing members for changed pages. Refer to Chapter 33, "Long-Term

Monitoring," to learn how to quickly view excessive negotiations that could be causing problems. The group buffer pool is used to support data coherency for inter-DB2 read/write interest among members.

P-locks are held to protect the coherency of cached objects and are held for as long as the object remains cached. However, you may experience performance problems if there are too many P-locks or excessive P-lock negotiation occurs. The accounting and statistics reports can show you the number of P-locks taken, IFCID 0251 can show you information about P-lock negotiation requests, and IFCID 0259 can help monitor page P-locking without a full lock trace.

You also can experience inconsistencies if you use group buffer pool duplexing. If duplexing is active, there may be a period when the primary and secondary group buffer pools become unsynchronized. This occurs when a changed page in the primary group buffer pool is not reflected in secondary group buffer pool. IFCID 0252 can provide information on group buffer pool duplexing.

The LPL (logical page list) error status is not new to data sharing, but data sharing provides new ways for pages to go into LPL status. Some reasons for LPL pages in data sharing include these situations:

- Errors occur for "must complete" operations, where DB2 must read a page during restart to apply an UNDO or REDO log record or where DB2 must read a page to apply an UNDO log record because an application issued a ROLLBACK or the UR ABENDed.
- A page is updated and then purged out of the virtual and group buffer pools (possibly due to thresholds). A transaction then requests a back-out. The page that was written needs to be back in the buffer pool.
- A force-at-commit write failure occurs when a write request fails and all updated pages are not written to the GBP. This can occur if a group buffer pool is not available when all the updated pages need to be written at commit.
- A group buffer pool castout failure occurs, and the pages in the GBP cannot be written to disk.
- A group buffer pool shortage occurs, where a write to the GBP gets a "structure full" condition after about five attempts (depending on MVS level).
- A restart with the DEFER option causes all retained locks to be converted to LPL.

To see what pages are on the LPL list, you can issue the DISPLAY DATABASE LPL command (figure 32.4). The LPL condition must be resolved on these pages, of course, before they can be used any member. Often this is done by a START DATABASE command, which can be issued by any DB2 member in the data sharing group, but if there is also a retained lock, the holding member must be up; a START command cannot override this.

If a group buffer pool structure fails, the pages in the GBP become GRECP (group buffer pool recover pending) and are unavailable to all members when the structure is rebuilt. You need to resolve the GRECP status to use the pages. To see what pages are in GRECP status, you can use the DISPLAY DATABASE GRECP command (figure 32.5). In version 5, an automatic rebuild takes care of the GRECP condition. If you are using

-DISPLAY DATABASE(db) SPACE(sp) LPL

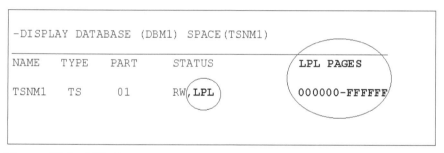

```
-DISPLAY DATABASE (DBM1) SPACE (TSNM1)

NAME     TYPE    PART     STATUS          LPL PAGES

TSNM1    TS      01       RW, LPL         000000-FFFFFF
```

Figure 32.4   LPL Pages

```
-DISPLAY DATABASE (DBM1) SPACE (TSNM1) LPL

NAME     TYPE    PART     STATUS          LPL PAGES

TSNM1    TS      01       RW, LPL, GRECP  000000-FFFFFF
```

Figure 32.5   GRECP Status

group buffer pool duplexing, DB2 switches immediately to the secondary GBP and should not have any page in GRECP status.

Application Error Checking

Rumor has it that you do not have to make any changes to application code for data sharing. Well, did you know that if you get a –904 (resource unavailable) error code, it may be due to a coupling facility structure being unavailable? If the environment is configured correctly, the outage will be very short (i.e., a lock structure rebuild usually takes a matter of seconds). You may want to code retry logic in your application instead of letting it ABEND.

Long-Term Monitoring

Several items need to be continuously monitored after data sharing has been implemented. These include group buffer pools, locking activity, XES activity, and coupling facility activity. This monitoring helps reduce the chance of eventual system performance degradation due to changing workload, additional system activity, and so on. The monitoring process should be ongoing, just as in a normal environment. It is very important in a data sharing environment, especially when a new application that uses shared data is implemented. New applications can play nicely, or they can impair the processing of all of the applications in the data sharing group. It is important to have baselines for comparison.

Group Buffer Pools

DISPLAY GROUPBUFFERPOOL Command

The characteristics of Group buffer pools that need to be monitored include reclaims due to directory entries, cross-invalidations, appropriate size, write failures due to lack of storage, and overhead associated with pseudo-close. The -DISPLAY GROUPBUFFERPOOL command can assist with monitoring these items (figures 33.1 and 33.2).

Cross-Invalidations and Reclaims

Tuning for reduction of reclaims often requires an increase to the group buffer pool and to the RATIO parameter. This can be done by an ALTER GROUPBUFFERPOOL command. Cross-invalidations occur when a changed page is written out to the GBP. If a

```
-DISPLAY GROUPBUFFERPOOL(GBP0) GDETAIL

-DB2P DISPLAY FOR GROUP BUFFER POOL GBP0 FOLLOWS
-DB2P DB2 GROUP BUFFER POOL STATUS
       CONNECTED                                    =YES
       CURRENT DIRECTORY TO DATA RATIO              =5
       PENDING DIRECTORTY TO DATA RATIO             =5
-DB2P CLASS CASTOUT THRESHOLD                       =10%
       GROUP BUFFER POOL CASTOUT THRESHOLD          =50%
       GROUP BUFFER POOL CHECKPOINT INTERVAL        =8 MINUTES
       RECOVERY STATUS                              =NORMAL
-DB2P MVS CFRM POLICY STATUS FOR DSNDB2P_GBP0       =NORMAL
       MAX SIZE INDICATED IN POLICY                 =17920
       ALLOCATED                                    =YES
-DB2P ALLOCATED SIZE                                =16128 KB
       VOLATILITY STATUS                            =VOLATILE
-DB2P NUMBER OF DIRECTORY ENTRIES                   =16103
       NUMBER OF DATA PAGES                         =3220
       NUMBER OF CONNECTIONS                        =4
```

Figure 33.1   -DISPLAY GROUPBUFFERPOOL

```
-DB2P INCREMENTAL GROUP DETAIL STATISTICE SINCE 14:20:44
-DB2P GROUP DETAIL STATISTICS
       READS
       DATA RETURNED                           =6618
-DB2P  DATA NOT RETURNED
       DIRECTORY ENTRY EXISTED                 =511
       DIRECTORY ENTRY CREATED                 =413
       DIRECTORY ENTRY NOT CREATED             101,0
-DB2P  WRITES
       CHANGED PAGES                           =14256
       CLEAN PAGES                             =0
       FAILED DUE TO LACK OF STORAGE           =0
       CHANGED PAGES SNAPSHOT VALUE            =26
-DB2P  RECLAIMS
       FOR DIRECTORY ENTRIES                   =0
       FOR DATA ENTRIES                        =2950
       CASTOUTS
-DB2P  CROSS INVALIDATIONS
       DUE TO DIRECTORY ENTIRES                =0
       DUE TO WRITES                           =7195
```

Figure 33.2   -DISPLAY GROUPBUFFERPOOL (cont.)

copy of the changed page exists in a local buffer pool, it is marked as invalid. You do not want to see cross-invalidation due to reclaims. This means that the directory is not large enough, so a directory had to be "stolen" in order for a page to be registered. The page that belongs to the directory entry that was stolen is then invalidated and, if needed, must be read back in from disk. When tuning to decrease the number of directory reclaims due to cross-invalidations, a certain amount of balancing must be performed to increase the ratio enough, but not so high that it interferes with the castout process. The individual buffer pools should be sized minimally to hold only what is required by the system processing.

Castout Efficiency

When a castout write finishes, it issues an UNLOCK CASTOUT request to the coupling facility for each page written with that I/O. These "locks" are taken to protect a page from being written by two processes (CLASST and GBPOOLT thresholds met). For example, if only two pages were written, the PAGES CASTOUT would be 2, and the UNLOCK CASTOUT would be 1. This is not a good scenario, and it points to a problem in the class castout threshold (CLASST) for a particular page set. Refer to figure 33.3 for an example

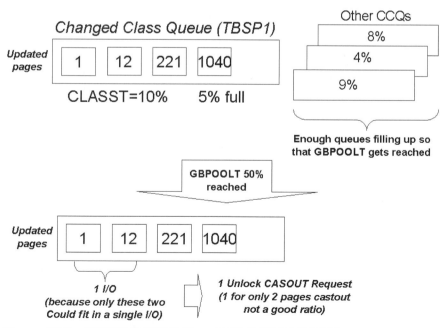

Figure 33.3 PAGES CASTOUT and UNLOCK CASTOUT

of how this works. In this example, there are too many nonreference random pages left in the class queue for a particular page set, and the CLASST threshold is not met. However, there is enough update activity in the other class queues that the GBPOOLT threshold is met. When the writes begin, only pages 1 and 12 are successfully written to disk because they could fit in one I/O, then one UNLOCK CASTOUT is issued. If the CLASST was lower and these random pages were written more often, the unlock request would better match the I/O requests (PAGES CASTOUT). The number of PAGES CASTOUT and the number of UNLOCK CASTOUTs should be less close (figure 33.4). You can get this information by issuing a -DISPLAY GROUPBUFFERPOOL MDETAIL command.

Inter-DB2 Interest

Improvements have been made in the -DISPLAY BUFFERPOOL command in Version 6 that provide a lot of good information for data sharing (figure 33.5). Many tuning issues involve the amount of intersystem sharing among the DB2 members. With the new

```
-DB2P    CASTOUTS
         PAGES CASTOUT              = 200
         UNLOCK CASTOUT             = 25
         READ CASTOUT CLASS         = 45
         READ CASTOUT STATISTICS    = 45
         READ DIRECTORY INFO        = 250
```

The number of **UNLOCK CASTOUTs**
should be much less that the
PAGES CASTOUT; else there is
a problem with the **CASTOUT** thresholds

Figure 33.4   Monitoring Castout Efficiency

Group bufferpool
Dependency
(Inter-system interest)

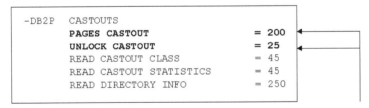

```
---------PAGE SET/PARTITION LIST INFORMATION---------------
                                      ------DATA SHARING INFO---
                          TS  GBP  MEMBER  CASTOUT   USE   P-LOCK
DATABASE  SPACE NAME PART IX  DEP  NAME    OWNER    COUNT   STATE
========  ========== ==== ==  ===  ======  =======  =====  =======
MYDB      MYTS        001 TS   Y   DB2P       Y        0      IS
```

Figure 33.5   Viewing Intersystem Sharing Information

enhancements, you can view this interest by using the -DISPLAY BUFFERPOOL (*) LIST(*) command. It provides a view of objects and how they are shared across the members. You can see which members by partition have interest in an object, the level of interest (P-lock state), and whether or not the member is the castout owner.

Viewing ALTER Effects

The -DISPLAY GROUPBUFFERPOOL command shows your current settings on the group buffer pool. You can also use IFCID 0256 to show the attributes of a GBP before and after an ALTER. This is helpful if a change is made that has a negative effect on performance and you need to find out what the prior settings were.

Statistics Report

You can also monitor group buffer pools by using the DB2 statistics report. Figures 33.6 and 33.7 show some statistics that are useful for monitoring the effectiveness of the group buffer pools.

```
GROUP BP1                      QUANTITY /MINUTE  /THREAD  /COMMIT
---------------------------    --------  --------  -------  ---------
SYN.READS(XI)-DATA RETURNED    3001.0    299.0     460.0    .20
# OF READS TO GBP BECAUSE PAGE WAS INVALIDATED IN VBP

SYN.READS(XI)-R/W  INTEREST    0.00      0.00      0.00     0.00
# OF READS TO GBP BECAUSE PAGE WAS INVALIDATED IN VBP AND HAD TO READ FROM DASD TO
    GET PAGES. OTHER MEMBERS INTEREST ALSO CAUSE DB2 TO CREATE A DIRECTORY ENTRY
    FOR THE PAGE BECAUSE IT DID NOT EXIST

SYN.READS(XI)-NO R/W INTER.    0.00      0.00      0.00     0.00
# OF READS TO GBP BECAUSE PAGE WAS INVALIDATED IN VBP, BUT NO R/W INTEREST,
    THEREFORE NO PAGE REGISTRATION

SYN.READS(NF)-DATA RETURNED    20.00     2.00      4.00     0.00
# OF READS TO GBP BECAUSE PAGE WAS NOT IN THE MEMBERS VBP

SYN.READS(NF)-R/W  INTEREST    15.00     1.00      2.70     0.00
# OF READS TO GBP BECAUSE PAGE WAS NOT IN THE MEMBERS VBP AND HAD TO READ FROM DASD
    TO GET PAGES. OTHER MEMBERS INTEREST ALSO CAUSE DB2 TO CREATE A DIRECTORY ENTRY
    FOR THE PAGE BECAUSE IT DID NOT EXIST

SYN.READS(NF)-NO R/W INTER.    0.00      0.00      0.00     0.00
# OF READS TO GBP BECAUSE PAGE WAS NOT IN THE MEMBERS VBP, BUT NO R/W INTEREST,
    THEREFORE NO PAGE REGISTRATION
```

Figure 33.6 Statistics Report for Monitoring GBP Activity

```
GROUP BP1                        QUANTITY /MINUTE  /THREAD /COMMIT
----------------------------     -------- -------- ------- ---------
CLEAN PAGES SYNC.WRITTEN           0.00     0.00     0.00    0.00
CHANGED PAGES SYNC.WRITTEN        5600.0   520.30   900.00   0.30
# OF CHANGED PAGES WERE SYNC. WRITTEN TO GBP FROM VBPs.
CLEAN PAGES ASYNC.WRITTEN          0.00     0.00     0.00    0.00
CHANGED PAGES ASYNC.WRITTEN        0.00     0.00     0.00    0.00
# OF CHANGED AND CLEAN PAGES ASYNC. WRITTEN TO GBP FROM VBPs
REG.PAGE LIST (RPL) REQUEST        0.00     0.00     0.00    0.00
CLEAN PAGES READ AFTER RPL         0.00     0.00     0.00    0.00
CHANGED PGS READ AFTER RPL         0.00     0.00     0.00    0.00
REGISTRATION OF PAGES FOR PREFETCH ACTIVITY

PAGES CASTOUT                    1030.00   99.00   200.00   0.05
CASTOUT CLASS THRESHOLD           10.00     1.00     2.00    0.00
GROUP BP CASTOUT THRESHOLD         0.00     0.00     0.00    0.00
CASTOUT ENGINE NOT AVAIL.          0.00     0.00     0.00    0.00
WRITE ENGINE NOT AVAILABLE         0.00     0.00     0.00    0.00
CASOUT ACTIVITY FOR GBP TO DASD FOR BOTH # PAGES READ AND # TIMES THRESHOLDS REACHED
READ FAILED-NO STORAGE             0.00     0.00     0.00    0.00
WRITE FAILED-NO STORAGE            0.00     0.00     0.00    0.00
INDICATE STORAGE PROBLEMS IN THE CF (INCREASE GBP IF NOT DUE TO A SURGE ONLY)
```

Figure 33.7   Statistics Report for Monitoring GBP Activity

Reads and Invalidations

If you compare the SYN.READS(XI) -DATA RETURNED with SYN.READ(XI) -R/W INTEREST and SYN.READS(XI) -NO R/W INTEREST in figure 33.6, you can get some interesting information about the hit ratio. Add all of them together and divide by the SYN.READS(XI) -DATA RETURNED. Between 50% and 90% is a good hit ratio. What you are looking at is the hit ratio for the synchronous reads that occurred due to buffer invalidations, which occur when a page is requested and found to be invalid, but it is found in the group buffer pool so that a request does not have to be made to disk to retrieve it. If the ratio is below 50%, your pages are being cast out before being used, and your group buffer pool is possibly too small.

Virtual Pool Issues

You can also look at the SYN.READ -NF with the GETPAGEs for the virtual buffer pool to see whether possibly your virtual buffer pool is too small (or the thresholds are set incorrectly), in which case pages are stolen from the virtual pool even though they are still cached in the group buffer pool.

Storage Problems

Keep an eye on the write failures due to lack of storage. If you constantly see a nonzero value here, not just periodically during a surge, you may have a problem with your castout process. A nonzero value shows that data is not getting written out to disk in a timely manner because a nonzero value indicates that a write of a changed page was attempted to the group buffer pool, but the pool was full.

Castout Efficiency

To evaluate castout efficiency, you can monitor how many times each threshold is reached (CLASST and GBPOOLT) in CASTOUT CLASS THRESHOLD and the GROUP HP CASTOUT THRESHOLD, respectively. As with any write process, you want to see the CLASST threshold hit more often, because this keeps the write flow more constant, whereas if the GBPOOLT is hit more often, a lot more pages are written at a time, possibly causing surges in I/O. You also risk running out of castout engines, which is indicated in CASTOUT ENGINE NOT AVAIL.

Locking

Activity

You can monitor lock activity online to periodically view the type of locking activity that occurs during processing. The -DISPLAY DATABASE LOCKS command (figure 33.8) shows what member is holding a lock, on which object the lock is held, and information about the lock. You can view both P-locks and L-locks. A corresponding CONNID and CORRID for the transaction holding the lock are shown, and a P-lock shows the level of interest in the page set.

Contention

Another key area in long-term monitoring is locking contention, including global lock contention, false lock contention, and XES contention.

Global (Real) Contention

Global lock contention is the total number of suspends caused by contention. You can calculate the amount of global lock contention by using the statistics report (figure 33.9).

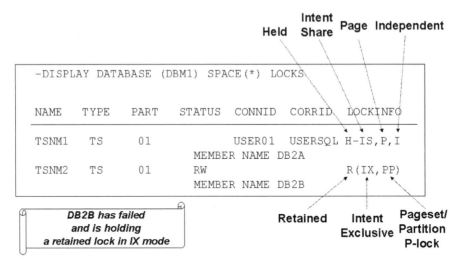

Figure 33.8 Monitoring Lock Activity Online

```
DATA SHARING LOCKING              QUANTITY /MINUTE /THREAD /COMMIT
-----------------------------     ------- ------- ------- -------
GLOBAL CONTENTION RATE (%)
FALSE CONTENTION RATE (%)
CONTENTION RATES
LOCK REQUESTS (P-LOCKS)
UNLOCK REQUESTS (P-LOCKS)
CHANGE REQUESTS (P-LOCKS)
TOTAL NUMBER OF LOCK-RELATED REQUESTS FOR P-LOCKS
SYNCH.XES - LOCK REQUESTS
SYNCH.XES - CHANGE REQUESTS
SYNCH.XES - UNLOCK REQUESTS
TOTAL NUMBER OF LOCK-RELATED REQUESTS (L-LOCKS AND P-LOCKS) PROPAGATED TO XES SYNC
ASYNCH.XES - RESOURCES
NUMBER OF LOCKS PROPAGATED TO XES ASYNC.
SUSPENDS - IRLM GLOBAL CONT
NUMBER OF REAL CONTENTIONS AS DETECTED BY THE IRLM
SUSPENDS - XES GLOBAL CONT
NUMBER OF REAL CONTENTIONS AS DETECTED BY XES (NOT IRLM LEVEL)
SUSPENDS - FALSE CONTENTION
NUMBER OF FALSE CONTENTIONS
```

Figure 33.9 Statistics Report: Locking

Add up the number of synchronous XES requests (lock requests + change requests + unlock requests) and divide this sum by the total amount of contention (IRLM global contention + XES global contention + false contention). Then divide this figure by the total number of requests to XES times 100. You can also view this figure in the GLOBAL CONTENTION RATE field. The total should be under 2%; if it is not, the amount of locking needs to be reduced, especially the number of P-locks propagated to the coupling facility. Lock avoidance though application tuning can help in this situation. The goal is to keep the total number of lock, change and unlock requests from exceeding 98% of the total number of lock.

Global locks cause conflicts on lock requests between members in a data sharing group when an attempt is made to serialize resources with shared interest. Global contention can be real or false. Real contention occurs when two processes (on the same or different subsystems) try to obtain the same lock. Real contention depends on the workload characteristics and is tuned the same as in a single-subsystem environment (commits, concurrency of processes, etc.).

False Contention

False contention occurs when multiple locks hash to the same indicator but there is no real contention. A lock requester can be suspended until the contention is determined to be false or not. As false contention increases, it can cause transactions to terminate and response time to increase. The indicators are contained in the lock table. The lock table is contained in the lock structure of the coupling facility. The lock structure needs to be sized for optimal performance and is used by the IRLM for lock control. It should always be kept in a separate coupling facility from the GBP structure. The lock table control locks, and the other item in the lock structure, the record list, contains the modified and retained locks. This increase assumes an even and efficient hashing algorithm. Decreasing the granularity of locks to reduce false contention has its own implications, such as for applicability to processing needs, and of course, it increases the possibility of real contention. When two elements point to the same lock entry by different subsystems that use the lock structure and lock negotiation must be performed, this is known as a synonym. If the number of users connected to the lock structure decreases, more lock entries can fit on the structure; however, this is usually not a feasible option.

You can also calculate the false contention in the statistics report by taking the number of unlock requests and dividing it by the total number of requests and dividing that number by 100. You can also view this number in the FALSE CONTENTION RATE field. The total needs to be kept under 50% of the calculated total global contention. If it is not, there are a few options:

1. Increase the lock table. More entries allowed in the lock table decreases the chance of two lock requests hashing to the same entry.

    Note: It is important to point out that a dynamic increase of the lock structure via a SETXCF ALTER command will not *resize the lock table portion of the lock structure, only the modify lock list, which will not help with false contention. You must rebuild the lock structure with and SETXCF REBUILD command.*

2. Decrease the granularity of the locks taken (e.g., table or table space locks).

3. Decrease the number of users connected to the lock structure, although this is usually not a viable option.

XES Contention

XES contention can occur for both L-locks and P-locks when a lock, unlock, or change request is made against an object with inter-DB2 interest. Contention occurs when truly compatible locks are viewed by XES as being in contention for the same resource. This occurs because XES views locks as only S or X, whereas the IRLM is actually issuing IS or IX locks. XES is used to determine whether contention for a resource is real or not. A lock requester may or may not be suspended until this determination is made, depending on whether or not it can run a process in parallel with this activity.

To reduce this type of contention, you need to reduce the amount of table-space locking. The best help for this type of contention is to bind your packages with RELEASE(DEALLOCATE) and to drive thread reuse (for more information on this, refer to Chapter 30, "Application Tuning"). By doing these two things, the intent locks on the table space are held through a commit and are not continually propagated to the coupling facility through XES, which interprets them as S and X. You thus prevent the opportunity for XES contention to occur.

A statistics report shows the amount false contention, IRLM contention, and XES contention. An RMF (resource management facility) also shows the asynchronous and synchronous requests for each structure, as well as the number of real and false contentions for the lock structure.

Coupling Facility Resources

Coupling facility resources can be monitored in the RMF reports. Some items to monitor are structure activity, resource usage, link contention, and service times.

Structure Activity

You can measure activity for all structures in the coupling facility by using the RMF coupling facility structure activity report (figure 33.10). In this example, you can see how to monitor global and false contention. You can also monitor directory reclaims for the group buffer pool structures in the coupling facility usage summary portion of the report.

Resource Usage

You can observe this in an RMF report in the coupling facility usage summary. Look for the AVERAGE CF UTLITIZATION (%BUSY). It is important for performance and availability reasons that this remain low. If you are constantly 30% busy (or busier), you may want to consider upgrading your coupling facility. Remember that once a coupling facility is over 50% busy, the performance of requests to the coupling facility seriously degrades. Generally, this degradation is not gradual; it is immediate and harsh.

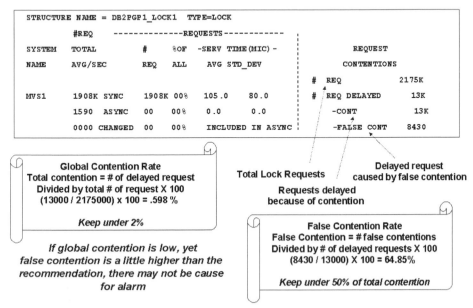

Figure 33.10 Coupling Facility Structure Activity Report

Link Contention

Coupling facility links (or channels) can get busy when a lot of requests are being issued. You need to monitor in particular the links for requests that are being delayed. You also need to see whether contention on the links is getting too high. Figure 33.11 shows and example of the subchannel activity section from an RMF report. Note that the percentage of TOTAL DELAYED REQUESTS was 0.9%. This is fine. You should keep this number below 10% for best performance. To help alleviate channel contention, if it is present, you may want to consider reducing the number of requests over the links, in other words, the amount of sharing between members on the same objects. This can be done by redistributing the workload, possibly by using some affinity processing. You can also consider upgrading the link. Also, if you notice that the BUSY COUNT for the PTH is high, you may want to evaluate the dedication of paths to the MVS subsystem, because there is too much contention.

Service Times

You can keep an eye on service times for each of your structures through the structure activity section of the RMF report (figure 33.12). The field SERV TIME(MIC) shows the average service time for synchronous requests. The example shows a lock structure for which the service time is 105.0. This is an okay service time. You should keep the time for lock structure requests below 150 microseconds. This number, of course, depends on the level of your coupling facility hardware. For a group buffer pool structure, you should keep the time under 250 microseconds. Since requests for the SCA are so few, don't sweat it.

```
SUBCHANNEL ACTIVITY
        #REQ                            --------DELAYED REQUESTS-----------
SYSTEM  TOTAL      --BUSY--                 #        % OF
NAME    AVG/SEC    -COUNTS-                 REQ      REQ


MVS1    81241      PTH 0           SYNC     0        0.0%
        90.3       SCH 0           ASYNC    724      0.9%
                                   TOTAL    724      0.9%
```

Figure 33.11   CF Link Contention RMF Report

```
STRUCTURE NAME = DB2PGP1_LOCK1   TYPE=LOCK

        #REQ      -------------REQUESTS-----------
SYSTEM  TOTAL        #     %OF   -SERV TIME(MIC) -              REQUEST
NAME    AVG/SEC      REQ   ALL   AVG    STD_DEV               CONTENTIONS
                                                    #   REQ              2175K
MVS1    1908K SYNC   1908K 00%   105.0  80.0        #   REQ DELAYED        13K
        1590  ASYNC  00    00%   0.0    0.0             -CONT              13K
        0000  CHANGED 00   00%   INCLUDED IN ASYNC       -FALSE CONT       8430
```

Figure 33.12   Coupling Facility Service Times RMF Report

Conclusion

Some final remarks about data sharing and performance. Performance tuning in DB2, data sharing or not, is still an art, not a science. However, with data sharing, tuning is critical for the performance of not only one subsystem, but of all subsystems in the data sharing group. A performance problem can be magnified greatly in this environment. Problem diagnosis now involves researching new components and processes for identification of problem sources. Data sharing also provides us with several new problem areas and opportunities for tuning. Most important for a smooth implementation is to evaluate and tune the current environment for compliance with standard recommendations before migrating subsystems to the data-sharing group. Long-term monitoring has even more importance than before. It is critical to keep current on maintenance. DB2 data sharing has a large number of benefits to offer us in terms of availability and performance, and the number of data sharing sites continues to grow. Just keep in mind that your performance tuning efforts are key to making it deliver.

Index

A

Access, 295–96

Access paths, 32
  hints for, 568–72
    monitoring and diagnosing, 572–73
  selection of
    influencing, 556–57
    OPTIMIZE FOR *n* ROWS, 557–68
    statistics on, 545–548

ACCTSEQ, 301

ACQUIRE option of BIND, 220–21

Active logs
  dual/placement, 38
  sizing, 37

Active triggers, 403

Addressability, extended, 20

Address space
  in OS/390, 56
  priority in, 49

Affinity processing, 642

AFTER triggers, 406

Aggregated columns, 165–66

ALTER, 60

ALTER BUFFERPOOL command, 83

ALTER TABLE statement, 306

Ambiguous cursors, 260

Application analysis, 591

Application databases, 249

Application design, 255–78
  application-enforced referential integrity, 262–63
  commit strategies, 269
    heuristic control tables, 269–70
  dynamic SQL, 264–66
  isolation levels, 277
  logging, 278
  plans and packages, 263–64

program functionality, retry logic, 268

program structure, 255–56
  cursors, 258–62
  I/O modules, 257–58
  logic in SQL, 255–56
  retrieval, 256

savepoints, 272–76
  establishing, 272–74
  releasing, 276
  restoring, 274–76

in SQL, 46

Application-enforced referential integrity, 262–63

Application error checking, 666

Application hangs, 660–62

Application programming change with hints, 572

Application tuning, 649–52
  bind parameters, 650–52
  lock avoidance, 649–50

Archived data, restoring, 241–43

Archive logs, 38

Archiving, 141

Arrays, column-forced, 167–69

Ascending sequence, 141

ASCII server, DB2 as, 365

AS clause of CREATE VIEW statement, 293

AS IDENTITY attribute, 305, 306

Asynchronous data movement facility (ADMF), 65

Asynchronous read, 21

Audit, performance, 43

Auditing, 152–53

Automatic restart manager (ARM), 637

Availability, 291

Available pages, 63

AVGSIZE, 105